THE
NORTH
AMERICAN
INDIAN

A twenty-one-volume set
Each volume edited with an introduction
by a major scholar

GENERAL EDITOR
David Hurst Thomas

ADVISORY EDITORS
Richard I. Ford
Charles M. Hudson
Bruce G. Trigger
Waldo R. Wedel

A GARLAND SERIES

THE NORTH AMERICAN INDIAN

The Antiquity and Origin of Native North Americans
CLARK SPENCER LARSEN, editor

A Northern Algonquian Source Book: Papers by Frank G. Speck
EDWARD S. ROGERS, editor

An Iroquois Source Book
Volume 1: Political and Social Organization
Volume 2: Calendric Rituals
Volume 3: Medicine Society Rituals
ELISABETH TOOKER, editor

The Early Prehistoric Southeast: A Source Book
JERALD T. MILANICH, editor

The Late Prehistoric Southeast: A Source Book
CHESTER B. DePRATTER, editor

Ethnology of the Southeastern Indians: A Source Book
CHARLES M. HUDSON, editor

A Creek Source Book, WILLIAM C. STURTEVANT, editor

A Choctaw Source Book, JOHN H. PETERSON, editor

A Seminole Source Book, WILLIAM C. STURTEVANT, editor

The Southern Caddo: An Anthology, H. F. GREGORY, editor

A Plains Archaeology Source Book: Selected Papers of the Nebraska State
Historical Society
WALDO R. WEDEL, editor

A Blackfoot Source Book: Papers by Clark Wissler
DAVID HURST THOMAS, editor

The Dunbar-Allis Letters on the Pawnee, WALDO R. WEDEL, editor

A Jean Delanglez, S. J., Anthology: Selections Useful for Mississippi
Valley and Trans-Mississippi American Indian Studies
MILDRED MOTT WEDEL, editor

A Great Basin Shoshonean Source Book, DAVID HURST THOMAS, editor

The Prehistoric American Southwest: A Source Book
History, Chronology, Ecology, and Technology
RICHARD I. FORD, editor

The Ethnographic American Southwest: A Source Book
Southwestern Society in Myth, Clan, and Kinship
RICHARD I. FORD, editor

An Ethnobiology Source Book: The Uses of Plants and Animals by
American Indians
RICHARD I. FORD, editor

Native Shell Mounds of North America: Early Studies
BRUCE G. TRIGGER, editor

THE SOUTHERN CADDO

AN ANTHOLOGY

Edited with an introduction by
H. F. Gregory

Garland Publishing, Inc.
New York & London
1986

Library of Congress Cataloging-in-Publication Data

The Southern Caddo.

  (The North American Indian)
  Bibliography: p.
  1. Caddo Indians—History.   I. Gregory, Hiram F.
II. Series.
E99.C12S68   1986   973'.0497   83-47626
ISBN 0-8240-5886-0 (alk. paper)

The volumes in this series are printed on acid-free,
250-year-life paper.
Printed in the United States of America

CONTENTS

Socio-culture

Linguistics

Physical Anthropology

Archaeology

Material Culture and the Arts

Overview

SOURCES

Bolton, Herbert E.
1908   The Native Tribes about the East Texas Missions. *Texas State Historical Association Quarterly* 2(4):249–76.

Chafe, Wallace L.
1977   Caddo Texts. *International Journal of American Linguistics, Native American Texts Series,* Douglas Parks, ed. 2(1):27–44. Reprinted by permission of The University of Chicago Press.

Dorsey, George A.
1905   *Traditions of the Caddo.* Carnegie Institution of Washington Publication 41. 136 pages. Reprinted by permission of the Carnegie Institution.
       Caddo Customs of Childhood. *Journal of American Folk-Lore* 18:226–28.

Douglas, F. H.
1932   *The Grass House of the Wichita and Caddo.* Denver Art Museum, Department of Indian Art Leaflet 42. Reprinted by permission of the Denver Art Museum.

Fletcher, Alice C.
1907   "Caddo" and "Kadohadacho." *Bulletin of the Bureau of American Ethnology* 30:179–82, 638–39. Reprinted by permission of the Smithsonian Institution Press from *Reports and Bulletins of the Bureau of American Ethnology,* Smithsonian Institution, Washington, D.C.

Glover, William B.
1935   A History of the Caddo Indians. *The Louisiana Historical Quarterly* 18(4):872–946.

Gray, Margery P., and William S. Laughlin
1960   Blood Groups of Caddoan Indians of Oklahoma. *American Journal of Human Genetics* 12(1):86–94. Reprinted by permission of The University of Chicago Press.

Heflin, Eugene
1953   The Oashuns or Dances of the Caddo. *Bulletin of the Oklahoma Anthropological Society* 1:39–42. Reprinted by permission of the Oklahoma Anthropological Society and Eugene Heflin.

Lesser, Alexander
1979   Caddoan Kinship Systems. *Nebraska History* 60(2):260–71. Reprinted by permission of the Nebraska State Historical Society.

Lesser, Alexander, and Gene Weltfish
1932   Composition of the Caddoan Linguistic Stock. *Smithsonian Mis-
       cellaneous Collections* 87(6):1–15.

Mooney, James
1896   The Caddo and Associated Tribes. *Fourteenth Annual Report of the
       Bureau of American Ethnology for 1892-1893,* part 2. Pp. 1092–1103.
       Reprinted by permission of the Smithsonian Institution Press from
       Reports and Bulletins of the Bureau of American Ethnology,
       Smithsonian Institution, Washington, D.C.

Sibley, John
1806   Historical Sketches of the Several Indian Tribes in Louisiana.
       American State Papers, Class II, Indian Affairs 1:721–31.

1879   Vocabulary of the Caddo Language. *American Naturalist*
       13(12):787–90.

Spier, Leslie
1924   Wichita and Caddo Relationship Terms. *American Anthropologist*
       n.s. 26:258–63. Reprinted by permission of the American Anthro-
       pological Association.

Story, Dee Ann
1978   Some Comments on Anthropological Studies Concerning the Caddo.
       In *Texas Archaeology: Essays Honoring R. King Harris,* Kurt
       House, ed. Pp. 46–68. Dallas: Southern Methodist University Press.
       Reprinted by permission of SMU Press.

Tanner, Helen H.
1974   The Territory of the Caddo Tribe of Oklahoma. In *Caddo Indians
       IV.* Pp. 66–104. New York and London: Garland Publishing.

Taylor, Alan R.
1963   The Classification of the Caddoan Languages. *Proceedings of the
       American Philosophical Society* 107(1):51–59. Reprinted by permis-
       sion of the American Philosophical Society.

Webb, Clarence H.
1940   House Types among the Caddo Indians. *Bulletin of the Texas
       Archeological and Paleontological Society* 12:49–75. Reprinted by
       permission of the Texas Archeological Society.

1978   Changing Archeological Methods and Theory in the Trans-
       mississippi South. In *Texas Archeology: Essays Honoring R. King
       Harris,* Kurt House, ed. Pp. 27–45. Dallas: Southern Methodist
       University Press. Reprinted by permission of SMU Press.

Wedel, Mildred Mott
1978   *La Harpe's 1719 Post on Red River and Nearby Caddo Settlements.*
       University of Texas at Austin, Texas Memorial Museum Bulletin
       30. 20 pages. Reprinted by permission of the Texas Memorial
       Museum.

Williams, Stephen
1964 The Aboriginal Location of the Kadohadacho and Related Tribes. In *Explorations in Cultural Anthropology,* Ward Goodenough, ed. Pp. 545–70. New York.

Wyckoff, Don G., and Timothy G. Baugh
1980 Early Historic Hasinai Elites: A Model for the Material Culture of Governing Elites. *Midcontinental Journal of Archaeology* 5(2):225–88. Reprinted by permission of the Kent State University Press.

INTRODUCTION

Today the Caddo Indians live near Binger and Fort Cobb, Oklahoma. The tribal name Caddo is an Anglicization of a French corruption of an individual tribal/linguistic label: Kadohadacho (Story 1978, this volume). It has been in general usage since it was coined by Anglo-Americans (or Texans) in the 19th century.

The Caddo themselves recognize two main linguistic groups: Hasinai and Kadohadacho, in that order. Those two old dialects are today still spoken by some, and older people recall a time when others were spoken: Yatasi, Hainai, Nadarko and Natchitoches. While outsiders perceived the Caddo as being one tribe, there were actually many. But given a common geography and culture history, these groups have in time managed, adroitly, to integrate themselves into a single group while maintaining their separate identities.

In any overview of ethnographic (and other) anthropological writing about a group it seems necessary to discuss the nature of various interests reflected in that literature. In terms of the Caddo a number of things are apparent:

1. There are at present *no* studies of the Caddo written by a Caddo. But it should be pointed out here that such a study has been started, and, when complete, should offer new points of view.
2. The overwhelming majority of literature on the Caddo tribe is historical and/or archaeological. The socio-cultural descriptive material from first-hand ethnographic description is sparse when compared with the ethnohistorical sources gleaned by John R. Swanton (1942), Herbert E. Bolton (1908, this volume, 1914), and William B. Glover (1935, this volume).
3. Ethnographic and ethnohistorical materials have often been used as analogies for "explaining" archaeological data. This earlier approach has been recently revived (Wedel 1978, this volume; Bell et al. 1970). Moreover, while some (Story 1978) strongly recommend a more thorough search of ethnohistorical data, few seek ethnographic analogies within living Caddo tradition.
4. Ethnographic studies of cultural continuity have been noted as potentially valid by E. C. Parsons (1941), John Swanton (1942),

Helen H. Tanner (1974, this volume), and Hiram F. Gregory (1974), but eschewed by more recent works (Story 1978; Pertullo 1980). Apparently the anthropological community remains divided about their models of culture change. As it is popularly phrased, the question is: "Can Indians stay Indians if they begin to live within white men's society?"

Elderly Caddo have generally recognized tribal history in terms of major events—not dates, but events. For example, the late Sadie Weller, in a series of tapes made for Claude Medford, Jr., pointed out that Caddo music and songs could be traced back to the time they were in "Louisiana." She further noted that Caddo music eventually incorporated the Ghost Dance, and the Peyote songs. Her emphasis was on the maintenance and continuity of music, noting the preservation of the old alongside the new.

E. C. Parsons (1942:5) observed the same persistence of Southeastern Indian culture traits among the Caddoan notes she obtained from her informant, White Moon, and John Swanton (1942:121) mentions a similar persistence of earlier fire rituals, Catholic influences, and the use of peyote in the Big Moon rituals.

James Mooney (1896, this volume) A. C. Fletcher (1907, this volume), Leslie Spier (1924, this volume), and Alexander Lesser and Gene Weltfish (1932, this volume) noted the maintenance of kinship terms and structures, including the clan and clan taboos. Helen Tanner (1974) noted that at the time of her research contemporary older Caddo recalled the *tamma* and the function of that office.

While these workers (ethnologists and archaeologists) and the Caddo sought and found continuity, more recent works have indicated, by pointing out the impact of European contact: disease, relocation, and technical change, that continuity is not all there is to Caddo history (Pertullo 1980).

Archaeological data (Story 1978) are beginning to be evalutated in terms of their own strengths, and a greater emphasis is being placed on ethnohistory in close association with this effort. Moreover, new stimuli are coming to bear from outside the disciplines of anthroplogy and history. Litigation over land claims, by establishing the social conditions and locations of the Caddo through time and space, have drawn new attention to these old problems. In addition, salvage ethnography has had some attraction to recent workers (Gregory 1974; Webb and Gregory 1978; Tanner 1974).

Answers to many structural questions, even historical questions, have yet to be sought among the Caddo.

C. H. Webb and H. F. Gregory (1978) have modeled the Caddo trade system archaeologically and attempted to demonstrate its effect on the development of French and Spanish trade strategies. The archaeological paradigm for research is shifting to deductive modeling while keeping traditional pursuits and theoretical issues in mind.

The Caddo themselves, are attempting to maintain their language, even to the point of teaching formal classes in the language to children. The earliest work was historical in nature. Prompted by President Thomas Jefferson's widespread interest in dialectology, John Sibley (1879:787–790, this volume) attempted to collect the "tribal" or "band" dialects. As late as the 1920s and 30s Lesser and Weltfish (1932:1–5) attempted to establish a descriptive frame for the Caddoan "stock" or family of languages. Alan Taylor (1963a:51–59, this volume, 1963b:113–31) has updated and revised that effort, and, from his research, a generally accepted comparative model of language relationships is now available. Wallace Chafe (1973) has done virtually all the recent analysis and description of the Caddoan language proper. His textual material (1977, this volume) is a major source, and his discussion of the structure and grammar (1973) remains virtually the only work on the subject. These traditional language studies have only recently begun to have an effect on tribal language maintenance programs.

Tribal traditionalists have organized at least two dance grounds —one at Binger and another near Hinton, Oklahoma (now disorganized)—where the separate factions of the Caddo have attempted to maintain their songs and dances. Many of these "go back to Louisiana." Still, some younger Caddo are losing the language, and the need for language maintenance programs is still evident.

As in kinship studies and archaeological and archival research, the linguistic research has been predominantly historical. For example, in the Kadohadacho and Hasinai dialects still spoken at Binger, there are two words for spoon: in Kadohadacho it is a word that means "horn" and in Hasinai it is a word that means "shell". Such correspondences might easily be tested against artifact distributional data for the Caddoan area. If numbers of such differences can be translated into artifactual data, linguistic boundaries might be established for the archaeological past. Further, certain glotto-chronological determinations might be tested archaeologically.

As in research on Indians elsewhere, physical anthropology has principally served as a handmaiden of archaeology in Caddoan research. Osteological studies far outnumber other approaches to Caddo biology. In an early attempt to relate Caddo physical anthropology to environment, Colquitt and Webb (1940) and Webb (1941) have pointed out some physical dental effects related to early dietary shifts postulated for the Louisiana Caddo. As summarized by D. A. Story (1978:55), the physical anthropology of the Caddo was virtually *all* osteology, although her own comments about physical anthropology reflect the current archaeological-osteological approach.

In the mountains near Hinton, on the dance ground at the Binger "Y", the Caddo sing their old songs and cherish their old ways. The test of continuity likely rests upon all *three* sets of data: contemporary Caddoan traditions, ethnohistorical accounts, *and* the archaeological record. Wedel (1978) has recommended the "direct historical approach" in the solution of this problem. Others (Wyckoff 1970:64–134) have integrated the historical and archaeological data to reconstruct prehistoric Caddoan settlement sequences and to evaluate the long-term development of their policy.

Dee Ann Story (1972) had addressed the depth of Caddoan chronology in her work on the western ceremonial center, the George C. Davis Site (Newell and Krieger 1949). Clarence H. Webb (1978:32–33) has discussed Caddoan origins in Louisiana, and Frank Schambach (1971 Unpublished Caddo Conference Paper) sees Caddo roots in earlier complexes in southwestern Arkansas and northwestern Texas. What seems clear now is that the Caddoan archaeological complexes date to the outer edges of the Temple Mound pattern which was so widespread across the southeastern woodlands.

Other questions of archaeological importance may be asked about the origin of Caddoan ceremonialism, ceramic styles, and/or social structure.

For example, Don G. Wyckoff and his associates have discussed the ethnohistorical models of the Xenesi or Caddo elite in the light of archaeological data (Wyckoff and Baugh 1980, this volume).

Growth studies, especially longitudinal studies of children, epigenetic studies, and other approaches to physical anthropology are notably missing from Caddoan studies. A single exception to this is a rather extensive blood study done with the cooperation of Caddoan tribal authorities (Gray and Laughlin 1960:86–94, this volume). Concentration on living Caddoan physiology and genetics—something that might be a prelude to the development of relevant medical anthropology and tribal program development—has a long way to go. No programs in medical anthropology, mental health, or other studies relevant to the contemporary Caddo have been undertaken. This neglect is not necessarily a consequence of the more functional analysis of Caddo socio-cultural development.

At a Caddoan Conference held at Natchitoches, Louisiana in 1971, the late Caddo tribal chairman, Melford Williams, asked for cooperation from the anthropologists in attendance. He asked that examples of material remains from Caddo sites—pottery points, etc.—be made available to the Caddo provided that they could curate them safely. A number of institutional representatives and some private collectors assented. However, more than a decade has passed since Williams' request and the Caddo children still see the classic artifacts of their culture in pictures in books, or in museums at Fayetteville, Norman, Tulsa, Idabel, Natchitoches, or Austin.

Art, for the Caddo, has been strongly influenced by the Plains tradition diffused to Indian communities via the schools set up by the Collier Administration of the Bureau of Indian Affairs. Traditional arts and crafts—silverwork, basketry, and ceramics—have not developed out of the 18th century or earlier tribal traditions because these were often defunct by the early 19th century.

A single amateur paper (Heflin 1953:39–42, this volume) has described traditional Caddoan dances as these persist. The dress styles, silverwork, and other contemporary Caddoan art styles reflect the pan-Eastern diffusion of certain European styles in the early part of the 19th century. To date these have been studied only briefly (Parsons 1942), and the beautiful artwork of the 1930-1980 period has yet to be adequately studied. As with structural and biological studies, Caddoan material culture studies have almost exclusively been done in relation to archaeology. Clarence H. Webb and Ralph McKinney (1975:39–127) have described the "river cane" basketry of the tribes, an art apparently lost in the Plains, where cane (*Aruindinana* sp.) is virtually absent. The few twilled baskets—made of willow and other kinds of wood—have yet to be studied and compared to older ethnographic specimens or archaeological fragments.

The 1800 to 2000 Caddo who live today in Oklahoma have little or no real knowledge of the anthropology or history of their tribe. They have not yet searched Caddoan literature for relevant items which they could use for self-maintenance and development. It is hoped that this anthology of articles on them and their ancestors will allow them, and others, to begin the arduous path of translating anthropology into their daily life.

H. F. GREGORY

References

Bell, Robert E., Edward B. Jelks, and W. W. Newcomb, eds.
1967   A Pilot Study of Wichita Indian Archeology and Ethnohistory. *Final Report for Grant GS-964, National Science Foundation.*

Bolton, Herbert Eugene
1908   The Native Tribes about the East Texas Missions, *Texas State Historical Association Quarterly* II(4):249–276.

1914   *Athanese de Mezieres and the Louisiana-Texas Frontier 1768–1780.* 2 vols. Cleveland: Arthur H. Clark

Chafe, Wallace
1973   Siovan, Iroqovian and Caddoan. In *Current Trends in Linguistics,* T. A. Sebeok, ed. *Linguistics in North America* 10:1164–1209.

1977   Caddoan Texts. *International Journal of American Linguistics, Native American Texts Series,* Douglas Parks, ed. 2(1):27–44.

Colquitt, W. T., and C. H. Webb
1940   Dental Diseases in an Aboriginal Group. *Tri-State Medical Journal* 12(4):2414–2417.

Fletcher, A. C.
1907a   Caddo, *Bulletin of the Bureau of American Ethnology* 30:179–182.

1907b   Kadohadacho. *Bulletin of the Bureau of American Ethnology* 30:638–639.

Glover, W. B.
1935   A History of the Caddo Indians. *Louisiana Historical Quarterly* 18(4):872-946.

Gray, Margery, and William S. Laughlin
1960   Blood Groups of the Caddo Indians of Oklahoma. *American Journal of Genetics* 12:86–94.

Gregory, Hiram F.
1974   Eighteenth Century Caddoan Archaeology: A Study in Models and Interpretation. Unpublished Ph.D. dissertation. Dallas: Southern Methodist University.

Heflin, E.
1953   The Oashuns or Dances of the Caddo. *Bulletin of the Oklahoma Anthropological Society* I:39–42.

Lesser, Alexander
1979   Caddoan Kinship Systems. *Nebraska History* 60(2):260–272.

Lesser, Alexander, and Gene Weltfish
1932   Composition of the Caddoan Linguistic Stock. *Smithsonian Miscellaneous Collections* 87(6).

Mooney, James
1896   The Caddo and Associated Tribes. *The Annual Report of the Bureau of American Ethnology for 1892–1893.* Pp. 1092–1103.

Parsons, E.C.
1941   Notes on the Caddo, *Memoirs of the American Anthropological Association* 57.

Pertulla, Timothy K.
1980   The Caddo Indians of Louisiana: A Review, *Louisiana Archaeology* 7, pp. 116–121.

Shambach, Frank
1971   The Trans-Mississippi South: The Case for a New Natural Area West of the Lower Mississippi Valley and East of the Plains. Unpublished paper given at the Caddo Conference.

Sibley, John
1832   Historical Sketches of the Several Indian Tribes in Louisiana. *American State Papers, Class II, Indian Affairs* I:721–731.

1879   Vocabulary of the Caddo Language. *American Naturalist* 13(12):787–790.

Spier, Leslie
1924   Wichita and Caddo Relationship Terms. *American Anthropologist* 26:258–263.

Story, Dee Ann
1972   *A Preliminary Report of the 1968, 1969, and 1970 Excavations at the George C. Davis Site, Cherokee County, Texas.* Report of Field Research Conducted Under National Science Foundation (GS-273 and 3200) and Interagency Contracts between the University of Texas at Austin, the Texas Building Commission, and Texas Historical Committee.

1978 Some Comments on Anthropological Studies Concerning the Caddo.
      In *Texas Archaeology: Essays Honoring R. King Harris*, Kurt
      House, ed. Dallas: Southern Methodist University Press. Pp. 46-68.

Swanton, John
1931 The Caddo Social Organization and Its Possible Historic Signifi-
      cance. *Journal of the Washington Academy of Sciences* 21:203–206.

1942 Source Material in the History and Ethnology of the Caddo Indians.
      Bulletin of the Bureau of American Ethnology 132.

Tanner, Helen Hornbeck
1974 The Territory of the Caddo Tribe of Oklahoma. In *Caddo Indians
      IV*. New York: Garland Publishing. Pp. 6-104.

Taylor, Alan R.
1932a The Classification of the Caddoan Languages. *Proceedings of the
      American Philosophical Society* 107:51–59.

1963b Comparative Caddoan. *International Journal of American
      Linguistics* 29(2):113–131.

Webb, Clarence H.
1940 House Types among the Caddo Indians. *Bulletin of the Texas
      Archeological and Paleontological Society* 12:49–75.

1945 A Second Historic Caddo Site at Natchitoches, Louisiana. *Bulletin
      of the Texas Archeological and Paleontological Society* 16:52–83.

Webb, Clarence H., and H. F. Gregory
1978 The Caddo of Louisiana. *Anthropological Study No. 2*. Louisiana
      Archaeological Survey and Antiquities Committee. Department of
      Culture, Tourism and Recreation, Baton Rouge.

Webb, Clarence H., and Ralph McKinney
1975 Mounds Plantation (16 D 12), Caddo Parish, Louisiana. *Louisiana
      Archaeology* 2:39–127.

Wedel, Mildred Mott
1978 LeHarpe's 1719 Post on Red River and Nearby Caddo Settlements.
      Bulletin of the Texas Memorial Museum 30. University of Texas at
      Austin.

Williams, Stephen
1964 The Aboriginal Location of the Kadohadacho and Related Tribes. In
      Explorations in Cultural Anthropology, Ward Goodenough, ed. Pp.
      545-570. New York.

ETHNOHISTORY

THE NATIVE TRIBES ABOUT THE EAST TEXAS MISSIONS.

HERBERT E. BOLTON.

INTRODUCTORY.

The history of the Spanish *régime* in the Southwest is very largely the history of an Indian policy in its military, political, and religious phases, and to understand it aright it is manifestly necessary to know something of the people over whom the Spaniards extended their authority and upon whom they tried to impose their faith and their civilization.

The purpose of this paper is to furnish a partial introduction to the early history of the Spaniards in eastern Texas—the scene of their first systematic activities between the Mississippi and the upper Rio Grande—by presenting some of the main features of the organization of the compact group of tribes living in the upper Neches and the Angelina River valleys, the first and the most important group with which they came into intimate contact. These tribes furnished the early field of labor especially for the Franciscans of the College of Santa Cruz de Querétaro, who worked for fifteen years in the region and founded in it five missions, while one was founded there and maintained for more than half a century by the College of Nuestra Señora de Guadalupe de Zacatecas. ·It is hoped that this paper will throw new light on the all too obscure history of these interesting establishments, particularly with respect to their locations.[1]

The Names "Texas" and "Hasinai."

The tribes in question commonly have been called the Texas, but more properly the Hasinai. Concerning the meaning and

[1]The authoritative presentation of the general history of the beginnings of these establishments is that contained in the excellent articles by Dr. R. C. Clark, published in this journal, Vol. V, 171-205, and Vol. VI, 1-26. In their bearings upon Indian organization and tribal names they are marred to some extent by the use of corrupt copies of the sources instead of the originals, as will be seen by comparing them with what follows. It is but fair to state that in the revision and extension of these articles, about to appear as a Bulletin of the University of Texas, Mr. Clark has corrected some of the errors.

For facts concerning the individual tribes mentioned in the course of this article, see the *Handbook of American Indians*, edited by F. W. Hodge (Bulletin of the Bureau of American Ethnology, No. 30, Part I, 1907; Part II in press).

usage of these terms I shall only present here somewhat dogmatically part of the results of a rather extended study which I have made of these points and which I hope soon to publish.[1]

The testimony of the sources warrants the conclusion that before the coming of the Spaniards the word Texas, variously spelled by the early writers, had wide currency among the tribes of eastern Texas and perhaps over a larger area; that its usual meaning was "friends," or more technically, "allies"; and that it was used by the tribes about the early missions, at least, to whom especially it later became attached as a group name, to designate a large number of tribes who were customarily allied against the Apaches. In this sense, the Texas included tribes who spoke different languages and who were as widely separated as the Red River and the Rio Grande. It seems that the Neches-Angelina tribes designated did not apply the term restrictively to themselves as a name, but that they did use it in a very untechnical way as a form of greeting, like "hello, friend," with which they even saluted Spaniards after their advent. I may say, in this connection, that the meanings "land of flowers," "tiled roofs," "paradise," etc., sometimes given for the name Texas, I have never seen even suggested by early observers, or by anyone on the basis of trustworthy evidence.

The name Texas has been variously applied by writers, but it was most commonly used by the Spaniards, from whom the French and the English borrowed it, to designate those tribes of the upper Neches and the Angelina valleys, and this in spite of their knowing full well that among the natives the word had the wider application that has been indicated. There are many variations from this usage in Spanish writings, it is true, but this, nevertheless, is the ordinary one. As a tribal name the term was sometimes still further narrowed to apply to a single tribe. When this occurred, it was most commonly used to designate the Hainai, the head tribe of the group in question, but sometimes it was applied to the Nabedache tribe. As a geographical term, the name Texas was first extended from these Neches-Angelina tribes to their immediate country. Thus for the first quarter of a century of Spanish occupation, the phrase "the Province of Texas" referred only to the country east of the Trinity River; but with the founding of the San Antonio settlements the term was extended westward, more in harmony

[1] The present paper embodies some of the results of an investigation of the history of the Texas tribes which the writer is making for the Bureau of American Ethnology.

with its native meaning, to the Medina River, and then gradually to all of the territory included within the present State of Texas.

While the name Texas, as used by the tribes in the eastern portion of the State, was thus evidently a broad and indefinite term applied to many and unrelated tribes occupying a wide area, it is clear that the native group name for most of the tribes about the missions in the Neches and Angelina valleys was Hasinai, or Asinai.[1] Today the term Hasinai is used by the Caddoans on the reservations to include not only the survivors of these Neches-Angelina tribes, but also the survivors of the tribes of the Sabine and Red River country. It seems from the sources, however, that in the early days the term was more properly limited to the former group. In strictest usage, indeed, the earliest writers did not include all of these. A study of contemporary evidence shows that at the first contact of Europeans with these tribes and for a long time thereafter writers quite generally made a distinction between the Hasinai (Asinai, Cenis, etc.) and the Kadohadacho[2] (Caddodacho) group; these confederacies, for such they were in the Indian sense of the term, were separated by a wide stretch of uninhabited territory extending between the upper Angelina and the Red River in the neighborhood of Texarkana; their separateness of organization was positively affirmed, and the details of the inner constitution of both groups were more or less fully described; while in their relations with the Europeans they were for nearly a century dealt with as separate units. Nevertheless, because of the present native use of the term and some early testimony that can not be disregarded, I would not at present assert unreservedly that the term formerly was applied by the natives only to the Neches-Angelina group. If, as seems highly probable, this was the case, in order to preserve the native usage we should call these tribes the Hasinai; if not, then the Southern Hasinai.

The name Hasinai, like Texas, was sometimes narrowed in its application to one tribe, usually the Hainai. But occasionally the notion appears that there was an Hasinai tribe distinct from the

---

[1] The Spaniards ordinarily spelled this name Asinai or Asinay, and the French writers Cenis. Mooney, the ethnologist, who knows intimately the survivors of these people living on the reservations, writes the name by which they now call themselves Hasinai, or Hasini, preferably the former. His spelling has been adopted as the standard one by the Bureau of American Ethnology. See the *Fourteenth Annual Report of the Bureau of American Ethnology*, 1092 (1896).

[2] I use here also the spelling adopted by the Bureau of American Ethnology.

Hainai. This, however, does not seem to have been the case. As now used by the surviving Hasinai and Caddos, Hasinai means "our own folk," or, in another sense, "Indians."[1]

Ethnological Relations: Historical Importance.

The Hasinai belonged to the Caddoan linguistic stock. This family, which was a large one, was divided into three principal geographic groups of tribes: the northern, represented by the Arikara in North Dakota; the middle, comprising the Pawnee confederacy, formerly living on the Platte River, Nebraska, and to the west and southwest thereof; and the southern, including most of the tribes of eastern Texas, together with many of those of western Louisiana and of southern Oklahoma.[2] Of this southern group the tribes about the Querétaran missions were one of the most important subdivisions. They, together with the related Caddo tribes to the north, represented the highest form of native society between the Red and the upper Rio Grande rivers, a stretch of nearly a thousand miles: This fact gave them from the outset a relatively large political importance. While it has been clearly shown by writers that the immediate motive to planting the first Spanish establishment within this area was French encroachment, little note has been made of the fame and the relative advancement of the Hasinai Indians as factors in determining the choice of the location. LaSalle's colony, which first brought the Spaniards to Texas to settle, was established on the Gulf coast; and had the natives of this region been as well organized and as influential among the tribes as the Hasinai, and, therefore, as likely to become the theater of another French intrusion, the logical procedure for the Spaniards would have been to establish themselves on the ground where the first intrusion had occurred, and within relatively easy reach from Mexico both by water and by land. But the Karankawan tribes of the coast proved hostile to the French and Spaniards alike, and, while their savage life and inhospitable country offered little to attract the missionary, their small influence over the other groups of natives rendered them relatively useless as a basis for extending Spanish political authority. These considerations entered prominently into

[1]See Mooney, *op. cit.*

[2]Powell, "Indian Linguistic Families," in the *Seventh Annual Report of the Bureau of American Ethnology*, with map; *Handbook of American Indians* (Bureau of American Ethnology, Bul. No. 30), 182.

the Spaniards' decision to establish their first Texas missions far in the interior, at a point difficult to reach from Mexico by land and wholly inaccessible by water. Events justified their estimate of the importance of the Hasinai as a base of political operations. But, while the control of these tribes and their Caddo neighbors remained for a century or more a cardinal point in the politics of the Texas-Louisiana frontier, it was soon learned that the less advanced and weaker tribes of the San Antonio region, nearer Mexico and farther removed from the contrary influence of the French, afforded a better field for missionary labors.

THE PRINCIPAL TRIBES.

Since Indian political organization was at best but loose and shifting and was strongly dominated by ideas of independence, and since writers were frequently indefinite in their use of terms, it would not be easy to determine with strict accuracy the constituent elements of this Neches-Angelina confederacy at different times. However, a few of the leading tribes—those of greatest historical interest—stand out with distinctness and can be followed for considerable periods of time.

De León learned in 1689 from the chief of the Nabedache tribe, the westernmost of the group, that his people had nine settlements.[1] Francisco de Jesús María Casañas, writing in 1691 near the Nabedache village after fifteen months' residence there, reported that the "province of Aseney" comprised nine tribes (*naciones*) living in the Neches-Angelina valleys within a district about thirty-five leagues long. It would seem altogether probable that these reports referred to the same nine tribes. Those named by Jesús María, giving his different spellings, were the Nabadacho or Yneci (Nabaydacho), Necha (Neita), Nechaui, Nacono, Nacachau, Nazadachotzi, Cachaé (Cataye), Nabiti, and Nasayaya (Nasayaha).[1] The location of these tribes Jesús María points out with some definiteness, and six of them at least we are able to identify in later times without question. Moreover, his description of their governmental organization is so minute that one feels that he must have had pretty accurate information. The testimony of a number of other witnesses who wrote between 1687

---

[1]"Poblaciones." Letter of May 18, 1689, printed in Buckingham Smith's *Documentos para la Historia de la Florida;* evidently that cited by Velasco, in *Memorias de Nueva España,* XXVII, 179. Concerning the *Memorias,* see note 3, p. 256.

[1]Relación, August 15, 1691, MS., 107, 108, 112.

and 1692 in the main corroborates that of Jesus María, particularly in the important matter of not including the Nasoni tribe within the Hasinai.[1]

It so happens that after 1692 we get little intimate knowledge of the Hasinai until 1715. When light again dawns there appear in common usage one or two additions to Jesus María's list. Whether they represent an oversight on his part or subsequent. accretions to the group we can not certainly say. Of those in his list six, the Nabadacho, Neche, Nacogdoche, Nacachau, Nacono, and Nabiti are mentioned under the same names by other writers. Cachaé is evidently Jesus María's name for the well known Hainai, as will appear later, while the Nabiti seem to be San Denis's Nabiri and may be Joutel's Noadiche (Nahordike). For the Nechaui we can well afford to accept Jesus María's explicit statement. Besides these nine, the Spaniards after 1716 always treated as within the Hasinai group the Nasoni, Nadaco, and the Nacao. Judging from the localities occupied and some other circumstances, it is not altogether improbable that two of these may be old tribes under new names, as seems to be clearly the case with the Hainai. The Nasayaya, named by Jesus María, may answer to the Nasoni, well known after 1716,[2] and the Nabiti may possibly be the Nadaco, also well known after that date. If both of these surmises be true, we must add to Jesus María's list at least the Nacao, making ten tribes in all; if not, there were at least eleven or twelve. Putting first the best known and the most important, they were: the Hainai, Nabedache, Nacogdoche, Nasoni, Nadaco, Neche, Nacono, Nechaui, Nacao, and, perhaps, the Nabiti and the Nasayaya. This is not intended as a definitive list of the Hasinai at any one time,

---

[1]See Joutel, in Margry, *Découvertes*, III, 341, 344, *et seq.* (French's version of Joutel's Journal, printed in the *Historical Collections of Louisiana*, is very corrupt, and must be used with the greatest care); Terán, Descripción, in *Mem. de Nueva España*, XXVII, 48, *et seq.*

[2]The Nasayaya are placed by Jesus María in a location corresponding very closely to that later occupied by the Nasoni. Yet, the facts that though Jesus María named the Nasoni he did not include them in the Hasinai group while he did include the Nasayaya, and that Terán explicitly excludes the Nasoni from the Hasinai, make it seem probable that the Nasoni and the Nasayaya were distinct. The strongest ground for rejecting this conclusion is the fact that the latter tribe never appears again under a recognizable name, unless they are the Nacaxe, who later appear on the Sabine. The Nabiti might possibly be the Nadaco, but this does not seem likely, for the locations do not correspond very closely, while as late as 1715 San Denis gave the Nabiri and Nadoco as two separate tribes.

but it does include those known to have been within the compact area about the Querétaran missions and commonly treated as within the Hasinai group. By following the footnotes below it will be seen that "Nacoches," "Noaches," and "Asinay," which have been given, with resulting confusion, as names of tribes where early missions were established, are simply corruptions of "Neche," "Nasoni," and "Ainai," as the forms appear in the original manuscripts, whose whereabouts are now known.

The Ais, or Eyeish, a neighbor tribe living beyond the Arroyo Attoyac, at whose village a Zacatecan mission was founded in 1717, seem to have fallen outside the Hasinai confederacy. Only recently have they been included by ethnologists in the Caddoan stock, and, although they are now regarded as Caddoan, there are indications that their dialect was quite different from that of their western neighbors, while their manners and customs were always regarded as inferior to those of these other tribes.[1] Moreover, there is some evidence that they were generally regarded as aliens, and that they were sometimes even positively hostile to the Hasinai. Thus Jesus María includes them in his list of the enemies of the Hasinai; Espinosa, a quarter of a century after Jesus María wrote, speaks of them as friendly toward the "Assinay," from which by implication he excludes them, but says that the Hasinai medicine men "make all the tribes believe that disease originates in the bewitchment which the neighboring Indians, the Bidais, Ays, and Yacdocas, cause them," a belief that clearly implies hostility between the tribes concerned,[2] while Mezières wrote in 1779 that the Ais were hated alike by their Spanish and their Indian neighbors.[3]

The Adaes, or Adai, in whose midst the mission of Nuestra Señora de los Dolores was founded in 1717, lived beyond the Sabine, and belonged to the Red River group of Caddoans, or the Caddo. They, therefore, do not fall within the scope of this paper.

THEIR LOCATION.

For determining the location of these tribes our chief materials are the Journal of Joutel (1687), the Relación of Fiancisco de

[1] On the subjects of their languages see the *Handbook of the American Indians*, under "Eyeish."
[2] *Crónica Apostólica*, 428.
[3] *Expedición*, in *Mem. de Nueva España*, XXVIII, 240.

Jesus María Casañas (1691), De León's diary of the expedition of
1690, Terán's for that of 1691-2, those of Ramón and Espinosa
for the expedition of 1716, Peña's for that of Aguayo (1721),
Rivera's for his *visita* of 1727, Solís's for that made by him in
1767-8, and Mezières's accounts of his tours among the Indians
in 1772, 1778, and 1779. Two only of these are in print, while
two of them have not before been used.[3] Besides these and
numerous supplementing documentary sources, there are (1) the

HASÍNAI VILLAGES.

I Nabedacha
II Neche.
III Hainai
IV Nasogdoche
V Nasoni
VI Nadaco
VII Nacachau
VIII Nacono
IX Nechaui
X Nabiti
XI Nacao

early surveys showing the Camino Real, or Old San Antonio Road,
whose windings in eastern Texas were determined mainly by the

---

[3]Of the diaries of De León and Espinosa I cite only the manuscripts in
the Archivo General y Público, Mexico. These, I believe, are not otherwise available, and have not before been used except by Mr. R. C. Clark,
who has recently had access to my transcripts. Of Jesus María's Relación
I follow an autograph manuscript, which, however, appears to be a copy
instead of the original. Of the diaries of Terán and Ramón I have had
access to the originals, and of the Mezières manuscripts either to the originals or to certified official copies. My copy of the Rivera diary is from
the edition printed in 1736. For the Peña and Solís diaries I have had
to depend upon the copies in the *Memorias*. On comparing *Memorias*
transcripts, in general, with the originals I have found that they are very
corrupt and that numerous mistakes have resulted from their use. But
in cases where there are no essential differences, I cite the *Memorias*
copies, because they are more generally accessible; otherwise I cite the
originals.

location of the principal Indian villages where the Spaniards had settlements, (2) certain unmistakable topographical features, such as the principal rivers and the Neche Indian mounds, and (3) geographical names that have come down to us from the period of Spanish occupation.

It will be interesting, before studying the location of each one of the tribes separately, to read the general description of the group given by Jesus María in 1691. Speaking of the Great Xinesi, he said, "To him are subject all of these nine tribes: The Nabadacho, which, for another name, is called Yneci. Within this tribe are founded the mission of Nuestro Padre San Francisco and the one which I have founded in Your Excellency's name, that of El Santíssimo Nombre de María. The second tribe is that of the Necha. It is separated from the former by the Rio del Arcangel San Miguel [the Neches]. Both are between north and east.[1] At one side of these two, looking south, between south and east, is the tribe of the Nechaui, and half a league from the last, another, called the Nacono. Toward the north, where the above-mentioned Necha tribe ends, is the tribe called Nacachau. Between this tribe and another called Nazadachotzi, which is toward the east, in the direction of the house of the Great Xinesi, which is about . . . half way between these two tribes,[2] comes another, which begins at the house of the Great Xinesi, between north and east, and which is called Cachaé. At the end of this tribe, looking toward the north, is another tribe called Nabiti, and east of this a tribe called the Nasayaha. These nine tribes embrace an extent of about thirty-five leagues and are all subject to this Great Xinesi."[3] This description will be convenient for reference as we proceed.

It may be noted here that the average league of the old Spanish diaries of expeditions into Texas was about two miles. This should be kept in mind when reading the data hereafter presented.

[1]Meaning north and east of the point where he was writing, near San Pedro Creek, Houston County, as will appear below.

[2]My text (see note 3, p. 256) may be correct here. It reads "q esta, Como almediodia y enel Medio de las dos Naciones." It is possible that the copyist first wrote *almediodia* by mistake for *enel Medio de* and then wrote the latter correctly, but neglected to erase the words written by mistake. Other data seem to bear out this supposition.

[3]Relación, 107-108.

The Nacogdoche Tribe and the Mission of Guadalupe.

A starting point or base from which to determine the location of most of the tribes is the founding of the mission of Nuestra Señora de Guadalupe at the main village of the Nacogdoches in 1716, for it can be shown that this mission remained on the same site until it was abandoned in 1773; that the modern city of Nacogdoches was built at the old mission site; and, therefore, that the location of this city represents the location of the principal Nacogdoche village. The evidence briefly stated is as follows: Ramón, whose expedition founded this mission, wrote in his *Derrotero* that nine leagues east-southeast of the principal Hasinai village (the Hainai), on the Angelina River, he arrived at the "village of the Nacogdoches," and that on the next day he "set out from this mission," implying clearly that the mission was located where he was writing, at the Nacogdoche village.[1] As is well known, all of the missions of this section were abandoned in 1719 because of fear of a French invasion. Peña reports in his diary of the Aguayo expedition of 1721 that Aguayo, who rebuilt the abandoned missions, entered "the place where stood the mission of N. S. de Guadalupe de Nacodoches," and rebuilt the church. The inference is that the site was the old one, more especially since in one instance in the same connection where a mission site was changed Peña mentions the fact.[2] This mission was continued without any known change till 1773, when it was abandoned. But when in 1779 (not 1778, as is commonly stated) Antonio Gil Ybarbo laid the foundations of modern Nacogdoches with his band of refugees from the Trinity River settlement of Bucareli, he found the Nacogdoches mission buildings still standing, settled his colony near them, and apparently reoccupied some of them.[3] Hence it is clear that the city of Nacogdoches represents very closely, perhaps exactly, the site of the main village of the Nacogdoche tribe at the opening of the eighteenth century. If more

[1] *Derrotero*, original in the Archivo General y Público, Mexico. The copy in *Mem. de Nueva España*, Vol. XXVII, is very corrupt. At this point a generous addition is made by the copist. See folio 158.
[2] Peña, Diario, *op. cit.*, XXVIII, 40, 43, 44.
[3] Antonio Gil Ybarbo to Croix, May 13, 1779, MS. See Bolton in THE QUARTERLY, IX, No. 2, for the story of the beginning of modern Nacogdoches.

evidence were necessary, the presence within the city of Nacogdoches till recent times of four ancient Indian mounds would
strengthen the conclusion.[1] With this as a starting point, it is
not difficult to indicate the approximate location of the most
prominent of the remaining tribes. Starting with the Nacogdoche
involves the disadvantage of reading the diaries backwards, it is
true, but has the great advantage of enabling us to proceed from
a well-established point.

The Hainai Tribe and the Mission of Concepción.

On the east bank of the Angelina River, a little north of a
direct west line from the Nacogdoche village, was that of the
Hainai.[2] This tribe, whose lands lay on both sides of the Angelina,[3] was the head of the Hasinai confederacy, and for that
reason was sometimes called Hasinai. It is to this tribe, also, that
the name Texas was usually applied when it was restricted to a
single one. Within its territory was the chief temple of the group,
presided over by the great Xinesi, or high priest.[4] At its main
village the mission of La Puríssima Concepción was founded in
1716.

After the Relación of Jesus María, our first sources of
specific information on the location of this village are the diaries.
Ramón tells us that he entered the "Pueblo de los Ainai" just
east of the Angelina River, and that nine leagues east-south-east
of this village he reached the "Pueblo de los Nacogdoches."[5] The

[1] Information furnished in 1907 by Dr. J. E. Mayfield, of Nacogdoches.
He writes: "Four similar mounds once existed at Nacogdoches, located
upon a beautiful site about three hundred yards northeast of the old
stone fort or stone house that has recently been removed from the main
city plaza. . . . These have been razed and almost obliterated. To
the east of them is a hole or excavation from which the earth may have
been taken for the construction of these mounds."

[2] I follow the spelling of Mooney, which has been adopted by the Bureau
of American Ethnology. The more common Spanish forms were Aynay
and Ainai. English writers frequently spell it Ioni.

[3] Espinosa, *Crónica Apostólica*, 425; Diario, 1716; MS. entry for July
12; Mezières, Carta, *Mem. de Nueva España*, XXVIII, 241.

[4] Jesus María, Relación; Espinosa, *Crónica Apostólica*, 423.

[5] Derrotero, entries for July 7 and 8. Original in the Archivo General
y Público, Mexico. The copy in *Memorias de Nueva España* (XXVII,
157-8) changes "Ainai" to "Asinay" and "Nacogdoches" to "Nacodoches."
It is such errors as the former, evidently, that gave rise to the idea that

missionary fathers who accompanied Ramón, in their Representation made at the same time reported the distance as eight leagues east-south-east. Peña (1721) says the distance was eight leagues east-north-east from the *presidio* founded near the mission, and nine from the mission. Rivera (1727) found the mission just east of the "Rio de los Aynays," or the Angelina, and nine leagues west of the Nacogdoches mission.[1] These witnesses tally in the main with each other and also, be it noted, with the testimony of the San Antonio Road, as its route is now identified in the old surveys. According to the best information obtainable it ran from Nacogdoches a little north of west to the Angelina, passing it about at Linwood Crossing.[2] Espinosa tells us that he founded the mission of Concepción a mile or two east of the place where the highway crossed the Angelina, near two springs, in the middle of the Hainai village. This site could not have been far from Linwood Crossing.[3]

This Hainai tribe, as has been stated, was evidently the one which Jesus María called the Cachaé or Cataye. He said that between the Nacachau and the Nacogdoche, about midway, was the lodge of the Great Xinesi, and—if we get his meaning here—that immediately northeast of this lodge was the Cachaé tribe. From other data we learn that the Xinesi's house was within or on the borders of the Hainai territory, about three leagues from the Concepción mission, and apparently west of the Angelina.[4] The Cachaé thus correspond, in location and relations, to the Hainai, while, moreover, the latter are the only tribe that appear in this locality after 1716. Considering with these facts the probability that Jesus María would hardly have left the head tribe unmentioned in so formal a description as is his, and the fact that

there was an Asinay tribe. Similarly, the *Memorias* copy of the Representación of the "Padres Misioneros" dated July 22, 1716 (Vol. XXVII, 163) states that the mission of Concepción was founded for the "Asinays," whereas the original of that document, as of Espinosa's diary, reads "Ainai." This error has been copied and popularized.

[1]Ramón, Derrotero, in *Memorias de Nueva España*, XXVII, 158; the "Padres Misioneros," Representación, Ibid., 163; Peña, Diario, *Ibid.*, XXVIII, 43-44; Rivera, Diario, leg. 2142.

[2]Maps of Cherokee and Nacogdoches counties (1879), by I. C. Walsh, Commissioner of the General Land Office of Texas, compiled from official data.

[3]Espinosa, Diario, entries for July 6 and 7; Ramón, Derrotero, op. cit.

[4]Espinosa, *Crónica Apostólica*, 424; Morfi, *Mem. Hist. Texas*, Bk. II, MS.

the Hainai is clearly the head tribe, it seems reasonably certain that the Cachaé and the Hainai were identical.

The Neche Tribe and the Mission of San Francisco (Second Site).

Southwest of the Hainai village, nearly straight west of the Nacogdoche, was the Neche village, near the east bank of the Neches River, and near the crossing of the Camino Real. The diaries usually represent the distance from the Neche to the Hainai as about the same as that from the Hainai to the Nacogdoche—some eight or nine leagues.[1] The air line distance was evidently somewhat less in the former case than in the latter, but the route was less direct, since between the Neches and the Angelina rivers the road bowed quite decidedly to the north. The usual crossing of this highway at the Neches, as now identified, was at Williams's Ferry, below the mouth of San Pedro Creek.[2] Archæological remains help us to identify this crossing and give certainty to the approximate correctness of our conclusions. These remains are the Indian mounds east of the Neches River. The first mention of them that I have seen is that by Mezières, in 1779. His record is important. Passing along the Camino Real on his way to the Nabedache, he noted the large mound near the Neches River, raised, he said, by the ancestors of the natives of the locality "in order to build on its top a temple, which overlooked the pueblo near by, and in which they worshiped their gods—a monument rather to their great numbers than to the industry of their individuals."[3] This mound and its two less conspicuous companions still stand in Cherokee County about a mile and a half from

[1]Espinosa tells us that the mission was near a spring and also near an arroyo that flowed from the northeast. He gave the distance from the mission from the camp near the Neches River as one league, and that to the mission of Concepción, east of the Angelina, eight leagues, going northeast by east, then east (Diario, entries for July 2 and 6). Ramón gave the distance to the mission of Concepción, from the camp near the Neches apparently, but possibly from the mission, as nine leagues east-northeast (Derrotero, in *Mem. de Nueva España*, XXVII, 157-158).

[2]See maps cited above, and also the Map of Houston County, copied from a map by Geo. Aldrich, by H. S. Upshur, Draughtsman in the General Land Office, 1841.

[3]Letter to Croix, August 16, 1779, MS., in the Archivo General y Público, Mexico. This letter was written at the "Village of Sn. Pedro de los Navedachos," just after Mezières passed the mounds. The *Memorias* copy of the letter gives the name of the place, erroneously, San Pedro Nevadachos" (Vol. XXVIII, 241).

the river and five miles southwest of Alto, in a plain known to some as Mound Prairie, undoubtedly the true Mound Prairie whose whereabouts has been debated. They are on land now the property of the Morrill Orchard Company, once a part of the original grant made to the romantic Pedro Ellis Bean. The Old San Antonio Road, as identified in the oldest surveys, ran about three hundred yards north of the largest, which is also the northernmost mound.[1] This mound, standing by the old highway, is an important western landmark for the location of the early tribes and missions, just as the site of Nacogdoches is an important eastern landmark. With the evidence of these mounds, the name San Pedro attached to the creek joining the Neches just above the crossing, and the early maps of the Camino Real, there is no doubt as to the approximate location of the old crossing, and, consequently, of the sites of the Neche and the Nabedache villages, with their respective missions, on opposite sides of the river.

The mission of San Francisco de los Texas, reëstablished in 1716 at the Neche village,[2] appears from the diaries to have been some one or two leagues—from two to four miles—from the crossing. Peña's diary puts it at two leagues. The entry in his diary for August 3, 1721, is as follows: "The bridge [over the Neches] having been completed, all the people, the equipage, and the drove, crossed in good order, taking the direction of east-northeast, and camp was made near the mission of San Francisco, where the *presidio* was placed the second time it was moved in 1716. The march was only two leagues."[3] Rivera gives the distance from the crossing as more than a league.[4] The other diaries are indefinite on this point, but the conclusion is plain that the mission and the

[1]Information furnished by Dr. J. E. Mayfield, of Nacogdoches. The original Austin map (1829) in the Secretaría de Fomento, Mexico, shows the mound on the north side of the road.

[2]On the authority of the corrupt copy of Ramón's itinerary in the *Memorias* (XXVII, 157) it has been stated that this mission was founded at the "Nacoches" village, a tribal name nowhere else encountered. The original of the itinerary, however, gives the name "Naiches," thus agreeing with the other original reports and clearing up a troublesome uncertainty. The official name of the mission was San Francisco de los Texas, but, because of its location at the Neche village, it came to be called, popularly, San Francisco de los Neches.

[3]Diary, in *Mem. de Nueva España*, XXVIII, 38. The *presidio* had been temporarily placed in 1716 on the west side of the Neches, near a small lake, and then moved across the river.

[4]Rivera, Diario, 1727, leg. 2140.

Neche village were close to the mounds, the mission, at least, being apparently farther from the river.

The Nabedache Tribe and the Mission of San Francisco (First Site).

The westernmost tribe of the group was the Nabedache. The main village was a short distance—perhaps six miles—west of the Neches River, above the crossing, near a stream that early became known as San Pedro, and at a site that took the name San Pedro de los Nabedachos. It is this name San Pedro, in part, that has caused some persons to think, groundlessly, that the first mission of San Francisco was founded at San Antonio.

The exact point at which the main Nabedache village stood I can not say, not having examined the locality in person, but certain data enable us to approximate its location pretty closely.

First is the testimony of the diaries and other early documents. De León reported in his itinerary (1690) that from the camp half a league from the Nabedache chief's house to the Neches River, going northeast, it was three leagues.[1] The site examined on the river at this point was deemed unsuitable for the mission "because it was so far out of the way of the Indians"; consequently the mission was established close to the camp "in the middle" of the village.[2] In their reports to the home government Massanet and De León seem to have stated that the mission was some two leagues from the Neches;[3] while Terán in 1691 reported it to be only a league and a half from the Mission of Santíssimo Nombre de María, which was evidently close to the Neches.[4] Jesus María and Espinosa said that the village was about three leagues from

[1]Entry for May 26. He recorded the distance going and coming as six leagues.

[2]De León, Derrotero, entry for May 27; Massanet, Letter, in THE QUARTERLY, II, 305.

[3]This is an inference from the instructions given in 1691 to Terán and Salinas, which required them to examine the large stream two leagues, more or less, from the village where the mission of San Francisco had been established the year before. (Ynstrucciones dadas, etc., January 23, 1691, in *Mem. de Nueva España*, XXVII, 19; Ynstrucción que han de observar el Capp. D. Gregorio Salinas, etc., April 13, 1691. Archivo General, Provincias Internas, Vol. 182. This document has not before been used.)

[4]See note 2, page 266.

this river, the former adding that it was right across the stream from the Neche tribe.[1] Joutel and Ramón called the distance from center to center of the two villages about five leagues.[2] In comparing these estimates with those that follow we must remember that it was somewhat further from the village to the crossing of the river than to the river at its nearest point, for as early as 1691 it was found that the best crossing was down stream a league or more.[3] Keeping these things in mind, it may be noted that Peña's diary makes the distance from San Pedro to the crossing four leagues. In his entry for July 27, 1721, he says, "The Father President F. Ysidro Felix de Espinosa went ahead with the chief of the texas, who wished to go to arrange beforehand the reception *in the place where the first mission had been."* In his entry for the next day he says, "Following the same direction of east-northeast, the journey was continued to the place of S. Pedro . . . *where the Presidio and Mission had been placed (for the Spaniards did not go beyond this point) in the year '90."* Here the reception was held, and presents were made to Aguayo by the Indians of the "ranchos which are near by," the point being, according to Peña's diary, fifteen leagues northeast from the crossing of the Trinity,[4] and four from the crossing of the Neches, passing by the site of the *presidio* as it was first established in 1716. Rivera's diary makes the distance from San Pedro to the crossing something over four leagues, or six to the mission on the other side. His record is interesting. He writes, on August 5, "I camped this day near a prairie which they call San Pedro de los Nabidachos, formerly occupied by Indians of the tribe of this name, but at present by the Neches tribe, of the group of the Aynays, head tribe of the Province of Texas." His next entry begins, "This day, the sixth, . . . continuing the march in the same direction [east-one-fourth-northeast] I traveled six leagues, crossing the Rio de los

[1]Relación, 2, 6.
[2]Relation, in Margry, *Découvertes,* III, 341-344; Ramón, Derrotero, *op. cit.*
[3]Terán, Descripción y Diaria Demarcación. *Mem. de Nueva España,* XXVII, 47, 61.
[4]Diario, in *Mem. de Nueva España,* XXVIII, 34-35. The Italics are mine. It may be noted that Peña and Rivera give quite commonly shorter leagues than the others.

Neches. At more than a league's distance from it I found some huts where a religious of the Cross of Querétaro resides, destined . . . to minister to these Indians . . . with the name of San Francisco de Nechas," that is, the mission having this name.[1] Solís, going northeast in 1767, tells us that San Pedro de los Nabedachos was beyond the San Pedro River. He may possibly have meant that it was on the north side, but I am inclined to think that he meant that it was east of one of the southern branches.[2]

Our inference from the diaries would thus be that the first site of the mission of San Francisco, in the village of the Nabedache, was from one and a half to three leagues—from three to six miles—distant from the Neches River at its nearest point, a league or more farther from the crossing, and still another league—in all some ten miles—from the Neches village on the other side of the river.

The information of the diaries is here supplemented by geographical names and the old surveys of the Camino Real or the San Antonio Road. San Pedro Creek, which joins the Neches River in the northern part of Houston County still bears the name that was early given to the vicinity of the Nabedache village and the first mission of San Francisco. This occurred as early as 1716 from the fact that Espinosa and Ramón celebrated the feast of San Pedro there. The celebration took place at a spot which, according to both Ramón and Espinosa was thirteen leagues northeast of the crossing of the Trinity.[3] That the name was continuously applied to the place until after the middle of the eighteenth century is sufficiently established by the citations already made. To show its continued use thereafter there is an abundance of evidence.[4]

---

[1]Rivera, Diario, leg. 2140. Ramón's Derrotero makes the distance four leagues from San Pedro to his camp near the Neches or to the mission site across the river, but it is not clear which, although the former is probably his meaning. (*Mem. de Nueva España*, XXVII, 155-157.) Ramón's Representación makes the distance between the first mission of San Francisco, and the second of this name, at the Neche village, five leagues. *Ibid.*, 159.

[2]Diario, in *Mem. de Nueva España*, XXVIII, 279.

[3]Ramón, Representación, in *Mem. de Nueva España*, XXVII, 159. Ramón and Espinosa, Diaries, entries for June 29-30.

[4]See Ramon, Derrotero, and Espinosa, Diario (1716), entries for June 29-30; Peña, Diario (1721), in *Mem. de. Nueva España*, XXVIII, 34; Rivera, Diario (1727), leg. 2140; Ereción de San Xavier, 5 (1746); De Soto Vermudez, Investigation (1752); Solís, Diario, in *Mem. de Nueva*

Next comes the testimony of the Camino Real, or the Old San Antonio Road. There seems to be no good topographical reason why this old highway should not have run directly from Crockett to the Neches at Williams's Ferry, and the long curve to the north between these points must be explained as a detour to the Nabedache village and the missions located nearby. The surveys represent this highway as running always south of San Pedro Creek, never crossing it, but definitely directed toward it at a point some six or eight miles west of the Neches crossing.[1] The point corresponds closely to that designated in the diaries. Near here, quite certainly, were the Nabedache village and the first mission of San Francisco, while not far away, but nearer the Neches, was the second mission established in that region, that of El Santíssimo Nombre de María, founded about October, 1690.[2]

The Nacachau, Nechaui, and Nacono Tribes.

Across the Neches from the Nabedache, only a few leagues away, and adjoining the Neche tribe on the north, was the relatively little known tribe called by Jesus María the Nacachau, and by Hidalgo the Nacachao. We have seen that Jesus María described the Neche tribe as being separated from the Nabedache only by the Neches River. Later he says, "Toward the north, where the above-mentioned Necha tribe ends, is that called the Nacachau." The Neche and Nacachau villages were thus close together. Near them the second mission of San Francisco was founded in 1716. Ramón says that the mission was founded in the village of the Naiches,

España, XXVII, 279; Mezières, Cartas (1778-1779), in *Mem. de Nueva España,* XXVIII, 270; Cordoba to Muñoz, December 8, 1793. Béxar Archives, Nacogdoches, 1758-1793. It may be noted that while the post-office village of San Pedro preserves the name of the general locality, it is too far west to answer to the site of the mission of San Francisco and the Nabedache village.

[1] See Upshur's map, cited above.

[2] This mission was close to or on the bank of the Neches River. According to Terán's itinerary (1691) it was a league up stream from the crossing and a league and a half northeast of the mission of San Francisco (Descripción, in *Mem. de Nueva España,* 45, 47, 61; Jesus María said that it was on the bank of the river (Relación, 104).

and the "Padres Missioneros" say that it was for the "Naicha, Nabeitdâche, Nocono, and Nacâchao."[1]

Southeast of the Neche and the Nabedache villages, according to Jesus María, were two villages half a league apart, called the Nechaui and the Nacono. Of the Nechaui we do not hear again, but from Peña (1721) we learn that the Nacono village, which he called El Macono, was five leagues below the Neches crossing. This would put the Nechaui and the Nacono villages five leagues down the Neches River, perhaps one on each side.[2]

The Nasoni Tribe and the Mission of San José.

Above the Hainai, on the waters of the Angelina, were the Nasoni. Joutel, in 1687, reached their village after going from the Nabedache twelve leagues eastward, plus an unestimated distance north. Terán, in 1691, found it twelve leagues northeast of the Neche crossing below the Nabedache village.[3] The founding, in 1716, of a mission for this tribe and the Nadaco gives us more definite data for its location. The missionaries who took part in the expedition, in their joint report, called the distance from the Hainai to the Nacogdoche eight leagues east-southeast, and that from the Hainai to the Nasoni mission seven northeast. Peña, who called the former distance nine leagues east-northeast, esti-

---

[1]Jesus María, Relación, 1691, 107-108; Ramón, Derrotero (1716), in *Mem. de Nueva España*, XXVII, 158; Padres Missioneros, Representación (1716), *Ibid.*, 163; Peña, Diario (1721), *Ibid.*, XXVIII, 38-41; Rivera, Diario (1727), leg., 2140; Bonilla, *Breve Compendio*, 1772, in THE QUARTERLY, VIII, 35, 38. As I have indicated above, the *Memorias* copy of Ramón's itinerary states that the mission was founded in the village of the "Nacoches," a miscopy for "Naiches." The map on page 256 was made before I discovered this error in the copy, which I had first used. My opinion now is that, with this correction, the sources would not be violated by placing the Nacachau tribe somewhat farther north than I have there represented it.

[2]Jesus María, Relación, 108; Peña, Diario, *op. cit.*, 36. As the Nacono visited Aguayo on the west side of the Neches, I have represented the village on that side in my map. Of course, the reason is a very slight one.

Espinosa in his diary says that the Nasoni mission was founded for the Nacono, but this seems to be a form of Nasoni, for by others it is uniformly called the mission of the Nasoni or of the Nadaco, or of both. See, Hidalgo, letter to Mesquia, October 6, 1716, in the Archivo General.

[3]Joutel, Relation, in Margry, *Découvertes* III, 337-340; Terán, Descripción, in *Mem. de Nueva España*, XXVII, 47-48.

mated this as eight north. Espinosa put it at seven northeast.[1]
Thirty years later Espinosa said that the mission was founded in
the Nasoni tribe and ten leagues from mission Concepción.[2] This
increase in his estimate of the distance may be due to lapse of time
and his long absence from the country.

The direction of the Nasoni mission from that of Concepción
was, therefore, evidently northeast, and the distance about the
same, perhaps a trifle less, than that to the Nacogdoche village.

Espinosa, who in 1716 went over the route from the Hainai
to the Nasoni to establish the mission of San José recorded in
his diary that on the way there were many Indian houses
(*ranchos*), and that the mission was situated "on an arroyo with
plentiful water running north." We must look, therefore, for a
point some fifteen or more miles northeast of the Hainai on a
stream running northward. These conditions would be satisfied only by one of the southern tributaries of Shawnee Creek,
near the north line of Nacogdoches County. In this vicinity,
clearly, was the Nasoni settlement in 1716. It seems not to have
changed its location essentially since it had been visited by Joutel
and Terán, a quarter of a century before, and it remained in the
same vicinity another third of a century, for in 1752 De Soto
Vermudez found the Nasoni village eleven leagues northward
from the Nacogdoches mission.[3] The mission of San José remained
near the Nasoni until 1729, when, like those of San Francisco, at
the Neche village, and Concepción, at the Hainai village, it was
removed to San Antonio.

The Nadaco.

For the rest of the tribes in this group our information is less
definite. The Nadaco, though a prominent tribe, can not be located
with certainty until 1787, when they, or at least a part of them,
were on the Sabine River, apparently in the northern part of
Panola County.[4] But in 1716 they were clearly near the Nasoni,

[1]Padres Missioneros, Representación, 1716, in *Mem. de Nueva España*,
XXVII, 163; Peña, Diario, 1721, *Ibid.*, XXVIII, 44; Espinosa, Diario,
1716, entry for July 10.
[2]*Crónica Apostólica*, 418.
[3]Investigation, 1752, MS.
[4]Francisco Xavier Fragoso, Diary, in the General Land Office, Austin,
Texas, Records, Vol. 68, p. 174.

and sometimes the two tribes seem to have been considered as one. Hidalgo, who must have known, for he was on the ground, distinctly states that the mission of San José was founded for the Nasoni and the Nadaco.[1] Although the mission was commonly known to the Spaniards as that of the Nasoni, the French writers, in particular, including San Denis, sometimes called it the Nadaco[2] mission. Frequent references made by La Harpe in 1719 to the Nadaco show that he is either speaking of the Nasoni or of a tribe in their immediate vicinity, more probably the latter, since in other instances the tribes are so clearly distinguished. For instance, he tells us that when at the Kadohadacho village on the Red River, not far from Texarkana, "they assured me that sixty leagues south was the village of the Nadacos, where the Spaniards had a mission, and that they had another among the Assinais, in the Amediche [Nabedache] tribe, which was seventy leagues south-one-fourth-southwest from the Nassonites [which were near the Kadohadacho]."[3] In 1752 the Nadaco were only a short distance

[1]Letter to Mesquia, October 6, 1716, in the Archivo General de Mexico, MS. The *Memorias* copy of Ramón's itinerary (XXVII, 158) calls this mission that of the "Noachis," but the original reads plainly "Nasonis."

[2]Thus, La Harpe noted in his journal that San Denis, who conducted the expedition of 1716 that founded the missions "proposed, sometime after his arrival, that he should be the conductor of nine missionaries to the tribes of the Adayes, Ayches, Nacocodochy, Inay and Nadaco" (Extrait du Journal manuscrit du voyage de la Louisiane par le sieur de La Harpe et de ses découvertes dans la partie de l'Ouest de cette colonie, in Margry, *Découvertes*, VI, 194). San Denis himself regarded the mission as having been founded in the Nadaco tribe. This is the inference from a correspondence carried on in 1735-1736 between him and Sandoval, governor of Texas. Sandoval wrote to San Denis on March 10, 1736, acknowledging a letter of December 2, 1735, in which San Denis outlined the basis of French claims to country west of the Red River. Judging from Sandoval's summary of the letter (I have not seen the letter) he alleged that, with Bienville, he had explored the country as far back as 1702; that in 1715 he had journeyed from the "Asinais" to Mexico, seeing on the way only vestiges of the old Spanish settlements; that he conducted Ramón into the country, "the result of which was the foundation [of missions], which it was requested of your lordship should be established among the Nacogdoches, Nadaco, Ainais, and Naicha, and the subsequent ones among the Ays and Adais, maintaining the ministers of the Gospel at your expense." (Triplicate of Sandoval's letter, in the Archivo General, Sección de Historia, Vol. 524, formerly in Indiferente de Guerra. With this letter there are several original letters of San Denis.

[3]La Harpe, Relation du Voyage, in Margry, *op. cit.*, VI 262. See also *Ibid.*, 266.

northward from the Nasoni, apparently northeast, and the two tribes then had a single chief.[1]

Supposing the Nadaco and the Nasoni to have lived in clearly distinct settlements at the early period, the Nadaco could hardly have been near the highway from the Nasoni to the Kadohadacho, for, as we have seen, the Nasoni always figure as the last station on the way to the Kadohadacho. It seems more probable, considering this last fact with the statements made about the mission of San José, that the two tribes lived in a settlement practically continuous, to which sometimes one and sometimes the other name was given. An upper branch of the Angelina is now called Anadarko (Nadaco) Creek, and it is possible, in spite of the above considerations, that this stream was the home of the Nadaco at the coming of the Spaniards and the French, but it seems more probable that it was applied in later times as a result of the removal of the tribe to that neighborhood.

It is clear, at any rate, that in the early eighteenth century the Nadaco village was very near that of the Nasoni.

Other Tribes.

Of the location of remaining tribes we know even less than of the last, and can only record the few statements made of them by the early writers. Three leagues west of the Nasoni Joutel entered the village of the Noadiche (Nahordike)[2] who, he said, were allies of the Cenis, and had the same customs. This location corresponds with that assigned by Jesus María to the Nabiti, and the tribes may have been identical. The site designated was apparently west of the Angelina River and near the southwestern corner of Rusk County. Similarly, the Nasayaya, put by Jesus María east of the Nabiti, may possibly have been the Nasoni. If they were a separate tribe they must have been in the same neighborhood. If separate, too, they early disappear from notice, unless possibly they may be the Nacaxe, who later are found in the same latitude, but farther east. All that we can say of the location of the Nacao is that they were northward from the Nacogdoche, and probably closer

---

[1]This is on the well-founded assumption that the Nadote discussed by De Soto Vermudez were the same as the Nadaco (De Soto Vermudez, Investigation, MS.).

[2]Relation, in Margry, *op. cit.*, III 388.

to the Nacogdoche than to the Nasoni, since they were attached to the Nacogdoche mission. A reasonable conjecture is that they were in the neighborhood of Nacaniche Creek, in Nacogdoches County.[1]

Thus, with varying degrees of precision and confidence, we are able from a study of the documents to indicate the early homes of the tribes usually included in the Hasinai group. Five of the sites, at least, are reasonably well established, and these are historically the most important, for they were the sites of Spanish establishments, while the others were not. I refer, of course, to the villages of the Nabedache, Neche, Hainai, Nacogdoche, and Nasoni. A careful examination of the topography of the country and of the archaeological remains would doubtless enable one to verify some and to modify others of the conclusions here set forth.

GENERAL CHARACTER OF THE SETTLEMENTS.

It will be helpful, as a means of conveying an idea of the true nature of the work attempted by the early Spaniards, to present a brief sketch of the general character of these Indian settlements and of their numerical strength.

They were a people living in relatively fixed habitations, and would be classed as sedentary Indians, in contrast with roving tribes, such as the neighboring Tonkawa west of the Trinity. They subsisted to a considerable extent by agriculture, and lived, accordingly, in loosely built agricultural villages, for miles around which were detached houses, located wherever there was a spot favored by water supply and natural or easily made clearings. Their dwellings were large conical grass lodges, which accommodated several families. In all of the tribes concerning which we have relatively full data there seems to have been a main village, which the surrounding communal families regarded as their tribal headquarters. It is these central villages that I have represented on the map.

The arrangement of the settlements may be most safely learned from the accounts of some of the early eye-witnesses. Joutel tells

---

[1] Jesus María puts the Nacogdoche tribe east and the Nacau tribe northeast of his mission. He says in another passage that the Nacao constituted a province distinct from the Aseney and thirty leagues from the Nabedache.

us, in 1687, that from the edge of the Nabedache village, west of the Neches River, to the chief's house in the middle of the settlement, it was a "large league," and that on the way there were "hamlets" of from seven to fifteen houses each, surrounded by patches of corn. From this village to that of the Neche tribe on the other side of the river it was some five leagues, but in fertile spots between them there were similar "hamlets," sometimes a league apart. So it was with the country to the northeast. When he left the Neches River at a point above the Neche village he wrote, "We pursued our route toward the east, and made about five leagues, finding from time to time cabins in 'hamlets' and 'cantons,' for we sometimes made a league and a half without finding one."[1] Between the Trinity River and the main Nabedache village De León, in 1690, encountered only one settlement. It consisted of "four farms (*haciendas*) of Indians who had planted crops of maize and beans, and very substantially built houses, with high beds to sleep on."[2] On the edge of the Nabedache village he "arrived at a valley occupied by many houses of Texas Indians, around which were large fields of maize, beans, calabashes, and watermelons. . . . Turning to the north by a hill of oaks, about a quarter of a league further on we came to another valley of Texas Indians, with their houses, their governor telling us that his was very near. We pitched our camp on the bank of an arroyo, and named this settlement San Francisco de los Texas."[3] The "governor's" house was about half a league from the camp.

Of the country beyond the Neches Terán wrote in 1691, "We continue our march [from the Neches]. . . . The country is very rough with frequent open groves, but no openings larger than a short musket shot across. In these openings, some in the lowlands, and some in the sand, their houses are located."[4] Joutel, in describing his passage from the lodge of one Nasoni chief to that of another, says, "Those who had escorted us went ahead and conducted us to his house, about a quarter of a league away, where his cabin was located. Before reaching it we passed several others, and on the way found women and children cultivating their

[1]Relation, in Margry, *op. cit.*, 341, 344, 387.
[2]Derrotero, MS., entry for May 20.
[3]*Ibid.*, entry for May 22.
[4]Descripción y Diaria Demarcación, *op. cit.*, 48.

fields." In 1716 Ramón referred to the Hainai settlement on the Angelina River as the "pueblo of the Ainai, where there is an infinite number of houses (*ranchos*) with their fields of corn, watermelons, melons, beans, tobacco," etc. As we have already seen, in his passage from the Hainai to the Nasoni in 1716 Espinosa noted many houses on the way.[1]

After several years' residence among these tribes, Espinosa, having in mind the dismal failure to reduce them to civilized life, described the Hasinai settlements in general thus: "These natives do not live in congregations reduced to pueblos, but each of the four principal groups where the missions are located are in *ranchos* [separate houses], as it were, apart from each other. The chief cause of this is that each household seeks a place suitable for its crops and having a supply of water."[2] In another place he tells us that in their ministerial work among the Indians the *padres* had to travel six or seven leagues in all directions from each of the four missions.[3]

It is thus evident that the Hasinai settlements by no means corresponded to the Spanish notion of a pueblo, built in close order. To induce the natives to congregate in such pueblos, as a means of civilizing them, was a chief aim of the government and the missionaries, and failure to accomplish this was a primary cause of the abandonment, after fifteen years of effort, of all but one of the missions of the group.

NUMBERS.

It is easy to gain an exaggerated notion of the numerical strength of the native tribes. Popular imagination, stimulated by the hyperbole of writers for popular consumption, has peopled the primitive woods and prairies with myriads of savages. Students, however, have shown that this is an error, and that the Indian population has always been, in historical times, relatively sparse. In their efforts to counteract these exaggerated notions, they, indeed, have leaned too far in the opposite direction.

[1]Joutel, in Margry, *op. cit.*, III 392; Ramón, Derrotero, in the Archivo General y Público, Mexico, entry for July 7; Espinsoa, Diario, entry for July 10.
[2]*Crónica Apostólica*, 440 (1746).
[3]*Ibid.*

The Hasinai, apparently one of the most compact native populations within an equal area between the Red River and the Rio Grande, numbered only a few thousands at the coming of the Europeans. What I have already said about the nature of their villages has, perhaps, prepared the reader to believe this assertion. While our statistical information on this point does not constitute entirely conclusive evidence, it does, nevertheless, give us a basis for plausible conjecture.

The earliest estimate that might be called general is that contained in a *mémoire* of 1699, printed by Margry, and based apparently upon the report of one of the survivors of the La Salle expedition. The *mémoire* states that from "Bay Saint-Louis [Matagorda Bay] going inland to the north-northwest and the northeast there are a number of different tribes. The most numerous is the Cenys and Asenys, which, according to the opinion of a Canadian who has lived several years among them, form but one village and the same nation. He estimates that they do not exceed six hundred or seven hundred men. The Quélancouchis [Karankawa], who live on the shores of the sea about Bay Saint-Louis, are four hundred men."[1]

It would seem that in this passage the term "Cenys et Asenys" corresponds closely with the term Hasinai as I have used it, unless, as is probable, the Nasoni are excluded; but, since this is not certain, the estimate, though based on long experience, would not be conclusive without corroborating testimony. This we get in 1716. Ramón tells us that the four missions founded by his expeditions, which were within easy reach of all the tribes described, "would comprise from four thousand to five thousand persons of all ages and both sexes."[2] In the same year Espinosa recorded in his diary his opinion that the Indians grouped around the three Querétaran missions, not including the mission among the Nacogdoche and the Nacao, would number three thousand; and after a residence there of some years he estimated the number of persons within range of each mission at about one thousand.[3] This estimate must have

[1]Mémoire de la Coste de la Floride et d'une partie du Mexique, in Margry, *op. cit.*, IV 316.
[2]Derrotero, in *Mem. de Nueva España*, XXVII, 160.
[3]*Crónica Apostólica*, 439.

had a good foundation, for we are told that the *padres* kept lists of all the houses and of the persons in each.[1]

Assuming that the *mémoire,* Ramón, and Espinosa include the same tribes in their estimates, it will be seen that the first is somewhat the more conservative. This fact strengthens the probability that, like other early reports, the *mémoire* did not include the Nasoni in the Hasinai.

So much for general estimates for the whole group. Detailed information concerning some of the individual tribes appears in 1721. When Aguayo in that year re-established the missions that had been abandoned some two years before, he made a general distribution of presents and clothing among the Indians at the different villages. At the mission of San Francisco de los Neches he gave the Neche chief the Spanish *baston,* token of authority, and "clothed entirely one hundred and eighty-eight men, women, and children." Never before had they received "such a general distribution." West of the Neches Aguayo had been visited by a hundred Nacono from down the river. At the mission of Concepción he requested the Hainai chief, Cheocas by name, to collect all his people. This took some time, as they were widely scattered, but several days later they were assembled, and Aguayo gave clothing and other presents to four hundred, including, possibly, eighty Kadohadachos, who happened to be there on a visit. Similarly, at the Nacogdoche mission he provided clothing "for the chief and all the rest," a total of three hundred and ninety; and at the Nasoni mission for three hundred.[2] This gives us a total of less than fourteen hundred Indians who came to the missions during Aguayo's *entrada* to take advantage of the ever welcome presents. This number apparently included the majority of the five most important tribes, and probably included some from the neighboring smaller tribes attached to the missions.

The conclusion is that the estimates of Ramón and Espinosa, which put the total number of inhabitants included in 1716 in the ten or more tribes about the four missions at four or five thousand are sufficiently liberal. If this conclusion is true, the tribes could not have averaged more than three or four hundred persons each.

[1] *Crónica Apostólica,* 439.
[2] Peña, Diario, in *Mem. de Nueva España,* XXVIII, 36, 39, 41, 43, 44.

The territory then occupied by perhaps four thousand Indians now supports one hundred thousand people.[1] Kept down by epidemics, crude means of getting food, and to some extent by war, the number of these natives was small. But few then, they are incomparably fewer today, for the descendants of all these tribes, now living on the reservations, do not exceed two hundred or three hundred souls.[2]

[1]The surviving Caddo and Hasinai together numbered 551 persons in 1906 (Data given by Dr. Mooney in a communication of April 23, 1908).
[2]Estimate based on the United States Census for 1900.

TRADITIONS OF THE CADDO

COLLECTED UNDER THE AUSPICES OF THE
CARNEGIE INSTITUTION OF WASHINGTON

BY

GEORGE A. DORSEY
CURATOR OF ANTHROPOLOGY, FIELD COLUMBIAN MUSEUM

WASHINGTON, D. C.:
Published by the Carnegie Institution of Washington
1905

CARNEGIE INSTITUTION OF WASHINGTON

PUBLICATION No. 41

WASHINGTON, D. C.
PRESS OF JUDD & DETWEILER (INC.)
1905

CONTENTS.

INTRODUCTION.

THE Caddo tales here presented were collected during the years
1903–1905, under the auspices of the Carnegie Institution of
Washington, and form part of a systematic investigation of the religious system and ceremonial organization of the tribes of the Caddoan
stock.

The Caddo, numbering 530 in 1903, are of Caddoan stock, and since
1859 have lived in western Oklahoma between the Washita and Canadian rivers, where they have been closely associated with the Wichita.
They retain practically nothing of their ancient culture. Their early
home was in Louisiana, on the lower Red River. Later they migrated
toward the Texas border, and still later to Brazos River in Texas. They
met the whites as early as 1540, and throughout their history have
maintained a friendly attitude toward the whites. Like the Wichita,
their early habitations were conical grass lodges, and they were agri-
culturists, hunting the buffalo only within comparatively recent times.

The comparison of the Caddo tales with those of other tribes is deferred until the completion of the present investigation.

GEORGE A. DORSEY.

Chicago, July 31, 1905.

5

TRADITIONS OF THE CADDO.

1. THE CREATION AND EARLY MIGRATIONS.*

In the beginning the sun, stars, moon, and earth did not exist as they are now. Darkness ruled. With the lapse of time came a man, the only living being. Soon after his arrival a village sprang into existence with many thousands of people, and the people noticed that the man seemed to be everywhere. For a time he disappeared, and when he came back he had all kinds of seeds. He called all the people together and told them that the seeds were for them to eat, and gave them to every one. He told them that soon Darkness would go, and the people would see, for Darkness had promised that they should have a man by the name of Sun, and that he should be given power by the Great-Father-Above; that whenever his time should come to give them to the Sun he should be called or taken away from his mother, from our great mother Earth below; that the direction where the Sun should come from should be called "east," and the way of its going down should be called "west." He also announced to the people that he was the first being created and that he had been given power by the same Great-Father-Above, and that he had to carry out his work. He then told the people that it was very necessary that they should have one man abler and wiser than any other man among them, to be their head man; that they should call him "chief;" that whatever the chief should command should be done by the people; that they should look upon him as a great father. The unknown man told the people to return to their homes, hold a council among themselves, and select a chief.

When they had returned and assembled there was in the council a man by the name of Coyote, who told the people that the unknown powerful man should be called Moon, because he was the first man created on earth. The people decided that the Moon should be their head man or chief. Finally the Moon called the people together again and asked them if they had selected their head man or chief. Coyote told him that they had decided that he should be their head man, and that they had named him "Moon." After Moon came to be chief he selected another man, whom he called the Errand-Man, to be his helper,

---

*Told by White-Bread.

7

and to go around among the people to call them together whenever he might want them.

One time the errand-man was sent out to tell the people that the chief wanted them to assemble ; that he had very important news to tell them, and that they should come as quickly as they could.   When they had come together the chief told them that they would all have to move away from the world that they were living in to another and better world ; that he was going to lead them through, for he knew the way.   The village which they were going to leave was called Old-Home-in-the-Darkness.   Before the people were ready to leave, the chief sent the errand-man around among them to tell them that they were to be divided into groups, because there were so many of them ; that each group must have a leader, and he would give each leader a drum.   The people began to form in groups and select their leaders. After the groups were all formed and each selected their leader, the chief called all the leaders together and gave each a drum, and then they were ready to start.   The chief told all the leaders that they must sing and beat their drums as they were moving along ; that none of them should ever look back the way they came, lest the people should be stopped and have to stay where they were—in darkness.

The people began moving westward, and they came out of the ground to another world.   While they were yet coming out Coyote happened to be out.   He began to look around, then told the chief that the world was too small for the people ; then he turned around and looked back in the direction from which they had come.   The people had not all come out, and so half of them went back, but the others kept on going westward.   Finally the chief picked up some dirt and threw it in front of him and formed very high mountains.   When the people came to the mountains they stopped and began to make their first homes and villages.   Moon went to the top of the mountain and looked about and found that the people had not all come the way he had come, but had scattered and gone in different directions.   At the time when the people were all together they spoke but one language, the Caddo ; but after they had scattered out in groups each group spoke a different language. For this reason the many tribes of the present time speak different languages.   When Moon came to his people, the few he had left, he told them the name of the place in the ground from which they had come. He told them that the direction to their right-hand side should be called north, or cold side, and the direction to their left-hand side should be called south, or warm side.   While Moon was talking the Sun came up out of the east, passed them, and went down in the west.   He went too fast to do them any good at all.   Coyote announced that he was going to stop the Sun from going so fast. He started eastward early in the morning, and when he came to a good place to stop he waited for the Sun to come up. When the Sun came up he found Coyote waiting for him. Coyote told the Sun that he had come there for the purpose of seeing him ; that he wanted to talk with him, for he was in trouble. The Sun said that he had not very much time to stop and talk. Coyote told the Sun that he would go with him and talk to him as they went along. They started on, walking very slowly. Coyote kept telling about things that had lately happened. When the Sun was nearing the west Coyote told him that he was going to defecate, and asked him to wait a while. He started out behind the bushes, and just as soon as he was behind them, where the Sun could not see him, he ran away from the Sun and the Sun stood there waiting for him to return. After a while the Sun grew tired of waiting and started on very slowly, looking back every little while and watching for Coyote to catch up with him, but Coyote did not appear. The Sun went down very slowly, still waiting for Coyote. This is the reason that the Sun lingers and goes down very slowly.

The people's first village in this new world was called Tall-Timber-on-Top-of-the-Hill, for the place was in black-jack timber near the top of a high hill. There was the beginning of the real people. Moon called the people together for the first time in the new world and said : " Soon there will be a child born of a certain woman. He is on the way. He shall have more power than any one else, for Great-Father-Above has sent him down to his mother, the earth, to be among the people and teach them right and wrong. When the child comes he shall name himself after the former chief, Medicine-Screech-Owl, and he shall have with him bow and arrows.''

When the child came he had with him the bow and arrows. When his birthday came his father and mother were talking about what name should be given him ; but before his mother or father could give him a name the young child spoke and named himself, saying, "My name shall be Medicine-Screech-Owl.'' He said to the people : "The bow and arrows are for the men only, to be used in killing game. The time is coming when we shall have to use these things, especially the bow and arrows.'' Later on the people began to learn that this child was going to be a powerful man. He went around among the people and taught them how to make bows and arrows. In those times the animals talked to human beings and the human beings could talk to the animals, and they understood one another. Time passed and some of the human beings began to turn into animals. Medicine-Screech-Owl knew that some of these people were not real human beings. He knew that if

2D

some of the people should turn into animals it would be very bad, as
the people would be destroyed by them, and as he knew just what animals
were the most ferocious he went and made them a visit in behalf of the
people.   Some of the animals were opposed to Medicine-Screech-Owl
and hated him, and when he came to certain ones they would try to kill
him, and that is how he came to kill some of them.

In those times the people had little to eat.   There were two people,
a man and a woman, known to the people as the Buzzards, who lived
at the north end of the village, and the people noticed that they always had plenty of meat and other things to eat, and they wondered
how they got it.   Time passed until finally Coyote came among the
people and told them that he was going over to visit the two people
and find out where and how they got so much meat and so many other
things to eat.   In those times the animals that were living with the
people had some magic powers, and Coyote had power.   He said:
"In order to find out where and how the Buzzard people get their
food, I must scheme."   After studying he resolved that he would imi-
tate a dog, and so before he came to the Buzzard home he turned himself into a very small and fine-looking dog.   He stayed away from the
Buzzards and watched his opportunity to place himself where they
would find him.   One time the Buzzards had gone out some distance
from their home for some purpose and were returning, when they
found the little dog by the trail.   The woman liked the dog, but the
man said that it was not a real dog, but some one else.   The woman
did not believe him.   The man allowed her to take the dog home with
them.   When they reached home he told her that they must find out
whether this was a real dog or not.   He told her to pinch the dog's
ear and see if it would howl like a real dog.   The woman pinched the
dog's ear and it howled like a dog.   Still the man did not believe that
it was a dog.   He told the woman to go and get some meat and give it
to the dog, saying that if a dog it would take its time, but if it were
not a dog it would eat fast ; that then he would know whether or not
to believe it was a dog.   The woman gave some meat to the dog.
Coyote took his time in eating it, and so Buzzard believed what the
woman had said, and they kept the dog.   Coyote stayed with them
until their meat gave out, then he watched them very closely.   Finally
the Buzzards began to talk about going after more meat.   Coyote listened.   At length they started out and left their dog at home.   They
thought the dog would stay at home until they returned.   But Coyote
had a scheme, so he followed at some distance, so that they could not
see him, and he watched them very closely.   When they came to the
place where they usually found their meat, Coyote found out all about

how and where they got it, then ran back to their home and lay down, so that when the Buzzards returned to their home they found their little dog lying there fast asleep. Coyote stayed with them two days longer, and the third day he made up his mind that he must carry out his work. Early one morning he started out straight to the place where he had seen the Buzzards at work. It was a large cave or hole in the ground. The door of the place was a large rock. When he came to the place he opened it and out came thousands and thousands of buffalo. They came out so fast that before long they had spread over the western prairies before the Buzzards knew it. It was quite a time before Buzzard discovered what had happened. First he heard a strange noise like thunder. He went and looked for the little dog, but in vain, for the dog had already gone. He heard Coyote howling in the distance. Buzzard went out and found that nearly all the buffalo had escaped.

When Coyote went to his home he told the people to hurry and make some bows and arrows, for the buffalo were coming. He told them just what had happened and how he had schemed.

Buzzard was very angry at his wife and scolded her. He told her that she ought to know by this time that they were not the only ones that had powers, and that henceforth the only way that they could make a living was to go around and look for dead meat. In order to do this they turned into birds and became real buzzards. They flew around and looked for dead things to eat.

From that time on the people began to make bows and arrows, which were given to mankind for their use in killing game. Time passed on and the people noticed that their chief, Moon, paid no attention to them and seemed to have nothing to say. He did not call them together any more, but stayed at his home all the time. The people began to think there must be something wrong, and so there was, for Moon himself was doing very wrong things. He knew that he was setting his people a bad example, and he believed the people had already found out something about him. Medicine-Screech-Owl knew all about this, for he had more powers than Moon himself. Moon was living with his family near the center of the village ; he was the chief, unmarried, and lived with his father and mother and one very young sister. Here was the beginning of his mistakes. Unknown to his father and mother, for a long time he kept going by night to see his own sister, not letting her know that he was her own brother. He abused her and treated her very meanly sometimes. For a long time she did not know who he could be, for she had no one to tell her. It finally occurred to her that it might be her brother. One night she made up her mind to find out who he was. She put some black paint on her fingers, and that night when the man came she passed her painted fingers across his forehead and made black marks, which the man knew nothing about until the next morning. In the morning, when he came in, she saw the marks on his forehead, and she knew that he was the man who had abused her. When he learned that the people were finding out about him he became so ashamed of himself that he wished to leave his people. He remembered that when he came into the world the Great-Father-Above had promised him that some day he should call him away from his people ; that he should be placed where the people could see him at night, and that he should be with the people all the time. He knew that the time was now approaching when he should be called away from his people, and soon he was called away from them. Great-Father-Above took him away and placed him far above, where the people could see him and the shame-marks on his forehead.

Medicine-Screech-Owl grew to be a man, and after Moon was gone the people gathered again to select another chief, and they selected the powerful Medicine-Screech-Owl. His first announcement to the people was that they must move on farther west. The people began moving westward, climbing the mountains. When they had got on top of them they saw a large lake, and they wondered where the water came from. Medicine-Screech-Owl called the people's attention to it, and they all came and gathered along the banks of the lake. He then spoke to the people, saying : '' These waters which are before you are the tears of your great chief, Moon, for before he was taken up into the heavens he came up to this mountain and shed tears for the wrongs he had done to his people. So we shall call this mountain Moon's-Tears-on-the-Mountain.'' The people kept on moving westward until they found a place where they wanted to locate their second village. They commenced making bows and arrows, which they used in killing game. They began to go out a long distance from their village to hunt buffalo and other animals. There were several kinds of dangerous animals in the country, and at one place near by the people dared not go, because there in the water was the most ferocious animal that ever lived. Medicine-Screech-Owl told the people that he had some power and that he was going to try to kill the animal. One day when he was alone he decided to go and destroy the animal. He went out, and when he came near the place where the animal was he stopped for a short time at the edge of the timber, for he could not locate the animal exactly. The name of the animal was Cannibal. The lake was large and all around were swamps and thickets. By the aid of his power and with a certain motion, Medicine-Screech-Owl made a narrow place

like a road through the thicket, through which he could see the animal. He had brought with him from his village his bow, but no
arrows, and some corn, which he was to use in killing the animal.
When he made the opening in the thicket he took out two tall canes
from the ground, with the roots and the dirt that was on them, to be
used as arrows. The corn that he had with him he threw in the air,
and it became blackbirds, which flew straight over the head of the animal. When the animal arose to draw the blackbirds down to him
Medicine-Screech-Owl shot it with the cane arrows, first from the right
side through the heart and out the left, then from the left side through
the heart and out to the right. The animal fell near the edge of the
water and died. Medicine-Screech-Owl went over to see the place
where the animal was. He saw all kinds of bones lying around the
place. Not long after this the lake dried up. When the people learned
what had happened and what their chief had done, they were no longer
afraid of the place.

Now Coyote became a very bad man. The people noticed that
he had done to them several things that he had no right to do. He
would go from place to place, sometimes very early in the morning and
sometimes very late in the evening. He made all kinds of trouble
among the people. Whenever he did anything that was wrong he
would blame some one else, and in some way he would escape the
consequences. Finally Medicine-Screech-Owl sent for Coyote and
told him that he must leave the people and go on his way ; but Coyote,
being a great schemer, told the chief that he was going to stop doing
mean tricks among his people, and that he was not yet ready to leave.
Medicine-Screech-Owl allowed him to stay with the people until he
should be captured or killed at any time.

2. THE ORIGIN OF DAY AND NIGHT.*

In the beginning the people all lived in darkness. After a time they
became dissatisfied and wanted light. They called a council to discuss
how they could get light. Coyote was the first to speak, and he said :
" We have had enough darkness ; we must now have light. It is right
that we should have both and not all darkness." There was a man at
that time who was a prophet, and Coyote said that he appointed the
prophet to investigate and see how the people might obtain light. The
prophet thought over the question and then reported :

" There are yellow, black, spotted, half-spotted, and white deer upon
the earth. These deer are here for some purpose. If you kill the yellow

---

* Told by Wing.

deer, everything shall be yellow all the time. If you kill the white deer, everything shall be white all the time. If you kill the spotted one, everything shall be spotted and very bad. If you kill the black one, everything shall be black as it is now. But if you kill both the black and the white deer, then we shall have day and night. During the day everything will be white, and we can go about and hunt and visit, and during the night we can return to our homes and rest.''

The people accepted the prophet's words and started out and hunted until they killed the black and white deer, and from that time we have had day and night.

3. THE ORIGIN OF ANIMALS.

The people and animals all lived together and were the same in the beginning of the world. After a time they became too numerous and there was not food enough for all. A council was held and the chiefs determined that some should become animals and live apart from the people and be hunted by them for food. Some of the people, who lived where the big fire had burned off the grass, were rolled about in the black ashes until they became black. Again they were rolled and then they took on the form of bears. Long pieces of white stone were put upon their feet for claws and in their mouth for teeth. They were given ten lives. When killed the first time, the second life was to arise from the blood that was spilled upon the ground, and so the third life was to arise from the blood that was spilled when the bear was killed for the second time, and so on through the other lives up to the tenth. During the first life the bear was not to be fierce, but as often as he was killed and passed to another life he was to become fiercer and fiercer, until, when he came to the tenth life, he would fight, and even eat, human beings.

Some other people who lived where the long grass grew were rolled upon the earth, and when they arose they had the form of buffalo, and the grass had stuck to them and hung all like a beard under their necks. They, too, were given ten lives and then put upon the prairie to live, where man could hunt them. The deer were then made in the same way, and after them all the other animals were made.

4. COYOTE REGULATES LIFE AFTER DEATH.*

The people had many councils from time to time. The errand man went all round to call the people to these councils. At one council Coyote arose and said : '' First, we must change our rule about death, because all are not being treated alike. Now when some die they come

---

* Told by White-Bread.

back to their people, and then others die and never see their people again. I propose to make another rule, so that we may all be treated alike after death. This is the rule that I wish to propose : When any one dies let him be dead forever, and let no living person ever see him again. Our Great-Father-Above made a place there where every one of us may go after death. Now when any one dies he shall go from the living forever, but we shall still keep up the fire for six days." All the people were well pleased with Coyote's rule, and so from that time on, even to the present day, the same rule is kept, and when anybody dies he is gone forever, never to return again. The people are taken to the sky when they die and become the stars that we see at night.

Morning Star, who freed the earth from bad animals, had three brothers, and he was the oldest one and the leader of all the tribe. In the beginning he had been the errand man, and during war expeditions he had to get up early in the morning, hours before dawn, to go around the camps and wake the people, so that the enemy would not find them. That is the reason he gets up so early now. In the evening one of his brothers would go back a long distance to see if the enemy were coming on their trail, and so the man was named Evening Star. The other two brothers were named North Star and South Star, and these four brothers always had something to do. North Star always had to camp in the North and watch for the enemy lest they should approach from that direction ; South Star had to camp in the South and watch lest the enemy should approach from that direction. Their father's name was Great Star, and he was the chief of the people. Now the people think that when any one dies he goes up to the sky, where he turns around and looks back and becomes one of the stars, and so they believe every one when he dies goes up to the sky.

5. COYOTE AND THE ORIGIN OF DEATH.

In the beginning of this world there was no such thing as death. Every one continued to live until there were so many people that there was not room for any more on the earth. The chiefs held a council to determine what to do. One man arose and said that he thought it would be a good plan to have the people die and be gone for a little while, and then to return. As soon as he sat down Coyote jumped up and said that he thought that people ought to die forever, for this little world was not large enough to hold all of the people, and if the people who died came back to life there would not be food enough for all. All of the other men objected, saying that they did not want their friends and relatives to die and be gone forever, for then people would grieve and worry and there would not be any happiness in the world.

All except Coyote decided to have the people die and be gone for a little while, and then to come back to life.

The medicine-men built a large grass house facing the east, and when they had completed it they called all of the men of the tribe together and told them that they had decided to have the people who died come to the medicine-house and there be restored to life. The chief medicine-man said that he would put a large white and black eagle feather on top of the grass house, and that when the feather became bloody and fell over, the people would know that some one had died. Then all of the medicine-men were to come to the grass house and sing. They would sing a song that would call the spirit of the dead to the grass house, and when the spirit came they would cause it to assume the form that it had while living, and then they would restore it to life again. All of the people were glad when the medicine-men announced these rules about death, for they were anxious for the dead to be restored to life and come again to live with them.

After a time they saw the eagle feather turn bloody and fall, and so they knew that some one had died. The medicine-men assembled in the grass house and sang, as they had promised that they would, for the spirit of the dead to come to them. In about ten days a whirlwind blew from the west, circled about the grass house, and finally entered through the entrance in the east. From the whirlwind appeared a handsome young man who had been murdered by another tribe. All of the people saw him and rejoiced except Coyote, who was displeased because his rules about dead were not carried out. In a short time the feather became bloody and fell again. Coyote saw it and at once went to the grass house. He took his seat near the door, and there sat with the singers for many days, and when at last he heard the whirlwind coming he slipped near the door, and as the whirlwind circled about the house and was about to enter, he closed the door. The spirit in the whirlwind, finding the door closed, whirled on by. Death forever was then introduced, and people from that time on grieved about the dead and were unhappy. Now whenever any one meets a whirlwind or hears the wind whistle he says: "There is some one wandering about." Ever since Coyote closed the door the spirits of the dead have wandered over the earth, trying to find some place to go, until at last they find the road to spirit land.

Coyote jumped up and ran away and never came back, for when he saw what he had done he was afraid. Ever after that he ran from one place to another, always looking back over first one shoulder and then over the other, to see if any one was pursuing him, and ever since then he has been starving, for no one will give him anything to eat.

6. THE SECOND MAN WHO CAME OUT OF THE EARTH.*

In the beginning, when the people first came out of the earth into the world, Moon was the first man to enter the world.   The second man was Tonin, and he was even greater than Moon and more powerful. He was only about four feet high and rode a bay horse that was no bigger than a dog.   He had the power to turn darkness into light, and to wish for anything and have his wish fulfilled at once.   If he wished to go a long distance, no sooner did he wish than he was there, no matter how far, and if he wished to kill any kind of game, all he had to do was to point to it with his forefinger and it lay dead before him. From time to time he disappeared and the people did not know where he went, until one time they saw him going as though on wings up into the blue sky.   He was able to tell what would happen in the future, and so one time he sent the errand man to go out and call all the people to come to the meeting place, for he had something that he wanted to say to them.   When the people were all assembled, he came and talked to them for half a day.   He talked to them about this world in which they were living, and then he told them that in six days he was going away, and that he would be gone six winters and seven summers.   He told them that he did not know exactly where he would go, but that he wanted them all to come in six days and see him start on his journey. The people went home and on the sixth day came again, and after they were there a little while Tonin came.   He began to sing a song, the song of death, and then he was gradually lifted from the earth and taken into the sky.   All the people wept for fear he would not come back, but they remembered his promise to return, and so took courage.

Time passed and the people remembered Tonin and his words for about three summers and three winters ; then they began to forget about him and his words.   Time passed on and it was time for him to return ; then the world began to change.   The stars became brighter and larger.   Tonin had several brothers, and one of these brothers had remembered what he promised the people, so he knew that it was time for him to return.   When the day came this brother gave the sign to his people that Tonin was about to return by beating six times on the drum ; but some of the people had so completely forgotten Tonin that they did not even know what the sign meant.   Toward evening a large star came up and shone very bright in the east, and all the people came and gathered together to watch it.   When Tonin came back to earth he was pleased to see the people all there to meet him, and he

---

* Told by White-Bread.

told them about the future.　He told them that strange people were coming into the land, and that they would frighten away the buffalo, the deer, and the bear.　He stayed on earth some time, then called the people together and told them that he was going as he had gone before, but that this time he was not to return.　Then he went up into the sky.

7. SNAKE-WOMAN DISTRIBUTES SEEDS.

The Great Father gave the seeds of all growing things to Snake-Woman.　He taught her how to plant the seeds and how to care for the green things that grew from them until they were ripe, and then how to prepare them for food.　One time, when Snake-Woman had more seeds than she could possibly care for, she decided to give some to the people.　She called her two sons and asked them to help her carry the seeds.　Each put a big bag full of seeds on his back, and then they traveled all over the world, giving six seeds of each kind of plant to every person.　As Snake-Woman gave each person the seeds she told him that he must plant them, and must care for the plants that grew from them, but must allow no one, especially children, to touch them or even point to them as they grew.　She said that until the seeds were ripe they belonged to her, and if any one gathered them too soon she would send a poisonous snake to bite him.　Parents always tell their children what Snake-Woman said, and so they are afraid to touch or go near any growing plants for fear a snake will come and bite them.

8. THE FLOOD.*

One time a long, hot, dry season came and all the waters of the earth dried up.　The people wandered from place to place, trying to find water, and after many days they became crazed and did many foolish things.　They went to the dried-up river beds and there found many dead fish and turtles and animals that dwelt in the water, and the people cut them to pieces and threw them about, for they thought that these animals and fish were in some way responsible for the waters disappearing.　While they were acting foolishly they looked up and saw a man in the sky coming toward them from the west.　A wind blew, and the man approached and lighted on the ground before them.　In his hand he carried a small green leaf.　He told the people that they had not acted wisely and had abused him, and that he was angry with them.　He motioned the leaf in four directions and drops of water fell from it.　Soon the waters grew in volume and arose all over the world, even to the tree-tops, and the highest mountains except one.　To this

---

* Told by Wing.

high mountain the man led a few of the people whom he chose, and they stayed on the mountain for four days, while the water rose higher and higher. As the waters rose the man caused the mountain to rise with them. He could do this because he had greater power than the spirit of Cold or Heat. After a time the waters began to go down, and green things appeared upon the earth again. Then he led the people down from the mountain. They found that many people who had been left in the water during the flood had not drowned, but had turned into alligators and other water animals.

9. THE EFFEMINATE MAN WHO INTRODUCED STRIFE.

One time there lived among the people a man who always did the women's work and dressed like the women and went with them, and never went with the men. The men made fun of him, but he did not care, and continued to work and play only with the women. A war broke out with some other tribe, and all of the men went to fight but this man, who stayed behind with the women. After the war party had gone, an old man, who was too old to go with them, came to him and told him that if he would not go to fight he was going to kill him, for it was a disgrace to have such a man in the tribe. The man refused to go, saying that the Great Father did not send him to earth to fight and did not want him to. The old man paid no attention to his excuse, and told him if he did not go to fight he would have the warriors kill him when they returned from battle with the enemy. The man said that they could not kill him, that he would always come to life, and would bewitch people and cause them to fight and kill one another. The old man did not believe him, and when the war party came home he told the men that they would have to kill the man because he was a coward, and they could not let a coward live in the tribe. They beat him until they thought he was dead, and were just ready to bury him when he jumped up alive. Again they beat him until he fell ; then they cut off his head. He jumped up headless and ran about, frightening all of the people. They were just about to give up killing him when some one noticed a small purple spot on the little finger of his left hand. They cut that out ; then he lay down and died. Soon after many people began to fight and quarrel, and some even killed their own brothers and sisters and fathers and mothers. The other people tried to stop the fighting, but could not, because the people were bewitched and could not help themselves. Then the old man remembered what the coward had said, and he told the people, and they were all sorry that they had killed him.

10. THE ORIGIN OF THE MEDICINE-MEN.*

In days of old people knew the animals and were on friendly terms with them. All of the animals possessed wonderful powers and they sometimes appeared to people in dreams or visions and gave them their power. Often when men were out hunting and were left alone in the forest or on the plains at night, the animals came to them and spoke to them in dreams and revealed their secrets to them. The man who had had a dream of this kind woke up and went home. There he remained several days in silence, refusing to talk to any one, thinking only of the things that had been revealed to him. After a time he called some of his friends and the old men of the tribe to his lodge and told them of his powers and asked them if they would be taught his secrets. If they agreed the man taught them his songs and dances. After he had taught them all the necessary things they declared themselves ready to give a Medicine-Men's dance, and gave themselves the title of medicine-men. Then if any one was sick in the village and sought the aid of the medicine-men they prepared to hold the dance in behalf of that person, that they might try their powers of healing on him. They built a large grass lodge, and the dance was held in this lodge for six days and nights.

The first medicine-men ever to receive power and give the dance were two young brothers. These boys were brave hunters, and one time when they were out on the hunt night overtook them far from any habitation. They made a camp in the lonely woods and laid down to sleep, for they were very weary. In their sleep they both had a dream and in their dreams each met the other, and they dreamed that they were walking together toward the east. On their way they saw a man coming toward them, and he was walking rapidly toward the west. They met him and he stopped and talked with them in their language. After they had talked long, the man revealed a bag that he carried and said, " Choose from this any kind of medicine that you want. If you wish to live long and be hard to kill, take this," and he handed them certain medicine. When the boys had accepted it he said, " Now that you have the same power that I have, I will show you how to use it." He spent a long time teaching them how to use the medicine and then he continued his journey toward the west. At break of day both boys woke up, and each remembered his dream, but said nothing to the other or to any one, but thought long on what the man had taught him. After many months each began to try his powers.

* Told by Wing.

After two winters war broke out with the Chickasaw people, and many were killed and yet many more were taken prisoners. The victorious Chickasaws marched home with their prisoners and booty, and every night when they made camp they held war dances and danced about their prisoners, who, bound, were placed in the center of the large ring of dancers. One night, after the dancing was over and the prisoners lay exhausted and cold, one of them, a young man, escaped. It was nearly morning and he had not gone far when the sun came up, and he heard the Chickasaws coming after him. He did not know what to do and was about to give up when he saw a hollow log. He crawled into it and the Chickasaws came to the log and went on by. He stayed in the log all day, and in the evening, after he had heard the Chickasaws return, he crawled out and went on toward his home. After two days he reached his village and there told his story. There were many men in the village who had been away when the Chickasaws made their attack, and among them were the two brothers who had received power in their dreams. By that time the Chickasaws were about five days on their way, but the men started to pursue them. The elder brother, whose name was Strong-Wind, was chosen to take the lead. After several days' marching they overtook the enemy. They came upon their camp at night, and they could hear the beat of the drums and the songs of victory before they found the camp. The night was very dark, and so the men had to wait until dawn before they could attack the camp. At the first light they rushed into the camp and killed many Chickasaws and rescued their prisoners. Strong-Wind and his brother were equal to ten men apiece, and so wonderful were their powers that they alone rushed into the midst of the enemy and killed many and took many women as prisoners. The Chickasaws were powerless before them, and even their own people stopped fighting to stare in wonder at the brave deeds of the two young men. The few Chickasaws who were left fled in terror and the party returned home rejoicing.

After many years, during which time the brothers practiced their powers in times of war, they died and the tribe was left without any medicine-men. Finally there was a very young man, who became a medicine-man through powers given him by the Black-Mountain-Bear. One time while he was out hunting he wandered far in quest of game, and before he realized it the sun was down and it was growing dark. He thought of his home and knew that he could not reach it before night. He made a shelter, lay down to sleep, and dreamed that he was walking on a narrow trail leading eastward. He looked ahead and saw a man sitting by the wayside with his head down. As he approached, the man raised his head, looked at him, and said · "My boy, I want to give you some medicine, for I want you to have powers like mine." The old man took out many roots and told the boy to choose six of them. He took six of the roots; then the old man told him that he would have to go before six men, each of whom would explain the power of one medicine and how to use it. The boy did not want to go to so many men for fear he would not have time, and so he gave back four of the roots. Then he thanked the old man and started on his way. Soon he saw another old man sitting by the trail, and as he approached, the man arose, and when he came up to him he began to talk to the boy and explained the use of his medicine. While he was yet on the way, going toward the third man, he awoke. He returned to his mother's lodge, but kept silent, and spoke to no one for many days, thinking always about his dream and the things that had been taught him. He wandered about alone, looking always for the medicine roots he had seen in his dream. After many months he found the plant.

Soon after there was a man in another village who was about to die, and when the young man heard of the sick man he determined to go and see him and try his powers. He called the medicine-men together and taught them the medicine dance-song that had been taught him in the dream; then they all went to the lodge where the sick man was. All the people wondered why the young man should call the men to sing medicine dance-songs for him, for they never thought of him as having power. He was with the sick man a long time before he could find out what was the matter with him. First, the dancers danced very slowly, and gradually increased the movement, as was their custom. So long was the young man in finding out what was the matter with the sick man, that the dancers were dancing as fast as they possibly could before he decided. Thus they danced for six days and nights, and many of the dancers dropped to the ground exhausted. Finally the young man began to talk in a tongue no one understood, and he began to dance slowly. Then the others knew that he had discovered what ailed the man. He fell to the ground and began to crawl like a mad bear. He crawled up to the sick man and, placing his mouth on the place where the greatest pain was, drew the pain out by blowing his breath on the place, and the pain was gone. The people knew then that the boy was in truth a medicine-man, and by his actions they knew that the Black-Mountain-Bear had given him power. It was the Bear who had appeared to the young man as an old man in his dream. From that time he was called Black-Mountain-Bear-Medicine-Man. Then the chief of the medicine-men's society announced that all the medicine-men were going to hold a dance, and they wanted the young man to be present and show his powers, if he had any. The dance was held and every one attended. Black-Mountain-Bear-Medicine-Man sat and watched the dancers until the last, the sixth night of the dance; then he arose and joined in the dance. He danced faster and faster, and after a time went over and picked up a gun. He took the bullet out, then he showed it and the powder to all the people. Then he put them in the gun again and gave it to his helper. He continued dancing, and after he had danced a long time and very fast he fell to the ground. After a while he arose on his knees and spread out his arms. His helper shot him through the breast and he fell over in a faint. Soon he arose and began dancing again, and as he danced he showed the bullet to the people and also bared his breast, and they could see no marks. He had caught the bullet in his hands. After that he became a member of the medicine-men's society.

After a time another young man appeared with wonderful power, also given him by the Mountain-Bear. He appeared at the medicine-men's lodge one night, where they were having a dance, and he joined in and did many wonderful things. He had a bear's skin that he could cause to turn into a young bear, which would follow him about, and then he would turn the animal back into a piece of skin.

There are two kinds of medicine-men. One kind has power to doctor and heal the sick; another has the power to prevent any one from being hurt or harmed, and can charm away all danger. The latter are supposed to be more powerful than the first kind of medicine-men, for they can perform their magic without medicine and have power to bewitch people who are afar off, and thus make them lose their minds and not know what they are doing. They have a song of death, and when they sing the song before a dying person they frighten away death and the person lives. There are few people who ever receive this power, which is generally given by the sun, moon, stars, earth, or storm, but some very wild and ferocious animals can also give the power to people.

II. THE GIRL WHO MARRIED A TURTLE.

A girl lived alone with her two brothers. They were famous hunters and were away all day hunting. While they were gone the girl often played down by the water, and there she came to know Turtle. One day he came up to her and asked her if she would have him for her husband. She said that she would, and after that she met him whenever she went to the lake. Often her brothers wanted to carry the water for her, but she would never let them, but would always go herself and stay a long time with Turtle. One time her brothers went away to be gone many days. She told Turtle that they were gone and that she was going to take him to her house and keep him there. He was glad, for then he could be with her all of the time. She went home and built a high bed, and when she had finished it she carried Turtle home and put him in the bed. She asked him what he liked best to eat, and he said that he liked potatoes better than anything else. Every day she went out to hunt potatoes and prepared a big bowl full and put it up in the bed for him to eat. After several days her brothers came home, and so she thought she would take Turtle back to the river, but he begged so hard to stay that she yielded to him, though she knew that she took a risk. She told Turtle that he must always stay up in the bed where her brothers could not see him and must not move when they were about, for they would hear him and look for him and would surely kill him if they found him. The boys noticed the high bed when they returned, but their sister told them that she had made it because she felt safer in it while they were gone. Then they thought nothing more about it until they noticed that their sister regularly filled a large bowl with potatoes and put it in the bed and then took it out empty. They began to suspect something, but said nothing. One day they said that they were going to hunt. The girl watched them until they were out of sight ; then she took her digging stick and started after more potatoes for Turtle. The boys only pretended to go hunting and soon came back. They slipped up to the house and peeped in. When they found that their sister was gone they went in and climbed up to the bed to see what was there. They found Turtle and killed him, then ran away. When the girl came home and found her husband dead, she knew at once that her brothers had killed him and she started after them.

The boys ran until they came to a river. There they met many white ducks playing on the water. In those days all birds were white. The boys offered to paint the ducks all different colors if they would carry them and their little bob-tailed dog that was with them across the river and not tell any one that they had seen them or helped them across. The ducks agreed, and so the boys painted their feathers. Then the ducks took them on their backs and flew across the stream with them. Soon the girl came along and asked the ducks if they had seen anything of two young men and a white bob-tailed dog. They said that they had not seen them, and the girl was about to turn back when one white duck, whom the boys had forgotten to paint, flew up and told her that her brothers and their dog had just passed, and that the other ducks had lied to her, because the boys had painted their feathers if they would not tell her the truth. The white duck carried the girl across the river and she began again to pursue her brothers. They saw her coming and were afraid that she would overtake them, when they met three white doves. They asked the doves to take them and their dog on their backs and carry them to the sky. The doves agreed and flew to the sky with them and left them there. As the doves were flying down they flew through so much smoke that their white feathers became gray. The girl met the doves and asked them where her brothers and the little bob-tailed dog were. The doves pointed to three bright stars in the southern part of the sky. The girl looked, and when she saw that her brothers and their dog had become stars she fell dead.

12. THE MAN AND THE DOG WHO BECAME STARS.

A young man had a Dog which he always took with him whenever he went to hunt. When he was at home he did not pay much attention to the Dog, and the Dog acted like any other dog, but when they were off alone the Dog would talk to his master just as if he were a man. He had the power of a prophet and could always tell what was going to happen. One time, while they were out hunting, the Dog came running back to his master and told him that they were about to come to a very dangerous place. The young man asked where the place was, and the Dog said that he did not know just where it was, but that he knew it was not far away. In another instant the Dog scented a deer and started out on its trail, and the man followed. Soon they came upon the deer. The man shot it, but only wounded it, and it continued to run until it reached the lake, and then jumped into the water. The Dog jumped in after it and soon caught it, because he could swim faster than the wounded deer. He held it while the young man threw off his clothes and swam to his assistance. Soon they killed the deer, and then the man put it on his shoulders and started to swim to the shore. All at once the Dog cried out, "Look out!" There before them and all around them were all kinds of poisonous and dangerous water animals. The man thought that they would surely be killed, for the animals were so numerous that they could not possibly swim past them. He began to pray to the spirits to help him, and as he prayed the water leaped up and threw them on the shore. The young man felt so grateful to the spirits who had saved his and his Dog's lives that he cut some of the flesh from the deer and threw it into the water as a sacrifice. Then he and the Dog decided that they would not stay longer in this dangerous world, and so they went to the sky to live. There they can be seen as two bright stars in the south. The one to the east is the young man, and the one to the west is the Dog.

3D

13. EVENING-STAR AND ORPHAN-STAR.

A poor orphan boy lived with a large family of people who were not kind to him and mistreated him. He could not go to play or hunt with the other boys, but had to do all of the hard work. Whenever the camp broke up the family always tried to steal away and leave the boy behind, but sooner or later he found their new camp and went to them because he had no other place to go. One time several families went in boats to an island in a large lake to hunt eggs, and the orphan boy went with them. After they had filled their boats with eggs they secretly made ready to go back to the mainland. In the night, while the orphan boy was asleep, they stole away in their boats, leaving him to starve on the lonely island.

The boy wandered about the island, eating only the scraps that he could find around the dead camp fires, until he was almost starved. As he did not have a bow and arrows, he could not hunt, but he sat by the water's edge and tried to catch fish as they swam past him. One day as he sat on the lonely shore he saw a large animal with horns coming to him through the water. He sat very still and watched the animal, for he was too frightened to run away. The monster came straight to him, then raised his head out of the water and said : " Boy, I have come to save you. I saw the people desert you, and I have taken pity upon you and come to rescue you. Get upon my back and hold to my horns and I will carry you to the mainland." The boy was no longer afraid, but climbed upon the animal's back. " Keep your eyes on the blue sky, and if you see a star tell me at once," the animal said to him. They had not gone far when the boy cried, " There in the west is a big star." The monster looked up and saw the star, then turned around at once and swam back to the island as fast as he could. The next day he came and took the boy again, telling him, as before, to call out the moment that he saw a star appear in the sky. They had gone a little farther than they had the day before when the boy cried out, " There in the west is a star." The animal turned around and went to the shore. The next day and the next four days he started with the boy, and each time he succeeded in getting a little farther before the boy saw the star. The sixth time they were within a few feet of the opposite shore when the boy saw the star. He wanted to reach the shore so badly that he thought he would keep still and not tell the monster that he saw the star, for he knew that he would take him back to the island at once if he did. He said nothing, and so the monster swam on until they were almost in shallow water, when the boy saw a great black cloud roll in front of the star. He became frightened and jumped

off of the animal's back and swam to the shore. Just as he jumped
something struck the animal with an awful crash and he rolled over
dead.   When the boy came upon the shore a handsome young man
came up to him and said : "You have done me a great favor.   For a
long time I have tried to kill this monster, because he makes the water
of the lake dangerous, but until now I could never get the chance.
In return for what you have done, I will take you with me to the sky,
if you care to go."   The boy said that he wanted to go, as he was alone
and friendless upon the earth.   The man, who was Evening-Star, took
him with him to the sky, and there he may be seen as Orphan-Star
who stands near Evening-Star.

14. THE GIRL WHO MARRIED A STAR.*

One time a maiden slept in an arbor, and as she lay under the blue
sky she watched the stars.   One star especially she watched, and she
wished that it would become a man and marry her, for she did not care
for any of the young men of the village.   She went to sleep wishing
that the star would marry her.   When she awoke she saw no stars, but
an old man sitting by the fireside.   "Where am I?" she asked.   "Your
wish is granted ; you are the Star's wife.   I am the Star."   She began
to cry, for the man was old and homely and she was young and beautiful,
and so she had dreamed that her husband would be.   The Star's sister
was preparing something to eat, and she told the girl to stop crying and
come and eat.   After a while the two women went out to dig potatoes.
They saw one big potato, and the girl asked the Star's sister what the
big potato was for.   She answered that it was the door of heaven,
and that it covered the entrance to the world beneath.   Then the girl
cried again and begged the woman to let her go back to her people.
She told her how unhappy she was and what a mistake she had made
in wishing to marry the Star.   The woman told the Star all that his
wife had said, and so the Star agreed to let her return to her people in
six days.   The two women went out to gather bark from young elm
trees to make a rope for the girl to climb down to earth on.   After
they had gathered the bark they began to make the rope and the Star
helped them.   After six days the rope was only half long enough, and
so the old man said she would have to wait six more days until they
could complete the rope.   On the eleventh day the rope was finished,
and the Star's sister cooked some corn meal for the girl to eat on the
way and filled a squash vessel with water for her.   The Star told her
to start early the next morning, for it would take her ten winters and

---

*Told by Wing.

summers to get to the earth.   They fastened her to the end of the rope
and then removed the potato and let her through the hole and gradually
let the rope slip out.   At first she could see nothing but darkness; then
after a long time she could see the earth.   After she had traveled
through many waves of warm and cold air, she knew she had been on
her way many summers and winters.   Her food was almost gone and
still she was a long way from the earth.   Suddenly the rope ceased to
slip and she hung swinging back and forth.   She had come to the end
of the rope.   It was not long enough.   She hung there for a long time
and was about to die from hunger and weariness when she saw Buzzard
circling around below her.   She called to Buzzard to come and help her
He came, and after she had told him her story he told her to get on his
back ; that he would take her down to earth.   Buzzard flew for a long
time and the girl was heavy, so that he nearly gave out.   He saw Hawk
flying below him, and he called Hawk and asked him to help him take
the girl home.   Hawk flew with the girl until they could see the mountains and the rivers ; then he gave out.   Buzzard took the girl on his
back again, and thanking Hawk for his help, told him to go his way; that
he could take the girl on to her home.   Buzzard flew on and on until
they could see the trees, and soon they were even with the tops of the
highest trees.   Then Buzzard told the girl to go into her lodge when
she went home and not to let any one but her father and mother see
her.   She was so thin that she was little more than skin and bones.
Buzzard flew to the ground and lighted very gently just outside the
girl's village.   He pointed out her parents' lodge to her and then said
good-bye and flew away.

The girl rested for a while and then began to walk very slowly to
the lodge, for she was weak and exhausted.   On the way she saw a
woman coming toward her.   She hid behind a bush, but the woman
saw her and screamed, for the girl was so thin that she frightened her.
The girl told the woman not to be afraid and told her who she was.
Then the woman recognized the lost maiden and helped her to her
lodge.   Her mother did not know her at first, but when she found
that the girl was her daughter she threw her arms about her and wept.
The news of the girl's return spread throughout the village, but her
parents obeyed her wish and refused to let any one see her until after
the tenth day.   Then they came to her tipi and she told them her
story and especially about the kindness shown her by Buzzard.

After that the people always left one buffalo for the buzzards after a
big killing.

15. THE GIRL WHO MARRIED A STAR. *

Long ago there lived a large family—father, mother, and eight children, four girls and four boys. They were all beautiful children, especially one of the girls, who was exceptionally beautiful. The time came when three of the girls were married, but the youngest and most beautiful would not receive the attention of any one. The girl was peculiar in her tastes and roamed around alone. She wished to go away somewhere, for she was tired of her home. One time while she was walking alone she began praying to the spirits to help her, that she might go wherever she wished. That night she was outside the lodge watching the stars, and she found that the stars were not all alike ; that some were bright and some were very dim. Finally she saw one, the North Star, that was very bright, and then again she began to pray to the spirits to help her, and she wished that she might marry the star and become his wife. She ceased praying and did not know where she was for a while, and the first thing she saw was a very old man sitting by the fireside with his head down. She stood for a long while watching him. At first she could not believe herself, and she thought that she was only dreaming, but finally the old man looked up at her and said : " You are the young woman who wished to marry me and you have your wish ; you are now in my home as my wife, as you wished." She did not like the looks of the old man, and she wished that she might get away from him ; but her wish was not granted and she had to stay. She tried many ways to get away, but all failed, and she was about to give up when she thought of a great big round stone that the Star had told her not to move, for it was very dangerous to move it. One time when the Star was away on a visit she thought she would go over and lift the stone and see what was there. She lifted the stone and found that she could look clear down to the earth, and then she began to wonder how she could get down to the earth. She put the stone back in its place, and when the Star came back he asked her where she had been, and she told him that she had been at home all the time. When night came she went to bed, and as she was wondering how to get down to the earth she thought about making a long rope out of soapweeds, for she had heard the old story about the people making such a rope long ago. When the Star went away for his nightly trip she would go out and cut soapweeds ; but when he came back he would always find her at home, and so he never thought of her doing anything of the kind. Finally she had enough weeds cut, and then she began to make the rope. It took her a long while before she had the rope finished.

* Told by Annie Wilson.

One day she thought she had rope enough to reach down to the earth. She went and lifted the stone to one side and dropped the rope down just as fast as she could. She finally came to the end of the rope ; then she fastened it to the rock and placed the rock over the hole again and went back home. When the man came she was at home, but the next time he went away she went to the hole and began to climb down. It took her a long while before she could see the land plainly, and before she came to the tops of the trees she came to the end of the rope, and she did not know what to do. She was getting very tired, but she hung there for some time, and after a while she heard a noise near her and she looked and saw a bird. The bird passed under her feet several times, and when he passed the fourth time he told her that he would take her down and carry her home if she would step on to his back. She stepped on the bird's back, and he asked her if she was ready, and she said that she was ; then he told her to let go of the rope. She did so, and the bird began to fly downward very easily. The bird asked if she would let him take her on to her home, and she said that she would. The bird then took her to her home, and when they came near, the bird let her down and told her that he had to go back to his home ; but before leaving her he told her that he was Black Eagle.

16. LIGHTNING AND THE PEOPLE.

In the beginning Lightning lived upon the earth with the people, but he became so powerful and killed so many of the people that they feared and hated him. One time after he had become angry and killed a number of the people, the chiefs of the tribe called a council to determine what to do with him. They decided that he could no longer live with the people, but would have to go away. Lightning pleaded to stay, but the chiefs would not change their decision and told him that he would have to go.

Not long after Lightning had gone a great monster that lived underground among the rocks began to carry away the people. They tried in every way to kill him, but could not, for he always disappeared under the ground where they could not reach him. Lightning appeared to them and told them that he would kill the monster if they would let him come back and live with them. He said that he wanted to come back to earth, and that he would kill all monsters and make the earth a safe place for the people to live on, and would not do any more harm himself if they would let him come back. The people decided to let Lightning come, because there was no one else powerful enough to kill the great monster.

17. THE BROTHERS WHO BECAME LIGHTNING AND THUNDER.*

When the world was new there lived among the people a man and his wife and one child, a boy of about twelve years.   The people called the man "Medicine-Man."   Now and then he went out on the hunt, and never was known to come home without killing a deer, and almost every time he came home with a big buck.   One time when he was out hunting he killed a deer and then started back for home, and when he reached home he found his little boy there alone and not as usual, for he looked weary and frightened.   When his father asked him where his mother was he began to cry and said he did not know ; that all he knew was that she took a water bucket and went down toward the creek.   He said that he had run over there two or three times calling his mother, but no answer came.   Then both the little boy and Medicine-Man went down to the place where the woman usually went to get water, but they could not find her.   They found foot-prints at the edge of the water, and then the Medicine-Man knew that his wife and the mother of his only child was dead and gone ; that something had taken her life ; so they came back to their home and mourned for her six days.   They built a fire and watched it and stayed by it for six days and nights.

The seventh day Medicine-Man told his son that he was going hunting, for their meat was about out.   He went out to hunt and the little boy stayed at home alone.   While his father was gone the boy would play around the house, shooting with his bow and arrows.   When Medicine-Man came home he found his little son there waiting for him.   Medicine-Man went out to hunt the second and the third time and found the boy safe on his return.   The fourth time he went out. While he was gone the little boy went out to play.   While he was shooting with his bow and arrows he saw some one coming toward him.   He was not a man, but a boy of his own size, and had with him a bow and arrows.   Medicine-Man's boy was afraid of him, and was about to run and cry when the unknown boy spoke to him, saying : "Don't be afraid of me, brother ; I know you don't know me.   I am your elder brother."   The unknown boy looked queer to him.   He had a rather long nose and very long hair, but Medicine-Man's boy was not afraid of him since he had spoken.   He continued : "I know you are lonely ; that is why I thought of coming down here to see you. Every time our father goes out for a hunt I will come to see you, but you must not tell him that I came to see you while he is gone.   Say nothing to him about me.   Now, brother, let us see who is the best

* Told by Wing.

shot with the bow and arrows.'' They began to play. Finally he said to his brother, ''Father is coming and I must go,'' and he ran back to the woods. Medicine-Man was far from home when the boy saw him coming, and when he came the boy was gone, and his son did not say anything about his having been there.

Again Medicine-Man went to hunt, the second time and the third and the fourth time. When he came home in the evening after he had been out the fourth time the boy seemed troubled. They ate and then went to bed. About midnight the boy woke up and thought of his secret brother, and he thought at once that he must tell his father about his brother. He woke his father and said : ''Father, I have something to tell you, although I was told not to say anything about it to you.'' Medicine-Man gave very close attention. ''Father, somebody comes here every time you go out to hunt, and he is not very big ; he is about my size. When he first came he frightened me and I started to run, but did not know where to go, and I began to cry and the boy told me not to be afraid of him, for he was my brother. He has a long nose and wears long hair and has a bow and arrows, and we always play around here every time you go out to hunt and he treats me kindly. He seems to see you, no matter where you are, and when you start home he knows when you are coming, and then runs for the woods, and when you get here he is gone.'' ''Well, my boy,'' said Medicine-Man, ''we must capture the boy some way. You must go out there and play just as if I had gone away again, and whenever he asks you where I am, tell him I am out hunting. I will turn into a very small insect and stay behind the door.''

The little boy ran out next morning with the bow and arrows and began to play at the usual place. Finally the other boy came, but before he came near he spoke and asked Medicine-Man's boy where their father was, and the boy said that he had gone out hunting again. The boy began to look around, and finally he said : '' Who is that man behind the door ? '' at the same time running back to the woods.

Again the next day the boy went out to play ; this time Medicine-Man placed himself at the edge of the roof of the grass house. When the boy came he asked his brother where their father was. He answered that he had gone out hunting, but the boy would not come near. He began to look around, and finally he said : '' Who is that man under the roof ? '' and he ran back into the woods again. Then Medicine-Man said : '' We must catch him some way. When he sits down near to you, tell him that something is crawling in his hair, and then he will let you look in his hair. Then catch hold of a small bunch of his hair and tie it up four times ; then call me and I will be there just as soon as I can. You must not let him go until I get there." The little boy understood.

The other boy had already run away twice and this was the third attempt. This time Medicine-Man placed himself in the middle of the fire. The boy went out and began to play. Soon the other boy came. He asked the boy where their father was and he told him he went out to hunt. The unknown boy began to look around, and finally he said : "Who is that man in the fire?" and then he ran back to the woods. The next day the boy went out and began to play and the unknown boy came again, and asked the boy the same question. The boy answered that their father had gone out to hunt. This time Medicine-Man had placed himself behind another door, and the unknown boy found him again and went back to the woods. And so the fifth time came, and this time Medicine-Man placed himself in the air, and when the unknown boy came he found him again and went back to the woods.

Medicine-Man tried once more. If he failed the sixth time he could do nothing more, for he would have used all his powers. He told his boy to go out again to play as usual, and this time his own boy did not see which way he had gone. Finally the other boy came and asked where their father was, and he told him that he was out hunting. This time the unknown boy believed him, and so he came near and sat down by him and the little boy got hold of his hair and said : "There is something crawling up in your hair, brother," and then the boy told him to get the bug out of his hair ; and the boy began to do as he had been told, and when he got through he called out, "All ready, father." Medicine-Man jumped out from the grass house, and then they captured the boy and took him into the grass house and held him there for six days. At the end of the sixth day the little boy boiled some water and they washed the other boy, and Medicne-Man cut his nose off and made it look like a human nose. Medicine-Man said : "You have been coming here when I am absent and have been playing with my son and you call him brother. Now you may be his brother and stay with him and go out and play with him." The boys went out to play, and before Medicine-Man went to hunt again he went over to see the boys and told them he was going to hunt, and told them to stay at home and not to go to a certain place in the timber, where some very large squirrels lived, for they often killed little children. After their father was gone the unknown boy told his young brother they would go there and see the squirrels, and so they started. They could not find the place for a while, but finally they did, and they stood there for a good while watching the big hole in the tree.

After a while one of the big squirrels came out, and sticking his tongue out like a snake, took the younger brother into the tree.   The other boy stood there watching the squirrel take his brother into the hole.   He did not try to help his brother, for he knew he could get him out of the hole whenever he wanted to.   After the boy had disappeared he went back to their home, and when he got there he found their father already returned from the hunt.   The father asked him where his son was, and the boy told him that his brother and he were making lots of arrows, and that he came home after fire to dry the arrows with it.   He took the fire and carried it to the timber, where he placed it near the tree where the large squirrel was.   Then he brought some hard, red stones and put them in the fire, and when the stones were very hot he took one of them and threw it into the hole, and then another one.   While he was standing there watching the hole he saw the large squirrel come out from the hole and drop down on the ground dead.   Then he went over and cut the squirrel's stomach open and found his brother in there, still alive.   He took him down to the river and washed him and then they both went home.

Sometimes these two boys would go out to make arrows.   One time when they went out the unknown boy made two arrows for his young brother ; one he painted black and the other he painted blue.   They made a small wheel out of bark of the elm tree.   One of the boys would stand about fifty yards away from the other, and they would roll this little wheel to each other and would shoot the wheel with the arrows. They played with the wheel every day until finally Medicine-Man's boy failed to hit the wheel, and the wheel kept rolling and did not stop until it went a long way from them, and they never found it again. The boy felt very bad, and he wanted to get the wheel back, and so the unknown boy said : "Don't worry, brother, for we can get the wheel back again."   And so they started out, and they did not let their father know where they were going, nor how long they would be away from home.   They went a long way and they could see the trace of the wheel all the way.   Finally the unknown boy said : "Well, brother, we are about half way now, and we must stop for a rest."   They began praying to the spirits to help them.   The unknown boy had two pecan nuts, and he told his brother to watch, that he was going to put one of the nuts in the ground.   Then they began to pray again, and while they were praying the pecan nut began to sprout, and it grew taller and larger. Finally the tree grew so tall that it went clear up into the sky, and then the unknown boy told his brother that he was going up on this tree, and that he must sit near to the tree, but must never look up to the sky, but down on the earth, and that he was going to be gone for a good while, until he dropped all the bones that he had in his body ; that at the last he would drop his head, and then the boy must gather all the bones up, put them on a pile, cover them with buffalo calf's hide, take the black arrow and shoot it up just as hard as he could, and when he heard the arrow coming down to tell him to get out of the way, that the arrow was coming right on him, and that the pile of bones would get out of the way. Then he started climbing up the tree and the little boy sat on the ground looking down. After quite a while he saw one of the bones drop, and then another and another, and so on until all the bones had dropped, and then he gathered them up and piled them together and covered them with the buffalo calf's hide. Then he shot the black arrow just as he was told, and when he heard the arrow coming down he cried out : " Look out, brother, the arrow is coming down right on you. Get out of the way." His brother jumped out from the buffalo calf's hide, and the arrow struck right where the hide was. He said, " My father gave me very dangerous power, and so, brother, you must climb up the tree and he will give you power, too." The little boy climbed the tree, and he went clear up as far as the other boy had gone. He did not know where he was, and it seemed like a dream to him, and when the bones began to fall from his body he did not know it. All he remembered was that there was some one talking to him, but he did not see who it was, and the next thing he heard was, " Look out, brother, the arrow is coming right down on you. Get out of the way." He jumped out of the way and saw his brother standing there. His brother asked him what kind of a power he had received, and he told him that it was a great power. The boy told his brother to show him what kind of a power he had, and then the little boy began making a loud noise that sounded like thunder when it rains, and then the unknown boy let his tongue out and it looked like a flash of lightning.

They went on until they came to a large lake, and when they looked near to the edge of the water they saw the trace where the wheel had passed into the water, but they could not find any place to cross. They sat down on the bank of the lake and began to pray again, and the boy planted another pecan nut, and soon a large tree sprang up ; but this time the tree did not grow upward, but bent over across the lake to the opposite bank, and so made a bridge for them to cross upon. They went across the lake, and when they got across they saw the trace of the wheel, and a little way from the landing place they saw a narrow road leading toward the east, and a little way from the end of the road they saw that the trace of the wheel was gone. A little way from there they saw an old man going toward the lake, and then the boy who had the power of lightning said : "We must kill this man, because we know he is a bad man ; he is a cannibal." When they met this old man Lightning boy said to Thunder boy : "This is the old man who took our wheel, and he has it with him now, and it is in his right side." They killed the old man and found the wheel and took it, and then they went on and they saw, a long distance from them, a smoke, and they went there and found many people. The people did not know who they were at first ; they thought they were the old man, for this old man whom they had killed was their head man ; and so these two brothers killed all the rest of the people. They began to look all around and finally they came to a pile of human bones. They found the bones of the wife of Medicine-Man. Only one little finger was missing. They piled the bones together and covered them with the buffalo calf's hide, and Lightning boy shot the black arrow up, and when they heard the arrow coming down they said : "Look out, mother, the black arrow is coming right on you. Get out of the way," and the woman jumped out of the way. The boys greeted their mother, and then they all started back for their home, and when they came near to their home Lightning boy said that he was going on ahead. The other boy and his mother came on behind. Lightning boy got there first and found their father a very old man, and still weeping for his children. The yard around the grass house was overgrown with tall trees and weeds and grass, for the old man was not able to work any more. Lightning boy told him that his son and his lost wife were coming. The old man was glad, and went out to meet them. They all lived happily for a number of years ; then the father and mother died. The boys were lonely then, and so they decided to leave this world. They went up in the sky, and now when the clouds gather together for a storm Lightning and Thunder, which are these two boys who once lived on the earth and killed the monsters that lived here, are seen in their midst.

18. SPLINTER FOOT BOY.

An orphan boy who lived alone with his grandmother was a famous hunter and often went out on a long hunt with his friends. One time, while they were a long way from home, the boy was wounded by a stick that pierced his leg and broke off inside of it. His leg festered and swelled up so that he could not walk and his friends had to carry him home. His leg continued to swell until it was as large as his body ; then the skin broke, but instead of the stick coming out, a child came. The boy was angry and would not look at the child or have anything to do with it. His grandmother took pity upon the baby and cared for it.

One day while she was away the boy took the child and carried it to the lake, where he left it to starve or be eaten by the wild animals. He was afraid to return to his grandmother's home for fear she would know that he had thrown his child away, and so he went far off and lived alone. The child lay on the shore of the lake for a long time, and as he lay there he grew to be a good-sized boy. Finally many birds flew over the lake, and when they were about half way across the lake, the water appeared to leap up to the sky and draw the birds down. Every day the boy saw the water leap up to the sky whenever any birds flew past, and one time he saw a big water monster in the water. He saw the monster draw so many birds into the water that he was afraid it would kill all the birds in the land, and he wished that he could kill it. While he was thinking about a way to kill the monster, he felt some one hit him on the back. He turned around and there behind him stood a boy about his own age. He was Medicine-Screech-Owl, but the boy did not know who he was or anything about him. Medicine-Screech-Owl asked the boy what he was thinking about, and the boy told him that he was thinking how he could kill the water monster that ate up all of the birds. Medicine-Screech-Owl told the boy that he would help him kill the monster. He showed him where the old woman, his grandmother lived, and then he told him to go to her house and get six arrows and a bow and six grains of corn from six kinds of corn and then return to the lake.

When the boy went to the old woman's house she was surprised and happy to see him, for she had been very lonely since the orphan boy and his son had disappeared, and had given up all hope of ever seeing them again. The boy told her what he wanted, and she gave him all he asked for. Then he returned to the lake, where he found Medicine-Screech-Owl waiting for him. Medicine- Screech-Owl took three grains of each of the six kinds of corn and threw them into the air. They became birds and flew out across the water, and the water monster leaped up to draw them down. As he leaped up Medicine-Screech-Owl cried to the boy to shoot it. He shot the first arrow, but it did not go near the monster. The second went nearer, and so did the third, fourth, and fifth, and the sixth pierced it through. The great monster rolled over on its side and floated on the water, and then they could see how large it was. Medicine-Screech-Owl said that it was the largest water monster in the world. He told the boy to take his bow and pull the animal to dry land, but the boy knew that he could not move the monster with his little bow, and so did not try. To his surprise Medicine- Screech-Owl took his bow, that was even smaller, and pulled the great monster to the bank. When he had done this he disappeared, and then the boy went back to his grandmother's house and told her about the boy he had met at the lake and how they had killed the big water monster. The old woman knew that the boy's companion was Medicine-Screech-Owl, and she also knew that he had given the boy wonderful power, though she said nothing.

The next day the boy went to the lake again. He found the water very low, since the monster had been pulled out of the lake, and it was so clear that he could see many fish swimming about. He dived down to catch some of the fish, and a big sword-fish swam up to him and went right through him. The boy, though severely wounded, did not die, but shot the fish with his bow and arrow. The next day he again went to the lake to fish, but found that all the water had gone. In the mud he saw two large shells. He carried them home and cut them so that he could put them over the holes that the sword-fish had made when it cut its way through him. He wore one in front and one behind, so that no one could see the wounds that the fish had made. The shells had the power to hear any sound in the whole world, and whenever he wanted to hear anything he removed the shells from the holes and put them to his ears. With the power of hearing every sound in the world and the power given to him by Medicine-Screech-Owl, he became a great medicine-man and the people began to fear him and planned to kill him. When he heard that they were going to kill him he told his grandmother that they would leave the people, but that he would do them harm some time because they had planned to kill him, and so made it necessary for him and his grandmother to leave. They went to a high mountain near the village, and made their grass house on the very top of it. He found two fierce dogs and placed them at his door to guard the house.

The boy knew who the people were who had planned to kill him, because he had heard them talking by means of his wonderful shells. Soon they died, one after another, until the people of the village began to suspect that the boy was bewitching them and causing them to die. Many of the warriors tried to steal up to his home on the mountain and kill him, but with the magic shells he could always hear them coming, and would set the dogs on them, so that they could never approach.

He kept on bewitching so many people that finally Medicine-Screech-Owl decided that he would have to interfere. He started up the trail to the boy's house, but first he blew his breath so hard that it took the magic power of sound from the shells, so that the boy could not hear him coming. When he was almost at the top of the mountain he blew his breath again and the dogs rolled over asleep, and when he passed them they were so sound asleep that they did not wake up and bark or give any warning of approach. He passed the dogs ; then he blew his breath again and the old woman fell over asleep. Again he blew his breath, and the boy fell down asleep. Medicine-Screech-Owl then entered the house and took the shells off of the boy. He walked around, looking at everything, then went away. When he was almost down the mountain he blew his breath and the boy woke up. He missed his shells at once and began to look everywhere for them. He called his grandmother to come and help him look, but she did not wake up. Finally he shook her so hard that he shook all of Medicine-Screech-Owl's breath out of her, and then she woke up and helped him look for his shells. He went outside and found the dogs asleep ; then he knew that some one had been to his house and stolen his shells. He called the dogs, but could not wake them, and so he took a club and knocked the breath out of them. They woke up and at once scented Medicine-Screech-Owl's tracks and started after him. The boy followed, and they soon came to a big circle of fire. In the midst of the burning circle stood Medicine-Screech-Owl, and he was wearing the shells. The boy had no power that would take him through fire, and so he had to return without his shells. Medicine-Screech-Owl kept the shells for some time, and then he took them back to the boy, but before he gave them to him he made him promise that he would not bewitch the people any more.

19. MEDICINE-SCREECH-OWL. *

Medicine-Screech-Owl was born at Long-Timber-on-the-Top-of-the-Hill. His father and mother were very old and lived near the center of the village. When his first birthday came he was given bow and arrows. His father and mother were asking each other what name they should give to their child, but before they could name him he spoke and said, "My name shall be Medicine-Screech-Owl." His mother scolded him, because at this time there was also a man by the name of Medicine-Screech-Owl, and he was an ex-chief ; but he said that he would have no other name, and so his parents named him Medicine-Screech-Owl. One night some one passed near the village and heard the child's mother calling him by the name of the ex-chief. When the man came to the ex-chief's place he told him that the child's name was the same as his. When the ex-chief heard this he was angry, and told the people that he was going to kill the boy if he did not do as he should tell him to do. He sent for him, and when the boy came to his lodge he gave him watermelon seed and said : " Go back and plant this watermelon seed this evening. In the morning go and

---

* Told by White House (Caddo Jack).

bring to me a great big watermelon to eat." "All right," said young Medicine Screech-Owl. He took the seed, went back to his village, and told his father and mother what the ex-chief had told him to do. That evening the boy went out a short distance from his lodge, threw the seeds upon the ground, and there sprang up a large watermelon plant. He then went back to the lodge and told his father and mother what had happened. Early in the morning he went out to his watermelon vine, and he found many large watermelons on it. He took one of the melons to the ex-chief, who was surprised, and he thought that surely the boy was going to be a wonderful man. He was so jealous of him that he determined to destroy him, for he thought that if he did not young Medicine-Screech-Owl would get ahead of him in every way, and that the people would no longer pay him any attention. The boy went back to his village and told his father and mother all about what had happened. The ex-chief sent for the boy the second time, and the boy again went to his lodge. The ex-chief had brought the boy a large bull to milk. He told him to take the bull to his lodge and to bring the milk over the next morning. The boy took the bull over to his village, but instead of milking it when morning came he took an axe and went out near the ex-chief's lodge to chop some wood, and when the ex-chief saw him chopping wood he went to him and asked him if he had already milked the bull. The boy told the ex-chief that he had not milked the bull, but that he was in a hurry to cut some wood to take home. The ex-chief asked him why he was taking the wood home. "Well," said the boy, "my father is going to have a child." The ex-chief laughed at the boy and asked him if he ever had seen a man have a child. The boy said, "No; I never have." Then he asked the ex-chief if he ever had seen a man milk a bull or a bull give milk. The ex-chief was very angry. The boy returned to his lodge and told his father and mother what had happened. The third time the ex-chief sent to have the boy come over to his lodge, informing him that he and some of his friends were going to have a fine time and a big dinner. In the meantime the ex-chief and the others were digging a big hole in the ground, in which they were going to throw the boy. They dug the hole about fifty feet deep and about four feet in diameter and covered it with a buffalo robe. When the boy came the ex-chief told him that he had already fixed a place for him to sit. Young Medi-cine-Screech-Owl never left his bow and arrows, but always had them with him everywhere he went. When he entered the ex-chief's lodge they told him to be seated. He laid down his arrows and bow and went and sat down on the hide, and down he went into the hole. The ex-chief was very glad, for he thought surely he had killed the boy. He commenced filling the hole with heavy stones and dirt until he supposed that the boy was dead.

One evening the same person, who had passed the lodge and heard the boy's mother calling him by the ex-chief's name, passed again, and again heard her calling the same name, and he heard young Medicine-Screech-Owl answering her. The man went to the ex-chief's lodge and told him that the boy was still living, because while he was passing by his lodge he had heard his mother calling him and had heard him answering. When the ex-chief heard this he became very angry, and said that he was going to try once more, and if he failed to kill the boy this time he would leave him alone. He sent for the boy the fourth time. He came, and found that they had built up a big fire. The ex-chief told the boy to go right into the middle of the fire and sit down, for he wanted to see if he had any powers at all; that if he had any powers he would not burn up. The boy went into the midst of the fire and sat down for a long time, until the fire burned out; then he arose unharmed. When he had come out of the fire he made another big fire and told the ex-chief that it was his turn to go into the fire, to show whether or not he had any power. The ex-chief went in and the fire burned him to death.

From that time on the boy would go from place to place. Finally he grew to be almost a man in size. Many times he would run away from his father and mother, and when he returned his mother would scold him. Still he continued to go off wherever he pleased. The reason why his mother scolded him so much when he went anywhere was because she knew that there were many people who were envious of his power and would try to kill him; but the boy did not care for that. There was one place where three of his enemies were living, who were always talking about killing him. Medicine-Screech-Owl heard these men talking about him, and so one day he determined to visit them. He quietly stole away from his father and mother, for he dared not say anything to them about going, for fear they would not let him go. When he came to the place he found the three men at home, and when they saw him coming they all came out from their lodge and were very glad to see him, for they had been wishing for a long time that he would come. They asked him where he was going. He replied that he had come over for a visit to his friends. They asked him to go into the lodge. Young Medicine-Screech-Owl knew that he was to go in first, and that all the others would come in and attempt to kill him. The door they had to enter was very small, although big enough for one man at a time to enter. When Medicine-Screech-Owl had entered he stood by the door and waited for the others to come in.

His only chance was to kill them. He stood by the door waiting and ready to strike the first to enter. As the first man entered, he struck him on the head and killed him, then pulled him in just as quickly as he could, to make it appear that the man had entered without anything happening. Thus he killed the second and the third man. Then he returned home and told his mother and father all that had happened.

Another time there was a man called Snow-and-Cold, living with his family far away in the north. When anybody went over there on a visit and happened to stay over night, he would be frozen before morning. Medicine-Screech-Owl heard all about this man and made up his mind to go and visit him and his family. One day he started out. It took him a long time to reach the place, for he had to go across a large lake. When he came to the water he stood on the edge of the bank. He wore on his head an eagle feather, and he took the eagle feather off from his head and placed it on the water and placed himself on the eagle feather. The feather began to sail across the water. On the other side of the water were many geese, and when any one came across the water the geese would make so much noise that the people at the home of Snow-and-Cold would know at once that somebody was coming. When young Medicine-Screech-Owl went across to visit old man Snow-and-Cold the geese did not see him when he landed on the other side. He stepped off from his eagle feather and placed it on his head again and walked straight to the place where Snow-and-Cold lived. All this time nobody had seen him. Medicine-Screech-Owl went into the lodge where Snow-and-Cold was and found him lying down, asleep. Medicine-Screech-Owl spoke to him and asked him how he was getting along. When Snow-and-Cold awoke he looked around, but could see no one. Again Medicine-Screech-Owl spoke to him, and this time Snow-and-Cold arose from his bed and began to look around. He could find no one in the room. When he started to lie down again Medicine-Screech-Owl spoke to him and showed himself. Snow-and-Cold was surprised to see Medicine-Screech-Owl there and asked him what he wanted. Medicine-Screech-Owl replied that he had come over on a visit, because he had heard so much of the place. When evening came Snow-and-Cold told the boy to sleep right there, in a bed which had nothing but snow on it. After they had gone to bed Snow-and-Cold did not go to sleep, but kept watching the boy, for he thought he would surely freeze to death in a little while; but every time Snow-and-Cold looked over to see him he would see a light right next to his head. He wondered what it could be. Medicine-Screech-Owl had his feather sticking straight up on his pillow during the night. Snow-and-Cold arose, reached for the cane which he had placed at the foot of his bed next to a place that seemed like a fireplace. Medicine-Screech-Owl watched him all this time, but he did not know that he was being watched. Snow-and-Cold took the cane and punched the snow where it seemed like a fireplace, and the fire sprang out from the snow. When he had warmed himself he covered the fire and went back to his bed. Soon he saw Medicine-Screech-Owl get out of his bed, go for the cane, and punch the place, and out came the fire. When Medicine-Screech-Owl was through warming himself he walked back to his bed. Snow-and-Cold did not know what to think of Medicine-Screech-Owl. The next morning Snow-and-Cold called to Medicine-Screech-Owl to get up from his bed. He thought he had been frozen to death, but the boy jumped up and said that he had had a fine sleep. After he was through talking to Snow-and-Cold he said he would have to go back home ; that his mother would not like it if he should stay out another day. He started back, and when he reached home he told his mother all about it.

20. MEDICINE-SCREECH-OWL.*

In a village there lived an old man, his wife, and one child, a beautiful girl. The girl had never been known to have a male acquaintance, and was always modest and well-beloved. Nevertheless, in some way she became pregnant. Her father and mother noticed this and called her attention to the fact, and asked her how it had happened and who was the father of the child. In those days it was the custom to find out all about such matters. The girl herself did not know how she had come to be in that condition and could not answer their questions. Her people were angry at her and much ashamed, but could not get her to answer any of their questions. She went as usual with the girls of the village to dig potatoes, but she could never find any and always returned without any. One time, after her mother had scolded her for never bringing home any potatoes, she was wandering slowly about trying to find some when she heard a voice cry, "Mother." She looked about, but could see no one. Again she heard the cry, and then she knew that it was the child in her womb that was crying. The voice told her to go to a certain place and dig. She obeyed and found many large potatoes. When the other girls saw them they wondered, for they knew that she was never successful in finding them.

The child was born and, at his own request, was called Medicine-Screech-Owl. The mother and child lived apart from the others and were very poor and often hungry, for they had no one to hunt food for them, and all they had to eat was what people gave to them. The child grew rapidly and was soon large enough to play with the other

---

* Told by Wing.

little boys. There was a lake near the village where the men fished, and the children were accustomed to go to the lake and watch them. One time Medicine-Screech-Owl asked his mother if he could not fish too. She only laughed at him and told him that he was too little ; but he begged so hard that she finally said he might go and try. He went, taking his little bow and arrows, and soon returned with a big fish. His mother was greatly surprised and gave her consent for him to go the next day. Again he came home with a big fish, and again and again, until his fame as a fisherman spread throughout the village.

There were many who did not like the boy because they did not know who his father was, and when they heard about his success they began to fear him and decided to kill him. There was among the people a powerful Medicine-Man, and they asked him to use his powers against the boy and kill him.

One day, while the boy was at the lake fishing, he saw the reflection of a big, black cloud in the water. He knew that the Medicine-Man was sending Thunder to try to kill him, but he did not fear. He walked into the water until it was up to his knees. Then came a peal of thunder and a shaft of lightning. He raised his bow over his head and the lightning rolled from it into the water. Again and again the lightning shafts struck at him, but every time he caught them on his bow and hurled them into the water. At last the Medicine-Man realized that the boy had more power over Thunder than he had, and so he gave up. That evening the boy returned home with a big fish and told his mother what had happened.

Nothing more happened for a long time, but one day while the boy was lying in his lodge resting it occurred to him that something was going to happen to him. He arose from his bed, took his bow and arrows, went back to his bed, lay down and began to sing. Soon he heard a great noise, and he knew that the Medicine-Man was sending Cannibal monster to destroy him. He heard the monster's roar, that sounded like thunder, but he lay still and sang as though he had nothing to fear. As the monster came nearer he could feel its hot breath, but he did not move until it leaped upon his lodge and fell through with an awful crash. Then he arose and killed it.

After that Medicine-Screech-Owl started out to travel, and he went from place to place, killing monsters and ferocious animals and healing the sick. Where he was, death could not come, and so powerful was his touch that people were healed if he placed his hand on the diseased place. Finally, after he had been with the people for a long time, he called them together and told them that he was going to leave them. He disappeared and has not been seen since.

21. THE ORPHAN BOY WHO BECAME A WRESTLER.*

A boy lived alone with his old grandfather. His mother and father died when he was only a baby, and there was no one to care for him but his grandfather. They lived together, and the old man cared for the child as best he could until he had become old enough to play around. The grandfather was looking forward to the time when he could make bows and arrows for the boy and teach him to hunt, but before that time came the old man died and the boy was left alone. He went from lodge to lodge and begged, and whatever the people gave him he ate and was grateful. At night he returned to his lonely lodge and cried, for he was poor and alone and afraid. The boys of the village came to his lodge to see him, and they teased him and laughed at him because he was sad and did not know how to play as they did. He was brave and did not lose courage. When he was larger he made himself a bow and some arrows and went out to hunt. He brought back small game at first and was happy, because he no longer had to beg.

One time when he was out alone far in the timber he heard a voice singing and calling to him to wait. He waited and a strange boy came running through the bushes. The stranger was homely, but so full of fun and energy that the poor orphan boy determined to make him his friend. They played together, and finally they tried to see which was the stronger. The stranger looked much stronger than the orphan, but, to his surprise, he found that he could easily throw him. The orphan boy could not understand how he could throw the strong-looking boy so easily, for all the boys in the village made fun of him because they could so easily throw him. The strange boy arose and smiled and said: "I have given you my power. I am a wonderfully strong man. I have given that power to you. Now you can go back to your village and throw any one you please. I have been watching you and seeing how the boys teased you. I have decided to give you power. Now you are one of the strongest men in the world and can throw any one."

The stranger disappeared. The boy lay down to rest, for it had grown dark and he could not find his way home. The sun arose and the boy waked and started on to hunt. He killed three deer and started home with them. His load was heavy and he could not go fast. When he was far from home darkness came again. He lay down on some soft grass to rest until daylight. Soon he heard a voice, and looking up he saw the same stranger who had appeared to him the night before. The

stranger asked the boy if he would not go to the meeting place where
he and all his friends met to wrestle.   The boy said that he would go.
The stranger helped him carry his meat, and soon they were at the place.
There were many boys and men there.   One stepped forward and asked
the orphan boy to wrestle with him.   The boy easily threw him.   A
second, third, fourth, and fifth came forward, and he threw one after
another.   Then the strong men began to fear the boy, and they all went
away and left him alone with only the one who had given him the power.
While they sat down to rest, the strong man told the boy more things
about the wonderful power he had given him and how to use it.   When
the sun arose the strong man disappeared and the boy took up his
meat and returned home.   He had been home but a few days when it
was noised about the village that the boys were going to have some
wrestling matches.   He went to watch the wrestling, but stood far out
from the ring among the spectators.   Soon a young man from the ring
called him to come in, if he were not a coward.   He only shook his head.
Again the young man called, not thinking that he would come, but only
to tease him.   The boy at once threw off his blanket and ran into the
ring.   In a short time he threw the man and killed him.   Then he
asked for another to come and fight with him.   None came.   All were
afraid of his great strength.   The report of his deeds soon spread among
the people, and it was not long before he had the respect and fear of all.

22. THE DANGEROUS WATER MONSTER.*

When the world was new and not well known it was a dangerous
place to live in.   One time when there were many people camping
near a small creek one of the men went down to the creek to get
water.   After he had finished drinking he looked into the water and
saw a large animal that looked like a snake.   It was slowly moving
up the creek and he saw that it was very long.   He ran up the creek
to see how long it was, and he ran about two miles before he came
to its head.   Then he started for the camp, and when he arrived
he went to his grandfather, who was always at home, because he was
a very old man and could not hunt with the others.   He told him
what he had seen, and when he finished telling him the grandfather
said: ''You have seen some wonderful thing, my son, that has been
sent as a sign to our people.''   He did not know what the sign was
and so he called for the errand man, and when he came the old man
told him to call all the people together at his lodge, for he had something
to tell them.   When the people came in he at once told them about
what his grandson had seen.   Some of the men would not believe him,

*Told by Wing.

but most of them went down to the creek and there saw the water monster and knew that the man had told the truth. They all wondered why it had come and whether it was a good or evil omen. The old men tried to recall the past, to find out if the people had ever had a similar sign sent to them, but could not remember any. There was one man in the camp who was old and blind, and he knew many wonderful things ; and so the people went for him, and when he came the chief asked him if he knew what the appearance of the water monster meant. The old man sat there for a while without a word, and every one was very quiet. "Well," he said, finally, "the sign is a very bad one, for it signifies that the waters shall rise in a short time." It was not long until the waters rose and formed a large lake. The lake was very dangerous. When one crossed it he had to cross without saying a word to any one.

One time there were four men who went out hunting on the other side of the lake, and after they had killed much game they started back again. They crossed the lake without making any noise and were within a short distance of the opposite shore when one man, who was very brave, thought he would see what the water would do to them if he spoke. He began to talk very loud, and in a little while the water rose up in a cloud over their heads and they were all drowned but the one man who had told that the water was very dangerous and warned the man not to talk. He went home empty-handed, for his bow and arrows had been washed away. He called some other men together and told them what had happened and asked them to go with him to search for the bodies of the men. Two of the bodies were found, but the body of the man who made the noise could not be found.

23. SLAYING THE MONSTERS BY FIRE.*

In the olden time the world was full of all kinds of wild animals who ate people and tame animals. In those times Coyote called all the people together to a council to see what could be done with the wild animals, because they were getting so bad that the people could not go away from their homes to hunt food or to visit each other. At the council they decided to set fire to all the grass, which was as high as trees, and so burn the wild animals and everything on the earth. They chose White-Headed-Hawk and Crow, because they were the swiftest of all the people, to fly to some bright Star and tell the Star that they were coming to his home to live. The Star told them that there was room for the people in the heavens if they could get up there. The messengers returned and reported to the people. They decided to make a long

---

* Told by White-Bread.

rope out of soapweed and go to heaven on that.   They began to gather
the soapweed and twist it into a strong rope.   The rope was finished ;
then White-Headed-Hawk and Crow took it and again flew to the
heavens.   They gave the end of the rope to the Star, who put one end
of it under a big stone and let it hang down.   It was so long that it
reached the earth, and the people saw it hanging ready for them to
crawl up when the time came.   They appointed two men, Gray and
Black Snakes, to carry the fire over the world.   One was to carry the
fire to the east, then to the south ; the other was to carry it to the west,
then to the north.   Soon the people noticed a cloud of smoke, and then
the sun began to fade and look dim, and a great noise of all the wild
animals arose.   The people saw the fire coming nearer, and so they
began to climb the rope.   After all the people were on the rope and had
climbed up a little way the wild animals came and began to climb up.
The people saw the animals coming up, and so they appointed Bat to
cut the rope just above the wild animals, and they gave him sharp teeth
to cut the rope with.   Bat began to fly around as though looking for a
place on the rope to stay.   Finally he asked the first wild animal to let
him in by him, and he did.   After a while the animal noticed that Bat
was eating something, and he asked him what it was, and Bat said that
he was eating a parched grain of corn that his grandmother had given
him.   He kept on chewing the rope when the animal was not looking,
and finally the rope broke and let all of the wild animals down and
many were killed.   Bat went down to make sure that all were killed
or burned.   He saw an immense animal on the ground and all the other
animals crawling into it to escape the fire.   Bat went into the animal's
nose and pulled out some hairs.   This made the animal sneeze and blow
all of the other animals out and they burned to death.   Bat flew up to
tell the people that all the wild bad animals were killed, and so they all
came down the rope again.

24. SLAYING THE MONSTERS BY FIRE.*

In the beginning of the world there were animals that lived with
human beings and were kind and friendly, but there were other animals
that were very strong and dangerous.   At that time, when the earth
was new, the grass was taller than the highest trees are now, and many
wild animals prowled through the high grass, and that was the reason
why the world was so very dangerous.   One time the people met in
council to make plans to kill all the dangerous animals in the world,
and Morning Star, who was one of the head men in the council, arose
and said: ''There is only one way to kill these animals and that is to

---

* Told by Wing.

burn the grass all over the world. I know how large the world is and what a big task we have, but we must do it.''

As every one was willing to try Morning Star's plan, he told a man who was present at the council that most of the work would fall to him, but that he would appoint two men to help him carry out the work. The man's name was Fire, and the first man appointed to help Fire was the fastest runner in the world, and his name was Black Snake ; the second man was the slowest in the world, and his name was Skunk. Fire took hold of Black Snake's tail and put fire on the end of it, and then took hold of Skunk's hind foot and placed fire between his toes. They both started out at the same time, the one going to the north, the other around to the south, so as to meet somewhere in the west, since they started in the east. While these two were on their way the people decided to make a long rope out of soapweeds that would reach up to the sky. Everybody helped make the rope, and as they worked Pigeon would go up into the blue sky to see how near the fire had approached. After a time the people could see that the sky was getting very dark on account of the smoke from the fire, and so they worked hard and fast to get their rope long enough. Finally they had the rope finished, and they appointed Crow to take it up to the sky. Crow took the rope and flew and flew until he was out of sight, and it was a long time before he returned, but when he came he assured the people that he had the rope firmly fastened to the sky. The fire was approaching rapidly, and so the people began climbing up the rope. After the people had climbed up, all kinds of animals came and began to get hold of the rope, and all the bad animals came, and then the rope began to move upward. After the people were high up they sent a man down the rope as far as the first bad animal. This man's name was Bat, and because he had very sharp teeth he was sent to cut the rope. The animal saw him chewing something and asked him what he was eating. Bat said that his grandmother had parched some corn for him and that he was eating it. He kept on cutting the rope, and finally it broke and let the bad animals fall down. When the animals dropped down to the ground Bat followed them down to see what would become of them. He saw a large animal and heard it call all the other animals to enter his body through his nose, ears, and mouth. These animals went in, and so large was the big animal that it had room inside of it for all the bad animals. After all the others were in, Bat slipped in and began to pull out some hair from the animal's nose. That made the animal sneeze, and he sneezed so hard that he threw all the other animals out through his nose. The animals were scattered every place and burned, for the fire was upon them.

Bat flew up where the people were, but he was scorched a little before he could get there, and that is the reason bats are yellowish in color. After the bad animals had all been burned the people returned to the world again, and ever since the world has been a good place to live upon.

25. HOW THE BUFFALO CEASED TO EAT HUMAN BEINGS.*

When the world was new there were many wild and fierce animals, and the buffalo were among the fiercest, for they ate human beings. In those days the buffalo were many-colored and roamed the plains in great herds, and were so numerous that men could not go out on the plains alone for fear of being caught by them. There was one great man who received power from the Father, and he had the power to go right into the midst of these terrible animals and kill them without being hurt. That man was Buzzard, and he was the only man who possessed such power. All the other people had to live in villages together that they might protect each other and hunt together. One time some men went out in the timber alone to hunt turkey and deer. They wandered far, and when they started home they found that they had to cross a long stretch of lonely prairie. While they were hurrying across the vast stretch of country they saw a black cloud arise in the west and come nearer and nearer, until at last they knew that a great herd of buffalo was sweeping down upon them. They threw the game from their backs, threw away their bows and arrows, and ran as fast as the wind. The buffalo, dangerous as they were, were not good runners, and so the men reached the timber before them and ran into the dense thicket.

After these men succeeded in escaping, the people took courage and ventured farther away from home. One time four men went out to hunt bear. They went into the timber that lay between two mountains and there they found the fresh tracks of a bear. They trailed it all through the timber and over the mountain, and found it at the edge of the timber at the foot of the mountain. The bear ran out to the open plain and the men pursued and killed it. While they were cutting it up to carry home they heard a great noise, like thunder, coming across the plains. They looked and saw that the buffalo were upon them. They tried to escape, but it was too late. The buffalo caught all but one man, who succeeded in gaining the timber and climbing a tall tree. All day the buffalo surrounded the tree and tried to butt it down, but could not. Night came on, then they returned to the plains and the man climbed down and ran to his home. He told all the

---

* Told by White-Bread.

people how the buffalo had surprised them and had killed his three companions.   The people hastened to the place, but found nothing but a few bones scattered about.   From that time on the buffalo ate many people, until Coyote came.   Then the people left this dangerous country and went into another.   They went through the gate to the new country, and Coyote went with them.   He was the last to go through the gate, and as he went he shut the gate, so no dangerous animals could enter, and he let through only a few buffalo who had never tasted human flesh and so were not dangerous.

26. THE GIRL WHO HAD POWER TO CALL THE BUFFALO.

A girl who had power to call the buffalo lived with her six brothers. The brothers were stars, and every night they left the girl to travel through the sky.   Every morning after they had returned from their nightly journey they put the girl in a swing of lariat rope that hung down from the sky and swung her through the air.   As she swung through the air the buffalo saw her and came.   The boys killed all that they wanted, and then the rest of the herd went away.   In this way the girl called the buffalo for her brothers, and so they always had plenty to eat.

One time Coyote came to visit them, and, finding that they always had meat, he decided to come and live with them.   The brothers did not think much of Coyote, but they decided to let him stay.   Every morning he watched the boys put their sister in the swing and swing her until the buffalo came.   Before the brothers would let Coyote watch them swing her they made him promise that he would never try to do the same while they were gone, because if any one else tried to swing the girl he would swing her too hard and she would swing to the sky and never return.   Coyote promised, but one day while all of the brothers were gone he called the girl to come and get into the swing. She refused, but he threatened her and made her obey him.   She climbed into the swing and Coyote pushed her.   The buffalo did not come, and so he pushed her again and caused her to go higher and higher through the air until she disappeared.   Coyote became frightened and called to her to come down, saying that if she did not come he would jump up and pull her down.   The girl did not come, and he could not see her.

When the brothers came home they missed their sister and asked Coyote where she was.   He said that he did not know, but that he thought some monster had carried her away.   The brothers knew that Coyote had lied, and that he had been the cause of her disappearance. They drove Coyote away, telling him that he and his children would always be hungry because he had disobeyed them. Then they held a council among themselves and decided to go to the sky and live there with their sister.

27. THE OLD WOMAN WHO KEPT ALL THE PECANS.*

There lived an old woman who was mother to all the pecan trees. She owned all of the trees and gathered all the nuts herself. When people went to her lodge she would give them a few pecans to eat, but would never allow them to take any away. The people were very fond of pecans and they wanted some for their own use, but the old woman would not let them have any. One time the people were very hungry and the old woman had everything in her lodge filled with pecans, but she would give them only a few when they went to see her and she made them eat them before going away. This made the people angry and they decided that something must be done.

There was in the village an old man who had four little sons who were very troublesome and meddlesome. The people—they were the field Rats—thought that these four little boys would be the right ones to go over to the old woman's house some night to try to steal some of the nuts. They chose the four boys both because they were small and quiet and sly and because they were such a nuisance around the village that they would be no great loss to the people if the old woman killed them. The Rats were willing to go because they were always glad to be meddling. They chose one to slip over and make sure that the old woman was asleep. He went to her lodge and peeped in through a small crack and saw that she was still at work. He waited until she finished her work and went to bed ; then when he heard her snore he ran back home to tell his brothers to come. When he went inside his father's lodge he saw a stranger sitting there. The stranger was Coyote. He had come to tell the Rats not to trouble about stealing pecans from the old woman, for he was going over the next day and kill her. Coyote was afraid to trust the Rats. He wanted to go himself, so he could get the most of the pecans. The next morning he went over to see the old woman and acted very friendly. The old woman gave him some pecans and he sat down and ate them all up. Then he asked her for some more, and as she turned around to get them he pulled out his stone knife and struck her on the head. She died, and ever since then the pecan trees have grown everywhere and belong to all of the people.

---

* Told by Wing.

28. THE COWARD, THE SON OF THE MOON.*

In the beginning, when the people first came out of the earth, a little boy was taken out with his grandparents, but his mother and father were left behind in the earth. The old people loved the child dearly and cared for him, but because they were old they were poor, and so the boy was often hungry. Sometimes other little boys took him to their lodges and fed him, and then the old people were happy ; for they did not mind being hungry themselves, so long as their grandson had something to eat. He grew rapidly and soon became old enough to hunt game ; then the old people always had plenty to eat, for he was successful on the hunt. One time, when he came home from a long hunt, he found his grandmother sick, and in a few days she died. The boy grieved for his grandmother, but remained with his grandfather to comfort and provide food for him. One day the grandfather, who was an old man, dropped dead. Then the boy, left all alone, gave up to his grief and spent days and nights in mourning. He wandered far away into the timber to mourn, and in his grief and loneliness he prayed that he might die. While he was praying one evening, just as the sun was going down, he heard some one calling him. He turned and saw a man coming, and when the man came near he opened out his arms to embrace the boy, and said : "I will be your father, and I will look upon you as my own son. One time you wished for me, and now I have come to claim you as my own. I am the Moon, who keeps watch over everything in this world. Go back to your people now and some time I will come for you. In the meantime remember that I will always watch over you and give you power."

The young man went back to his home and wept no more, for he did not feel so lonely and forsaken, now that he had a father. After a time a girl came to his lodge and asked to become his wife. He accepted her and they lived together. One time while they were at dinner he said : "Some one is coming with news for the chief." The person was then several days' journey from the village, and so his wife saw that her husband had great power. One time he was told by a mother to watch her child while she went out to get water. She told him that the child was asleep, and if it woke up to give it a buffalo bone to suck. When the mother was gone he woke the child up and cut its leg off. When the mother returned she saw her child lying dead upon the blankets, and saw the young man sitting beside it playing with its

---

* Told by Caddo George.

leg. She ran and called the people and they came and killed the young man. Soon after they heard that he was living with another family not far away. The people went to the place where they had buried him and saw that he had come out of the grave. Then they went to the family with whom it was reported he was living, and they found him there alive and looking just the same as before they had killed him.

One time the tribe went on the war-path and fought another tribe. All the men went except this man. The chief asked him why he did not go with the others to fight the enemy and kill a man instead of a little child. Coward, for so the people called him, said that his father had not told him to have trouble with people. The chief asked him who his father was, but he did not answer. He arose, took up a war club, and went out to fight. The enemy shot many arrows at him, but soon they saw that the arrows flew off from him, and they knew that he was wonderful and could not be killed. They turned to run, and as they ran he killed many with his war club. The next day he became sick and began to shake all over. Finally he vomited all the arrow heads that had pierced his body, then he bathed himself and was well. After that the people knew that he had some great power. Many years after he told his people that he was going away, and that evening when the Moon came up he pointed to it and said: "There is my father." Then he arose from the earth and went up to the Moon.

29. THE FIRST WAR PARTY.*

When the people came into the world there were so many that they had to be divided into groups, and each group was given a different name, although they all belonged to the same tribe. After a time the tribes began to fight with each other, and the Caddo fought the Kiowa and Comanche. The Caddo gathered one time in council and the chief told the errand-man to cry out for all the young men to come to the council. The young men came and the chief asked all of those who wanted to fight the other tribes to sit in a circle. After the circle was formed the chief brought the largest buffalo hide that he had and laid it upon the ground in the center of the circle. Then he gave each man a stick and they all beat the buffalo hide with the sticks and sang a war song. They began singing at sunset and continued until Morning Star drove the other stars away.

In the meantime the chief and his assistants went ahead to choose a good place with water near by to make a camp. At dawn all the men

---

*Told by Wing.

arose and marched out to the place, continuing their war song as they went. They were not allowed to go back to their homes, but had to march all together out of the village. They waited until noon at the place the chief had chosen, so that others who decided late to join the party would have time to catch up with them. They all stopped their songs and ate, and, while they were eating, the chief made the following speech :

" I want to make certain rules for you, my men, for if you are to become great warriors you must learn to obey. First, I want all to move forward in one body and want none to stop by the way. I will appoint two men who shall be water-carriers, and I want each man to drink only when water is brought by the water-carriers, and not to stop and drink at every spring or stream. A drink of water three times a day is enough for each man. We will also eat three times a day. March on, now, and remember to keep in one body, that we may overcome the enemy."

They marched by day and made camp by night. The chief always camped about a hundred yards in advance of the others, facing the enemy's country. When the men were near the enemy's country the chief appointed four men to go on ahead as spies and to come back at night and report. They went out in all directions, but before going they arranged a meeting place, so that if any one saw the enemy he could go to that place, give the signal, and the other spies could join him and all race back to tell the leader that they had seen the enemy. When they reached camp they stood in line and waited for the water-carriers to give them a drink before they began to speak.

They went on until they found the enemy and fought them, but scalped only one, for that was enough to show that they had been victorious. When the battle was over the warriors were all left to do as they pleased. The chief sent word to their homes that they had defeated the enemy and were bringing back a scalp. The people decked themselves in paint and feathers and went out to meet the returning war party. When the people met the party the chief told the man who had the scalp to put it on a pole, and then all the young men raced for it, and the one who got it ran on until some one overtook him ; then that one took the scalp and ran on until some one overtook him, and so they raced home. The people at home were waiting for them, and when they arrived they all joined in a big war dance.

So it was with the first war party, and so it has been with all war parties since that time.

30. THE POWER OF THE CYCLONE.*

A boy sat down on the banks of the river to rest after his morning bath, and as he sat there watching the sun come up and listening to the water and trees, a voice from some place spoke in his ear and said : "Boy, I have been watching you at your bath every morning. I know that your grandmother has sent you here every day in winter and in summer to plunge into the water, no matter how cold, that you might gain strength and become a strong man, hardened to endure. I have come to give you that strength that you desire, and even more."

The boy looked about him through the trees and in the water, but for a long time he saw nothing. After he had gazed into the water for a long time he saw slowly arising to the surface a man. The boy was not frightened, but sat still on the bank and waited. The man came close and spoke to him, saying : "Dive into the water four times, and as you dive always face the west." After the boy had dived four times and again sat on the bank, the unknown person said : "I am the power of the Cyclone. Once I was so strong and powerful that I held all the Winds in my control, and all people feared me, but now I am growing old and my strength is going from me. For some time I have been looking over the world to find some one to take my place and to whom I could intrust my powers. As I was looking and almost despairing of finding a worthy young man, I found you. From that time I have been watching you, and now at last I am come to give my power to you. Swing your arms about." The young man began to swing his arms, and soon a big, black cloud rolled up in the north. It passed to the west, and then, as the boy threw his arms about faster, the wind broke from the cloud and passed through the forest, tearing up trees by the roots and tossing the waters in fury as it went. At last the man cried in a loud voice that was barely heard above the roar of the winds, "Stand still !"

The boy dropped his arms at his sides and stood breathless and panting with the exertion. The man said : "You have received my power. Take care that you never abuse it, and send the cyclone only in the spring, when it is necessary. I give you the name 'Path-of-the-Cyclone' to be yours, and people shall know you by that name." Then the man disappeared. Years after the people came to know the power the boy possessed when they saw him carried through the air to the sky on the breast of the cyclone.

---

*Told by Wing.

31. HOW THE CANNIBAL WAS DESTROYED.*

In the beginning of this world there lived many kinds of fierce animals. Among these animals was one especially that was called by the people living in those times the cannibal.

One time there were three men who went out hunting. They went a long way from home and kept on going farther and farther in search of game. One day they came to a country timbered with many large trees. They came to one of these trees and saw that something had been climbing on the tree, and near the base there was a large hole. The men thought that a bear must have made the hole, and that the bear was in the hole. They gathered dry leaves and grass and made it up into a small bundle, and they set the bundle on fire and tied it to the end of a long pole and thrust the burning bundle into the hole. They kept on dropping bundles into the hole until they thought it about time the bear should come out. One of the bundles which was put into the hole dropped out from the hole, and then they knew that the bear was coming out. Finally some strange animal came and peeped out from the hole, and it was not a bear, but a cannibal.

As soon as they saw and knew what kind of animal it was, they ran. The smoke cleared away and the cannibal came down from the tree and smelled around until he scented the tracks of the men, and then he began to follow them. These men were on foot and the cannibal was very swift, and so it was not long until he overtook one of the men and killed him. Then the animal took the man back to the woods, to the large tree, and went back after the other two men. After running a long way he overtook the second man. He killed him and carried him back and placed him by the side of the first man. Then he returned for the third man. When the third man was almost overtaken, and was running with all his might, he saw something flat on the ground in front of him, but he did not stop. He saw that it was a mountain-lion, lying there watching and waiting for the approaching cannibal. The man ran on a way, then turned around and looked back to see what the mountain-lion would do. The cannibal did not see the mountain-lion lying there, and before he knew anything the mountain-lion jumped upon him and seized him by the throat. Finally the cannibal was overpowered and killed, and then the man started on for his home. When he got home he told his people what had happened to the other two men. When they all heard this they started down where he last saw the cannibal, and when they got to the place they found nothing

* Told by Annie Wilson.

but many white and black wolves, which had already eaten the body, and there was nothing left but the bones of the cannibal. The men went on to the tree where the cannibal had lived. The tree was not burning, and so the men began to cut the tree down, and when it fell they found two bodies. They took the bodies out from the tree and buried them a short distance away.

32. THE YOUNG MEN AND THE CANNIBALS.*

Ten boys lived with their grandmother. One day the oldest went out to hunt and did not return. The grandmother worried about him, and so the next day one of his brothers went to look for him. He did not return, and so the next brother went out to look for his brothers. He did not return and another went, and so on until the ninth boy went out, leaving his little brother at home with his grandmother. They waited long, but none of the brothers returned and no news came of them. They worried and grieved and became sadder each day, until at last the youngest boy declared that he was going to look for his brothers. His grandmother begged him not to go and leave her alone, for she felt that the same evil fate would befall him that had come to his brothers; but the boy was determined and prepared to go. He went out and prayed for help and put an eagle feather in his hair just before starting, thinking that it might have some hidden power. The boy traveled far, and after a time he saw a tipi. He approached the tipi, and as he went near he heard some one laugh and say : "Another one is coming. Cook some corn and we will soon have the meat." The boy understood the meaning of this, but he was so sad and weary that he thought he would as soon die as live, and so he went on to the tipi. An old man came out of the tipi and said to him : "Are you looking for your nine brothers?" "Yes," the boy answered. Then the man said : "I know where your brothers are and I will put you on the right path to find them, but first you must do some work for me. Lift that big log there and put it on the fire. I will give you four trials, and then if you can not do it you must lie down upon the log and let me lift it."

The boy did not believe anything the man said, but thought he would try to lift the log and see if some power would not come to his aid in answer to his prayers. He tried four times, but could not move the log; then he lay down upon it. The old man was just about to spear him with the iron nose of the mask he wore, when some unseen power pulled the boy off the log, and the iron nose of the mask caught

---

* Told by Wing.

in the log and held the old man fast. A voice said to the boy : " Run to the tipi and take the pounder away from the woman who is pounding corn, bring it here, and beat the old man to death." The boy obeyed, and when the old man was dead, the voice said : " Gather up all of your brothers' bones. I will help you, for I know the bones of each boy, and put them in nine piles." A strange man, the possessor of the voice, appeared and helped the boy gather up the bones. When they had them all piled up the man said : " Put your robe over them, shoot an arrow up in the sky, then cry : ' Look out, brothers, the arrow will hit you!'" The boy obeyed, and as he cried " Look out, brothers, the arrow will hit you !" his brothers jumped out from under the robe. The man then told them to burn the tipi with the man and his wife in it and to scatter the ashes. After they had done all that, the man said : " Return now to your grandmother. I am the Sun and I have helped you destroy the cannibals." Then he disappeared. The brothers all returned to their grandmother, who had almost grieved herself to death. They told their story, and the youngest boy told how the Sun had taken pity on him and helped him ; and from that time all the people knew that the Sun was their friend and always willing to help them in times of trouble.

33. COYOTE AND THE SIX BROTHERS.

An old woman lived alone with her seven sons. They were all good hunters and kept her busy preparing the game that they killed. One day the oldest son went out to hunt and did not return. After several days his dogs came back, but he did not come. The second son decided to go to search for his brother, and so he took the dogs and started out. After several days the dogs came back, but the second son did not come. The third son decided to go after his missing brothers. Again the dogs returned alone, and the brothers did not come. The fourth, the fifth, and the sixth sons in turn went to search for their missing brothers, but each time the dogs came back alone. The youngest son wanted to go, but his mother could not give him up, for she feared that he, too, would go, never to return. One day, after the brothers had been gone a long time, the little boy saw a raccoon in a tree. He asked his mother if he could not take his bow and arrow and kill it. She said that he could, and gave him his bow and arrow. He chased the raccoon from one tree to another until it had led him far into the thick timber. Finally it ran down a hollow tree and he climbed the tree to get it out. While he was in the tree he heard some one speak, and, turning around, he saw a little old woman standing by the tree. " Throw the raccoon down here, and I and the dogs will kill it," she said. He threw the raccoon down and the old woman killed it and one of the dogs. Then she said, ''There is another raccoon in the tree.'' He pulled out another raccoon and threw it down. She killed it and another one of his dogs. He saw another raccoon in the tree and he pulled it out, and again she killed it and another dog. He continued to pull raccoons out of the tree until he had pulled six, and each time the old woman killed the raccoon and another dog. As the boy was about to pull the seventh raccoon out, it spoke to him and said: ''Boy, when you get me out, throw me just as far as you can. I will run away and the old woman will chase me. While she is chasing me, you must jump and run home as fast as possible. She has already killed all of your dogs, and she will kill you next. She is a witch, and is the one who has killed all of your brothers. You must run from her.'' The boy said that he would, and then he threw the raccoon just as far as he could. While the old woman was chasing it he jumped out of the tree and started to run home. The old woman killed the raccoon, then returned to the tree, and when she found the boy gone she was angry, and started after him as fast as she could run, but he was too far ahead, and she could not catch him.

When the boy reached home he told his mother all that had happened. That night he had a strange dream, in which he dreamed that he met Coyote, and Coyote told him that his brothers were not dead, but were with some bad people who made them work so hard that they would soon die if they did not get away, and Coyote promised to help him rescue his brothers. The next morning he told his mother his dream, and she told him that his dream would probably come true. That very afternoon the boy went out to hunt, and while he was walking along he met a man, and the man told him the same thing that the man in the dream had told him. The boy returned to his home and the man went on through the timber until he met Flying Squirrel. He was one of the bad people's slaves and had to work for them. Coyote, for he was the man, began to talk to Squirrel and asked him about the bad people. Squirrel told him that the bad people made slaves of all of the people that they could catch alive, and that they ate all that they killed. Coyote asked about the six brothers, and Squirrel told Coyote that they were slaves like himself and could not get away, but had to work. Coyote said that he would like to help them, and that he thought he could, for he was very cunning and had a good deal of power. Squirrel told Coyote if he could only find some way to kill the wicked chief that there would be no more trouble. Coyote said that he thought he could plan to kill him if he could only get to him, but that he lived across the river and had no way of getting across. Flying Squirrel said that he would take him across if he thought he could hold on to his tail as he flew. Coyote said that he could, and so they started. When they were almost to the other bank Coyote let go Squirrel's tail and fell into the water. He hid in the tall grass until he thought of a plan. When he had made up his mind what he was going to do, he turned into a nice, new corn mill, and floated out on the water where he would be in plain sight. Soon a woman came down to the river to get some water. She saw the mill and tried to get it, but could not. She ran back and told the chief about the nice, new mill, and asked him to get it for her. He told her that he was afraid it was Coyote, or some one trying to play a trick on them, but the woman said that it could not be anything but a fine corn mill and that she wanted it. The chief sent some one to get it, and then all of the women came to pound their corn in the new mill. They used it for several days, and all thought it was the best mill they had ever had. One day some one put some fine sweet corn in it, and after she had ground a little while all of her corn was gone. She ran to the chief and told him. He said that the corn mill was Coyote, as he had feared, and he told the people to bring it to him. They brought it, and he placed it on the big log where he always speared people with his long, spiked nose. He raised his head high, then dropped it, and his nose stuck in the log so that he could not get loose. The corn mill had rolled off the log and turned into Coyote. He grabbed the chief by the head and held him there while he called all the slaves to come and kill him. With the others came the six brothers. After they had killed the chief, Coyote told all that they were free, and to go to their homes. The six brothers returned to their home, and ever after that whenever they killed any game they always left some for Coyote.

34. THE DEATH OF THE CANNIBALS.*

There was a village called Tall-Timber-on-Top-of-Hill, and the people decided to move from that village to another. They were all ready to go when a baby was born to a young woman whose husband had died. The woman could not make the long journey with the new baby, and the people were unwilling to wait for her, so they decided to go on and leave her to follow when she was strong enough to carry the child. The woman remained alone in the deserted village for many days. She was afraid to be there alone, and counted the days until she could start to the new village. One night as she sat with only her child in the grass lodge she heard some one outside, and a strange voice begged admission. She was frightened, but let the man in, and said: "Are

*Told by Shorter.

you from my people?" "No," said he, "though I often go around their village at night. Do not be frightened, and I will tell you who I am. People call me Spotted-Wolf. I have come here to see you and your child and to beg you not to start too soon on your journey, for there are many dangerous animals on the way." The woman replied : "I know, but I want to go to my people. It is lonely here, and I am afraid." Spotted-Wolf said : "I am afraid something will happen to you if you go now. Take this tobacco, and if you meet danger and need help throw some of it to the four directions and call to me, and I will come and help you." The woman took the tobacco ; then Spotted-Wolf arose and went to his home.

After a few days the woman decided to start on her journey. She put her child on her back and started. After she had traveled three days she saw in her way a strange-looking being. She went on, and as she came nearer she was not certain whether it was a wild animal or a person ; but in a moment it dropped on the ground and rolled over twice, and then she saw that it was a wild animal. Again she looked and saw that it had taken the form of a person. Then she knew that it was a cannibal, for those creatures first appear as human beings ; then they turn into wild animals and eat people. She was frightened so that she could not go on, for she thought that she and her child would be eaten by the cannibal. She thought of Spotted-Wolf and took some tobacco out of her bag and threw it to the south, the east, the west, and the north ; and as she threw it she prayed that Spotted-Wolf would come and help her. Soon she heard the howl of a wolf in the south, then another in the east, another in the west, and another in the north. The cannibal stopped growling at her and looked frightened. In a moment big spotted wolves were coming from the four directions. They killed the cannibal, and the wolf from the south conducted the woman and her child in safety to the village of her people.

There is another kind of cannibal, though not so dangerous as the one who first appears as a human being, then turns to an animal. These cannibals live as human beings and eat people only after they are dead. Whenever they hear of any one who is sick and about to die they pretend to be sick, too, and when they hear that the sick person is dead, they pretend to die, too, and are buried ; but in the night they jump out of their graves and steal the dead person before the spirits can take him away.

One time there was an old medicine-man and he had noticed how certain people got sick whenever they heard of any one else being sick, and how they died when the sick person died, and then how they always came to life again. He watched one of these beings for a long time ;

then he pretended to be very sick and caused it to be rumored about that he was about to die. Soon he heard that the person he had been watching was sick. Then the medicine-man pretended that he was dead, but before he pretended to die he told his sons to put a bow and some arrows in his grave, and told them not to put much earth over him when they buried him. As soon as the person heard that the medicine-man was dead, he pretended to die also, and was buried. That night he jumped out of his grave and went to get the medicine-man. The medicine-man heard him coming, and so he jumped out of his grave and shot an arrow through the cannibal and killed him, so that he never came back to life again. Then the medicine-man told the people what he had done, and ever since that bows and arrows are always put in the graves with the dead, that they may shoot the cannibal.

35. THE MAN WHO MADE ARROWS FOR GHOST.*

Two men arose and went out to hunt before daybreak, and they were a long way from their village when the sun came up. They hunted all day and far into the evening, but did not find anything. They decided to stay in the timber and sleep that night, so they might hunt next day, for they hated to go home empty-handed. They threw themselves down on a soft, grassy place and slept soundly, for they were weary. After they had been asleep for a long time both awoke with a start and listened. Soon they heard a voice whooping, the same that had awakened them. One of the men was so frightened that he jumped up and ran for home through the dark. The other man was brave and was ashamed to run, for he had not run from anything in all his life. He arose and stood his ground. Soon a dead person stood before him. He asked the man if he could help him get into Spirit Land. He said : " I have been trying for a long time, but can not get any farther, for my bowstring has a knot in it. Can't you give me a bowstring and make me two new arrows?" The man said that he would, and so he sat down to make the arrows. Then he put a new string on the dead person's bow. The dead person shot the arrows and went up in the air with them. Before going he told the man that he would whoop when he was high up in the air, to let him know that the arrows had carried him up all right, and he wanted the man to whoop back, to let him know that he had heard him. The man listened and soon he heard a whoop. He answered it, and then he heard nothing more, so he knew that the man had entered Spirit Land. The next day he returned to his people and told them the story, and ever since that time bows

---

* Told by Wing.

and arrows are always made and buried with the dead, so that they can go to Spirit Land at once and not have to wander about. But no one ever makes bows and arrows at night, because they are afraid some of the ghosts might come for them and cause a death in the family, for whenever a ghost appears it is a sign of death.

36. THE LAZY BOYS WHO BECAME THE PLEIADES.*

Long, long ago, in the beginning of this world, there lived an old woman with seven children, who were all boys. The boys were full of life and fun and they would go away from the others and play all the day long, and would not work, nor take time to eat but twice a day—morning and evening. When they came home in the evening their mother would scold them, and one evening when they came home late for their supper their mother would not let them have anything to eat. The boys were very angry and went back to their play and determined on the morrow to go away where they would never trouble her any more. The next morning early they went down to their playground before breakfast and began to go round and round the house, praying to the spirits to help them. At last their mother noticed and heard what they were saying, and as she watched them she noticed that their feet were off the earth, and then she knew that something was wrong, and she ran out trying to get her children, but it was too late. With every round they rose higher and higher in the air, and were soon above the roof of the house. They circled higher and higher until they went up to the sky, where we can see them now as the Seven Stars. These seven boys who were taken to the sky were very indolent, and when the work time came they would always slip off and play. That is the reason that during the winter months the Seven Stars can be seen ; but at the beginning of the spring months, at the work time, the Seven Stars are gone.

37. THE LOST TIMBER SPIRITS.†

When the world was new the old man, Coyote, decided that if a man, woman, or child died they should return to the earth again after ten days. Finally Coyote made another rule, and that was that when anybody died and was buried within six days he should stay under the ground, but if not buried by the seventh day he might escape. If caught before he succeeded in getting away he was to be brought back home. When the person was caught, a fire was kindled all around him ; but finally he threw off the fire from him, and then was taken back to his home,

---

* Told by Wing.　　　† Told by Short-Man.

where he was kept for six days and nights. At the end of the sixth day some old woman washed him, and then they let him go, and he became a real person again.

When a person dies they dig a hole in the ground about four or five feet long and about three or four feet wide—according to the size of the person—and the body is laid head toward the west and feet toward the east. One of the family builds a fire at the feet of the person, and this fire should be kept up for six days and nights. Very often the person forgets to keep up the fire and lets it go out before the end of the sixth day, and when this happens they find that the grave is open and tracks are seen leading toward the east. They follow the tracks sometimes and overtake the dead person, but generally he gets away from them when they do overtake him. They build the fire all around the dead person; the wood for that purpose is cedar and mulberry trees, and the sparks from the fire get on the person. At first the dead person pays no attention, but the people keep on building up the fire until the dead person begins to look around and tries to escape the sparks from the fire. Then they know the dead person is coming to life again, for he is beginning to feel, and then they take hold of him and bring him back home, where he is kept for six days and nights. At the sixth day, in the early evening, some one of the family would bathe him, and then he would live again. When the dead person is not caught he becomes something like a very large monkey, and lives in the thickets and timber. Whenever the people meet a dead person he talks to them, and so the people think that dead people are crazy people. They do not know where their homes are or who their relatives are, and so they go off and stay in the woods or among the wild animals. That is the reason that large monkeys are called "the last people in the thickets." When any one or two people go out to hunt in the thickets or woods they always meet these monkeys, and monkeys always ask for a wrestling match. They are very strong little men, and if the people do not pay any attention to them, they bother them all night long. These creatures are still living, but they do not talk as they did when the world was new.

38. THE MAN WHO TURNED INTO A SNAKE.*

One time two boys who were close friends went out hunting. They met a large snake, and one of the boys killed it and cooked it. The other boy begged him not to eat it, but to eat the buffalo meat that he had prepared ; but the boy would not listen to him and ate the snake meat. That was in the evening. The next morning the boy who had

---

* Told by Wing.

eaten the snake meat began to turn into a snake. After another day and night he had completely turned into a snake. He told his friend to go to the mountain and find a hole for him to live in. The friend found a hole and carried the snake to it. The snake told him to go to their village and tell his people what had happened to him, and to tell them that whenever they went to hunt to stop and offer presents to him and he would help them in the hunt. The snake lived there for many years, until the lightning killed him.

39. THE WOMAN WHO TURNED INTO A SNAKE.*

A long time ago there lived a man and his wife and a dog. At that time the animals talked like human beings, and so the dog talked to the man and woman. Every day the man went out to hunt, and as soon as he was gone his wife always went away and never returned until evening, just before her husband came. He did not know that she left home in his absence until one time his dog said : "I believe you ought to know that your wife goes away and stays all the time that you are gone." The man told his dog to follow her the next time she went away. Early the next morning the man started out hunting and the woman left home as usual. The dog followed her, but stayed a good distance behind, so that she did not know that he had followed her. She went to the large timber and stopped at one of the large trees and stood there looking up, and then after she had stood there for some time she whistled once, and then again and again. The third time she whistled the dog saw something moving out from a large hole in the tree, and finally the dog saw that it was a big snake. The snake came down to the ground and went straight to the woman, and began crawling up on her and coiling round and round her body. Finally the snake began to move away from her and crept back to the hole in the tree. That night the dog told the man what he had seen. The next day the man made many arrows and told his wife that he and the dog were going out fishing. Instead of going down to fish they went to the place where the snake was, and when they were there the man went near to the tree and whistled three times. The snake began to creep out, and when it had reached the ground the man shot it and killed it, and then cut it up in very small pieces, so that the pieces looked like pieces of fish. They went down to the river and began to fish, and they caught a few small fish and took them home. When they arrived at their home the man told his wife that he was going to cook the fish himself, and told her to go in the grass house until the dinner was brought to her. She went,

---

*Told by Annie Wilson.

and the man began to cook the fish and the snake flesh. When he was through he took the snake flesh to his wife for her dinner. He and the dog ate the fish. He sent the dog into the grass house to see what his wife was doing, and the dog saw that she was eating the snake. He was sent in the second time, and he saw that she was scratching herself all over her body. Every place she scratched herself the skin would turn the color of the snake skin, until she finally turned into a snake. She crept away from the grass lodge and went to find the snake, for she did not know that he was dead. Some time after, the man went out hunting and he came to a large tree. He heard something making a noise inside of the tree and finally saw a large snake come out from the tree. He knew that it was his wife, but he passed on.

40. HOW OWL FOOLED THE GIRLS WHO WANTED TO MARRY THE CHIEF.*

One time there lived an old man and woman who had two beautiful twin daughters. These girls heard of a chief who lived in another village, and rumors of his great wealth and his fame as a great chief had traveled far. The girls asked their parents if they might not go to the chief and offer themselves in marriage. Their parents consented, and so the girls started to the chief's village. They did not know just where the village was, but they started in the direction that they thought it was, and decided to ask the first person they met to direct them. They traveled along for a time and then met a man with a turkey in his hand coming down the road. They stopped him and began to talk to him. "We want to marry this famous chief, for we hear that he is good and very wealthy, but we do not know him. We have never seen him, we have not even been to his village, and perhaps we would not know him if we should see him." The man grinned to himself and said: "I am the chief and I live just a little way from here; I have been away attending a council. Well, I must say that I am willing, but wait here while I run on home and tell my grandmother."

The girls waited. They thought it strange that so great a chief should have to tell his grandmother, but they said nothing. The man, who was no other than Owl, ran on to his home, and calling his grandmother, said: "Clean up the lodge and put it in order. I am going to bring home two girls whom I am playing a joke on. They think I am the rich chief and want to marry me." After they had cleaned the lodge, for it was very disorderly, Owl said: "I am going to put this turkey which I have brought home over my bed; when you get up in the morning ask me which turkey you shall cook and pretend to point

---

*Told by Wing.

to one, and I will say, 'No, take this.' Then the girls will think that we have many turkeys and many good things to eat."

Owl went back for the girls and brought them to his grandmother's lodge. They were pleased, for everything looked neat and nice, and so they married Owl. Every day Owl came in with a turkey, and he always pretended to have been out hunting. Really he had been at the council, and the chief gave him the turkey for allowing him to sit on his back. At all the councils the chief always sat on Owl's back, and so he gave Owl a turkey every time to repay him for his trouble and the pain of holding him so long. After many moons the twins grew weary of nothing but turkey and they began to suspect something, so one day they followed Owl when he went away. They followed and saw him go to a large grass lodge. They peeped through an opening, and there they saw Owl sitting in the middle of the lodge with the chief sitting on his head. They gave a scream. Owl recognized their voices and jumped up, throwing the chief off his head, and ran home. He gave his grandmother a terrible scolding for letting the girls follow him and find him out. The girls felt so ashamed when they discovered how they had been fooled, that they slipped off to their home and told their father and mother their experience.

Owl sat in his lonely lodge and thought for a long time about the twin sisters, and the longer he thought the more angry he became, because he had been fooled at his own joke. Finally, he said to his grandmother : "We must kill the people, and in order to do that we must gather all the water, from the smallest to the largest rivers and the springs and the lakes. We will have to dig a big hole here, and when we finish the hole we will begin to dam the waters out from all the rivers, springs, and lakes." They worked long and hard, and the people did not notice that the creeks, lakes, and springs were getting low until they were dry.

The water was gone and the people were dying of thirst, while Owl splashed and swam about in the water in the big hole where he had all the waters of the earth. Every one went out to search for water, and Crow, who was snow white then, went with the others. He came to a field where the grass was all dried and withered for want of water, and big grasshoppers were jumping about in the grass. Crow ran after them and made such a loud noise in trying to catch them that all the people heard. They thought that he had found water, and so they ran in great haste. When they found that Crow had not found water they were all disappointed and angry at him for fooling them. Coyote jumped on Crow and rolled him about in the black earth until he was black, and ever since that time the crow has always been black as night. After that

Coyote made a rule that if any one made a loud noise and aroused the people's expectations he must either lead them to water or take a hard whipping. Turtle was traveling along one day searching for water, as they all were. He went down to the river bed, where the water had been, and he fell into a large crack in the dried mud. He began to halloo for help. The people heard him and all ran down to the river bed, for they thought surely he had found water ; but when they found he was only calling for help, Coyote took him out of the crack and gave him a hard whipping. He whipped him so hard that he cracked his shell, and to this day turtles bear the markings of the cracks on their shells.

One time some one was going along looking for water, when he heard a big splashing noise, and he knew that it was the sound of water. He went until he came to the hole where Owl sat playing in the water. He went back and told the people. They gathered in council to decide how they could get the water from Owl. They were about to give up when Flea said that he would go to Owl's lodge and try to free the water. He went, and as he entered the lodge Owl's grandmother was about to take a bath. She had a big jar full of water sitting in front of her. Flea slipped up to her, crawled up her leg, and bit her ; she gave a big kick and upset the jar. When Owl saw the water running in every direction he opened his eyes wide in astonishment, and they have always looked that way ever since. All the people felt very grateful to Flea, and Coyote put him on his back that he might have a good warm home.

41. THE POOR HUNTER AND THE ALLIGATOR POWER.*

One time the hunters went out on a two months' hunt. They took their wives with them. After they had gone a long distance from home they camped. Among these hunters was a poor man and his wife who were hungry and starving, while every one else was killing plenty of game and having an abundance to eat. The poor man would go out to hunt from early in the morning till sundown and come home with nothing to eat. He continued to hunt day after day, expecting to find deer or some game, but always returned without anything. The people would not give him anything to eat and would make fun of the unfortunate man because he could not kill anything. One morning he arose early and started out and hunted all morning. About noon he heard some one calling him, and the person was a long distance away. He started to see who it was and what was the matter with

---

* Told by White-Bread.

him, and when he got there he asked the person why he called. "Well," said the person, "I want to find out where there is water." The hunter told him there was some water a short distance from where they were. He did not know who the man was, for there was no such person among his people. The unknown person asked the man to carry him to the water, so the hunter told him to get on his back and he would carry him. When they reached the water the unknown man told the hunter to take off his clothes, and so he did, and then the unknown man told him to get on his back, saying: "It is now my time to carry you on my back. Shut your eyes and do not open them until I say so." The man obeyed, and when the unknown person told him to open his eyes he did not know where he was. Then the unknown person told him that he wanted him to come and see what he had. The hunter looked and saw the heads of all kinds of animals. "Now," said the unknown person, "there is what I have killed, and I will tell you why I brought you here. I am going to give you some of my powers that you may kill game as I do. Point out the heads of the animals that you want to kill." The man pointed to the largest deer head, bear head, etc. "And now," said the unknown person, "you must not tell any one how and where you obtained your powers. All people call me Alligator, and I will give you these powers as long as you are able to hunt." Alligator then told him to shut his eyes, and when he told him to open them he saw that he was upon dry land once more. Alligator told him to go hunting, and so after he put on his clothes he started out to hunt.

He did not go very far until he saw four big deer coming toward him and he killed every one of them. He dressed them carefully and then left them while he went to his camp. When he reached his camp he found his wife there, but nothing to eat. He went out and led up two of his horses and asked his wife to go with him. They arrived at the place and found the four deer. The man put two of the deer on one horse's back and two on the other one, and they started back to their camp. As they came into camp with their horses loaded with meat, everybody at the camp saw them and wondered, for they did not think the man could ever kill a deer. After that time he never failed to bring back much meat when out hunting. When the people started back to their homes they discovered that this man, whom the people had always made fun of, had been the most successful of all the hunters. He had killed the most deer, and besides he had killed the largest deer that was ever seen by the people, and he had killed the most bears and the most of every other kind of game.

The people named him Deer-Head, because of his braveness in killing big deer. Deer-Head lived with the people many years and was well known among his tribe, but one time he disappeared. It was but a short time until the people noticed that he was missing, and they wondered what had become of him.

Deer-Head had only one younger brother, and when the people would go and ask Deer-Head's wife where he was she could not tell, for she did not know where he was or what had become of him. Finally one of the men went where Deer-Head's little brother was, and he asked him if he knew where his big, brave brother was, and he replied that his brother had gone home ; that some one came after him during the night and had taken him away that same night. Then they asked him if he knew which direction they took, and he said that he did not know where he went, but that he said he was going home.

While out hunting a long time after this one of the men found a large deer and the deer did not try to get away from him. When he came near he shot the deer, but the deer kept on walking very slowly and the man followed until the deer finally went over the hill where the man could not see him, and then he heard some one calling him to come on, and it was the deer that was talking. The man did not keep on, but turned and started back home. When he got home he told the whole story of the deer, and then the people thought the story of the deer was true, and that Deer-Head had changed into a deer.

42. THE BOY WHO MARRIED A MOUNTAIN-LION.*

A little boy often told his parents that he was a red mountain-lion. No one believed him, but they called him Red-Mountain-Lion. When he grew to manhood he was a successful and famous hunter. He went off alone for days at a time and always brought back much game. One time it was noticed that he acted queerly when he returned from the hunt, and so the next time he went his brother followed him. He tracked him through the timber up the rocky side of a mountain. He heard voices among the rocks, but could not see any one. He climbed on until he saw just above him a cave in the side of a steep wall. He looked in and saw his brother in there with a female mountain-lion. He went home and told what he had seen. After a few days Red-Mountain-Lion came home and acted stranger than ever. One time he heard some men talking about going to the cave and killing a mountain-lion that some of them had seen there. The man started out at once and alone to hunt, and he went straight toward the cave.

_____

* Told by Wing.

The men started out to hunt the next day, and when they came to the cave they saw the foot-prints of a man and a mountain-lion leading away from it. They tracked them down the mountain and up another, and then they gave up and returned to their homes. The man did not return to his people, but many years afterward he was captured by a hunting party and carried to his home. He decided to stay at his home then. One autumn he and his brother decided to form a war party. The brother was to be the leader, and so he went off to get some power before starting. He wandered about alone until he found a rattlesnake skin and a red mountain-lion's tail. He took them and then prayed to the rattlesnake and red mountain-lion for their powers. Then he returned home and hid the skin and mountain-lion tail, for he did not want his brother to know what he had. For some reason or another the war expedition was given up. Then the man should have thrown away the skin and tail, for the animals always want their gifts returned if they are not used for the purpose they have given them. If they are not used or returned something always happens to the man who has received them or to some member of his family.

A long time after the war party had been given up Red-Mountain-Lion awoke one morning and heard a turkey cackling. He slipped out to catch the turkey, and while he was slipping upon the turkey he heard a rattlesnake by the side of him. He moved away and heard another. Again he jumped aside and heard still another.

The woman prepared the morning meal and waited a long time for Red-Mountain-Lion to return; then his brother was sent to look for him. His brother found him unconscious and called some men to help carry him to the lodge. Red-Mountain-Lion was scalped, but the only tracks that could be found were those of a mountain-lion, and they were only around his head, and did not come from or lead to any place. They sent for the medicine-man. He came and after he had examined Red-Mountain-Lion he asked his brother if he had not planned a war expedition and prayed for power and received gifts from the animals. The brother admitted that he had. The medicine-man told him to return the gifts to the woods where he had found them, and told him that his brother should have known better than to have kept them. The man obeyed, and then they took Red-Mountain-Lion to the creek and bathed him, and he recovered, but he was always foolish. He lived to be an old man, but some one had to kill him in his old age, because he became more foolish and did many evil things.

43. BUFFALO WOMAN.*

In a village there lived a cannibal at that time and the people called him Snow-Bird-with-White-Wings. He had a handsome son, who would not marry any of his own tribe. The father named his son Braveness because he was very brave in hunting. Whenever he went out to hunt he brought home many kinds of game that he had killed. Many of the young girls tried to win him as a husband, but Braveness would pay no attention to any of them. One night he decided to go hunting the next day. Early the next morning he started out toward the west. While he was going along looking and watching for wild animals he saw some one sitting ahead of him under a small elm tree. He approached the person and saw that it was a woman. She called him to come where she was, and he obeyed and saw that she was very beautiful and very young. She told him that she knew he was coming there and so she had come to meet him. He listened eagerly to hear what she had to say. She asked him if she could stay with him, and if he would take her to his home and let her become his wife. He told her that he would take her to his home, but that she must ask his parents if she could stay with him. They started for his home at once, and when they arrived the girl asked the old people to let her become the young man's wife, and they consented. After that the young man had some one to love and they lived happily for a long time ; but one time while they were alone she asked him if he would do whatever she said, and he finally said that he would. She asked him to go with her to her home and told him that they would return again some day.

A few days after, they started to her home and she led the way. After they had gone a long way they came to high hills, and all at once she stopped and turned around and looked at her husband and said : "You have promised me that you will do anything that I say." "Yes," said he. "Well," said she, "my home is on the other side of this large hill which is before us. I will tell you when we get to my mother. I know there will be many people coming there to see who you are, and they will bother you and try to get you angry, but do not get angry at any of them. The young men will try to kill you in some way. Listen to what I am about to tell you. I was just like you when I met you. I knew you, but you did not know me. I was the one who made you come there to find me. I have said that some of the young men will try to get you angry, and when they get you angry at them one of them will jump on you, and when they see that you are going to try to

*Told by White-Bread.

fight they will all get after you and will not let you go until they have
killed you. They are jealous of you. The reason is that I have refused many of them when they have asked me. I have told you what
to do when we get there, and now I want you to lay down on the
ground and roll over twice." The man did, and when he arose he had
changed into a Buffalo. The woman sat there watching him for a
moment ; then she did the same thing and became a Buffalo. They
started on climbing the high hill, and when they reached the top of the
hill the Buffalo man looked down toward the west. He saw thousands
and thousands of Buffalo. Then the woman told him that they were
her people. When the herd saw these two coming they began to move
to one certain place, as though to wait there and see who was coming.
The woman kept on leading Braveness. He followed her until she came
to an old Buffalo cow and then they stopped, and Braveness knew that
she was the mother of his beautiful wife. They stayed there for a
long time. Every now and then four or five of the young Buffalo
would come around and bother Braveness, and so they decided to go
back again to Braveness' home. On the way they stopped at the place
where they had turned themselves into Buffalo. The Buffalo woman
told him to do the same thing that he had done before, and so he rolled
over twice and became as he was before, and then she did the same.
While they were going she told him not to mention the transformation
or her people to any one. When they reached home his father, Snow-
Bird-with-White-Wings, asked him where he had been, and he told his
father that he had been hunting and then had gone down to his wife's
home, and his father did not ask him any more questions.

They stayed at home about one year, and then they made up their
minds to go again and see the woman's mother. After they had been
living with the Buffalo a long time his wife told him that the old people
were talking about killing him ; that they were going to have a foot
race and that they intended that he should run in this foot race. When
he heard all this he was worried and did not know what to do. That
night he could not sleep, and he went out to take a long walk. He
went a long way and walked very slowly. He heard some one calling,
but could not see the person, for it was a very dark night. The unknown
person said to him : " You are very young, but you must remember you
can not beat those Buffalo running without my help, and I know what
they are going to do with you when the race is over. If they beat you
running they are going to kill you, and so I am going to help you to
win. If I do it there are others who will also help you. If you win
the race they will let you have this woman all to yourself and will not
bother you any more." Then the unknown person told Braveness to

hold out his hand, and when he did this the unknown person placed a small medicine root in it and said : "At the start you will leave them a long way behind, but finally some one of them will catch up with you, but he will not stay with you long. Remember, whenever he comes up with you, to throw this medicine down behind you and you will leave him again a long way behind. Then some one else will catch up with you again, and here is another medicine to throw behind you when the second man overtakes you. This medicine is mud, and you must throw it down when they come too close to you. Soon after you have thrown the mud you will be near the stopping place ; there I will meet you."

The next day was the day of the race. At about sunrise Braveness saw the Buffalo coming in from all directions to see the race. While he stood watching them, an old Buffalo came and told him that the young Buffalo would like to have him run in a foot race with them. He went with the old man to the place where the runners started. When the young Buffalo saw him coming they all made fun of him. When he joined them they lined up for the race. Braveness placed himself in their midst and they started. Braveness left the Buffalo a long way behind at the start, and they had to run long and hard before they could come near him. When he saw them gaining on him he threw the root behind him that the unknown person had given him. He was almost winded and thought he could not run any more, when he saw that he was far ahead of all of them again. The next time it took them longer to come up to him, but finally he gave out, and then one of the Buffalo began to gain on him. When the Buffalo was about to catch up, Braveness threw the mud, his last medicine, down behind him and soon he was far ahead again. He knew that he had used all of his medicine, and he knew not what would happen to him next, but he kept on running. When he was nearing the goal, he could hear the others coming close behind him, for some of them were gaining on him and he was giving out. He did not know what to do, but just as one of the Buffalo was about to catch up with him, a heavy wind came up and greatly assisted and kept the Buffalo far behind him until he crossed the goal and won the race. Because wind had helped him at the last moment, he knew that it was wind that had talked to him and had given him the medicine and thus saved his life. After the race he stayed with the Buffalo people for a long time and no one ever molested him again.

Finally he and his wife went back to live with his people. They had one child, and when it was about one year old they decided to go again to see the wife's people, so that her parents might see their grandson. They went and remained with the Buffalo three years, and then they returned to Braveness' home. The child's mother would not let him go out and play with the other boys, for she was afraid he might do things that he ought not to do; but one time, while she was cooking dinner, the boy slipped away from her and went down where the other boys were playing. When he joined them they began to play that they were Buffalo. The little boy began to play with them. He laid down to roll like a Buffalo, and when he rolled over twice he got up a real Buffalo calf, and the boys began to run from him. Just at this time his mother had missed him and she looked down where the boys were playing. She saw them running and thought something must be wrong. She went to see what the trouble was and there she found her son changed into a Buffalo calf. She took him and ran down the hill, and then she dropped down on the hill and became a Buffalo, and then ran away before her husband came back from hunting. When he came back he could not find his wife or his son, and then some one told him what had happened while he was gone. At first he could not believe what he heard, but soon he went down to the place where they had rolled and saw their tracks, and then he believed the story. He never heard of them again.

44. THE GIRL WHO MARRIED WILD-CAT.*

A father and mother had three sons and a daughter. The girl was very beautiful, but very proud, and refused the attentions of the many young men who came to court her. One time a handsome youth came to their home and ate with them and talked to her father and brothers, but paid no attention to her. After he had spent the evening he arose and went home. The girl thought she had never seen so handsome a young man, and she wondered why he had not sought her as all the others had. She went to bed and thought of him for a long time; then she fell asleep and dreamed of him. She dreamed that she saw him coming to her, and finally she awoke and lay still for a long time listening and waiting to see if her dreams were true. She heard a faint noise, and she closed her eyes and prayed that her dream would come true. When she opened her eyes the young man was bending over her, begging her to go with him. She arose and followed him out into the darkness.

When they were a long way from home the man told her that he was not a real person, but an animal, the Wild-Cat, and he told her that if she wanted to go home he would take her back. She refused to go back, saying that she wanted to go with him, no matter what he was. Then he told her that her three brothers were already on their

---

* Told by Wing.

trail, and that they were very angry with him for taking her off. They hurried on until they came to the mountains. They climbed a high mountain, and then Wild-Cat told the girl to wait there for him. He went away and disappeared among the trees and rocks, but soon returned with another large Wild-Cat, who he said was his grandfather. While the three sat down to rest and talk they heard voices, and the girl knew that they were her brothers' voices. They arose and ran deep into the forest, but still they could hear the voices from the three brothers, who were gaining on them. At last they caught up with them and were very angry. They were going to fight the Wild-Cats, who, of course, were dressed like men, so the brothers did not know that they were Wild-Cats. The sister cried and promised her brothers that she would soon return to her home if they would go and leave them. The brothers at last yielded to her requests and went back home and told her father and mother all that had happened. The father became very angry and swore that he would find his daughter and kill her or the man. He went to the mountains and wandered about in search of her for many days, without food or drink or sleep, until he died.

45. THE WOMAN WHO TRIED TO KILL HER SON.*

At the beginning of this world the people and animals could understand each other and visited each other. There lived in those times a man and wife and one child, a boy about seven years of age. The people called the man Hunter, because he was very fond of hunting and hunted from morning until evening. While he was out, his wife, who was a very cross woman, abused her own boy, as she always did, because she disliked him. She told the boy to stay at home while she went away for a short time. She went out and was gone for a long time. Finally she came back and told the boy to go along with her. While she was gone she had been working hard digging a deep hole in the ground, and when she went after the boy she took him to the hole and threw him in. The hole was so deep that it was impossible for the boy to get out. She put some brush over it to keep any one from finding him. When Hunter returned home he asked his wife where his son was, and she told him she did not know where he was; that she had been looking for him all day long. Then they both went out to look for the boy, but she would not take the man near the place where the hole was, and so they did not find him. They looked until night, and again the next day and the next.

---

* Told by Annie Wilson.

In the meantime the boy was growing very hungry, and so he began to cry. Finally he heard some one making a noise at the edge of the hole, but he could not see who it was, and so kept quiet, for he was afraid. Some one spoke to him, saying: "Boy, you are weary and hungry and I have come down to help you out of this hole. Now, do not be afraid of me, but catch hold of my tail and climb up." The boy obeyed, and when he came out of the hole he found that the person was Coyote. Coyote asked the boy if he would go along with him, and the boy said that he would, and so they went on to Coyote's home. He was kept there for three or four years and was kindly treated and was happy. One day he asked Coyote to let him go home and see his father. He said: "I do not want to see my mother; I am very angry at her, and I am going to try to kill her, but I want to see my father, for he loved me and was kind to me. I am going to tell my father how my mother treated me, and then he will help me kill her. I will take my father and mother on a buffalo hunt when I get home, and toward evening we will kill a buffalo. I want you and your children to come near and howl, and then I will tell my mother to come with me to give you some meat. When we go among you I will push her over, and then I want you and your children to jump upon her and kill her."

Coyote consented, and so the boy went to his home. He arrived one evening and his father was very glad to see him. He asked his father if they could go out buffalo hunting on the next day, and he told his father all about what he was going to do with his mother. The next day they went out buffalo hunting, and he and his father found a herd of buffalo and killed one that evening. They made a camp near by, and while the woman was cooking their supper they heard the Coyotes howling. After they had eaten their supper the boy told his mother to get some meat and come with him to feed the Coyotes. He told her to carry the meat on her back. She put the meat on her back, and then they started out toward the Coyotes, and the boy walked behind his mother. The woman was afraid, for it was almost dark, but the boy told her not to be frightened, for there was no danger ahead of them and that nothing would hurt her. They kept on going until they came to the Coyotes. The boy told his mother not to be afraid, but to go among them and give them the meat. As she took another step forward the boy pushed her down, and then the Coyotes jumped upon her. The boy came back to his father and told him all that had happened. The father and son lived together for many years.

46. THE JEALOUS HUSBAND.*

One time the people decided to go on the war-path, and when they were about to start they selected one man to be their leader. They started out and they had to go a long way before they could find the enemy. After they had traveled several days, the head man selected from eight to twelve men to go ahead and spy and see if they could locate the enemy. When any of these men located any of the enemy they would go back and tell what they had seen, and then all the others would ride out to fight the enemy. The leader chose for spies two men who were very close friends and who would always go together from place to place. One of these two was married and the other was single. One day they went out for some distance, and after they had gone about two miles, climbing up and down the hills, they came to a high hill, almost like a mountain. They decided to climb up this mountain so they could look far out over the country. They found on top a big hole in the rock that looked like an old well, and when they looked down into the hole they saw water. The married man told his friend to go down in the hole to get some water, for they were very thirsty. They had a long buffalo-hide rope and on this he descended. When he got to the bottom, he cried out to his friend to pull him up. Instead of pulling him up he threw the rope down the hole and went away and left him. He started for the camp, and when he reached there he told the head man that some of the enemy pursued them and that his friend was killed. It was a custom for the war party to continue the journey until they met the enemy in open battle, but if anything happened to a member of the party, or if any member should die through sickness or be killed, otherwise than in open fight with the enemy, then the expedition was given up and the entire party returned home. When the man told the head man that his friend had been killed, the camp broke up and all prepared to start home. When they returned to their homes, the errand-man was sent by the chief to all the camps to call the people together. When the people came the chief told them what had happened.

The man in the hole was starving, for he had been in there several days without food. Whenever any birds passed over him he would ask for help and pray them to take him out of the hole, but the birds did not seem to take any notice of him. One day, after he had been in the hole nine days, there was a certain kind of bird passed over the hole and the man asked it for help. The bird went on, but finally flew

---

* Told by Wing.

over the hole, and the man again asked for help. The bird passed on again, and yet again, but the fourth time it lit on the ground and came near to the edge of the hole and peeped over the rim and saw the man. This bird was Buzzard, and Buzzard told the man not to be worried, that he would help him out, but that he must wait until he went back home after some of his medicine which he required. Buzzard went away, but came back and flew down to the bottom of the hole. Then Buzzard spoke to the man, saying that he was going to take him to the home of the Buzzards until he was able to walk home. The man was told to shut his eyes and then take one step forward. When he did this he stepped on Buzzard's back. Then Buzzard began to fly upward and out of the hole. Then Buzzard told him to open his eyes, and he did so and saw that he was on land again. The man was not able to walk at all, and so Buzzard told him to shut his eyes again, and they began to fly away from the place. After a while the man tried to open his eyes a very little, but Buzzard knew what he was doing and told him not to do it again. In a short time they arrived at the home of Buzzard, and while he was there the young man was treated kindly. After he had been there several days Buzzard asked him if he would like to see his people, and the man told him that he would, and then Buzzard called the man over to where he was, and when he got there Buzzard opened a very small place which was near where he was sitting. The man looked down below him and could see many Buzzard people. Two days after this the man was able to walk around and to do anything, and then Buzzard told him that he was going to take him to his home to see his people once more. Then Buzzard told the young man that his friend was jealous of him, and that the reason he had maltreated him was that he had been told he was going to take his wife away from him. Buzzard said : '' I am going to take you home, and we will reach your home about dark, and when we reach a place that is near to your home I will have to let you off. Then you will hear your friend singing in his lodge, which is near to yours. When you go into your lodge you will find all of your people there, and when they see you, tell them not to cry or make any kind of noise. Your own sister will be there and you must tell her to go after your friend's wife. She will not refuse your sister, but come right along with her.'' They started out and Buzzard told him to shut his eyes again. When Buzzard told him to open them he could hear his friend singing, and he knew it was he because he recognized his voice. When they came near to his home Buzzard told him to get off of his back. He did, and went straight to his lodge, and when he went in his sister was the first one to meet him. When she came to him she began to cry. He told her not to cry, but to keep quiet. He told them how his friend had treated him and how Buzzard had taken pity on him and rescued him. When he had finished he told his sister to go and tell the woman to come. She went and told the woman that she was wanted. She did not hesitate, but went along with the girl, and they both came in and the woman saw her husband's friend, whom she thought was killed, sitting with the others. The woman stayed with this man and did not care to go back to her former husband any more.

The husband was very sorry that he had told the stories to the head man and the chief. Many times after this these men went out on the buffalo hunt, and some of the others always watched him closely to see that he did not harm any one else. Finally they noticed that every time they went out he killed one buffalo first, and then did not take any of the meat, but would cut it up or dress it as though he were going to take it, and then would scatter the meat as though he were dividing it out to some people. The people began to wonder what he did that for. After he had prepared and scattered the meat of the first buffalo he had killed he would go on and kill another one, and then he would take his meat home. After people had seen him leave the meat of the first buffalo many times some one asked him why he did that. He would not tell, but one time his uncle came and asked him why he had done that so many times, and he told him all about it. He said he had lived with the woman many years, and when he should die his wife should drop dead, too.

47. THE TURTLE WHO CARRIED THE PEOPLE AWAY.*

One time the people broke camp and were traveling about looking for a village site. They traveled far until they came near the big water, and there they saw what they thought was a large rock. They decided to make their village near the rock, so they could use it as a dancing place. They had several dances on the rock, but not all of the people were there. One time, after they had been at the village for some time, they sent the crier to announce a big dance. All the people came and danced on the smooth, flat rock. While they were dancing they noticed that the rock began to move. They watched it and soon saw a big head and legs appear from under it. Then they knew that they were not on a rock at all, but on a big turtle. They tried to get off, but found their feet stuck tight. They cried and called for help, but the turtle carried them down into the water and drowned them.

* Told by Wing.

48. WHY DOGS HAVE LONG TONGUES.*

A long time ago, when the animals were like people, dogs were noted for telling everything that they knew. In those days there were not so many dogs as now, but the best families always had a few hounds to take with them on the hunt. A man, Running-Water, who was a great hunter, wanted a dog to help him hunt, but he would not have one, because he hated to have some one always tattling on him and telling everything that he did. One time he saw four little pups and he decided to take one of them and try to teach him not to talk so much. He took the pup home, and every day, when he played with him, he would talk to him and try to teach him not to be a tattler like other dogs. The pup grew and was soon big enough to be taught to hunt. Running-Water began to take him out to hunt rabbits and small game. Every time the man killed any game the dog would sneak home and tell ; then he would return to Running-Water in a circuitous way and come up to him from behind, as though he had been hunting all the time. Running-Water knew that the dog was trying to deceive him, and he whipped and scolded him. After each whipping he would stop running off and tattling for a little while, but soon he would begin again.

After a time the dog was big enough to go far away into the high timber to hunt with his master. One day Running-Water told his mother to prepare a large quantity of food, for he and his dog were going to the mountains to hunt and would be gone many weeks. He loaded several horses with provisions and started out, with his dog for his only companion. After three days of traveling they came to the mountains and made camp. They hunted several weeks and killed many big animals, and then started home. After a day's journey Running-Water missed his dog. He called him and searched for him and then went back to camp, thinking that he had perhaps gone back. He could not find him there, and so he gave him up for lost and again started home. He did not think the dog had gone on home ahead of him, for he thought that he had broken him of the habit of running home and telling everything ; but when he came home he found the dog there. He had been there a long time and had told many big stories about the number of bears, mountain-lions, deer, coyotes, and other animals that they had killed. Running-Water was more angry than ever before, and he said, '' I will make that dog stop tattling so much.'' He caught the dog, gave him a hard whipping, and told him he would

* Told by Hinie.

pull his tongue out the next time he came home and told everything. Then, being still angry, he caught hold of the dog's tongue and pulled it as hard as he could, and then he ran a stick across his mouth. Ever since then dogs have had long tongues and big mouths.

49. WHY HAWKS HAVE THIN LEGS.*

Chicken-Hawk was a poor hunter and never succeeded in bringing his family more than a little mouse or some game that he had begged from another hunter. One time he met Eagle and asked him if he would not help him kill an antelope that he had seen not very far away. Hawk pretended that he had killed many such big game before, and acted as if he were being kind to Eagle in asking him to help him. Eagle said he would if he could have half of the meat. Hawk said that he could, and so they agreed to go hunting for the antelope the next morning. Hawk went on home, and when he arrived he told his family that he had shot an antelope through the head, but that he could not kill him, and so he had run him into a place for the night, and that he would return in the morning and kill him. Hawk arose the next morning and went to the place where he was to meet Eagle. They started on the hunt and hunted half a day. They found the antelope in the mountain. Eagle killed it, and then Hawk came down and they divided the meat. Eagle took his meat and went away. Hawk took his meat and went straight home to show it to his family, for he was very proud of it. He told them that he had met a person who had never tasted antelope meat and who was a poor hunter, and so he had given him part of his meat, but that the person promised to pay him back some day. His family were so well pleased that they told every one what a good hunter Hawk was. One time, after the antelope meat was gone, a friend, who had heard what a good hunter Hawk was, came to visit him, especially to see if the reports were true. Hawk hunted all one day, but returned with only a mouse. The friend refused to eat the mouse. Again Hawk hunted all day, but could not find anything. As he was returning home he felt so ashamed, that he cut some of the meat off of his legs to take home for his friend to eat, rather than admit that he had not found any game. For that reason hawks have no meat on their legs.

---

* Told by White-Bread.

50. THE POWER OF BUFFALO AND BEAR.*

One time when the animals spoke many languages, and yet under-stood one another, Bear and Buffalo met. They commenced telling each other about the powers that each received from the Father and when these powers should be used. Said the Bear: "Once upon a time I was a human being and lived like a human being, and went with the people from place to place. When they camped in the open, my family always made a camp near by in the timber or mountains, for we liked to climb the trees and play among the rocks. One night I had a dream. I dreamed that I was as you see me now, and I heard some one telling me of the many things that I had within my power to do. I was shown the place where I should stay, and I was given the paws and claws and the sharp teeth which I now possess. Then I dreamed that a human being was pursuing me and shooting at me with his arrows, and I knew that he was trying to kill me for food, as he does any other animal. I awoke from sleep and found that all I had dreamed was true, and from that time I have been as I am now. I left the people and began a new life in the mountains and woods, and from that time the people have hunted me and have tracked me with dogs. Now they call me Bear, meaning 'the mountain animal.' I have told you all." Buffalo began to speak: "I, too, was like a human being and my ways were like their ways when we first came to dwell upon the earth. My people were called the Buffalo people because our oldest chief was named Buffalo. One time our chief was taken away from us and we never knew what became of him, though we were told that the Great-Powerful-One had taken him to another world, and that some day we were all going to that other world, and that we would meet our chief there. We lived with the people and traveled with them, going behind them. The people began to enter this world, but we were forbidden to enter because some one had made a mistake that caused us to stay back where we came from. We found out that the person who had made this mistake was Coyote, and so our people began at once to pray that the Father would give him powers and teach him so that he might enter the world and take us along, that we might be with the people. We do not know how we came to be as we are now, but we know that in order to be in the same world as the people are we had to change into wild animals, and that for the love of the people we had to be their game, and we were to be killed and eaten by them. Then we were given powers to be dangerous, and these horns on our heads were given to us to fight with."

---

* Told by White-Bread.

Then Bear asked Buffalo if he could show just what he did when he was very angry or when he wanted to hurt or kill any one. Buffalo began to throw up the earth and strike the ground with his sharp horns. Bear sat watching him, and all at once, before he knew what had happened, he was falling to the ground and Buffalo was coming at him again. When he had fallen to the ground a second time Buffalo asked him if he saw him when he first started after him. "No," said Bear. "Well," said Buffalo, "I think you ought to show me how you use your powers when you get angry." Bear began to go through his movement, and Buffalo sat watching him. Bear began to walk back and forth and look at Buffalo with angry eyes. Finally he began to move very slowly toward a small tree which was near by, and when he reached the tree he grabbed hold of it and with his sharp teeth cut it down. Before Buffalo knew what had happened Bear was upon him and he was trying to get up from the ground, but Bear held him down until he was ready to give up. Finally Bear let him go, saying, "That is the way I do when I get very angry, but I would treat you worse than that if I wanted to kill you." Bear and Buffalo parted and went to their homes.

51. HOW RABBIT STOLE MOUNTAIN-LION'S TEETH.*

One time when Rabbit's grandmother had gone off and left him alone he decided to wander about and see what he could see. He went along until he came to the home of Mountain-Lion. Mountain-Lion was not at home, so Rabbit went in and hunted about. He finally found Mountain-Lion's teeth and he took them and ran home with them. He was glad to find them, for the other animals were afraid of Mountain-Lion on account of his sharp teeth. Rabbit showed the teeth to his grandmother when he reached home, and said : "Now, grandmother, Mountain-Lion will soon be after his teeth, and we must fool him some way or he will kill us." Rabbit thought for a while ; then he said : "Build a fire just outside the door, put a big kettle of water on the fire, and then put some stones into the water and boil them. When Mountain-Lion comes he will ask what you are going to do with those stones. Tell him that I have a guest in the lodge who is going to eat them. I will talk to myself in the lodge as though I were entertaining a friend, and when Mountain-Lion asks who my friend is, say 'Chief of all the beasts.'" The grandmother made a big fire and put the stones on to boil. Finally they heard a big noise, and Mountain-Lion came tearing through the bushes and came straight to the old woman. He asked her if Rabbit was at home, and she told him that he was inside talking to his friend and guest.

---

* Told by Wing.

Then he asked what she was going to do with the stones, and she told him what Rabbit had told her to say. He asked who the friend was, and she told him, "Chief of all the beasts." "Oh, yes, I know him," he said, and at the same time backed off a little, and then he turned on his heels and ran as fast as he could.

52. RABBIT AND THE DANCING TURKEYS.*

One time while Wild-Cat was out hunting he came upon Rabbit in the tall grass. Rabbit and Wild-Cat were enemies, and so they began to fight. Soon Wild-Cat had Rabbit down and was about to kill him, when Rabbit said : " How would you like some nice Turkeys to eat ? " " That is just what I have been looking for," said Wild-Cat. " Well, I know where there are some, and I was just about to catch some when I met you. Now, if you kill me they will all get away. You had better spare my life until I show you how to catch the Turkeys ; then you may do what you please with me." Wild-Cat agreed, and so Rabbit told him to stand still while he sang the Turkey dance song. After he had sung a little, he told Wild-Cat to lie down and pretend to be dead ; that he would tell the Turkeys that he had killed Wild-Cat, and wished them to dance around him with closed eyes. While they danced, Wild-Cat was to jump up and grab all he wanted. Soon the Turkeys heard the song and came to see what it was about. Rabbit told them that he had killed the great turkey-eater, Wild-Cat, and that he wanted them to dance a victory dance around him. Rabbit continued his song, and as he sang the Turkeys danced. Wild-Cat peeped and saw one big one dancing near him. He jumped to get it, and as he grabbed the Turkey, Rabbit ran away through the grass, and so escaped from Wild-Cat.

53. ADVENTURES OF COYOTE.†

In the beginning of the world there were many, many people, and the people held councils to decide how things should be. There was one man, named Coyote, who always had something to say on every subject. At one council this question came up : " How and what kind of rain should be in the world ? " One of the men said that it should rain in the form of lead balls, which would be very dangerous, and so when the rain came the people would have to stay at home. Then Coyote arose from his seat and said : " If it should rain nothing but lead it would be very dangerous for my people, because they do not stay at home very much, and as for myself, I might be carrying a big deer to my family to eat when the rain begins to fall and I would cer-

---

* Told by Wing. † Told by Moon-Light.

tainly be killed. I say, let it rain in drops of water. Then we can be caught out in the rain and get very wet, but we will soon be dry again, and the wetting will be good for us." The people accepted Coyote's suggestion, and so it is that it rains in the form of water.

When the council was all over and the people went to their homes, Coyote made up his mind to go out and visit some of his friends. He traveled until he came to the mountains. He saw smoke coming up among the mountains, as though some one was making up a big fire, and he thought he would go up and see who was living there. When he came near to the place he saw some one sitting by the fire. It was the great, powerful Bear. Coyote went closer, and Bear asked him if he was the person who was called Coyote, and Bear told him that if he was that he was going to kill him, for he had heard many bad things about him. Coyote told Bear he was not the person, but that he was the son of a great and powerful medicine-man. Bear did not believe him and decided to kill him. When he was about to kill him, Coyote told him to wait until his father saw him, for he might have something to say to him before he died. This happened at sunrise, and when the sun was just peeping over the hilltops Coyote said to Bear : '' Now you may kill me or do as you please with me, because my father is watching me.'' Then Bear began to back away, and as he did so, Coyote• began to go nearer and nearer to Bear. Finally he began to push him with his elbow, at the same time saying : ''Now kill me while my father is watching me.'' Bear thought that he must be a great man, if he was the son of the Sun, and he wondered how he received his powers from the Sun. He became frightened and gave Coyote many things to eat, and then Coyote told Bear to come and make him a visit some time, whenever he felt like going anywhere. A long while after this, Bear found out that the person who made a visit to him was not the son of the Sun, but that he was the man Coyote, whom he wanted to kill. Bear was more angry at him than ever, and so he thought he would fool Coyote some way by going and visiting him and killing him if he could find his home. Bear did not find his home, because Coyote was always moving from place to place, for he knew that Bear was after him, and that he would kill him if he could catch him.

While Coyote was moving from one place to another he came down to a large lake of clear, cool water, and after he had been there for some time he started off a little way from the lake. While gone he saw some one coming up toward him and, as he was very cowardly, he started to run away. The person was not his enemy, but a friend of his, Moun-tain-Lion. He called Coyote back, and so he came, and he told his friend that he was very hungry, for he had had nothing to eat for a long while.   Mountain-Lion asked him to go along with him, saying that he would find something for him to eat soon.   They both went to the lake, and when they came down to the water Mountain-Lion told Coyote that he was going to kill a young horse.   In those times there were many herds of wild horses, and at the lake there was a certain place where the wild horses drank.   Near the place where the road led to the water there was a large tree, and the horses passed under the tree as they went down to the water.   Every day at about noon Mountain-Lion would climb the tree and then pounce down on a young horse and kill him.   As Mountain-Lion and Coyote drew near to the tree Mountain-Lion told Coyote to place himself where the wild herd of horses could not see him, and so he did, and Mountain-Lion climbed the tree.   Soon Coyote saw dust rise up from the ground and he heard something like thundering, and later he saw many hundreds of horses coming down to the water.   As the horses were passing under the tree, Coyote saw Mountain-Lion jump out of the tree and pounce upon a young horse and kill it.   Then Mountain-Lion and Coyote both had a fine dinner.   That day, after they had eaten, Mountain-Lion told Coyote to continue on his way; but Coyote did not want to leave his friend, and so he asked Mountain-Lion if he could give him power so that he could kill a horse, too, and eat it when he was hungry.   Mountain-Lion told him he would.   They stayed there until the next day, and at about noon they both went down to the lake again, and went to the tree, and then Mountain-Lion showed Coyote how and what to do when the horses should come.   He taught him how to climb the tree, and then he went out to place himself where the horses could not see him.

Soon they began to come from different directions, and as they filed down to the water Coyote picked out a fat young horse, and as they were coming up from the water he jumped on it and killed it.   They had another fine dinner, and then Mountain-Lion said to Coyote : '' Do not try to kill a three or four year old horse.   If you jump on one that is three years old you can not kill him and you may lose your own life.   Try to kill one that is one or two years old and you will succeed every time.''   Coyote left his new friend and went on his way.   The next day, while he was alone, he began to get very hungry, and so at about noon he went down to the lake to kill a horse.   While he was on the tree he said to himself : '' I wonder if it would be dangerous for me to kill one of the large horses.   I may be stronger than Mountain-Lion, and so I will try to kill the largest horse and I will show Mountain-Lion that I am not so small as I look to him.''   The horses began to go down to the water, and Coyote waited and waited for the chance to jump upon the largest horse in the herd.   Finally a large horse came, and when he was right under the tree Coyote jumped upon him. It was but a short time until the horse threw Coyote off from his back, and when Coyote was down on the ground the horse kicked him under the jaws and went off. As Coyote was about to die, Mountain-Lion, who had been watching Coyote all the time, came up to see what was the matter with him, and when he came up to him he saw his jaws to one side. Mountain-Lion asked Coyote what he was laughing about, and asked him if he was able to kill another five-year-old horse. Coyote lay there for a long time before he was able to move. Finally he arose and decided to leave the place, never to return to it. As he was going along a small stream he heard some one up in a persimmon tree, and so he thought that he would go over and see who it was. He found Opossum in the persimmon tree eating persimmons. Coyote went under the tree and asked Opossum to throw down some persimmons to him. Opossum refused and laughed at Coyote and began to play with him. Opossum would take one persimmon and eat it, and then he would throw the seeds down to Coyote. Finally Coyote became angry at Opossum and wished he could get him down from the tree. Sometimes Opossum would get on a small limb of the tree, and then drop down as though he was going to fall to the ground, but he would always catch himself by wrapping his tail around the limb. He kept on doing this to torment Coyote for a long time, until he climbed out on a dry limb. He threw himself off the limb again and said to Coyote : "I am falling off, sure. I am coming down," and just as he let himself off of the limb it broke off and down came Opossum. Coyote was upon him and gave him a good beating, and then he left him to die. Opossum fooled Coyote, for he was not hurt at all, and when Coyote went away Opossum jumped up and climbed the persimmon tree again. After a while Coyote looked back to see if Opossum was dead. He could not see him, and so he went back and found that Opossum was gone. He looked up in the tree, and there he saw him laughing at him again.

54. COYOTE ESCAPES AN IMAGINARY FOE.*

One time Coyote went out hunting buffalo. While he was going through the timber he found Turkey up on the top of a tall tree. He told Turkey that he was going to kill him if he did not get down from the tree. He said: "If you don't come down I will climb the tree. If you fly to another tree, I will break it down at once, and will certainly kill you; but if you fly toward the prairie I can not harm you, for I have no powers to kill anything on the prairie." Turkey believed

---

* Told by Wing.

all that Coyote said and started out toward the prairie. Coyote was right under Turkey all the time. At first Turkey flew up so high that Coyote thought he was going to lose him, but after a long flight Turkey kept coming down lower and lower, and finally came down on the ground. Then Coyote was not very far behind and he caught up with him and killed him. While Coyote was eating Turkey, he happened to look around to make sure that no one was watching him. He thought that he saw somebody standing behind him making motions as if trying to strike him. He started to run without learning who it was. Every now and then he would look back to see if he were out of his reach. Every time he looked back he thought he saw the man right after him, ready to hit him. He ran with all his might, trying to get away from him. Coyote had been given power at the beginning of the world to run without decreasing his running powers. Coyote began to think that some great, powerful man was behind him and that he had to die. He had run eight times. The ninth time he thought he would run farther than usual. Again he looked around, right and left, and thought he saw the man just about to hit him. He started to run his best again, but his running powers were decreasing continually. He was then running for the tenth time ; but it was all in vain, for the man seemed to be right up with him. Then Coyote thought he would fool the man, so he kept dodging right and left, but the man seemed to be near him all the time. When he started to run the twelfth time he had not gone far when he gave out. He rolled and turned over on his back and begged not to be killed. He fell over on his face, then heard something crack, and he thought it was one of his teeth, but it was only a turkey feather which had stuck between two of his upper teeth, and it stuck up nearly straight and level with his head back of his right eye. At first when he looked back he had thought surely that some one was standing behind him ready to strike him. When he found that he had been fooled by only a turkey feather, and had been running himself almost to death for nothing, he was very angry. Ever since, Coyote has looked wild, and when he runs he starts out very slowly for fear he may have to run a long distance, and when he runs he first looks around to the right and then to the left to see if anybody is near him. Most often he looks to his right side while running. When Coyote reached home he told his family and others that he had been running after a great big mountain-lion, and that he had killed it. He said: "If there had not been so many trees I would have brought it home."

55. COYOTE GOES FISHING.*

One time Coyote went out hunting along the river and saw some one walking along its banks, carrying something on his back. When he came nearer he saw that it was a man carrying a fish. Coyote came to him, and said : '' How do you do, my friend ? Where are you going? Where have you been ? Where did you get that big snake ?'' '' Well,'' said the man, '' I have been out fishing nearly all night, and finally I caught this fish. I was so tired that I did not care to catch another.'' '' What !'' said Coyote, ''do you call that a fish ? How did you get hold of it ?'' '' Well,'' said the man, '' I will tell you how to get them. When evening comes go down along the edge of the river and break a place in the ice just big enough to put your tail in, and stay there until I come to see you again.'' That same evening Coyote went to the place and found the man waiting for him. It was getting dark. The man told Coyote to sit down by the edge of the water, while he was breaking the ice. Coyote did as the man told him. He did not know that this was a man whom he had tricked some time before and that he was trying to get revenge. The man left Coyote sitting by the bank fishing all that cold night. Toward the middle of the night the water began to freeze on Coyote's tail, and toward morning the ice got thicker and thicker, and when morning came Coyote tried to get up from his seat, for he was very tired, but he could not. There he was, trying in every way to get free, but he could not move. When the man came he said to Coyote : '' How are you getting along ? Are you catching any fish ?'' Coyote replied : '' I think I have caught two or three of them, but can you help me to get them out on dry land ?'' '' Yes,'' said the man, ''of course I will, although I want to talk to you before we get the fish out of the water. You remember that a long time ago you were one of my best friends, but finally you tricked me, and now I am getting even with you. You will have to die, for I am going to kill you.'' '' My friend,'' said Coyote, '' I think you are mistaken. I do not think I am the man who played the mean trick on you. You know very well that I never betray my friends while I am able to see. If you will let me go this time I will go and bring the man you are looking for, and I will come back to-morrow evening and assure you that I am your friend.'' '' But,'' said the man, '' I do not see how you are going to get loose to go, do you ? I will look for the other man myself, and I will do to him just as I am going to do to you.'' The man went back to his lodge to get his bow and arrows. When he returned to Coyote he took one of the arrows

---

*Told by Wing.

out and showed it to him and said, "You see this?" He began to sing the song that warriors sing just before they kill their enemies. When he had finished the song he shot and killed Coyote.

56. COYOTE HUNTS GEESE.*

Coyote was once a man and lived with the people. His great-grandfather named him Coyote, but because he did wrong the people came to dislike him and began to call him coward. The reason the people did not like him was because he was always scheming and trying to cheat some one. One time he went out to visit his best friend, and when he arrived at his friend's lodge he found that his friend had been feasting on white geese. "Where did you get these white geese?" "Well," said his friend, "I catch them every evening near the lake. Would you like to go with me this evening to catch a few of them?" "Yes," said Coyote. His friend then said : "You go on home and come back this evening. We will then go together and I will show you where the geese always come in the evening, and I will see that you have a good time, too." "Oh, you do not have to show me how to get them ; I can get them all right. All you have to do is just to show me where they are," said Coyote. "All right," said his friend, and Coyote was pleased, for he thought he was going to have a very fine, fat bird for supper that evening. He danced all the way from his friend's home to his own. As soon as Coyote was out of sight the friend began to carry out ashes from the fire and place them near the lake, where he formed them in the shape of white geese. Just before it was evening he went out and put some coals under the ashes, and in a little while the coals burned up, but the fire could not be seen from the outside. When Coyote came to his friend he found him laughing and feeling in high spirits. "Well," said Coyote, "are you ready to go and catch a few white geese? I am ready to make a long jump and I think I can get two at once." "Well," said the friend, "I am ready, too. We will go now." They started out, and as they approached the place the friend began to go slowly, taking the lead, and when they came to the place he pretended not to see the first pile of ashes. Finally Coyote saw the first pile, came closer to his friend and began punching him in the back. Both stopped and Coyote said : "I guess I will have to kill this first one, and if I catch him I will take him for my supper." "All right," said the friend. Coyote began to get down next to the ground, going nearer and nearer to the pile of ashes. When he was about to jump, the friend began to laugh. Coyote paid no attention, but jumped on the pile of hot ashes and burned himself. He began to run from the place. He was burned so badly that he ran until he killed himself.

---

* Told by Wing.

57. COYOTE IMITATES HIS HOST.*

In the days of old, when animals were like people and talked and visited each other, Coyote and Raven were great friends. One day after Coyote had grown weary of hunting for game and finding none, he went up to the top of the mountain to see his friend Raven. Raven had control of the buffalo and was always seen with the herds. (Now, since the buffalo has gone from the earth, Raven has disappeared and is seldom seen any more.) Raven invited Coyote to enter, and when he saw Coyote weary and sad and silent he arose, took an arrow, shot it up into the air, and then stood waiting for it to come down. It came down and pierced him under the right arm. He drew the arrow out and with it came buffalo meat and fat. He gave the meat to Coyote, who ate heartily. Then Coyote smacked his mouth, arose, and said that he must be going, but before he went he gave Raven an urgent invitation to come over and make him a visit, and Raven promised to come.

When Coyote went home he began making a bow and arrow, and when he had finished them he put them away until Raven should visit him. One day Raven bethought himself of his promise, and so he left his home in haste to pay Coyote a visit. Coyote received him with joy. After they had talked about many things Coyote said : " I have no meat, for I did not expect you, but if you will wait I will soon have some for you." Coyote took his bow and arrow and shot the arrow into the sky, then stood waiting for it to come down. Raven watched him and said never a word. The arrow came down and struck in Coyote's thigh. He ran away screaming with pain and left his guest alone. Raven waited a while and then went home without any meat, but in very high spirits notwithstanding, for Coyote's performance amused him greatly and he chuckled to himself as often as he thought of it. Coyote continued to run until he pulled the arrow out of his thigh ; then he took the arrow and broke it to pieces. He never went back to see Raven, and time passed on and none of Coyote's friends saw him, and they all wondered what had become of him. At last he grew so hungry that he had to go out for food. He found none, and so he went to visit another one of his friends, for he had many. Black-Mountain-Bear received him graciously when he came to his home and asked him in. Bear said : " I regret that I have no meat to offer you." As he spoke he leaned against a persimmon tree that was weighted down with many ripe persimmons, and as he leaned against the tree the ripe fruit fell to the ground. Bear smiled and asked his friend to eat. Coyote ate many,

---

* Told by Wing.

for he was very hungry. When he had finished he thanked Bear and said that he must be going, but before he went he insisted that Bear come to see him, and Bear promised to come soon.

Coyote wandered all about looking for a persimmon tree. He could not find one with any fruit on it, and so he decided to take one without fruit. He cut the tree down and carried it to his home, where he set it up; then he went out to look for persimmons. He had stolen some from Bear's home, but he had not stolen enough. When he found more persimmons he took them home, and climbing the tree he placed the persimmons all over the tree, so that they looked as though they had grown there.

Black-Mountain-Bear was out hunting one day, and as he was near Coyote's home he remembered his promise to visit him, and so he ran over to see him. Coyote was glad to see him and asked him in. "I am so sorry I have no meat for you," he said, "but if you will wait I will try to get you something to eat." Coyote began to bump against the tree with his head. He hit harder and harder, but the persimmons would not fall. Finally he arose and shook the tree with his hands, though it embarrassed him to have to do this. He gave the tree a big shake and over it fell, hitting him on the head. He pretended that it did not hurt and went about gathering up the fruit for Bear, though he could hardly see for pain. Bear ate, though he could hardly swallow for laughing, for Coyote's head kept getting bigger and bigger. After a little while Bear said that he must be going, for he was afraid to stay longer for fear Coyote would see him laugh. After he had gone Coyote sat down and held his sore head, but he felt happy notwithstanding, for he had furnished food for Bear.

58. COYOTE IMITATES HIS HOST.*

One morning while Coyote was out looking for something to eat he came to a grass lodge. Thinking that there might be food inside, he decided to go in and pay his respects to its owner if he should be there; if not, help himself to food. He entered and saw a man walking about with a light on his head. At once Coyote called out: "Say, friend, your head is on fire, and you and your house will burn up if you don't look out." The man smiled and replied in a calm voice: "I have always worn this light on my head. It was given to me in the beginning. It will not burn anything." Then the man, who was Woodpecker, gave Coyote something to eat. After Coyote had eaten all he could, he arose and said that he must go. He asked Woodpecker to

---

* Told by Wing.

come over and make him a visit, and Woodpecker promised that he would. Some time later Woodpecker remembered his promise and so started out to find Coyote's lodge. He found it, and Coyote, much pleased, invited him to come in and be seated. Woodpecker entered and was surprised to see a big bunch of burning straw on Coyote's head. "Ah, take that off. You will burn your head." Coyote only smiled, and replied in a calm voice: "Oh, no; that will not burn my head. I always wear it. I was told in the beginning that I would wear a light on my head at nights so that I can do whatever I like to while others are in darkness." He had no more than finished speaking when the hair on his head caught fire. He began to scream and try to put it out, but could not. He ran out of his lodge screaming for help. Woodpecker waited for him to return, but he did not come.

59. COYOTE, THE DEER, AND THE WIND.*

One time when Coyote was out hunting something to eat he met Deer. Deer asked Coyote where he was going, and Coyote told him that he was going out hunting. Deer asked Coyote how he killed his game, for he noticed that he carried no bow and arrows. "I can kill anything I can get my hands on," said Coyote. "But how do you get close enough to get your hands on your game?" Deer asked. "Sometimes I run the game down, sometimes I catch them asleep." Deer said: "I am considered good food; even the human beings are very fond of my flesh. If you can catch me I will let you kill me and eat me." Deer started to run, and Coyote started after him, but soon lost sight of him and gave out. He went on home, but he could not help thinking of Deer's offer, and wondering how he could catch him. He wandered about trying to find him asleep, but never did. One time, after Coyote had been out searching to find Deer asleep, he grew very tired and lay down in the tall grass to take a nap. When he awoke he heard some one singing near by. He was badly frightened and sat up straight and rubbed his eyes and peeped about. He saw no one, but as he sat still and listened again he heard his name mentioned in the song. He jumped up and ran as fast as he could; yet he always heard the voice singing in his ears, just as near as when he woke up. He ran as fast and far as he could; then he dropped down to die. While he was panting, he heard the voice again, and it was so near that he heard these words: "If Coyote ever kills a Deer he shall be as fleet as he, and I who am singing am going to give him power to catch a Deer. I am the Wind." Coyote's fear vanished, and he arose and barked at

---

* Told by White-Bread.

the Wind in a loud voice, to give thanks. His weariness left him and he started out to find Deer. He traveled all day, but could not find him. At night he came to a camp, where he stole a buffalo robe. He put the robe over him and then went on to look for Deer. Down by the river he thought he saw him. He went another way and slipped round a bend in the river until he came close to Deer. He reached out his hands to grab him and said, as he caught hold of him : "I have you ; I thought you said I could not get you." To his surprise he found that he did not have Deer, but the man whose robe he had stolen.

The man took Coyote home with him and made him work for him and his sister, and treated him very cruelly, because he had stolen his robe. One time while the man was out hunting, Coyote went into the lodge and said to the sister in a loud, angry voice : "Pack up your clothes ; I am going to take you to my home as prisoner, and you will have to work there as I have worked here. Your brother is killed and now you must come with me." The girl was frightened and obeyed. They started toward Coyote's home. Coyote went behind the girl with a long stick in his hand, and whenever she stopped or fell he hit her with the stick. The girl went on, though she was so tired and frightened that she could hardly move, and as she went she prayed that her brother was not dead, but would come and help her.

In the meantime the man returned home and found his sister and Coyote gone. He knew at once what had happened and started after them and soon caught up with them ; for he had the power to travel as fast as the fleetest arrow, though Coyote did not know it. When he was almost up with them he shot an arrow in front of his sister. She saw it and knew that her brother was coming to help her ; then she began to cry the more from joy. Coyote whipped her for crying and made her travel faster. The man saw Coyote strike his sister and heard the cruel words that he spoke to her. He went on a hill and then shot another arrow. Coyote looked up and saw him and became frightened even more than the girl had been. He dropped his stick and ran to the girl and begged her to let him carry her bundle of clothing, and begged her not to cry. The man came down from the hill and asked Coyote where he was going with his sister. Coyote said that the people had treated them so badly he had decided to take the girl to another village, where the people would be kind to her. He said that he was helping her along the way and had been kind to her. The brother of the girl did not believe Coyote, for he had seen his treatment of her. He told Coyote to take the bundle of clothes and put it on his back ; then he told his sister to sit on the bundle. He put his bow-string through Coyote's mouth and gave the ends to the girl. She sawed the strings back and forth and the man ran along by the side of Coyote, whipping him, and thus they returned to their home. This man was the Wind, who had become angry at Coyote for stealing his robe and trying to catch Deer with it, instead of waiting for him to give him power.

60. COYOTE DIVES FOR MEAT.*

One time when Coyote was out hunting she killed a big deer. She cut the deer up and hid it in a tree while she went home to get her children to come and help her carry the meat home. Wild-Cat saw her kill the deer and hide it, and as soon as Coyote was gone he stole the meat and climbed a tree on the bank of the river, where Coyote could not see him. After a little while Coyote returned with all of her happy and hungry children. They looked every place for the meat. The children were angry at their mother and said that she had lied to them. While they were abusing her, she saw the reflection of the meat in the water, and, thinking that it was the meat, she told her children to sit still while she dived for it. She told them that it had fallen into the water, but that she could very easily get it if they would only be quiet and wait. She dived and struggled in the water, reaching for the meat, but never getting it. Finally she sat down upon the bank to rest, wondering how she could dive deep enough to get the meat. After she had rested she told the little Coyotes to bring her some stones. She tied the stones about her neck and dived again. The Coyotes waited a long time for their mother to come up, but she did not come. After a while they saw some excrement on the water, and they laughed, for they thought it was the meat their mother had thrown up. When they laughed Wild-Cat laughed at their foolishness. They looked up in the tree, and there saw Wild-Cat and all of the meat. Wild-Cat told them that their mother was drowned. Then they began to cry, but Wild-Cat told them not to cry, that he was going to come down and take care of them. He climbed down and brought the deer meat with him. He gave the little Coyotes all they wanted and then took them home. After that, whenever he killed any game he always took some over to the Coyote children, and fed and cared for them until they were grown.

61. COYOTE, THE GEESE, AND THE WOODPECKERS.*

Coyote was returning home after an unsuccessful hunt. He was going along sad and discouraged, when he heard some one laughing and playing. He listened for a while, then decided to go and enter into the fun, so that he might be cheered up. He ran over a little hill, and there on

* Told by Wing.

the other side was a big lake, and on the surface several white Geese were playing. He sat down behind some brush to watch them. They were trying to see which was the strongest. One would get on the back of another and fly, trying to see which could fly the farthest. Coyote decided not to enter into their play, but to try to catch them and take them home to his family. The Geese had seen Coyote coming, for they have power to see a long distance, but they pretended that they had not seen him and did not know that he was hiding behind the brush.

Coyote watched them for a long time, trying to think of some plan whereby he could catch all of them. Finally he began to grin to himself, for he had thought of a plan that he thought would work splendidly. He limped out from the bushes, pretending that he had been hurt and was almost dead. The Geese, hearing him crying, turned and saw him come limping toward them, and they all began to swim out into the water. When they were out far enough for safety one turned and asked Coyote what was the matter with him. He answered: "I am going to be killed if I do not get across the water. I must get across, not so much on my own account as others, for if I am killed all the rivers and lakes will dry up and there will be no water for any one. I should hate to die and cause all of this to happen."

The Geese thought for a while, and then decided to take Coyote and throw him into a deep hole; for the Geese were very smart people in those days and they knew that Coyote was lying to them. One old Goose, who was very strong, went to the bank and told Coyote to get on his back if he wanted to go across the water. Coyote said that he was too heavy for one to take him across; that he would not trust himself to one. The Goose told him to get on if he wanted to go across the water; that they did not have much time to fool away with him. There was nothing else to do, so Coyote got on the old Goose's back. The Goose flew up in the air so quickly that Coyote did not know what had happened until he was away up in the air. All the other Geese flew up, and they all took turns in carrying him. They flew over a timbered country back from the lake, and when they were directly over a large hollow trunk of a tree they dropped Coyote. He fell into the hollow trunk and could not get out. He began to pray for power, and asked everything all around for help, for he was frightened almost to death and thought he would never get out. A Fly flew into the hollow tree, and he prayed to him to give him any power that he had which would help him out of the tree. The Fly said that his power was too weak to help Coyote, but that he would go to a friend of his and bring him to help Coyote. The Fly flew away and soon returned, saying that his friend was coming. Finally he heard a bird on a tree near by, and he peeped out of a small hole in the tree and saw that the bird was a Wood-pecker. The Woodpecker called to Coyote and asked him if he really wanted to get out. Coyote answered in a weak voice that he did. The Woodpecker said that he had to go and get some one to come and help him. Soon Woodpecker returned with some of his brothers, and they began to peck a hole in the hollow tree. At last the hole was big enough for Coyote to get out. He told them to stick their heads in and see if they thought he could get out all right. They stuck their heads in and Coyote bit their heads off. After he had eaten all the Woodpeckers who had worked to make the hole for him, he escaped.

62. COYOTE AND RABBIT KILL A BUFFALO.*

Rabbit and his grandmother lived by themselves, and Rabbit often went out to hunt to get something for them to eat. He began to go pretty far from home, and his grandmother scolded him and told him not to go so far, but to remember that he was little and might be killed. Rabbit did not pay any attention, for he knew that he was a good run-ner. One time he went far away, but could not find any game, and so he turned around to go home. As he went he played along the way and sang to himself. Coyote was out the same day looking for some-thing to eat. He was just about to give up and go home when he heard some one singing. He looked all about and saw Rabbit. He grinned to himself and quietly slipped up behind Rabbit. When he knew that he was so close that Rabbit could not get away, he yelled "Bo!" at Rabbit and made a grab for him. Rabbit was badly frightened, but he determined not to give up. He said : "Coyote, don't kill me yet and I will tell you how to kill some good game. I can not do it alone, and I have just been wishing that you would come and help me with my scheme." "What is it?" asked Coyote, very much interested. "I know where there is a big fat buffalo that we can kill if you will go with me." Coyote went, first telling Rabbit that if he lied to him he would kill him at once. Rabbit led the way to a place where an old buffalo stood. They went up to the buffalo, and Rabbit told Coyote to climb into its anus. Coyote obeyed and Rabbit followed. When inside, Rabbit told Coyote to begin to bite and eat the buffalo's sides. They both began and soon the buffalo fell dead. Then an old man ran up to the buffalo and began to butcher it. Rabbit told Coyote to hide in an intestine, and he hid in the bladder. When the man had cut up the buffalo he placed the intestines to one side, but threw the bladder away in the bushes. Rabbit crawled out of the bladder and escaped, but Coyote was discovered and killed.

---

* Told by Wing.

63. COYOTE, MOUNTAIN-LION, AND RABBIT.*

One time, when Coyote was out hunting for something to eat, he heard something crying like a child. He ran to some rocks from whence the sound came, and there he found Mountain-Lion's den and her young left there alone. He determined to devour them, for he was very hungry, but he hesitated because he feared Mountain-Lion. At last hunger got the better of his judgment, and, saying to himself that he was not afraid of old Mountain-Lion, he killed and ate all of her children.

When the mother came back from the hunt with food for her young ones, she could not find them. She looked every place, and soon discovered Coyote's foot-prints. She knew at once what had happened. She started out to find Coyote, but he always escaped her. After she had followed him many days, she sat down on the bank of the river to rest. Not far away she saw some one and she at once recognized Rabbit. She determined to call Rabbit and ask him to help her catch Coyote, for he was the enemy of both. Mountain-Lion called to him in a gentle voice so as not to frighten him, and asked him to come to her, for she wanted to speak to him. Rabbit was afraid at first, but when Mountain-Lion told him that she wanted him to help capture Coyote, Rabbit came. They started along the river together. Soon they found a deer. Mountain-Lion told Rabbit to wait while she killed the deer. She followed the deer into the thicket, killed it, and then called Rabbit to come and help her cut it up. When they had butchered it, Mountain-Lion told Rabbit to cover her face with fat so that she could not be recognized ; then to put the deer on her back. After Rabbit had done that, Mountain-Lion told him to get on top of the deer and to drive her around until they met Coyote. While they were crossing the prairie they heard some one calling, "Rabbit, where did you get your fine horse?" But Rabbit did not answer, and went on as though he had not heard the voice. Again the voice called, "Rabbit, did not you hear me? Wait, I say, I want to see your horse." Rabbit went on until Coyote, for it was he, had caught up with him ; then he said, "This fine horse was given to me." Coyote said : "Get right off. That horse is mine. I lost it and you have found it. Get right off." Rabbit pretended to be afraid and jumped off. Just as Coyote was about to get on the horse, he stopped to bite a piece of fat off of its face. Then he recognized Mountain-Lion and started to run for his life, but it was too late. Mountain-Lion sprang upon him and killed him.

---

* Told by Wing.

64. COYOTE BECOMES A BUFFALO.*

While Coyote was out hunting something to eat he met Buffalo, who was very powerful among his tribe. He was eating grass and looked fat and well fed. Coyote asked him if he would give him power to turn into a Buffalo and eat grass as he did. Buffalo said: "Yes, I will give you the power which was given to me by the Great-Father-Above, but when I give you the power you must not use it every chance you get, but only when very necessary." He told Coyote to stand facing the other way and not to move, but to be brave as he was. Coyote stood still, wondering what was going to happen to him. Buffalo began to throw up dirt with his hoofs and to act very angrily. He told Coyote to keep his eyes closed. Then he made a plunge toward him, and when he was about to strike him with his horns, Coyote jumped out of the way, and Buffalo passed him without touching him. He did this the second, third, fourth, fifth, and sixth times, but the seventh time he stood there without moving. He could hear Buffalo coming at him, but he stood there awaiting what would happen to him. Buffalo struck him and rolled him under his stomach with his horns and threw him up into the air. When he came down on his feet he was turned into a very young Buffalo. He began to eat green grass at once. Then the old Buffalo told him that if he wanted to turn into a Coyote again, he must find a Buffalo wallow, roll himself over two or three times, and then he would arise a Coyote. Again Buffalo cautioned him not to use his power too often, telling him that the power was good for only seven times, and he also told him that he must not give the power to any one else, especially to any of his own race. Before they parted the real Buffalo told Coyote to change back into a Coyote, and he did so, and then they both went on their way. Before Coyote had gone far from Buffalo, he wanted to try his power to see if he could use it alone. He did, and became a Buffalo. During that same day he tried his power three or four times, and before he had met any one he had tried it six times, and had turned himself into a Buffalo for the seventh time. While he was a Buffalo he met one of his own people, a famous Coyote, and so he went up to him and said : "Do not you want me to give you some of my power, so that you can eat grass as I do? You look as though you were very hungry." "Yes," said Coyote. "Well, all right," said Coyote-Buffalo. "Go off a short distance from me and stand there and face the other way. Do not run, but be brave as I am. Close your eyes. Now, I am

* Told by White-Bread.

ready,'' and so he started at him, but the other Coyote jumped out of the way every time until the last time came. Then Coyote stood his ground, and Coyote-Buffalo rolled him under his stomach, and they both went up in the air and came down on their feet. They were both Coyotes, and they stood looking at each other for a time; then they separated and went off.

65. COYOTE AND THE TURKEYS.*

Coyote was looking for something to eat, for he was hungry as ever. Finally, on his way, he heard a noise. He thought to himself, '' Some people must be having lots of fun,'' so he made up his mind to go and enjoy himself with them. He went in the direction of the noise and he found many Turkeys. They were having fun by getting into a large sack and rolling down a steep hill. When the Turkeys saw him coming they said that they were going to put him in too. Coyote came and wanted to take part in the fun, for he thought it a good chance to kill some of the Turkeys. He let the Turkeys roll him down the hill two or three times; then he thought that his time had come to carry out his plan. He told all the Turkeys to get into the sack and he would roll them down the hill. Every one of them crawled into the sack, and then Coyote tied it fast at each end, so that they could not get out, and put it on his back and started for home. He had four young sons at home, and calling them to him he opened the sack and took out one of the Turkeys, saying: '' You see this. I have that sack full of Turkeys. Build a big fire and we will have a feast.'' They built a fire, but did not have enough wood to make a big, hot fire. '' We will go to the timber for wood, and you,'' speaking to his youngest son, ''stay here and watch the sack.'' '' Be careful not to untie the strings,'' said Coyote. Then he and his three sons started for the wood. After they had been gone a little while young Coyote thought he would look into the sack and see what the Turkeys were doing. He untied the strings, and just as soon as he untied the strings the Turkeys all ran out and flew away. Young Coyote did not know what to do, but finally he decided to put some dirt in the sack and fool his father that way. He went to work and filled the sack with dirt. His father returned and said, '' Now, children, we will have a fine feast,'' and went to the sack to kill three or four more of the Turkeys; but when he opened the sack he found nothing but dirt in it. Coyote was very angry at his son, and he asked him how he had let the Turkeys get away, and the boy told him all about it. Coyote killed his young son and ate him in place of the Turkeys.

---

* Told by White-Bread.

66. COYOTE'S EYES ARE REPLACED BY BUCKEYES.*

One time Coyote was out hunting something to eat, and on his way he heard a noise and he said to himself, "I think those are some Turkeys that escaped from me some time ago. They will not get away this time, for I will kill them before I get home." And so he made up his mind to go and see what they were doing, and to catch them. When he went to the place, he found Ducks playing about in the water. When they saw Coyote coming they knew him at once, for they had often heard about him. They came out of the water and stood on the bank, and when he came up they asked him if he would like to play with them. He said, "Yes, that is just what I want to do, and I will show you some of my tricks after you show me some of yours." They debated what to play, and one of the Ducks spoke up and said : "We will play in the water. We will take one man and take his eyes out and let him dive into the water just as long as he can hold his breath, and as soon as he goes under the water we will throw his eyes into the water after him, and when he comes out from under the water his eyes will be in their place. How do you like that?" the Duck asked Coyote. "That is all right," said Coyote. "Well, we will commence now." The first Duck had his eyes taken out, and then he dived into the water and his eyes were thrown in after him, and when he came up he had them in their place. Then another took his turn, and so on until every one of the Ducks had tried, and then Coyote's turn came. His eyes were taken out and thrown into the water after him, and he came out with his eyes in their place. The Ducks were given power to do most anything that they wanted, but they had the power to do each thing only once. Coyote wanted to try the trick once more, but the Ducks did not want him to try it again, for they knew that their power was limited to one time. Coyote kept begging them, and finally the Ducks let him try the trick again, and so they took his eyes out and he dived into the water. The Ducks knew that they could not put the eyes in place again, and so they flew away and left Coyote. While he was going along he was talking and crying. He was asking some one who had greater powers than he to help him out of his trouble and to give him eyes again. Finally a man found him and he told him that he would help him all he could, and told him to wait there until he returned. He went off to find something with which to make Coyote some new eyes. He was gone for a while, and when he returned he had some green buckeye balls.

---

* Told by White-Bread.

He told Coyote to be brave once more, that he was going to hit him where the right eye was with the buckeye ball, and then where the left eye was with another ball, and then he would be able to see ; and so he did, and thus Coyote's eyes were restored.

67. COYOTE AND TURTLE RUN A RACE.*

One time, as Coyote was returning from a long and unsuccessful hunt for game, he passed the home of his old friend Turtle. Being weary and hungry and in no hurry, he decided to stop and make Turtle a visit. Turtle invited him in and offered him something to eat, as Coyote had hoped that he would. While Coyote ate, Turtle stretched himself out to rest, saying, "I am tired out. I have just come back from the races." Coyote asked what races. "Our people have been having foot races down by the river. Have not you heard of them?" Coyote smiled at the thought of Turtle's racing and said that he had not heard of the races, and if he had he surely would have been there. "Who won?" he asked. "I did," said Turtle. "I have never yet been beaten in a race with my people." Coyote answered, "I have never been beaten either. I wonder how a race between us would come out." "The way to find out is to have a race," Turtle said. "I am willing, if you are. When shall we have it?" Coyote answered. They determined to run the race two days hence. In the meantime Coyote had finished eating, and so, promising to come on the second day to run the race, he departed.

When he arrived home Coyote sent his son to call all of the Coyote people and announce to them that his father was going to run a race with Turtle, and that he wanted them all to come and bet heavily on the race, for of course he would defeat Turtle. As soon as Coyote had gone Turtle sent his son out to announce that his father was going to run a race with Coyote, and that he wanted all of the best runners to come to his lodge. They all came and listened to Turtle's plan to beat Coyote in the race. Turtle arose when they came in and said : "We all know that Coyote is a good runner, but he is also a cheat. He has cheated us in many ways. Let us now cheat him out of this race. Will you help me do it?" Every one present agreed to help him. Then he continued : "This is my plan. I want each one of you to put a white feather in your hair just like the one I wear, and paint yourselves to look just like me. Then station yourselves at intervals along the course. Coyote will run with his head down, as he always does. One of you will start with him, but when he has left you far behind drop down in the grass. Then the next one will jump up and run. Coyote will look up and see you ahead, then he will run until he passes you. Then the next one will jump up and run, and so on until the last one. I will be the last, and beat him over the goal." The Turtles talked over the plan, then arose and went home to prepare for the race.

The first day passed, and then the day came when they had to run the race. Early in the morning the Turtles stationed themselves along the way in the tall grass, and soon Coyote came. They began to discuss the distance they should run. Turtle wanted to run a long distance, but Coyote did not want to go a very long distance ; he thought that he could beat Turtle in a short distance just as easily as in a long distance, and he did not care to tire himself. Turtle insisted, and so Coyote said that he would agree to any distance that he would mention. Many Coyotes came and began to bet on Coyote.

They started to run and all the Coyotes began to laugh, for their man was far ahead, but soon to their surprise Turtle was ahead. Coyote overtook Turtle, and then they began to laugh again. Soon they heard the Turtles cheering, and to their amazement Turtle was far in the lead. Again Coyote overtook Turtle, and again Turtle came up far in the lead. The Coyotes cheered one moment and the Turtles the next. Just as Coyote had passed Turtle and was near the goal, Turtle crossed the line, and all the Turtles set up a loud cheer. Coyote ran off in the grass, and is wondering yet how Turtle beat him in the race, and all the other Coyotes are angry at him because he lost the race and caused them to lose so many bets.

68. COYOTE, WILD-CAT, AND THE OLD WOMAN.

An old, blind woman lived all alone. Her home was far away, and no one ever came to see her and few people even passed by. Though she was blind and old she somehow always had plenty to eat and seemed to get along as well as any one else. She always had her pot full of meat, and those who passed could smell it cooking, and they wondered who brought the meat to her. Whenever she sat down to eat she would always say, "All ready for dinner," just as though she were calling some one to come and eat with her ; then she would say, " Orphan, I was only talking to myself."

One day Wild-Cat happened to come to her house while he was out looking for something to eat. He smelled the cooking meat, and so decided to stop a while. When he went in he saw that the old woman was blind. He slipped quietly to a corner and sat with one eye on the boiling pot and the other on the old woman while he tried to make a plan to steal the meat.   After a while the old woman took the pot off of the fire and sat down to eat, but first she called, "All ready for dinner.   Orphan, I was only talking to myself."   Wild-Cat sprang up ready to run, for he thought that she saw him and was talking to him. When she did not say anything more, but began to eat, he forgot his fright and slipped over and began to eat, too.   He ate very quietly, being careful not to crack any bones or to make any noise in chewing or swallowing.   He ate until there was only a little left in the pot ; then he slipped quietly out.   After that he came there every day and ate so much that he grew slick and fat.

One day Coyote met Wild-Cat and said : " You always seem to have plenty to eat, and yet I never see you kill any game.   Where do you get so much to eat ? "   Wild-Cat told Coyote how he went to the old woman's home and ate from her pot every day.   Coyote wanted to go along, and so Wild-Cat agreed to take him, but first he made him promise to keep very quiet and to do only what he was told.   Coyote promised, and so they started to the old woman's place.   When they came near Coyote smelled the cooking meat and started to run on ahead, but Wild-Cat pulled him back.   They slipped inside and sat near the door while the meat was cooking.   When the old woman took the pot off of the fire and called, "All ready for dinner," Coyote jumped up, and it was all Wild-Cat could do to hold him back.   When the old woman began to eat, Wild-Cat and Coyote slipped up and quietly stole meat out of the pot.   Coyote put a big piece in his mouth and began to chew so hard that he forgot all about keeping quiet.   His jaw came down on a bone and it cracked so loud that the old woman jumped up. Wild-Cat saw his jaw coming down on the bone and was out of the house by the time the old woman jumped up.   She ran to the door and closed it, and then took a long spear that stood in the corner and began to poke around in the room.   Coyote slipped about for some time, but finally the spear pierced him and he cried out with pain. Then the old woman knew for sure that some one was in the house, and so she kept on poking until she killed him.   Wild-Cat came back next day and found Coyote dead.   He was sorry, not because he cared for Coyote, but because he was afraid to go in the old woman's house again to eat, for fear she would kill him.

69. COYOTE CHALLENGES THE SNAKE.*

One time while Coyote was out hunting something to eat he decided to go where Snake lived.   He started in the direction he thought Snake lived and went to many places, but he could not find him.   He went

---

* Told by Annie Wilson.

along talking to himself, saying, "I thought so; Snake is not so poisonous as people think, and if I ever find him I will show him my power." He kept going from place to place. Finally he came to one place and thought he would stop and rest for a while. He was not there very long when he heard some one calling him. He arose and looked around and saw Snake coming toward him. When Snake came up to him, Coyote asked him how he was getting along in the world, since he had been made so small. "You look so small that I do not think you can do very much harm to any one, though I have heard many times that you have much poison. They say that you are more dangerous than I, and so that is the reason I have gone from place to place looking for you. Now that I have met you I want you to show me in what way you are more powerful and dangerous than I am." Snake said: "Yes, I look very small to you, but you know that although I am small I am given power by our Father, and by his aid I have done many things in this world. I have killed many animals, large and small. Now you have come to see me, and whatever you want me to do I will do it; but first tell me what you want me to do." "Well," said Coyote, "I want to see which of us has the most power." "All right," said Snake, "you may bite me just once anywhere you like, and I will bite you, too, and in that way we will see who has the more power." "But you have to bite me first," said Coyote. "All right," said Snake, and went up to Coyote and bit him on the top of his nose, and then said: "That is all I can do." Coyote stood there as though he was not hurt at all. He asked Snake if that was all he could do, and Snake said: "That is the best I can do to show you my power." Coyote said: "Well, it is my time to show you my power." "Yes," said Snake, and so Coyote came up to Snake and bit him nearly in two. Snake cried out and begged Coyote to let him go. "Now," said Coyote to Snake, "you lie there and I will lie here. We will call to each other every now and then, so that we can see who will live the longer." Snake went a little way off and laid down, acting as though he were about to die. Coyote also went off a little way and lay down. He was thinking Snake would die in a little while, and so he called out to him. Coyote could just hear him answer in a weak voice, as though he was almost dead. After a while he heard Snake calling him and he answered with a big voice. They kept on calling to one another all night. Toward daylight Snake called Coyote, but no answer came from him. He called again, but still no answer. The third and fourth times he called, but there was no answer. Snake went over to see what was the matter, and when he got there he found Coyote all swollen and dead. Snake was more dangerous than Coyote.

70. COYOTE TURNS INTO A CORN MILL.*

The women made their corn mills from the trunk of an old tree. They cut a piece about two feet through and three or four feet high and hollowed it about twelve inches deep in one end. There they placed their corn and ground it to meal with a pounder. There were many of these mills, but one that was very old and smooth the women liked best.

One day a woman went to use the old corn mill, and as she pounded her corn she saw that it was diminishing too fast, and when she had it ground she saw that she had only a little. She gathered up her meal and said nothing, but watched the next woman pound her corn. It disappeared in the same way, and so did the corn of the third and the fourth women who came to use the mill. They all wondered what could be the matter with the mill, and they examined it carefully and saw that it was not the old mill that they had always used. One of the women cried out to get an axe and cut it and see where their corn had disappeared. As one of the women ran to get an axe the mill fell over and began to roll about, and Coyote jumped up from the place where the mill had been and ran away. Coyote had turned into a corn mill and hidden the old one so that he could get all he wanted to eat.

* Told by Wing.

ABSTRACTS.

1. THE CREATION AND EARLY MIGRATIONS.

In beginning darkness rules. Man comes, and soon there is village with thousands of people. Man disappears; returns with seeds. He says Sun is coming and will be given power by Great-Father-Above. Unknown man tells people to select chief. In council is Coyote, who tells people to call unknown man Moon, because he is first created man on earth. People make Moon chief, and he selects errand-man to summon people, and chief tells them they are to move to better world. They divide into groups and select leaders, and chief gives each leader drum and tells them to sing and beat their drums. None of them is to look back, lest they should be stopped and stay in darkness. People move westward and come out of ground to another world. Coyote tells chief world is too small, and looks back. Half go back and others go on west. Chief throws dirt in front of him and forms high mountains. People come to mountains and there make their first homes. Moon goes to mountain top and sees people have scattered in different directions. When together they spoke Caddo; now each group speaks different language. Moon says direction to right is north, or cold side; that to left south, or warm side. Sun comes up from east and goes down in west. He goes too fast to do any good, so Coyote starts eastward and tells Sun he wants to talk with him. They walk together slowly, and when half way to west Coyote tells Sun he is going to defecate and asks him to wait a while. Coyote goes behind bushes and then runs away. Sun waits; then starts on slowly, still waiting for Coyote. Beginning of real people was in village called Tall-Timber-on-Top-of-the-Hill. Moon calls people together first time in new world, and says child will soon be born of woman and will have more power than any one else. He will name himself Medicine-Screech-Owl, after former chief, and have with him bow and arrows. Child comes and has bow and arrows. On his first birthday he names himself Medicine-Screech-Owl. He says bow and arrows are for men to kill game. He teaches people to make bows and arrows. In those times animals talked to human beings and they understood one another. Afterward some human beings turned into animals. Medicine-Screech-Owl visits most ferocious animals in behalf of people. People have little to eat, except man and woman known as Buzzard, who have plenty of meat. Coyote, in order to find out where they get so much meat, turns into dog. Buzzards find little dog. Man says it is not real dog. To find out whether it is real dog, woman pinches its ear and it howls like dog. Man tells woman to give dog some meat to see whether it eats fast. She does so, and Coyote takes his time in eating it. So Buzzard believes woman and they keep dog. Coyote stays with them until meat gives out and then watches them. Buzzard starts out after more meat, leaving dog at home. He follows and finds out where they get their meat. Three days afterward he goes to cave with rock as door, where he had seen Buzzards at work. He opens place and out come thousands of buffalo. Buzzard discovers what has happened, but dog has gone. Coyote tells people to make bows and arrows, as buffalo are coming. Buzzards now have to look for dead meat; so they become real buzzards. As time passes on, people notice that Moon pays no attention to them and stays at home. He is unmarried and lives with his father and mother and one very young sister. Unknown to his father and mother, Moon goes by night to see his own sister. She does not know who he is ; but one night she put black paint on her fingers, and when man comes she passes fingers across forehead and makes black marks. In morning she sees marks on his forehead. When Moon learns that people are finding out about him, he is ashamed and wishes to leave them. Father-Above takes him away and places him far above, where people can see his shame marks on his forehead. After Moon has gone, people select Medicine-Screech-Owl as chief. He makes them move westward, climbing mountains. At top they see large lake, and Medicine-Screech-Owl says waters are tears shed by Moon for wrongs he had done his people. People keep moving on westward and make bows and arrows. They go long distance to hunt buffalo and other animals. One place they dare not go to, as in water there is most ferocious animal. Medicine-Screech-Owl goes to kill animal. He makes narrow road through thicket and sees animal. He has bow and some corn to use in killing it. He throws corn into air and it becomes blackbirds, which fly over head of animal. When animal rises to draw blackbirds down, Medicine-Screech-Owl shoots it through heart, first from right, then from left side. Animal falls and dies. Coyote now becomes bad man and makes all kind of trouble among people. Medicine-Screech-Owl tells Coyote he must go, but on Coyote's saying he is going to stop his mean tricks, chief allows him to stay until he should be captured or killed at any time.

2. THE ORIGIN OF DAY AND NIGHT.

In beginning people live in darkness. They discuss how they can get light. Man who is prophet is appointed by Coyote to investigate. Prophet reports that there are yellow, black, spotted, half-spotted, and white deer. He says that if they kill both black and white deer they will have day and night. They hunt until they kill black and white deer, and from that time we have had day and night.

3. THE ORIGIN OF ANIMALS.

People and animals live together and are same in beginning. After a time there is not food for all. Council is held and chiefs determine that some shall become animals and be hunted for food. People living near burnt grass are rolled in ashes until they become bears. They are given ten lives. When killed first time, second life is to arise from blood spilled upon ground, and so on through other lives up to tenth, bear to become fiercer each life, and finally to eat human beings. People living near long grass are rolled and become buffalo. They are given ten lives and put to live upon prairie. Deer are made in same way, and after them all other animals.

4. COYOTE REGULATES LIFE AFTER DEATH.

Coyote proposes rule that when any one dies he shall be dead forever and no living person ever see him again. People are well pleased, and from that time when anybody dies he is gone forever. People are taken to sky and become stars. Morning-Star has three brothers, and he is leader. He gets up early now, because formerly he was errand-man and had to rise early. His brothers are Evening-Star, North-Star, and South-Star. They watch lest enemy should approach. Their father was Great-Star and was chief of people. They believe every one when he dies goes up to sky.

5. COYOTE AND THE ORIGIN OF DEATH.

In beginning there is no death, but there are so many people that there is no room for any more. Coyote thinks people should die for good, but all others decide that people shall come back. Medicine-Men build a grass lodge and tell people that when white and black eagle feather on top becomes bloody and falls over, they will know some one has died. Then Medicine-Men will sing and call spirit to grass house and they will restore it to life again. Sign shows that some one is dead. Medicine-Men sing, and in ten days whirlwind blows from west, circles about, and finally enters by east. From it appears handsome young men. People rejoice, except Coyote, who is displeased. After feather becomes bloody and falls, Coyote goes to grass house and sits near door with singers. When he hears whirlwind coming and it is about to enter, he shuts door. Spirit finding door closed whirls on by. Death forever was then introduced. Ever since then spirits of dead wander over earth until they find road to spirit land. Coyote runs away, and ever since he runs from one place to another, looking back to see if he is being pursued. He starves, as no one will give him food.

6. THE SECOND MAN WHO CAME OUT OF THE EARTH.

Moon first man to come out of earth into world. Second man is Tonin, who is greater than Moon and more powerful. He is four feet high and rides horse no bigger than dog. He can turn darkness into light and have anything he wishes for. By wishing he can go any distance, and he can kill any game by pointing his forefinger at it. From time to time he disappears into sky. He can foretell future. He calls people together and tells them about this world, and says in six days he is going away and will be gone six winters and seven summers. He wishes them to come and see him start. On sixth day Tonin sings death song, and is gradually lifted up from earth to sky. When it is time for him to return, stars become brighter and larger. When day comes and Tonin's brother gives sign that he is about to return, large stars come up in east and Tonin comes back to earth. He tells people about future, and that strange people will come and frighten away buffalo, deer, and bear. After some time he tells people he is going as before, but that he will not return. He goes up into sky.

7. SNAKE-WOMAN DISTRIBUTES SEEDS.

Great-Father gives seeds of all growing things to Snake-Woman. Afterward she and her two sons travel over world to carry seeds to people. They give six seeds of each kind of plant to every person. Snake-Woman says they are not to allow any one, especially children, to touch them or ever point to them as they grow. If any one gathers seeds too soon she will send poisonous snakes to bite them.

8. THE FLOOD.

Waters of earth dry up. People become crazed and cut to pieces dead animals that dwelt in water, thinking them responsible for water disappearing. They see man in sky coming from west. Wind blows and man lights on ground, carrying small green leaf. He tells people they have abused him and he is angry. He motions leaf in four directions and water falls from it. Waters grow in volume and rise all over world to highest mountains except one. To this mountain man leads few of people, and they stay four days. As waters rise man causes mountain to rise. When green things appear on earth again, he leads people down from mountain. They find many people have been turned into alligators and other water animals.

9. THE EFFEMINATE MAN WHO INTRODUCED STRIFE.

Man works and dresses like women and goes with them. War breaks out, and all men go to fight but this one. Old man threatens to kill him if he will not fight. Man refuses to go, and when old man threatens to have him killed by warriors on their return, he says they can not kill him and he will bewitch people and cause them to fight and kill one another. Old man incites warriors to kill man as coward, and they beat him until they think he is dead. He jumps up alive and they cut off his head. He runs about headless. People notice spot on little finger of left hand. They cut it out and man lies down and dies. Soon after, people begin to fight and quarrel and kill each other. Then old man tells people what coward had said, and they are sorry they killed him.

10. THE ORIGIN OF THE MEDICINE-MEN.

In days of old, people and animals are on friendly terms. Animals possess wonderful powers and give people power in dreams or visions. Man who has had dream remains several days in silence. He then calls friends and old men to lodge and teaches them his songs and dances. They all call themselves medicine-men, and if any one is sick they hold dance in grass lodge for six days and nights. First medicine-men to receive power and give dance are two young brothers. They are brave hunters. In sleep in lonely woods both have dream, in which they walk together toward east. They see man coming rapidly toward them. He stops and after long talk reveals bag and asks them choose any kind of medicine. He gives them medicine for long life and teaches them how to use it. When boys wake up, each remembers dream, but says nothing. After many months each begins to try his powers. War breaks out with Chickasaw and many are killed or taken prisoners. Chickasaw on way home have war dances and dance around prisoners. Young man escapes, and when Chickasaw come after him he crawls into hollow log. After they return he crawls out and goes home. Many men are away when Chickasaw make attack, among them two brothers with power. Men start to pursue Chickasaw and overtake them. At first sight they run into camp, kill many Chickasaw, and rescue prisoners. Strong-Wind and his brother exhibit wonderful powers. After many years brothers die and tribe has no medicine-man. Finally very young man is given powers by Black-Mountain-Bear. While out hunting, darkness comes and he lays down to sleep in shelter. He dreams that he is walking on narrow trail eastward and sees man sitting with head down. Man tells him he wants to give him medicine, and takes out many roots, of which boy is to choose six. He takes six roots, but old man tells him he must go before six men, who will explain their use. He gives back four. He sees old man sitting by trail, who explains use of his medicine. While going toward third man he awakes. He returns home and keeps silent. He wanders about, looking for roots seen in dream. At last he finds plant. Soon after man is about to die. Young man calls medicine-men together and teaches them dance song he has been taught in dream. They all go to sick man's lodge. They dance six days and nights before young man finds out what is matter with him. Finally young man begins to talk in strange tongue and dances slowly. He falls to ground and begins to crawl like mad bear. He places mouth on place where greatest pain is, draws pain out by blowing breath on place, and pain is gone. People know Black-Mountain-Bear has given him power. He is now called Black-Mountain-Bear-Medicine. Medicine-men's society holds dance and wants young man to show his powers. Sixth night he joins dance. He dances faster and faster and picks up gun. He takes out bullet and powder and puts them back again and gives gun to helper. He dances again, falls, kneels, and spreads out arms. Helper shoots him through breast and he falls in faint. He rises, dances again, and shows bullet to people. He has caught it in his hands. Another young man has wonderful power given him by Mountain-Bear. He has bear's skin that he causes to turn into young bear, which follows him about. Then he turns animal back into skin. There are two kinds of medicine-men. One has power to heal sick ; another has power to prevent any one from being hurt or harmed. The latter are more powerful than others, as they can perform without medicine and can be with people afar off. They have a song of death which frightens away death. This power is generally given by Sun, Moon, Stars, Earth, or Storm, and also by some very wild and ferocious animals.

11. THE GIRL WHO MARRIED A TURTLE.

Girl lives with two brothers, who are famous hunters. Girl plays by water and gets to know Turtle. He asks to be her husband. She consents and sees him as often as she can. Brothers go away for many days. Girl builds high bed for Turtle ; carries him home and puts him in it. Every day she puts bowl of potatoes in bed for him to eat. Brothers come home, and she wants to take Turtle back to river, but he begs to stay. Boys notice high bed, but suspect nothing until they see sister take bowl full of potatoes to bed and take it out empty. They pretend they are going hunting, and soon return. Girl goes to dig potatoes. Boys find Turtle in bed and kill him, and then run away. Girl finds husband dead and runs after them. Boys come to river, where many white ducks are playing. Boys offer to paint ducks different colors if they will carry them and bob-tailed dog across river. Ducks carry them across and soon girl comes. Ducks say they have not seen boys and dog. White duck, whom boys have forgotten to paint, says boys and dog have just passed. Duck carries girl across. Brothers see her coming. They meet three white doves, who, at their request, fly to the sky with them and dog. Smoke makes doves' white feathers gray. Girl asks doves where brother and dog are. They point to three bright stars in southern part of sky. Girl looks at stars and falls dead.

12. THE MAN AND THE DOG WHO BECAME STARS.

Man has dog who when they are off alone hunting talks as if he were man. He can always tell what is about to happen. Once Dog comes running back and tells master they are coming to dangerous place. Dog scents deer and starts on trail. Man shoots deer, which runs to lake and jumps into water. Dog jumps in and holds deer until man comes. They kill deer, and man swims toward shore with it on his shoulders. Dog cries out. They are surrounded by poisonous and dangerous water animals. Man prays to spirits to help them, and water leaps up and throws them on shore. Man in gratitude throws some of deer's flesh into water as sacrifice. Man and dog decide to leave this dangerous world and go to sky to live. They are two bright stars in south.

13. EVENING-STAR AND ORPHAN-STAR.

Poor orphan boy lives with large family who mistreat him. He goes with people to island in large lake to hunt eggs. They go away while he is asleep and leave him to starve. He lives for time on scraps he finds around dead camp fires.

He sits by water's edge and tries to catch fish as they swim past. Large animal with horns comes to him through water. He tells boy he will carry him to mainland. He climbs upon animal's back and animal says he is to tell him if he sees star. They have not gone far when boy says there is big star in west. Monster sees it, turns and swims back to island. For five days he starts with boy and swims back again because boy sees star, but each day he gets little farther. Sixth time he is within few feet of opposite shore when boy sees star. Boy says nothing and monster swims on until they are near shallow water. Boy sees great black cloud roll in front of star. He jumps off animal's back and swims to shore. Something strikes animal with awful crash and he is killed. Handsome young man comes and thanks boy for what he has done. He has long tried to kill monster, because he made waters of lake dangerous. Man, who is Evening-Star, takes boy to sky and he stands near him as Orphan-Star.

14. THE GIRL WHO MARRIED A STAR.

Maiden sleeps in arbor and watches stars. She goes to sleep, wishing one star especially would marry her. When she awakes she sees old man sitting by fireside. He tells her she is Star's wife. She begins to cry. Star's sister is preparing food, and tells her to stop crying and come and eat. Women go out to dig potatoes. Big potato is gate of heaven and covers entrance to world beneath. Girl tells Star's sister she wants to go back again. Sister tells Star and he agrees to let her return in six days. They begin to make rope of young elm bark. In six days rope only half long enough. It is finished on eleventh day. Next morning girl is fastened to end of rope and let through hole. Rope is gradually slipped out, and after long while she sees earth. She travels many summers and winters. Her food is almost gone and she is far from earth. Rope ceases to slip and she hangs there long time. She sees Buzzard circling around below her and she calls to him. He takes her on his back and flies until he nearly gives out. Hawk helps him and flies with girl until he gives out. Buzzard takes her again and alights with her near village. Girl is weak and exhausted, and woman helps her to lodge. Mother does not know her at first. After tenth day people come to tipi to see her. She tells them her story, and especially about kindness of Buzzard. After that, people always leave one buffalo for buzzards after big killing.

15. THE GIRL WHO MARRIED A STAR.

Very beautiful girl, whose three sisters marry, will not receive attention. She is tired of home and prays spirits to help her go wherever she wishes. She watches stars and wishes she may become wife of North Star. She sees very old man sitting by fireside and thinks she is dreaming. Old man tells her she is in his home as his wife, as she wished. She does not like looks of old man, but has to stay. She tries to get away and thinks of big stone North Star has told her not to move. She goes and lifts stone and finds she can look down to earth. She wonders how she can get down, and thinks of rope of soapweeds. When North tar is out at night she cuts soapweeds, and when she has enough she begins to make rope. When rope finished she fastens it to rock, and next time man goes away she climbs down. She comes to end of rope before she comes to tree tops. She hears noise, and bird passes under her feet. When passing fourth time he tells her to step on his back and he will take her home. She gets on bird's back and he flies with her to her home. Before leaving her he says he is Black-Eagle.

16. LIGHTNING AND THE PEOPLE.

Lightning lives upon earth with people, but he becomes so powerful and kills so many people that he is sent away. Great monster lives under ground and begins to carry away people. They can not kill him, as he always disappears under ground. Lightning tells them he will kill monster if they will let him come back. He will kill all monsters and make earth safe place for people to live. People let Lightning come back.

17. THE BROTHERS WHO BECAME LIGHTNING AND THUNDER.

Medicine-Man has wife and child twelve years old. He kills many deer. One day on returning from hunting he finds boy alone. He asks where mother is, and child says she took water bucket and went toward creek. They go and can not find her. There are footprints at edge of water, and man knows something has taken his wife. They go back to house and mourn for six days. Seventh day Medicine-Man goes hunting. While he is gone, boy plays with bow and arrows. Fourth time father goes, and while boy is playing, unknown boy with long nose and very long hair comes. He says he is boy's elder brother, and will always come to see him when father goes hunting, but he is not to tell father. They play with bows and arrows, and unknown boy runs back to woods when he sees Medicine-Man coming. Medicine-Man again goes to hunt, and after fourth time boy wakes father at midnight and tells him about his brother. Father says they must capture boy and tells son he must play as though he had gone away, and he will turn into small insect and stay behind door. Boy comes, but sees man behind door and runs away. Next day father places himself at edge of roof of grass house, but boy again sees. Third day father tells boy to tie other boy's hair, and then places himself in middle of fire, but unknown boy finds him out and runs back to woods. Next day man goes behind another door, and fifth time he places himself in air, but boy each time finds him. Sixth time boy does not see which way father goes, and when he says father has gone hunting, other boy believes him and sits down by him. Little boy gets hold of his hair and says there is something in it. Boy tells him to get it out, and little boy ties hair as father had said. He calls and father jumps out of grass house. They capture boy and keep him in grass house six days. Then they wash boy, and Medicine-Man cuts his nose off and makes it look human. Before going hunting again, Medicine-Man tells boys not to go to place where large squirrels live, for they kill little children. They go to place and big squirrel comes out of hole in tree, sticks tongue out like snake, and takes young brother into tree. Other boy goes home and brings fire. He puts hard red stones into fire, and when hot throws two stones into hole. Large squirrel comes out and drops on ground dead. Boy goes and cuts open squirrel's stomach and finds brother alive. Boys go to make arrows. Unknown boy makes two arrows for his brother and paints one black and other blue. They make small wheel of thin bark. They roll wheel to each other and shoot it with arrows. They play with wheel every day until Medicine-Man's boy misses it and wheel keeps rolling and they can not find it. They start out after wheel, and when they have gone long way, they stop for rest. They pray to spirits to help them. Unknown boy puts pecan nut in ground. It sprouts and tree grows up to sky. Boy tells brother he is going up tree, and will be gone until he has dropped all bones in his body and his head, and that brother must gather bones in pile, cover with buffalo calf's hide, and shoot arrow up as hard as he can. When he hears arrow coming he is to tell him to get out of way, and bones will do so. Boy then climbs tree, and after a while his bones drop, and little boy piles them together as he was told, and shoots black arrow, and brother jumps from calf hide. He says his father has given him very dangerous power, and that brother must climb tree to get power. Little boy climbs tree with like result. Little boy has power of thunder and other boy power of lightning. They go on until they come to large lake and see place where wheel has passed into water. They pray again, and boy plants another pecan, and large tree springs up and it bends over lake and makes a bridge. They cross and find trace of wheel. They follow it and see old man. Lightning boy tells Thunder boy that old man took wheel and has it in his right side. They kill man and find wheel. They go on and find old man's people, whom they kill. They come to pile of bones and they are bones of Medicine-Man's wife. They cover them with buffalo calf hide, and bring her to life again by means of black arrow. They all start for home. Lightning boy gets there first and finds father very old man and still weeping for his children. He goes out to meet his wife and son. All live happily for number of years, and then father and mother die. Boys are lonely and decide to leave world. They go up in sky, and when clouds gather in storm, Lightning and Thunder are seen in their midst.

18. SPLINTER FOOT BOY.

Orphan boy who lives with grandmother is famous hunter. While long way from home stick pierces his leg and breaks off inside. Leg swells and friends have to carry him home. Leg continues to swell and finally skin breaks and child comes. Boy is angry, but grandmother cares for baby. While she is away boy takes child to lake and leaves it. Child lays there until it grows to be good-sized boy. Many birds fly over lake, and when they are half way cross, lake leaps up and draws them down. Boy sees this, and one day sees big water monster in water. He wishes he could kill water monster, and while thinking about it some one hits him on back. He turns, and there is Medicine-Screech-Owl, boy about his own age. Medicine-Screech-Owl says he will help him to kill monster, and tells him to go to grandmother's and get six arrows, bow, and six grains from six different kinds of corn. Grandmother surprised to see him and gives him all he asks for. He returns to lake and Medicine-Screech-Owl throws three grains of each kind of corn into air. They become birds and fly across water. Water monster leaps up to draw them down, and boy shoots at monster. Sixth arrow pierces it through and it rolls over and floats on water. Medicine-Screech-Owl says it is largest water monster in world. He takes bow and pulls monster to bank. He disappears and boy goes to grandmother's house and tells her what they have done. Boy goes again to lake. Water is very low, and so clear he sees fish swimming about. He dives to catch fish, and sword-fish goes right through him. Boy shoots fish with bow and arrow. Next day all water gone, but boy sees two large shells. He takes them home and cuts them so that he can put them over holes made by sword-fish. He wears one in front and one behind. Shells have power of hearing any sound in whole world. Whenever boy wants to hear anything he puts shells to his ears. He now becomes great medicine-man, and people plan to kill him. He and grandmother go to top of high mountain near village and make grass house there. He places two fierce dogs at door to guard house. Boy knows people who are planning to kill him by means of his shells. They die one after another, and people suspect boy is bewitching them. Many warriors try to steal to his home to kill him, but he hears them coming and sets dogs on them. Finally, Medicine-Screech-Owl decides to interfere. He starts up trail to boy's house, and blows so hard that it takes magic power of sound from shells. Near top of mountain he blows breath again, and dogs roll over asleep. He passes dogs and blows again, and old woman falls asleep. He does same with boy. He enters house and takes shells off boy, walks around, and then goes away. When almost down mountain he blows breath and boy wakes up. He misses shells and begins to look for them. Grandmother will not wake up and he shakes Medicine-Screech-Owl's breath out of her. Dogs will not wake and he knocks breath out of them with club. Dogs wake up and scent Medicine-Screech-Owl's tracks. They start after him and come to big circle of fire. In midst stands Medicine-Screech-Owl wearing shells. They can not get through fire, and return without shells. Medicine-Screech-Owl keeps them some time, and then takes them back to boy and makes him promise not to bewitch people any more.

19. MEDICINE-SCREECH-OWL.

On Medicine-Screech-Owl's first birthday he is given bow and arrows. He names himself Medicine-Screech-Owl and will not have any other name, although there is ex-chief by that name. Ex-chief hears that child's name is same as his, and says he will kill boy if he does not do what he tells him. He sends for boy and gives him watermelon seed and tells him to plant it that evening and in morning to bring him big watermelon to eat. Boy takes seeds and throws them on ground near his lodge. Watermelon plant springs up and in morning many large watermelons are on it. Boy takes melon to ex-chief, who is surprised and determines to destroy boy. Ex-chief again sends for boy and tells him to take large bull to his house and bring milk the next morning. Boy takes bull and in morning goes near to ex-chief's lodge to chop wood. Ex-chief sees him and asks him if he has already milked bull. Boy says he has not, but is in hurry to cut some wood, as his father is going to have child. When ex-chief asks if he has ever seen man have child, boy asks him if he has seen bull give milk. Third time ex-chief sends for boy, saying he and some friends are going to have fine time. They dig very deep hole and cover it with buffalo robe. Boy is told to sit on hide, and he goes down into hole, which ex-chief fills with stones and dirt until he supposes boy is dead. Man tells ex-chief that boy is still living, and ex-chief sends for him fourth time. He tells boy to go and sit down in middle of big fire. Boy does so and sits until fire burns out. He then arises unharmed. Boy makes big fire and tells ex-chief it is his turn to go into fire to show whether he has any power. Ex-chief goes in and is burned to death. Boy now goes from place to place, although mother knows that people envious of his power would try to kill him. He hears three men talking about him and determines to visit them. They welcome him and ask him to go into lodge. He goes in first and then stands near door, which is very small, and kills the three men as they enter, one at a time. He hears of Snow-and-Cold, who lives far away in the north and whose visitors, if they stay over night, are frozen before morning. He starts to visit him and sails over lake on eagle feather he wears on his head. Geese on other side of water make noise, when any one crosses, to warn Snow-and-Cold's people. They do not see Medicine-Screech-Owl, who goes to Snow-and-Cold's lodge and finds him asleep. Medicine-Screech-Owl speaks and Snow-and-Cold looks around, but can see no one. Finally, boy shows himself and tells Snow-and-Cold he has heard so much of that place he has come on visit. In evening

Snow-and-Cold tells boy to sleep on bed of snow. He watches boy and sees light near his head. Boy has feather sticking straight up on pillow. Snow-and-Cold arises and punches snow in place that seems like fireplace with cane, and fire springs out. When he has warmed himself he covers fire and goes back to bed. Soon boy does same thing. In morning Snow-and-Cold calls to boy to get up. He thinks boy has been frozen to death, but he jumps up and says he has had fine sleep. After talking to Snow-and-Cold, boy goes back home.

20. MEDICINE-SCREECH-OWL.

Beautiful girl, who had no male acquaintance, becomes pregnant. She can not explain it. She goes with other girls to dig potatoes, but can never find any. She hears voice cry, "Mother," and it is that of child in womb. It tells her where to dig and she finds many large potatoes. Child is born, and at his own request is called Medicine-Screech-Owl. Child grows rapidly, plays with other children and goes to watch them fish. He tries and catches big fish. Soon he acquires fame as a fisherman. Persons begin to fear him, and employ powerful medicine-man to kill him. One day while fishing he sees reflection of big cloud in water and knows medicine-man's intention to send Thunder to try to kill him. He walks into water, and when Thunder and Lightning come he raises bow over his head and Lightning rolls into water. This occurs again and again, and medicine-man, realizing that boy has more power over Thunder than he has, gives up. Long afterward, while resting in lodge, boy thinks something is going to happen to him. He gets his bow and arrows, lays on bed, and sings. Soon he hears great noise and he knows that medicine-man is sending cannibal monster to destroy him. He hears its roar and feels its hot breath and it leaps on his tipi and falls through. Then he arises and kills it. Afterward Medicine-Screech-Owl goes from place to place killing monsters and ferocious animals and healing sick. Where he is, death can not come. He heals sick by touch of his hand. Finally he tells people he is going to leave them, and disappears.

21. THE ORPHAN BOY WHO BECAME A WRESTLER.

Boy lives with old grandfather, who dies before he can teach boy to hunt. Boy begs from lodge to lodge, and at night returns to his lodge and cries. Boys come and tease him. He is brave, and when larger he makes bows and arrows and goes to hunt small game and has no longer to beg. When in timber he hears voice calling him. Strange boy comes and they play together. They try to see which is stronger, and orphan boy easily throws stranger. Orphan boy can not understand it. Strange boy says he is strong man and has given boy his power; that he is now one of strongest men in world. Stranger disappears and next morning boy starts to hunt. He kills three deer and starts home with them. Load is heavy and he can not go fast. At night he hears voice and sees stranger again. He goes with stranger to place where his friends meet to wrestle. He wrestles and throws every one. They fear him and leave him with stranger. Strong man tells boy how to use his power and then disappears. Boy returns home and soon afterward boys have wrestling match. Young man calls him to come into ring. At first he declines. On second call he runs into ring and soon throws man and kills him. Others are afraid of his strength. People hear of his deeds, and soon he has respect and fear of all.

22. THE DANGEROUS WATER MONSTER.

Man goes to creek to get water. He sees large animal like snake. It is moving slowly, and man runs two miles up creek before he comes to its head. He goes home and tells grandfather. He calls people together and tells them. They wonder whether it is good or evil omen. Old and blind man is sent for, and after a while he says sign is very bad, as it signifies waters will rise. Soon waters rise and form large lake. Lake is very dangerous. When crossing it no word must be said. Four men hunt on other side of lake. They start back and cross lake without making any noise. When near opposite shore one man, to try it, talks very loud. Lake rises and drowns all men but one who warned man not to talk. He calls others and they search for bodies. Two are found, but body of man who made noise can not be found.

23. SLAYING THE MONSTERS BY FIRE.

In olden times world was full of wild animals who ate people. Coyote calls council to see what can be done with them. It is decided to set fire to grass and burn wild animals and everything on earth. White-Headed-Hawk and Crow are sent to Star to say that people are coming to his house to live. Star says there is room for people if they can get up there. Long rope of soapweed is made, and White-Headed-Hawk and Crow fly up with it and give end to Star, who puts end under big stone. Rope is so long it reaches to earth. Gray and Black Snakes carry fire over world. When fire comes near, people begin to climb rope. Then wild animals come and begin to climb up. Bat is sent to cut rope just above wild animals. Bat chews rope and rope breaks, letting all wild animals down. Many are killed. Bat goes down and sees immense animal on ground, and all others crawling into it to escape fire. Bat pulls hairs out of animal's nose. Animal sneezes and blows all other animals out and they burn to death. Bat tells people all bad wild animals are killed, and they come down rope again.

24. SLAYING THE MONSTERS BY FIRE.

In beginning some animals live with human beings and are friendly ; others are strong and dangerous. Grass is taller than trees are now, and wild animals prowl through it. Morning-Star in council of people says only way to kill all dangerous animals is to burn grass all over world. Fire is man to do work, and Morning-Star appoints two men to assist him, Black-Snake, the fastest runner in the world, and Skunk, the slowest. Fire puts fire on end of Black-Snake's tail and between toes of Skunk's hind foot. They start in east, one going north, other south, to meet in west. People make rope of soapweeds to reach the sky. Pigeon goes up into sky to see when fire approaches. When rope finished, Crow takes rope and fastens it firmly to sky. As fire approaches, people begin to climb up rope. Bad animals get hold of rope and it moves upward. People send Bat, who has sharp teeth, to cut rope. Finally it breaks and lets bad animals fall down. Bat follows and sees animal so large he has room for all bad animals. These go in and Bat follows. He pulls hair from animal's nose. It sneezes and throws all animals out through nose. Animals are burned. Bat flies up to people, but is scorched, becoming yellowish. People return to world again, and ever since it has been good place to live upon.

25. HOW THE BUFFALO CEASED TO EAT HUMAN BEINGS.

At first Buffalo ate human beings. They were many-colored and were so numerous that men dared not go on plain alone. Buzzard is only man who has power to go in midst of them and kill them without being hurt. Other people live in villages and hunt together. Some men hunting turkey and deer, while crossing prairie, see black cloud coming and know it is great herd of Buffalo sweeping down upon them. They throw away everything and, running very fast, take refuge in dense thicket. People now take courage and venture farther from home. Four men go to hunt bear. They trail bear. It runs into open plain and men kill it there. They hear noise like thunder and see Buffalo upon them. Buffalo catch all but one man, who gains timber and climbs tall tree. Buffalo try to butt it down, but can not do so. At night man climbs down and runs home. People hasten to place where companions killed, but find only few bones scattered about. Buffalo eat many people until Coyote comes. Then people go into another country. Coyote is last to go through gate, and shuts it, so no dangerous animals can enter. He lets through only few Buffalo who have not tasted human flesh and so are not dangerous.

26. THE GIRL WHO HAD POWER TO CALL THE BUFFALO.

Girl who has power to call Buffalo lives with six brothers. They are stars, and every night leave girl to travel through sky. In morning they put girl in swing hung from sky and swing her through air. Buffalo see her and come, and boys kill all they want. Coyote comes to live with them. Boys tell him to stay, but make him promise never to try to swing girl. One day while all brothers gone Coyote makes girl get into swing and he pushes her. Buffalo do not come, and he pushes her higher and higher, until she disappears. Coyote tells brothers monster has carried her off. They drive him away and tell him he and his children shall always be hungry. They decide to go to sky and live with their sister.

27. THE OLD WOMAN WHO KEPT ALL THE PECANS.

Old woman is mother of pecan trees. She gives few pecans to people who go to lodge, but will not let them take any away. People are very hungry and decide something must be done. Old man has four little sons who are very troublesome. People are field rats and they chose four boys to go to old woman's to steal some nuts. One goes to see if old woman is asleep. When she goes to bed and snores he goes back home to tell brothers. Then he sees Coyote, who tells rats not to trouble about stealing pecans, as next day he will kill old woman. In morning Coyote goes to see her, and as she is getting him some pecans, Coyote strikes her on head with stone knife and kills her. Old woman dies, and ever since pecan trees grow everywhere.

28. COWARD, THE SON OF THE MOON.

When people first come out of earth, little boy is taken out by grandparents who are poor. Boy is fed by other boys and grows rapidly. He becomes successful hunter. His grandparents die and boy wanders away into timber to mourn. Man comes and embraces him. He is Moon, and says he will be boy's father, watch over him, and give him power. Boy goes home and weeps no more. Girl comes and asks to become his wife, and they live together. Wife sees husband has great power. Woman asks him to watch her child, who is asleep, while she goes to get water. When she has gone he wakes child up and cuts its leg off. When she returns child is dead, and young man is playing with leg. She calls people, and they come and kill young man. He comes out of grave and looks just the same as before he was killed. All men go on war-path except Coward, as people call him. When asked by chief why he does not go, he takes war club and goes out to fight. Arrows fly off from him and enemies see he can not be killed. Men run, and he kills many with war clubs. Next day he is sick, and vomits all arrow-heads that have pierced his body. He bathes and is well. Many years after he tells people Moon is his father. Then he arises and goes up to Moon.

29. THE FIRST WAR PARTY.

When people came into world they were divided into groups, and each group was given different name. Tribes began to fight each other, and Caddo fought Kiowa and Comanche. Caddo gather in council and chief sends errand-man to call all young men. Chief asks all who want to fight other tribes to sit in circle. Chief lays large buffalo hide in center of circle. He gives each man stick, and they beat hide with sticks and sing war song. They sing until Morning-Star drives other stars away. Chief and assistants go ahead to choose good place near water for camp. At dawn men march out, continuing war song, to place where they wait until noon, so that others who decide late may join party. While they are eating, chief makes speech, giving them rules for their conduct. They march by day and camp at night, chief in advance. When near enemy's country chief appoints four men as spies to go in all directions. They go on until they find enemy, and fight them, but scalp only one to show they have been victorious. When battle is over warriors leave and do as they please. Word is sent home, and people deck themselves with paint and feathers and go to meet war party. Scalp is put on pole and young men race for it. When they arrive at home all join in war dance.

30. THE POWER OF THE CYCLONE.

As boy sits on bank of river resting after his morning bath, voice speaks to him. He sees nothing, but, after gazing into water for long time, he sees man slowly rising to surface. Man comes and tells him to dive into water four times and to always face west. He does so, and man says he is power of Cyclone, but is growing old and his strength is going, and he has come to give boy his power. He tells boy to swing his arms about. He swings his arms and black cloud rolls up, and as he throws his arms farther, wind breaks from cloud and passes through forest, tearing up trees by roots and tossing waters in fury. At last man tells him to stand still, and boy drops his arms breathless and panting with exertion. Man tells him he has received power which he is to exercise only in spring, and calls him " Path-of-the-Cyclone." Then man disappears. Years after people see boy carried through air to sky on cyclone.

31. HOW THE CANNIBAL WAS DESTROYED.

Three men out hunting come to large tree on which something has been climbing. Near the base is large hole. Thinking bear is in hole, they thrust into it bundle of burning leaves and grass. Finally strange animal peeps from hole, and it is cannibal. Men run, and cannibal scents their tracks and follows them.

9D

He overtakes one man, kills him, and carries him back to tree. He returns and overtakes second man, whom he kills and carries back. Third man is almost overtaken, but Mountain-Lion lies in wait for cannibal, seizes him by throat, and kills him. When man gets home he tells people what has happened. Cannibal's body is eaten by white and black wolves, and when people go they find nothing but his bones. They go to tree where cannibal lived, cut it down, and find two bodies, which they bury.

32. THE YOUNG MEN AND THE CANNIBALS.

Ten boys live with grandmother. Oldest goes hunting and does not return. Next day one of his brothers goes to look for him. He does not return, and next brother goes in search of him, and so on until ninth boy goes, leaving little brother at home with grandmother. At last youngest boy goes in search of brothers, putting eagle feather in his hair. After looking far, boy sees tipi and hears voice referring to him as meat. Old man comes out and asks if he is looking for his brothers. He says he will put him on path to find them, but boy must first do some work for him. He tells boy to put log on fire. He is to have four trials, and if he fails he is to lie on log and let man lift it. Boy can not move log, and lays down on it. Old man is about to spear him with iron nose of mask he wears, when unseen power pulls boy off log, and iron nose catches in log and holds man fast. Voice tells boy to take pounder from woman who is pounding corn and beat old man to death. Boy obeys, and, when old man dead, voice tells him to gather up his brothers' bones and put them in nine piles. Strange man appears and helps him, and then tells him to put his robe over bones, shoot arrow up in sky, and tell brothers to look out lest arrow hits them. Boy does so, and brothers jump out from under robe. Man tells them to burn tipi with man and his wife and scatter ashes. Man then says he is Sun and has helped them to destroy cannibals. Then he disappears. They return home to grandmother and tell story. People then know that Sun is their friend and willing to help them.

33. COYOTE AND THE SIX BROTHERS.

Old woman has seven sons. They are good hunters. One day oldest son goes to hunt and does not return. Several days after, his dogs come back, but he does not. This happens to six sons in turn. Mother will not let youngest son go. Long time afterward he sees Raccoon in tree. He chases it, and it leads him far into timber. It runs down hollow tree, and he climbs tree to get it out. Old woman tells him to throw Raccoon down, and she and his dogs will kill it. He throws Raccoon down and she kills it and one of dogs. Then she says there is another Raccoon in tree. He pulls it out and throws it down. She kills it and another of his dogs. This happens until he has pulled six Raccoons out of tree. As boy is about to pull seventh Raccoon out, it tells him to throw it as far as he can. While old woman is chasing him, boy is to run home as fast as possible, as old woman is witch and has killed all his brothers. He does so. When old woman finds boy is gone she starts after him, but can not catch him. That night boy dreams that he meets Coyote, who tells him his brothers are not dead, but are working for bad people and will so on die if they do not get away. Coyote promises to help him to rescue them. Next day he meets man, who tells him something. Man goes on and meets Flying-Squirrel, who is one of bad people's slaves. Coyote asks him about six brothers and hears they are slaves. Coyote says he would like to help them, and Flying-Squirrel suggests that wicked chief be killed. Flying-Squirrel carries Coyote across river hanging to his tail. Coyote lets go of tail and falls into river. He hides until he thinks of plan. Then he turns into corn mill and floats out on water. Woman persuades chief to get it, although he is suspicious. Woman uses mill, but one day all corn is sour. She tells chief, who says mill is Coyote. Chief has it placed on big log to spear it with his long, spiked nose. His nose sticks in log and corn mill turns into Coyote. Coyote knows chief and tells slaves to kill him. Slaves are free and brothers return home. Afterward when killing game they leave some for Coyote.

34. THE DEATH OF THE CANNIBALS.

People of village Tall-Timber-on-Top-of-Hill decide to move to another. Young woman whose husband is dead gives birth to baby and has to stay until she can carry child. She remains in deserted village many days. One night she hears some one outside and strange voice begs admission. She lets man in and he says he is Spotted-Wolf. He says he has come to beg her not to start on journey too soon, for there are many dangerous animals in way. She says she is lonely and wants to go to her people. Spotted-Wolf then gives her some tobacco and tells her if she meets danger and needs help to throw some of it to four directions and call to him ; then he will come and help her. After few days woman starts with baby on her back. After traveling three days she sees in her way cannibal. She is much frightened and takes tobacco and throws it to four directions, praying that Spotted-Wolf would come. Soon big spotted wolves come from four directions and kill cannibal. Wolf from south conducts woman and child safely to her people. Another kind of cannibal lives as human being and eats dead people. They pretend to be sick when they hear of one who is about to die, and when he dies they pretend to die and are buried. In night they jump out of graves and steal dead person before spirits can take him away. An old medicine-man watches one of these beings for long time. Then he pretends to be very sick and spreads news that he is about to die. Soon he hears that watched person is sick, and then he pretends to die, first telling his sons to put bow and arrows in his grave and not to put much earth over him when buried. Person pretends to die also and is buried. At night he jumps out of grave and goes to get medicine-man. Medicine-man hears him and jumps out of his grave and shoots an arrow through cannibal and kills him. Ever since bows and arrows are put in graves with dead, that they may shoot cannibal.

35. THE MAN WHO MADE ARROWS FOR GHOST.

Two men hunt all day without finding anything. They stay in timber to hunt next day and go to sleep. They are awakened by voice whooping. One man is frightened and runs away. Other man stays, and soon dead person comes and asks if he can help him get into spirit land. He wants bow-string and two arrows. Man makes arrows and puts new string on bow. Dead person shoots arrows and goes up with them. He whoops to let man know that arrows have carried him up all right. Ever since bows and arrows are always made and buried with dead, that they may go to spirit land at once.

36. THE LAZY BOYS WHO BECAME THE PLEIADES.

In beginning of world lives old woman with seven sons. They are full of fun and play all day long. They will not work, and eat only in morning and evening. Mother scolds them, and one evening will not give them anything to eat. Boys are angry, and next morning they go to playground and go around and around house, praying to Spirits to help them. With every round they rise higher and higher in air, and at last go up to sky, where they are "The Pleiades." These stars are seen during winter, but at beginning of spring, at work time, they are gone.

37. THE LOST TIMBER SPIRITS.

When world is new, Coyote decides that people dying return to earth after ten days. Finally he makes rule that if anybody dies and is buried within six days he shall stay under ground. If not buried by seventh day he may escape. If caught he is to be brought home. Fire is to be kindled all around him, and after being kept at home six days and nights he is to be washed by some old woman and he becomes real person again. At death body is laid in hole, head toward east and feet toward west. Fire is made at feet and kept up six days and nights. If fire goes out grave is found open and tracks seen toward east. When they follow tracks and overtake dead person, fire is built all around him until he tries to escape sparks. He is then coming to life again and is taken home, and in evening of sixth day bathed and will then live again. When dead person not caught he becomes like large monkey and lives in the thickets. These monkeys talk to people and they are thought to be crazy. When people meet them they always ask for wrestling match. They are still living, but do not talk as they did when world was new.

38. THE MAN WHO TURNED INTO A SNAKE.

Two boys go hunting. One of them kills snake and eats snake meat instead of buffalo. He turns into snake and tells friend to find hole for him to live in. Friend carries snake to hole. Snake tells him that when people go to hunt they are to offer presents to him and he will help them. Snake lives there many years until lightning kills him.

39. THE WOMAN WHO TURNED INTO A SNAKE.

Man has wife and dog. At that time animals talk, and dog talks to man and woman. Every day man goes to hunt, and as soon as he has gone woman goes out and does not return until evening. Dog tells husband, and he says dog is to follow woman next time. Dog does so and sees woman go to large tree and whistle three times. Third time big snake comes from large hole in tree, goes to woman, and coils round her body. Finally it goes back to hole. Dog tells man, and next day he makes many arrows and tells wife that he and dog are going fishing. Instead of fishing they go to place where snake is. Man whistles three times and snake creeps out. When it reaches ground man shoots and kills it. He then cuts it into very small pieces to look like pieces of fish. They go to river and catch few small fish. Man tells wife he is going to cook fish and she is to go in grass house. Man cooks fish and snake flesh. He then takes snake flesh to wife for her dinner. He and dog eat fish. Man sends dog to see what wife is doing and he sees she is eating snake. Second time dog sees she is scratching herself all over. When she scratches, skin turns color of snake skin, until finally she turns into snake. She creeps away from grass lodge and goes to find snake. Some time after, when out hunting, man hears voice inside large tree and large snake comes out of tree. He knows it is his wife, but he passes on.

40. THE GIRLS WHO WANTED TO MARRY THE CHIEF.

Two twin daughters hear of chief in another village and obtain parents' consent to go and offer themselves in marriage to him. They start in search of chief's village. They meet man with turkey and tell him. He says he is chief, and is willing, but asks them to wait until he runs home and tells his grandmother. Man is Owl. He runs home and tells grandmother to clean up lodge, as he is bringing home two girls on whom he is playing joke. In morning she is to ask which turkey she is to cook, that girls may think there are many turkeys and good things to eat. Owl goes for girls, who are pleased with things, and marry Owl. Every day he comes in with turkey; as he goes to council and chief gives him turkey for allowing him to sit on his back. Finally twins grow weary of turkey and begin to suspect. They follow Owl and peep through opening in grass lodge and see Owl sitting in middle with chief on his head. Girls scream. Owl recognizes their voices, jumps up, throwing chief off his head, and runs home. He scolds grandmother for letting girls follow him, and they slip off and return home. Owl, angry at being fooled by his own joke, tells grandmother they must kill people. They gather all water by digging big hole and draining waters out from all rivers, springs, and lakes. Water is all gone, and people are dying of thirst, while Owl is splashing about in big hole. Every one goes in search of water. Crow, who was snow white then, comes to field where grass is all withered and big grasshoppers are jumping about. He runs after them, and makes so much noise that people think he has found water. They run in great haste, and are so angry with Crow for fooling them that Coyote rolls him in black earth until he is black. Coyote makes rule that if any one makes loud noise and arouses people's expectations he must either lead them to water or take hard whipping. Turtle falls in great crack in dried mud and halloos for help. People run, thinking he has found water, and Coyote takes him out of crack and gives him so hard a whipping that his shell cracks. Turtles still bear marks of cracks on their shells. Some one hears big splashing noise. He goes on and comes to hole where Owl sits playing in water. He tells people, and they consider how they can get water from Owl. Flea goes to Owl's lodge and enters as his grandmother is about to take bath. She has big jar full of water in front of her. Flea crawls up her leg and bites her. She gives big kick and upsets jar. When Owl sees water running in all directions he opens eyes wide in astonishment, and they have been that way ever since. All people are grateful to Flea. Coyote puts him on his back that he may have warm home.

41. THE POOR HUNTER AND THE ALLIGATOR POWER.

Hunters go on two months' hunt and take their wives with them. Among them are a poor man and wife who are starving. Poor man hunts day after day, but returns without anything. One day, after hunting all morning, he hears some one calling him. He goes and sees person who wants to find water. When hunter tells him there is water short distance off, unknown person asks man to carry him. He does so, and when they reach water person tells hunter to take off clothes and to get on his back. Man shuts eyes, and when he opens them he sees heads of all kinds of animals. Unknown person tells man to point out heads of animals he wants to kill. He does so, and person, who is called Alligator, gives him powers, and when he is again on dry land tells him to go hunting. He kills four big deer, dresses them, and goes to camp. He takes his wife, with two horses, and finds deer, which he puts on horses. Everybody wonders when they see horses loaded with meat. After that, man never fails to bring back much meat when out hunting. When people start back home, they find that man they had made fun of is most successful of all hunters. They name him Deer-Head, because of his bravery in killing big deer. After many years he disappears, and his younger brother says some one came during night and took him away home. Long time afterward hunter shoots large deer, which walks very slowly, and after going over hill calls to him to come on. Man starts back home and people think Deer-Head has changed into deer.

42. THE BOY WHO MARRIED A MOUNTAIN-LION.

Little boy tells parents he is Red-Mountain-Lion, and they so call him. He becomes a successful hunter. Once he acts queerly when he returns from hunt, and next time brother follows him. He tracks him to mountain cave, where he sees brother with female mountain-lion. When Red-Mountain-Lion comes home he acts stranger than ever. Hearing some one talking about going to kill mountain-lion in cave, he starts off alone to hunt. When men come to cave they see footprints of man and mountain-lion leading away from it. Man does not return to his people, but years afterward he is captured by hunting party and is carried home, where he stays. He and brother form war party, and he goes off to get power. He finds rattlesnake skin and mountain-lion's tail. He takes them and prays to rattlesnake and mountain-lion for their powers. War expedition is given up and man neglects to throw away skin and tail. Long time afterward Red-Mountain-Lion one morning hears turkey cackling. He goes to catch it and hears rattlesnakes by his side. As he does not return, brother goes for him. He is found unconscious and scalped. Tracks of mountain-lion are found. Medicine-man comes and tells brother to return animal's gifts to the woods, where Red-Mountain-Lion had found them. Man obeys, and then takes brother to creek and bathes him. Red-Mountain-Lion recovers, but is always foolish. He becomes more foolish in old age and does many evil things, and so is killed.

43. BUFFALO WOMAN.

Cannibal has handsome son who will not marry. He is called Braveness for his bravery in hunting. He goes hunting and sees young and beautiful woman sitting under elm tree. She calls him and says she has come to meet him. She asks him to take her to his home to be his wife. They start for his home at once, and old people let girl become son's wife. They live happily together for long time. Then girl tells him to do whatever she asks. When he promises, she asks him to go with her to her home. They start, and when they come to high hills, she says her home is on other side, and that people will bother him, but he is not to get angry. If he does, young men will kill him, as they are jealous of him. She then asks him to lay on ground and roll over twice. He does so, and is changed into Buffalo. Then woman does same, and becomes Buffalo. When they reach top of hill, they see thousands of Buffalo. They are woman's people. Braveness follows woman until they come to old Buffalo cow, her mother. They stay long time, and as young Buffalo bother Braveness, they go back to his home. On way they become human again. Woman asks man to say nothing about transformation. They stay at home a year, and then decide to go and see woman's mother. After living with Buffalo long time, wife tells husband old people are thinking of killing him. He is to run in foot race. He is worried and goes out for walk. Unknown person tells him if he is beaten at running, he is to be killed, and so he is going to help him to win. He gives Braveness medicine root, which he is to throw behind him when one catches up with him, and he will leave him long way behind. Then he gives Braveness mud to throw behind him when second man overtakes him, after which he will soon be at stopping place. There person will meet him. Next day is day of race. Old Buffalo takes him to place where runners start. Young Buffalo make fun of him, but he places himself in their midst. Braveness leaves Buffalo long way behind at start, but they gain on him. He throws root, and he is far ahead again. He gives out and one Buffalo gains on him. He throws mud, and he is far ahead again. When nearing goal Buffalo is about to catch up with him, when heavy wind comes up and keeps Buffalo back until he reaches goal and wins race. He knows it is Wind who has saved his life. After race, no one molests him again. Afterward he and wife go to live with his people. When child year old, they go again to see wife's people. They remain three years, and then return to Braveness' home. Mother will not let child go out to play with other boys. He slips away and joins boys. They play buffalo, and when little boy rolls over twice, he gets up real buffalo calf. Boys run, and mother seeing them, goes out and finds son changed into buffalo calf. She runs down hill with him, becomes buffalo, and they run away before husband comes from hunting. He can not find his wife and son, and some one tells him what has happened. He does not believe story until he sees their tracks. He never hears of them again.

44. THE GIRL WHO MARRIED WILD-CAT.

Beautiful girl refuses attention of young men. Handsome youth comes and talks with father and brother, but pays no attention to her. Girl dreams of him when asleep; sees him coming to her. She awakes and hears faint noise. She closes eyes and prays that dream may come true. She opens eyes and young man is bending over her. He begs her to go with him and she does so. When long way from home man tells her he is Wild-Cat, but she refuses to go back. They climb high mountain, and Wild-Cat leaves girl to fetch his grandfather Wild-Cat. Girl's brothers overtake them, and want to fight Wild-Cats, who are dressed like men. Sister cries and promises brothers she will soon return home. They go back and father is very angry. He goes in search of daughter and wanders about until he dies.

45. THE WOMAN WHO TRIED TO KILL HER SON.

Abut has wife and boy seven years old. He is always hunting. Wife dislikes boy and abuses him. She digs deep hole and throws him in, putting brush over it. Abut returns and asks for son. She says she has been looking for him all day. They look for him several days and can not find him. Boy grows hungry and cries. Coyote comes, helps him out of hole, and takes him to Coyote's home. He remains several years; then he tells Coyote he wants to go and see his father. He says he will tell father what happened, and that they will go on buffalo hunt, and that Coyote and family are to kill mother when she brings them meat. Coyote lets boy go home. He tells father what he is going to do with mother. Next day they go hunting and kill buffalo. While woman is cooking supper they hear Coyotes howling. After supper boy tells mother to get meat and come with him to feed Coyotes. She carries meat on back. When near Coyotes, boy pushes her down and Coyotes jump upon her. Father and son live together many years.

46. THE JEALOUS HUSBAND.

People go on war-path and spies are sent out to locate enemy. Leader chooses for spies two who are very close friends and always go together. One is married and other single. One day they come to high hill. They climb it and find on top big hole, like well, with water. Married man tells friend to go down in hole to get some water. He descends on long buffalo-hide rope. Instead of pulling him up again his friend throws rope into hole and goes away. He starts for camp and tells head man that his friend was killed by enemy who pursued them. Camp therefore breaks up and people return home. Man in hole asks birds passing over to take him out, but they take no notice of him. After nine days Buzzard flies over hole and man again asks for help. Bird passes again and again, and fourth time lights on ground. He peeps over rim of hole and tells man he will help him out, but he must first go for some medicine. Buzzard goes away, but comes back and flies to bottom of hole. He tells man to shut his eyes and take step forward. He is then on back of Buzzard, who flies upward out of hole. Bird takes man to home of Buzzard, and there he remains until he can walk around. Buzzard tells him his friend maltreated him because he had been told he was going to take his wife away. He then says he is going to take man home, and tells him what to do there. They start and Buzzard tells man to shut his eyes. When near home he gets off Buzzard's back and goes to his lodge. He tells how his friend had beaten him and how Buzzard had rescued him. He then sends his sister to fetch friend's wife. Woman returns with sister and stays with man, refusing to go back to former husband. Afterward, whenever they go on buffalo hunt, husband kills one buffalo first, cuts it up, and scatters meat ; then he kills another one and takes meat home. When asked why he did that, he will not tell ; but once his uncle comes and asks him, and he says he had lived with woman many years and when he dies she shall drop dead, too.

47. THE TURTLE WHO CARRIED THE PEOPLE.

People travel about looking for village site. They come near big water and see what they think is large rock. They make village near rock, which they use as dancing place. After some time crier announces big dance. While all people are dancing on rock it begins to move. They see big head and legs appear from under it ; then they know they are on big turtle. They try to get off, but their feet are stuck tight. Turtle carries them into water and drowns them.

48. WHY DOGS HAVE LONG TONGUES.

When animals were like people, dogs were noted for telling everything they knew. Running-Water is great hunter, and wants dog to help him who is not tattler. He tries to teach young pup not to talk so much. When big enough, Running-Water takes it to hunt small game. Every time man kills game, dog sneaks home and tells, returning circuitous way, as though he has been hunting all time. After time Running-Water goes for long hunt and takes dog with him. They kill many big animals and start for home. Running-Water misses dog and returns to camp for him. Dog is not there, and when Running-Water gets home he finds dog. He has told many big stories about animals they have killed. Running-Water is very angry and gives dog good whipping. He then catches hold of dog's tongue, pulls it as hard as he can, and then runs stick across his mouth. Since then dogs have long tongues and big mouths.

49. WHY HAWKS HAVE THIN LEGS.

Chicken-Hawk is poor hunter. He meets Eagle, and, pretending he has killed many big game before, asks him if he will help him to kill antelope. Eagle promises on condition he can have half meat. Hawk goes home and tells family he has shot antelope in head and is going in morning to kill him. Hawk and Eagle go hunting together and find antelope in mountain. Eagle kills it and they divide meat. Hawk takes meat home and tells family he has given part of meat to poor hunter who had never tasted antelope. Family tell every one what good hunter Hawk is. Friend visits him to see if reports true. Hawk hunts all day and returns with only mouse, which friend refuses to eat. He hunts next day and can not find anything. He is so ashamed that he cuts meat off of his legs to take home for friend to eat. This is why hawks have no meat on their legs.

50. THE POWERS OF BUFFALO AND BEAR.

Once, when animals understood one another, Bear and Buffalo met. They told each other of their powers. Bear says he was once human being and went with people. One night he dreamed that he became Bear and that human being was pursuing him and shooting him with arrows. When he awoke he found all was true. He left people and began new life in mountains and woods. Buffalo then speaks and says he, too, was like human being. His people were called Buffalo after oldest chief. When people began to enter this world Buffalo people were forbidden to enter, because some one had made mistake. They found out it was Coyote, and they prayed that Father would give him powers, so that he could enter world and take them along. They had to change into wild animals, and for love of people to be their game. Then they were given powers to be dangerous and horns to fight with. Then Bear asks Buffalo to show what he does when he wants to hurt or kill any one. Buffalo watches him, and before he knows what has happened he is falling to ground and Buffalo is coming at him again. Buffalo asks Bear if he saw him when he first started after him. He says, "No," and Buffalo asks him to show how he uses his powers. Bear walks back and forth looking at Buffalo with angry eyes, then moves slowly toward small tree, which he grabs and cuts down with his sharp teeth, and before Buffalo knows, Bear is upon him, and he is trying to get up from ground. Bear holds him down until he is ready to give up. When Bear lets him go they part and go to their homes.

51. HOW RABBIT STOLE MOUNTAIN-LION'S TEETH.

Rabbit, in absence of grandmother, goes to house of Mountain-Lion. He is not at home. Rabbit finds Mountain-Lion's teeth and takes them home. Rabbit tells grandmother Mountain-Lion will come after his teeth and they must fool him. He tells her to build fire outside of door and put on it kettle of water, and to put some stones into water and boil them. When Mountain-Lion comes she is to tell him that she is boiling stones for "Chief of all the beasts," who is Rabbit's guest. Mountain-Lion comes, and when he hears what grandmother says, he runs away as fast as he can.

52. RABBIT AND THE DANCING TURKEYS.

Rabbit and Wild-Cat meet and begin to fight. To save his own life, Rabbit says he will show Wild-Cat how to catch Turkeys. He tells him to stand still while he sings Turkey dance song. Rabbit sings, and then tells Wild-Cat to lie down and pretend to be dead. Turkeys hear song and come to see what it is about. Rabbit tells them he has killed Wild-Cat and they are to dance victory song. Turkeys dance and Wild-Cat jumps up and grabs big Turkey. As he does so Rabbit runs away and escapes.

53. ADVENTURES OF COYOTE.

In beginning of world people held councils to decide about things. Question comes up, what kind of rain there shall be. Rain in form of lead balls is proposed. Coyote objects, as lead would be dangerous, and suggests drops of water. This is accepted. Coyote goes traveling and comes to place where great powerful Bear lives. Bear says if he is Coyote he will kill him. Coyote pretends to be son of powerful medicine-man. Bear decides to kill him, and Coyote tells Bear to wait until his father sees him. This is at sunrise, when Sun peeps over hill. Coyote says Bear can kill him, as father is watching him. Bear thinks Coyote must be great man and becomes frightened. He gives Coyote many things to eat. Long after, Bear discovers that he has been deceived and tries to find Coyote's home to kill him, but without success. Coyote moves from place to place and meets Mountain-Lion near lake. He tells him he is very hungry, and they go together to lake. Mountain-Lion climbs the tree and tells Coyote to hide. Wild horses come to water, and Mountain-Lion jumps and kills young horse, which they have for dinner. Mountain-Lion teaches Coyote how to kill horse. Next day he does so. Mountain-Lion tells him not to try to kill three or four year old horse. Coyote leaves his friend and next day goes to lake and thinks he will try to kill largest horse. He jumps from tree on large horse, which throws him off and kicks him under jaws. Mountain-Lion comes and Coyote asks him what he is laughing about. Coyote is not able to move for a long time and then leaves place. He hears some one in persimmon tree and finds Opossum eating persimmons. He asks Opossum for some, but Opossum laughs at him. While pretending to fall from tree, limb breaks and Opossum comes to ground. Coyote gives him good beating and leaves him to die. Opossum fools him, and when Coyote goes away Opossum climbs tree again and laughs at him.

54. COYOTE ESCAPES AN IMAGINARY FOE.

Coyote goes hunting buffalo. He sees Turkey on top of tall tree and threatens to kill him if he does not get down. Turkey starts out toward prairie, as Coyote says he has no power to kill anything on prairie. When Turkey comes to ground Coyote catches up with him and kills him. While eating Turkey, Coyote looks around to see that no one is watching him. He thinks he sees somebody standing behind him, making motions as if to strike him. He starts to run, every now and then looking back to see if he is out of reach. He thinks he sees man right after him, ready to hit him, and runs with all his might. Coyote was given power at beginning of world to run without decreasing his running powers. He has run eight times, and ninth time he runs farther than usual. Again he looks around and thinks he sees man about to hit him. When running tenth time his powers are decreasing, and he dodges from right to left to fool man. Coyote gives out when running twelfth time. He turns on his back and begs not to be killed. He falls over on his face and hears something crack. It is turkey feather, which had stuck between his teeth and is nearly straight up above his right eye. He finds he has been fooled by turkey feather and is very angry. Ever since he has looked wild, and when he runs first looks around to right and then to left to see if anybody is near him. When he reaches home Coyote says he has killed Mountain-Lion.

55. COYOTE GOES FISHING.

Coyote goes hunting along river and meets man carrying fish. Coyote asks him how he got fish. Man, who has been tricked by Coyote, tells him to go to edge of river in evening and stay until he comes to see him. Coyote goes and finds man waiting for him. Man tells Coyote to sit by edge of water while he breaks ice. Coyote does as man tells him and sits by bank fishing all night. Water freezes on Coyote's tail, and in morning he can not move. Man comes and asks if he is catching any fish. Coyote says he thinks he has caught two or three, and asks man to help him to land them. Man reminds Coyote of his trickery and tells Coyote he is going to kill him. Coyote denies trickery and offers to go and bring one that man is looking for. Man goes to lodge for bow and arrows, and on return sings death song, and then shoots and kills Coyote.

56. COYOTE HUNTS GEESE.

Coyote once man. People dislike him and call him coward, as he is always trying to cheat some one. He visits his best friend and finds he has been feasting on white geese. Coyote asks friend where he got them. Friend tells him to come back in evening and he will show him where geese come. When Coyote is out of sight, friend carries ashes from fire and forms them in shape of geese near lake. Just before evening he goes and puts coals under ashes. Coals burn up, but fire can not be seen from outside. When Coyote comes they go to place, friend taking lead. He pretends not to see first pile of ashes. When Coyote sees it he prepares to jump, and friend laughs. Coyote pays no attention, but jumps on pile of hot ashes and burns himself. He runs away, but is burned so badly that he runs until he kills himself.

57. COYOTE IMITATES HIS HOST.

In old days, when animals talked and visited each other, Coyote and Raven were great friends. Coyote, weary of hunting without success, goes to Raven, who has control of buffalo. Raven, seeing Coyote sad and silent, shoots arrow into air and waits for it to come down. It pierces him under right arm. He draws arrow out, and with it comes buffalo meat and fat. He gives meat to Coyote, who eats heartily. Before he goes he invites Raven to visit him. Coyote makes bow and arrows and puts them away until Raven comes. Raven pays Coyote visit. After talking, Coyote says he has no food, but will soon have some. He takes bow and arrow; shoots arrow into sky. When it comes down it strikes him in thigh. He runs away, screaming with pain. After waiting a while Raven goes home without any meat, but much amused at Coyote's performance. Coyote's friends wonder what has become of him, but he grows very hungry, and not finding any food he goes to visit Black-Mountain-Bear. Bear regrets to have no food, but leans against persimmon tree and ripe fruit falls to ground. Coyote eats many, and before going insists that Bear come to see him. Coyote can not find persimmon tree with fruit on it.

He cuts down tree without fruit and takes it home, where he sets it up. He then takes persimmons he has stolen from Bear's home and others he finds and places them all over tree as though they have grown there. Black-Mountain-Bear goes to visit Coyote, who bumps head against tree, but persimmons will not fall. Finally he arises and gives tree big shake with hands, and it falls over, hitting him on head. He pretends not to be hurt and gathers up fruit for Bear. Bear can hardly swallow for laughing, as Coyote's head keeps getting bigger and bigger. Bear soon goes, and Coyote holds his sore head, but is happy for having furnished food for Bear.

58. COYOTE IMITATES HIS HOST.

Coyote, looking out for something to eat, comes to grass lodge. He enters and sees man walking about with light on his head. Coyote calls out to him that his head is on fire. Man smiles and says he has always worn light, and it will not burn anything. Man is Woodpecker. He gives Coyote something to eat. Coyote goes, after eating as much as he can, and asks Woodpecker to make him a visit. Some time afterward Woodpecker goes to Coyote's lodge and is surprised to see im with big bunch of burning straw on his head. Woodpecker tells him to take it off, but Coyote says he always wears it at night. As he finishes speaking, his hair catches fire, and he runs out of lodge screaming for help. Woodpecker waits for his return, but he does not come.

59. COYOTE, THE DEER, AND THE WIND.

Coyote meets Deer, who asks him how he kills his game. Coyote replies he can kill anything he can lay his hands on. Deer tells Coyote if he can catch Deer he may kill and eat him. Coyote tries to catch Deer, but without success. One day, after trying to find him asleep, he lays down in grass to take nap. When he awakes, he hears some one singing near by. He is frightened and peeps about, but sees no one. He hears his name mentioned in song, and jumps up and runs as far as he can; then he drops to die. He hears voice again, and it says that he is Wind, and is going to give Coyote power to catch Deer. Coyote arises and barks thanks. He starts out to find Deer and travels all day, but can not find him. He comes to camp where he steals buffalo robe. He puts robe over him, and goes on to look for Deer. He thinks he sees him near river, goes round another way to get close, and grabs him. To his surprise, he has man whose robe he has stolen. Man takes Coyote home and makes him work for him and his sister, treating him cruelly because he has stolen robe. One time while man out hunting, Coyote makes sister pack her clothes and go away with him, saying her brother is killed. They start for Coyote's home. Coyote goes behind girl, and whenever she stops or falls hits her with stick. Man returns, and finds sister and Coyote gone. He starts after them and soon catches up with them. He shoots arrow in front of sister. She sees it and knows her brother is coming to help her. She cries for joy and Coyote whips her. Man goes on hill and shoots another arrow. Coyote sees man and is frightened. He pretends to be kind to girl, and tries to deceive man when he comes down hill and asks where Coyote is going with sister. Man makes Coyote put bundle of clothes on his back, and tells sister to sit on bundle. He puts bow-string through Coyote's mouth and gives ends to girl. She saws string back and forth, and man runs alongside of Coyote, whipping him, thus returning home. Man is Wind, who has become angry at Coyote for stealing his robe and trying to catch Deer with it, instead of waiting for power.

60. COYOTE DIVES FOR MEAT.

Coyote kills big deer, which she hides in tree while she goes for her children. Wild-Cat sees her, and when she has gone, steals meat and climbs tree on bank of river. Coyote returns with children, but can not find meat. While children are abusing her she sees reflection of meat in water and thinks it is meat. She dives into water and reaches for meat, but can not get it. She ties stones about her neck and dives again. Coyotes wait long for mother, and after a while they see excrement on water and think it is meat. They laugh, and Wild-Cat laughs at them. They look up and see Wild-Cat and meat in tree. Wild-Cat tells them that mother is drowned. They cry, and Wild-Cat climbs down and gives little Coyotes all they want to eat and takes them home. He cares for them until they are grown.

61. COYOTE, THE GEESE, AND THE WOODPECKERS.

Coyote, returning home after unsuccessful hunt, hears laughing and playing. He runs over hill, and on other side is big lake, with several white geese playing on surface. Coyote watches them from bushes until he thinks of plan whereby he can catch them. He limps out from bushes, pretending he has been hurt. Geese hear him and swim out into water. One then asks Coyote what is the matter, and he answers that he will be killed if he does not get across water, and then all rivers and lakes will dry up. Geese know that Coyote is lying and decide to take him and throw him into deep hole. Old Goose tells Coyote to get on his back. Coyote at first objects, but at last does as he is told, and Goose flies up in air. Other Geese follow and take turns in carrying Coyote. They fly over timbered country away from lake and drop him into hollow trunk of tree. He can not get out, and is frightened almost to death. Fly comes and Coyote prays to him for power. Fly goes and brings Woodpecker, who, finding Coyote really wants to get out, fetches some of his brothers. They peck big hole in tree. Coyote tells them to stick their heads in and see if he can really get out, and then bites their heads off. After he has eaten Woodpeckers, Coyote escapes.

62. COYOTE AND RABBIT KILL A BUFFALO.

Rabbit hunts for food, and one day goes far away without finding any game. He is going home playing and singing when Coyote sees him. Coyote steps behind Rabbit, yells "Bo!" and makes grab for him. Rabbit is frightened, but tells Coyote not to kill him, as he knows where is good fat buffalo. Rabbit leads way to where old buffalo stands. Rabbit tells Coyote to climb into animal. Coyote obeys, and Rabbit follows. They then begin to eat buffalo's side, and soon it falls dead. Old man comes and begins to butcher buffalo. Rabbit tells Coyote to hide in intestines, and he hides in bladder. Old man places intestines on one side, but throws bladder in bush, where Rabbit crawls out and escapes. Coyote is discovered and killed.

63. COYOTE, MOUNTAIN-LION, AND RABBIT.

Coyote hears crying like child. He finds Mountain-Lion's den and young there alone. He is hungry, and kills and eats them all. Mother comes back with food for young and can not find them. She follows Coyote many days, and when sitting on bank of river to rest sees Rabbit. She calls him and asks him to help her to capture Coyote. They go along river together and find deer. Mountain-Lion kills it. When they have butchered it she tells Rabbit to cover her face with fat and then put deer on her back. Rabbit then gets on top of deer. While crossing prairie some one calls out asking Rabbit where he got his fine horse. Rabbit pretends not to hear, and voice again calls to him. Rabbit goes on until Coyote catches up with him and tells him to get off, as horse is his. Rabbit jumps off, and as Coyote is about to get on he stops to bite piece of fat off its face. He recognizes Mountain-Lion and starts to run. Mountain-Lion springs upon him and kills him.

64. COYOTE BECOMES A BUFFALO.

Coyote meets Buffalo and asks him for power to turn into Buffalo and eat grass. Buffalo consents, and tells Coyote to stand facing other way and not to move. Buffalo throws up dirt with hoofs and makes plunge toward Coyote, who jumps out of way. This is repeated six times, but seventh time Coyote stands firm and Buffalo throws him up into air. When he comes down on feet he is very young Buffalo. He begins to eat grass at once. Old Buffalo tells him he can become Coyote again by rolling over two or three times in Buffalo wallow. He cautions him that power is good for only seven times, and that he must not give power to any one else. Buffalo then makes him change back into Coyote and leaves him. Coyote soon begins to try his power, and before meeting any one has tried it six times and has turned into Buffalo seventh time. He meets Coyote and asks him if he does not want some of his power. He tells him to stand facing other way with eyes shut. He starts at him and at last attempt they both go into air and they both come down Coyotes.

65. COYOTE AND THE TURKEYS.

Coyote is looking for something to eat and hears voice. He goes and finds Turkeys having fun by getting into sack and rolling down hill. Coyote lets Turkeys roll him down hill several times. Then he tells Turkeys to get into sack and he will roll them down. All crawl into sack and Coyote ties it fast at each end and starts for home with it. He calls his four sons and takes Turkey out of sack. He tells sons to build big fire and they will have feast. They go to timber for wood and leave sack in charge of youngest son. Coyote tells him not to untie strings. Young Coyote unties strings and looks into sack to see what Turkeys are doing. Turkeys all run out and fly away. He does not know what to do, but finally fills sack with dirt. Father returns and says they will have fine feast. When he opens sack he finds only dirt. He is very angry and kills young son and eats him instead of Turkeys.

66. COYOTE'S EYES ARE REPLACED BY BUCKEYES.

Coyote is hunting and hears voices. He thinks they are turkeys making noise and goes to catch them. He finds Ducks playing in water and they ask him to join them. He consents to play at taking eyes out. First Duck has eyes taken out, then he dives into water and his eyes are thrown after him. When he comes up he has them in place. All Ducks take turns. Then Coyote goes through same performance and comes out all right. Ducks have power to do almost anything, but to do it only once. Coyote wants to try trick again, but Ducks object. At last they take his eyes out and he dives into water. Ducks all fly away and leave

Coyote. He goes along talking and crying. Man finds him and goes to get something to make him new eyes. He returns with green buckeye balls. He hits place of right eye with buckeye ball, and then place of left eye with another ball, and Coyote's eyes are restored.

67. COYOTE AND TURTLE RUN A RACE.

Coyote, returning from unsuccessful hunt for game, passes home of Turtle. Turtle invites him in and offers him something to eat. Turtle is tired and says he has just come back from races. Coyote and Turtle arrange to have race two days hence. Coyote sends son to announce race to Coyote people and tell them to bet heavily, as he would defeat Turtle. Turtle sends son to announce race, and that best runners are to come to his lodge. They come, and Turtle asks them to help him to cheat Coyote out of race. Each is to put white feather in his hair and to paint himself to look like Turtle. They are to station themselves at intervals along course. One is to start with Coyote and when far behind is to drop into grass. Then next one is to jump up and run, then next one, and so on until last. Turtle will be last and beat Coyote over goal. On day of race Turtles station themselves along way in tall grass. Coyote comes and wants to run short distance, but Turtle insists on long distance. Many Coyotes come and bet on Coyote. They start and Coyotes laugh, for their man is far ahead. Soon to their surprise Turtle is ahead. Coyote overtakes Turtle, and they laugh again. They hear Turtles cheering and Turtle is far in lead. The race then goes on, and just as Coyote has passed Turtle and is near goal, Turtle crosses line and all Turtles set up loud cheer. Coyote runs off in grass and is wondering yet how Turtle beat him. All other Coyotes are angry because he makes them lose so many bets.

68. COYOTE, WILD-CAT, AND THE OLD WOMAN.

Old blind woman lives alone. She always has plenty to eat. Whenever she sits down to eat she speaks as though talking to some one. Wild-Cat smells meat and goes in. He sees old woman is blind and slips quietly to corner. She speaks, but then begins to eat ; so Wild-Cat slips over and begins to eat, too. He is careful not to make noise, and when little left in pot quietly slips away. He comes there every day and grows sleek and fat. Coyote meets him and asks where he gets so much to eat. Wild-Cat tells him and agrees to take him, on his promise to keep very quiet. They go and sit near door while meat cooking. They steal meat out of pot. Coyote forgets all about keeping quiet and cracks bone so loud that old woman jumps up. Wild-Cat gets out of house. Old woman runs to door and closes it. She takes long spear and pokes around room. Spear pierces Coyote. He cries out with pain, and she continues poking until she kills him. Wild-Cat comes next day and finds Coyote dead. He is sorry, because he is afraid to go to house again to eat.

69. COYOTE CHALLENGES THE SNAKE.

Coyote goes from place to place to find Snake. He stops to rest and soon hears some one calling him. Snake comes up, and Coyote, after referring to Snake's supposed power, says he wants to see which of them has most power. Snake agrees and suggests that they bite each other once. Coyote says snake is to bite first. Snake goes up to Coyote and bites him on top of nose. Coyote asks if that is all Snake can do, and says he will show his power. He comes to Snake and bites him nearly in two. They go little way off and lie down. Coyote calls to Snake and hears him answer in low voice. Snake then calls to Coyote, who answers with big voice. They keep calling to one another all night. Toward daylight Snake calls Coyote and no answer comes. After calling fourth time, Snake goes to see what is the matter and finds Coyote all swollen and dead.

70. COYOTE TURNS INTO A CORN MILL.

Women make corn mills from trunk of old tree. There are many such mills, but one very old and smooth, women like best. Woman pounds corn in old mill and when ground she sees she has only little. She watches other women and corn disappears in same way. They examine mill and woman suggests that they cut it with axe to see where corn has gone. Mill falls over and Coyote jumps up and runs away. He has turned into corn mill, so that he can get all he wants to eat.

Caddo Customs of Childhood

CADDO CUSTOMS OF CHILDHOOD.

THE following brief and imperfect notes on Caddo customs of childhood were obtained from an old man named White-Bread.

The lodge is always placed so that it faces the east. This is done that the sun, as it arises out of the east to shine upon another day and bless all things, may bless the inmates of the lodge. When a child is born it is carried to the door of the lodge and held there as the sun rises that it may see the child and bless it. Then, if the child be a boy, the father places a tiny bow and arrow in his hands that it may grow to a good hunter and ward off dangers. Before the child is born a bright fire is kindled and kept burning for ten days and nights after the birth to keep away evil. There is a great animal with wings who eats human beings, especially babies, but the animal cannot come near the light. A greater monster than this is the cannibal person. In every tribe there are some of these wicked people. They look like any one else, but at night, when it is dark, they set forth and steal human children to eat. Like the animal who eats human beings, they cannot go near the light, and so people keep the fire kindled to frighten them away. Then, too, the fire is related to the sun, because it gives heat and light, and so it gives a blessing to the child.

At the end of the tenth day the mother and father carry the child to the river, and all bathe. After that the fire is allowed to smoulder, but it is not put out entirely until after the child is two years old. From that time until the child is eight or ten it is allowed to play and grow in its own way. Then the grandmother, or some old person, calls the child into the lodge and, telling it to sit still and behave, she teaches it. If the child is a boy, she tells him how to take care of himself so that he will grow up to be a strong man. She tells him how to act that he will gain the good will of the tribe, and she tells him stories about boys who would not listen to the teachings of their grandmothers, and the trouble that they caused when they grew to be men. And she tells him about boys who have listened to their grandmothers, and how they grew up to be great and wonderful men. Then she tells the boy to go to the river every morning to swim and bathe, no matter how cold the water is. He is taught to say this prayer to the water: "Grandfather, make me strong to endure all things, that heat and cold, rain and snow may be as nothing to my body." As he returns to the lodge he is taught to pick up a stick and carry it to the fire, saying: "Grandfather, help me to live and become a good man, and to help others to live." To the rising sun he is taught to pray:

"Grandfather, protect me, keep me from dangers and give me a long life and success."

At another time the boy is taught that there are many bad and dangerous places on the road leading to the spirit-land, and that he will be caught in some of these places if he does not heed what is taught him. She says, "There are six bad places on the way to the spirit-land. The first place is where the dogs stay. If you whip or mistreat or kill a dog, the dog, when it dies, goes to its people and tells what you have done. When you die, you have to pass the place of the dogs, and the chief of the dogs goes and sits by the road and waits for you. When you come he tells you to look for fleas on his head, and when you find one he tells you to bite it. When you bite it, you become a dog. Then he takes you to where the dogs stay, and there they mistreat you as you mistreated them on earth. They keep you there and never let you get away, so that you cannot continue your journey. For this reason we place a bead on the little finger of a dead person, so that he may bite it instead of the flea and so fool the dog and escape him. Along the road there is another place where you hear some one calling you. If you form the habit during life of standing about talking about people, you will turn your head and wait for the person who is calling. Then you will stand and say mean things about some one until you forget that you are going on a journey and become a tree by the roadside. If you learn to go through life attending to your own affairs, you will not pay any attention to the voice, but go straight ahead. Soon you will come to a place where there are two large rocks pounding each other. You will have to pass between these rocks. If you listen well to all that you are told, and remember that you were told about the rocks, you can pass through. If you forget what you have been told, you will be crushed by the pounding rocks. Next you will come to a stream of water that looks very small; but it is not small, for the banks stretch away, and it becomes a great river. If you are quick to do all that you are told in this world, you will reach the stream when the banks are close together and you can jump across; but if you are slow to do what you have to do on this earth, you will reach the river after the banks have spread and you will be too late to jump across, but will fall into the water and become a fish. As you journey on the other side of the river, should you get across, you will come to persimmon-trees. If in this world you want everything you see and always try to get things that you do not need, just because some one else has them, you will stop under a tree to gather persimmons. Then you will wander to the next tree and the next, until you lose your way and forget that you are on a journey. Then you will become a raccoon and live forever among the trees. Should you escape the persimmon-trees, you will soon meet a person along the road. He will ask you to help him to do some work. If you are forgetful in life and begin one thing and do not finish it, but go off about something else, you will forget that you are on a journey and you will stop and help this man. You will work until you are nothing but skin and bone. Then you will die, but you will soon come to life only to work yourself to death again. Then you will come to life again, and so on. There is no end. This is the last danger that you meet on the way."

After the boy has been taught about all the dangers that beset him on the way, and entreated to follow closely the teaching of his elders that he may escape those evils, he is taught what is in store for him when at last he reaches the end of his journey. All this is done to encourage him to lead a good life and grow up to be a good man.

George A. Dorsey.

Caddo (contracted from *Kä'dohädä'cho*, 'Caddo proper,' 'real Caddo,' a leading tribe in the Caddo confederacy, extended by the whites to include the confederacy). A confederacy of tribes belonging to the southern group of the Caddoan linguistic family. Their own name is Hasínai, 'our own folk.' See *Kadohadacho*.

History.—According to tribal traditions the lower Red r. of Louisiana was the early home of the Caddo, from which they spread to the N., W., and S. Several of the lakes and streams connected with this river bear Caddo names, as do some of the counties and some of the towns which cover ancient village sites. Cabeza de Vaca and his companions in 1535–36 traversed a portion of the territory occupied by the Caddo, and De Soto's expedition encountered some of the tribes of the confederacy in 1540–41, but the people did not become known until they were met by La Salle and his followers in 1687. At that time the Caddo villages were scattered along Red r. and its tributaries in what are now Louisiana and Arkansas, and also on the banks of the Sabine, Neches, Trinity, Brazos, and Colorado rs. in E. Texas. The Caddo were not the only occupants of this wide territory; other confederacies belonging to the same linguistic family also resided there. There were also fragments of still older confederacies of the same family, some of which still maintained their separate existence, while others had joined the then powerful Hasinai. These various tribes and confederacies were alternately allies and enemies of the Caddo. The native population was so divided that at no time could it successfully resist the intruding white race. At an early date the Caddo obtained horses from the Spaniards through intermediate tribes; they learned to rear these animals, and traded with them as far N. as Illinois r. (Shea, Cath. Ch. in Col. Days, 559, 1855).

During the 18th century wars in Europe led to contention between the Spaniards and the French for the territory occupied by the Caddo. The brunt of these contentions fell upon the Indians; the trails between their villages became routes for armed forces, while the villages were transformed into garrisoned posts. The Caddo were friendly to the French and rendered valuable service, but they suffered greatly from contact with the white race. Tribal wars were fomented, villages were abandoned, new diseases spread havoc among the people, and by the close of the century the welcoming attitude of the Indians during its early years had changed to one of defense and distrust. Several tribes were practically extinct, others seriously reduced in numbers, and

ANTELOPE, A CADDO

a once thrifty and numerous people had become demoralized and were more or less wanderers in their native land. Franciscan missions had been established among some of the tribes early in the century, those designed for the Caddo, or Asinais, as they were called by the Spaniards, being Purísima Concepción de los Asinais and (for the Hainai) San Francisco de los Tejas (q. v.). The segregation policy of the missionaries tended to weaken tribal relations and unfitted the people to cope with the new difficulties which confronted them. These missions were transferred to the Rio San Antonio in 1731. With the acquisition of Louisiana by the United States immigration increased and the Caddo were pushed from their old haunts. Under their first

treaty, in 1835, they ceded all their land and agreed to move at their own expense beyond the boundaries of the United States, never to return and settle as a tribe. The tribes living in Louisiana, being thus forced to leave their old home, moved s. w. toward their kindred living in Texas. At that time the people of Texas were contending for independence, and no tribe could live at peace with both opposing forces. Public opinion was divided as to the treatment of the Indians; one party demanded a policy of extermination, the other advocated conciliatory methods. In 1843 the governor of the Republic of Texas sent a commission to the tribes of its N. part to fix a line between them and the white settlers and to establish three trading posts; but, as the land laws of the republic did not recognize the Indian's right of occupancy, there was no power which could prevent a settler from taking land that had been cultivated by an Indian. This condition led to continual difficulties, and these did not diminish after the annexation of Texas to the United States, as Texas retained control and jurisdiction over all its public domain. Much suffering ensued; the fields of peaceable Indians were taken and the natives were hunted down. The more warlike tribes made reprisals, and bitter feelings were engendered. Immigration increased, and the inroads on the buffalo herds by the newcomers made scarce the food of the Indians. Appeals were sent to the Federal Government, and in 1855 a tract near Brazos r. was secured and a number of Caddo and other Indians were induced to colonize under the supervision of Agent Robert S. Neighbours. The Indians built houses, tilled fields, raised cattle, sent their children to school—lived quiet and orderly lives. The Comanche to the w. continued to raid upon the settlers, some of whom turned indiscriminately upon all Indians. The Caddo were the chief sufferers, although they helped the state troops to bring the raiders to justice. In 1859 a company of white settlers fixed a date for the massacre of all the reservation Indians. The Federal Government was again appealed to, and through the strenuous efforts of Neighbours the Caddo made a forced march for 15 days in the heat of July; men, women, and children, with the loss of more than half of their stock and possessions, reached safely the banks of Washita r. in Oklahoma, where a reservation was set apart for them. Neighbours, their friend and agent, was killed shortly afterward as a penalty for his unswerving friendship to the Indians (Ind. Aff. Rep. 1859, 333, 1860). During the civil war the Caddo remained loyal to the Government, taking refuge in Kansas, while some went even as far w. as Colorado. In 1872 the boundaries of their reservation were defined, and in 1902 every man, woman, and child received an allotment of land under the provisions of the severalty act of 1887, by which they became citizens of the United States and subject to the laws of Oklahoma. In 1904 they numbered 535.

Missions were started by the Baptists soon after the reservation was established, and are still maintained. Thomas C. Battey, a Quaker, performed missionary work among them in 1872. The Episcopalians opened a mission in 1881, the Roman Catholics in 1894.

Customs and beliefs.—In the legend which recounts the coming of the Caddo from the underworld it is related: "First an old man climbed up, carrying in one hand fire and a pipe, and in the other a drum; next came his wife with corn and pumpkin seeds." The traditions of the people do not go back to a time when they were not cultivators of the soil; their fields surrounded their villages and furnished their staple food; they were semisedentary in their habits and lived in fixed habitations. Their dwellings were conical in shape, made of a framework of poles covered with a thatch of grass, and were grouped about an open space which served for social and ceremonial gatherings. Couches covered with mats were ranged around the walls inside the house to serve as seats by day and beds by night. The fire was built in the center. Food was cooked in vessels of pottery, and baskets of varying sizes were skilfully made. Vegetal fibers were woven, and the cloth was made into garments; their mantles, when adorned with feathers, were very attractive to the early French visitors. Living in the country of the buffalo, that animal and others were hunted and the pelts dressed and made into clothing for winter use. Besides having the usual ornaments for the arms, neck, and ears, the Caddo bored the nasal septum and inserted a ring as a face decoration— a custom noted in the name, meaning "pierced nose," given the Caddo by the Kiowa and other unrelated tribes, and designated in the sign language of the plains. Tattooing was practised. Descent was traced through the mother. Chieftainship was hereditary, as was the custody of certain sacred articles used in religious ceremonies. These ceremonies were connected with the cultivation of maize, the seeking of game, and the desire for long life, health, peace, and prosperity, and were conducted by priests who were versed in the rites and who led the accompanying rituals and songs. According to Caddo belief all natural forms were animate and capable of rendering assistance to man. Fasting, prayer, and occasional sacrifices were observed; life was thought to continue after death, and kinship groups were supposed to be reunited in the spirit world. Truthfulness, honesty, and hospitality were inculcated, and just dealing was esteemed a virtue. There is evidence that cannibalism was ceremonially practised in connection with captives.

Divisions and totems.—How many tribes were formerly included in the Caddo confederacy can not now be determined. Owing to the vicissitudes of the last 3 centuries only a remnant of the Caddo survive, and the memory of much of their organization is lost. In 1699 Iberville obtained from his Taensa Indian guide a list of 8 divisions; Linares in 1716 gave the names of 11; Gatschet (Creek Migr. Leg., I, 43, 1884) procured from a Caddo Indian in 1882 the names of 12 divisions, and the list was revised in 1896, by Mooney, as follows: (1) Kadohadacho, (2) Hainai, (3) Anadarko, (4) Nabedache, (5) Nacogdoches, (6) Natchitoches, (7) Yatasi, (8) Adai, (9) Eyeish, (10) Nakanawan, (11) Imaha, a small band of Kwapa, (12) Yowani, a band of Choctaw (Mooney in 14th Rep. B. A. E., 1092, 1896). Of these names the first 9 are found under varying forms in the lists of 1699 and 1716. The native name of the confederacy, Hasinai, is said to belong more properly to the first 3 divisions, which may be significant of their prominence at the time when the confederacy was overlapping and absorbing members of older organizations, and as these divisions speak similar dialects, the name may be that which designated a still older organization. The following tribes, now extinct, probably belonged to the Caddo confederacy: Doustionis, Nacaniche, Nanatsoho, and Nasoni(?). The villages of Campti, Choye, and Natasi were probably occupied by subdivisions of the confederated tribes.

Each division of the confederacy was subdivided, and each of these subtribes had its totem, its village, its hereditary chieftain, its priests and ceremonies, and its part in the ceremonies common to the confederacy. The present clans, according to Mooney, are recognized as belonging equally to the whole Caddo people and in old times were probably the chief bond that held the confederacy together. See *Nasoni*.   (A. C. F.)

Acinay.—Tex. St. Arch., Nov. 17, 1763. Ascanis.— La Harpe (1719) in Margry, Déc., VI, 289, 1886. Asenys.—Iberville (1699), ibid., IV, 316, 1880. A-Simaes.—French, Hist. Coll., II; 11, note, 1875. Asimais.—Kennedy, Repub. Texas, I, 217, 1841. A-Simais.—Yoakum, Hist. Texas, I, 28, note, 1855. Asinaes.—Kennedy, Repub. Texas, I, 217, 1841. Asinais.—Mezières (1778) quoted by Bancroft, No. Mex. States, I, 661, 1886. Asinay.—Teran (1691), ibid., 391. Asoni.—Barcia, Ensayo, 278, 1723. Asseni.—Charlevoix, New France, IV, 78, 1870. Assinais.—Pénicaut (1712) in Margry, Déc., v, 499, 1883. Assinay.—La Harpe (ca. 1717) in French, Hist. Coll. La., III, 48, 1851. Assine.—Gatschet, Creek Migr. Leg., I, 43, 1884. Assinnis.—Boudinot, Star in the West, 125, 1816. Assoni.—Joutel (1687) in Margry, Déc., III, 311, 1878. Assony.—Joutel, ibid., I, 147, 1846. Assynais.—Pénicaut (1716) in Margry, Déc., v, 539, 1883. Ceneseans.—Boudinot. Star in the West, 126, 1816. Cenesians.—Hennepin. New Discov., pt. 2, 25, 1698. Cenis.—Joutel (1687) in French, Hist. Coll. La., I, 148, 1851. Cenys.—Joutel (1687) in Margry, Déc., III, 266, 1878. Ceries Assonys.—French, Hist. Coll. La., II, 11, note, 1875. Cneis.—Drake, Bk. Inds., vii, 1848. Coeni.—Hennepin, New Discov., map, 1698. Cœnis.—De l'Isle, map, 1700. Couis.—Morse, N. Am., map, 1776 (misprint). Hasinai.—ten Kate, Reizen in N. Am., 374, 1885 (own name). Iscanis.—Bull. Soc. Geog. Mex., 504, 1869. Nasoni.—For forms of this name, see Nasoni. Senis.—Cavelier (1687) quoted by Shea, Early Voy., 31, 1861. Tiddoes.—Keane in Stanford, Compend., Cent. and So. Am., 539, 1878 (same?). Yscanes.—Tex. State Arch., Nov. 15, 1785. Yscanis.—Census of Nacogdoches urisdiction, ibid., 1790.

Kadohadacho (*Kä'dohadä'cho*, 'real Caddo,' 'Caddo proper'). A tribe of the Caddo confederacy, sometimes confused with the confederacy itself. Their dialect is closely allied to that of the Hainai and Anadarko, and is one of the two dialects dominant to-day among the remnant of the confederacy.

The Kadohadacho seem to have developed, as a tribe, on Red r. of Louisiana and in its immediate vicinity. and not to have migrated with their kindred to any distance either N. or S. Their first knowledge of the white race was in 1541, when De Soto and his followers stayed with some of the subtribes on Washita r. and near the Mississippi. The Spaniards never penetrated during the 16th and 17th centuries to their villages in the lake region of N. W. Louisiana, but the people came in contact with Spanish soldiers and settlers from the w. by joining the war parties of other tribes. Various articles of European manufacture were brought home as trophies of war. The tribe was not unfamiliar with horses, but had not come into possession of firearms when the survivors of La Salle's party visited them on their way N. in 1687. For nearly two years La Salle had previous direct relations with tribes of the Caddo confederacy who were living in what is now Texas, so that when the approach of the French was reported the visitors were regarded as friends rather than as strangers. The chief of the Kadohadacho, with his warriors, taking the calumet, went a league to meet the travelers, and escorted them with marks of honor to the village on Red r. On arrival, "the women," says Douay, "as is their wont, washed our heads and feet in warm water and then placed us on a platform covered with very neat white mats. Then followed banquets, the calumet dance, and other rejoicing day and night." The friendly relations then begun with the French were never abandoned. A trading post was established and a flour mill built at their village by the French early in the 18th century, but both were given up in a few years owing to the unsettled state of affairs between the Spaniards and the French. These disturbances, added to the enmity of tribes who were being pushed from their homes by the increasing number of white settlers, together with the introduction of new diseases, particularly smallpox and measles, brought about much distress and a great reduction in the population. During the last quarter of the 18th century the Kadohadacho abondoned their villages in the vicinity of the lakes in N.W. Louisiana, descended the river, and settled not far from their kindred, the Nachitoches. By the beginning of the 19th century their importance as a distinct tribe was at an end; the people became merged with the other tribes of the confederacy and shared their misfortune. In customs and ceremonies they resembled the other Caddo tribes.

The tribes of the Caddo confederacy, including the Kadohadacho, have 10 clans, according to Mooney, viz.: Suko (Sun), Kagahanin (Thunder), Iwi (Eagle), Kishi (Panther), Oat (Raccoon), Tao (Beaver), Kagaih (Crow), Nawotsi (Bear), Tasha (Wolf), Tanaha (Buffalo). The Buffalo clan was sometimes called Koho (Alligator), " because both animals bellow in the same way." The members of a group did not kill the animal from which the group took its name, except the eagle, whose feathers were necessary for regalia and in sacred ceremonies; but the bird was killed only by certain men initiated to perform this ceremonial act. The rituals and songs attending the rite of preparation for the killing of eagles have passed away with their last keeper, and the people have now to depend on other tribes for the needed feathers (see Mooney in 14th Rep. B. A. E., 1093, 1896). (A. C. F.)

At'-ta-wits.—ten Kate, Synonymie, 10, 1884 (Comanche name). Cadadoquis.—Tonti (1690) in French, Hist. Coll. La., I, 73, 1846. Cadaquis.—Joutel (1687) in Margry, Déc., III, 409, 1878. Cadaudachos.—Barreiro, Ojeada, 7, 1832. Cadaux.—Sibley, Hist. Sketches, 136, 1806 (so called by the French). Caddo-dacho.—Espinosa (1746) quoted by Buschmann, Spuren, d. aztec. Spr., 417, 1854. Caddoe.—Nuttall, Jour., 288, 1821. Caddokies.—Gallatin in Trans. Am. Antiq. Soc., II, 116, 1836. Caddons.—Keane in Stanford, Compend., 504, 1878. Caddoques.—Sibley, Hist. Sketches, 66, 1806. Caddoquies.—Ibid., 105. Caddoquis.—Brackenridge, Views of La., 80, 1815. Caddos.—Sibley, Hist. Sketches, 66, 1806. Caddow.—Sen. Ex. Doc. 21, 18th Cong., 2d sess., table, 5, 1825. Cadeaux.—Sibley, Hist. Sketches, 162, 1806. Cadloes.—Keane in Stanford, Compend., 504, 1878. Cado.—Long, Exped. Rocky Mts., II, 310, 1823. Cadodaccho.—Hennepin, New Discov., pt. 2, 41, 1698. Cadodache.—Drake, Bk. Inds., vi, 1848. Cadodachos.—De l'Isle, map, 1700. Cadodaguios.—Carver, Trav., map, 1778. Cadodakis.—Güssefeld, Charte U. S., 1784. Cadodaquinons.—Keane in Stanford, Compend., 504, 1878. Cadodaquio.—Joutel (1687) in French, Hist. Coll. La., I, 168, 1846. Cadodaquiou.—Joutel (1687) in Margry, Déc., III, 408, 1878. Cadodaquioux.—Pénicaut (1701) in French, Hist. Coll. La., n. s., I, 73, 1869. Cadodaquis.—Joutel (1687) in Margry, Déc., III, 409, 1878. Cadoes.—Ker, Trav., 83, 1816. Cadogdachos.—Morfi, Mem. de Texas, 1792. Ca-do-

ha-da-cho.—Pénicaut (1701) in French, Hist. Coll. La., n. s., I, 73, note, 1869. Cadojodacho.—Linares (1716) in Margry, Déc., VI, 217, 1846. Cadoux.—Lewis and Clark, Jour., 193, 1840. Cadrons.—Schoolcraft, Ind. Tribes, VI, 34, 1857. Candadacho.—Altamira (1714) quoted by Yoakum, Hist. Texas, I, 386, 1855. Caodacho.—Tex. State Arch., Nov. 17, 1763. Catcho.—Joutel (1687) in Margry, Déc., III, 409, 1878. Chadadoquis.—Sibley, Hist. Sketches, 134, 1806. Coddoque.—Brackenridge, Views of La., 87, 1815. Codogdachos.—Morfi quoted by Shea in Charlevoix, New France, IV, 80, note, 1870. Dä'sha-i.—Mooney in 11th Rep. B. A. E., 1092, 1896 (Wichita name). Datcho.—Joutel (1687) in Margry, Déc., III, 409, 1878. Dĕ'sa.—Mooney, op. cit. (another form of Dä'sha-i). Édawika.—Gatschet, MS., B. A. E. (Pawnee name, sing.). Érawika.—Ibid. Kaado.—Möllhausen, Journ. to Pac., 95, 1858. Ka'-di.—Gatschet, Caddo and Yatassi MS., B. A. E. ('chief': original name). Kado.—Bruyère (1742) in Margry, Déc., VI, 483, 1886. Kadodakio.—Gravier (1701) quoted by Shea, Early Voy., 149, 1861. Kadodakious.—Bruyère (1742) in Margry, Déc., VI, 474, 1886. Kadodaquious.—Ibid., 483. Kä'dohädä'cho.—Mooney in 14th Rep. B.A.E., 1092, 1896 (own name). Ka-lŏ꜓-la'-tce.—ten Kate, Synonymie, 11, 1884 (Choctaw form). Kalu-꜓nádshu.—Gatschet, Tonkawa MS., B. A. E. (Tonkawa form). Karo-꜓nádshu.—Ibid. Kásséya.—Ibid. (Tonkawa name). Kasseye'-i.—Ibid. (Tonkawa name). Kul-hül-atsī.—Grayson, MS. B. A. E., 1885 (Creek name). Ma'se'p.—Mooney in 14th Rep. B. A. E., 1092, 1896 ('pierced nose': Kiowa name). Mósi.—ten Kate, Reizen in N. Am., 375, 1885 (Kiowa name). Ni'ris-häri's-ki'riki.—Mooney in 14th Rep. B. A. E., 1092, 1896 (another Wichita name). Otá's-itä'niuw'.—Ibid. ('pierced-nose people': Cheyenne name). Quadodaquees.—Boudinot, Star in the West, 128, 1816. Quadodaquious.—Le Page du Pratz, Hist. La., map, 1758. Quodadiquio.—Barcia, Ensayo, 288, 1723. Soudayé.—La Harpe (1722) in Margry, Déc., VI, 363, 1886 (Fr. form of Quapaw name). Su'-dĕé.—Dorsey, Kwapa MS. vocab., B. A. E., 1891 (Quapaw name). Tani'bänĕn.—Mooney in 14th Rep. B. A. E., 1092, 1896 ('pierced-nose people': Arapaho name). Tani'bänĕnina.—Ibid. Tani'bätha.—Ibid. Táshash.—Gatschet. Wichita MS., B. A. E. (Wichita name). Táwitskash.—Ibid. (Wichita name for a Caddo). U-tai-si'-ta.—ten Kate, Synonymie, 9, 1884 ('pierced noses': Cheyenne name). Utásĕta.—Gatschet, MS., B. A. E. (Cheyenne name). Witúne.—Gatschet, Comanche MS.vocab., B.A.E., 9, 1884 (Comanche name).

A History of the Caddo Indians

A HISTORY OF THE CADDO INDIANS*

By WILLIAM B. GLOVER

PREFACE

In a study of the history of Caddo Parish, Louisiana, an interest was developed in the Caddo Indians who were aborigines of the parish, and since no adequate study had been made of these interesting people it became my purpose to give an account of them from the time when first met by the white man until about 1845.

The region inhabited by the Caddo Indians when they were first met by the whites, soon became the disputed territory between France and Spain, and later between Spain and the United States. From the outset the Caddoes were border Indians, therefore their relations with the Europeans and later with the Americans were somewhat different from that of tribes inhabiting undisputed territory. Because of the strategic importance of the Caddo country, each of the different nations under whose jurisdiction the natives lived, employed certain methods in dealing with them. Often in order to maintain control of the natives, the nations involved in controversy made a complete change in their policy and these policies had a decided influence on the Indians.

Inasmuch as the native background as expressed in customs, traditions, and location affected the general relations of the natives with the white man it seems necessary to put together such information as is available concerning the tribes for the period before the white man came into their territory. The available information came largely through reports made by the French and Spanish who first came in contact with these Indians.

*Presented to the Faculty of the Graduate School of the University of Texas in Partial Fulfillment of the Requirements for the Degree of MASTER OF ARTS, August, 1932.

Among those who have given me help in the preparation of this work I wish to thank Miss Harriet Smither, archivist of the Texas State Library, and I am especially grateful to Mrs. Mattie Austin Hatcher and Miss Winnie Allen of the University of Texas Library staff for their kindness and helpfulness in making available the materials of the library.

To Dr. William Campbell Binkley of Vanderbilt University, I wish to express my gratitude for his scholarly advice and helpful criticisms during the development of this study.

TABLE OF CONTENTS

CHAPTER I

EARLY HISTORY OF THE CADDO

I.

SKETCH OF THE TRIBES

The Caddo Indians are the principal southern representatives of the great Caddoan linguistic family, which include the Wichita, Kichai, Pawnee, and Arikara. Their confederacy consisted of several tribes or divisions, claiming as their original territory the whole of lower Red River and adjacent country in Louisiana, eastern Texas, and Southern Arkansas.[1]

Caddo is a popular name contracted from Kadohadacho, the name of the Caddo proper, as used by themselves. It is extended by the whites to include the Confederacy.[2] Most of the early writers, and even many of the later ones used different names for the Kadohadacho. Chevalier de Tonti, a French explorer, called them Cadadoquis, M. Joutel, historian for La Salle's exploring party, called them Cadaquis, and John Sibley, Indian agent at Natchitoches, called them Caddoes.[3] They were called Masep by the Kiowa, Nashonet or Nashoni by the Commanche, Dashai by the Wichita, Otasitaniuw (meaning "pierced nose people") by the Cheyenne, and Tanibanen by the Arapaho.[4]

The number of tribes formerly included in the Caddo Confederacy can not now be determined. Only a small number of the Caddo survive, and the memory of much of their tribal organization is lost. In 1699 Iberville obtained from his Taensa Indian guide a list of eight divisions; Linares in 1716 gave the names of eleven; Gatschet procured from a Caddo Indian in 1882 the names of twelve divisions,[5] and the list was revised in 1896, by Mooney, as follows: Kadohadacho (Caddo Proper), Nadako (Anadarko), Hainai (Ioni), Nabaidacho (Nabedache), Nakohodotsi (Nacogdoches), Nashitosh (Natchitoches), Nakanawan,

---

[1] James Mooney, in the *Fourteenth Annual Report of the Bureau of American Ethnology*, Part II, 1092.
[2] Alice C. Fletcher, in Frederick Webb Hodge (editor), *Handbook of American Indians*, I, 179.
[3] *Ibid.*, I, 639.
[4] Mooney, in the *Fourteenth Annual Report of the Bureau of American Ethnology*, Part II, 1092.
[5] Fletcher, in Hodge, *Handbook*, I, 181.

Haiish (Eyeish, Aliche, Aes), Yatasi, Hadaii (Adai, Adaize), Imaha, a small band of Kwaps, and Yowani, a band of Choctaw.[6] A more recent study by Dr. Herbert E. Bolton, of the University of California, reveals the fact that there were two confederacies of the Caddoan linguistic stock inhabiting northeastern Texas, instead of one, as indicated by Mooney and Fletcher.[7] Bolton says that the Caddo whose culture was similar to the Hasinai, lived along both banks of the Red River from the lower Natchitoches tribe, in the vicinity of the present Louisiana city of that name, to the Natsoos and Nassonites tribes, above the great bend of the Red River in southwestern Arkansas and southeastern Oklahoma. The best known members of this group were the Cadodacho Grand Cado, or Caddo proper, Petit Cado, upper and lower Natchitoches, Adaes, Yatasi, Nassonites, and Natsoos.[8] On the Angelina and upper Neches rivers, lived the Hasinai, that comprised some ten or more tribes, of which the best known were the Hainai, Nacogdoche, Nabedache, Nasoni, and Nadaco.[9]

Of the names mentioned by the different writers nine tribes named by Mooney in his list are found under varying forms in the lists of 1699, by Iberville, and 1716, by Linares.[10] It will be noticed from the above lists that both Mooney and Bolton included the Cadodacho, Natchitoches, Yatasi, and Adai in the Caddo Confederacy. It appears from the evidence at hand that during the eighteenth century two confederacies existed instead of one as indicated by Mooney. In this paper the Yatasi, Adai, Natchitoches, Natsoos, Nassonites, and Cadodacho will be considered as the tribes that belonged to the Caddo Confederacy.

It is impossible at the present time to identify all the tribes that belonged to the Caddo Confederacy, but a sketch of the best known tribes that inhabited the Louisiana territory will be undertaken. The Natchitoches lived on Red River, near the present city of Natchitoches, Louisiana. Whether the army of De Soto

---

[6] Mooney, in the *Fourteenth Annual Report of the Bureau of American Ethnology*, Part II, 1092. The spelling used is that adopted by the Bureau of American Ethnology.

[7] Herbert E. Bolton, *Texas in the Middle of the Eighteenth Century*, 2. Bolton says that Mooney and Fletcher in writing on the "Caddo and Associated Tribes", based their articles largely on English sources and on recent conditions and traditions (among Caddo) without the knowledge of their early history that has since come to light through a study of the Spanish sources, hence they fail to distinguish with sufficient clearness the Hasinai and the Caddo. Bolton, *Athanase De Mézières and the Louisiana Texas Frontier, 1768-1780*, I, 22.

[8] Bolton, *De Mézières*, I, 21-22. In this paper these names will be used in referring to the Caddo tribes.

[9] Bolton, *Texas in the Middle Eighteenth Century*, 2.

[10] Fletcher, in Hodge, *Handbook*, I, 181.

came in contact with them is unknown, but the companions of La Salle, after his death, traversed their country, and Douay speaks of them as a powerful nation.[11] In 1730 according to Du Pratz, the Natchitoches villages near the trading post at Natchitoches numbered about two hundred cabins. The population rapidly declined as a result of the wars in which they were forced to take part, and the introduction of new diseases, particularly small pox and measles.[12]

In 1805 Dr. John Sibley, Indian agent at Natchitoches, in a report to Thomas Jefferson relative to the Indian tribes in his territory said:

> There is now remaining of the Natchitoches but twelve men and nineteen women, who live in a village about twenty-five miles by land above the town which bears their name, near the lake, called by the French Lac de Muire. Their original language is the same as the Yattassee, but speak Caddo, and most of them French.
>
> The French inhabitants have great respect for this nation, and a number of very decent families have a mixture of their blood in them. They claim but a small tract of land, on which they live, and I am informed, have the same rights to it from Government, that other inhabitants in their neighborhood have. They are gradually wasting away; the small pox has been their great destroyer. They still preserve their Indian dress and habits; raise corn and those vegetables common in their neighborhood.[13]

The Yatasi tribe is first spoken of by Tonti, who states that in 1690 their village was on the Red River, northwest of Natchitoches. In the first part of the eighteenth century, St. Denis invited them to locate near Natchitoches, in order that they might be protected from the attacks of the Chickasaw who were then waging war along Red River. A part of the tribe moved near Natchitoches, while others migrated up the river to the Kadohadacho and to the Nanatsoho and the Nasoni.[14]

At a later date the Yatasi must have returned to their old village site. John Sibley, in a report from Natchitoches, states that they lived on Bayou River (Stony Creek), which falls into

11 Alice C. Fletcher and John R. Swanton, in Hodge, *Handbook*, I, 37.
12 *Ibid.*, II, 27.
13 *Annals of Congress*, 9 Cong., 2 Sess., II, 1084.
14 Fletcher, in Hodge, *Handbook*, II, 993.

Red River, Western division, about fifty miles above Natchitoches. According to Sibley's report they settled in a large prairie, about half way between the Caddoques (Cadodacho) and the Natchitoches, surrounded by a settlement of French families. Of the ancient Yattassees (Yatasi) there were then but eight men and twenty-five women remaining. Their original language differed from any others, but all of them spoke Caddo. They lived on rich land, raised plenty of corn, beans, pumpkins, and tobacco. They also owned horses, cattle, hogs, and poultry.[15]

The Adai village was located on a small creek near the present town of Robeline, Louisiana, about twenty-five miles west of Natchitoches. This was also the site of the Spanish Mission, Los Adaes.[16] The first historical mention of the Adai was made by Cabeca de Vaca, who in his "Naufragios", referring to his stay in Texas, about 1530, called them Atayos. Mention was also made of them by Iberville, Joutel, and some other early French explorers. In 1792 there was a partial emigration of the Adai, numbering fourteen families, to a site south of San Antonio de Bejar, southwest Texas, where it is thought they blended with the surrounding Indian population. The Adai who were left in their old homes at Adayes, numbered about one hundred in 1802.[17] According to John Sibley's report in 1805 there were only twenty men of them remaining, but more women than men. Their language differed from that of all other tribes and was very difficult to speak, or understand. They all spoke Caddo, and most of them spoke French also. They had a strong attachment to the French, as is shown by the fact that they joined them in war against the Natchez Indians.[18]

The Cadodacho (real Caddo, Caddo proper), seem to have lived as a tribe on Red River of Louisiana from time immemorial. According to tribal traditions the lower Red River of Louisiana was their original home, from which they migrated west and northwest.[19] Penicaut reported in 1701 that the Caddo lived on the Sabloniere, or Red River, about one hundred and seventy leagues above Natchitoches, which places them a little above the big bend

---

[15] *American State Papers, Indian Affairs*, I, 721-722.
[16] Winslow M. Walker, "A Reconnaissance of Northern Louisiana Mounds", in *Explorations and Field-Work of the Smithsonian Institution in 1931*, (Publication 3134), 169.
[17] J. W. Powell, in the *Seventh Annual Report of the Bureau of American Ethnology*, 45-46.
[18] *American State Papers, Indian Affairs*, I, 722.
[19] Fletcher, in Hodge, *Handbook*, I, 179, 638.

of Red River near the present towns of Fulton, Arkansas, and Texarkana.[20] In 1800 the Caddo moved down the Red River near Caddo Lake, which placed them about one hundred and twenty miles from the present town of Natchitoches. Sibley says:

> They formerly lived on the south bank of the river, by the course of the river 375 miles higher up, at a beautiful prairie, which has a clear lake of good water in the middle of it, surrounded by a pleasant and fertile country, which had been the residence of their ancestors for time immemorial. They have a traditionary tale, which not only the Caddoes, but half a dozen other smaller nations believe in, who claim the honor of being descendants of the same family; they say, when all the world was drowning by a flood, that inundated the whole country, the Great Spirit placed on an eminence, near this lake, one family of Caddoques, who alone were saved; from that family all the Indians originated.[21]

In 1719 the Assonites (Nassonites), and Natsoos, dwelt along Red River, often on both sides of the channel about one hundred and fifty leagues northwest of Natchitoches. They lived near the Cadodacho and were related to them.[22]

The Cadodacho was the leading tribe in the Caddo Confederacy. This nation wielded a great influence over many of the tribes belonging to the Southern Caddoan family. In 1805 their influence extended over the Yatasi, Nandakoes, Nebadaches, Inies, or Tackies, Nacogdoches, Keychies, Adai, and Natchitoches, who looked up to them as their father, visited and intermarried among them, and joined them in all their wars.[23]

It is impossible to determine with exactness the population of the Caddo during the early period, for no record of a census is available until after the Louisiana Purchase in 1803. Fletcher says that before the coming of the French and Spanish they were no doubt a thrifty and numerous people.[24] One writer states that during their early history they must have numbered about ten thousand.[25] No doubt this estimate included both the Caddo and Hasinai Confederacies. According to a report from the Indian

---

[20] M. B. Harrington, *Certain Caddo Sites in Arkansas,* 140-141.
[21] *American State Papers, Indian Affairs,* I, 721.
[22] Weston Arthur Goodspeed, *The Province and the State,* I, 181.
[23] *American State Papers, Indian Affairs,* I, 721.
[24] Fletcher, in Hodge, *Handbook,* I, 180.
[25] Maude Hearn O'Pry, *Chronicles of Shreveport,* 50.

agent at Natchitoches made in 1805 the tribes of the Caddo confederacy at that time numbered approximately six hundred, not including children.[26]

All the tribes of the Confederacy spoke the Caddoan language. However, the language of the Adai differed from all the others and was very difficult to speak.[27] The Caddoes had a very convenient way of communicating with each other and with other tribes, through the medium of a sign language. Their tribal sign was made "by passing the extended index finger, pointing under the nose from right to left." When they wanted to accuse someone of telling a lie, or falsehood, they did that "by passing the extended index and second fingers separated toward the left, over the mouth".[28]

II.

THE MANNERS AND CUSTOMS OF THE CADDO

The Caddoes were cultivators of the soil. They planted fields around their villages in corn, pumpkins and vegetables that furnished their staple food.[29] They would not allow idleness; there was always something to be done, and those who would not work were punished. They worked hard in their fields when the weather was good, but when the cold rain fell and the north wind blew they would not come out of their houses. Yet they were not idle; they sat around the fire employing themselves with handiwork. It was then that they made their bows and arrows, their necessary clothing and tools with which to work. The women worked making mats out of reeds and leaves, and pots and bowls out of clay.[30]

Joutel gives an interesting account of the agriculture of the Caddo tribes in his day. He says:

> I noticed a very good method in this nation (Cenis), which is to form a sort of assembly when they want to turn the soil in the fields belonging to a certain cabin, an as-

---

[26] *American State Papers, Indian Affairs*, I, 721, 722, 724.
[27] *Ibid.*, I, 721-724.
[28] Garrick Mallery, in the *First Annual Report of the Bureau of American Ethnology*, 345.
[29] Fletcher, in Hodge, *Handbook*, I, 181.
[30] Mrs. Lee C. Harby, "The Tejas, their Habits, Government and Superstitions," *Annual Report of the American Historical Association*, 1894, p. 68. Mrs. Harby collected her information principally from the report of Fray Francisco de Jesus Maria Cesana who was a missionary among the Hasinai. These Indians were living south and southwest of the Cadodacho. Their customs were almost the same says Joutel who made observations among both tribes.—Harrington, *Certain Caddo Sites in Arkansas*, 147. Bolton says, "The Caddo and the Hasinai were similar in culture."—Bolton, *Athanase De Mézières*, I, 21-22. Other authorities state that the culture and customs of both confederacies were similar. Therefore, I feel free to use some descriptions given of the Hasinai to fill out the picture of the life of the Caddo.

sembly in which may be found more than a hundred persons of both sexes. When the day has been appointed, all those who were notified come to work with a kind of Mattock made of a buffalo's shoulder-blade, and some of a piece of wood, hafted with the aid of cords made of the bark of trees. While the workers labor, the women of the cabin for which the work is being done, take pains to prepare food; when they have worked for a time, that is, about midday, they quit, and the women serve them the best they have. When someone coming in from the hunt brings meat, it serves for the feast; if there is none, they bake Indian bread in the ashes, or boil it, mixing it with beans, which is not a very good dish, but it is their custom. They envelop the bread that they boil with the leaves of the corn. After the repast, the greater part amuse themselves the rest of the day, so that, when they have worked for one cabin, they go the next day to another. The women of the cabin have to plant the corn, beans, and other things, as the men do not occupy themselves with this work. These Indians have no iron tools, so they can only scratch the ground, and can not pick it deep; nevertheless, everything grows there marvelously.[31]

The Caddo also hunted and fished for a living. M. de la Harpe mentions the fact that the Cadodaquious (Cadodacho) and their associates prepared a feast for him which included among other things, the meat of bear, buffalo, and fish. Another evidence that they fished and hunted for a living, was brought to light by Harrington, field worker for the Heye foundation, in excavations made near Fulton, Arkansas, in the old Caddo villages. In their digging they found the bones of deer, racoons, turkeys, and many other creatures, mixed with the ashes of ancient camp fires, showing that hunting was one of their principal means of gaining a livelihood. They also found fish and turtle bones and stone sinkers for nets, all of which indicated that they used fishing as another means of making a living.[32]

The tribal organization among the Caddo was similar to that of the Hasinai. Fortunately, Father Jesus Maria left a good account of the Tejas or Aseney (Hasinai) tribes. Each group of the Tejas Indians was apparently under the command of a great chief called Xinesi. Each tribe had a chief or governor called a Caddi, who ruled within the section of country occupied by his

---

[31] Harrington, *Certain Caddo Sites in Arkansas*, 235-236.
[32] *Ibid.*, 232-234.

tribe, no matter whether it was large or small. If large, they had a sub-chief called Canahas. The number of sub-chiefs depended on the size of the tribe ruled by the Caddi. The number ranged from three to eight. It was their duty to relieve the Caddi and to publish his orders. One of these gave orders for preparing the chief's sleeping place while on the buffalo hunt and the war-path, and filled and lighted his pipe for him. They also frightened the people by declaring that, if they did not obey orders, they would be whipped and punished in other ways. There were other subordinate officers called Chayas, who carried out orders issued by the Canahas. There were petty officers under the Chayas, called jaumas, who promptly executed orders. They whipped all the idlers with rods, by giving them strokes over the legs and belly. When the Caddi wished to have a council meeting, the Canahas had to summon the elders.[33] This organization must have worked well, for Father Jesus Maria states that during his stay of one year and three months among them he had not heard any quarrels.[34] It is certain from the evidence at hand that their life was more or less communal, for we are told that eight or ten families often lived in one dwelling, and cultivated the land about it in common. It appears that the food supply was kept in common, for Joutel says:

> The mistress, who must have been the mother of the chief, for she was aged, had charge of all the provisions, for that is the custom, that in each cabin, one woman holds supremacy over the supplies, and makes the distribution to each, although there may be several families in the cabin.[35]

We are told by Jesus Maria that if the house and property of one of the tribesman were destroyed, all the rest of the tribe joined in helping provide him with a new home.[36] This communistic practice was common among the early white settlers, and will be found among the farmers in the rural sections of Louisiana today.

The Caddo lived in two kinds of houses, the grass thatched, and earth covered. The grass houses were conical in shape, made of a framework of poles covered with a thatch of grass. They were grouped around an open space which served for social and

---

[33] Harrington, *Certain Caddo Sites*, 149.
[34] Hatcher, in *Southwestern Historical Quarterly*, XXX, 216.
[35] Harrington, *Certain Caddo Sites*, 150.
[36] *Ibid.*, 151. Harby, "The Tejas", *Annual Report of the American Historical Association*, 1894, p. 68.

ceremonial purposes. Arranged around the walls inside of the house were couches covered with mats, that served as seats during the day and as beds at night. In the middle of the house was the fire, which was kept burning day and night.[37]

The earth houses were erected by constructing a frame, probably in the form of a low dome of very stout poles upon which were placed smaller ones at right angles. These in turn were covered with brush and cane, and then with sage grass on which was placed a heavy coating of earth.[38]

The Caddoes wore very few clothes during the early period as reported by Joutel. During the winter months they covered themselves with animal skins. They hung these skins around their bodies reaching about half way down their legs. During the warm months nearly all of them went without clothing.[39]

They loved ornaments such as beads, ear-pendants, and ear-plugs. Father Jesus Maria states that at festive times they did not lack for ornaments such as collars, necklaces, and amulets, which resembled those the Aztecs wore, with the one difference that the Tejas Indians knew nothing of gold and silver.[40]

If a man wanted to marry, he took the maiden of his choice the best and finest present he could afford. If the father and mother gave their permission for her to receive the gift, it meant that the man had their consent to take her. However, she was not taken away until notice was given to the Caddi. If the woman was not a maiden, all that was necessary was her consent to receive the presents. Often the agreement was made only for a few days. At other times they declared it binding forever. Only a few of them kept their word. When a woman found another man who was able to give her better things she went with him and there was no punishment for this conduct. Few men ever remained with their wives very long, but they never had but one wife at a time.[41]

Another custom of interest among the Hasinai was the war dance. Before going to war they usually sang and danced for

[37] Fletcher, in Hodge, *Handbook*, I, 181.
[38] Harrington, *Certain Caddo Sites*, 257-258.
[39] B. F. French, *Historical Collection of Louisiana*, I, 150.
[40] Harrington, *Certain Caddo Sites*, 244-245.
[41] Mrs. Mattie Austin Hatcher, "Description of the Tejas or Asinai Indians," in *Southwestern Historical Quarterly*, XXX, 283.284.

seven or eight days, offering to their God such things as corn, tobacco, bows, and arrows. Each offering was hung on a pole in front of the place where they were dancing, and near the pole was a fire before which stood a wicked-looking person who made the offering of incense by casting tobacco and buffalo fat into the fire. Each man gathered around the fire collected smoke and rubbed his body with it, believing that by performing this ceremony his God would give him whatever he requested. They prayed to nature, and to the animals for courage and strength to defeat the enemy. They asked the water to drown their enemies, the fire to burn them, the arrows to kill them, and the wind to blow them away. On the last day the Caddi came forward and encouraged the men by telling them that if they really were men, they must think of the wives, their parents, their children, but not to let them be a handicap to their victory.[42]

Ethnologists agree that the Caddoes follow nearly the same mode of burial as the Wichitas.[43]

When a Wichita dies the town crier goes up and down through the village and announces the fact. Preparations are immediately made for the burial, and the body is taken without delay to the grave prepared for its reception. If the grave is some distance from the village, the body is carried thither on the back of a pony, being first wrapped in blankets and then laid prone across the saddle, one person walking on either side to support it. The grave is dug from three to four feet deep and long enough for the body. First blankets and buffalo robes are laid in the bottom of the grave, then the body, being taken from the horse and unwrapped, is dressed in its best apparel and with ornaments is placed upon a couch of blankets and robes, with the head toward the west and the feet to the east; the valuables belonging to the deceased are placed with the body in the grave. With the man are deposited his bows and arrows or gun, and with the woman her cooking utensils and other implements of her toil. Over the body sticks are placed six or eight inches deep and grass over these, so that when the earth is filled in, it need not come in contact with the body or its trappings. After the grave is filled with earth, a pen of poles is built around it as a protection from the wild animals. The ground on and around the grave is left smooth and clean.[44]

42 *Ibid.*, 214.
43 H. C. Yarrow, in the *First Annual Report of the Bureau of American Ethnology*, Part I, 102-103.
44 *Ibid.*, I, 102-103.

If a Caddo is killed in battle, the body is never buried, but left to be devoured by beasts or birds of prey, and the condition of such individuals in the other world is considered to be far better than that of persons dying a natural death. This practice resembles that of the ancient Persians who threw out the bodies of their dead on the roads, and if they were promptly devoured by wild beasts they esteemed it a great honor, and if not, a terrible misfortune."

Not much is known about the religious beliefs of the Caddo, but the early writers tell us that they believed in a "great spirit," known under the name of Ayanat Caddi, or as Ayo-Caddi-Aymay. Manzanet says that their ceremonial leader "had a house reserved for the sacrifices, and when they entered therein they behaved very reverently, particularly during a sacrifice. They never sacrificed to idols, but only to him of whom they said that he has all power, and that from him came all things. Ayimat Caddi, in their language, signifies the great captain. This was the name he gave to God."" In spite of these remarks there is evidence that the Caddo and their relatives worshipped a number of minor spirits and powers. This may be inferred from Douay's statement that the Caddo adored the Sun. He says, "Their gala dresses bear two painted suns; on the rest of the body are representations of buffalo, stags, serpents, and other animals."" Harrington says, "it even appears that they thought everything in nature had some sort of spirit or power, which could be prayed to, reasoned with, and led to assist the supplicant, so they 'solicited the deer and buffalo, that they should allow themselves to be slain; the maize, that it would grow and let itself be eaten; the air, that it would be pleasant and healthful.' ""

III.

THE CADDO COUNTRY AND RANGE

According to a tradition of the Caddo which has parallels among other tribes, their original home was on lower Red River in Louisiana. The story says that they came up from under the ground through the mouth of a cave on a lake close to the south

---

45 *Ibid.*, I, 103.
46 Harrington, *Certain Caddo Sites*, 263.
47 John Gilmary Shea, *Discovery and Exploration of the Mississippi Valley*, 221-222.
48 Harrington, *Certain Caddo Sites*, 264.

bank of Red River, just at its junction with the Mississippi. From this place they spread out toward the west, following up the course of Red River, along which they made their principal settlements.[49] Bolton states that during the eighteenth century they extended along both banks of the Red River from the present city of Natchitoches, Louisiana, to the Natsoos and Nassonites tribes, above the great bend of the Red River in southwestern Arkansas and southeastern Oklahoma.[50]

No definite boundary lines can be given for the territory claimed by the Caddo previous to eighteen hundred. Good authority establishes the fact that they claimed a very extensive tract of country on both sides of Red River extending from the present city of Shreveport to the cross timber, a remarkable tract of woodland, which crosses Red River more than a thousand miles above its mouth.[51] This tract of country claimed by the Caddo was one of the finest sections within the bounds of North America.[52]

The topography of the country made it suitable for agriculture, stock raising, fishing, and hunting. The Caddo uplands are marked by numerous bayous and lakes and are undoubtedly excellent in quality. The river lands are of the richest alluvial soil and of wonderful fertility. The soil of the valley in many places is a black, deep soil of unsurpassed fertility.[53] At intervals along the Red River from Shreveport to the timber line there are numerous lakes and spring-brooks, flowing over a fertile soil, here and there interspersed with glades and small prairies, affording a fine range for the wild animals that inhabited the Indians' happy hunting ground.[54]

[49] Mooney, in the *Fourteenth Report of the Bureau of Ethnology*, II, 1093-1094.
[50] Bolton, *Athanase De Mézières*, I, 21-22.   The Natsoos tribe was about one hundred seventy leagues above Natchitoches.
[51] Jedidiah Morse, *A Report to the Secretary of War on Indian Affairs*, 257. Sibley to Secretary of War, May 18, 1812, 27 Cong., 2 Sess., *House Reports*, Doc. 1035, p. 105. In speaking of the cross-timber, Marcy says, "This extensive belt of woodland, which forms one of the most prominent and anomalous features upon the face of the country, is from five to thirty miles wide, and extends from the Arkansas River in a southwesterly direction to the Brazos, some four hundred miles. . . . This forms a boundary line, dividing the country suited to agriculture from the great prairies, which for the most part, are arid and destitute of timber. . . . It seems to have been designed as a natural barrier between civilized man and the savages, as, upon the east side, there are numerous spring-brooks, flowing over a highly prolific soil, with a superabundance of the best of timber, and an exuberant vegetation, teeming with the delightful perfume of flowers of the most brilliant hues; here and there interspersed with verdant glades and small prairies, affording inexhaustible grazing, and the most beautiful natural meadows that can be imagined."—Randolph B. Marcy, *Explorations of the Red River of Louisiana in the Year 1852*, p. 84-85.
[52] Sibley to Secretary of War, May 18, 1812, *House Reports*, 27 Cong., 2 Sess., Doc. 1035, p. 106.
[53] The Southern Publishing Company, *Biographical and Historical Memoirs of Northwest Louisiana*, 9-10.
[54] Marcy, *Exploration of the Red River of Louisiana in 1852*, pp. 84-85.

The range of the Caddo was far beyond the territory that they claimed. It undoubtedly extended east from the Red River near the present city of Shreveport to the Ouachita River, and north to the Arkansas River, northwest to the source of the Red River and west to the Sabine River.[55]

Since the Caddo hunted, traded, and often went to war with adjacent tribes, it appears necessary at this time to give a sketch of the tribes bordering on the territory claimed by the Caddo. To the west and southwest of the Caddo on the Angelina and upper Neches rivers lived the Hasinai Confederacy, that comprised some ten or more tribes, of which the best known were the Hainai, Nacogdoche, Nabedache, Nasoni, and Nadaco. They were a settled people, who had been living in the same region certainly since the time of La Salle, and probably long before. They dwelt in scattered villages, practiced agriculture to a great extent, and hunted buffalo on the western prairies.[56] In manners, customs, and social organization the tribes of the confederacy were similar to those of the Caddo.[57]

The Wichita, comprising another group of the Caddoan tribes, lived northwest of the Caddo, on the upper Red, Brazos, and Trinity Rivers. They were known to the Spaniards of New Mexico as Jumano and to the French as Panipiquet or Panis. They are now collectively called by ethnologists the Wichita.

> The civilization of the Wichita was essentially like that of the Caddo and the Hasinai, though they were more war-like, less fixed in their habitat, and more barbarous, even practicing cannibalism extensively.[58]

The Arkansas (Quapaw) lived north of the Caddo on the south side of the Arkansas River about twelve miles above the Arkansas post. They claimed all the land along the river for about three hundred miles above them. They were friendly with

---

[55] Sibley to Dearborn, April 10, 1805, in *American State Papers, Indian Affairs*, I, 725-730.

[56] Bolton, *Texas in the Middle Eighteenth Century*, 2. Fletcher and Mooney listed most of the Hasinai tribes as belonging to the Caddo Confederacy. Bolton discovered Spanish documents that revealed the fact that two confederacies existed during the greater part of the Eighteenth Century instead of one.—Bolton, "The Native Tribes about the East Texas Missions," in Texas State Historical Association, *Quarterly*, XI, 249-276.

[57] Fletcher, in Hodge, *Handbook*, I, 52, 524.

[58] Bolton, *De Mézières*, I, 23-24.

the Caddo tribes, but at war with the Osage who lived farther up the river.[59] They were active tillers of the soil, and also made pottery of the finest design.[60]

East of the Caddo across Red River on Bayou Chicot was a Choctaw village. Marshall says that as early as 1763, and perhaps earlier, some of the Choctaw left their homes in Mississippi and Georgia, and migrated west of the Mississippi where they evidently encroached upon the Caddo, for in 1780 some of them were at war with that nation."[61]

These are the principal tribes and confederacies found along the borders of the territory claimed by the Caddo Indians during the eighteenth century.

CHAPTER II

CADDO RELATIONS WITH THE FRENCH AND SPANISH

I.

FRENCH AND SPANISH RELATIONS BEFORE 1762

In order to understand the history of the Caddo Indians it is not only necessary to have a knowledge of their traditions, customs, and location but also to know something about their relations with the Europeans. The Caddo was one of the groups located on the frontier between Louisiana and New Spain.[1]

France and Spain began a contest to control these frontier tribes from the first moment of contact until 1762 when Louisiana was ceded to Spain. The principal weapon used by the French was the trader, and by the Spaniards, the Franciscan missionary, each backed by a small display of military force.[2] One of the reasons for a desire to control the frontier tribes was to secure possession of their territory. Both France and Spain realized that the best way to accomplish this was to establish an influence over the

---

[59] *American State Papers, Indian Affairs*, I, 725.
[60] Cyrus Thomas, in Hodge, *Handbook*, I, 335.
[61] Thomas Maitland Marshall, *A History of the Western Boundary of the Louisiana Purchase, 1819-1841*, 132.
[1] Bolton, *De Mézières*, I, 18-19.
[2] *Ibid.*, I, 30.

natives of the district desired. Another reason to control the tribes was to foster trade. A third was a desire of the mission-aries to bring them to the knowledge of the Christian faith.[3]

From the outset both the French and Spanish governments regarded the Caddo country as a strategic point of great import-ance. Likewise, both countries began to make a bid for control of the individual tribes before the close of the seventeenth century. The first contact made by the French was with the Cadodacho who were visited by the survivors of the La Salle party in 1687, and the friendly relations established by this visit were never abandoned. In 1689 Tonti, while searching for La Salle's colony, visited the tribe and further strengthened the amicable relations already existing between them and the French.

The first Spanish explorer to reach the Cadodacho country was Domingo Teran. His attempt to explore the region was a complete failure and it was not until 1717 when another unsuc-cessful attempt was made by Father Margil to establish missions for the Cadodacho and the Yatasi.[4]

In 1718 a large grant of land was made to Bernard de la Harpe, a French colonizer, in the Cadodacho country.[5] In 1719 a garrisoned trading post was established on Red River by La Harpe between the Cadodacho and Nassonite villages. This post was maintained part of the time with a garrison until after the Louis-iana cession. It checkmated every attempt made by the Spaniards to penetrate the Cadodacho country. Later, depots were established at the village of the Petit Cados and Yatasi.[6]

Bolton says:

> These trading establishments at Natchitoches and in the villages of the Cadodacho, Petit Cado, and Yatasi, together with the influence of the remarkable St. Denis, who in 1722 became commander at Natchitoches, and who till his death in 1744 remained the master genius of the frontier, were the basis of an almost undisputed French domination over the Caddo tribes. More than once the Spanish authorities contemplated driving the French out of the Cadodacho vil-lage and erecting there a Spanish post, but each attempt failed.[7]

---

[3] *Ibid.*, I, 28-29.
[4] Bolton, *De Mézières*, I, 43.
[5] Francois Xavier Martin, *History of Louisiana*, 127.
[6] Bolton, *De Mézières*, I, 44-45. The Petit Cado lived near Caddo Lake on Red River.
[7] *Ibid.*, I, 45.

The first relations with the Natchitoches began in 1690 when Tonti reached these tribes from the Mississippi and made an alliance with them. In 1700 Iberville sent his brother, Bienville, on a visit to their country from the Taensa villages. Bienville as an ambassador must have accomplished his ultimate aim, for, from the date of his visit to the close of the eighteenth century the tribe never broke faith with the French. In 1712 they helped St. Denis establish a post on the Red River at Natchitoches as a protection against the intrusions of the Spanish, and also in the hope of establishing trade relations with Spain.[8]

In 1701 Bienville and St. Denis visited the Yatasi tribes and made an alliance with them. That the friendship formed by this alliance was permanent, was shown by the fact that the Yatasi refused to close the road between the Spanish province and the Red River settlement, after the Spanish had demanded that it be closed.[9]

The French maintained control over all of the Caddo tribes with the exception of the Adai, among whom the Spanish were located from the very beginning. In 1715 Domingo Ramon, a Spanish colonizer, with a company of Franciscans, made settlements in the Adai territory. The mission of San Miguel de Linares was founded among them in 1716.[10]

In 1719, when France and Spain were at war, orders were given to Blondel, the commandant at Natchitoches, to drive the Spaniards from Texas. In carrying out these orders Blondel, with Natchitoches and Caddo allies, took possession of Los Adaes, and the Indians were allowed to destroy the buildings. The Adai tribe because of their allegiance to the Spanish, were removed from their lands by the French and treated as enemies.[11]

In 1721 the Marquis de Aguayo, a Spanish general, was sent with the strongest military force that had ever entered Texas to re-establish the presidios of Texas and the abandoned missions. He established a new presidio in the Adai tribe beside the Mission of San Miguel. This new presidio was located where the present town of Robeline, Louisiana, now stands.[12] About 1735 a military

---

[8] Fletcher, and Swanton, in Hodge, *Handbook*, II, 37.
[9] Fletcher, in Hodge, *Handbook*, II, 993. The Yatasi were located between the Sabine and Red Rivers in disputed territory, near the present city of Shreveport.
[10] *Ibid.*, I, 13.
[11] *Ibid.*, II, 450. Bolton, *De Mézières*, I, 39.
[12] Eleanor Claire Buckley, "The Aguayo Expedition into Texas and Louisiana, 1719-1722", in Texas Historical Association, *Quarterly*, XV, 50-51.

post called Nuestra Senora del Pilar was established, and five years later this garrison became the Presidio de los Adayes. Afterwards, when the country was districted for the jurisdiction of the Indians, the Adai tribe was placed under the division having its official headquarters at Nacogdoches.[13] Although Spain had established the political rule over the Adai, she had not stopped the French trade that had won the hearts of the natives. These Indians and associated tribes along the frontier looked to the French for their weapons, ammunition, and other articles of trade, for which they exchanged their peltry, and often their agricultural products.[14]

As a result of the wars between France and Spain the Adai had suffered severely, one portion of their villages being under French control, the other being under Spanish control. The ancient trail between their villages became the noted "contraband trail" along which traders and travelers journeyed between the French and Spanish provinces. One of their villages was on the road between the French fort at Natchitoches and the Spanish fort at San Antonio. The adverse influences of the whites, together with the conflict between France and Spain, almost exterminated this ancient tribe of Indians.[15]

II.

The Spanish Indian Policy after 1762

From this time the Caddo tribes were under Spanish control; therefore the outcome of the Indians will be largely determined by the Spanish Indian policy. The three fundamental purposes of the early Spanish policy were to convert the natives to the Christian faith, to civilize them, and to use them in the development of the frontier. In order to accomplish these desires the encomienda system was devised. It was soon learned that before the savage could be civilized, converted, or made a useful being, he must first be controlled. To provide such control, the land and Indians were distributed among the colonizers who held them in trust, or in encomienda. It was the duty of the trustee to provide for the protection, the conversion, and the civilization of his sub-

---

13 Fletcher, in Hodge, *Handbook*, I, 13.
14 Bolton, *De Mézières*, I, 40-41.
15 Fletcher, in Hodge, *Handbook*, I, 13.

jects; in return he was given the privilege to exploit them. The encomendero, or guardian, was required to support friars, whose duty it was to instruct the Indians in the Christian religion, in citizenship, and in the industrial arts. This plan led to the establishing of great monasteries in the territory conquered by the Spanish colonizers.

It was also learned that in order to instruct and exploit the Indian properly, he must be made to remain in a specified place of residence. Thus it soon became a law that Indians must be congregated in pueblos, and kept there by force if necessary. The encomienda system was so badly abused that it placed the Indians in a state of slavery. The trustees, yielding to the desire of the flesh, thought only of the usefulness of the natives in terms of dollars and cents. They disregarded the primary objects for which the system was designed; to convert and civilize the natives. The encomienda system was gradually replaced by the missions. During the seventeenth and eighteenth centuries many missions were planted on the expanding frontiers of Spanish America. These missions were in the hands of priests whose first duty was to teach the Christian religion to the heathen, and to teach the Spanish language and civilization. The missionaries were not only religious agents but they also served as political agents for Spain. They explored the frontiers, promoted their occupation, defended them and the interior settlements from foreign influences and savage tribes, and often served as diplomatic agents. The Spanish Indian policy prior to the Louisiana cession, although tinged with mercenary aspirations, was designed for the preservation of the Indians rather than for their destruction.[16]

In 1762 France ceded Louisiana to Spain but the transaction was not completely carried into effect until 1769.[17] The Indians were very angry when they learned of the treaty of cession. They did not believe that the King of France had a right to transfer them to any white or red chief in the world, and to dispose of them like cattle; thus they threatened resistance to the execution of the treaty.[18]

---

[16] Bolton, "The Mission as a Frontier Institution in the Spanish-American Colonies," in *The American Historical Review*, XXIII, 42-61; Anna Muckleroy, "The Indian Policy of the Republic of Texas," in *The Southwestern Historical Quarterly*, XXV, 243-244.
[17] Charles Gayarre, *History of Louisiana*, III, 1.
[18] *Ibid.*, II, 95.

Spain now had a new Indian problem. She had the difficult task of winning the loyalty of the Indian tribes that had been living peaceably under the influence of the French in the contested territory. The new policy adopted was similar to that employed by the French, a "method of control," Bolton says, "Through the fur trades and presents, a good many modifications in the directions of greater equity for the white men and greater humanity toward the natives."[19]

III.

RELATIONS WITH THE SPANISH AFTER THE LOUISIANA CESSION

After the Louisiana cession Antonio de Ulloa, first Spanish governor in Louisiana, and Hugo O'Conor, ad interim governor in Texas, issued proclamations threatening death to any Frenchman trading in Texas. Later, O'Conor claimed that by this means all such trade was suppressed.[20] Ulloa soon concluded, however, that the French system of trade and presents for the friendly Indians must be continued. He reached this conclusion in December, 1767, after an attempt was made to suppress the trade with the Yatasi tribe. On his way to the village, Du Buche, a trader who had been stopped by orders of O'Conor, caused the tribe to rise in rebellion. They held a meeting and planned to attack one of the Texas presidios, but were deterred by Guakan, head chief of the Yatasi nation. Guakan was pacified and trade allowed to continue. French traders were allowed to go freely to the tribes of Louisiana and Texas without restrictions as to time or place.

When Alexander O'Reilly became governor of Louisiana in 1769, he continued the trade with the friendly tribes, but attempted to discontinue trade with the enemies.[21] Athanase de Mézières, lieutenant governor at Natchitoches, was instructed by O'Reilly to continue the annual presents to the Cadodacho, Petit Cado, and Yatasi tribes.[22] De Mézières was also instructed to choose traders of good habits to send into the Indian villages and to encourage the savages to work and not to remain idle. He selected Alexis Grappe, Dupin, and Fazende Moriere to reside in the villages of

---

[19] Bolton, *Athanase de Mézières*, I, 67, 70.
[20] *Ibid.*, I, 88.
[21] *Ibid.*, I, 89.
[22] O'Reilly to De Mézières, January 22, 1770, in Bolton, *De Mézières*, I, 132.

the Cadodacho and Yatasi. The instructions which they were to observe specified that the savages must be furnished satisfactory merchandise for the ordinary trade price; no English merchandise should be introduced among the Indians; goods should be sold and distributed only to friendly nations; the traders should arrest all French and Spanish wanderers or vagabonds, and confiscate their effects, demanding, if necessary, the forcible aid of the Indians; the chiefs were requested to bring such rovers to the post; English traders should not be allowed to trade with the Indians or even to go into their villages; they were pledged to maintain peace and harmony among the tribes allied with Spain; they were to teach the natives to be loyal subjects; they were to tell the hostile nations that the French and Spanish were united and if they did not refrain from violence they would be treated as their cruel enemies; but if they made true ·signs of repentance they would be added to their list of allies; it was recommended to the traders that no adult or infant Indian in danger of death should be without the blessing of holy baptism[23]

Traders having been selected, and instructions having been given to the traders, De Mézières proceeded to make an agreement with the Caddo tribes. He informed Tinhiouen, chief of the Cadodacho, and Cocay, chief of the Yatasi, of their selection as medal chiefs,[24] and arranged for a meeting at Natchitoches. The chiefs of the Cadodacho and Yatasi met De Mézières at Natchitoches on April 21, 1770. They ceded their lands to the king, agreed to receive the presents and the traders, and to use their influence in controlling and making peace with the tribes of the north. In writing about this agreement De Mézières said: :

> . . . They have ceded him (the King) all proprietorship in the land which they inhabit, have promised him blind fidelity and obedience, and have received his royal emblem and his august medal with the very greatest veneration. They have engaged to aid with their good offices and their persuasion, in maintaining the general peace, and, in consequence, not to furnish any arms or munitions of war to the Naytanes, Taovayaches, Tuacanas, Quitseys, etc.; to

---

[23] Instructions for the traders of the Cadaux d' Acquioux and Hiatasses, February 4, 1770, in Bolton, *De Mézières*, I, 248-250.

[24] Distinguished chiefs were appointed captains and dignified by decoration with great and small medals. One of these chiefs, and the most influential Indian among the allies was Tinhiouen, Capique of the Cadodacho, another was Cocay, head chief of the Yatasi, and possibly Guakan, chief of the Yatasi.—Bolton, *De Mézières*, I, 74.

employ themselves peacably in their hunting, both for their entertainment and for their subsistence; and to arrest and conduct to this post all coureurs de bois and persons without occupation whom they may meet in the future, protesting that they will never forget their promise, which is just and very conformable to the harangue which has been brought to them by us, in the name of the captain-general of this province. . . . [25]

On February 3, 1770, De Mézières made a contract with Juan Piseros to furnish the goods for the traders. He was to deliver them at Natchitoches on a year's credit, and to receive in payment deer skins of good quality at thirty-five sous apiece, bear's fat at twenty-five sous a pot, and buffalo hides, good and marketable, at ten livres each. Piseros purchased the goods in New Orleans, and on their arrival at Natchitoches, they were divided among the licensed traders who had been appointed to distribute them. [26]

In the fall of 1770, De Mèzières went to the village of the Cadodacho, [27] on the Red River, to undertake the task of winning the friendship of the nations of the north. On his journey from Natchitoches he passed through the villages of the Adai, Yatasi, and Petit Cado. The Caciques and principal men of these villages, gladly accompanied him to the Cadodacho village. De Mézières met at the appointed place the chiefs of the Taovayas, Tawakoni, Yscanis, and Kichai tribes who were hostile to the Spanish and made peace with them. De Mézières said, "I am indebted to the Cacique Tinhiouen and that of the Yatasi, called Cocay, both decorated with his majesty's medals, and alike devoted to our nation, for seconding my discourse with forceful arguments." [28]

In 1779 the first chief of the Cadodacho decided to visit New Orleans. De Mézières informed Governor Bernardo de Galvez of the chief's intention of visiting him. He said:

---

[25] Agreement made with the Indian nations in Assembly, April 21, 1770, in Bolton, *De Mézières*, I, 157-158.

[26] Contract of Juan Piseros with De Mézières, Natchitoches, February 3, 1770, in Bolton, *De Mézières*, I, 143-146. The traders selected were men of proved conduct, and men of wealth. Thus if they departed from their instructions they were able to pay in goods as well as personal punishment.

[27] The village of San Luiz de Cadodachos was one hundred leagues from the fort of Natchitoches and eighty from the Arkansas post. With respect to neighboring foreigners this location was considered the master-key of New Spain.—Bolton, *De Mézières*, I, Doc., 69, p. 208.

[28] Report by De Mézières of the Expedition to Cadodachos, October 29, 1770, Bolton, *De Mézières*, I, 207-208, 211. The Taovayas, Tawakoni, Yscanis, and Kichai tribes belonged to the Wichita confederacy.—*Ibid.*, I, 211.

The first chief of the Cadauz-dakioux, who has never gone down to that capital, has decided to make this long journey, attracted by your reputation and moved by the strongest desire to see you and know you. This Indian (of whom I have had the honor of reporting to you) is friendly, and is very commendable both because of an inviolable fidelity to us as well as by reason of a courage which never fails. It is to him principally that we owe in this district a constant barrier against the incursions of the Osages; moreover, it is to the love and respect which the villages of the surrounding district show him that we owe the fact that they generally entertain the same sentiments for us . . . As the Cadaudakious nation is very much enfeebled by the continual war of the Osages, and since the last epidemic has still more diminished its numbers, it has created a faction amongst them who desire to abandon the great village. This would leave the interior of the country exposed to incursions of foreigners and its Indian enemies, a design so fatal that it will not succeed if Monsieur the Governor uses his prodigious influence to frustrate it. . . . The medal chief being accompanied by all the principal men of the nation . . . it will be well for your Lordship to treat them kindly, and to recommend them to love both our nation and their chief. . . . Since many hunters of the Arkansas River are introducing themselves among the Cadaudakioux, to the prejudice of their creditors; I pray your Lordship to remedy this abuse by intimating to the medal chief not to receive them in the future, and even to force them to appear in this post, because this sort of hunters, seeking only to flatter the Indians, very often give them very bad impressions. . . . Your Lordship will make known how interested you are in maintaining peace among the Caddodoukioux, the Arkanas, and other allies.[29]

On June 1, 1779, Galvez replied to De Mezieres' letter as follows:

The head chief of the Cados nation who came to this capitol to visit me, I received with all the affection and kindness merited by the fidelity, love, and other qualities which you indicate, I keeping in mind in the conversation which I had with him, everything which you suggested to me; and after remaining here some days he returned to his country with a present of considerable importance which I gave him, and decorated with the large medal.[30]

---

[29] De Mézières to Galvez, May 1779, Bolton, *De Mézières*, II, 248-251.

[30] Galvez to De Mézières, June 1, 1779, in Bolton, *De Mézières*, II, 253. The Medals given to chiefs for distinguished services were made of silver weighing about an ounce. On one side was the royal portrait with these words: "Carlos, III, King of Spain and emperor of the Indies." On the other, and between laurels: "for merit".—Bolton, *De Mézières*, I, 211.

The Caddo tribes were satisfied with the new Spanish Indian policy as advocated and put into operation by De Mézières. They were loyal to the Spanish government, and served faithfully to maintain peace at all times. The Spanish had won their support by making money and presents the basis of all negotiations with them.

CHAPTER III

THE CADDO IN LOUISIANA, 1803-1835

In 1803 the Caddo Indians after having been under the jurisdiction of the French and Spanish for nearly a century passed under the yoke of American domination. The French, who were the first whites to come in contact with the Caddo, had controlled them from the first quarter of the eighteenth century until Spain actually took possession of Louisiana in 1768. The Spanish exercised control over them until the Louisiana Purchase in 1803. At the time of this transaction the Caddoes were living in the same territory that they had inhabited when first met by the white man. The different tribes of the confederacy had wandered up and down Red River at different periods, and finally during the first quarter of the nineteenth century consolidated in the Sodo Creek region in the present state of Louisiana.

I.

MIGRATION OF THE CADODACHO AND AMALGAMATION
OF THE TRIBES

During the last quarter of the eighteenth century the Cadodacho abandoned their villages in the prairies along the great bend in Red River, descended the river, and settled about thirty-five miles west of the main branch of Red River, on a bayou, called by them, Sodo. The new settlement was about one hundred and twenty miles by land in nearly a northwest direction from Natchitoches.[1] They were driven from their old homes by the Osages

---

[1] *American State Papers, Indian Affairs*, I, 721. This new location was near the present city of Shreveport. The Petit Caddo lived in the Sodo Creek region, near Caddo Lake to the south of Red River.

who were constantly making excursions into their territory, killing their warriors, and stealing their horses.[2]

The land on which they now lived was a prairie of a white clay soil. The country around them was hilly, covered with a growth of oak, hickory, and pine trees, interspersed with prairies of a rich soil, very suitable for cultivation. They raised corn, beans, and pumpkins, as they had done in their old villages.[3]

By the beginning of the nineteenth century the importance of the Cadodacho as a distinct tribe was at an end; the people became merged with the other tribes of the confederacy and shared their misfortune.[4] In 1776 De Mézières recommended that presents no longer be given to the Natchitoches and Yatasi tribes, since they had disbanded and scattered among other bands.[5] In 1805 the Natchitoches numbered fifty. Shortly afterwards, they ceased to exist as a distinct tribe, having been completely amalgamated with the other tribes of the Caddo Confederacy. The Yatasi tribe was practically destroyed by the wars and new diseases of the eighteenth century. These had such an effect on the Yatasi that by 1805, according to Sibley, they had been reduced to eight men and twenty women and children. They, too, merged with the other members of the Caddo Confederacy. All of the Adai, Natsoos, and Nasonnites disappeared as distinct tribes by the close of the eighteenth century. The Adai were absorbed by the Caddo, and it is thought the Natsoos, and Nasonnites were also merged with their kindred.[6] By the close of the eighteenth century with the exception of a few scattered bands, the Caddo villages in the vicinity of the present Caddo Parish, Louisiana, represented the remnants of the old Caddo Confederacy. Tribal wars and diseases had spread havoc among them, and they, who were once a thrifty and numerous people had become demoralized and were more or less wanderers in their native land.[7]

The peaceful Caddoes who had lived under the French and Spanish regimes soon learned that they were subjects of a new

---

[2] O'Pry, *Chronicles of Shreveport*, 54. Bolton, *De Mézières*, II, 131. The Osage Indians lived on Arkansas River and were traditional enemies of the Caddoan confederacies.—Bolton, *De Mézières*, I, 167.

[3] *American State Papers, Indian Affairs*, I, 721.

[4] Fletcher, in Hodge, *Handbook*, I, 639.

[5] Bolton, *De Mézières*, II, 120.

[6] Hodge, *Handbook*, I, 13, 23, 35, 37, 50, 993. *American State Papers, Indian Affairs*, I, 722, 724.

[7] Fletcher, in Hodge, *Handbook*, I, 180.

master. Before the Americans took possession of Louisiana, Sibley reported the Caddoes as anxiously inquiring about their coming, for their presence meant higher prices for furs.[8]

II.

CADDO RELATIONS WITH THE UNITED STATES

On February 4, 1804, Edward Turner was given a commission as civil commandant of the District of Natchitoches. He was placed in full charge of the post by Governor William C. C. Claiborne. In the letter informing him of his appointment, Claiborne said, "On the waters of the Red River there reside two small nations of Indians the Paunies (Panis) and Caddoes, who trade at the post of Natchitoches. You will receive these people with friendly attention and have a regard to their interest. No person is to be permitted to trade with them, who has not been heretofore licensed under the Spanish Authority, and the period for which such license was granted has not expired, or who shall not produce a license in writing from myself."[9]

A few months after Captain Turner took charge of the post, he wrote Governor Claiborne that he had received a visit from the Caddo Indians, who had said that the Spaniards gave them a present each year, and they wished the same from the Americans.[10] Turner further stated that he gave them a few presents that satisfied them temporarily, and promised to let the chief know later what he could expect in the way of presents. Turner also suggested that it would not be a wise policy to let the Indians become dissatisfied, for the Spaniards were exerting every means to induce them to be unfriendly.[11] On November 3, Claiborne advised Turner to do everything in his power to gain the good will of the Caddoes and keep them friendly with the United States. He advised him to furnish rations to the honest, well disposed Indians that visited the post, but stated that he had not been authorized to make presents to them generally. He instructed Turner to give

[8] Isaac Joslin Cox, *The Early Exploration of Louisiana*, 75. Dr. John Sibley, of North Carolina, migrated to Louisiana early in 1803, and while the country was still a Spanish possession, mad? a personal investigation of the Red River as far as the vicinity of Natchitoches, for the purpose of selecting a suitable spot to locate as a ranchman.—*Ibid.*, 14.
[9] Claiborne to Turner, February 25, 1804, in Rowland (ed), *Official Letter Books* of W. C. C. Claiborne, I, 386.
[10] Cox, *Early Explorations of Louisiana*, 75.
[11] Turner to Claiborne, October 13, 1804, Rowland, *Letter Books*, II, 385.

presents to the Caddo chief and his principal men, but these presents were not to exceed two hundred dollars in value.[12]

While the Caddo Indians were under Spanish control they had been given presents annually from the post at Natchitoches, and they expected the American government to continue this system. Inasmuch as the United States government was making a bid for the control of the Caddo who were again living within contested territory, it was imperative that it continue the Spanish policy of giving presents.

In 1803 Turner recommended the immediate establishment of American factories at Natchitoches to attract the Indians from the Spaniards. Turner and Sibley informed Claiborne of the privilege enjoyed by Murphy and Davenport in trading with the Spanish Indians. As this trade included the privilege of supplying them with ammunition, the Americans, in case of difficulty with the Spaniards, might feel its evil effects. Accordingly they thought that if the trade could be turned into the proper channel, and be supplied from a post on Red River the Indians might become loyal friends of the Americans.[13]

In 1804 Sibley was asked by Secretary of War Henry Dearborn to act occasionally as agent for the United States in holding conferences with the various Indians of his vicinity. He was to keep them friendly towards the American government by the distribution of some three thousand dollars worth of merchandise. On May 23, 1805, Secretary Dearborn instructed Sibley to use all means, at all times, to conciliate the Indians, and especially those natives that might, in case of a rupture with Spain, be useful, or mischievous to the government. He said "they may be assured that . . . (they) will be treated with undeviating friendship as long as they shall conduct themselves fairly and with good faith towards the government and the citizens of the United States."[14]

As Indian agent, Sibley was very active, holding numerous conferences with the Indians of his territory, and counter acting

---

[12] Claiborne to Turner, November 3, 1804, Rowland, *Letter Books*, II, 390.

[13] Cox, *Early Explorations of Louisiana*, 75-76.

[14] Cox, *Early Explorations of Louisiana*, 77-78. Sibley was first employed as a contract surgeon to care for the troops stationed at Natchitoches. In 1805 he was commissioned as Indian agent for Orleans territory and the region south of the Arkansas. He held this position until 1815.—G. P. Whittington, in *Louisiana Historical Quarterly*, X, 471.

the efforts of the Nacogdoches traders to move the Caddo and other friendly Indians into Spanish territory.[15]

In 1805 Governor Claiborne informed Thomas Jefferson that, in his opinion, the Indians west of the Mississippi would give them very little trouble. He said that the Caddo nation had a decided influence over most of the tribes in lower Louisiana, and they would be easily managed. He stated also that their disposition toward the United States was already friendly, and with the proper treatment, he was persuaded their friendship could be preserved.[16] Sibley in a report to President Jefferson in 1805 said, "The whole number of what they call Warriors of the Ancient Caddo, is now reduced to about one hundred, who are looked upon somewhat like Knights of Malta, or some distinguished military order. They are brave, despise danger or death, and boast that they have never shed white men's blood."[17] The Caddo Indians were so brave, peaceful, diplomatic, and influential that it is not surprising the Spanish officials refused to admit that they lived on American soil or to give them up without a controversy. On one side of the border Sibley was working faithfully to keep the Caddoes friendly, while on the other side Captain-General Salcedo was issuing instructions to prevent the removal of Indians from Texas into Louisiana, and by every means possible to keep them faithful to Spanish allegiance. In 1805 from each group of frontier officials, came accusations against the unfair dealings of the other in dealing with the Indians in the disputed territory.[18]

The Spanish officials disliked the fact that the Caddoes rendered assistance to the Freeman-Custis expedition in exploring Red River. They also disliked the fact that the Caddoes, instead of displaying the Spanish flag in their villages, had replaced it with an American flag given them by members of the Freeman-Custis party. The Spanish force sent to stop the Freeman-Custis exploring party entered the Caddo village, cut down the American flag, insulted their chief, and threatened to kill the Americans if they resisted their attempt to stop them. In consequence, Claiborne immediately communicated with Simon de Herrera, commander of the Spanish troops east of the Sabine River, saying,

---

[15] Whittington, in *Louisiana Historical Quarterly*, X, 470.
[16] Claiborne to Jefferson, July 14, 1805, Rowland, *Letter Books*, III, 125.
[17] *American State Papers, Indian Affairs*, 1, 721. The number of warriors given represents only those belonging to the Cadodacho tribes.
[18] Cox, "The Exploration of the Louisiana Frontier, 1803-1806," in *Annual Report of the American Historical Association*, 1904, pp. 165-166.

On my arrival at this port, (Natchitoches), I learned with certainty that a considerable Spanish force had crossed the Sabine, and advanced within the territory claimed by the United States. It was hoped, Sir, that pending the negotiations between our respective Governments for an amicable adjustment of the Limits of Louisiana, that no additional settlement would be formed, or new Military Positions assumed be (by) either Power, within the disputed territory; a Policy which a conciliatory disposition would have suggested and Justice sanctioned; but since a contrary conduct has been observed on the part of certain officers of his Catholic Majesty, they alone will be answerable for the consequences which may ensue.

The above proceeding, Sir, is not the only evidence of an unfriendly disposition which certain officers of Spain have afforded. I have to complain of the Outrage lately committed by a Detachment of Spanish Troops, acting under your Instructions, towards Mr. Freeman and his party, who were ascending the Red River under the Orders of the President of the United States. . . . Mr. Freeman and his party were assailed by a Battalion of Spanish Troops, and commanded to return. . . .

This Detachment of Spanish Troops . . . (committed) another outrage, towards the United States, of which it is my duty to ask an explanation. In the Caddo Nation of Indians, the Flag of the United States was displayed and commanded from the chief (and) warriors all the respectful venerations, to which it is entitled. But your troops are stated to have cut down the Staff on which the Pavilion waved; and to have menaced the Peace and safety of the Caddo's should they continue their respect for the American Government, or their friendly Intercourse with Citizens of the United States.

I experience the more difficulty, in accounting for this transaction, since it cannot be unknown to your Excellency that while Louisiana appertained to France, that the Caddo Indians were under the protection of the French Government, and that a French Garrison was actually established in one of their villages: hence it follows, Sir, that the cession of Louisiana to the United States, with the same extent which it had when France possessed it, is sufficient authority for the display of the American Flag in the Caddo village, and that the disrespect which that Flag has recently experienced, subjects your Excellency to a serious responsibility."

[19] Claiborne to Herrera, August 26, 1806, in Rowland, *Letter Books,* III, 383-384.

On August 28 Herrera replied to Claiborne's letter in part as follows: "I think as your Excellency does that all the country which his Catholic Majesty has ceded to France belongs to the United States, but the Caddo's nation is not upon it and on the contrary the place which they inhabit is very far from it and belongs to Spain. . . . "[20] Herrera further stated that he informed the Caddoes that if they wished to continue to live under the domination of the United States, they would have to pass into their territory, but if they wanted to remain where they were, they would have to take down the American colors.[21] On August 31, Claiborne replied to Herrera's letter, as follows: "You have not denied, Sir, that the French when in possession of Louisiana, had established a garrison on the Red River, far beyond the place where Mr. Freeman and his associates were arrested on their voyage, or that the Caddo Indians were formerly considered as under the protection of the French Government. The silence of your Excellency on these points, proceeds probably from a knowledge on your part of the correctness of my statements."[22] It appears that this letter ended the official correspondence between Claiborne and the Spanish relative to the control of the Caddo Indians. It also appears that the American agents were making progress in their bid for the control of the Caddoes. The Americans were now put to the task of holding the advantages they had already gained.

Governor Claiborne had invited the chief of the Caddo nation to meet him in Natchitoches. On September 5, 1806, the grand chief of the Caddoes, accompanied by twelve or fifteen of his warriors, arrived at Natchitoches, and on the following day Governor Claiborne, in the presence of the officers of the army, and many respectable citizens, gave an address to the chief of the Caddo Nation. In this address he said:

> That great and Good Man, the president of the United States esteems you and your people. Like the rising sun that gives light and comfort to the world, expands the cares of the American chief, and his desire is to promote the happiness of all mankind. He is particularly solicitous to better the condition of his red children; he wishes them to

---

[20] Herrera to Claiborne, August 28, 1806, Rowland, *Letter Books*, III, 392.
[21] *Ibid.*
[22] Claiborne to Herrera, August 31, 1806, Rowland, *Letter Books*, III, 394.

know war no more; to live in peace with their neighbors; to pursue the deer in safety; to cultivate their little fields of corn without fear, and that no enemy should disturb their sleep at night. . . .

Brother! Let your people continue to hold the Americans by the hand with sincerity and Friendship, and the chain of peace will be bright and strong, our children will smoke together, and the path will never be colored with blood. . . .

The talk (at this time) is not straight between the United States and Spain; but I hope no mischief will ensue, for a council fire is now burning, and the beloved men of the two nations are endeavoring to settle the dispute. But if it should so happen that the Americans must bid their Swords to leap from the scabbard, we wish not your tomahawks to rise. When white people enter into disputes, let the red men keep quiet, and join neither side.[23]

Claiborne further told the chief that the Americans and Spaniards were disputing over the boundary line, and that the Americans purchased the country from the French and claimed all the land which the French formerly possessed. He requested the chief to tell what he had heard to the traveler and to the hunter.[24]

After the ceremonies of smoking the pipe were solemnized, the chief returned the following answer:

I am highly gratified at meeting today with your Excellency and so respectable a number of American officers, and shall forever remember the words you have spoken.

I have heard, before, the words of the President, though not from his own mouth:—his words are always the same; but what I have this day heard will cause me to sleep more in peace.

Your words resemble the words my forefathers have told me they used to receive from the French in ancient times. My ancestors from chief to chief were always well pleased with the French; they were well received and well treated by them, when they met to hold talks together, and we can now say the same of you, our new friends.

If your nation has purchased what the French formerly possessed, you have purchased the country that we occupy, and we regard you in the same light as we did them. . . .[25]

[23] Claiborne's Address to the Caddo Chief, September 5, 1806, Rowland, *Letter Books.* IV, 2.3.
[24] *Ibid.,* IV, 4.
[25] Caddo chief's reply to Claiborne's address, September 5, 1806, Rowland, *Letter Books,* IV, 4.

This speech from the grand chief of the Caddo nation assured Claiborne that the United States could rely on the Caddoes being friendly and loyal subjects.

The Caddo chief acted as ambassador for Sibley to the other Indian tribes of east Texas and north Louisiana by inviting and conducting a delegation composed of the head men of seven different nations to a council meeting at Natchitoches. After the delegation had been seated in the great council room, and the calumet and council fire had been lighted, Sibley delivered a talk, and in the course of this talk he said:

> By the treaty with France and Spain we have become your neighbors, and all the great country called Louisiana as formerly claimed by France belongs to us; the President of the United States is your friend and will be as long as you are friendly to him; we should live together in peace; the boundaries between our country and Spain are not yet fixed, but you may rest assured whether your lands fall within our boundaries or not, it will always be our wish to be at peace and friendship with you; we are not at war with Spain, and do not ask you to be unfriendly to Spain; I caution you against opening your ears to bad talks of any people who wish to make us enemies, but remember that we have not come to this country to do harm to any of our Red brothers, but to help them; it is the wish of your great and good father, the President of the United States, that you should live together in peace.[26]

Sibley gave presents to the different delegations, and extended them an invitation to trade at Natchitoches, promising to exchange articles of merchandise for horses, mules, robes, and silver ore.[27]

During the War of 1812 between the United States and Great Britain the allegiance of the Caddoes to the United States was tested. The Creeks who had attacked the Americans sent war talks to the Caddoes and other tribes along the Louisiana-Texas frontier endeavoring to stir up an insurrection. Claiborne, realizing the gravity of the situation, visited Natchitoches and delivered a war talk to the Caddoes saying that seven years ago they had held a conference at Natchitoches and had mutually agreed to keep the path between their two nations white, and he hoped that they

---

[26] Annie H. Abel, "A report from Natchitoches in 1807," in *Indian Notes and Monographs*, Heye Foundation, XXV, 55-60.
[27] *Ibid.*

and the chiefs who followed would endeavor to keep the chain of friendship bright and so strengthen it that their children would live together as neighbors and friends. He further told them that Doctor Sibley was agent for the president and whatever he said they should receive as the president's own words. He reminded them also that seven years ago they had told him they had but one enemy, the Osages, and he was sorry to learn that they were still at war with them. He further said, "In the vast hunting grounds where the great Spirit has placed a sufficiency of Buffalo, Bear and Deer for all the red men, the Osages, I hear have already robbed the hunters of all the nations, and their chiefs wage war to acquire more skins." The English, whom he said were like the Osages, were taking many Americans who were peacefully navigating the seas, and compelling them to serve on board of war canoes and fight against their friends and countrymen. Claiborne further told them that the English were unwilling to fight the Americans man to man but had appealed to the red people for assistance by telling them lies and making unfair promises which they would not and could not fulfill. He warned them that the English would be unable to shield the Creeks whom they had already incited to acts of hostility against the Americans. In conclusion he said:

> I hear the Creeks have sent runners with war talks, to the Conchattas and other tribes, your neighbors, but I hope all these people will look up to you, as an elder brother, and hold fast your good advice. When your father was a chief, the paths from your Towns to Natchitoches was clean, and if an Indian struck the people of Natchitoches—It was the same as to strike him. To a chief, a man and warrior, nothing could be more acceptable than a sword. . . . I have therefore directed, that a sword be purchased at New Orleans, and forwarded to Doctor Sibley, who will present it to you (Caddo Chief) in my name.[28]

Although war talks had been sent to the Caddoes by the Creeks, their friendship and loyalty could not be shaken in their determination to remain at peace with the United States.[29]

It appears that Claiborne not only suspected the English of meddling with the border Indians, but also anticipated trouble again from the Spanish. On October 21, 1814, he wrote John Per-

---

[28] A talk from William C. C. Claiborne to the great chief of the Caddo Nation, October 18, 1813, in Rowland, *Letter Books*, VI, 275-279.
[29] Claiborne to Armstrong, October 25, 1813, in Rowland *Letter Books*, VI, 278.

kins, that, according to information ascertained at Natchitoches, the Spanish authorities of the province of Texas had made peace with several of the Indian tribes, lately their enemies, and were again likely to acquire an influence in their councils;[30] also, it was reported that eight hundred Spanish regulars were advancing toward Nacogdoches, and no doubt would attempt to occupy the post at Bayou Pierre. He further added, that in case of an invasion of Louisiana, the Caddo and other Indian friends would be needed and. . . . "I pray you to keep them prepared for a prompt cooperation."[31] In a letter to Andrew Jackson, who was at this time commander of the American forces at New Orleans, Claiborne said, "The chief of the Caddoes, is a man of great merit, he is brave, sensible and prudent.—But I advise, that you address a talk immediately to the chief, he is the most influential Indian on this side of the River Grande, and his friendship sir, will give much security to the western frontier of Louisiana."[32]

The Caddoes and other friendly tribes had already informed Sibley that they were willing to take up arms in defense of their American brothers and had been ordered by General Jackson to assemble at Natchitoches. Thomas Gale, late judge advocate of the seventh military district, succeeded Sibley as Indian agent, and, being a military man, was appointed commander of the Caddoes, and other Indians assembled at Natchitoches.[33] From further information it was learned that the Caddoes and other friendly Indians were held in readiness at Natchitoches to be used against the English, if needed, or to help maintain peace along the Spanish border.

In 1816 John Jamison was appointed Indian agent at Natchitoches and was informed by Claiborne that "the policy of the government has been to keep the Indians at their homes, to guard against those impositions to which they were exposed by an indiscriminate trade and intercourse with the whites, to introduce among them, husbandry and the art of civilization, finally by supplying all their wants to impress them with grateful and friendly sentiments."[34] After this policy was stated, Jamison was further in-

---

[30] In the revolution of 1813 in Texas, a nation of Indians, called the Lapans, or Cances were driven to the Louisiana frontier, because they took a stand against the Royalists— Claiborne to Macarty, October 16, 1813, *Ibid.*, VI, 274.

[31] Claiborne to John Perkins, October 21, 1814, Rowland, *Letter Books*, VI, 283.

[32] Claiborne to Jackson, October 28, 1814, Rowland, *Letter Books*, VI, 293-294.

[33] Claiborne to Macarty, October 16, 1813, Rowland, *Letter Books*, VI, 274. Claiborne to James Monroe, December 20, 1814, *Ibid.*, VI, 328.

[34] Claiborne to Jamison, May 18, 1816, Rowland, *Letter Books*, VI, 401.

structed to enforce strictly the act of Congress regulating trade and intercourse with the Indian tribes; to permit no traders to reside among the Indians, but such as had been licensed according to law; to impress upon the minds of the Indians the benefit derived by exclusively trading with the factory; to discourage and try to prevent the Indians from exchanging their peltry with the whites for ardent spirits; to prosecute those who should wilfully sell ardent spirits to the Indians; to encourage the tribe to live in peace with all nations; to protect and treat with kindness not only their own Indians but individuals of other tribes who lived outside the bounds of the United States that might visit the agency; to endeavor to ascertain the policy observed by the Spanish authorities towards the Indians residing on Red River.[35] It appears that the continued success of the federal Indian policy among the tribes along the Red River depended on the enforcement of these regulations, for if the unlicensed traders were allowed to carry on commerce without restrictions the natives would soon be looking to them for advice instead of looking to the Indian agents.

In as much as the war Department expected the Indian Agents to enforce the trade and intercourse laws,[36] and inasmuch as it expected the factories[37] to supply the goods necessary to keep the Indians friendly and satisfied, it became necessary to establish agencies nearer the Caddo villages. With this in mind, George Grey, who had been appointed agent in 1819, established an agency in 1821 at Sulphur Fork, Red River, in the vicinity of Long prairie. In 1825 the agency was moved to Caddo prairie and remained there about six years when, on account of overflows caused by the great raft in Red River, it was removed below Lodo Lake (Sodo Lake) near the Caddo villages, only a short distance west of the present city of Shreveport. The agency remained at this place until the Caddo Treaty in 1835 after which it was no longer needed and was abolished.[38]

---

[35] Claiborne to Jamison, Rowland, *Letter Books,* VI, 402.

[36] From the outset acts were passed to regulate trade and intercourse among the Indian tribes. Among the acts were those of 1790, 1793, 1796, 1799, 1802, 1816, and 1834. These acts in general required licenses of traders, imposed fines for illegal hunting on the lands of the Indians, forbade foreigners from securing licenses, and prevented the sale of liquor to the Indians.—Henry Ford White, *The Economic and Social Development of Arkansas prior to 1836,* MS., Dissertation, University of Texas, 89.

[37] By the term, "factories", is meant an agency for supplying goods to the Indians at cost.

[38] Extract of a letter from Grey, to Calhoun, June 16, 1831, in *House Reports,* 27 Cong., 2 Sess., Doc. 1035, p. 106. The Caddo Indian agents were John Sibley 1805-1815, Thomas Gales 1815, John Jamison 1816-1818, George Grey 1819-1828, Thomas Griffith 1828-1830, Jehiel Brooks 1830-1835.—Collected from materials studied.

Soon after George Grey became agent he was informed by the Secretary of War that the law of intercourse should be rigidly enforced against all white persons trespassing upon the Indians' lands. Those hunting were liable to prosecutions, fines, and imprisonment, and could be removed by military force. The agent had the authority to get soldiers to aid in the execution of his duty from the nearest military post.[39] Although rigid enforcement of the intercourse laws was required, and the use of military force was suggested, it seemed almost impossible to stop the liquor traffic. The character of the illegal traders was portrayed in a communication from Brooks to Judge E. Herring, commissioner of Indian affairs, in which Brooks said:

> There are hovering all around the Indian borders, smuggling dealers, watching, with a packhorse laden with two skins filled with whiskey and a few worthless toys besides, for an opportunity to wheedle the Indian out of every thing acquired by the chase. He is here today and there tomorrow, as necessity, fear, or interest may suggest. They are an irresponsible and almost intangible race of beings, generally without homes or country; cunning in all the little intrigues and arts of their vocation, well acquainted with the prohibition of the laws of Indian intercourse; and skillful in evading the rules of evidence which bring them into action. Some of the Indians deprecate this traffic while others become the willing recipients, and are often employed to help disseminate the spirits in smaller quantities.[40]

The Indians were usually friendly to the traders. The relations of the traders to the Indians were different from those of their rivals, the American backwoodsmen. The traders wanted to acquire wealth by trapping and trading and did not want the land, but only wanted a free pass through it. The purpose of the American frontiersmen was settlement, permanent occupation, and the dispossession of the natives. Naturally the Indians welcomed the one party as a friend and saw in the other an enemy.[41]

---

[39] Extract from a letter, Secretary of War to Grey, November 27, 1820, *House Reports*, 27 Cong., 2 Sess., Doc. 1035, p. 115.

[40] Brooks to Herring, November 25, 1833, *House Reports*, 27 Cong., 2 Sess., Doc. 1035, pp. 112-113.

[41] Annie Heloise Abel, "The History of Events Resulting in Indian Consolidation West of the Mississippi," *Annual Report of the American Historical Association*, 1906, I, 265.

CHAPTER IV.

THE TREATY OF 1835 WITH THE UNITED STATES

I.

THE CADDO DECIDE TO SELL THEIR LAND

At the beginning of the second quarter of the nineteenth century the Caddoes informed Brooks, their agent, that they were willing to sell their lands.[1] Why they decided to dispose of the territory that had been inhabited by their ancestors from their earliest time is of immediate concern. At least three factors had a direct influence on their decision. First, the white settlers were moving down Red River valley from the Arkansas territory settling on the Caddo lands regardless of the federal laws prohibiting such action. In 1823 George Grey was ordered by the war department to remove all settlers from the Caddo lands.[2] In 1825 Grey wrote the war department as follows: "I enclose you a list of the names of persons that were ordered off the Caddow lands, by order of the former Secretary of War, who have since laid in claims for donations on the Caddow lands. I mention this that our Government may be apprized of their improper claims to the Caddow lands." The names of persons claiming donations under the donation act of Congress on the Caddo lands were Leonard Dyson, Samuel Norris, B. Paira, Henry Stockman, Peter Stockman, Philip Frederich, Moses Robertson, James Faris, Caesar Wallace, John Armstrong, Old Lay, James Wallace, James Coats, Charles Myers, and Manuel Treshall.[3] The whites continued to settle in the Caddo prairies, regardless of government and Indian titles, and when removed from the land became hostile towards the agent commanded to perform the act.[4] In a letter from Brooks to the Commissioner of Indian affairs, he said:

> I am informed that persons are engaged at Natchitoches taking the depositions of every old resident from this quarter, to prove that the Caddo nation have no right to the country they occupy, two of these settlers who have thus de-

---

[1] *House Reports,* 27 Cong., 2 Sess., Doc. 1035, p. 99.
[2] *Ibid.,* p. 107.
[3] *House Reports,* 19 Cong., 1 Sess., Doc. 33, pp. 5-6.
[4] Brooks to Herring, July 1, 1834, in *House Reports,* 27 Cong., 2 Sess., Doc. 1035, pp. 113-114.

posed, hold settlement rights themselves that would be good under the laws, provided, the government decide that the nation has no claim.

This matter is already exciting unfriendly feeling among the Caddoes, who are instigated, by some of the parties concerned, to lay the blame entirely on me.

Thus, between the Indians on the one hand, and the evil minded whites on the other, I consider my present situation quite embarrassing.[5]

Not only were settlers from the United States moving into the Caddo region, but individuals from Texas seemed determined to divide the country among themselves in the face of repeated warnings from the officials in charge. Brooks as agent attempted to discharge his duties faithfully, but was looked upon by these frontiersmen as an enemy to the settlement and improvement of the region. When Brooks informed the Caddoes of the various claims set up by white men to portions of their lands, where located, and of the attempts made to settle thereon, they unconditionally objected, and requested that their objections be communicated to the government.[6]

Another factor that influenced the Caddoes to sell their lands, was the government policy of settling in the territory claimed by the small bands of Indians driven from other sections by the westward expansion of the whites. At first the Caddoes permitted small bands such as the Coshattos, Delawares, Cherokees, and Alabamas, who had migrated from east of the Mississippi to settle in their territory, hoping to use them as allies against their common enemy, the Osages.[7] As early as 1763, and perhaps earlier, some of the Choctaw left their homes in Mississippi and Georgia, and migrated west of the Mississippi where they evidently encroached upon the Caddo, for in 1780 some of them were at war with that nation. About 1809 a Choctaw village was known to exist on Bayou Chicot and by 1820 another existed near Pecan Point,[8] both villages being located in the Caddo Country. In 1805 Sibley said, "The Caddoques (Caddo) complain of the Choctaws encroaching upon their country; call them lazy, thievish, etc. There

---

[5] Brooks to Herring, April 9, 1833, in *House Reports*, 27 Cong., 2 Sess., Doc. 1035, p. 110.

[6] *Ibid.*, pp. 111-114.

[7] Morse, *A Report of the Secretary of War on Indian Affairs*, 257. *House Reports*, 27 Cong., 2 Sess., Doc. 1935, p. 106.

[8] Marshall, *The Western Boundary of the Louisiana Purchase, 1819-1841*, p. 132.

has been a misunderstanding between them for several years, and small hunting parties kill one another when they meet."⁹   The Caddoes did not seem to object to small bands from different nations settling in their country if they were well behaved and served as allies.

On January 19, 1825, the Quapaw tribe made a treaty with the United States giving up all their lands in Arkansas and agreeing to move to the Caddo territory.   Article four of the treaty reads as follows, "The Quapaw tribe of Indians will hereafter be concentrated and confined to the district of country inhabited by the Caddo Indians, and form a part of said tribe.   The said nation of Indians are to commence removing to the district allotted them before the twentieth day of January, eighteen hundred and twenty-six."¹⁰   A short time after this agreement the Quapaw chiefs visited the Caddoes and with the consent of the Caddo chief selected a location on which to settle, about half a mile from the Red River agency on Treache Bayou.¹¹   To facilitate removal the United States agreed to furnish them corn, meal, meat, and salt for six months.   By March, 1826, the Quapaws began moving to Louisiana under the direction of Antoine Barraque.   As soon as they reached the Red River country they suffered reverses.   The Caddoes refused to amalgamate with them and had given them a poor location near the Red River raft.¹²   They were nearly drowned by successive floods, and most of them wandered back to their old haunts in a starving condition.   They were temporarily taken care of, but by a final treaty in 1833 the last foot of ground they owned among the Caddoes was given up and they agreed to move to the Indian Territory.¹³   The Quapaws lived nearest the whites in the Arkansas territory and were removed from their lands because their presence was a bar to the white men's going there.   Immediately after their removal, their country was thrown open to settlement and when they returned to Arkansas they were considered as intruders.¹⁴

George Gray advocated the settling of all the small bands in Louisiana on the Caddo lands for this would place them away

⁹ *American State Papers, Indian Affairs*, I, 721.
¹⁰ *Ibid.*, II, 530.
¹¹ *Ibid.*, II, 706.
¹² White, *The Economic and Social Development of Arkansas Prior to 1836*, 59-60.
¹³ Myra McAlmont Vaughn, "Habitat of the Quapaw Indians", in Arkansas Historical Association *Publications*, II, 529-530.
¹⁴ White, *The Economic and Social Development of Arkansas, Prior to 1836*, p. 59.

from the influences of the white settlers. He talked with the Caddo chief relative to the proposition and found that he voiced no objections to their settling on his lands, as it was the wish of the government. The chief said that he had never sold any land to the government, but had permitted the Quapaws and other Indians that had sold their lands to reside among his people, and he thought the government should give him a small annuity, for which he would be thankful. Grey stated that in his opinion a small annuity to the old chief would have a good effect, as his influence among the small bands of Indians both in Louisiana and in the Spanish provinces was great. On November 16, 1825, McKenny, commissioner of Indian affairs, instructed Grey to defer assembling the small bands of Indians in Louisiana, as he had proposed, in order to secure their assent to a removal upon Caddo lands, but if they accepted the invitation extended to them by the Caddo chief to receive them as a part of the charge of his agency. The secretary also authorized Grey to give the Caddo chief an annuity of fifty dollars, and to tell him that it was as a token of the good will of his greatfather, the president of the United States, as a small return for his kind feelings towards the Quapaw, in giving them a home upon his lands, and for the offer he had made the bands now in Louisiana to come and join them.[15] This idea of consolidating the small tribes was carried out, for in 1829 practically all of the small bands in Louisiana were living in the country claimed by the Caddo between Red River and the Mexican border. The Caddo still exercised considerable influence over the tribes near them.[16] These small bands of Indians, together with thousands of individuals of different and discordant tribes that the federal government had settled on the Red and Arkansas rivers, soon exhausted the game supply within the Caddo territory, so by 1835 the Caddoes wanted to retire from their old homes, because it was almost impossible to procure enough food from the chase to maintain their existence.[17]

A third factor that influenced the Caddoes to dispose of their lands was the insistence on the part of the Spanish, that they move to Texas. Pierre Rublo and Joseph Valentin, farmers and inhabitants of Natchitoches parish, reported that in 1821 the Gover-

---

[15] *American State Papers, Indian Affairs*, II, 106-707.
[16] Henry A. Schoolcraft, *Indian Tribes*, III, 596.
[17] *House Reports*, 27 Cong., 2 Sess., Doc. 1035, p. 33.

nor of Monterey sent a messenger express to the Caddo tribe, inviting them to move to that country, and offered liberal pay to any whites that would conduct them into Texas. In August, 1821, according to Rublo and Valentin they accompanied a deputation of eighty-three Caddoes to Monterey. During a conference with them the governor learned that they were willing to migrate into Texas, and desired a tract of land on which to settle, and, according to Rublo, made them an assignment on the Guadalupe River, commenacing where the upper road from San Antonio to Nacogdoches crosses that stream, and running up the Guadalupe to its source. Valentin said that the reason the Caddoes did not move immediately was because of the Texas Revolution and the illness of one of the old Indians, much respected, whom they did not want to leave behind. He further stated that they had decided to go when Brooks became agent, but their departure was checked because Brooks offered inducements to them to remain.[18] In 1826 Sibley wrote to Austin, saying:

> Our government is placing above us on the waters of Red River and Arkansas more than fifty thousand Indians of different and discordant tribes. I do not like the Policy, not for the reason only, that it will hasten their extinction. The Caddos and Quapaws, are going to settle above you on the same River.—They will be peaceable, but unprofitable neighbors.[19]

From the contents of this letter it seems that Sibley was aware of the fact that the Caddoes had been granted land in Texas. In 1835 Colonel Many, an officer stationed at Fort Jesup, reported that he understood from good authority, that the Caddoes had been granted land by the Mexican government, and that a number of them had already gone into that country to settle. He said that he had been informed, and did not doubt the truth of the information, that these Indians were more attached to the Spaniards than to the Americans, and that the only thing that had kept them from going into the Spanish country was the few presents they had received, and the work that had been done for them by the gunsmith furnished by the United States.[20] Colonel Brooks in a

---

[18] *Ibid.*, pp. 33-35. This information is taken from depositions of Pierre Rublo and Joseph Valentin who were witnesses in house investigations of charges of fraud brought against Brooks in negotiating the treaty with the Caddoes.

[19] Sibley to Austin, September 15, 1826, in Barker (ed), *The Austin Papers*, I, 1455-1456.

[20] *House Reports*, 27 Cong., 2 Sess., Doc. 1035, p. 96.

communication to the Secretary of War stated that he was enclosing a paper which he had obtained from the Caddo chief, purporting to be a grant of land made to the Caddo nation of Indians by a former governor at San Antonio.[21] The fact seems to be well established that the Spanish authorities had assigned a tract of land to the Caddo Indians, and that the Caddoes had been desirous of going since 1820, but their departure had been delayed by the presents given, and the promises made them by United States Indian agents.

During the first quarter of the nineteenth century the Caddoes were urged to remain on American soil, but by 1830 conditions had changed and they were then urged to sell their lands. In 1834 Brooks, in a letter to Judge E. Herring, commissioner of Indian affairs, said:

> Since the practicability of removing the obstructions to the navigation of Red River has been established, much excitement has been manifested respecting the river lands throughout the region of the raft, embracing a considerable scope of the Caddo territory, and is already a fruitful source of trouble to me and uneasiness to the nation. This state of things was anticipated by me from the first, and was the occasion of my suggesting to the President, when last at Washington, the necessity of extinguishing the Indian title to all such land prior to the removal of the raft. . . .
>
> As I have reason to believe that some branch of the Government has been addressed in regard to the lands, and as there are frequent attempts of late to encroach upon them, I have felt it my duty to apprise the register of lands for this district of the occurances, and now take leave to renew the suggestion, through you, whether it would not be best to negotiate for these lands at once, before the further progress of the work shall open the eyes of the tribe, as to their importance to the whites, or before their true interest shall be surrendered to the cupidity of the evil advisers who surrounded them.
>
> I beg, further to suggest that, if the Government approve of the above views, I believe the safest and best course of accomplishing the object will be between the Secretary of War and a delegation of the nation, at Washington City. By such a course of procedure, justice may be done between

---

[21] Brooks to Cass, November 9, 1835, in *House Reports*, 27 Cong., 2 Sess., Doc. 1035, p. 114. This paper was not found with the letter.

the parties without any of the embarrassments sure to attend a negotiation here."

In another letter to the commissioner of Indian affairs dated July 1, 1834, Brooks informed the commissioner that in anticipation of the speedy opening of the river navigation, speculators were flocking to, and settlements were being made on, the Caddo lands, regardless of government and Indian titles." Evidently Colonel Brooks had been urging the Caddoes to sell their lands in order to relieve the embarrassing situation that he related in his letters of March 20, and July 1, to the commissioner of Indian affairs, for in January 1835 they sent a memorial to the President of the United Stated indicating that they would sell their lands. In this memorial they informed the President that according to their traditions they were living in the same region they had inhabited since the first Caddo was created; that they had been promised by the French, the Spanish, and later the Americans that no white man would ever be permitted to settle on their lands; that the agent at Natchitoches in their first council with representatives of the United States had told them that they could not sell their lands to anybody except their great father, the President; that Brooks had informed them that they would no longer have an agent, gunsmith, or blacksmith and that he was at a loss to know what the government intended to do with them. In reply they said:

> This heavy news has put us in great trouble; we have held a great council, and finally come to the sorrowful resolution of offering all our lands to you which lie within the boundary of the United States for sale, at such price as we can agree on in council one with the other. . . ."

The Caddoes further urged that the President would expedite measures to treat with them in order that they might obtain relief from their deplorable condition.

---

²² Brooks to Herring, March 20, 1834, in *House Reports*, 27 Cong., 2 Sess., Doc. 1035. p. 113.
²³ *Ibid.*, p. 114.
²⁴ *Ibid.*, pp. 98.99.

II.

MAKING THE TREATY OF 1835

In March 1835 Colonel Brooks received instructions to treat with the Caddoes for their land. The instructions said:

> You will endeavor to procure a cession of their right to any land in that state. After considerable search and inquiry, I have not been able to ascertain, with precision, either the extent of the country occupied by them or the tenure by which it is held. The report of Colonel Many, a copy of which is enclosed, contains the best information in the possession of this Department on the subject.[25] It appears probable, from this report, and from an examination of the map, that after the boundary line between the United States and Mexico is permanently established, the district of country occupied by these Indians may contain from six hundred thousand . . . to one million . . . of acres. It is believed that the Caddo Indians are desirous of removing from the state of Louisiana, and their condition would be no doubt benefited by such removal.[26]

On June 3, 1835, Brooks employed Larkin Edwards who was interpreter for the Caddoes, to visit the Caddo villages and inform the chiefs and people of the Caddo nation of his arrival at the agency-house with instructions to treat with them for the purchase of their land; and that he had brought a great many presents for them, and expected them to assemble at the agency-house. On June 25, the Caddoes assembled to the number of four hundred and eighty-nine, men, women, and children, and, as instructed by Brooks, selected a council to represent them in negotiating the treaty. On June 26, the head chief, Tarshar, and underchief, Tsauninot, with twenty-three chosen councillors, met Brooks at twelve o'clock, and presented themselves as the chosen representatives of the Caddoes assembled, to listen to whatever he had to say

---

[25] Many's report said: "The result of my inquiries I now proceed to state: These Indians formerly lived higher up the river, in the vicinity of Kio Michie, but were driven from thence by the Osage Indians, upwards of thirty years since, when they set'led where some of them still reside. During Captain Grey's agency, he assigned to these Indians, by order of the Secretary of War, a tract of country lying on Red River, between the Sulphur fork and the Cypress bayou, and extending up those streams to their sources, and thence west to the Sabine. The Cypress bayou lies below Sulphur fork about sixty miles in a direct line. These Indians were to hold these lands during good behavior; they have no other claims to them that I can learn, except the occupancy of the thirty years. . . ."—Many to Kentz, January 6, 1835, in *House Reports,* 27 Cong., 2 Sess., Doc. 1035, pp. 95-96.

[26] Extract from the instructions to Colonel Jehiel Brooks, dated March 25, 1835, to treat with the Caddo Indians, in *House Reports,* 27 Cong., 2 Sess., Doc. 1035, p. 95.

to them, and to make such replies as justice to themselves might seem to require.   The council pipe was lighted and passed around, and Brooks proceeded without further ceremony to state the object of his present mission.

He told them that the President was pleased to hear that they were desirous of selling their lands, and had delegated him to arrange for a council and to make the transaction, provided they could reach an agreement as to the price and conditions of payment; that in the event of an agreement (as the land was to be purchased for the white settlers), the Caddoes would be required to remove within a reasonable time after the President had approved the bargain; that he had come prepared to make them an offer that would place them in a state of independence, compared with their present destitution; that he was aware of the fact that many people purporting to be their friends, had advised them not to depart with their lands, but he said, "I have never deceived you, and am again sent, as your friend, to obtain that from you which is of no manner of use to yourselves, and which the whites will soon deprive you of, right or wrong."[27]

After Brooks had informed them that his business had been stated, and that he awaited a reply, Tsauninot, underchief of the Caddoes in the absence of the chief, addressed them:

> Brothers: We salute you, and through you, our great father, who has sent you again with words of comfort to us.   We are in great want, and have been expecting you to bring us relief; for you told us, before you departed last fall, that you had no doubt our great father would treat with us for our country, and would supply us with things of much more value to us than these lands, which yield no game. . . . It is true that we have been advised by many not to make a treaty at all; that we would be cheated out of our land, and then driven away like dogs; and we have been promised a great deal if we refused to meet you in council. But we have placed no reliance on the advice and promises of these men, because we know what they want, and what they will do; and we have warned our people, from time to time, not to heed such tales, but wait and see what our great father would do for us.   We now know his wishes, and be-

---

[27] A journal of the proceedings at the agency-house, Caddo Nation, Louisiana, in forming and completing a treaty for the cession of land, between the Commissioner on the part of the United States and the Caddo nation of Indians, in *House Reports*, 27 Cong., 2 Sess., Doc. 1035, pp. 116-117.

lieve he will deal justly with us. We will therefore go and consult together, and let you know tomorrow morning what we are willing to do.[28]

After the council adjourned Brooks exhibited samples of goods intended for them, in the event they agreed to the treaty. In the afternoon he gave them presents, and informed them they were tokens of friendship, which had nothing to do with the bargain he wished to make for their land.

On June 27, the council convened at ten o'clock in the morning, and Tsauninot informed Brooks that when he communicated the proceedings of the council of June 26 to his people they hung down their heads and were sorrowful, after which their head chief, Tarshar, rose and said:

> My Children: For what do you mourn? Are you not starving in the midst of this land? And do you not travel far from it in quest of food? The game we live on is going farther off, and the white man is coming near to us; and is not our condition getting worse daily? Then why lament for the loss of that which yields us nothing but misery? Let us be wise then, and get all we can for it, and not wait till the white man steals it away, little by little, and then gives us nothing.[29]

After Tarshar's talk they all sprang to their feet with cries of satisfaction and voiced their agreement to sell their lands.

The Caddo council, having secured the consent of their people, were now ready to continue treaty negotiations. According to Brooks they requested him to make a reservation of four leagues of land in the southeast corner of their territory, bordering on the Red River to the heirs of Francois Grappe, and a reservation to Larkin Edwards anywhere within their territory that Edwards should select.[30]

Brooks informed the Caddoes that their great father, the President, and his head men were opposed to Indian reservations,

---

[28] *Ibid.*, p. 117.
[29] *Ibid.*, pp. 117-118.
[30] *House Reports*, 27 Cong., 2 Sess., Doc. 1035, pp. 117-118. In a memorial to the President previously referred to in this paper the Caddoes stated that many years ago they had made a gift of four leagues of land to Francois Grappe and his three sons, situated on the lowest corner of their land on Red River; that this gift was in writing, and ratified by the Spanish authority of Natchitoches.

for there were always bad men seeking every opportunity to cheat the Indian out of everything they possessed, but he would state their wishes relative to the grant in such a form that, if not approved, they would not effect the main bargain. Then Brooks and the Caddoes tried to reach an agreement on the price to be paid for their land, but as an agreement could not be reached at this time, the council adjourned until June 28.

On the morning of June 28, white men of suspicious characters were found within the Indian encampment, and were warned to depart. Captain Thomas J. Harrison, of the third regiment of United States infantry, was directed to post a chain of sentinels around the camp to guard it from all intrusions of the whites, and to allow no one to enter without a pass signed by the commissioner. A white man, Francois Bark,[31] was arrested soon afterward but discharged, on his promise that he would immediately depart, and not return among the Indians while they were engaged in making the treaty.[32]

On July 1, 1835, Brooks and the Indian council reached a satisfactory agreement on the price to be paid for their possession. This was the first treaty that the Caddoes had ever made with the United States. By agreement the Caddoes were to relinquish to the United States all their land contained in the following boundaries:

> Bounded on the west by the north and south line which separates the United States from . . . Mexico, between the Sabine and Red River wheresoever the same shall be defined and acknowledged to be by the two governments. On the north and east by the Red river, from the point where the said north and south boundary line shall intersect the Red river whether it be in the territory of Arkansas or the State of Louisiana, following the meanders of the said river down to its junction with the Pascagoula bayou. On the south by the said Pascagoula bayou to its junction with Bayou Wallace, by said Bayou and Lake Wallace to the mouth of the Cypress bayou thence up said bayou to the point of its intersection with the first mentioned north and south lines, following the meanders of the said water-courses; but if the said Cypress be not clearly definable, so far then from

---

[31] Francois Bark was an old Frenchman, who had spent the greater part of his life with the Caddoes, but not to their benefit. He was very hostile to the Anglo-Americans.—*Ibid.*, p. 119.

[32] *Ibid.*, p. 119.

a point which shall be definable by a line due west, till it intersects the first mentioned north and south boundary line. . . ."[33]

They further agreed to remove at their own expense from the boundaries of the United States within one year after the signing of the treaty. The United States agreed to pay the Caddoes eighty thousand dollars, thirty thousand to be paid in goods on the signing of the treaty, and ten thousand dollars in money on September 1, 1836, then ten thousand dollars per year for four years.

In the articles supplementary to the treaty it was agreed that the legal representatives of Francois Grappe, deceased, and his three sons Jacques, Dominique, and Belthazar Grappe, should receive four leagues of land located in the southeast corner of the lands ceded to the United States. It was further agreed that Larkin Edwards and his heirs should receive one section of land to be selected from the lands ceded to the United States by the Caddo Indians.[33]

John W. Edwards, the interpreter, translated the treaty and supplementary treaty into the Caddo language. After he had finished, each member of the council was asked if he understood the interpreter clearly, and if he was ready to sign his name to the document, all of which being answered in the affirmative, the formality of signing was concluded in the presence of several witnesses. After the pipe was passed around, and congratulations exchanged between Brooks and the Caddo representatives on having concluded the treaty, they shook hands and separated in friendship.[34]

By July 10, all the goods and horses, amounting to thirty thousand dollars, had been delivered to the chiefs and head men of the Caddo nation, in compliance with the third article of the treaty. Brooks said that the Indians appeared to be well satisfied with the goods received, and with the whole proceeding, from the beginning to the end.[35] The treaty was ratified by the United States Senate on January 26, 1836, and signed by President Andrew Jackson, on February 2, 1836.[36]

---

[33] *Senate Documents*, 57 Cong., 1 Sess., Doc. 452, p. 320.
[33] *Ibid.*, pp. 320-322.
[34] *House Reports*, 27 Cong., 2 Sess., Doc. 1035, p. 120.
[35] *Ibid.*
[36] *Ibid.*, pp. 77-78.

III.

RESULTS OF THE TREATY

On February 6, 1840, Samuel Norris, an inhabitant of Rush Island, brought a charge of fraud against Jehiel Brooks who had negotiated the treaty with the Caddo Indians July 1, 1835. The cession which had been made to the Grappes was used by Norris as a basis for this charge. He claimed that at the time of the treaty this land was inhabited by Samuel Norris, Lefroy Dupree, and other persons. He also asserted that a short time after the treaty was negotiated, the whole of the reservation made in favor of the Grappes, had been purchased from them by Jehiel Brooks for six thousand dollars. This reservation, it was alleged by Norris, was a fraud upon the United States and on those who occupied the land at the time of the treaty. He charged that Rush Island, on which the reservation in favor of the Grappes was located by the treaty, was not within the limits of the country claimed by the Caddoes; that no land had ever been granted by the Caddoes to the said Grappes, and the reservation of the four leagues of land was fraudulently introduced into the treaty without the knowledge or consent of the Indians.[37]

In a memorial of the chiefs, head men, and warriors of the Caddo nation, dated September 19, 1837, and addressed to the Senate of the United States, they stated that the treaty made between them and Brooks had recently been interpreted to them and they discovered that the boundaries and limits of the treaty were not the same as understood by them in 1835; that the lands sold by them were:

> Bounded on the west by the north and south line which separates the United States from Mexico (running) between the Sabine and Red rivers, wheresoever the same shall be defined to be by the two goverments; on the north and east by the Red river, from the point where the aforesaid north and south boundary line shall intersect said Red river, following the western waters of said Red river down to where the bayou Cypress empties into the said river; thence up the bayou Cypress, following the meanders of the stream, to the western boundary line.[38]

---

[37] *Ibid.*, pp. 1-2.
[38] *House Report*, 27 Cong., 2 Sess., Doc. 1035, pp. 103-104.

They further stated that they had never claimed any of the low lands between Bayou Pierre (the western channel of Red River) and the main Red River; that they knew the land between Bayou Pierre and the main channel of the Red River had for a long time been exclusively settled and claimed by the white people. They further stated that the Caddo Indians did not make a reservation in favor of the Grappes within the limits of land they claimed or sold to the United States.[39]

The committee on Indian affairs, after a thorough investigation of the charges brought against Brooks, reported that the tract of land called Rush Island, described in the treaty with the Caddoes, was never a part of their territory. They recommended that the question of fraud involved in making the reservation to the Grappes be referred to the courts.[40]

The treaty was allowed to stand and by it the United States government obtained a cession from the Caddoes of about one million acres of land.[41]

This land was purchased for the white settlers who were already encroaching upon the Caddo country regardless of the trade and intercourse laws. The cession was no doubt highly regarded by the settlers, but it left in the minds of the Caddoes a contempt for the whites who had made it necessary that they dispose of their territory.

CHAPTER V.

THE CADDO IN TEXAS, 1836-1845

With the acquisition of Louisiana by the United States, and with the removal of the great raft on the Red river, immigrants flocked into the Caddo country and pushed the Indians from their old haunts. According to the treaty of 1835 the Caddo ceded all their land and agreed to move at their own expense beyond the boundaries of the United States, never to return and settle as a

---

[39] *House Reports*, 27 Cong., 2 Sess., Doc. 1035, pp. 103-104.
[40] Extract from the Journal of the Committee on Indian Affairs of the House of Representatives, July 23, 1842, *House Reports*, 27 Cong., 2 Sess., Doc. 1035, p. 19.
[41] *Senate Documents*, 24 Cong., 2 Sess., Doc. 1, p. 424.

tribe. Thus the tribes living in Louisiana, being forced to leave their old home, gradually moved southwest and joined their kindred living in Texas.

I.

RELATIONS WITH THE TEXAS COLONISTS

The second article of the treaty of 1835 stipulated that the Caddo should move without the boundaries of the United States within one year after the signing of the treaty. Their plan to move into Texas was interrupted by the outbreak of the Texas revolution in October, 1835, and by the request of the Texans that the United States government prohibit the Caddoes from moving into their country.[1] In March, 1836, John T. Mason of Nacogdoches wrote Major Nelson, commander at Fort Jesup, as follows:

> Travis and all his men captured and murdered. An apprehension of a serious character exists here that the Indians are assembling to fall upon this frontier, particularly those from the United States. I have taken pains to inform myself of the facts, and I have no doubt they have been prepared to move in the event of Santa Anna's success. He is determined to wage a war of extermination against Texas, and has engaged the Indians to aid him. The Committee of Vigilance here will address you on the subject of the threatened danger from the Indians. Is it not in your power to send a messenger to them, particularly the Caddoes, to make them keep quiet? To the extent of your authority, every principle of humanity and safety to the inhabitants of both borders requires an exertion of your powers to avert the disaster of an Indian war; and I have no doubt you will exert all your energies to that end.[2]

General Edmund P. Gaines, who had been ordered by the Secretary of War to the western frontier of the state of Louisiana to take charge,[3] arrived at Natchitoches on April 4, 1836, where he at once began an investigation of border conditions.[4] He said:

---

[1] Hodge, *Handbook*, I, 180. In October, 1835, actual hostilities were begun between the Texans and a Mexican force. On March 2, 1836, a convention of delegates definitely declared Texas to be independent of Mexican control.

[2] Mason to Nelson, March 20, 1836, *House Ex. Docs.*, 25 Cong., 2 Sess., Doc. 351, pp. 773-774.

[3] Jones to Gaines, February 22, 1836, *House Ex. Docs.*, 25 Cong., 2 Sess., Doc. 351, p. 767.

[4] Marshall, *The Western Boundary of the Louisiana Purchase, 1819-1841*, p. 148.

The 33d article of the treaty with Mexico requires both
the contracting parties to prevent, by force, all hostilities
and incursions on the part of the Indian nations living within their respective boundaries, so that the United States of
America will not suffer their Indians to attack the citizens
of the Mexican States.

He had been instructed to enforce the provisions of that
article, and to make known to the Indians inhabiting that part
of the United States along the Red and Arkansas rivers, the determination of the government to prevent any hostile incursions
into Texas. He had learned from citizens that Manuel Flores,
a Mexican resident of Spanish Town near Natchitoches, had been
lately commissioned by persons professing to act by the authority
of the Mexican government, to persuade the Indians in the western
prairies on the United States side of the boundary line to join
Mexico in the war in Texas; and that with this in view, Flores,
accompanied by a stranger, had lately passed up the valley of the
Red River, and had already produced considerable excitement
among the Caddo Indians. He further stated:

> These facts and circumstances present to me the im-
> portant question, whether I am to sit still and suffer these
> movements to be so far matured as to place the white settle-
> ments, on both sides of the line, wholly within the power of
> the savages; or whether I ought not instantly to prepare
> the means for protecting the frontier settlements, and, if
> necessary, compelling the Indians to return to their own
> homes and hunting grounds? I cannot but decide in favor
> of the last alternative which this question presents; for
> nothing can be more evident than that an Indian war, com-
> mencing on either side of the line, will as surely extend to
> both sides as that a lighted quick-match thrust into one
> side of a powder-magazine would extend the explosion to
> both sides.[5]

The Indian situation on both sides of the border caused a
great deal of fear and excitement. The Cherokees and their associated bands of eastern Texas, who had been for a long time legal
contestants of the whites for lands, were very restless. A fear
that the Caddo and other tribes from north of Red River would
join the Texas Indians was an added terror, it being known that

---

[5] Gaines to the Governors of Louisiana, Mississippi, Alabama, and Tennessee, April 8,
1836, *House Ex. Docs.*, 25 Cong., 2 Sess., Doc. 351, pp. 770-771.

Manuel Flores had been among the Red river Indians trying to incite them to attack the settlements. The committee of vigilance and safety at San Augustine reported to the citizens that large bodies of Caddo, Shawnee, Delaware, Kickappo, Cherokee, Creek, and other tribes were assembling at the three forks of the Trinity to make war on the inhabitants of the frontier. On April 1, Mason wrote to Gaines that the settlers had no protection except that afforded by the soldiers of the United States. All of the tribes of the Missouri and Arkansas frontier, as well as the immigrant Indians of Texas who had been deprived of their lands, would be glad to enter into a war against the whites.[6]

The committee of vigilance and safety at Nacogdoches appointed C. H. Sims, William Sims, and M. B. Menard as agents to visit the tribes north of Nacogdoches and ascertain their intentions. C. H. Sims stated that he had visited the Cherokee, thirty miles west of Nacogdoches, and found them hostile and prepared for war, and they had informed him that a large body of Caddo, Kichai, Inies, Towakanas, Waco, and Comanche were to attack the settlements. News also came from James and Ralph Chesher, who were in command of a military company, that a Mexican and Indian force conducted by the Caddo had already crossed the Trinity river and that Nacogdoches was in danger. R. A. Irion, acting commandant of Nacogdoches, notified Mason that the news of the movements of the Indians had been confirmed, and that on April 10, a large force led by the Caddo, had encamped at the Sabine sixty miles north of Nacogdoches. The inhabitants were leaving the town and were planning to assemble at Attagas or San Augustine.[7]

While these conditions prevailed at Nacogdoches, Gaines was making an effort to find out the true state of affairs among the Caddoes. J. Bonnell, a lieutenant in the Third Infantry, was sent to the Caddo villages to ascertain facts relative to reports concerning the conduct of these Indians. On April 20, Bonnell reported at Camp Sabine after he had visited the Caddo villages, where he was informed by the Caddo chief and warriors, through his interpreter, that Manuel Flores had recently been among them en-

---

[6] Marshall, *The Western Boundary of the Louisiana Purchase, 1819-1841*, pp. 148-150.
[7] *Ibid.*, 150, 152, 153. Depositions of C. H. and William Sims, Menard, and letter of James and Ralph Chesher to the Committee of Vigilance and Safety of Nacogdoches, all of April 11, 1836, *House Ex. Docs.*, 25 Cong., 2 Sess., Doc. 351, pp. 775-776. Irion to Mason, April 12, 1836, *ibid.*, 781.

deavoring to persuade them to go with him into Texas to kill and plunder the white inhabitants. Flores told them that he held a commission from the Mexican government and promised them free plunder if they would go with him; that the Spaniards (Mexicans) wished all the Americans (white inhabitants of Texas) destroyed; that all the Americans in Texas were deserters from their own country. At the first village Bonnell found only two or three squaws and a few children, the warriors having gone to the prairies because Flores had told them that the Americans were going to kill them. Bonnell sent for the few warriors who were found in the neighborhood and assured them that the Americans were their friends, and wished them to return to their villages and live in peace, and hunt on their own grounds as usual. The Indians declared that Flores had made no impression on their loyalty and that they had heard so many reports they did not know what to believe; they were now glad to know the truth.

At the second village, twelve miles further, Bonnell found Chief Cortes and several warriors who said that when the principal chief led the men to the prairies to hunt, he (Cortes) had told them not to disturb the whites. He promised to notify the Indians on the prairies and requested that Gaines be informed that if the Caddoes should see the Americans and Spaniards fighting, they would not take part on either side. Cortes further said that when the Caddoes left for the prairies to hunt they were friendly to the whites.

When Bonnell returned to the first village he learned that Flores had passed through the village accompanied by "a thick, short man, about middle-aged, who had formerly lived at Nacogdoches," and that there were three Mexicans then on the prairies hunting with the Indians. One Indian said that had it not been for the lies that Flores told them, the Caddoes would long since have returned and planted their corn. This Indian said that the tribe would not wage a war against the whites, but admitted that Flores was then hunting with the Caddoes on the prairies, that he had gone with them since he could not prevail upon them to go with him.[8]

---

[8] Bonnell to Gaines, April 20, 1836, *House Ex. Docs.*, 25 Cong., 2 Sess., Doc. 351, pp. 774-775.

Marshall says:

> Three of the circumstances brought out in Bonnell's report tend to confirm the opinion that the Caddo were in league with the Cherokee in spite of all their friendly protestations; the first striking fact is the absence of the warriors; the second, that the Indians had done nothing toward their corn planting, an operation which the squaws usually performed; and third, the fact that the Mexican emissaries were admitted to be with the warriors.[9]

If the Caddoes had promised the Cherokees to join them against the settlers of Texas, Bonnell's visit evidently influenced them to change their minds, for on May 13, the Caddo chiefs requested Larkin Edwards who had lived among them for thirteen years and had been their interpreter for six years, to write to Gaines in their behalf. In this letter Edwards said:

> A Mexican or Frenchman named Manuel Flores, an emissary of the Mexican Government, has been for some time past residing among the Caddo Indians, and by promises of large sums of money attempted to embroil the Indians in the war between the Mexican Government and Texas. This I know to be the fact, as he is commissioned by the Mexican Government for the purpose of exciting·the Caddoes to war against the Texians. . . . The emissary, Manuel Flores, informed them that the American Government intended to exterminate them. . . . The Cherokees of Texas, they [Caddoes] also inform me, have attempted to make them a part with them against the Texians.[10]

Flores remained among the Caddoes and Sterling C. Robertson reported that his promises of Mexican gold had a great deal to do with inciting them to acts of hostility against the settlers. On June 16, several depredations occurred in the Robertson colony. James Dunn, the regidor of the municipality of Milam, testified that having heard of the massacre at Parker's fort, on the Navasota River in which several persons had been killed by the Kiowa and Comanche Indians, he prepared to move to Nashville, on the Brazos, with a view of "forting" and that he, with Henry Walker and William Smith, were attacked by about fifty Indians. They wounded Smith, killed his horse, killed many cattle and drove the

---

[9] Marshall, *The Western Boundary of the Louisiana Purchase, 1819-1841*, p. 156.
[10] Edwards to Gaines, May 13, 1836, *House Ex. Docs.*, 25 Cong., 2 Sess., Doc. 351, pp. 814.815.

remainder away. Half of the Indians proceeded about a mile and a half away and attacked other settlers in the neighborhood killing two of them.

It was Dunn's belief that about half the Indians who attacked them were Caddoes because the Caddoes wore shirts which were rarely worn by any of the tribes of Indians living in Texas; they had a peculiar manner of wearing their hair, having it cut closely on both sides of the head, and leaving a "top-knot," which was generally worn in a silver tube, "and that they had silver in their nose;" furthermore, he recognized Douchey, a Caddo chief, among the assailants. Montgomery B. Shackleford, one of the settlers who had been attacked, confirmed the testimony given by Dunn. Robertson sent the depositions of Dunn and Shackleford to Gaines, calling attention to the fact that the Caddoes, whom the United States by treaty obligations should restrain from lawless violence, rapine, plunder, and murder, were participants, if not leaders, in the attacks that had recently been made upon the citizens of the frontier. Robertson further said that many citizens had been murdered and much property had been taken by the Caddoes, and that helpless women and children were now in their possession as prisoners, subject to their cruel treatment. He appealed to the sympathies of Gaines,—"Already we hear from lisping infancy and weary and withered age throughout this wide-spreading republic, that you are a friend of Texas. If the facts as stated will justify your march against the Caddoes, the country, we trust, will shortly be relieved from Indian hostility."[11]

On June 22, Gaines answered Robertson's letter, saying that the depositions established beyond a doubt the lamentable fact that the murders to which they referred had been perpetrated by the Indians of Texas or its vicinity, but it was not clear that the Caddoes were among the offenders; yet he thought the evidence sufficient to justify an immediate investigation of the matter.[12]

Spy Buck, an Indian of the Shawnee tribe, testified before a meeting of the committee of safety at Nacogdoches that he had heard from his uncle that a number of Indians, including the Kichai, Towakanas, and Caddoes, had recently killed, at one time,

---

[11] Robertson to Gaines, June 16, 1836, with copies of the depositions of Dunn and Shackleford of June 15, in *House Ex. Docs.*, 25 Cong., 2 Sess., Doc. 351, pp. 792-794.
[12] Gaines to Robertson, June 22, 1836, *House Ex. Docs.*, 25. Cong., 2 Sess, Doc. 351, p. 794.

eight Americans, four or five miles below the old Delaware town on Red River.[13]

As a result of these reported hostilities an effort was made by Bonnell and the Texan Indian agent Menard to ascertain the true Indian situation. On August 9 Menard reported to Samuel Houston at Nacogdoches that the Cherokee, Biloxi, Choctaw, Alabama, and Caddo were very hostile, and he believed they would soon begin incursions against the settlements.[14] Bonnell sent the reports of Menard to Gaines, adding that they had been confirmed by Michael Sacco, a Frenchman.

Major B. Riley was sent among the Caddo to make a thorough investigation. He visited four of the Caddo villages or settlements and saw between one hundred and twenty and one hundred and thirty men of the different villages. Riley found them peaceably inclined, very much degraded, and addicted to the use of liquor, and if they had committed depredations on the inhabitants, or their property, it was caused by the use of too much whiskey, which appeared to be in abundance in and about their villages. They seemed to be "a poor, miserable people, incapable of the smallest exertion, either as it regards living, or any thing else except liquor." The Caddo chief, Tarshar, or the "Wolf", told Riley that they wanted to live in peace with the whites and did not want to go to war. He said that Flores had been trying to persuade his nation to move to Texas, but they had refused to go.[15]

After July 1, 1836, it appears that the Caddoes proceeded to carry out their treaty obligations with the United States. Until that time Gaines had insisted that they remain in their old villages near Shreveport and refrain from committing depredations on the settlements in Texas. Some of the bands immediately migrated into Texas, while others, taking advantage of the unsettled state of the boundary between Texas and the United States, and of the unsettled conditions in Texas as a consequence of the revolution, continued to live in the Caddo Lake region until about 1840 when they, too, joined their brethren in Texas. The Caddoes associated themselves with the prairie Indians in Texas and combined with

---

[13] Raguet to Bonnell, July 19, 1836, *House Ex. Docs.*, 25 Cong., 2 Sess., Doc. 351, pp. 797-798.

[14] Marshall, *Western Boundary of the Louisiana Purchase, 1819-1841*, pp. 180-181.

[15] Riley to Gaines, May 13, 1836, *House Ex. Docs.*, 25 Cong., 2 Sess., Doc. 351, pp. 815-818.

them in waging warfare against the white settlements.[16] In August, Henry M. Morfit appointed by President Jackson to ascertain the political, military, and civil condition of Texas, reported that about five hundred Caddoes "have lately migrated from the borders of the United States towards the Trinidad, and who, a few weeks ago, destroyed the village of Bastross."[17]

In January, 1837, according to Kenney, a force of Caddoes, estimated at more than a hundred, invaded the settlements on Little River, west of the Brazos, where they were encountered by Captain Erath with fourteen men. The white men surprised their camp on the bank of Elm Creek at daylight and killed several. The Caddoes being armed with rifles made a counter attack in which they defeated the whites, killing three, and wounding several others, besides losing ten of their warriors. They were forced to retreat because of a great storm of sleet and snow; but, being disappointed because they had failed to get scalps and plunder, they soon returned and murdered several settlers along the frontier as far west as the Colorado.[18] Another report stated that they had murdered Captain Beaston and several persons who were in company with him on the Guadalupe River. It was also reported that a family consisting of an old man, his wife, and several children, living thirty miles north of Nashville had been killed by the Caddoes.[19]

In a report to Memucan Hunt, dated September 20, 1837, Irion said:

> The line of the Sabine and Red River frontier is not the scene of the depredations of the Caddoes; their acts of violence are perpetrated on the Trinity, Brazos, Colorado, Guadalupe, etc., far distant from the place of their ordinary abode. In almost every skirmish that occurs on our western frontier Caddoes are recognized. They have in several instances, been shot in the act of stealing horses and murdering the Texians. They are not formidable on account of numbers but from their influence with the prairie tribes.[20]

---

[16] Jones to Forsayth, December 31, 1836, *Senate Doc.*, 32 Cong., 2 Sess., Doc. 14, pp. 11-12.

[17] *Congressional Debates*, XIII, Pt. 2, app., 87.

[18] M. M. Kenney, "The History of the Indian Tribes of Texas," in Dudley G. Wooten, *A Comprehensive History of Texas, 1685-1897*, I, 749.

[19] Henderson to Wharton and Hunt, January 21, 1837, in Garrison (Ed.) *Texan Diplomatic Correspondence*, I, 178.

[20] Irion to Hunt, September 20, 1837, *ibid.*, I, 260.

According to Kenney, the Caddoes murdered the Goacher family (in what is now Lee County) in 1837 and took a Mrs. Crawford with an infant two months old and two other children as captives to their villages on Red River. He related the following incident concerning these captives:

> Becoming tired of hearing the infant cry, they snatched it from its mother and threw it into a deep pool of water. The mother followed and brought it out. The Indians seized it and threw it back, and, amused at the frantic efforts of the mother to save it from drowning, continued the sport for some time. At length one of them took the babe and, drawing back its head, told another to cut its throat, which he was about to do, when the mother, nerved by desperation, seized a billet of wood, which chanced to be near at hand, and knocked him down. She expected instant death, but, instead of the expected resentment, the Indians laughed loudly at their fallen comrade, and one of them gave her the child, saying, "Squaw too much brave . . . take your pappoose and carry it yourself." They did not attempt to injure it afterwards. After two years the captives were ransomed from them at Coffee's trading-house on Red River and returned to their kindred.[21]

In 1837 Colonel Many sent an officer to make inquiries concerning the robberies and murders supposed to have been committed by Indians from the United States. This officer reported that all the depredations committed had been by Indians in the interior of Texas, and by small straggling bands, none of whom belonged to the United States, except the Caddoes; and "that he did not know why they had been regarded as United States Indians, as their principal villages had always been considered within the limits of Texas." He further reported that the Caddoes denied having committed any depredations on the whites, and appeared very anxious to be on friendly terms with them; "that there were but two well-attested cases against the Caddoes—one of robbery, and the other of murder—for which they had provocation in (the fact that) several of their tribe had been killed by the whites."[22] Colonel Many and the officer he sent to the Caddo village failed to take into account the fact that more than half of the Caddoes had already migrated into Texas.

---

[21] Kenney, "The History of the Indian Tribes of Texas," in Wooten, *History of Texas,* I, 749.

[22] Abstract of correspondence and documents on file in the Department of Indian Affairs, Washington, D. C., *Senate Documents,* 32 Cong., 2 Sess., Doc. 14, p. 59.

II.

CADDO RELATIONS WITH THE REPUBLIC OF TEXAS

Houston wrote to the Secretary of State of Texas on March 1, 1837, requesting him to urge upon the United States the necessity of keeping the Caddoes peaceful.

> The Secretary of State will write to the Government of the United States, and urge in the strongest terms the necessity of sending a force, and at least two companies of mounted men, from the United States, to keep the Caddoes in check besides an infantry force at Nacogdoches.
> The last treaty between them, and the United States, threw them upon us, with feelings of hostility against all Americans. They regard us as a part of the American family.
> The treaty (with Mexico, 1831) demands all we solicit. Our demand should be heard.[23]

On June 26, R. A. Irion, Secretary of the State of Texas, wrote Memucan Hunt, Minister at Washington, that the Caddoes were intruders in Texas, that they were allowed to come in flagrant violation of treaty stipulations between Mexico and the United States, and that they seemed to be the leaders of the hostile bands. He instructed Hunt to solicit the early attention of the United States government to this subject, and to endeavor to get the Caddoes removed from Texas. He said, "offer as a theater for military operations, should they attempt their removal from Texas, a free passage for troops as far as the Trinity; and the privilege of establishing depots, [and] Garrisons . . . anywhere east of that river."[24]

On September 20, 1837, a joint committee had been appointed by the Congress of Texas with instructions to report a bill for the protection of the eastern frontier. After having taken into consideration the suggestions of Houston and of the Secretary of War this committee recommended active operations against the hostile Indians of the borders.

> That several of the tribes near the extreme settlements have been and still are hostile, is too notorious to require a

---

[23] Muckleroy, "The Indian Policy of the Republic of Texas," in *Southwestern Historical Quarterly*, XXVI, 24.
[24] Irion to Hunt, June 26, 1837, in Garrison (ed.) *Texas Diplomatic Correspondence*, I, 233.

detailed statement of fact to prove it. Among those tribes are embraced the Caddos, Wacos, Tiwachanes, Keechies, Iones, and Pawnees, whose murders and depredations are of almost daily occurrence. The Caddos who exercise a controlling influence over these tribes, and with whom they are in some degree incorporated, recently received on Red River, from the agent of the United States government, ammunition and rifles, and immediately thereafter set off for Texas, to join their confederates on the Trinity and Brazos, which has doubtless inspired the latter with increased confidence. Within the last few days we have received from various sources, satisfactory information, that these Indians have penetrated even below the San Antonio road, having murdered several citizens on the Brazos, Trinity, and Neches rivers. Those incursions of late are becoming more daring, and we are decidedly of the opinion that unless the means of repelling their aggressions be not speedily increased . . . their attacks, robberies, and murders, will spread extensively, and probably in the end, if not checked by judicious measures, will shortly involve the whole country in a disasterous Indian war. To avert this state of things, your committee advise that an expedition, composed of a suitable force, sufficiently numerous to scour their country, thoroughly, be as soon as practicable sent against them.[25]

This report clearly shows the policy to be pursued towards the border Indians, especially the Caddoes. The Texas officials from the beginning considered the Caddoes intruders. This point is confirmed in a report from John Bell, Secretary of War, to Daniel Webster, Secretary of State.[26] The United States government had the same attitude towards the Republic that it had taken towards the Mexican government. In a communication dated October, 1835, it was stated that, "unless Indians migrating into Mexico manifested a hostile intent, it was doubtful whether, under the 33d article of the treaty (treaty with Mexico 1831), the intervention of the United States could be claimed or afforded; that if they went there with peaceable intentions, it was for the Mexican government alone to decide upon their admission or exclusion".[27] As a consequence of this declaration, the officials of the Republic of Texas endeavored to convince the officials of the United States

---

[25] *Journal of House of Representatives* (of Texas), 1 Cong., 2 Sess., 50-51.
[26] Report from Bell to Webster, September 11, 1841, in *Senate Ex. Docs.*, 32 Cong., 2 Sess., Doc. 14, pp. 59-66. This report contains an abstract of the correspondence between the war department and Texas officials relative to Indian intrusions into Texas from 1837 to 1841.
[27] Abstract of letter from Department of State to the Mexican Minister, October 22, 1835, in *Senate Ex. Docs.*, 32 Cong., 2 Sess., Doc. 14, p. 61.

that the Caddoes entered Texas with hostile intentions. The Secretary of State received a number of communications from the Republic of Texas during the years 1837 and 1838 on the subject of the murders and depredations committed on the white settlements by the Caddoes. In 1838 the Secretary of War of the United States received a communication from Felix Huston stating that the Caddo and other Indians had joined "the rebel Mexicans;" and that they were within one day's march of Nacogdoches. Colonel Many, who was in charge of the United States troops on the western frontier, having been instructed to make an investigation, said, "there had been good grounds for fearing such an attack, but the danger was over." He further reported that Indians from the United States had not been connected with the affair, but the Indians implicated had lived in Texas for several years.[28]

As the Texas officials failed to get action from the United States relative to the removal of the Caddoes, and as the Indians continued their intrusions into Texas, General Rusk decided to drive them out of Texas. General J. H. Dyer with eighty men marched near the Caddo village on the western fork of the Trinity on October 21, 1838. Very few Indians could be found, but in a skirmish he killed six Caddoes and two of his men were wounded. He declared that if necessary, he would summon his entire force to protect the frontier from the Caddoes and other tribes.[29]

H. McLeod, Adjutant General, under instructions from Rusk sent a communication to Charles A. Sewell, United States Indian agent at Shreveport, on November 21, saying, that he had been informed that the Caddo Indians had been paid their late annuity in arms and ammunition, that in several recent engagements with the Caddo in the territory of Texas it had been discovered that they had new United States arms in their possession. He further said:

> The fact that the Caddoes have for more than twelve months past, been depredating upon the lives and property of the people of Texas, cannot be unknown to you . . . and Sir, that you as agent of the United States Government, should, under such circumstances . . . furnish these savages

---

[28] Abstract of letter from Many to Secretary of War, August 18, 1838, *Senate Ex. Docs.,* 32 Cong., 2 Sess., Doc. 14, pp. 60-61. Many enclosed letter from Huston.
[29] Dyer to Mayfield, October 21, 1838, Gulick (ed), *Lamar Papers,* II, 257.

with the means of murdering the defenceless women and children, of Texas, is a matter of the greatest astonishment.[30]

On the same day McLeod wrote Lamar that Sewell had not only furnished arms to the Caddoes, but had said that he did not care if they murdered every woman and child in Texas, and that he would arm them and push them across the line.[31]

This controversy with Sewell, coupled with the hostilities of the Caddoes, influenced Rusk to invade the United States territory. Rusk and McLeod went from Nacogdoches to Clarksville, on Red River, on November 16, to join Dyer in a campaign to the head waters of the Trinity and Brazos Rivers. On their way, near Caddo Lake, they found Captain Tarrant on the march with his company to attack the Caddoes. He had been ordered by Dyer to expel them from Texas territory or destroy them. Rusk halted and took charge of the operation in person. When they reached the Caddo camp, the Indians fortified themselves for battle, but their chief said they wished to talk and not to fight. Rusk ordered him to advance and met him between the lines. The chief stated his ostracised condition, having been bought out and expelled by the United States, and now being denied a right to hunt or live in Texas. Rusk acknowledged the hardship of his case and offered to support his people in Louisiana until the Indian war in Texas was terminated. The chief agreed, but his horses and families being on the other side of the lake, he could not go at once. Rusk exchanged hostages with him, taking a Caddo chief and leaving McLeod in the Indian camp.

The next day Rusk and the chief met at the agency in Shreveport, and after some discussion and much opposition on the part of Sewell and citizens of Shreveport, the arrangement was concluded.[32] The Indians gave up their guns to Sewell with whom they were to remain until the war with their tribe on the frontier of Texas was terminated. Rusk bound the government of Texas to pay for the subsistence of the Indians until the two governments could settle the matter. The Caddoes were to remain in

---

[30] McLeod to Sewell, November 21, 1838, *Lamar Papers*, II, 296.
[31] McLeod to Lamar, November 21, 1838, *Lamar Papers*, II, 298-299.
[32] Rusk to Secretary of War, December 1, 1838; MS. in *Indian Affairs Papers*, Texas State Library.

Louisiana for such time as Sewell should direct. No Texas citizen, under any pretence, would be allowed to molest or destroy their property.[33]

This band of the Caddo tribe had been accused of making intrusions into Texas and retreating to the United States for protection. The larger part of the tribe had migrated to Texas under the leadership of Chief Tarshar,[34] and had joined the wild Indians at the three forks of the Trinity. After Rusk had made the agreement with the band of Caddoes at Shreveport, he proceeded to join Dyer for a campaign against the Indians on the Trinity River.[35] In January, 1839, he encountered the Caddoes in the cross timbers west of the Trinity River and burned their villages.[36]

Lamar's policy of extermination caused much suffering among the Caddoes, but it did not put an end to their acts of hostility. In 1839 a Mrs. Webster had been captured by the Comanches but finally made her escape and had arrived within thirty miles of Austin when she was recaptured by the Caddoes and delivered into the hands of those who had first taken her.[37] The Caddoes continued acts of hostility on the settlements, but no doubt the chastising they received from the operations of Rusk made them feel the horrors of war and welcome peace at any price.

III.

CADDOES MAKE PEACE WITH TEXAS

When Houston became president in 1841, most of the Caddoes and associated bands had retired east of the Red River whence they sent war parties to ravage and plunder the frontiers. He sent commissioners to that region for the purpose of establishing amicable relations with any and all Indians on the frontiers of Texas.[38] An indication that the time was ripe for negotiations is

---

[33] Treaty with Caddoes, November 29, 1838, at Shreveport, Louisiana, MS, in *Rusk Papers*, Archives, University of Texas.

[34] Tarshar was head chief of the Caddoes at the making of the treaty in 1835. He had persuaded his people to sell their lands, because he said that the white man was stealing them piece by piece.

[35] McLeod to Lamar, November 21, 1838, *Lamar Papers*, II, 298-299.

[36] *Map of Texas*, 1839, Compiled by Richard S. Hunt, and Jesse F. Handel, Archives, University of Texas.

[37] Extract of a letter from Liscomb to Bee, August 8, 1840, in Garrison (ed.) *Texas Diplomatic Correspondence*, I, 464.

[38] William Carey Crane, *The Life and Select Literary Remains of Sam Houston*, 314.

shown by a letter written to the Caddo Chief, Red Bear, by the
Muskogee chief, on July 20, 1842. He advised the Caddoes to be
friendly with the whites, and to prevail upon their neighbors to
cease hostility against the Texans.[39] Red Bear wrote to R. M.
Jones at Boggy Depot, Texas, inquiring about the possibility of
making peace with the government of Texas. Jones informed
him that Houston had already appointed commissioners for that
purpose:

> The Government of Texas by her commissioners propose
> to meet you and such other tribes as shall wish, and make
> a permanent peace, and will allow the Red men to return
> to their old Hunting Grounds in Texas, and will appoint
> agents for their different tribes to watch over their interest
> and will establish trading houses convenient to their Hunt-
> ing Grounds where they can barter their skins for clothing
> and other articles of comfort that they may need.[40]

Jones notified the commissioners that the Caddoes were anxious to make peace with Texas. Arrangements were made to meet
the chiefs, head men, and warriors of four different tribes at the
Caddo village above the Chickasaw nation. On August 26, 1842,
a treaty was made with the Indians. The four tribes present at
this council promised to visit the hostile tribes and to persuade
these to meet the President and the commissioners on October 26,
1842, at Waco village on the Brazos.[41]

The commissioners attended, but for some reason the Indians
were unable to attend. Houston believed that the high waters,
the inclemency of the weather, and the buffalo ranging further
south than usual explained the failure of the Indians to appear at
the appointed council grounds. Houston said, "If a treaty is once
concluded, and good faith maintained on the part of the people
of Texas, there can be no doubt that friendly relations will be
maintained with the Indians."[42] Finally arrangements were made
to hold a council at Tawakano Creek in the latter part of March,
1843. The commissioners representing Texas were G. W. Terrell,
J. S. Black, T. J. Smith, with T. Bryson as secretary, P. M. Butler

[39] Muskogee Chief to Caddo Chief, July 20, 1842, MS. in *Indian Affairs Papers*, Texas State Library.
[40] R. M. Jones to Red Bear, Caddo Chief, July 30, 1842, in MS. *Indian Affairs Papers*, Texas State Library; Muckleroy, "The Indian Policy of the Republic of Texas," in *Southwestern Historical Quarterly*, XXVI, 186.
[41] *Ibid.*, 187.
[42] Crane, *The Life and Select Literary Remains of Sam Houston*, 314.

representing the United States, with Burgenille as secretary. The Indian tribes represented were the Delawares, Caddoes, Wacos, Shawnees, Ionies, Anadako, Tawakano, Wichitas, and Kichai. On March 31, 1843, an agreement was signed by the different parties to hold a grand council at a date and place to be arranged and agreed upon later. Its purpose should be to conclude a definite and permanent treaty of peace, and friendship between the Republic of Texas and the Indian tribes residing within or near its limits. In the meantime all hostilities, and depredations of every kind should cease. Those Indians who desired were allowed to trade at the trading house on the Brazos River and to plant corn north of the trading house until a permanent line was established between Texas and the Indians. If a treaty were concluded at the Grand Council both parties were to give up all prisoners without ransom.[43]

In September, the Grand Council convened at Bird's Fort on the Trinity River, where a treaty of far reaching importance was concluded between the Republic of Texas and the Caddoes and associated tribes. Both parties agreed that they would forever live in peace and friendship, and that the President should make such arrangements and regulations with the several tribes of Indians as he might think best for their peace and happiness.

This treaty was approved by the Senate, January 31, 1844, and signed by Houston, February 3, 1844.[44]

In March 1844, the Caddoes and other tribes that had signed the Bird's Fort treaty visited President Houston at Washington. He made them a talk, gave them presents, and assured them of the friendship of the republic. The Indians promised to serve as ambassadors of peace to induce the Comanches and other wild tribes who had not signed the treaty to attend the council arranged to meet in April. The friendly tribes were not able to get the Comanches to the council until October. This council was held on the clear fork of the Brazos beginning October 7, and resulted in the formation of a treaty which was concluded October 9. There were representatives from the Comanches, Cherokees, Delawares,

---

[43] Minutes of Indian Council, March 28, 1843, Articles of Agreement between the Republic of Texas and Indian Tribes, March 31, 1843, MS. *Indian Affairs Papers*, Texas State Library.

[44] Muckleroy, "The Indian Policy of the Republic of Texas," in *Southwestern Historical Quarterly*, XXVI, 188-191.

Kichais, Wacos, Towakanos, Caddo, Ionies, Lipan, Anadakos, and Shawnees present at the meeting. The Texan commissioners were J. C. Neill, Thomas S. Smith, and E. Morehouse. Sam Houston, president of the Republic, and G. W. Terrell, attorney general, also attended the council. The treaty was similar to that concluded at Bird's Fort, September 29, 1844.

Both parties agreed that they would forever live in peace, and always meet as friends and brothers; that the government of Texas should permit no bad men to cross the line into the hunting grounds of the Indians; that the Indians should make no treaty with any nation at war with Texas; that they should not steal horses or other property from the whites; that they should not trade with any other people than the Texans so long as they could get such goods as they needed at the trading houses. It was further agreed that the government of Texas should establish trading houses for the benefit of the Indians, and such articles as they needed for their support and comfort should be kept for the Indian trade; that no whiskey or other intoxicating liquor should be sold to the Indians; that the President should send among them schoolmasters and families for the purpose of instructing them in the knowledge of the English language, and Christian religion, as well as other persons to teach them how to cultivate the soil.

This treaty was ratified by the Senate, January 24, 1845, and signed by the President, February 5.[45]

The peace agreements brought about a cessation of hostilities between the settlers and the Caddoes to a great extent but the Indians continued to suffer from natural causes such as famine and disease.

IV.

CONCLUSION

More than a century of contact and relationship with the Europeans and Anglo-Americans practically broke up the once powerful and influential Caddo Confederacy. The peaceful disposition and friendly attitude of the Caddoes towards the nations

---

[45] *Ibid.*, 193, 196. Here articles of the treaty will be found. Minutes of the Grand Council held near the Fall's of the Brazos between the Republic of Texas and the Indians, October 7, 1844, MS. in *Indian Affairs Papers*, Texas State Library.

under whose jurisdiction they happened to be, established early contact with the civilized people. Naturally this expedited the work of civilizing influences, but it proved disastrous for the natives, who were exposed to the contaminating vices which backward people generally acquire from contact with races more advanced.

The tribes belonging to the Caddo Confederacy were scattered from Natchitoches to the great bend of the Red River, thus they were so divided that at no time could they successfully resist the intruding white races. Never did they attempt to use violence against the white traders and settlers who penetrated the territory claimed by themselves, but always referred such acts of intrusion to the governmental agencies in charge.

During the first half of the eighteenth century the French and Spaniards were involved in a contest for the control of the Caddo country. Each nation endeavored to win the allegiance of the Caddoes, as they exercised a commanding influence over all of the border Indians. The Spanish policy of attempting to win the natives through the influence of the Franciscan missionary was no match for that of the French who operated through the agency of the trader. As a result the French soon established undisputed control over most of the Caddo tribes, but the brunt of these contentions fell upon the Indians. The trails connecting their villages became routes over which armed forces traveled, while some of their villages were converted into fortified posts.

The Caddoes suffered greatly from their contact with the Europeans. Tribal wars were fomented, villages were destroyed and abandoned, new diseases took their toll among the people, and by the end of the century a number of the tribes were practically extinct, while others were seriously reduced in numbers; and those tribes that had migrated north, being too few in numbers to resist the onslaught of the Osages who were being driven south by the whites, descended the Red River, and joined the other tribes of the confederacy.

With the purchase of Louisiana by the United States the Caddoes again became border Indians, and the bid for their control was now between the United States and Spain. The policy followed by the United States in winning the allegiance of the Caddoes was similar to that used by France. They gave presents and established trading houses whereby the Indians could be supplied with the necessities of life without having to travel a great distance in search of them.

As a result of the acquisition of Louisiana, immigration into the Caddo country increased, and it soon became impossible for the government to restrain the white immigrants from inhabiting the Caddo lands. The policy of the government had been not to allow settlements in the territory claimed by the Indians until their title had been extinguished. As the government agents realized that it was beyond their power even with military assistance to prevent intrusions into the Caddo country, they recommended the purchase of that country.

The United States Indian agent, taking advantage of the starving condition of the Caddoes, enticed them to sell their lands and to agree to leave the United States, never to return and settle as a tribe.

Thus it seems that they were to be forced into Mexican territory, but at that time the Anglo-Americans in Texas were waging a revolution and strenuously objected to Indians from the United States migrating into their territory. The Caddoes found themselves in a desperate situation, the United States Indian agent on one side of the border selling them guns and ammunition and urging them to enter Texas, while on the other side, the Texans threatened to exterminate them if they crossed into their country.

Although the Caddoes were forbidden to enter Texas, necessity compelled them to go into that region in search of game. The transfer of thousands of Indians from east of the Mississippi, and the westward migration of the whites had so taxed the resources of the old Caddo hunting grounds as to make stealing almost a necessity.

The Texans failed to make a distinction between friendly and hostile Indians. They thought that the only good Indian was a dead one, therefore they attempted to drive out or exterminate all of the Caddoes that had migrated into their country. As a result of this policy of extermination the Caddoes that were not killed were driven from Texas east of the Red River, where in retaliation for this cruel treatment they sent small bands into Texas to plunder and harass the white settlements.

By this time the friendly attitude of the Caddoes towards the whites had changed to that of hatred and distrust. They who had been ambassadors of peace under the rule of France, Spain, and the United States; they who had been promised as a reward for their allegiance that they would never be disturbed; they who were once a thrifty and influential people had become demoralized, and were now forced to fight for their actual existence. But when the party in Texas that had advocated conciliatory methods in dealing with the Indians returned to power, the Caddoes were invited to return into Texas, where a permanent peace was made that resulted in a cessation of hostilities.

BIBLIOGRAPHY

PRIMARY MATERIALS

MANUSCRIPT

Indian Affairs Papers, Texas State Library.
Rusk Papers, Archives of the University of Texas.

OFFICIAL DOCUMENTS

American State Papers, Indian Affairs, 2 vols., Washington, 1832-1834.
Annals of Congress, 9 Cong., 2 Sess., Vol. II, 1806-1807.
Congressional Debates, XIII, Pt. 2, Washington, 1837, (Report by Morfit on conditions in Texas, 1836.)
House Executive Documents, 25 Cong., 2 Sess., Doc. No. 351 (Serial 332). (Correspondence on Indian encroachments on the eastern frontier).
House Reports, 19 Cong., 1 Sess., Doc. No. 33 (Serial 125a). 27 Cong., 2 Sess., Doc. No. 1035 (Serial 411).
Senate Documents, 24 Cong., 2 Sess., Doc. No. 1 (Serial 297). 32 Cong., 2 Sess., Doc. No. 14 (Serial 660). (Correspondence on Indian intrusions in Texas). 57 Cong., 1 Sess., Vol. XXXV (Serial 4254). (Contains the Treaty of 1835 with the Caddoes).

Texas Congress, *House Journal,* 1 Cong., 2 Sess., 1837.

OTHER PRINTED SOURCES

ABEL, ANNIE H.—"A Report from Natchitoches in 1807, by Dr. John Sibley", *Indian Notes and Monographs,* Heye Foundation, New York, 1922.

BARKER, EUGENE C., editor.—*The Austin Papers,* 3 vols., vols. I and II, in American Historical Association, *Annual Reports for 1919 and 1922,* Washington, 1924-1928; vol. III, Austin, 1928.

BOLTON, HERBERT EUGENE—*Athanase de Mézières and the Louisiana Texas Frontier, 1768-1780,* 2 vols., Cleveland, 1914. (Contains much source material bearing on the Caddoes).

FRENCH, B. F.—*Historical Collections of Louisiana,* 4 vols., New York, 1846-53.

GARRISON, GEORGE PIERCE, editor.—*The Diplomatic Correspondence of the Republic of Texas,* 3 vols., in American Historical Association, *Annual Reports,* for 1907 and 1908, Washington, 1908-1911.

GULICK, AND SMITHER, editors.—*The Lamar Papers,* 6 vols., Austin, 1922-1927.

HARRINGTON, M. R.—*Certain Caddo Sites in Arkansas,* New York, 1920.

HATCHER, MATTIE AUSTIN—"Description of the Tejas or Asinai Indians, 1691-1722" in *Southwestern Historical Quarterly,* Vol. XXX, 206-218, 283-304.

MARCY, RANDOLPH B.—*Explorations of the Red River of Louisiana in the year 1852,* Washington, 1854.

MOONEY, JAMES—*The Ghost Dance Religion, Fourteenth Report of the Bureau of American Ethnology,* part I, Washington, 1896.

MORSE, JEDEDIAH—*A Report to the Secretary of War of the United States, on Indian Affairs, Comprising a Narrative of a Tour performed in the Summer of 1810,* New Haven, 1822.

ROWLAND, DUNBAR, editor.—*Official Letter Books of William C. C. Claiborne, 1801-1816,* 6 vols., Jackson, Miss., 1917.

ROYCE, CHARLES C., (Compiler)—"Indian Land Cessions in the United States," *Eighteenth Annual Report of the Bureau of American Ethnology,* 1896-1897, Washington 1899. (Used in compiling map of Caddo country).

SHEA, JOHN GILMARY.—*Discovery and exploration of the Missis-sippi Valley; with the Original Narratives of Marquette, Allouez, Membre, Hennepin, and Anastase Douay,* New York, 1852.

WALKER, WINSLOW M.—"A Reconnaisance of Northern Louisiana Mounds", in *Explorations and Field Work of the Smith-sonian Institute,* 1931.

YARROW, H. C.—"The Mortuary Customs of the North American Indians" in the *First Annual Report of the Bureau of Ameri-can Ethnology,* Part I, (1881), 91-203.

SECONDARY REFERENCES

ABEL, ANNIE HELOISE.—"The History of Events Resulting in In-dian Consolidation West of the Mississippi", *Annual Report of the American Historical Association,* 1906, Volume I.

BOLTON, HERBERT E.—*Texas in the Middle Eighteenth Century,* Berkeley, 1915.

BOLTON, H. E.—"The Mission as a Frontier Institution in the Spanish-American Colonies," in *The American Historical Review,* XXIII, 42-61.

BOLTON.—"The Native Tribes about the East Texas Missions," in Texas Historical Association, *Quarterly,* XI, 249-276.

BUCKLEY, E. C.—"The Aquayo Expedition into Texas and Louis-iana, 1719-1722," in Texas State Historical Association, *Quarterly,* XV, 1-65.

COX, ISAAC JOSLIN.—*The Early Exploration of Louisiana,* Cincin-nati, 1905.

COX, ISAAC JOSLIN.—"The Exploration of the Louisiana Frontier, 1803-1806," in *Annual Report of the American Historical Association* (1904), 151-174.

CRANE, WILLIAM CAREY.—*The Life and Select Literary Remains of Sam Houston,* Philadelphia, 1884.

GARRICK, MALLERY.—"Sign Language Among North American Indians," in the *First Annual Report of the Bureau of American Ethnology,* Part I, (1881), 269-552.

GAYARRE, CHARLES.—*History of Louisiana,* 4 vols., New York, 1854.

GOODSPEED, ARTHUR WESTON.—*The Province and the State,* 6 vols., Madison, Wisconsin, 1904.

HARBY, MRS. LEE C.—"The Tejas, Their Habits, Government and Superstitions," in American Historical Association, *Annual Report* (1894), 63-82.

HODGE, FREDERICK WEBB, editor.—*Handbook of American Indians*, Smithsonian Institution, Bureau of American Ethnology Bulletin 30, 2 vols., Washington, 1902-10. (Indispensable to student of Indians).

MARSHALL, T. M.—*A History of the Western Boundary of the Louisiana Purchase, 1819-1841*, Berkeley, 1914.

MARTIN, FRANCOIS XAVIER.—*History of Louisiana*, New Orleans, 1882.

MUCKLEROY, ANNA.—"Indian Policy of the Republic of Texas," in *The Southwestern Historical Quarterly*, XXV, 230-260, XXVI, 128-148, 184-206.

O'PRY, MAUDE HEARNE.—*Chronicles of Shreveport and Caddo Parish*, Shreveport, 1928.

POWELL, J. W.—"Indian Linguistic Families," in the *Seventh Annual Report of the Bureau of American Ethnology*, (1891), 7-142.

SCHOOLCRAFT, HENRY ROWE.—*History of the Indian Tribes of the United States*, 6 vols., Philadelphia, 1857.

SOUTHERN PUBLISHING COMPANY.—*Biographical and Historical Memoirs of Northwest Louisiana*, Nashville and Chicago, 1890.

VAUGHN, MYRA MCALMOUNT.—"Habitat of the Quapaw," in Arkansas Historical Association, *Publications*, II, 521-541.

WHITE, HENRY FORD.—*The Economic and Social Development of Arkansas Prior to 1836*. (Manuscript: Ph. D. Dissertation, University of Texas, 1931.)

WHITTINGTON, G. P.—"Dr. John Sibley of Natchitoches, 1757-1837," in *Louisiana Historical Quarterly*, X, 468-512.

WOOTEN, DUDLEY G.—*A Comprehensive History of Texas, 1685-1897*, 2 vols, Dallas, 1898.

Historical Sketches of the several Indian tribes in Louisiana, south of the Arkansas river, and between the Mississippi and river Grande.

CADDOQUES.—Live about thirty-five miles west of the main branch of Red river, on a bayou or creek, called, by them, Sodo, which is navigable for pirogues only, within about six miles of their village, and that only in the rainy season. They are distant from Natchitoches about 120 miles, the nearest route by land, and in nearly a northwest direction. They have lived where they now do, only five years. The first year they moved there, the small pox got amongst them, and destroyed nearly one half of them; it was in the winter season, and they practised plunging into the creek, on the first appearance of the irruption, and died in a few hours. Two years ago they had the measles, of which several more of them died. They formerly lived on the south bank of the river, by the course of the river 375 miles higher up, at a beautiful prairie, which has a clear lake of good water in the middle of it, surrounded by a pleasant and fertile country, which had been the residence of their ancestors from time immemorial. They have a traditionary tale, which not only the Caddoes, but half a dozen other smaller nations believe in, who claim the honor .of being descendants of the same family; they say, when all the world was drowning by a flood, that inundated the whole country, the Great Spirit placed on an eminence, near this lake, one family of Caddoques, who alone were saved; from that family all the Indians originated.

The French, for many years before Louisiana was transferred to Spain, had, at this place, a fort and some soldiers; several French families were likewise settled in the vicinity, where they had erected a good flour mill, with burr stones brought from France. These French families continued there till about twenty-five years ago, when they moved down and settled at Compti. on the Red river, about twenty miles above Natchitoches, where they now live; and the Indians left it about fourteen years ago, on account of a dreadful sickness that visited them. They settled on the river nearly opposite where they now live, on a low place, but were drove from there on account of its overflowing, occasioned by a jam of timber choking the river at a point below them.

The whole number of what they call warriors of the ancient Caddo nation, is now reduced to about one hundred, who are looked upon somewhat like Knights of Malta, or some distinguished military order. They are brave, despise danger or death, and boast that they have never shed white men's blood. Besides these, there are of old men, and strangers who live amongst them, nearly the same number: but there are forty or fifty more women than men. This nation has great influence over the Yattassees, Nandakoes, Nabadaches, Inies or Tackies, Nacogdoches, Keychies, Adaize, and Natchitoches, who all speak the Caddo language, look up to them as their fathers, visit and intermarry among them, and join them in all their wars.

The Caddoques complain of the Choctaws encroaching upon their country; call them lazy, thievish, &c. There has been a misunderstanding between them for several years, and small hunting parties kill one another when they meet.

The Caddoes raise corn, beans, pumpkins, &c. but the land on which they now live is prairie, of a white clay soil, very flat; their crops are subject to injury, either by too wet or too dry a season. They have horses, but few of any other domestic animal, except dogs; most of them have guns, and some of them have rifles. They, and all other Indians that we have any knowledge of, are at war with the Osages. The country, generally, round the Caddoes, is hilly, not very rich; growth, a mixture of oak, hickory, and pine, interspersed with prairies, which are very rich, generally, and fit for cultivation. There are creeks and springs of good water frequent.

YATTASSEES.—Live on Bayou river, (or Stony creek) which falls into Red river, western division, about fifty miles above Natchitoches. Their village is in a large prairie, about half way between the Caddoques and Natchitoches, surrounded by a settlement of French families. The Spanish Government, at present, exercise jurisdiction over this settlement, where they keep a guard of a non-commissioned officer and eight soldiers. A few months ago, the Caddo chief, with a few of his young men, were coming to this place to trade, and came that way, which is the usual road; the Spanish officer of the guard threatened to stop them from trading with the Americans, and told the chief, if he returned that way with goods, he should take them from him. The chief and his party were very angry, and threatened to kill the whole guard; and told them, that that road had been always theirs, and that, if the

Spaniards attempted to prevent their using it, as their ancestors had always done, he would soon make it a bloody road. He came here, purchased the goods he wanted, and might have returned another way, and avoided the Spanish guard, and was advised to do so, but he said he would pass by them, and let them attempt to stop him if they dare. The guard said nothing to him as he returned. This settlement, till some few years ago, used to belong to the district of Natchitoches, and the rights to their lands given by the Government of Louisiana, before it was ceded to Spain. Its now being under the Government of Texas, was only by an agreement between the commandant of Natchitoches and the commandant of Nacogdoches. The French formerly held a station and factory there, and another on the *Scbine* river, nearly a hundred miles northwest from the Bayou Pierre settlement. The Yattassees now say the French used to be their people, and now the Americans; but of the ancient Yattassees there are but eight men remaining, and twenty-five women, besides children; but a number of men of other nations have intermarried with them, and live together. I paid a visit at their village the last summer; there were about forty men of them altogether. Their original language differs from any other; but now, all speak Caddo. They live on rich land, raise plenty of corn, beans, pumpkins, tobacco, &c. have horses, cattle, hogs, and poultry.

NANDAKOES.—Live on the Sabine river, sixty or seventy miles to the westward of the Yattassees, near where the French formerly had a station and factory. Their language is Caddo; about forty men of them only remaining. A few years ago they suffered very much by the small pox. They consider themselves the same as Caddoes, with whom they intermarry, and are occasionally visiting one another in the greatest harmony; have the same manners, customs, and attachments.

ADAIZE.—Live about forty miles from Natchitoches, below the Yattassees, on a lake called Lac Macdon, which communicates with that division of Red river that passes by Bayou Pierre; they live at, or near, where their ancestors have lived from time immemorial. They being the nearest nation to the old Spanish fort, or mission of Adaize, that place was named after them, being about twenty miles from them, to the south. There are now but twenty men of them remaining, but more women. Their language differs from all other, and is so difficult to speak, or understand, that no other nation can speak ten words of it; but they all speak Caddo, and most of them French, to whom they were always attached, and joined them against the Natchez Indians. After the massacre of Natchez, in 1798, while the Spaniards occupied the post of Adaize, their priests took much pains to proselyte these Indians to the Roman Catholic religion, but, I am informed, were totally unsuccessful.

ALICHE, (commonly pronounced Eyeish.)—Live near Nacogdoches, but are almost extinct as a nation, not being more than twenty-five souls of them remaining; four years ago the small pox destroyed the most of them. They were some years ago a considerable nation, and lived on a bayou which bears their name, which the road from Natchitoches to Nacogdoches crosses about twelve miles west of Sabine river, on which a few French and American families are settled. Their native language is spoken by no other nation; but they speak and understand Caddo, with whom they are in amity, often visiting one another.

KEYES, or KEYCHIES.—Live on the east bank of Trinity river, a small distance above where the road from Natchitoches to St. Antoine crosses it. There are of them sixty men; have their peculiar native language, but mostly now speak Caddo, intermarry with them, and live together in much harmony, formerly having lived near them on the head waters of the Sabine. They plant corn, and some other vegetables.

INIES, or TACHIES, (called indifferently by both names.) From the latter name, the name of the province of Tachus or Texas is derived. The Inies live about twenty-five miles west of Natchitoches, on a small river, a branch of the Sabine, called the Natchez; they are like all their neighbors, diminishing; but have now eighty men. Their ancestors, for a long time, lived where they now do. Their language the same as that of the Caddoes, with whom they are in great amity. These Indians have a good character, live on excellent land, and raise corn to sell.

NABEDACHES.—Live on the west side of the same river, about fifteen miles above them; have about the same number of men; speak the same language; live on the best of land; raise corn in plenty; have the same manners, customs, and attachments.

BEDIES.—Are on the Trinity river, about sixty miles to the southward of Nacogdoches; have one hundred men; are good hunters for deer, which are very large and plenty about them; plant, and make good crops of corn; language differs from all other, but speak Caddo; are a peaceable quiet people, and have an excellent character for their honesty and punctuality.

ACCOKESAWS.—Their ancient town, and principal place of residence, is on the west side of the Colerado, or Rio Rouge, about two hundred miles southwest of Nacogdoches, but often change their place of residence for a season; being near the bay, make great use of fish, oysters, &c. kill a great many deer, which are the largest and fattest in the province; and their country is universally said to be inferior to no part of the province, in soil, growth of timber, goodness of water, and beauty of surface; have a language peculiar to themselves, but have a mode of communication by dumb signs, which they all understand. Number, about eighty men. Thirty or forty years ago, the Spaniards had a mission there, but broke it up, and moved it to Nacogdoches; they talk of resetting it, and speak in the highest terms of the country.

MAYES.—Live on a large creek, called St. Gabriel, on the bay of St. Bernard, near the mouth of Gaudaloupe river; are estimated at two hundred men; never at peace with the Spaniards, towards whom they are said to possess a fixed hatred; but profess great friendship for the French, to whom they have been strongly attached since Monsieur de Salle landed in their neighborhood. The place where there is a talk of the Spaniards opening a new port, and making a settlement, is near them, where the party, with the Governor of St. Antoine, who were there last fall to examine it, say they found the remains of a French block-house. Some of the cannon now at Labahie are said to have been brought from that place, and known by the engravings now to be seen on them. The French speak highly of these Indians, for their extreme kindness and hospitality to all Frenchmen who have been amongst them. Have a language of their own, but speak Attakapas, which is the language of their neighbors the Carankouas; they have likewise a way of conversing by signs.

CARANKOUAS.—Live on an island, or peninsula, in the bay of St. Bernard, in length about ten miles, and five in breadth; the soil extremely rich and pleasant, on one side of which there is a high bluff or mountain of coal, which has been on fire for many years, affording always a light at night, and a strong thick smoke by day, by which vessels are sometimes deceived, and left on the shoaly coast, which shoals are said to extend nearly out sight of land. From this burning coal there is emitted a gummy substance, the Spaniards call *Cheta*, which is thrown on the shore by the surf, and collected by them in considerable quantities, which they are fond of chewing; it has the appearance and consistence of pitch, of a strong aromatic, and not disagreeable smell. These Indians are irreconcileable enemies to the Spaniards, always at war with them, and kill them whenever they can. The Spaniards call them cannibals, but the French give them a different character, who have always been treated kindly by them, since Monsieur de Salle, and his party, were in their neighborhood. They are said to be five hundred men strong; but I have not been able to estimate their numbers from any very accurate information; in a short time, expect to be well informed. They speak the Attakapas language, are friendly and kind to all other Indians, and, I presume, are much like all others, notwithstanding what the Spaniards say of them, for nature is every where the same. Last summer an old Spaniard came to me from Labahie, a journey of about 500 miles, to have a barked arrow taken out of his shoulder, that one of these Indians had shot in it. I found it under his shoulder blade, near nine inches, and had to cut a new place to get at the point of it, in order to get it out the contrary way from that in which it had entered. It was made of a piece of an iron hoop, with wings like a fluke and an inch.

CANCES, are a very numerous nation, consisting of a great many different tribes, occupying different parts of the country, from the bay of St. Bernard, across river Grande, towards La Vera Cruz. They are not friendly to the Spaniards, and generally kill them when they have an opportunity. They are attached to the French; are good hunters, principally using the bow. They are very particular in their dress, which is made of neatly dressed leather, the women wear a long loose robe, resembling that of a Franciscan friar; nothing but their heads and feet are to be seen. The dress of the men is straight leather leggins, resembling pantaloons, and a leather hunting shirt or frock. No estimate can be made of their number.

Thirty or forty years ago, the Spaniards used to make slaves of them when they could take them; a considerable number of them were brought to Natchitoches, and sold amongst the French inhabitants, at forty or fifty dollars a head, and a number of them are still living here, but are now free. About twenty years ago, an order came from the King of Spain that no more Indians should be made slaves, and those that were enslaved should be emancipated; after which, some of the women, who had been servants in good families, and taught spinning, sewing, &c. as well as managing household affairs, married natives of the country, and became respectable, well behaved women; and have now, grown up, decent families of children, have a language peculiar to themselves, and are understood by signs by all others. They are in amity with all other Indians except the Hietans.

TANKAWAYS, or TANKS, as the French call them, have no land, nor claim the exclusive right to any, nor have any particular place of abode, but are always moving, alternately occupying the country watered by the Trinity, Braces, and Colerado, towards Santa Fé. Resemble in their dress the Cances and Hietans; but all in one horde or tribe. Their number of men is estimated at about two hundred; are good hunters; kill buffalo and deer with the bow; have the best breed of horses; are alternately friends and enemies of the Spaniards. An old trader lately informed me, that he had received five thousand deer skins from them in one year, exclusive of tallow, rugs, and tongues. They plant nothing, but live upon wild fruits and flesh. Are strong athletic people, and excellent horsemen.

TAWAKENOES, or THREE CANES. They are called by both names indifferently, live on the west side of the Braces, but are often, for months at a time, lower down than their usual place of residence, in the great plain on the Tortuga, or Turtle, called so, from its being a hill in the prairie, which, at a distance, appears in the form of a Turtle, upon which there is some remarkable springs of water. Their usual residence is about two hundred miles to the westward of Nacogdoches, towards Santa Fé. They are estimated at two hundred men; are good hunters; have guns, but hunt principally with the bow; are supplied with goods from Nacogdoches, and pay for them in rugs, tongues, tallow, and skins.

They speak the same language of the Panis, or Towiaches, and pretend to have descended from the same ancestors.

PANIS, or TOWIACHES. The French call them, Panis, and the Spaniards Towiaches; the latter is the proper Indian name. They live on the south bank of the Red river, by the course of the river upwards of eight hundred miles above Natchitoches, and by land, by the nearest path, is estimated at about three hundred and forty. They have two towns near together; the lower town, where the chief lives, is called Witcheta, and the other is called Towaahack. They call their present chief the Great Bear; they are at war with the Spaniards, but friendly to those French and American hunters who have lately been among them; they are, likewise, at war with the Osages, as are every other nation. For many hundreds of miles around them, the country is rich prairie, covered with luxuriant grass, which is green, summer and winter, with skirts of wood on the river bank, by the springs and creeks.

They have many horses and mules; they raise more corn, pumpkins, beans, and tobacco, than they want for their own consumption; the surplusage they exchange with the Hietans, for buffalo rugs, horses, and mules; the pumpkins they cut round in their shreds, and when it is in a state of dryness, that it is so tough it will not break, but bend, they plat and work it into large mats, in which state they sell it to the Hietans, who, as they travel, cut off, and eat it, as they want it. Their tobacco they manufacture and cut as fine as tea, which is put into leather bags of a certain size, and is, likewise, an article of trade. They have but few guns, and very little ammunition; what they have they keep for war, and hunt with the bow; their meat is principally buffalo; seldom kill a deer, though they are so plenty they come into their villages, and about their houses, like a domestic animal. Elk, bear, wolves, antelope, and wild hogs, are likewise plenty within their country, and white rabbits or hares, as well as the common rabbit; white bears sometimes come down among them, and wolves of all colors. The men go entirely naked, and the women nearly so, only wearing a small flap, of a piece of skin. They have a number of Spaniards amongst them, of a fair complexion, taken from the settlement of Santa Fé when they were children, who live as they do, and have no knowledge of where they came from. Their language differs from that of any other nation, the Tawakenoes excepted. Their present number of men is estimated at about four hundred. A great number of them, four years ago, were swept off by the small pox.

HIETANS OR COMANCHES, who are likewise called by both names, have no fixed place of residence; have neither towns nor villages—divided into so may different hordes or tribes, that they have scarcely knowledge of one another. No estimate of their numbers can well be made; they never remain in the same place more than a few days, but follow the buffalo, the flesh of which is their principal food; some of them occasionally purchase of the Panis, corn, beans, and pumpkins, but they are so numerous, any quantity of these articles the Panis are able to supply them with, must make but a small proportion of their food. They have tents made of neatly dressed skins, fashioned in form of a cone, sufficiently roomy for a family of ten or twelve persons; those of the chiefs will contain, occasionally, fifty or sixty persons. When they stop, their tents are pitched in very exact order, so as to form regular streets and squares, which, in a few minutes, has the appearance of a town, raised, as it were, by enchantment. And they are equally dexterous in striking their tents and preparing for a march, when the signal is given; to every tent, two horses or mules are alloted, one to carry the tent and the other the poles or sticks, which are neatly made of red cedar; they all travel on horseback; their horses they never turn loose to graze, but always keep them tied with a long cabras or halter, and every two or three days, they are obliged to move, on account of all the grass near them being eaten up, they have such numbers of horses. They are good horsemen, and have good horses, most of which are bred by themselves, and being accustomed, when very young, to be handled, they are remarkably docile and gentle. They sometimes catch wild horses, which are every where amongst them, in immense droves; they hunt down the buffalo on horseback, and kill them, either with the bow or a sharp stick like a spear, which they carry in their hands. They are generally at war with the Spaniards, after committing depredations upon the inhabitants of Santa Fé and St. Antoine, but have always been friendly and civil to any French or Americans who have been amongst them.

They are strong and athletic, and the elderly men as fat as though they had lived upon English beef and porter. It is said, the man who kills a buffalo catches the blood and drinks it while warm; they likewise eat the liver raw, before it is cold, and use the gall by way of sauce. They are, for savages, uncommonly cleanly in their persons; the dress of the women is a long loose robe, that reaches from their chin to the ground, tied round with a fancy sash or girdle, all made of neatly dressed leather, on which they paint figures of different colors and significations. The dress of the men is close leather pantaloons and hunting shirt or frock of the same. They never remain long enough in the same place to plant any thing; the small Cayenne pepper grows spontaneously in the country, with which, and some wild herbs and fruits, particularly a bean that grows in great plenty on a small tree resembling a willow, called *Musketo*, the women cook their buffalo beef, in a manner that would be grateful to an English squire. They alternately occupy the immense space of country, from the Trinity and Braces, crossing the Red river, to the heads of Arkansas and Missouri, to river Grande, and beyond it, about Santa Fé, and over the dividing ridge to the waters of the Western ocean, where, they say, they have seen large pirogues, with masts to them, in describing which, they make a drawing of a ship, with all its sails and rigging; and they describe a place where they have seen vessels ascending a river, over which was a draw bridge, that opened to give them a passage. Their native language of sounds differs from the language of any other nation, and none can either speak or understand it; but they have a language by signs, that all Indians understand, and by which, they converse much among themselves. They have a number of Spanish men and women among them, who are slaves, and who, they made prisoners when young. An elderly gentleman, now living at Natchitoches, who, some years ago, carried on a trade with the Hietans, a few days ago related to me the following story:

About twenty years ago, a party of these Indians passed over river Grande to Chawawa, the residence of the Governor General of what is called the Five Internal Provinces, lay in ambush for an opportunity, and made prisoner the Governor's daughter, a young lady going in her coach to mass, and brought her off. The Governor sent a message to him, (my informant) with a thousand dollars, for the purpose of recovering his daughter. He immediately despatched a confidential trader, then in his employ, with the one thousand dollars in merchandise, who repaired to the nation, found her, and purchased her ransom, but, to his great surprise, she refused to return with him to her father, and sent by him, the following message: That the Indians had disfigured her face, by tattooing it according to their fancy and ideas of beauty, and a young man of them had taken her for his wife, by whom she believed herself pregnant; that she had become reconciled to their mode of life, and was well treated by her husband; and, that she should be more unhappy by returning to her father, under these circumstances, than by remaining where she was. Which message was conveyed to her father, who rewarded the trader by a present of three hundred dollars more, for his trouble and fidelity, and his daughter is now living with her Indian husband in the nation, by whom she has three children.

NATCHITOCHES, formerly lived where the town of Natchitoches is now situated, which took its name from them. An elderly French gentleman lately informed me, he remembered when they were six hundred men strong. I believe it is now ninety-eight years since the French first established themselves at Natchitoches; ever since, these Indians have been their steady and faithful friends. After the massacre of the French inhabitants of Natchez, by the Natchez Indians, in 1728, those Indians fled from the French, after being reinforced, and came up Red river, and camped about six miles below the town of Natchitoches, near the river, by the side of a small lake of clear water, and erected a mound of considerable size, where it now remains. Monsieur St. Dennie, a French Canadian, was then commandant at Natchitoches; the Indians called him the Big-foot; were fond of him, for he was a brave man. St. Dennie, with a few French soldiers and what militia he could muster, joined by the Natchitoches Indians, attacked the Natchez in their camp, early in the morning; they defended themselves desperately for six hours, but were at length totally defeated by St. Dennie, and what of them that were not killed in battle, were drove into the lake, where the last of them perished, and the Natchez, as a nation, became extinct. The lake is now called by no other name than the Natchez lake.

There are now remaining of the Natchitoches, but twelve men and nineteen women, who live in a village, about twenty-five miles, by land, above the town which bears their name, near a lake called by the French, Lac de Muire. Their original language is the same as the Yattassee, but speak Caddo, and most of them French.

The French inhabitants have great respect for this nation, and a number of very decent families have a mixture of their blood in them. They claim but a small tract of land, on which they live, and, I am informed, have the same rights to it from Government, that other inhabitants, in the neighborhood, have. They are gradually wasting away; the small pox has been their great destroyer; they still preserve their Indian dress and habits; raise corn, and those vegetables common in their neighborhood.

BOLUSCAS, are emigrants from near Pensacola; they came to Red river, about forty-two years ago, with some French families, who left that country about the time Pensacola was taken possession of by the English. They were then a considerably numerous tribe, and have generally embraced the Roman Catholic religion, and were very highly esteemed by the French. They settled first at Avoyelles; then moved higher up to Rapide Bayou, about forty miles from Natchitoches, where they now live, and are reduced to about thirty in number. Their native language is peculiar to themselves, but speek Mobilian, which is spoken by all the Indians, from the east side of the Mississippi. They are honest, harmless, and friendly people.

APALACHIES, are likewise emigrants from West Florida, from off the river whose name they bear; came over to Red river, about the same time the Boluscas did, and have since lived on the river, above Bayou Rapide. No nation has been more highly esteemed by the French inhabitants; no complaints against them are ever heard; there are only fourteen men remaining; have their own language, but speak French and Mobilian.

ALABAMAS, are likewise from West Florida, off the Alabama river, and came to Red river about the same time of the Boluscas and Apalachies. Part of them have lived on Red river, about sixteen miles above the Bayou Rapide, till last year, when most of this party, of about thirty men, went up Red river, and have settled themselves near the Caddoquies, where, I am informed, they last year made a good crop of corn. The Caddoes are friendly to them, and have no objection to their settling there; they speak the Creek and Choctaw languages, and Mobilian: most of them French, and some of them English. There is another village, whose village is on a small creek in Opelousas district, about thirty miles northwest form the church of Opelousas; they consist of about forty men; they have lived at the same place ever since they came from Florida; are said to be increasing a little in numbers for a few years past; they raise corn, have horses, hogs, and cattle, and are harmless, quiet people.

CONCHATTAS, are almost the same people as the Alabamas, but came over only ten years ago; first lived on Bayou Chico, in Opelousas district, but, four years ago, moved to the river Sabine, settled themselves on the east bank, where they now live, in nearly a south direction from Natchitoches, and distant about eighty miles. They call their number of men one hundred and sixty, but say, if they were all together, they would amount to two hundred; several families of them live in detached settlements; they are good hunters, and game is plenty about where they are.

A few years ago, a small party of them were here, consisting of fifteen persons, men, women, and children, who were on their return from a bear hunt up Sabine; they told me, they had killed one hundred and eighteen, but this year, an uncommon number of bears have come down; one man alone, on Sabine, during the summer and fall hunting, killed four hundred deer; sold his skins at forty dollars a hundred. The bears, this year, are not so fat as common; they usually yield from eight to twelve gallons of oil, which never sells for less than a dollar a gallon, and the skin a dollar more; no great quantity of the meat is saved; what the hunters don't use when out, they generally give to their dogs. The Conchattas are friendly with all other Indians, and speak well of their neighbors, the Carankouas, who, they say, live about eighty miles south of them, on the bay, which, I believe, is the nearest point to the sea, from Natchitoches. A few families of the Choctaws have lately settled near them, from Bayou Bœuf. The Conchattas speak Creek, which is their native language, and Choctaw; and several of them, English, and one or two of them can read it a little.

PACANAS, are a small tribe of about thirty men, who live on Quelqueshoe river, which falls into the bay, between Attakapas and Sabine, which heads in a prairie called Cooko prairie, about forty miles southwest of Natchitoches. These people are likewise emigrants from West Florida, about forty years ago; their village is about fifty miles southeast of the Conchattas; are said to be increasing a little in number; quiet, peaceable, and friendly people; their own language differs from any other, but speak Mobilian.

ATTAKAPAS.—This word, I am informed, when translated into English, means man-eater; but it is no more applicable to them than any other Indians. The district they live in, is called after them; their village is about 20 miles to the westward of the Attakapas church, towards Quelqueshoe; their number of men is about fifty; but some Runicas and Humas, who have married in their nation, and live with them, make them altogether about eighty; they are peaceable and friendly to every body; labor occasionally for the white inhabitants; raise their own corn; have cattle and hogs; their language, and the Carankouas, is the same; they were at, or near, where they now live, when that part of the country was first discovered by the French.

OPELOUSAS.—It is said the word Appalousa, in the Indian language, means black-head, or black-skull. They are aborigines of the district called by their name; their village is about fifteen miles west from the Opelousas church; have about forty men; their native language differs from all others; understand Attakapas, and speak French; plant corn; have cattle and hogs.

TUNICAS.—These People formerly lived on the Bayou Tunica, above point Coupée, on the Mississippi, East side; live now at Avoyelles; do not, at present, exceed twenty-five men. Their native language is peculiar to themselves, but speak Mobilian; are employed occasionally by the inhabitants as boatmen, &c.; in amity with all other People, and gradually diminishing in numbers.

PASCAGOULAS.—Live in a small village on Red river, about sixty miles below Natchitoches; are emigrants from Pascagoula river, in West Florida; twenty-five men only of them remaining; speak Mobilian, but have a language peculiar to themselves; most of them speak and understand French; they raise good crops of corn, and garden vegetables; have cattle, horses, and poultry plenty; their horses are much like the poorer kind of French inhabitants on the river, and appear to live about as well.

TENISAWS, are likewise emigrants from the Tensaw river, that falls into the bay of Mobile; have been on Red river about forty years; are reduced to about twenty-five men. Their village is within one mile of the Pascogoulas, on the opposite side; but have lately sold their lands, and have, or are about moving, to Bayou Bœuf, about twenty-five miles south from where they lately lived. All speak French and Mobilian; and live much like their neighbors, the Pascagoulas.

CHACTOOS.—Live on Bayou Bœuf, about ten miles to the southward of Bayou Rapide, on Red river, towards Opelousas; a small, honest People; are aborigines of the country where they live; of men about thirty, diminishing; have their own peculiar tongue; speak Mobilian. The lands they claim on Bayou Bœuf, are inferior to no part of Louisiana, in depth and richness of soil, growth of timber, pleasantness of surface, and goodness of water. The Bayou Bœuf falls into the Chaffeli, and discharges through Opelousas and Attakapas, into Vermillion bay.

WASHAS.—When the French first came into the Mississippi, this nation lived on an island, to the southwest of New Orleans, called Barataria, and were the first tribe of Indians they became acquainted with, and were always friends; they afterwards lived on Bayou La Fourche; and from being a considerable nation, are now reduced to five persons only, two men and three women, who are scattered in French families; have been many years extinct as a nation, and their language lost.

CHOCTAWS.—There are a considerable number of this nation on the West side of the Mississippi, who have not been home for several years; about twelve miles above the post on Ouachita, on that river, there is a small village of them, of about thirty men, who have lived there for several years, and made corn; and likewise on Bayou Chico, in the northern part of the district of Opelousas; there is another village of them, of about fifty men, who have been there for about nine years, and say they have the Governor of Louisiana's permission to settle there. Besides these, there are rambling hunting parties of them, to be met with all over lower Louisiana. They are at war with the Caddoquies, and liked by neither red nor white People.

ARKANSAS.—Live on the Arkansas river, south side, in three villages, about twelve miles above the post or station. The name of the first village is *Tawanima*, second *Ousolu*, and the third *Ocapa*; in all, it is believed, they do not at present exceed one hundred men, and diminishing. They are at war with the Osages, but friends with all other People, white and red; are the original proprietors of the country on that river, to all which they claim, for about 300 miles above them, to the junction of the river Cadron with Arkansas; above this fork the Osages claim; their language is Osage. They generally raise corn to sell; are called honest and friendly people.

The forementioned, are all the Indian tribes that I have any knowledge of, or can obtain an account of, in Louisiana, south of the river Arkansas, between the Mississippi and the river Grand; at Avoyelles, there did live a considerable tribe of that name, but, as far as I can learn, have been extinct for many years, two or three women excepted, who did lately live among the French inhabitants at Washita. There are a few of the Humas still living on the east side of the Mississippi, in Insussees parish, below Manchac, but scarcely exist as a nation.

That there are errors in these sketches, is not to be doubted; but in all cases out of my own personal knowledge, I have endeavored to procure the best information, which I have faithfully related; and I am confident, any errors that do exist, are too unimportant to affect the object for which they are intended.

I am, sir, &c. &c.

JOHN SIBLEY.

Natchitoches, April 5, 1805.

General H. DEARBORN.

NATCHITOCHES, 10*th April*, 1805.

SIR:

You request me to give you some account of Red river, and the country adjacent; I will endeavor to comply with your request, to the best of my knowledge and capacity; my personal knowledge of it, is only from its mouth to about seventy or eighty miles above Natchitoches, being by the course of the river near four hundred miles. After that, what I can say of it is derived from information from others, on whose veracity I have great reliance, principally from Mr. Francis Grappe, who is my assistant, and interpreter of Indian languages; whose father was a French officer, and superintendent of Indian affairs, at a post or station occupied by France, where they kept some soldiers, and had a factory, previous to the cession of Louisiana to Spain; situated nearly five hundred miles, by the course of the river, above Natchitoches, where he, my informant, was born, and lived upwards of thirty years; his time, during which, being occupied alternately as an assistant to his father, an Indian trader and hunter; with the advantage of some learning, and a very retentive memory, acquired an accurate knowledge of the river, as well as the languages of all the different Indian tribes in Louisiana; which, with having been Indian interpreter, for the Spanish Government, for many years past, and (I believe) deservedly esteemed by the Indians, and all others, a man of strict integrity, has, for many years, and does now, possess their entire confidence, and a very extensive influence over them. And I have invariably found, that whatever information I have received from him, has been confirmed by every other intelligent person having a knowledge of the same, with whom I have conversed.

NOTE.—Contrary to geographical rules, as I ascended the river, I called the right bank the northern one, and the left the southern.

The confluence of Red river with the Mississippi is, by the course of the latter, estimated about two hundred and twenty miles from New Orleans. Descending the Mississippi, after passing the Spanish line at the thirty-first degree of north latitude, it makes a remarkable turn to the westward, or nearly northwest, for some distance before you arrive at the mouth of Red river, as though, notwithstanding the immense quantity of its waters, already, from its almost numberless tributary streams, it was still desirous of a farther augmentation, by hastening its union with Red river, (which perhaps is second only in dignity to it) that they might from above flow on, and join the ocean together, which for many leagues is forced to give place to its mighty current. But there are reasons for believing the Red river did not always unite with the Mississippi, as it does at present; and that no very great length of time has elapsed, since the Mississippi left its ancient bed, some miles to the eastward, and took its course westwardly, for the purpose of intermarrying with Red river. The mouth of the Chaffali, which is now, properly speaking, one of the outlets of the river Mississippi to the ocean, is just below, in sight of the junction of Red river with the Mississippi, and, from its resemblance to Red river, in size, growth on its banks, appearance and texture of soil, and differing from that of the Mississippi, induces strongly the belief, that the Chaffali was once but the continuation of Red river to the ocean; and that it had in its bed no connexion with the Mississippi. There is no doubt but the Mississippi has alternately occupied different places in the low ground, through which it meanders almost from the high lands of one side, to those of the other, for the average space of nearly thirty miles. These two great rivers, happening to flow from a distance through the same mass of swamp, that annually is almost all inundated, it is not extraordinary that their channels should find their way together; the remarkable bend of the

Mississippi at this place, to the westward, seems to have been for the express purpose of forming this union; after which, it returns to its former course.

In the month of March, 1803, I ascended Red river from its mouth to Natchitoches, in an open boat, unless, when I chose to land, and walk across a point, or by the beauty of the river bank, the pleasantness of its groves, or the variety of its shrubs and flowers, I was invited ashore to gratify or please my curiosity. On entering the mouth of the river, found its waters turgid, of a red color, and of a brackish taste; and as the Mississippi was then falling, and Red river rising, found a current from its mouth upwards, varying considerably in places, but averaging about two miles an hour, for the first hundred miles, which at that time I found to be about the same in the Mississippi; but when that river is high, and Red river low, there is very little current in the latter, for sixty or seventy miles. The river for that distance is very crooked, increasing the distance by it, from a straight line, more than two-thirds, the general course of it nearly west: that I was able to ascertain, from hearing the morning gun at fort Adams, for three or four mornings after entering the river, which was not at the greatest height by about fourteen feet, and all the low grounds, for nearly seventy miles. entirely overflowed, like those of the Mississippi, which in fact is but a continuation of the same. Some places appeared, by the high water mark on the trees, to overflow not more than two or three feet, particularly the right bank, below the mouth of Black river, and the left bank above it; the growth, on the lowest places, willow and cotton wood, but on the highest, handsome oaks, swamp hickory, ash, grapevines, &c. I made my calculation of our rate of ascent, and distances up the river, by my watch, noting carefully with my pencil the minute of our stops and settings off, the inlets and outlets, remarkable bends in the river, and whatever I observed any way remarkable. About six miles from the mouth of the river, left side, there is a bayou, as it is called, comes in, that communicates with a lake called lake Long, which by another bayou communicates again with the river, through which, when there is a swell in the river, boats can pass, and cut off about thirty miles, being only fourteen or fifteen through it, and about forty-five by the course of the river; and through the lake there is very little or no current, but the passage is intricate and difficult to find; a stranger should not attempt it without a pilot; people have been lost in it for several days; but not difficult for one acquainted; we, having no pilot on board to be depended on, kept the river. From the mouth of Red river, to the mouth of Black river, I made it thirty-one miles; the water of Black river is clear, and when contrasted with the water of Red river, has a black appearance. From the mouth of Black river, Red river makes a regular twining to the left, for about eighteen miles, called the Grand Bend, forming a segment of nearly three-fourths of a circle, when you arrive at the bayou, that leads into lake Long, which perhaps is in a right line, not exceeding fifteen miles from the mouth of the river. From bayou lake Long to Avoyelles landing, called Baker's landing, I made thirty-three miles, and the river is remarkably crooked. At this place the guns at fort Adams are distinctly heard, and the sound appears to be but little south of east; we came through a bayou called Silver bayou, that cut off, we understand, six miles; 'twas through the bayou about four miles. Until we arrived at Baker's landing, saw no spot of ground that did not overflow the high water marks, generally from three to fifteen feet above its banks. After passing Black river, the edge of the banks near the river are highest; the land falls from the river back. At Baker's landing I went ashore. I understood, from Baker's landing accross the point, to La Glass' landing, was only three or four miles, and by water fifteen; but I found it six at least, and met with some difficulty in getting from where I landed to the high land, at Baker's house, for water; though at low water, it is a dry cart road, and less than a mile. I found Baker and his family very hospitable and kind; Mr. Baker told me he was a native of Virginia, and had lived there upwards of thirty years. He was living on a tolerable good high piece of land, not prairie, but joining it; after leaving Baker's house, was soon in sight of the prairie, which I understood is about forty miles in circumference, longer than it is wide, very level, only a few clumps of trees to be seen, all covered with good grass. The inhabitants are settled all around the out edge of it, by the woods, their houses facing inwards, and cultivate the prairie land; though the soil, when turned up with the plough, has a good appearance, what I could discover by the old corn and cotton stalks, they made but indifferent crops; the timbered land that I saw cleared and planted, produced the best; the prairie is better for grass than for planting. The inhabitants have considerable stocks of cattle, which appear to be their principal dependence, and I was informed their beef is of a superior quality; they have likewise good pork; hogs live very well; the timbered country all round the prairie is principally oak, that produces good mast for hogs; corn is generally scarce; they raise no wheat, for they have no mills. I was informed that the lower end of the prairie, that I did not see, was much the richest land, and the inhabitants lived better, and were more wealthy: they are a mixture of French, Irish, and Americans, generally poor and ignorant. Avoyelles, at high water, is an island, elevated thirty or forty feet above high water mark; the quantity of timbered land exceeds that of the prairie, which is likewise pretty level, but scarcely a second quality of soil. La Glass' landing, as it is called, I found about a mile and a half from the upper end of the prairie; the high lands bluff to the river. After leaving this place, found the banks rise higher and higher on each side, and fit for settlements; on the right side, pine woods sometimes in sight; I left the boat again, about eight miles from La Glass' landing, right side, walked two and an half miles across a point, to Mr. Hoome's; round the point is called sixteen miles. I found the lands through which I passed, high, moderately hilly; the soil a good second quality. clay, timber, large oak, hickory, some short leaved pine, and several small streams of clear running water. This description of lands extended back five or six miles, and bounded by open pine woods, which continue for thirty miles to Ocatahola. I found Mr. Hoome's house on a high bluff, very near the river; his plantation the same description of lands through which I had passed, producing good corn, cotton, and tobacco, and he told me he had tried it in wheat, which succeeded well, but having no mills to manufacture it, had only made the experiment; Mr. Hoomes told me all the lands round his, for many miles, were vacant. On the south side there is a large body of rich, low grounds, extending to the borders on Opelousas, watered and drained by Bayou Robert and Bayou Bœuf, two handsome streams of clear water, that rise in the high lands, between Red river and Sabine, and, after meandering through this immense mass of low grounds, of thirty or forty miles square, fall into the Chaffeli, to the southward of Avoyelles: I believe, in point of soil, growth of timber, goodness of water, and conveniency to navigation, there is not a more valuable body of land in this part of Louisiana. From Mr. Hoome's to the mouth of Rapide Bayou, is by the river thirty-five miles; a few scattering settlements on the right side, but none on the left; the right is preferred to settle on, on account of their stocks being convenient to the high lands; but the settlers on the right side own the lands on the left side too. The lands on the Bayou Rapide are the same quality as those on Bayou Robert and Bœuf, and in fact are a continuation of the same body of lands. Bayou Rapide is somewhat in the form of a half moon, the two points or horns meeting the river about twenty miles from each other; the length of the Bayou is about thirty miles; on the back of it there is a large Bayou falls in, on which there is a saw-mill, very advantageously situated in respect to a never failing supply of water, plenty of timber, and the plank can be taken from the mill tail by water. This Bayou is excellent water; rises in the pine woods, and discharges itself each way into the river by both ends of Bayou Rapide. Boats cannot pass through the Bayou from the river, to the river again, on account of rafts of timber choking the upper end of it; but can enter the lower end, and ascend it more than half through it. On the lower end of the Bayou, on each side, is the principal Rapide settlement, as it is called. No country whatever can exhibit handsomer plantations or better lands.

The Rapide is a fall or shoal, occasioned by a soft rock in the bed of the river, that extends from side to side; over which, for about five months in the year, viz: from July to December, there is not sufficient water for boats to pass without lightening; but at all other seasons it is the same as any other part of the river. This rock, or hard clay, for it resembles the latter almost as much as the former, is so soft it may be cut away with a penknife, or any sharp instrument, and scarcely turn the edge, and extends up and down the river but a few yards; and I have heard several intelligent persons give it as their opinion, that the extraordinary expense and trouble the inhabitants were at, in one year, in getting loaded boats over this shoal, would be more than sufficient to cut a passage through it: but it happens at a season of the year when the able planters are occupied at home, and would make no use of the river, were there no obstructions in it; but, at any rate, the navigation of the river is clear a longer proportion of the year than the rivers in the northen countries are clear of ice. But this obstruction is certainly removable at a very trifling expense, in comparison to the importance of having it done; and nothing but the nature of the Government we have lately emerged from, can be assigned as a reason for its not having been effected long ago.

After passing the rapids, there are very few settlements to be seen, on the main river, for about twenty miles, though both sides appeared, to me, to be capable of making as valuable settlements as any on the river; we arrive, then, at the Indian villages, on both sides situated exceedingly pleasant, and on the best lands. After passing which, you arrive at a large, beautiful plantation, of Mr. Gillard; the house is on a point of a high pine woods bluff, close to the river, sixty or seventy feet above the common surface of the country, overlooking, on the east, or opposite side, very extensive fields, of low grounds, in high cultivation, and a long reach of the river up and down; and there is an excellent spring of water issues from the bluff, on which the house is situated, from an aperture in the rock, that seems to have been cloven on purpose for it to flow; and, a small distance, back of the house, there is a lake of clear water, abounding with fish in summer, and fowl in winter. I have seen, in all my life, very few more beautiful or advantageously situated places.

Six miles above Mr. Gillard's, you arrive at the small village of Bolusca Indians, where the river is divided into two channels, forming an island of about fifty miles in length, and three or four in breadth; the right hand division is called the Rigula de Bondieu, on which are no settlements; but, I am informed, will admit of being well settled; the left hand division is the boat channel, at present, to Natchitoches; the other is, likewise, boatable. Ascending the left hand branch, for about twenty-four miles, we pass a thick settlement, and a number of wealthy inhabitants; this is called the River-cane settlement, called so, I believe, from the banks, some years ago, being a remarkably thick cane brake.

After passing this settlement, of about forty families, the river divides again, forming another island, of about thirty miles in length, and from two to four in breadth, called the *Isle Brevel*, after a reputable old man, now living in it, who first settled it. This island is sub-divided by a bayou, that communicates from one river to the other, called also Bayou Brevel. The middle division of the river is called Little river, and is thickly settled, and the best channel; the westward division of the river is called False river; is navigable, but not settled; the banks are too low; it passes through a lake called *Lac Accassa.* When you arrive at Natchitoches, you find it a small, irregular, and meanly built village, half a dozen houses excepted; on the west side of that division of the river it is on, the high pine and oak woods approach within two or three hundred yards of the river. In the village are about forty families; twelve or fifteen are merchants, or traders, nearly all French. The fort built by our troops, since their arrival, called fort Claiborne, is situated on a small hill, one street from the river, and about thirty feet higher than the river banks; all the hill is occupied by the fort and barracks, and does not exceed two acres of ground. The southern and eastern prospects from it are very beautiful; one has an extensive view of the fields and habitations down the river, and the other a similar view over the river, and of the whole village. This town, thirty or forty years ago, was much larger than at present, and situated on a hill about half a mile from its present site; then, most of the families of the district lived in the town; but finding it inconvenient, on account of the stocks and farms, they filed off, one after another, and settled up and down the river; the merchants and trading people, finding being on the bank of the river more convenient for loading and unloading their boats, left the hill on that account; and others, finding the river ground much superior for gardens, to which they are in the habit of paying great attention, followed the merchants; after them, the priests and commandant; then, the church and jail, (or Callaboose) and now nothing of the old town is left, but the form of their gardens and some ornamental trees. It is now a very extensive common of several hundred acres, entirely tufted with clover, and covered with sheep and cattle. The hill is a stiff clay, and used to make miry streets; the river soil, though much richer, is of a sandy loose texture; the streets are neither miry, nor very dirty. Our wells do not afford us good water, and the river water, in summer, is too brackish to drink, and never clear; our springs are about half a mile back from the river; but the inhabitants, many of them, have large cisterns, and use, principally, rain water, which is preferred to the spring water; the planters, along on the river, generally, use rain water; though, when the river is high, and the water taken up and settled, in large earthern jars, (which the Indian women make, of good quality, and at a moderate price) it can be drank tolerably well, but makes bad tea.

Near Natchitoches, there are two large lakes, one within a mile, the other six miles, to the nearest parts; one of them is fifty or sixty miles in circumference, the other upwards of thirty; these lakes rise and fall with the river. When the river is rising, the bayous that connect with the lakes run into the lakes, like a mill tail, till the lakes are filled; and when the river is falling, it is the same the contrary way, just like the tide, but only annual. On these creeks good mills might be erected; but the present inhabitants know nothing of mills by water, yet have excellent cotton gins, worked by horses. I do not know a single mechanic, in the district, who is a native of it, one tailor excepted; every thing of the kind is done by strangers, and mostly Americans. Though Natchitoches has been settled almost one hundred years, it is not more than twelve or fifteen years since they ever had a plough, or a flat to cross the river with; both which were introduced by an Irish Pennsylvanian, under a similar opposition to the Copernican system. 'Tis almost incredible the quantity of fish and fowl these lakes supply; it is not uncommon, in winter, for a single man to kill from two to four hundred fowl in one evening; they fly between sun-down and dark; the air is filled with them; they load and fire, as fast as they can, without taking any particular aim, continuing at the same stand, till they think they have killed enough, and then pick up what they have killed; they consist of several kinds of duck, geese, brant, and swan. In summer, the quantities of fish are nearly in proportion; one Indian will, with a bow and arrow, sometimes, kill them faster, than another, with two horses, can bring them in; they weigh, some of them, thirty or forty pounds. The lakes, likewise, afford plenty of shells for lime, and, at low water, the greater of them is a most luxuriant meadow, where the inhabitants fatten their horses. All around these, above high water mark, there is a body of rich land, generally wide enough for a field; on the bank of one of them there is plenty of stone coal and several quarries of tolerable good building stone; at high water, boats can go out of the river into them. Similar lakes are found, all along Red river, for five or six hundred miles; which, besides the uses already mentioned, nature seems to have provided as reservoirs for the immense quantity of water beyond what the banks of the river will contain; otherwise, no part of them could be inhabited; the low grounds, from hill to hill, would be inundated.

About twelve miles north of Natchitoches, on the north east side of the river, there is a large lake, called *Lac Moir*; the bayou of it communicates to the Rigula de Bondieu, opposite Natchitoches, which is boatable the greater part of the year. Near this lake are the salt works, from which all the salt, that is used in the district, is made; and which is made with so much ease that two old men, both of them cripples, with ten or twelve old pots and kettles, have, for several years past, made an abundant supply of salt for the whole district; they inform me that they make six bushels per day; I have not been at the place, but have a bottle of the water, brought to me, which I found nearly saturated; the salt is good; I never had better bacon than I make with it. I am informed there are twelve saline springs now open; and by digging for them, for aught any one knows, twelve hundred might be opened. A few months ago, Captain Burnet, of the Mississippi territory, coming to this place by Washington, came by the salt works, and purchased the right of one of the old men he found there, and has, lately, sent up a boat, with some large kettles and some negroes, under the direction of his son; and expects, when they get all in order, to be able to make thirty or forty bushels a day. Captain Burnet is of opinion that he shall be able to supply the Mississippi territory, and the settlements on Mississippi, from Point Coupée, upwards, lower than they can get it in New Orleans and bring it up. Cathartic salts and magnesia might, likewise, be made, in large quantities, if they understood it. The country all round the Saline and Black lake is vacant; and from thence to Washita, a distance of 120 miles, which, I am informed, affords considerable quantities of well timbered good uplands, and well watered. There is a small stream, we cross, on the Washita road, the English call *Little river*, the French *Dogdimona*, affording a wide rich bottom; this stream falls into the Acatahola lake; from thence to Washita, it is called Acatahola river; its course is eastwardly, and falls into Washita, near the mouth of Tensaw, where the road, from Natchitoches to to Natchez, crosses it; from the confluence of these three rivers, downwards, it is called Black river, which falls into Red river, sixty miles below. There is a good salt spring near the Acatahola lake.

Ascending Red river, above Natchitoches, in about three miles, arrive at the upper mouth of the Rigula de Bondieu; there are settlements all along, plantations adjoining. From the upper mouth of the Rigula de Bondieu, the river is in one channel through the settlement of Grand Ecore, of about six miles; it is called Grand Ecore, (or, in English, the Great Bluff) being such an one on the left hand side, near one hundred feet high. The face, next the river, almost perpendicular, of a soft, white rock; the top, a grand loam, of considerable extent, on which grow large oaks, hickory, black cherry, and grape vines. At the bottom of one of these bluffs, for there are two near each other, is a large quantity of stone-coal, and, near them, several springs of the best water in this part of the country; and a lake of clear water within two hundred yards, bounded by a gravelly margin. I pretend to have no knowledge of military tactics, but think, from the river in this place being all in one channel, the goodness of the water, a high, healthy country, and well timbered all round it, no height, near it, so high, its commanding the river, and a very public ferry just under it, and at a small expense, would be capable of great defence with a small force. The road from it to the westward, better than from Natchitoches, and, by land, only about five miles above it, and, near it, plenty of good building stone. These advantages it possesses beyond any other place, within my knowledge, on the river, for a strong fort, and safe place of deposite. Just above the bluff, the river makes a large bend to the right, and a long reach nearly due east and west by it; the bluff overlooks, on the opposite side, several handsome plantations. I have been induced, from the advantages this place appeared to me to possess, to purchase it, with four or five small settlements adjoining it, including both bluffs, the ferry, springs, and lake, the stone quarries, and coal; and a field of about five hundred acres of the best low grounds, on the opposite side. After leaving Grand Ecore, about a mile, on the east side, comes in a large bayou, from the Spanish lake, as it is called, boatable the greater part of the year. This lake is said to be about fifty miles in circumference, and rises and falls with the river, into which, from the river, the largest boats may ascend, and from it, up the mouths of several large bayous that fall into it, for some distance; one, in particular, called bayou Dupong, up which boats may ascend within one and a half mile of old fort Adaize. Leaving this bayou about two miles, arrive at a fork or division of the river; the left hand branch bears westwardly for sixty or 80 miles; the eastwardly meeting the branch it left, after forming an island of about one hundred miles long, and, in some places, nearly thirty miles wide. Six or seven years ago, boats used to pass this way into the main river again, its communication with which being above the great raft or obstruction; but it is now choked, and requires a portage of three miles; but, at any season, boats can go from Natchitoches, about eighty miles, to the place called the point, where the French had a factory, and a small station of soldiers, to guard the Indian trade, and is now, undoubtedly, a very eligible situation for a similar establishment. The country bounded to the east and north, by this branch or division of the river, is called the bayou Pierre settlement, which was begun, and some of the lands granted, before Louisiana was ceded to Spain by France, and continued under the jurisdiction of the commandant of Natchitoches until about twenty years ago, when, by an agreement between a Mr. Vogene, the commandant of this place, and a Mr. Eliberbe, commandant at Natchitoches, the settlement called bayou Pierre was placed under the jurisdiction of the latter, and has so continued ever since. The settlement, I believe, contains about forty families, and, generally, they have large stocks of cattle; they supply us with our cheese entirely, and of a tolerable quality, and we get from them some excellent bacon hams.

The country is interspersed with prairies, resembling, as to richness, the river bottoms, and in size from five to five thousand acres. The hills are a good grey soil, and produce very well, and afford beautiful situations. The creek called Bayou Pierre (Stony creek) passes through the settlement, and affords a number of good mill seats, and its bed and banks lined with a good kind of building stone; but no mills are erected on it. Some of the inhabitants have tried the uplands in wheat, which succeeded well; they are high, gently rolling, and rich enough; produce good corn, cotton, and tobacco. I was through the settlement in July last, and found good water, either from a spring or well, at every house. The inhabitants are all French, one family excepted. A few miles to the westward, towards Sabine, there is a saline where the inhabitants go and make their salt. On the whole, for health, good water, good living, plenty of food, and every kind of animal, general conveniency, and handsome surface, I have seen few parts of the world more inviting to settlers.

Returning back again to the fork of the main river we left, for the purpose of exploring the Bayou Pierre branch, we find irregular settlements, including Compti, where a few families are settled together on a hill near the river, northeast side. For about twenty miles, the river land is much the same every where; but the Compti settlement is more broken with bayous and lagoons than any place I am acquainted with on the river; and for want of about a dozen bridges, is inconvenient to get to, or travel through. The upper end of this settlement is the last on the main branch of Red river, which, straight by land, does not exceed twenty-five miles above Natchitoches. At the Upper House, the great raft or jam of timber begins; this raft chokes the main channel for upwards of one hundred miles by the course of the river; not one entire jam from the beginning to the end of it, but only at the point, with places of several leagues that are clear. The river is very crooked, and the low grounds are wide and rich; and I am informed no part of Red river will afford better plantations than along its banks by this raft, which is represented as being so important as to render the country above it of little value for settlements. This opinion is founded entirely upon incorrect information. The first or lowest part of the raft is at a point or bend in the river, just below the upper plantation; at which, on the right side, a large bayou, or division of the river, called Bayou Channo, comes in, which is free of any obstructions: and, the greater part of the year, boats of any size may ascend it into lake Bistino, through which, to its communication with the lake, is only about three miles; the lake is about sixty miles long, and lies nearly parallel with the river; from the upper end of which it communicates again with the river, by a bayou called Daichet, about forty miles above the upper end of the raft; from the lake to the river, through bayou Daichet, is called nine miles; there is always in this bayou sufficient water for any boat to pass; from thence, upwards, Red river is free of all obstructions to the mountains. By lake Bistino and these two bayous an island is formed, about seventy miles long, and three or four wide, capable of affording settlements inferior to none on the river. From the above account you will perceive, that the only difficulty in opening a boat passage by this raft, through the lake, which is much shorter than by the course of the river, and avoid the current, and, indeed, was the river unobstructed, would always be preferred, is this small jam of timber at the point, just below the bayou Channo, as it is called. After the receipt of your letter, I had an opportunity of seeing some of the inhabitants who live near this place, who informed me that that small raft was easily broken, and that they had lately been talking of doing it. I persuaded them to make the attempt, and they accordingly appointed the Friday following, and all the neighbors were to be invited to attend and assist. They met accordingly, and effected a passage next to one bank of the river, so that boats could pass; but did not entirely break it; they intend to take another spell at it, when the water falls a little, and speak confidently of succeeding.

The country about the head of lake Bistino is highly spoken of, as well the high lands as the river bottom. There are falling into the river, and lake in the vicinity, some handsome streams, of clear wholesome water, from towards Washita, one in particular, called bayou Badkah by the Indians, which is boatable at some seasons; this bayou passes through a long, narrow, and rich prairie, on which, my informant says, five hundred families might be desirably settled. And from thence up to where the Caddoes lately lived, the river banks are high, bottoms wide and rich as any other part of the river; from thence, it is much the same to the mouth of the Little river at the left. This river is generally from fifty to a hundred yards wide, heads in the great prairies south of Red river, and interlocks with the head branches of the Sabine and Trinity rivers, and in times of high water is boatable forty or fifty leagues, affording a large body of excellent, well timbered, and rich land; the low grounds from three to six miles wide. But the quality of the water, though clear, is very inferior to that of the streams that fall into Red river on the north side. The general course of Red river from this upwards is nearly from west to east, till we arrive at the Panis towns, when it turns northwestwardly. After leaving the mouth of the little river of the left, both banks are covered with strong thick cane, for about twenty miles; the low grounds very wide, rich, and do not overflow; the river widening in proportion as the banks are less liable to overflow; you arrive at a handsome rich prairie, twenty-five miles long, on the right side, and four or five miles wide, bounded by handsome oak and hickory woods, mixed with some short leaved pine, interspersed with pleasant streams and fountains of water. The opposite, or left side, is a continuation of thick cane; the river, or low lands, ten or twelve miles wide. After leaving the prairie, the cane continues for about forty miles; you then arrive at another prairie, called Little Prairie, left side, about five miles in length, and from two to three in breadth; opposite side continues cane as before; low grounds wide, well timbered, very rich, and overflow but little; the river still widening. Back of the low grounds is a well timbered, rich, upland country, gently rolling, and well watered. From the little prairie, both banks cane for ten or twelve miles, when the oak and pine woods come bluff to the river for about five miles; left hand side, cane as before, then the same on both sides, from ten to twenty miles wide, for about fifteen miles, when the cedar begins on both sides, and is the principal growth on the wide, rich river bottom, for forty miles. In all the world there is scarcely to be found a more beautiful growth of cedar timber; they, like the cedars of Libanus, are large, lofty, and straight.

You now arrive at the mouth of the little river of the right. This river is about one hundred and fifty yards wide; the water clear as chrystal; the bottom of the river stony, and is boatable, at high water, up to the great prairies, near two hundred miles by the course of the river; the low grounds generally from ten to fifteen miles wide, abounding with the most luxuriant growth of rich timber, but subject to partial inundation at particular rainy seasons. After leaving this river, both banks of Red river are cane, as before, for about twenty miles, when you come to the round prairie, right side, about five miles in circumference. At this place, Red river is fordable at low water; a hard stony bottom, and is the first place from its mouth where it can be forded. This round prairie is high and pleasant, surrounded by handsome oak and hickory uplands; left side, cane as before, and then the same both sides for twenty miles, to the long prairie, left side, forty miles long; opposite, cane as before. Near the middle of this prairie, there is a lake of about five miles in circumference, in an oval form, neither tree or shrub near it, nor stream of water running either in or out of it; it is very deep, and the water so limpid that a fish may be seen fifteen feet from the surface. By the side of this lake the Caddoques have lived from time immemorial. About one mile from the lake is the hill on which, they say, the Great Spirit placed one Caddo family, who were saved when, by a general deluge, all the world were drowned; from which family all the Indians have originated. To this little, natural eminence, all the Indian tribes, as well as the Caddoques, for a great distance, pay a devout and sacred homage. Here the French, for many years before Louisiana was ceded to Spain, had erected a small fort, kept some soldiers to guard a factory they had here established for the Indian trade, and several French families were settled in the vicinity, built a flour mill, and cultivated wheat successfully for several years; and it is only a few years ago that the mill irons and mill stones were brought down. It is about twenty-five years since those French families moved down, and fourteen years since the Caddoques left it. Here is another fording place when the river is low. On the opposite side, a point of high oak, hickory, and pine land comes bluff to the river for about a mile; after which, thick cane to the upper end of the prairie; then the same on both sides for about twelve miles; then prairie on the left side for twenty miles; opposite side cane; then the same for thirty miles; then an oak high bluff three miles; cane again for about the same distance on both sides; then, for about one league, left side, is a beautiful grove of pecans, intermixed with no other growth; after which cane both sides for forty miles; then prairie, left side, for twenty miles, and from one to two miles only in breadth; about the middle of which comes in a bayou of clear running water about fifty feet wide; then cane again both sides of the river for about forty miles; then, on the right side, a point of high pine woods, bluff to the river for about half a mile; cane again fifteen or sixteen miles; then a bluff of large white rocks for about half a mile, near a hundred feet high; cane again about forty-five miles, to a prairie on the right side, of about thirty miles long, and twelve or fifteen miles wide; there is a thin skirt of wood along the bank of the river, that, when the leaves are on the trees, the prairie is, from the river, scarcely to be seen. From the upper end of this prairie, it is thick cane for about six miles, when we arrive at the mouth of Bayou Galle, which is on the right side, about thirty yards wide, a beautiful, clear, running stream of wholesome well-tasted water; after passing which, it is thick cane again for twenty-five miles, when we arrive at a river that falls in on the right side, which is called by the Indians Kiomitchie, and by the French La Riviere la Mine, or Mine river, which is about one hundred and fifty yards wide, the water clear and good, and is boatable about sixty miles to the silver mine, which is on the bank of the river, and the ore appears in large quantities, but the richness of it is not known. The Indians inform of their discovering another, about a year ago, on a creek that empties into the Kiomitchie, about three miles from its mouth, the ore of which, they say, resembles the other. The bottom land of this river is not wide, but rich; the adjoining high lands are rich, well timbered, well watered and situated. About the mine the current of the river is too strong for boats to ascend it, the country being hilly. After passing the Kiomitchie, both banks of the river are covered with thick cane for twenty-five miles, then, left side, a high pine bluff appears again to the river for about half a mile; after which nothing but cane again on each side for about forty miles, which brings you to the mouth of a handsome bayou, left side, called by the Indians Nahaucha, which, in English, means the Kick; the French call it Bois d'Arc, or Bow-wood creek, from the large quantity of that wood that grows upon it. On this bayou, trappers have been more successful in catching beaver than on any other water of Red river; it communicates with a lake, three or four miles from its mouth, called Swan lake, from the great number of swans that frequent it. It is believed that this bayou is boatable, at high water, for twenty or thirty leagues, from what I have been informed by some hunters with whom I have conversed, who have been upon it. The low grounds are from three to six miles wide, very rich; the principal growth on it is the bois d'arc. The great prairies approach pretty near the low grounds on each side of this creek; leaving which it is cane both sides for about eight miles, when we arrive at the mouth of the Vazzures, or Boggy river, which is about two hundred yards wide, soft miry bottom, the water whitish, but well tasted. Attempts have been made to ascend it in pirogues, but it was found to be obstructed by a raft of logs, about twenty miles up it. The current was found to be gentle, and depth of water sufficient; was the channel not obstructed, might be ascended far up it. The low grounds on this river are not as wide as on most of the rivers that fall into Red river, but very rich; the high lands are a strong clay soil; the principal growth oak. After leaving this river the banks of Red river are alternately cane and prairie; timber is very small and scattered along only in places; it is now only to be seen along the water courses. From the Boggy river to the Blue river is about fifty miles, which comes in on the right side. The water of this river is called blue, from its extreme transparency; it is said to be well tasted, and admired, for its quality, to drink. The bed of this river is lined generally with black and greyish flint stones; it is about fifty yards wide, and represented as a beautiful stream; pirogues ascend it about sixty or seventy miles. The low grounds of Blue river are a good width for plantations, very rich; the growth pecan, and every species of walnut. The whole country here, except on the margin of the water courses, is one immense prairie. After passing this river, copses of wood only are to be seen here and there along the river bank for about twenty-five miles, to a small turgid river, called by the Indians Bahachaha, and by the French Fauxoacheta; some call it the Missouri branch of Red river; it emits a considerable quantity of water; runs from north to south, and falls into Red river, nearly at right angles, and heads near the head of the Arkansas, and is so brackish it cannot be drank. On this river, and on a branch of the Arkansas, not far from it, the Indians find the salt rock; pieces of it have often been brought to Natchitoches by hunters, who procured it from the Indians.

From the mouth of this river, through the prairie, to the main branch of the Arkansas, is three days journey, perhaps sixty or seventy miles in a straight line; from this to the Panis or Towiache towns, by land, is about thirty miles, and by water, double the distance; the river is near a mile wide. The country on each side, for many hundreds of miles, is all prairie, except a skirt of wood along the river bank, and on the small streams; what trees there are, are small; the grass is green, summer and winter. In between thirty-three and thirty-four degrees of north latitude, the soil is very rich, producing luxuriantly every thing that is planted in it. The river from this upwards, for one hundred and fifty miles, continues at least a mile wide, and may be ascended in pirogues.

Mr. Grappe, to whom I am indebted for the foregoing accurate description of Red river, informed me, that his personal knowledge of it did not extend but little above the Panis towns; but Mr. Brevel, of the Isle Brevel, who was born at the Caddo old towns, where he was, had been further up it; and that whatever account he gave me, might be relied on.

I therefore sought an opportunity, a few days after, to obtain from Mr. Brevel the following narrative, which I wrote down from his own mouth as he related it:

"About forty years ago, I sat off on foot, from the Panis nation (who then lived about fifty leagues above where they now live) in company with a party of young Indian men, with whom I had been partly raised, on a hunting voyage, and to procure horses. We kept up on the south side of Red river, as near it as we could conveniently cross the small streams that fell in, sometimes at some distance, and at others very near it, in sight of it. We found the country all prairie, except small copses of wood, cedar, cotton or musketo, amongst which. a stick six inches in diameter, could not be found; the surface becoming more and more light, sandy, and hilly, with ledges of clifts of a greyish sandy rock, but every where covered with herbage. We found many small streams falling into the river, but none of any considerable size, or that discharged much water in dry seasons, but many deep gulleys formed by the rain water. After travelling for several days over a country of this description, the country became more broken, the hills rising into mountains, amongst which, we saw a great deal of rock salt, and an ore, the Indians said was my (meaning the white people's) treasure; which I afterwards learnt was silver; and that amongst these mountains of mines, we often heard a noise like the explosion of cannon, or distant thunder, which the Indians said was the spirit of the white people, working in their treasure; which I afterwards was informed, was the blowing of the mines, as it is called, which is common in all parts of Spanish America where mines exist. The main branch of the river becoming smaller, till it divided into large innumerable streams, that issued out of the valleys amongst these mountains; the soil very light and sandy, of a reddish grey color. We travelled on from the top of one mountain to the top of another, in hopes the one we were ascending was always the last, till the small streams we met with ran the contrary way, towards the setting sun, and the lands declined that way. We continued on till the streams enlarged into a river of considerable size, and the country became level, well timbered, the soil rich black loam; the waters were all clear and well tasted. Here we found a great many different tribes of the Hietan, Apaches, and Concee Indians; we likewise fell in with them frequently, from the time we had been a few days out from the Panis towns, and were always treated kindly by them.

" I believe the distance from the Panis towns to where we saw the last of Red river, is at least a hundred leagues; and that in crossing over the ridge, we saw no animals that were not common in all the interior of Louisiana, except the spotted tiger, and a few white bears. After spending some days on the Western waters, we set off for the settlements of Santa Fé; steering nearly a southeast course, and in a few days, were out of the timbered country into prairie; the country became broken and hilly; the waters all running westwardly; the country clothed with a very luxuriant herbage, and frequently passing mines of silver ore. We arrived, at length, at a small meanly built town, in the Santa Fé settlement, containing about one hundred houses, round which were some small cultivated fields, fenced round with small cedars, and musketo brush wattled in stakes; this little town was on a small stream of water that ran westwardly, that in a dry season did scarcely run at all; and that the inhabitants were obliged to water their cattle from wells; and I understand, that the Bayou upon which this town is situated, was no part of Rio Grande, but fell into the Western ocean; but of that I might have been mistaken. I understood that similar small towns or missions were within certain distances of each other, for a great extent southwardly, towards Mexico, and that the inhabitants were mostly christianised Indians and Maitiffs; that the mines in that settlement afforded very rich ore, which was taken away in large quantities, packed on mules, and had the same appearance of what we met with, about the head branches of Red river. After furnishing ourselves with horses at this place, we sat off again for the Panis towns, from whence we started; steering at first southwardly, in order to avoid a high mountainous country that is difficult to cross, that lies between Santa Fé and Red river; after travelling some distance south, we turned our course again northeastwardly, and arrived at the Panis towns in eighteen days from the day we left Santa Fé settlements, and in three months and twenty days from the time we started."

He is of the opinion that, from the Panis towns to Santa Fé, in a right line, is nearly three hundred miles; and all the country prairie, a few scattering cedar knobs excepted. After he had finished his narrative, I asked him how far Red river was boatable. He said, not much above the Panis old towns; not that he knew of any particular falls or obstructions, but that the head branches of the river came from steep mountains, on which the rain often poured down in torrents, and runs into the river with such velocity, sweeping along with it large quantities of loose earth, of which these hills and mountains are composed, that it rolls like a swell in the sea, and would either sink or carry along with it, any boat that it might meet in the river. But, he observed at the same time, that his opinion was founded on no experiment that he had ever known made. I asked him, if the Indians had no pirogues high up in the river. He told me, that the Indians there knew nothing of the use of them; for instead of their being, for hundreds of miles, a tree large enough for a canoe, one could scarcely be found large enough to make a fowl trough. I asked him what animals were found in the great prairies. He told me, that from Blue river, upwards, on both sides of Red river, there were innumerable quantities of wild horses, buffalo, bears, wolves, elk, deer, foxes, sangliers or wild hogs, antelope, white hares, rabbits, &c. and on the mountains, the spotted tiger, panther, and wild cat. He farther told me, that, about twenty-three years ago, he was employed by the Governor of St. Antoine, to go from that place into some of the Indian nations who lived towards Santa Fé, who were at war with the Spaniards, to try to make a peace with them, and bring in some of the chiefs to St. Antoine. He sat off from that place with a party of soldiers, and was to have gone to Santa Fé; they passed on a northwestwardly course for about two hundred miles, but after getting into the great prairie, being a dry season, they were forced to turn back, for want of water for themselves and horses, and that he does not know how near he went to Santa Fé, but believes he might have been half way.

The accounts given by Mr. Brevel, Mr. Grappe, and all other hunters with whom I have conversed, of the immense droves of animals that, at the beginning of winter, descend from the mountains down southwardly, into the timbered country, is almost incredible. They say the buffalo and bear particularly, are in droves of many thousands together, that blacken the whole surface of the earth, and continue passing, without intermission, for weeks together, so that the whole surface of the country is, for many miles in breadth, trodden like a large road.

I am, sir, &c.

JOHN SIBLEY.

To General HENRY DEARBORN, *Secretary of War.*

Distances up Red river, by the course of the river.

From the mouth of Red river to Black river,	Miles.		Miles.
From the mouth of Red river to Black river,	31	Through Bayou Diachet to the river again,	9
To Baker's landing, lower end Avoyelles,	51	Late Caddo villages, where they lived five	
La Glass' do. upper end do.	15	years ago, - - - -	80
Rice's,	6		— 197
Hoome's,	18	Little river of the left, - -	80
Nicholas Grubb's,	21	Long prairie, right side,	25
Mouth of Bayou Rapide,	15	Upper end of ditto, -	25
	— 157	Little prairie, left side, -	40
Indian villages,	22	Upper end, ditto,	40
Mount Pleasant, Gillard's place,	7	Pine bluff, right side, -	12
Mouth of Rigula de Bondieu,	6	Upper end, ditto, -	5
Mounett's plantation,	10	Cedars, - - -	15
Mouth of Little River,	24	Upper end ditto and mouth of Little river	
Bayou Brevel,	20	of the right, - -	40
Natchitoches, -	20		— 247
	— 109	Round prairie, right side (first fording	
Grand Ecore,	10	place) - - -	20
Compti, -	20	Lower end of long prairie, left side,	25
Bayau Channo,	15	Upper end ditto, -	40
Lake Bistino, through Bayou Channo,	3	Next prairie, same side, -	12
Through lake Bistino to the upper end of		Upper end of the same, -	20
Channo, - - -	60	Three mile oak and pine bluff,	30

	Miles.
Pecan grove, - - - - -	9
Upper end of the same, - - -	6
	— 162
Prairie next above the Pecan's,	40
Upper end of the same, - - -	25
Pine bluff right ride, - - -	45
White rock bluff, - - - -	15
Next prairie, right side, - - -	45
Uper end, ditto, - - -	30
Bayou Galle, right side, - - -	6
Mouth of Kiomitchie, or Mine river,	25
Pine Bluff left side, - - -	25
Bayou Kick or Bois d'arc, - -	40
	— 296
The Vazzures, or Boggy river, right side,	8
Blue river, right side, - - -	50
Faux Ouachita, a Missouri branch, -	25
Panis or Towiache towns, - -	70

	Miles.
Panis or Towiache old towns, -	150
Head branch of Red river, or dividing ridge,	300
	— 603
	1,771
To which may be added for so much the distance being shortened, by going through lake Bristino, than the course of the river,	60
	1,831
Computed length of Red river, from where it falls into the Mississippi, to which add the distance from the mouth of Red river to the ocean, by either the Mississippi or the Chaffeli, which was once probably the mouth of Red river, - - -	320
Total length of Red river, miles,	2,151

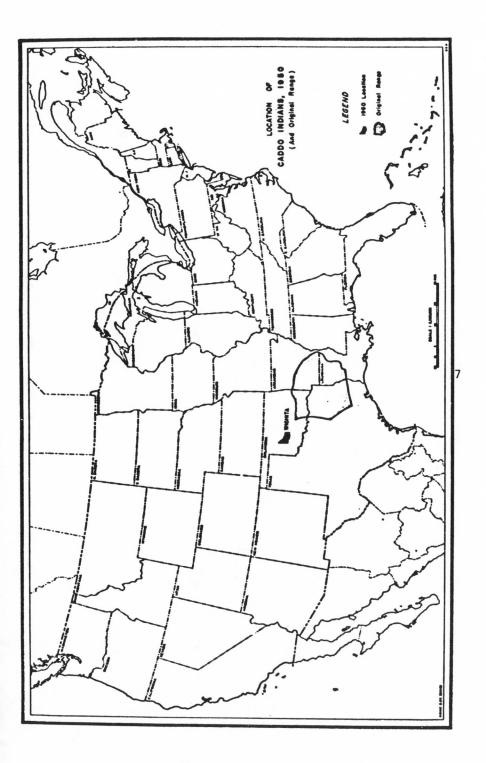

LOCATION OF
CADDO INDIANS, 1950
(And Original Range)

LEGEND

▰ 1950 Location
⬡ Original Range

WICHITA

SCALE IN MILES

7

8

THE TERRITORY OF THE CADDO TRIBE

OF OKLAHOMA

Helen Hornbeck Tanner
Ann Arbor, Michigan
1972

10

TABLE OF CONTENTS

11

12

Introduction

This ethnohistorical report concerns the aboriginal territory of the Caddo Tribe of Oklahoma, whose ancestors occupied a region now part of four American states: Texas, Louisiana, Arkansas and Oklahoma. The earliest data on Caddo occupancy in the four state region is derived exclusively from archaeological investigation and is summarized in a separate report, "The Caddoan Cultural Area: An Archaeological Perspective" by Don G. Wyckoff. (Plaintiff's Exhibit W-197, Dkt. 226.)

Written accounts of the various Caddo groups and their neighboring tribes date from the arrival of the first French and Spanish explorers and missionaries in the late seventeenth century, although some information has been gleaned from records of the DeSoto expedition in 1541. When first reported, the principal Caddo villages - with individual names - were located: on the big bend of the Red River of Texas and Arkansas, lower on the Red River near present-day Natchitoches, Louisiana, in the valleys of the Neches and Angelina rivers of Texas and on the Ouachita river of Arkansas and Louisiana. Other groups that have figured less prominently in Caddo literature were noted north of the Red river in eastern Oklahoma and on the Arkansas river.

13

The complete history of the widespread Caddo, covering a span of more than a thousand years, can be traced only by combining and cross-checking the results of archaeological fieldwork with date from maps and written records. Language study and tradition provide additional guides

to the reconstruction of tribal history. In recent years, the major contribution to the knowledge of Caddo culture has been made by archaeologists
working in the four state region who have held a series of informal conferences. To date, there has been no similar joint enterprise to assemble
and correlate historical documents from French, Spanish, Mexican and American archives.

The basic manual for investigating general Caddo history has been
John R. Swanton's pioneer study, Source Material on the History and Ethnology of the Caddo Indians, Bulletin 132 of the Bureau of American Ethnology published in 1942 and long out of print. Other contributions to
Caddo history have been regional in approach. Herbert E. Bolton's original
research, published between 1908 and 1916, emphasized Spanish Texas.
W.B. Glover's substantial article, "A History of the Caddo Indians" (1935)
concentrates on the Caddo of Louisiana, although it covers part of the
tribal history in Texas up tO 1845. The extensive documentary study of
William J. Griffith, The Hasinai Indians of East Texas as seen by Europeans,
1687-1772 (1954) again concentrates on neighboring Caddoan communities
clustered in a single state, Texas. A fourth authority, Grant Foreman,
views Caddo activities as part of the southwestern frontier history of
the Arkansas territory and modern Oklahoma.

One of the problems of following total Caddo history is the changing
European political jurisdictions over the area in which the Caddo had their
villages and hunting territory. Initially, the Caddo country of Louisiana
and Texas was a region of rivalry between France and Spain. The lower
Red river region was firmly in the hands of French traders, while the
territory on the Sabine river and further west was under Spanish jurisdiction

14

After French Louisiana was transferred to Spain, effective in 1769, the
entire region west of the Mississippi river came under the rule of Spain.
For thirty-five years, the Caddo were under a single European political
authority, even though Louisiana and Texas remained separate administrative districts within the Spanish empire.

The Caddo lived in comparative harmony with the French and Spanish, probably because they enjoyed the advantages of trade and presents,
and the European population was small. In this report, the aboriginal
territory of the Caddo will be described with reference to the situation
at the beginning of the nineteenth century, concurrent with the American
purchase of Louisiana territory in 1803.

With the advent of American sovereignty over Louisiana, the
Caddo found themselves in a region contested first by Spain and the
United States, and later by the Republic of Mexico and the United States.
On both sides of an uncertain international border, the Caddo became
unwillingly involved in the frequent disruptions of a chaotic frontier
zone until Texas was annexed to the United States in 1845. Among the
important events influencing regional history in the intervening years
were the:

15

   (1) Mexican War for Independence from Spain, 1810-1823
   (2) British-American War of 1812
   (3) The Adams-Onís Treaty of 1819 establishing the upper
       Red river as the boundary between Spain and the United
       States
   (4) Texas War for Independence from Mexico, achieved in 1836

The subsequent Mexican-American War, 1846-1848 was also part of the historical background. Simultaneous with these military and diplomatic events,
Caddoan occupancy of their aboriginal lands was affected by two great

waves of population: (1) immigration of Indians from east of the Mississippi river, followed by the wholesale transfer of tribal groups into
the territory north of the Red river implementing the Indian Removal Bill
of 1830, and (2) rapid influx of settlers into Louisiana and Arkansas
territories after the War of 1812, and into Texas after 1836.

The first treaty between the Caddo and the American federal government, in 1835, concerned only a small portion of Caddo lands in Arkansas and Louisiana. The area is identified at No. 202 on Charles C. Royce,
Indian Lands Cessions in the United States, Eighteenth Annual Report
of the Bureau of American Ethnology, Part II (1899). On July 1, 1835
just prior to the outbreak of the Texas Revolution, the Caddo signed a
16   treaty in Louisiana agreeing to remove from American territory and join
their related tribes in Texas. By this time, the Caddo had long been
involved in Indian affairs of Arkansas and Oklahoma, but not in land
cessions in those areas. Land cessions were taken from the Osage and
Quapaw, and designated for immigrant Indian tribes, by the Federal
government while the majority of Caddo were still based outside American
territory.

During the short life of the Texas Republic, the question of
Indian lands in Texas was never settled, but remained a critical issue.
Surveying continued while treaties were signed and tentative boundaries
between white and Indian territory were under discussion. The Caddo
and related tribes at times fought the encroaching white population and
at other times cooperated in negotiations with Texas authorities to fix
a line separating areas of white and Indian occupancy.

With the annexation of Texas in 1845, all the Caddo came under the protection of the United States. The problem of Texas Indian lands was still unresolved by the first American Treaty, signed May 15, 1846. Thereafter, under extreme pressure from the growing white population, the Caddo and their allies were confined to a reservation established on the Brazos river in 1854. Following an unprovoked massacre and threats of anihilation by militant Texas settlers, the surviving population was guided across the Red river into Oklahoma in 1859 by the United States agent.

The foregoing summary is but an outline, intended as a frame of reference for interpreting the complex history of the tribal groups whose present-day descendants are members of the Caddo Tribe of Oklahoma.

In place of lengthy footnotes, this report cites accompanying   17 exhibits by letter ("T" for Tanner), exhibit number and page number(s) within the specific exhibit. Citations to a separate "W" series indicate exhibits assembled for the archaeological report of Don G. Wyckoff.

18

I.

The Caddo: Beginning of Historic Era

A distinctive feature of the Caddo is their long history in the
same geographic region. The entire archaeological report (W-197) is
consequently considered as the beginning history of the contemporary
Caddo. Because this background is so important, attention is first directed to particularly significant parts of the conclusions reached by
Wyckoff:

> "From archaeological evidence it is possible to recognize
> some 800 or 900 years of prehistoric habitations believed
> integral to the Caddoan cultural tradition.... For some of
> the historically known Caddoan groups it is possible to see
> outlines of continuity which reach back through the entire
> time span.... Throughout the prehistoric periods, the
> greatest consistence and continuity of an overall cultural
> pattern seems represented by the sequent, regional manifes-
> tations found from the southern border of the Ouachitas to
> the middle reaches of such streams as the Ouachita, Red,
> Sabine, Angelina and Neches. The long tradition of sedentary
> villages along these streams would implicate that these were
> the homelands for the Caddoan peoples reported by the first
> European explorers and settlers." (W-197: 215-216.)

Although archaeological research concerned primarily with historic
Caddo has been in progress for only ten years, results to date have
identified five localities interpreted as manifestations of Caddo
affiliated occupation in the historic era. These are all on rivers
associated with Caddo culture history for long periods of time:

(1) Red river in the vicinity of Natchitoches

(2) Upper Sabine, Neches and Angelina rivers

(3) Big bend of the Red river, along with Little river and Sulphur
Fork

(4) Upper Ouachita river in the vicinity of Hot Springs, Arkansas

(5) Ouachita river near the Louisiana-Arkansas border.

These locations are plotted on Figure 6, "Components of Caddo Period V,"
(W-197: 201).

13

A detailed geographical description of much of the Caddoan
territory has been presented in the section of the Wyckoff archaeological report, "The Region: Physiographic and Ecological Characteristics." (W-197: 6-12) Since the area of historical occupancy does
not coincide completely with the area of archaeological investigation,
the differences should be noted. First of all, the Wyckoff map of the
Caddoan archaeological area (W-197: 9) included a region north of the
Ouachita Mountains and the Arkansas river where there is scant evidence
of Caddo occupation during the historic era. The divergent history of
the northern region beginning about 1400 A.D. has been discussed by
Wyckoff. (W-197: 211-212, 215) A second difference will be noted
between an archaeological map and the area of historical occupancy,
i.e. the archaeological map does not completely cover the region used
for hunting by the Caddo during the historic era. Archaeological research is directed more toward the location of village and ceremonial
sites rather than scattered hunting activity. Also, selection of sites
has been largely determined by imminent dam construction or highway
building.

20

Turning to historical documentation of the Caddo and their
territory, it is clear at the outset that a large region is involved.
An early indication of the dimensions of the Caddo country comes from the
writings of a Spanish priest who lived among the Hasinai tribes of East
Texas, learned their language during the period from 1715 to 1719, and
later returned in 1721. He wrote:

> "The Province of the Assinais, commonly called Texas, is
> more than five hundred leagues from the Imperial City of
> Mexico by the road which has been travelled by our Spaniards
> up to this time.... This nation of the Assinais contains
> many divisions which I do not list by their own names for
> the purpose of avoiding confusion. The nation extends for
> a distance of more than one hundred leagues in each of the
> principal directions. To the northward it reaches as far
> as the banks of the Missouri River [Arkansas] which flows
> into the River of the Palisades [Mississippi], where there
> are many civilized agricultural tribes." (T-61: 152)
> See also (T-60: 54-55)

Taking the eighteenth century land league as equal to 2.65
English miles, the above description indicates an area extending more

than 265 miles north and south, and an equivalent distance east and west.
(T-90: 68) These measurements can be interpreted geographically by referring to the Raisz topographic map (T-190). For example, the north-
south distance measures 300 miles, or 113 leagues, on a straight line
from Fort Smith, Arkansas on the Arkansas river at the Oklahoma-Arkansas
border, down to the confluence of the Neches and Angelina rivers at the
Kisatchie Wold. In an east-west direction, the same straight-line
distance reaches from Monroe, Louisiana to Forth Worth, Texas. In terms
of present-day highway mileage, the computed distance from Fort Worth,
Texas to El Dorado, Louisiana ["E" on T-190, the Raisz map] is 295 miles,
or 111.5 leagues. The same mileage on a north-south axis is equated to
the distance between McAlester, Oklahoma ["Mc.A" on T-190, the Raisz map]
and Trinity, Texas in southwest Trinity County about where the Trinity
river reaches Kisatchie Wold.

Bolton states that distances in early diaries were based on the
"Old Spanish League" which he equates to two English miles. Using this
scale, all the distances in the preceding paragraph would be reduced
twenty-five percent. On the other hand, the phrase "each of the principal directions" could easily be interpreted as the "four points of the
compass", or an overland distance of 800 miles for both the north-south
and east-west axes measured in "old Spanish leagues".

The territory of the Caddo encompassed rivers, lakes, mountains,
forests and prairies in the four state region of Louisiana, Arkansas,
Oklahoma and Texas. One of the main theatres of action, particularly
for French contact with the Caddo, was the section of the Red river valley
between Natchitoches, Louisiana and the "big bend" of the river in the
southwest corner of Arkansas. In this middle course of the Red river,
two well-known landmarks were the rapids above modern Alexandria and the
"Great Raft", a mass of tangled tree trunks and flood debris that ob-
scured the actual river course, impeding navigation for seventy miles
above Natchitoches. At intervals, portions of the "Great Raft" were
dislodged, but the mass tended to increase !n length over a long period
of time, creating lakes, swamps and bayous that formed alternative water
courses with frequent portages. (T-56: 770-711) (T-47: 253-254)

21

The first French accounts of the barrier describe the difficulties
of dragging heavy pirogues over the interlaced logs, or the fearful experience of struggling through the dark passageways under the tangled
branches, with the added menace of snakes and crocodiles. (T-88) The
"Great Raft" and a number of smaller rafts continued to create problems
on the Red river until Captain Henry Shreve systematically destroyed
the collected timber, a five-year job he commenced in 1833. The removal
of the raft improved drainage and brought some physical changes to the
Red river valley, as well as opening the stream for general transportation
and communication. (T-56: 772-773)

Within the section of the Red river between the rapids and the big
bend, two major tributaries enter from the west: the Big Cypress Creek
flowing through Caddo Lake above modern Shreveport, and the Sulphur
Fork flowing through modern Lake Texarkana to enter the Red river just
above the Louisiana-Arkansas border. The Sulphur river was also
called the Little river of the South. In many places, dam construction
has changed the face of the country sufficiently so that frequent reference must be made to historical maps.

Beginning at the big bend of the Red river, the important streams
within Caddo country all enter from the north. The Little river [of the
North] at modern Fulton, Arkansas provides the main southern drainage
from the Ouachita Mountains that rise to 2,600 feet above sea level near
the Oklahoma-Arkansas border. Oklahoma streams figuring in Caddoan
accounts are: The Kiamichi, Boggy, Blue and Washita rivers, all crossing
the prairies west of the Ouachita Mountains. The mouth of the Washita
river is within the region now submerged by the Denison Dam on the
central Oklahoma-Texas border. In early documents, the Washita was
often called the False Washita [Faux Ouachita to the French] because
its course had become confused with the Ouachita river of south-central
Arkansas.

A second theatre of action in Caddo history, important for
Spanish contacts with the Hasinai division, was the East Texas forest
land between the Sabine and Trinity rivers. The headwaters of the
Sabine river are not far from the often-mentioned "three forks of the

Trinity" at modern Dallas, Texas. Between these two main streams lie
the Neches river and a parallel tributary, the Angelina, meeting at
the edge of the Kisatchie Wold, the ridge separating interior Texas
from the coastal prairie. North of the Sabine river, the Sulphur Fork
of the Red river originates close to the creeks forming the East Fork
of the Trinity river.

West of the main course of the Trinity river in Texas and the
lower Washita river of central Oklahoma, the Cross Timbers formed an
important landmark for the Indian tribes of the region. (T-152a: 92)
(T-23: 77) (T-116: 537) South of the Red river, two separate timber
belts are distinguished with the Grand Prairie in between. (T-190, map)
The eastern Cross Timbers extend south to the Brazos river in the
vicinity of Waco, Texas. The broader Western Cross Timbers begin west
of Fort Worth, Texas. (T-65)

Early nineteenth century accounts indicate that the timber belt
crossed the Red river about forty of fifty miles above the mouth of the
Washita river, stretching northward with westward prongs. (T-66: 185)
The Cross Timbers were not represented consistently or accurately on
many early manuscript maps. At the South Canadian river, the western
edge of the timber belt was present-day Purcell, Oklahoma. Apparently,
there was some variation in the breadth of the Cross Timbers, in some
cases as a result of forest fires along the edge of the timberland.
Quite possibly, the Indian custom of burning over the prairies to produce a better crop of buffalo grass led to destruction of bordering
forested areas. Breadth of timber belt was estimated at five to thirty
miles, with a total length of 400 miles. (T-152a: 92)

Within the region called "Texas" by the Spaniards, including some
areas of French Louisiana, a number of villages and tribal divisions were
listed by the earliest reporters. Since the literature of the Caddo involves so many tribal names, particularly varied in the seventeenth Spanish and French sources, it may be useful to clarify terminology at the
outset. The modern English term "Caddo" is but a handy abbreviation of
a name that appears in its longest form at "Kadohadacho", shortened with
various spellings to "Cadodacho" by the Spanish and translated as

23

"Caddodoquieux" by the French. The name is derived from the native work
for an administrator of chief, "Kaadi" or "Caddi". (T-59: 216-217)

In this report, the general phrases "Caddo people" and "Caddo
country" are used in referring to all the tribal divisions that became
consolidated on the reservation of the Caddo Tribe in Oklahoma. The
spelling "Cadohadacho" will indicate only the tribe and regional grouping
at the big bend of the Red river, the "Caddo" of nineteenth century
Louisiana history. "Caddoan" most precisely refers to a linguistic
family including the Caddo, Wichita, Kichai and several other Indian
nations, but this term is also used by archaeologists with different
geographical and cultural connotations.

Modern descriptions of the Caddo people have usually identified
three regional "confederacies", but early accounts do not indicate definite political sub-divisions of this kind. (T-53: 875) (T-11: 2)
On the other hand, all the Caddo villages seem to have been affiliated,
although ties would naturally be closer among near-neighbors.

24   At the beginning of the historic era, the largest group of
Caddo was the collection of villages in modern East Texas, the "Hasinai
confederacy" in Bolton's terminology. (T-11: 2) Their population early
in the eighteenth century has been estimated at 4000 to 5000. (T-9: 276)
The Hasinai tribes called each other friends and allies, using the native
word "tejas" or "texas". (T-59: 286) The term was heard so frequently
that the Spanish described the territory east of the Trinity river as the
Province of Texas. (T-112: 4-5) As a geographical designation, much
enlarged first to cover the independent republic and later an American
state, "Texas" has endured to the present time.

The principal Hasinai settlements were found between the Trinity
and Sabine rivers, in the modern Texas counties of Nacogdoches, Cherokee,
Rusk and Houston. Bolton has discussed their earliest locations.
(T-9: 255-273, passim) The leading tribe was the Hainai, whom the
Americans later called the "Ionies" or even "Ironeyes". The names of
only four other of the original nine or eleven Hasinai divisions continued in use during the nineteenth century. Those most frequently
mentioned were the Nabedache, Nasoni, Nadaco whose English spelling
evolved into Anadarko, and Nacogdoches.

The Caddo group on the bend of the Red river were located in the heart of the Caddo country. Here were the Cadohadacho whose name signifies the "real chiefs", along with the Nanatscho, Nasoni and part of the Natchitoches. Total population for the four villages was probably about 2000. Early eighteenth century maps show three villages on the north side of the Red river, as well as a community of the southern bank. (T-193 and T-194)

The Cahinnio living northeast of the Red river bend in the vicinity of modern Arkadelphia, Arkansas appear to have been closely connected with the Cadohadacho. They were located about twenty-five leagues in an east-north-east direction. (T-36: 218) (T-77: 412-413, 420-421) (T-76: 169-172) Beyond the Cahinnio, their friends the Mento were nearer to the Arkansas river. Later, both tribes were reported on the Arkansas. (T-67: 1, 184) The most precise statement concerning the early location of the Mento was made by the French explorer, Tonti, in 1689. He reported that the Mento were ten leagues "inland" from a Quapaw village situated six leagues above the mouth of the Arkansas river. The Caddo were forty leagues from the Mento. (T-115: 278) These figures would place Caddo in the vicinity of Caddo Gap, the Little Missouri river or central Hempstead county, Arkansas.

25

Between the big bend of the Red river and Natchitoches, there were originally two more Caddo groups, the Yatasi and the Nacachae, according to the Le Maire map of 1716 (T-193) and Vermale map of 1717 (T-194). Another tribe on this part of the river was the Choy (T-112: 13) The Natchitoches had as a neighboring village the Doustioni. The Natchitoches also maintained ties with the Ouachita on the lower Ouachita river in central Louisiana. (T-112: 12) West of Natchitoches lived two tribes of more independent status, the Adai and Ais. The Adai had a village near the modern town of Robeline, Louisiana and camped north of the Natchitoches on the Red river. (T-112: 7) (T-196) The Ais, or Eyeish, were located west of the Adai near modern San Augustine, Texas. (T-197) (T-112:7)

The population distribution of Caddo north of the Red river has been difficult to establish, largely because geographical knowledge was

so incomplete and maps correspondingly difficult to interpret. Nevertheless, the Vermale map of 1717 bears the legend "Qualneo" at a point
upstream from the bend of the Red river, although the actual stream
may have been a northern tributary of the Red river. (T-144) Phonetically,
"Qualneo" is a reasonable approximation of "Cahinnio". The notation
suggests that there were Cahinnio Caddo further west of the Ouachita
river than the location where Joutel found them in 1687. Furthermore,
among Joutel's contacts was a chief entitled "Hinma Kiapemichi", a name
so close to the modern "Kiamichi" that it cannot be ignored. (T-77:421)
Kiamichi is the name of a Caddo division recalled by modern informants.
(T-85) On modern maps the name Kiamichi identifies a section of the
Ouachita Mountains, and a river whose course is from the mountain range
of eastern Oklahoma to the Red river. (T-190)

The Le Maire map of 1716 (T-193) and the Vermale Map of 1717
(T-194) also show a cluster of three villages situated between the Red
river and the Arkansas, at the head of the Ouachita river directly above
the bend of the Red river. One of these names, the Nabiti, is included
in Swanton's list of original Hasinai tribes. A second name spelled
"Ouhanahanhan", with the addition of the Caddo prefix "na" meaning
"upper", forms a reasonable version of the tribal division pronounced
"Nakahanawan" by Swanton's Caddo informant. A similar name was listed
by Mooney. (T-89: 1092)

These two French maps locate the Mento on the Arkansas river,
the northern frontier of the Caddo country at the beginning of the
historic era. In addition, the Vermale map of 1717 shows two villages
of "Outechitas": one on the lower course of the Ouachita river, and
another on the Arkansas river above the Mentos and near the "Panioussa".
The second location is difficult to explain.

The Naoudiche, whose identity was a puzzling problem for Swanton,
are clearly indicated on a manuscript map of 1716 at a point that appears
to be the juncture of the Red river and the Washita river of Oklahoma.
Since the legend "Assinai ou Namediche" appears on the same map, the
Naoudiche and Namediche are evidently different divisions of Caddo.
(T-192) The unsigned map is probably the work of St. Denis, a competent
engineer, who visited the Cadohadacho in 1700. (T-112: 50)

The foregoing discussion indicates the geographic spread of the Caddo communities in the region of the four adjoining modern states of Texas, Louisiana, Arkansas and Oklahoma at the beginning of the historic era. Swanton devoted considerably thought to the problem of resolving the various names of Caddo divisions found in descriptions of the early missionaries and explorers. (T-112: 8-13) See also (T-59: 288) Bolton likewise analysed the tribal names reported by the French and Spanish. (T-9: 253-255) Harby thought the total might add up to forty-five different units in several confederations. (T-55) Looking at the inconsistencies in lists of "allies" or "enemies" of the Caddo, an historian could well suspect some initial problems with the translation in the original interrogation of Indian informants. (T-77: 409-410) For example, it is quite possible to translate "go to war with" either "go to war in conjunction with", or "go to war in opposition to". Such misunderstandings could result in the same tribe being listed both as an ally and an enemy of the Caddo or Hasinai.

Although the Caddo people probably had passed their cultural peak   27
in the fifteenth century, they continued to be the most important native society between the Mississippi river and the Rio Grande. They were a highly religious and artistic nation, with a well-developed system of government and administration, and an economy based on agriculture, hunting and trade. Largely as a result of the extensive research of Herbert E. Bolton, the most detailed information about the internal organization, society and economy of the Caddo people refers to the Hasinai settlements in Texas. But the customs of the Hasinai and other Caddo groups were practically the same. (T-76: 168-169)

The Caddo did not congregate in compact villages, but were spread out in farming communities or hamlets. A dispersed population appears to have been common to all the Caddo people.

In 1685, a French priest accompanying the LaSalle expedition, viewed the Hasinai community, and later observed:

"This village...is one of the largest and most populous that I have seen in America. It is at least twenty leagues long, not that this is evenly inhabited, but in hamlets of ten or twelve cabins forming cantons, each with a different name. Their cabins are fine, forty or fifty feet high, of the shape of bee-hives." (T-65: 39)

His observation is corroberated by a Spanish report:

> "These natives do not live in settlements confined within
> the limits of a pueblo, but each division of the four
> principal tribes among whom the missions were located
> lives in ranchos some distance from each other. The
> principal reason for this is that each family seeks a
> place large enough for his crop and one where there is
> water at hand for household use and for bathing--which
> is very frequent among them." (T-65: 164)

A contemporary statement concerning the Cadohadacho on the Red river pointed
out that:

> "All the nations of this tribe speak the same language.
> Their cabins are covered with straw, and they are not
> united in villages but their huts are distant one from
> the other. Their fields are beautiful. (T-65: 43)

Similarly, the early Yatasee lived in cabins "scattered along the Red
river for two leagues. (T-65: 50)

Bolton drew on reports of Joutel in 1687, De Leon in 1690, and
Teran in 1691 in describing the dispersed population pattern of the Caddo
people. For example, between the edge of the Nabedache village and the
28 chief's house in the center, there were several "hamlets" surrounded by
patches of corn. But west of the village, toward the Trinity river there
was an additional settlement of four farms. (T-9: 272-273)

In fields adjacent to their thatched houses, the Caddo people
raised farm crops, principally corn, beans, squash and tobacco. More
information is available about Hasinai gardening, and the list of products
for that region is correspondingly more detailed. The tribes in Texas
planted sunflower seeds and watermelons, and by the late eighteenth century
had established orchards of peaches, apricots, plums, and other fruits.

They also gathered wild fruits and nuts: grapes, strawberries,
blackberries, mulberries, wild cherries, hickory nuts, walnuts, acorns,
pecans and chestnuts. (T-59: 210) (T-60: 55) (T-61: 153)

The Caddo were skilled artisans, chiefly famous for their exceptionally fine pottery. (T-94: 297) Their homes were furnished with
beds, benches, basket containers and reed mats. (T-60: 58) They used
dogs for hunting, and acquired Spanish horses through intermediate traders
before 1690. Hunting through the forests and water courses beyond their

fields, Caddo brought back turkeys, ducks, deer, wild pigs, rabbits, and
sometimes bear. (T-59: 211) They fished in the streams using trot-lines,
the same system used today in that region. (T-61: 153) On the longer
hunting expeditions, they went after buffalo. (T-60: 55) The seasonal
expeditions, ofter lasting three months took the Caddo far from their
homes and fields. (T-61: 157) In determining the total tribal territory
of the Caddo, it will be necessary to give attention to their hunting
grounds, about which little information is available prior to the
American era.

Over a long period of time, the Caddo had developed a stable system
of government. In describing the system in The Indians of Texas (1969)
W.W. Newcomb, Jr. observed:

> What we know of the Caddoes' political organization is much
> more intelligible to people of Western civilization than
> that of many other Texas Indians. This is not because it
> closely resembles modern democracies or other political
> systems, but because it was a bureaucracy, containing a
> series of graded offices--and officers, each with specific
> duties to perform. (T-94: 303)

29

All accounts of the Hasinai stress the importance of the priestly ruler,
carrying the title of the "Grand Xinesi", probably pronounced "shinesei",
an office that was hereditary in the male line. (T-59: 216) (T-60: 50)
The lower levels of the hierarchy are outlined by Newcomb as follows:

> Subordinate to the xinesi were the caddices. These men
> were the tribal chiefs, and, like the xinesi, gained their
> office through inheritance. If a caddi's tribe was a large
> one, there were a number of subordinate officials, termed
> canhas who assisted the caddi.... Another group of officials,
> the tammas, had duties roughly similar to those of sergeants-
> at-arms or sheriffs.... A war hero was called an amayzoya; he
> carried and wore special insignia and was set apart as a mem-
> ber of another distinguished group.... According to Casanas,
> "The peace and harmony among the officials described is so
> great that during the year and three months (we have been
> among them) we have not seen any quarrels--either great or
> small. But the insolent and lazy are punished."
> "Sometimes women had great authority, for among the
> Nabedaches, De Solis encountered a woman who was addressed
> by a title which meant 'great lady' or 'principal lady'. She
> lived in a house of many rooms and was much honored by her
> tribesmen, who continually brought her gifts.... Another re-
> ference to a 'queen' has been recorded for the Kadohadachos,
> and is reminiscent of the term 'white woman' among the Natchez
> --the mother of the heir apparent, sister of the ruler and often
> herself a person of great power." (T-94: 303-304)

As the religious leader, the "Gran Xinesi" presided at impressive ceremonies in the fire temple during which he served as mediator between his people and their gods. The perpetual fire was the most significant element of the Caddo's religious observance.

Special festivals and ceremonies were an integral part of Caddo society presided over by the Gran Xinesi. Among the most important was the ceremony marking the maturing of a new crop, an observance that appears to be identical to the "green corn" ceremony of the Creeks, Shawnee and other southern agricultural tribes. In describing the Hasinai festival William J. Griffith noted:

> The first fruits ceremony was apparently a universal practice, but it seems to have been performed separately for each house on a scale determined by the owner's wealth and position. (T-54: 76)

A more elaborate festival was celebrated after the harvest during the "waxing moon in September". The harvest festival featured an elaborate repast, a special drink brewed from wild olive leaves, ceremonial pipe-smoking, huge bonfires, singing and dancing. (T-54: 78-79) (T-59: 52) Racing and endurance contests were the main events at a spring festival held in May in preparation for warfare. (T-54: 81)

The Caddo were far from being an isolated people. Through intermediate traders, they had already come into possession of horses as well as material objects of Spanish origin by 1690. (T-209: 981, 983) Their horse-trading operations with French living in the Illinois country were definitely in existence before 1715. (T-88: 138) Furthermore, an important feature of Caddo society was inter-tribal visiting among the neighboring villages and more distant friends and allies. (T-77: 402, 412)

Ceremonialism played a less prominent part in Caddo life as the eighteenth century advanced. In fact, the general character of society altered as the Caddo--like neighboring tribes--became more dependent upon European goods procurable only in exchange for hides and skins. With increasing emphasis on long hunting expeditions, less time remained for living in the agricultural communities that had so long formed the basis for Caddo social organization. Nevertheless, eighteenth century Caddo were well aware of their long past history. Ceremonial mounds and

"eminences" held meaning for them. La Fora, who accompanied a Spanish
Inspection tour of Texas in 1767, learned the significance of an important mound near the Neches river:

> "It was here that the first Spaniards met the principal
> chiefs of this nation with whom they negotiated a peace
> observed without violation by the Indians ever since."
> (T-21b: 230)

This is probably a reference to the prominent mound now of major importance in Caddoan archaeology as part of the George C. Davis site near
Alto, Texas. (W-115) (W-197: 41-47)

Morfi, in his History of Texas, 1673-1779, noted that the
Cadohadachos living near the Red river also had a special attachment to
a particular piece of high ground:

> "They declare that in a hill, two leagues from their village,
> there appeared a woman whom they consider their goddess and
> called Zacado; that she reared their first parents, taught
> them how to hunt, fish, and make their houses, their dresses,
> and that when they had learned all these things she disappeared.
> The hill is still held in veneration by these Indians, and the
> Cadodachos are respected as the forefathers of the other nations.
> (T-90: 88)

31

No doubt this was the same feature of the landscape pointed out to John
Sibley, first American representative to the Caddo who arrived at
Natchitoches in 1803. In his account of the Red river, Sibley called
attention to the little lake and adjacent hill in the long prairie
above the Little river. He noted:

> "By the side of this lake the Caddoques have lived from time
> immemorial.... To this little natural eminence, all the
> Indian tribes, as well as the Caddoques for a great dis-
> tance, pay a devout and sacred homage." (T-105: 729)

Documents of the eighteenth and nineteenth centuries clearly indicate
that the mounds, hills and other landmarks in Caddo country were visible
reminders of a tradition that had its genesis in the archaeological past,
before the tenth century of the Christian era.

32

II.
French Trade and Spanish Missions

Tracing the history of the Caddo people through the first quarter
of the eighteenth century is largely a matter of shifting attention from
French traders advancing up the Red river to Spanish mission expeditions
advancing and retreating across the Trinity river. Spanish influence in
the Texas-Louisiana area was exerted only in response to evidence of
French activity. The preliminary event, however, was the unsuccessful
colonizing attempt of LaSalle on Matagorda Bay in 1685.

As soon as news of the LaSalle colony reached Mexico, the viceroy authorized an expedition in search of the French who were viewed as
illegal invaders of territory under the jurisdiction of Spain. Through
intermediate Indian traders, the Jumanes, the Spanish administration,
by 1676, had already learned of the "Great Lord of the Texas" who was
adverse to allowing strangers within his "kingdom". (T-21a: 214) (T-209)
Beginning in 1686, a series of expeditions into the region northeast of
the Rio Grande was led by a provincial governor, De Leon. On the fourth
"entrada" in 1689, De Leon found that coastal Indians had destroyed LaSalle's
fort and the remaining inhabitants.* He also was visited by a Nabedache
chief who asked for a mission among his people. Consequently, on a fifth
expedition, De Leon founded two Spanish missions--the first in Texas
near the Neches river in 1690. The Spanish authorities now designated
the region a new province, Texas. The first governor, Domingo Teran de
Los Rios, made his initial visit to the frontier region in 1691, advancing

33

---

*LaSalle and companions set out to get aid in Illinois in 1687.
En route, LaSalle was murdered probably near the Navasota river. About
a half dozen survivors made their way through the Hasinai, Cadohadacho
and Cahinnio settlements to the Arkansas post on the Mississippi river.
In 1689, Tonti descended from the Illinois river as far as the Nabedache
village hoping to rescue colonists left behind on Matagorda Bay.
(T-21a: 355)

as far as the Cadohadacho village at the big bend of the Red river.
(T-24: 9-11) Immediately following this expedition, a disastrous epidemic
spread throughout the region, but most serious in the vicinity of the
missions. (T-54: 88) In retrospect, it seems likely that the epidemic
of 1691 may have been responsible for the disappearance of some of the
original tribes of the Hasinai area. If the survivors of one community
were few, they might merge with another tribal division. Total population
loss was estimated at 3000, a figure probably including deaths among
the coastal and nearby tribes as well as the Caddo. There were 300
fatalities among the Hasinai. (T-54: 88) (T-59: 303) The Hasinai
associated the epidemic with the arrival of the Spaniards. The resulting
increasing in Indian hostility, plus a series of crop failures, are given
as causes for the abandonment of this first mission experiment in 1693.
(T-24: 11)

Shifting attention back to the French scene, we find that the
French established a base in the Biloxi-Mobile Bay area in 1699, only
34 two months after the Spanish founded Pensacola in late 1698. Gaining
a permanent foothold, French commanders advanced up the Mississippi and
Red rivers by 1700, renewing contact with the Caddo who still remembered
the previous visits of the French in the time of LaSalle. (T-24: 11)
This venture was the beginning of a lasting alliance between the French
and the Caddo.

The Natchitoches tribe living at the head of navigation on the
Red river was the first Caddo tribe to have extensive contact with the
French. (T-88: 150 fn) Following a disastrous harvest in 1702, or
perhaps 1705 or 1708, depending on the reporter, the Natchitoches were
taken down to Lake Ponchartrain to live with the Acolapissa tribe for
several years. (T-112: 51) During this interval, they became acquainted with French customs, imported tools and fabrics, violin music and
the minuet. In 1713, the Natchitoches returned to their native habitat,
found the Doustioni they had left behind, and all resettled in the
vicinity. Their first task was to help the French construct a log fort
signifying French sovereignty over the region. (T-88: 98, 106-107, 110,
145, 148-149) Natchitoches became the base for Indian trade far up the
Red river and across Spanish Texas.

The French base at Natchitoches in turn triggered a second attempt on the part of the Spaniards to establish control over the East Texas Indian tribes through missions. This part of the narrative of French and Spanish competition for influence among the Caddo tribes involves more biography than general history. In a frontier region sparsely populated with Europeans, individual personalities played an important role in international affairs. On this partucular scene, the dominant figure from 1700 to 1744 so far as both the French and Spanish were concerned was Louis Jucherau de St. Denis. He was actually involved with the establishment of the Spanish missions in 1716, as well as the founding of the base at Natchitoches in 1713.

A brief review of the sequence of events begins with a letter from a Spanish priest who correctly guaged that a "French threat" would goad Spanish authorities into renewed efforts to establish a mission frontier in Texas. In 1711, Father Hidalgo wrote a letter directed to the French governor in Louisiana. When the letter reached Cadillac in 1713, he immediately sent St. Denis, his most experienced Indian agent, in search of Hidalgo. St. Denis began by returning the Natchitoches tribe to their previous location on the Red river and setting up French trading headquarters nearby. Next, he set out overland toward Mexico but spent the next winter trading among the Hasinai, a factor he later tended to conceal from Spanish authorities. (T-88: 149-151) In 1714, he reached the Spanish presidio on the Rio Grande, only to find that Father Hidalgo was in the interior of New Spain. (T-7: 36-37)

35

Passing over many details from his dramatic experiences, including an interval in jail in Mexico City, we come to the important fact that St. Denis won the hand of the niece of the commandant at the Spanish fort on the Rio Grande, and subsequently became part of the Spanish expedition in 1716 to reestablish Spanish missions in Texas. (T-7: 37)

St. Denis' role in the reestablishment of the Spanish missions in Texas was actually not inconsistent with his responsibilities as a French official. This part of his career has been evaluated realistically by historian Robert Carleton Clarke:

"The Saint-Denis expedition, from the viewpoint of the
French was a business enterprise growing out of the commercial policy of Antoine Crozat and his agent, Cadillac;
it was in no sense military or political, but sought merely
to secure for the French of Louisiana a freer and more
profitable trade arrangement with Mexico. The same business motive no doubt led Saint-Denis, when he failed in his
first effort, to accept service with the Spanish and to assist to introduce their friars and soldiers into territory
which, with much justice, have been claimed as French. The
missionary and colonizing expedition of 1716 was the immediate result of the presence of Saint-Denis and his companions in Mexico; the rulers of New Spain [Mexico] were
again brought to fear that the French would supercede them
in the lands east of the Rio Grande." (T-28: 24-25)

St. Denis' marriage formed an alliance between high-ranking French
and Spanish families; an alliance that became the basis for personal influence over the Caddo tribes until 1780. It was also the basis for
Indian trading connections that continued in spite of commercial restrictions until the end of the Spanish era. (T-10: 85) St. Denis the
elder was clearly the most influencial man on the Lousiana-Texas frontier up to his death in 1744. (T-11: 41) His work was carried on by
his son and by his son-in-law, Athanése de Mezières, who first entered
the French service then transferred to the service of Spain after Spain
assumed sovereignty over Louisiana in 1769. (T-7: 82-85)

Following the establishment of the Spanish mission chain in
1716-1717, the next event in the series of French and Spanish reactions and counteractions was the addition of a military detachment
to the French post at Natchitoches in 1717. (T-83a fn) (T-107: 85)
That same year, Chickasaw warfare was a factor on the eastern frontier
of the Caddo country. In 1717, one part of the Yatasi joined the
Natchitoches and another part moved up the Red river near the
Cadohadacho, where they maintained a separate village up to the
advent of the American era in Louisiana. (T-107: 234) An earlier
incursion of Chickasaw had been responsible for the Ouachitas' moving
to the Red river to join the Natchitoches. (T-84: 303) In 1700,
the Ouachita village on the lower course of the Red river was already
reduced to five cabins. (T-112: 50) Although undocumented, the same
Chickasaw threat may have been the reason for the removal of the Nacache,

36

originally neighbors of the Yatasi. By 1716, the Nacaché were listed
among the Hasinai settlements of the Neches valley. (T-24: 13, 30 fn)
In 1719 they were no longer on the Red river.

The history of the missions is discontinuous. News of war
between France and Spain in 1719 created a frontier war scare, and
the Spanish missionaries withdrew from the region east of the Trinity
river. (T-15: 42-43) In 1721, Aguayo led a truly impressive expedition
to re-establish the missions. He found the Adaes, the most eastern
Caddo tribe, dispersed into the woodlands because of reported attacks
by the French, who carried off some of the Indians to slavery. In conference with Aguayo, St. Denis, French commandant at Natchitoches, agreed to limit French westward advance to the post at Natchitoches.
(T-32: 30; T-15: 44-45) To provide protection for the Adaes and to
strengthen the Spanish frontier, Aguayo built a presidio and established
a garrison at the Adaes mission. (T-15: 52; T-28: 23-24; T-32: 33)

After receiving an unfavorable progress report in 1727, three
of the missions among the Hasinai were transferred to San Antonio in
1730. San Antonio had been founded in 1718, the same year New Orleans
was established by the French. (T-5: 11) The mission at Nacogdoches
and the two near the Ais and Adaes remained in existence until 1773
when East Texas was evacuated by the Spanish. (T-11: 312)

Los Adaes, less than 20 miles from Natchitoches, served as
the Spanish capital of East Texas until 1773 when an administrative
reform ordered the abandonment of the country. (T-32: 37) (T-11: 377-378)
All accounts agree that relations were remarkably cordial between the
French and Spanish outposts that shared a common frontier for over a
half century. References were frequently made to the fact that Spanish
soldiers aided in the successful defense of Natchitoches, besieged by
Natchez Indians who revolted against the French in 1731. A Spanish
chaplain served both communities. (T-11: 40-41)

Although the missions were of negligible permanent influence,
the records of the missionaries and the location of the missions are
guides to the distribution of the Hasinai and allies in East Texas in
the eighteenth century. Missions were placed with a view of serving

37

nearby Indians. The six missions founded in 1716 and their locations
were: (1) San Francisco de los Texas above the site abandoned in 1693
on the Neches not far from Alto, Cherokee County; (2) La Purissima
Concepcion for the Hainai, not far from Linwood crossing of the
Angelina river in Nacogdoches County; (3) St. Joseph for the Nabedache
(also called the San Pedro Indians), the most western of the Hasinai
whose earliest location was near modern Weches, Houston County; (4)
Mission of Guadeloupe in Nacogdoches. These four were all within the
central core of the Hasinai region and have been represented on maps,
but the locations have not been verified by archaeological research.
(T-112: Map facing p. 8; T-28: 23) (T-9: 256 Map, 258, 263-269)

In 1717, the last two missions were established further east:
(5) Nuestra Senora de los Dolores for the Ais on Ayish bayou near
modern St. Augustine, and (6) San Miguel de Linares for the Adaes near
modern Robeline, Natchitoches Parish, Louisiana. (T-15: 40, 49-51)
The accounts of Spanish Texas frequently refers to the "Concepcion"
mission, or the "Linares" mission, consequently, it is helpful to be
familiar with the geographical locations of the mission centers.

38

In reviewing the Spanish missionary activity in East Texas,
it is clear that the program was not successful in spite of the dil-
igent efforts of the padres themselves and the intermittent support
of the political and military authorities. The missions were more
important among the coastal tribes and in the region more directly
subsidiary to San Antonio. The extensive literature regarding the
founding, support, removal, revival and final dissolution of the missions
is disproportionate to their role in the Indian history of the region.
For the Spanish, the missions were useful symbols of Spanish sovereignty,
but ultimately not worth the high cost of maintainance. Spanish missionaries never were able to congregate the Hasinai in compact settlements where they could be brought more under control. (T-10: 81)

Although the diaries and reports furnish valuable descriptions
of the Hasinai communities in the eighteenth century, even these accounts provide only a narrow view of life in the Hasinai region. The
reports are pretty well limited to observations along the road from

San Antonio to Los Adaes, "El Camino Real". The Hasinai obviously
enjoyed the ceremonious arrivals, formal receptions of Spanish dig-
nitaries, giving and receiving presents, the honors bestowed of chiefs
who were selected as "captains". (T-24: 74-75) (T-9: 275) Within
their own culture, inter-tribal visits and the receiving of ambassadors
or messengers was always accompanied by celebrations. (T-15; T-61: 151)
This kind of procedure was understandable, but they remained attached
to their own religion, customs and life style. The Cadohadacho, firmly
under French influence, never accepted Spanish missionaries. (T-83a:
199)

Turning to the northern section of the Caddo country in French
Louisiana, we find the paucity of information in the first decades of
the eighteenth century in striking contrast to the wealth of data about
the southern region. In the northern region, the historical theme is
the development of the Indian trade. The ultimate goal of the French
was to establish contact with Santa Fe and the highly advertised mineral
wealth of the Spaniards. In 1718, Louisiana was turned over to a new
company for commercial exploitation. In the interest of increasing
the trade of his company, Bernard LaHarpe led an expedition up the Red
river to the Cadohadacho region in 1719, then made his way northwest
across modern Oklahoma to the villages of "Toucara" on the South Canadian river. In 1719, he was able to make this exploration free of the
danger of foreign interference because the Spanish had received news
of war with France and retired beyond the Trinity river. (T-107: 374,
380)

Much attention is given to LaHarpe's journal because he made
the first eye-witness report of the mountain and prairie region on
the northwestern border of Caddo territory. Since varying interpretations have been made of the LaHarpe journal, his account will be
treated in considerable detail. (T-83a and T-107)

LaHarpe and his companions made their way up the Mississippi
then the Red river early in the year 1719, battling the strong spring
currents. After stopping at the settlements of the Natchitoches,
Doustioni and Yatasi on islands near the new French fort, they advanced

39

northward to the Cadohadacho region. (T-107, 81-85) Here, LaHarpe
determined to establish an advance post to serve as a trading center
for the frontier and to establish a foothold for France at a strategic
location on the Red river. He knew that the Spanish governor, Martin
de Alarcon, had his eyes on the same location for a Spanish outpost.
He arranged for a small land cession from the Nasonite chief and set
up his headquarters on the southside of the river opposite the Nassonite
village. The Nassonite village itself was near modern Ogden, Arkansas.
(T-107: 86, 253-255)

From the Cadohadacho and Nassonites, LaHarpe learned that several
migratory tribes would be found about 80 leagues further west in the
region north of the Red river. At a distance of 100 leagues northwest
on the banks of a great river, there was a group of powerful tribes,
the most important being the "Toucara" or "Tawakoni". (T-107: 252-253)
LaHarpe was accompanied by a geometrician, DuRivage, to check distances
and direction on the expedition. (T-107: 372) In his journal, LaHarpe
commented on the accuracy of the Indians' knowledge of the surrounding
territory. DuRivage made a preliminary excursion in June looking for
the "nomadic tribes", some of whom he encountered only seventy leagues
west of the Nassonites returning from a joint war expedition against
the Apaches. After a conference, the chiefs agreed to furnish two
guides who would come to the Nassonite village in a month to guide
LaHarpe to the locality of the Tawakoni. LaHarpe set out on this main
expedition on August 11, arrived at the Tawakoni on September 3, started
back on September 16 without adequate Indian guides, and after an interval of desperate confusion in the Ouachita mountains, arrived back
at the Nassonites on October 13, 1719. (T-107: 380, 525-528, 535)

LaHarpe's journal, like the first reports of the Hasinai and
Cadohadacho, records the names of several unfamiliar Indian tribes including some whose names do not appear in later literature. (T-107:
375-376) More important are the distances he gives, for these are
reliable guides to tribal locations at that time.

LaHarpe's base point was "the Nassonites" living in the vicinity of present-day Ogden, Arkansas. LaHarpe quoted distance in

40

'esgues, a French land league at that time being roughly equivalent
to 2.65 English miles. His distances were all in round numbers,
multiples of ten, probably representing his translation of the Indian
method of distance measurement, a day's travel. LaHarpe figured that
a day's travel 'n Indian terms was five leagues, or thirteen and a
quarter miles. By comparing modern highway mileage with the mileage
equivalent of LaHarpe's distances in leagues, it is possible to determine the location of the migratory tribes as well as the villages
at "Toucara". Among the names of the nine villages at "Toucara" are
four prominent in later literature: Tawakoni, Yscani, Taovayas and
Wichita. The Wichita village was rather unimportant. The name did
not become prominent or inclusive of other tribal groups until after
the middle of the nineteenth century.

Considering first the migratory tribes to the west, we learn
from LaHarpe's journal that DuRivage found them "70 leagues west and
a quarter northwest", (T-107: 375) although he had expected to find
them 10 leagues farther away. The meeting probably occurred near   41
the Washita river east of Ardmore, Oklahoma, using the following mileage
figures as the basis for computation:

(1) 70 leagues equals 185 miles

(2) 80 leagues equals 210 miles

(3) Ogden to Idabel, no direct road, estimated 50 miles

(4) Idabel to Ardmore, 148 miles on Oklahoma State Highway Map
1970-1971

The total distance of 198 miles from Ogden to Ardmore is equivalent
to 75 leagues. On this basis, the actual meeting of DuRivage and the
returning war parties would have been thirteen miles east, while his
anticipated meeting was thirteen miles further west. The latter location would have been near the western edge of the Cross Timbers.

LaHarpe reported that the distance from the Nassonites to
"Toucara", generally agreed to have been on the South Canadian river,
was 110 leagues, although he expected the distance to be 100 leagues.
(T-107: 534) He actually spent twenty-three days on the road. Using
as a guide the five leagues per day figure, a twenty-three day trip

at average Indian speed would cover 115 leagues. The distance of 110
leagues, or 281.5 miles, indicates that the Tawakoni and eight neighboring villages were west of Oklahoma City and north of Chickasha,
Oklahoma. This conclusion is based on the following calculations:

    (1)   276 miles, Ogden to Oklahoma City (50 mile estimate Ogden
            to Idabel, plus 226 official mileage Idabel to Oklahoma City)

    (2)   274 miles, Ogden to Chickasha (50 mile estimate Ogden to Idabel,
            plus 224 official mileage Idabel to Chickasha)

Because the east-west course of the South Canadian river near Bridgeport
fits the description of the natural setting of "Toucara" given by LaHarpe,
the Bridgeport vicinity appears to be a likely location, even though
actual mileage indicates a location lower on the river, near Union City.
The Bridgeport section of the Canadian river is close to speculatively
identified sites of the "Wichita", the archaeological classification
for the Tawakoni and allied villages. (T-215: 123-127)

        The preceding conclusions concerning the locations of the migra-
42   tory tribes and the villages of "Toucara" are supported by calculations
based on the fact that the "seventy league" figure was also given as
the distance from the Nassonites to the Nabedache village near modern
Weches, Houston County, Texas. A third check can be made using data
from LaHarpe's trip up the Arkansas river in 1722. His estimate that
at a point sixty leagues from the mouth of the Arkansas, he was 100
leagues from "Toucara" points to Union City, on the Canadian river
directly north of Chickasha, as the "Toucara" location. (T-86)

        LaHarpe further provides valuable information concerning
inter-tribal relations and recent history of the tribes in the modern
Oklahoma region. The migratory tribes numbered about 2500 and are
described as allies of the "Quichua", identified as the Kichai, who
lived south of the Red river between the Cadohadacho group and the
migratory tribes. (T-107: 378-379) In a rather histrionic "harangue"
with the mixture of fact and drama characteristic of Indian oratory,
the Cadohadacho chief told LaHarpe of a peace recently made with the
Naoudiche and other migratory tribes. (T-107: 251-252)

        At this point in the discussion, other data about some of the "migratory tribes" can be introduced. On an unsigned map of 1716, probably the work of St. Denis, the Naoudiche village was located just west of the mouth of the Washita river of Oklahoma, probably not far from the place DuRivage met the migratory tribes in 1719. (T-192) In the 1687 accounts of the LaSalle expedition, the Naoudiche were encountered three leagues from the "Assoni" village and were further identified as allies of these Hasinai. (T-76: 163) A Naoudiche who spoke the Nassonite language (or dialect) also understood the Tawakoni and served as interpreter for LaLarpe, along with a French soldier who understood Nassonite speech. (T-107: 526) In the Cadohadacho region in 1687, Father Anastasious Douay mentioned a village of Ouidiche, where there were visitors from the Cahinnio and Mento whose home was twenty-five leagues east-northeast. (T-36: 218)

The Kichai or "Quichua" themselves must have been recent arrivals in Caddo territory. Their language is identified as "between Pawnee and Wichita". (T-111: 321) The Vermale Map indicates a tribe in that geographic location as "Quichua--attcha ou les jambes courtes [the short legs]". Although the map is dated 1717 it represents information collected earlier. (T-194)

Putting together all the facts in the two preceding paragraphs suggests the following developments: (1) Between the Cadohadacho group on the Red river and the Tawakoni group on the Canadian, in the latter part of the seventeenth century there was a group of migratory tribes with names like Quichua, Quidehai, Oudiche, Naoudiche ["Upper" Ouidiche?] and others as well. (2) By the time of LaHarpe, 1719, some of these tribes--at least part of the Kichai, Ouidiche and Naoudiche--had joined the Cadohadacho and Hasinai although they usually remained on the fringe of the core communities.

LaHarpe's journal also indicates that eastern Oklahoma was a hunting ground used by the Naoudiche, Nassoni, Nadsoos and Cadohadacho. The buffalo country began twenty leagues or about fifty miles from the Cadohadacho. (T-107: 255) LaHarpe encountered a hunting party of Nassonites and Natsoos 130 miles northwest of the Nassonite village returning from a hunting expdeition. (T-107: 382) The Nassonites and

43

the Naoudiche were quite familiar with the territory and resources
of the Ouachita Mountain region for 100 miles north of the Red river,
but they recognized the danger of the Osage if they advanced too far.
(T-109: 371)

Additional evidence of changing status of tribes north of the
Red river in this early period concerns the Nabiti, or "Nabiri". This
tribe, placed north of the Red river on early maps and classed as an
enemy of the Hasinai in 1687, was also among the nine tribes in the
Hasinai mission area in the 1690's. (T-193, T-194) (T-36: 217)
(T-112: 8-10)

One further point of clarification must be made concerning
the migratory tribes met by DuRivage seventy leagues west of the
Nassonites. The joint war expedition included two Tonkawan tribes
belonging to an entirely separate cultural classification outside the
Caddoan language division. The Tonkawa were north-central Texas
tribes particularly persistent in maintaining primitive, migratory
habits. In the mid-eighteenth century, they were generally found
further south between the Trinity and Brazos rivers. (T-7: 289-290)

In the foregoing discussion, emphasis has been on events affecting the Caddo country in the first three decades of the eighteenth
century. Along the Red river, there was evidence of consolidation of
tribal groups: first, the transfer of the Ouachita to the Red river,
and second, movement of the Yatasi to Natchitoches and to the Cadohadacho.
The Chickasaw warfare, mentioned in 1717 as a factor in this region,
subsided as French colonists spread up the Mississippi river after the
founding of New Orleans in 1718. There is some evidence that the
Spanish missions may have drawn in outlying tribes such as the Nacaché
and the Nabiti. After 1731, the three Spanish missions remaining in
East Texas--at Nacogdoches, the Ais, and Adaes-- were rather inactive.
They had slight influence over the Caddo people.

In the northwestern section of the Caddo country, a few new
tribal troups belonging to the Caddoan linguistic family, i.e. the
Kichai and others, became affiliated with the Caddo by the opening
years of the eighteenth century and retained that status. During the

44

period under consideration, all Caddo became involved in French trading
enterprise. The most significant development was the extension of
French outposts beyond Natchitoches to the Cadohadacho and to the
Tawakoni village in 1719. The expedition of LaHarpe, responsible for
these accomplishments, revealed important information about the relative geographical location of Caddoan tribes north of the Red river.
LaHarpe's journal indicates that at the beginning of the eighteenth
century, tribes later called "Wichita" (Tawakoni, Yscani, Taovayas and
Oudesitas) were situated west of the Cross Timbers; while tribes later
grouped together under the "Caddo" heading occupied territory east of
the Cross Timbers. In other words, the Cross Timbers referred to so
commonly in the nineteenth century was an ancient topographical dividing
line.

46

III.

Caddo Alliances and Frontier Warfare

In planting French flags at the Cadohadacho and Tawakoni villages in 1719, LaHarpe not only extended the French trade network but also facilitated contacts between Texas-Red river Caddo and tribes on the Canadian river. By mid-century, the Tawakoni were among the Indian tribes mobilized under Hasinai leadership for an expedition against the Apache of central Texas. The projected campaign was not carried out, but reports from the San Ildefonso mission station on the San Xavier river [west of the Trinity] noted the tribes allied for joint warfare in August, 1750. Bolton summarized the situation:

> On August 2, the Ais and Hasinai tribes arrived, followed by some Cadohadacho, Nabedache, and Yojuane, saying that the "capitan grande", called Sanchez Teja, was near by bringing the Tawakoni, Yatasi, Kichai, Nazoni, Tonkawa and a multitude of others. (T-11: 232-233)

47

The governor of Louisiana in 1753 listed together as joint allies of the French, the Tawakoni, Yscani, Kichai, Hasinai and Cadohadacho. (T-7: 47)

For the Caddo people, the extension of alliances was probably a major development of the eighteenth century. Other developments of this period, considered in turn are: (1) changing European jurisdiction over the Caddo country, (2) an interval of intensive Osage warfare after 1770, (3) Choctaw hostilities after 1792, (4) the steady approach of the Anglo frontier beginning in 1763. Throughout the century, the Cadohadacho and Hasinai groups lived in their customary locations, but they were involved in both friendly and hostile activity along their territorial frontiers. Attention is first of all directed to the western frontier.

Closely connected with the extension of Caddo alliances in the eighteenth century was the southern movement of villages from "Toucara"

on the Canadian river, visited by LaHarpe in 1719. The southern
migration of the Tawakoni, Yscani, Taovayas and Wichita brought about
a new rearrangement of tribes on the western border of Caddo territory. The migration initiated a period of hostilities with the
Spanish in 1758, alleviated two years later through the intermediary
aid of the Hasinai chiefs. In 1771, these tribes, new to the Red
river region concluded their first treaties with representatives of
Spain.

In the chain of occurrences on the western frontier of the
Caddo country summarized in the previous paragraph, the first notable
event took place in 1757. In that year, the large Taovayas village
accompanied by a smaller Wichita contingent, moved to the Red river
and established twin villages on opposite sides of the river near
modern Spanish Fort, Texas. (T-58: 27) (T-159: 108) The Taovayas
move was attributed to harassment by the Osage, but better trading
opportunities on the Red river were probably another attraction. In
48 moving south, the Taovayas drive out the Lipan Apache who previously
lived there. (T-58: 278-279) Resenting Spanish support given the
Lipan through the San Saba mission, the Taovayas and allies attacked
San Saba in 1758. (T-158) (T-159: 108)

The Taovayas successfully repulsed the Spanish counterattack
in 1759 with the aid of allies, including the Yscani, who had concentrated near their village. One big accomplishment was the capture
of two Spanish cannon, the subject of much subsequent correspondence
in Spanish archives. (T-159: 109) (T-156: 109) (T-10: 101)

The year following the Spanish counterattack, the Tawakoni
and Yscani were on the Sabine river of East Texas. The date of their
arrival is not certain, but the Sabine river was their third location
in recent years and they had previously been on the Red river. (T-157:
124-125) In any case, their interest in making peace brought their
presence to the attention of a Spanish priest at Nacogdoches in 1760.
(T-156) Chiefs Canos and Sanchez of the Texas--as the Hasinai are
hereafter called--played an active role in peace negotiations. Captain
Canos accompanied the Tawakoni and Taovayas on later official visits

to Spanish authorities. (T-156: 110) (T-159: 103) While they were
living on the Sabine, the Tawakoni seem to have recognized the authority
of the "Texas" chiefs. (T-210)

The Yscani and Tawakoni remained only temporarily on the Sabine.
The Yscani rejoined the Taovayas on the upper Red river. (T-58: 288)
The Tawakoni moved across the Trinity, were reported near the headwaters
of the Navasota at a former Tonkawan location, and by 1778 had settled
on the Brazos river. (T-8: 193, 196) (T-7: 289, 292) Their shifting
locations have been plotted on Bolton's map, beginning with the dates
of 1760-1763 for their stay on the Sabine. (T-196)

While peace efforts were in progress in Texas in the early
1760's, peace negotiations with more far-reaching consequences for the
Indian tribes were being completed in France. European warfare and
treaty-making in the latter half of the eighteenth century resulted
in transfers of territory on the American continent that directly
affected the lives of all the Indian tribes. In the Mississippi valley
and Red river country, the first major change was the cession of French
Louisiana to Spain in 1762, a transfer regarded by the Indians as
very highhanded. (T-53: 892)

France and Spain had become close allies in the eighteenth
century through a series of "Family Compacts" between the Bourbon
rulers on both thrones. This diplomatic situation provided the basis
for greater cooperation between French and Spanish officials in the
Louisiana and Texas provinces. (T-157: 129) The administration of
Indian affairs involving the Cadohadacho, Texas tribes and their
neighboring Indians was further unified after Spain formally took
over the government of Louisiana in 1769. (T-68: 4)

Chief promoter of a new program of Indian alliances in
Louisiana and Texas was Athanése De Mezières who entered Spanish
service in 1769. De Mezières had several advantages: (1) He was a
highly respected Natchitoches citizen, son-in-law of the famous St.
Denis and consequently of both French and Spanish heritage, (2) He
was proficient in French and Spanish, and Latin as well! (3) He
already had an association with the Cadodacho through his interest

49

In Indian trade. (T-7: 82-85) His vigorous efforts to contact remote tribes and form alliances with those traditionally hostile to
Spain increased the unity and sense of a common bond among the Caddoan-
speaking people in Texas and Louisiana.

De Mezières' overtures to the "Nations of the North," as the
tribes north and west of the Cadohadacho and Texas were called, came
at a time when all these Indian nations suddenly felt the need for
assistance. In 1770, devastating raiders suddenly struck all along
the Red river region. The impetus behind the raids was not only the
Osage, but a derelict gang of European traders near the Arkansas Post.
This small station had been established in 1686 by LaSalle's expedition
at a point fifty miles above the mouth of the Arkansas river. (T-47:3)

De Mezières reported the new incursions as follows:

"I ought to tell you that the Osages, living on the river of
the same name, which empties into the Missuris, have from
time immemorial been hostile to the Indians of this jurisdiction; but on account of the immeasurable distance which
intervenes between their establishments and that of the
[Comanches, Taovayas, Yscanis, Tawakanis, Tonkawas and
Kichai], they formerly inflicted on these tribes only slight
injuries or damages, their mutual enmity being more in evidence through talk than through actual hostilities; and the
Osage being diverted in hunting to pay their creditors of
[Illinois], to which district they belong, and their enemies
being occupied in the same pursuit for the Frenchmen from
here, neither party aspired so much to be at war as to enjoy the pleasures of their respective trade.... But that
river of the [Arkansas] having become infested by...male-
factors...they soon came to know the Osages, and incited
them with powder, balls, fusils, and other munitions...to
attack those of this district, for the purpose of stealing
women, whom they would buy to satisfy their brutish appetites;
Indian children, to aid them in their hunting; horses on
which to hunt wild cattle; and mules, on which to carry the
fat and flest. Thus all at once, this district has become
a pitiful theater of outrageous robberies and bloody encount-
ers....In dispair the [Tawakonis, Yscanis, Tonkawas and
Kichai] have retreated toward the south until they are now
in the neighborhood of the presidios of San Saba, Bexar
[San Antonio] and Espiritu Santo.*" (T-7: 166-167)

50

---

*Brackets indicate modernized spelling or added identification.

De Mezières' first conference with the "Nations of the North"
was held at the principal Cadohadacho village in October, 1770. For
the successful handling of the frontier tribes, De Mezières felt greatly
indebted to Tinhioüen, the Cadohadacho chief, and to Coco, the Yatasi
chief. The conference was attended by only seven chiefs of the Taovayas,
Tawakoni, Yscani and Kichai, because the other members of the delegations still feared reprisal from the Spaniards because of the San
Saba incident, and refused to go further east than the Sabine river.
(T-7: 201-220)

The conference in October, 1770 paved the way for formal treaties
with "The Nations of the North", concluded in 1771 with the additional
help of the Texas chief and Spanish clerics acquainted with the distant
tribes. (T-7: 255) The governor of Texas reported the event as follows:

"They succeeded in bringing four chiefs of the Quitseis,
Yscanes, Tauacanas and Cainiones [Kichai, Yscanis, Tawakonis
and Cahinnio] who solemnly made peace in Natchitoches with
all the customary ceremonies, speaking also for the Tancaues
[Tonkawas], and Tauayares [Taovayas], who are the farthest
distant but also the most powerful and the ones who have
caused the most damage in this province. The...lieutenant,
Don Atanasio Demezières, as the representative of your Lordship, and the lieutenant of Los Adaes, as my representative,
together with the fathers and the Indian chiefs, covered
themselves with the royal banner, as a sign of the union of
all.... Having been given liberal presents, especially by
the lieutenant-governor of that post, all went away pleased
although they excused themselves from coming to ratify the
treaties in San Antonio, both on account of the distance
and because they had been called to go on an expedition
against their enemies the Osages." (T-7: 264-265)

51

The Texas chief and a delegation represented all the tribes
that fall in San Antonio, where they were rewarded by the governor
following the formal treaty ratification ceremony. Bigotes, the
Texas chief, was further given a new honorary name "Sauto" as well
as the title of "capitan grande" or head chief of "all these nations".
(T-7: 266) Later in the year, Tinhioüen of the Cadohadacho came to
Natchitoches with a delegation of five Taovayas including two chiefs
who made a separate treaty of peace on October 28, 1771. In the
opening paragraph of the treaty, the Taovayas are identified as

"mediators for the Comanches", with a further explanation, "Done in the presence of the great Cacique of the Cadodachos, Tin-hi-ouen, who guided and accompanied the Taouaiazes chiefs". (T-7: 256-259)

De Mezières followed up the treaties with journeys to the villages of the new allies of Spain. In 1772, and later in 1778 and 1779, he led expeditions that covered the country from Natchitoches through the little-known interior visiting the Kichai, Tawakoni, Wichita on the Brazos and the twin villages of the Taovayas on the Red river near Spanish Fort, Texas. From the Taovayas, he marched straight south to San Antonio. The correspondence and reports of De Mezières are valuable sources of information on tribal groups within the Caddo country and adjacent territory.* His routes of travel and the Indian tribes he encountered are marked on Bolton's map. (T-196)

Before leaving the De Mezières decade, 1769-1779, four factors merit special emphasis. First, the mention of the Cahinnio as party to the treaty of 1771 is the latest reference that has been found to the separate identification of this tribal division of Caddo. Possibly the Cahinnio were located closer to the Cadohadacho than in earlier reports, although their inclusion in "Nations of the North" still indicated a frontier position. The Cahinnio had always been found near the Mento, a tribe that was close to the Cadohadacho by 1742. Fabry, who ascended the Arkansas that year, reported that the Mento had left their ancient village four or five years earlier, i.e. 1737 or 1738, and moved near the Cadohadacho where they were living currently. Fabry met an Osage war party en route to attack the Mento. (T-42: 474, 483)

The next important factor affected population totals in the Caddo country. During the De Mezières decade, a second epidemic swept through the territory west of the Mississippi river, with a high fatality rate among both the European and Indian populations.

52

---

*For the 1772 expedition (T-7: 283-311), 1778 expedition (T-8: 187-233), 1779 expedition (T-8: 256-275).

(T-7: 84 fn) (T-10: 109) De Mezières' wife and two of his children
died within a single week. Among the Texas tribes, the Hasinai, Bidai
and Nabedache lost their chiefs. (T-8: 250, 303 fn) The epidemic
diminished the strength of the allied Caddoan-speaking tribes and
their neighbors as well. The epidemic struck Natchitoches and the
surrounding region in 1777. The following year the malady appeared
in more remote villages of the Kichai and Nasonis, passing to the
Takakoni, Taovayas and Cadohadacho. More than three hundred deaths
were reported. (T-8: 231-232)

In the third place, some comments should be made on De Mezières'
observations concerning the Kichai who usually were located in an
intermediary position between settlements of the Cadohadacho-Hasinai
[Texas] and the Tawakoni-Iscani. After visiting the Kichai,
De Mezieres described the Kichai relationship in two sections of his
report of 1772 as follows:

> The village of the Quitseys [Kichai]...is composed of thirty
> houses occupied by eighty men, most of whom are young. They
> maintain a <u>close union</u> with the neighboring Cadohadachos and
> Texas....(T-7: 285)

53

> The Quitsey [Kichai] nation is the one which has taken the
> least part in the hostilities waged against our presidios
> ....It is <u>closely allied</u> with the Iscanis, Tucanas,
> Taouaiazes, and Ouedsitas. (T-7: 286) [underline added - HHT]

The Kichai maintained a separate identity throughout the time they had
villages in Texas. Yet there are indications of a split in the tribe
in the 1770's with one group more closely associated with the Cadohadacho-
Hasinai, and another faction acting in concert with the Tawakoni and
Iscani. In the year 1770, De Mezieres reported that the Kichai, Tawakani,
Iscani and even the Tonkawa had retreated south to the vicinity of San
Saba and San Antonio because of an attack by malefactors living on the
Arkansas river. (T-7: 166-168) The following year, the year of the
peace treaty of "Nations of the North" in Natchitoches, these tribes
were reported to have taken refuge in the district of Los Adaes, i.e.
east of the Trinity river. In 1772, De Mezieres located the Kichai
group of thirty houses 30 leagues from San Pedro, the Nabedache village
on the Neches river. (T-7: 285)

One Kichai group split off about 1774 and settled eighteen
leagues north of Bucareli, the Spanish settlement existing 1774-1779
on the mid-Trinity river. (T-196 Map) (T-90: 89) The principal
Kichai village was fifteen leagues further west, but a contemporary
reported concluded: "The greater part of the nation joined the
Cadohadachos."

In his His<u>tory of Texas</u>, Morfi's account of the Kichai states:

A rancheria of Quitseis was established eighteen leagues
north of Bucareli by a group of these Indians that separated
themselves from their nation. It has about twenty warriors
....The principal village of this nation is fifteen leagues
beyond [to the west], the country between consisting of
rich woods and valleys in which the wild grapes, so much
admired by De Mezières for their delicate taste, abound.
The greater part of the nation joined the Cadodachos.
(T-90: 89)

A fourth development of the De Mezieres decade was the abandonment of East Texas on orders of the governor, a decision based on
results of an inspection tour in 1767-1768. (T-10: 85) In 1773, the
small number of settlers at Los Adaes and the last of the missionaries
left the region east of the Trinity river. (T-10: 82-85) East Texas
was completely vacated for only a short interval. In 1774, a few
former inhabitants began to filter back, first forming a short-lived
town named Bucareli on the Trinity river at Paso Tomas. (T-196) In
1779, the former residents of Los Adaes moved permanently to Nacodgoches,
but remained ignored and neglected for many years. (T-10: 99, 127)

De Mezieres died in 1779 before he was able to take over the
post of governor of Texas to which he had been appointed. (T-7: 84-85)
The alliances he made through joint Indian councils lasted for the
balance of the Spanish era in Texas-Louisiana history and into the
period of American sovereignty beginning in 1804.

The evacuation of Los Adaes in 1773 left Natchitoches as the
important point of contact for Indian tribes, and traders to the
Cadohadacho and Texas tribes, but officials in New Orleans took an
increasing interest in the Indian affairs of East Texas and Louisiana.
In 1779, Tinhiouen and his son made an official visit to New Orleans,

54

where the son was given a medal by Bernardo de Galvéz, a new and
talented governor. (T-8: 250, 252-253) Indian support was particularly
important at this juncture because Spain entered the warfare of the
American Revolution in 1779. The same year, Bernardo de Galvez launched
a military campaign up the Mississippi river to Natchez, and the following
year advanced along the Gulf Coast forcing the surrender of British
forts in Mobile and Pensacola. (T-68: 10-11)

A continuing problem of major importance to the Caddo and the
Spaniards alike was the danger posed by the Osage and the disreputable
element gathered around the Arkansas post, first reported by De Mezieres
in 1770. (T-7: 166-167) At the beginning of his career, De Mezières
had recommended that the Spanish government take measures to force
each tribe to remain within its own territory, the Osage to the north
and the Cadohadacho to the south of the Arkansas river. (T-9: 194)

De Mezières' advice was given following an incident that
occurred at the Arkansas Post in 1768. Chief Tinhioüen pursued a
band of Osage who had stolen horses from his villages. He caught up
with two Osage chiefs on the Arkansas river and realized that the
trader was furnishing supplies for the Osage incursions. In his anger,
Tinhioüen ordered his Cadohadacho warriors to kill the Osage chiefs,
and almost killed the French trader but was persuaded to spare his
life. The Osage later killed the trader and his family because he
had permitted his Osage guests to be killed in his presence. (T-7:
193-194)

Another firsthand account of Tinhioüen's battles against the
Osage reached De Mezières in the fall of 1777. On the Arkansas
river in July, Tinhioüen met four hunters who had been robbed by
the Osage of all their possessions, even to basic essentials for
subsistence. Tinhioüen trailed the "thieves", killed five and recovered the property. He also noted a new establishment of illegal
English traders on the Arkansas and asked permission to "dislodge
them". De Mezières approved this objective, but issued further
instructions that if Tinhioüen found them to be unlicensed Spanish
traders, he should bring them into headquarters and as a reward could

55

confiscate their property. (T-8: 141-142) Indeed, De Mezières expected both the Cadohadacho and Yatasi to exercise police power within
their territory. By agreement in April, 1770, they had the responsibility for arresting and bringing to the Natchitoches post any
"wandering" coureurs de bois [traders] Spaniards, French or blacks
found in the Indian villages. (T-7: 158)

  Although the Cadohadacho may have born the brunt of Osage
warfare, they were not alone in carrying the battles into Osage
territory. In 1773, the Texas chief Sauto, or Bigotes, stopped
fighting the Osage long enough to beg the Spanish not to abandon
East Texas. (T-10: 83) In 1777, the Kichai and Nadaco went to the
Arkansas river to plunder and arrest a renegade from Natchitoches who
was trading with the Osage. (T-8: 130 fn, 150)

  Spanish governors in New Orleans and commandants at the
Arkansas Post and St. Louis cooperated to bring the Osage under
control. In 1785, chiefs of the Cadohadacho and Osage went to New
56 Orleans to make a peace treaty in the presence of governor Miro.
(T-69: 253) When the Osage broke the peace the following year,
orders were given to withhold the annual presents from the tribe
as punishment. (T-69: 11, 100) (T-78: 170-173) (T-69: 1, 251)

  The Osage attacks had been aimed not only at the Cadohadacho,
their traditional Indian enemies to the south, but also toward the
European settlement at Natchitoches, as well as a number of tribes
up north in the Illinois district. (T-47: 19) In 1790, Osage raids
were directed at Santa Fe, New Mexico. (T-87: 105) The Spanish in
Louisiana depended on the Cadohadacho to fend off Osage attacks and
protect white settlers while defending their own villages and hunting grounds.

  In March of 1791, the commandant at Natchitoches pointed out
the valuable protection provided by the Cadohadacho:

> "The nation of the Caddo is the only one that stands in
> the way of the passage of the Osage to this post, and
> it is of the greatest importance to me to keep it satis-
> fied and always loyal to our monarch." (T-78: 407)

The formation of an alliance of immigrant Indians in the St. Louis and St. Francis river region, including newly arrived Cherokee, Shawnee and Delaware, was one factor in eventually curbing Osage aggressive warfare. (T-69: I, 53) The Osage problem was partially solved in 1794 when a trade monopoly with the tribe was given to Auguste Chouteau, veteran St. Louis trader, who established his home, a fort, and a series of trading posts in the Osage country. (T-69: II, 100-101) Except for sporadic outbreaks, the Osage were under Chouteau's control until his death in 1838.

Before the Osage menace was alleviated, a new problem developed on the eastern frontier of the Caddo country, creating a period of Caddo-Choctaw hostilities that continued to the beginning of the American period. The genesis of the Caddo-Choctaw conflict was a plan of the Spanish governor to move Choctaw across the Mississippi river because of a serious food shortage in their own territory in 1792. The governor knew that the Choctaw were accustomed to hunt on the western shores of the Mississippi, but now asked the Caddo allies as well as the Creek immigrants settled below Natchitoches to "invite" the Choctaw to share their hunting grounds. (T-16: 287-288)

57

The Choctaw created havoc west of the Mississippi, raiding north to the Osage territory and west beyond the Texas border. Both native Indian and white farmers protested the results. Efforts of the Spanish authorities to create peace were unsuccessful as each death required vengeance on the part of the other tribe. Although successful in early raids, the Choctaw begged the Spanish authorities to intercede for them and make peace with the Caddo, after a serious defeat in 1796. (T-187: 160)

The peak of violence was reached in 1797 when forty-eight Texas Indians were killed, and many thefts reported. The great chief of the Caddo nation was one of the casualties. (T-187: 163) A later encounter the same year resulted in the death of only eight Caddo, but twenty-five Choctaw warriors including two nephews of a great-medal chief. (T-187: 185) By this time, the Choctaw realized the advisability of ending the warfare. (T-187: 165)

Isolated attacks continued, however, and by 1800 the Choctaw were generally suspected of being under American influence. (T-22: 224) John Sibley, the first American Indian agent in Louisiana, brought the Caddo and Choctaw together for a peace treaty that was broken by the Choctaw in the spring of 1807. Sibley insisted that the Choctaw take measures to give satisfaction for the violation, and used his influence to create inter-tribal peace. (T-106: 23) One band of Choctaw at some point joined the Cadohadacho tribe, according to Mooney. (T-89) An interesting map of the Gulf Coast in 1806 shows a well-marked path from a Choctaw village, "Youanne", in Mississippi across to Natchitoches, indicating regular contact between these points. (T-198)

In the years following the De Mezières era, the Anglo frontier came steadily closer to the Caddo country. European wars, diplomacy and boundary treaties played a decisive role in this trend. (T-87: 33) The series of treaties in the latter half of the eighteenth century marking stages in the Anglo advance had begun with the Treaty of Paris in 1763, whose provisions brought the British border to the Mississippi river and the Gulf Coast. By terms of the 1763 treaty: (1) Spain ceded East and West Florida to England. (2) France ceded Canada and territory east of the Mississippi river to England. (3) France ceded Louisiana to Spain, a factor already mentioned in discussion of the De Mezières era.

58

The second Treaty of Paris in 1783 at the close of the American Revolution made the Mississippi river the border between Spain, an old colonial power, and an aggressive new republic, the United States of America, whose population passed the million mark by 1790. The same treaty returned East and West Florida to Spain, but with a controversial northern border. The Spanish held to the British provincial borderline, 32 degrees and 8 minutes; while the United States insisted on an earlier 31 degree line. The difference was a seventy-eight mile band stretching from Georgia to the Mississippi river through territory of southern Indian tribes. By the Treaty of San Lorenzo in 1795, the United States secured Spanish agreement to the 31 degree line and

also free navigation of the Mississippi river, a privilege previously
forbidden by Spanish law. (T-16: 289) (T-22: 210) By this treaty,
American territory extended south to the latitude of the mouth of
the Red river. The Caddo country consequently became far more accessible to American traders and to questionable entrepreneurs already
interested in Indian lands. (T-86: 206-207)

    Illegal trade, cutting into the financial return of licensed
Spanish traders, was a big problem in the latter years of the Spanish
regime in Louisiana. (T-78: 407) The Caddo became more dependent
upon American traders as Spanish traders became increasingly unable
to furnish customary supplies. The Caddo ousted unwelcome "vagabonds",
possibly illegal traders, from the Ouachita river in 1774. (T-7: 114)
By 1779, De Mezières suspected that traders were reaching the Caddo
by way of the Arkansas Post now in American territory. (T-8: 207)
Evidence for American trading is clear by 1799. (T-87: 105) Furthermore, by that time the American firm of Barr and Davenport was in
business in Nacogdoches. (T-212: 66, 72-73)   59

    The series of European treaties also brought about the trans-
fer of Indian tribes to the territory west of the Mississippi river.
First to migrate in the South were groups who did not want to be under
English domination after 1763. (T-16: 281) The advent of the American
republic in 1783 and settlement of the Florida boundary in 1795 brought
another wave of immigrants. As a result, by the end of the eighteenth
century fragments from a number of Creek affiliated tribes were gathered
in the district of Rapides below Natchitoches. (T-16: 289) These
Creek groups and the Choctaw, were the immigrant Indians located closest
to the Caddo.

    The next development in European diplomacy involving the Caddo
country was the retrocession of Louisiana to France in 1802. News
of the retrocession reached New Orleans just ahead of news of the
subsequent sale of Louisiana to the United States, so that the two
transactions were almost a single event. Formal ceremonies for the
retrocession took place in New Orleans on November 30, 1803, while
the transfer of Louisiana from France to the United States followed

on December 20 of the same year. (T-22: 230-231) (T-87: 227)

Looking back over the history of the Caddo country in the
latter half of the eighteenth century, it is clear that the note-
worthy events took place on the frontiers--western, northern and
eastern. On the western frontier, the era of fighting Apache diminished as the Tawakoni, Yscani and Taovayas moved south into
Texas and the Caddo acquired friendly allies on their western borders. On the northern frontier, traditional hostility with the
Osage flamed into a period of intensive warfare in 1770 that continued for two decades. On the eastern frontier, the Choctaw constituted a general menace for a fifteen year interval beginning about
1792, although some of the later depredations were attributed to
renegade members of the tribe. Immigrant Creeks moved less eventfully
into Louisiana, some of them collecting on the Red river in the Rapides
district bordering Caddo territory. On the seldom mentioned southern
frontier, the coastal tribes as always were peaceful neighbors.

60

Within the Caddo country, the tribal villages remained in their
respective districts near the Angelina, Neches, Sabine and Red rivers
throughout the eighteenth century. Reports of the De Mezières era
indicate that the Cadohadacho in the Red river region had two villages,
a principal village and a smaller village the French had named the
"Petit Caddo". (T-8: 71-72) The first was above the bend of the Red
river and the second was on Sodo Lake, or Caddo Lake, in Caddo Parish,
Louisiana, thirty-five miles west of the main branch of the Red river.
(T-122: 554 Map) In 1773, one small additional community of Caddo
was living on a prairie between the Petit Caddo and the principal
village. (T-8: 83) About 1790 or 1791, the inhabitants of the principal village also moved to Caddo Lake. (T-122: 551) Although the
Osage menace was stated as the immediate reason for transferring, the
move had been contemplated soon after the epidemic of 1777. (T-8: 250)

For the Caddo, hunting and warfare were often combined. Both
of these activities were pursued in the region between the Red and
Arkansas rivers. French establishments for handling the products of
the chase were located on the Kiamichi, a northern tributary of the

ı'ed river, according to Bolton's Map. (T-196) These "Casas de los
Franceses para carnear" were noted by LaFora during the inspection
trip of the province of Texas in 1767.

The Yatasi occupied a separate village, south of the Cadohadacho,
near modern Shreveport. (T-8: 71, T-7: 128-129) (T-122: 554 Map)
The Natchitoches, who originally had homes on an island in the Red
river, lived above the old French post at the turn of the century.
(T-122: 554 Map) (T-8: 252) The Adaes were located about a day's
journey from the Spanish presidio, Los Adaes, or twenty-five miles
west of Natchitoches. (T-8: 69) About fourteen families of the
Adaes moved to the San Antonio vicinity in 1792. (T-53: 878)

The principal location for the Ais was in the vicinity of
the old Dolores mission. (T-7: 309) (T-11: 442) An additional village,
the "Little Ais" or in Spanish "Ajitos", lived two leagues from the
Nacogdoches mission in 1754, and in 1777 were on the Sabine river.
(T-11: 312) (T-8: 257) The Nadaco village was situated on the upper
Sabine river, probably near Winona in Smith county in 1788. Twenty
miles east were rancherías of Bidai who lived with the Texas tribes.
(T-22: 166)

The main road from San Antonio to Natchitoches passed through
the better-known communities of the Nabedache on the "plain called
San Pedro" and the Nacogdoches near the mission of Guadalupe before
reaching the Ais. (T-7: 309) (T-196 Map) The Texas tribes, usually
discussed as a group, remained stable throughout the century.

As Bolton stated: "The Hasinai were a settled people, who
apparently had been long in the place where they were found at the
end of the seventeenth century, and where they remained with little
geographical change throughout the eighteenth." (T-7: 21) Morfi's
history, covering events through 1779, stated that eight Indian nations
inhabited the province of Texas [meaning East Texas]: the "Adaes,
Ais, Nacogdoches, Asinai, Nasones, Neches, Naconomes and Navedachos."
(T-90: 248)

In his description of Texas, LaFora summarized the Indian
population of an area larger than Morfi considered, beginning his

61

list with eight tribes of the familiar Texas "confederacy", essentially
the same as Morfi's: "Adaes, Ais, Ainais, Nacogdoches, Neches, Nazones,
Nabidachos, Naconomes...." The only variation is the substitution of
"Ainais", the name of the principal Texas or Hasinai tribe, for the
name "Asinai" in the Morfi list. Continuing his list with the names
of coastal and more western tribes in the Spanish province, LaFora
ended with the Tonkawa and Tawakoni, noting in addition that the
Taovayas and Iscani were further north. LaFora concluded with the
observation:

> All these tribes are allied with the Texas Indians and
> our safety in that province is entirely dependent upon
> their fidelity. They have little respect for the Spanish
> and we are admitted only as friends, but without any
> authority. (T-82: 185)

LaFora's judgement was rendered before De Mezières had worked
out the system of Spanish alliances among the Indian tribes in the
Texas hinterland in 1771. These alliances did not augment Spanish
authority, but did increase Spanish influence, although this influence
was dependent upon satisfactory trade arrangements, still handled by
French traders, and gifts including powder and ammunition. (T-7:
132-133) At the opening of the nineteenth century, the territory of
the Caddo was still Indian country. The two European communities,
the struggling Spanish settlement at Nacogdoches and French populated
Natchitoches, served the Indian tribes as trading centers.

62

IV.

Caddo Aboriginal Territory

Following the plan set forth in the introduction to this report, the tribal territory of the Caddo will be defined with reference to the status at the beginning of the period of American sovereignty in the Louisiana territory, a period which began in 1804. The description will necessarily include land in Texas at that time still under Spanish sovereignty. This technical problem is less serious since Americans almost immediately asserted that the boundary of Louisiana territory was the Rio Grande; and embarked on assorted courses to realize this objective. Regardless of the disputed borders, from 1804 the Caddo and their allies were in constant contact with American government officials and Indian agents.

63

In 1804, the interior of the Caddo country was generally unknown in spite of a century of European contact. No map of the area could be found by John Sibley, first American Indian agent at Natchitoches, who took over these responsibilities in 1805. (T-17: 72) Sibley had actually arrived in Louisiana two years earlier to inquire into the prospects for development of the region. (T-106: 6) In 1804, an American expedition explored the Ouachita river up to Hot Springs. (T-37) Two years later a projected American investigation of the Red River was stopped by a Spanish military detachment just above the bend of the Red river. (T-49)

The upper regions of the Red, Canadian and Arkansas rivers were still so little known that the boundary specified in the Treaty of 1819 with Spain could not be precisely stated. Even in 1833, the first official expedition from Fort Gibson across southeastern Oklahoma to the mouth of the False Washita river was considered a pioneer venture through the uncharted wilderness. (T-23: 44-45) Actual surveys of the upper territory north of the Red river, later Oklahoma, were not made until 1852 following the Mexican War. (T-47: 10)

On the other hand, the entire region was familiar home-
territory to the Indians themselves and to the traders who were closely
associated with the Indians. Each trader accumulated a vast knowledge
of Indian affairs, unrevealed unless he was interviewed by a literate and
interested individual. John Sibley's great contribution to ethnohistory
was to tap the reservoir of information collected by a Red river trader
and interpreter, François Grappé. Sibley's historic sketches of the
Indian tribes, written in 1805, is probably the basic document for
understanding the location of the tribes and the relation between the
tribes at the beginning of the American regime. (T-105) His historical
sketches are supplemented by extracts from a journal of Indian affairs he
kept for 1807, the year tribal representatives as far west as the Comanches
came to a big Indian council in Natchitoches to establish friendly relations
with the American government. (T-106) A second valuable account of the
Caddo Indians and their neighboring tribes is W.A. Trimble's 1817 report
also based on traders' information. (T-91) His report has the ring of
authenticity that characterizes the Sibley documents. Trimble's report
included immigrant tribes who were temporarily in Texas, as well as the
native tribes.

From Spanish sources, the report closest to this period is based
on information supplied by Samuel Davenport, Indian agent at Nacogdoches,
Texas, in 1809. His locations for Indian villages in the province of Texas
are found on a map (T-197) from Casteneda's detailed history of Texas.
Although dated considerably later, Berlandier's account of the Texas Indians
in 1830 includes historical background and footnote references to earlier
information. (T-6) Consequently, this source contains material pertinent
to a description of Caddo territory as early as the first decade of the
nineteenth century.

Freeman and Custis' account of the Red river in 1806 (T-49) and
the 1806 map (T-199) of the river course to the big bend are basic documents for describing that particular part of the Red river. The first
reliable map of the Louisiana region is the William Darby map of 1816,
drawn after two years of preliminary work. (T-200) For Texas, the
earliest map of the nineteenth century is Stephen Austin's sketch map of

64

1827, imprecise in drawing but useful for the legends of Indian tribes
and village locations, including the recent immigrant tribes. (T-201)

The documents and maps cited in the foregoing paragraphs are all
special references for understanding the Caddo country at the beginning
of the American regime. To establish territorial boundaries, data has
been assembled from a wider variety of sources. First of all, consideration
will be given to the eastern boundary, at the beginning of the historic
era set close to the Mississippi river.

On Newell and Krieger's archaeological map, a zig-zag line marks
the "approximate eastern limit of historic Caddo", dated at about 1700.
(T-191) This line commences near Alexandria, Louisiana and continues
northward between the Ouachita and Mississippi rivers across the Arkansas
river, ending in the vicinity of Little Rock. The line swings to the
east of three regional historic manifestations of the Caddo noted on
Wyckoff's map "Components of Caddo Period V",: the Lawton phase, Glendora
focus and Mid-Ouachita focus. (W-197, Figure 6) The proximity of Caddo
territory to the Mississippi river is indicated by Spanish correspondence
from the late eighteenth century. The Caddo were described as being so
close to the English that "only the Mississippi intervenes". (T-7: 270)

65

In describing the distribution of Indian tribes of the Arkansas-
Oklahoma frontier in 1803, Grant Foreman explained:

> The country adjacent to the west bank of the lower Mississippi
> was the home of the Caddo tribe that had been weakened by the
> continued struggle between the French and Spaniards. (T-27: 14)

Concerning only the modern state of Arkansas, Swanton stated simply:
"Tribes of the Kadohadacho Confederacy are the only ones known to have lived
in Arkansas." (T-111: 212) In making such a statement, he must have been
referring to a very early period before the Quapaw moved down the Mississippi river to the vicinity of the mouth of the Arkansas river. In his
map of tribal distribution Swanton noted the conventional location of the
Quapaw as well as the lower Mississippi valley tribes occupying territory
on the west bank of the Mississippi river. (T-111: map before 314)

An eastern line for Caddo territory near the Mississippi river
could be termed an "ancestral border", but it is clear that during the
course of the eighteenth century an adjustment was made along the eastern

flank of Caddo territory, principally because of Choctaw migration. In
1804, Choctaw hunters gathered to meet traders on the lower Ouachita river
near old Fort Miro, about the location of modern Monroe, Louisiana.
(T-103: 329, 331, 371) (T-200) In 1805, some of the dispersed and
wandering Choctaw had a temporary village near the Arkansas Post close
to the Quapaw. (See Royce Map "Arkansas 1")

An eastern boundary for Caddo territory must also conform to the
territorial extent of the Quapaw, northeastern neighbors of the Caddo in
Arkansas. These tribes were peaceful neighbors and there is no evidence
of friction along their mutual border. The Quapaw stated that their
territory extended west to the Saline river, and up the Arkansas river to
El Cadron, the water course serving as the county line between Faulkner
and Conway counties on the north side of the Arkansas river. Since the
extent of Quapaw territory has already been investigated, and the Saline
river boundary confirmed, no further discussion of this subject seems
necessary.

66   Choctaw encroachment and the Quapaw boundary are factors limiting
Caddo territory along the eastern flank, but attention must also be given
to positive evidence of Caddo claims to the balance of the territory in
northeastern Louisiana and southwestern Arkansas. At the north end of the
eastern boundary the Saline river dividing line can be used with confidence.
West of the headwaters of the Saline river, the Hot Springs vicinity is
traditional Caddo territory figuring in tribal tradition. (T-112: 28)
The headwaters of the Ouachita river, i.e. Hot Springs vicinity, were
reported to be the place where Caddo hunters met traders from the Arkansas
Post in the late eighteenth century. (T-78: 407) Although the reference
is vague, Claude C. Robin--a stranger visiting Louisiana in 1804--reported
that the headwaters of the Ouachita was a communication link between the
Arkansas river and the Red river. (T-103: 383)

The Caddo name is perpetuated in southwestern Arkansas, identifying
a section of the Ouachita mountains and a tributary of the Ouachita river.
In 1804, Caddo were considered residents of the area between the Ouachita
and Red rivers. (T-47: 25) Dunbar, ascending the Ouachita in 1804, noted
the point where he "arrived at the road of the Caddodoquis nation, leading

to the Arkansas nation." (T-37: 735) He reached the Caddo road two days
travel south of the mouth of the Little Missouri river, probably in the
vicinity of Camden, Ouachita county, Arkansas. This trading path is
probably the same one marked on Nicholas King's map of 1806 near the
Coushatta village. The same map also indicated a "pack route" crossing
the Red river near big bend, probably a branch of the Caddo road. (T-199)

A second pathway through eastern Caddo territory, the trace from
Natchitoches to Hot Springs shown on Darby's map (T-200), indicates
frequent travel within Caddo territory to that destination. The Hot
Springs region was safe from the Osage, according to Dunbar. He commented
that the area was inaccessible and unknown to the Osage because of the
perpendicular rock ridges on the face of the mountains to the north.
(T-37: 736) Although it is clear that Indians who must have come from
the south are hunting on the upper reaches of the Ouachita river and
tributaries such as the Little Missouri, specific identification is lacking.
(T-37: 735) Dunbar, like so many American observers, used only the general
terms "hunter" and "Indian", or on occasion "red and white hunters".
(T-37: 734) He was primarily interested in the flora and fauna of the
Ouachita river basin, and the chemical properties of the thermal waters.
By 1804, white hunters had penetrated the Arkansas wilderness, and whites
were visiting the Hot Springs.

67

An eastern boundary for the Caddo territory must also run east
of Lake Bistinau. The Caddo demonstrated their proprietorship of this
region by making land grants on the lake. (T-112: 84) There is no
indication that Caddo could not have made grants further east, but there
would probably be little demand for a land concession in the pine woods
beyond the water course.

Taking into consideration all the factors discussed in the foregoing
paragraphs, the eastern boundary for Caddo aboriginal territory has been
marked to include the Hot Springs region and headwaters of the Ouachita
river. The boundary next follows the dividing ridge between the upper
waters of the Ouachita river and the parallel Saline river, continuing
along the ridge to the east of the tributaries of the Red river that fall
into the Red river above the rapids. The rapids of the Red river were

located near Alexandria, Louisiana. The line just described strikes the
Red river at the modern town of Colfax, Grant Parish, Louisiana.

The Colfax boundary marker on the Red river has historical validity.
It conforms to the southern boundary of Caddo territory on the Red river
at the beginning of the eighteenth century, according to Swanton's map.
(T-80: 6) The village of the Avoyelles, original southern neighbors of
the Caddo tribes on the Red river, was located just above the rapids and
marked the upper boundary of the tribe. (T-41: 1119) The southern
boundary of the Caddo tribes on the Red river became the dividing line
between Natchitoches Parish and Rapides Parish in the Louisiana territory.

Under the Spanish regime, the influx of immigrant Muskhogean tribes
was into the Rapides district below the Caddo tribes occupying the
Natchitoches District. (T-16) Documents of the American era indicate
that Caddo permission was needed for tribes to move north out of Rapides
Parish. (T-91: 257) (T-20a: 92) The uppermost settlements of immigrant
tribes on the Red river were just south of the Parish boundary crossing
the river below the forks where the river split in two branches called the
Cane river and the Rigolet de Bon Dieru. (T-200 Map) The Rigolet is
called the "North Branch" on the Nicholas King map of 1806. (T-199) The
Indian villages below the forks are the Pascagoula village, located on
both banks of the river, and an Apalache village situated two miles further
down. (T-49: 9) (T-199 Map)

The location of the Pascagoula village is important to bear in
mind. This is the only Pascagoula location on the upper Red river. A
"Pascagoula Bayou" is given as a boundary marker for Caddo territory in
the Treaty of 1835, but placed opposite the Coushatta village for reasons
that cannot be satisfactorily explained. (See Royce Area 202, Louisiana)
Chronologically, a discussion of that treaty is out of place at this point
in the report and will be deferred until the next chapter. The Pascagoula
village was near the mouth of the Rigolet de Bon Dieu. This geographical
location can be verified on the Darby map of 1816. (T-200) Changes in
the drainage pattern of the Red river valley have eliminated the old Rigolet
from contemporary maps, but Colfax marks in former mouth of this branch
of the Red river.

In addition to having historical validity, the Colfax marker on
the Red river satisfies the topographical requirements for establishing

68

boundaries of Indian territory. Colfax is the point at which the Kisatachie Wold, defining the edge of the Gulf coastal plain, strikes the Red river. Consequently, this marker is harmonious with the southern boundary for Caddo territory.

The southern boundary of the Caddo country can best be established by considering general topography, and the location of the small Atakapan tribes along the Gulf Coast. (T-11: 2-3) (T-80: 6 Map) These tribes were on the fringe of the Caddo cultural area and their mutual boundary, well defined topographically, was entirely peaceful. The Atakapans occupied a strip of coastal prairie extending inland less than a hundred miles. The topographical guideline for this boundary, the Kisatchie Wold, is distinctly marked on the topographic map. (T-190)

The western limit of the southern boundary line for Caddo territory may be debatable. Although the Caddo territory has casually been described as the Texas timber region "east of the Trinity", research for this report indicates that the Caddo territorial boundary on the south should be drawn to include contiguous territory of the Bidai, particularly the Bidai Creeks west of the Trinity river in Walker, Grimes and Madison counties.

The Bidai were identified and affiliated with the Caddo from the beginning of the historic era. (T-59: 286) The Bidai spoke Caddo (T-105: 722) had customs similar to the Caddo (T-6: 106) and lived for a time in the late eighteenth century near the Nadaco village in northeastern Texas. (T-22: 166) Furthermore they were considered as part of the "Caddo confederation" in 1820 (T-19: 197-198); and as an "offshoot" of the Caddo in 1828. (T-6: 106) Finally, in 1854, the Bidai went to the federal reservation on the Brazos river for the Caddo and allied tribes. (T-94: 319) The above reasons are given to justify: (a) including a Bidai section within the total territory of the Caddo, and (b) extending the southern boundary west of the Trinity river to Bedias in northeastern Grimes County.

In considering the western boundary of Caddo territory, the line is drawn west of the Trinity to include Keechi Creeks in Leon and Freestone County. The reasoning is similar to the analysis of the Bidai situation.

69

One group of Kichai was affiliated with the Caddo tribes in the late
seventeenth century. (T-59: 286) By the late eighteenth century, two
groups of Kichai are mentioned. In the report of Indian tribes from the
Spanish Indian agent in 1809, (T-160) a "Quichain" village was located
six leagues west of the Trinity and ten above El Camino Real, in
southern Leon County. (T-197) Another village called "Aquichi" was
listed on the upper Red river with the "Tahuayas" and "Huichita".
(T-160: 2) (T-197 Map) Sibley included the Kichai among the tribes
"who all speak the Caddo language, look up to them as their fathers,
visit and intermarry among them, and join them in all their wars."
The other tribes were the Yatasi, Nadaco, Nabedache, Hainai or Texas,
Nacogdoches, Adai and Natchitoches. (T-105: 721) Specifically concerning the Kichai, Sibley stated that they "have their peculiar language,
but mostly now speak Caddo, intermarry with them, and live together in
much harmony, formerly having lived near them on the head waters of the
Sabine". (T-105: 722) The western boundary has been placed to include
the Kichai united with the Caddo. (T-7: 285) (T-78: 259)

70

     General statements of the western boundary of the Caddo country
mention the Trinity river and the Cross Timbers. The Trinity river references are from the writings of Bolton concerned only with Texas history.
Two quotations from his volume Texas in the Middle Eighteenth Century
describe the limits of colonial Texas in terms of the geographic extent
of the Hasinai confederacy:

    (1) "The original Texas was the territory of the Hasinai
        (Texas) Indians, between the Trinity and Red rivers,
        and included much of what is now Louisiana." (T-11:1)

    (2) The eastern tribes [in Texas, i.e. Hasinai] living
        between Adaes [Robeline, Louisiana] and the middle
        Trinity, were generally friendly to the Spanish...
        (T-11: 398)

Territorial claims of the Caddo themselves are recorded from the
beginning of the American era. They are phrased with reference to the
Red river country and indicate that the Caddo claimed lands on both sides
of the Red river as high as the Cross Timbers.

    Sibley, already interested in securing Indian land in 1812,
wrote the Secretary of War:

The Caddoes claim a very extensive tract of country
on both sides of the Red river for six or seven hundred
miles. (T-140: 106)

The most complete statement of this claim comes from the report of

W.A. Trimble, who collected his information from hunters and traders

while he was on the military frontier in 1817. He wrote:

> When the French established themselves on Red River
> in 1717, the Caddos formed the most numerous and warlike
> nation inhabiting that country, which they claimed to
> the sources of the Red River. This nation suffered
> greatly from small pox, and from their wars with the
> Osages, Towcash and Camanches; by whom they were driven
> from the sources of the Red River. They now reside on
> the waters of Lake [Caddo], about ninety miles north-
> west from Natchitoches, and they claim the country of
> Red River from Bayou Pierre and Lake Bistianeau, to the
> Cross Timber, a remarkable tract of wood land, which
> crosses Red River more than a thousand miles above its
> mouth. (T-91: 257)

The same impression is preserved in Schoolcraft's publication based on

1825 information. Accompanying a list of Caddo and some immigrant

tribes--a list outdated by the time of publication--he noted under

remarks:

71

> The Caddoes were the actual owners of the country,
> and their claim extends 1,000 miles up Red River. By
> war and the small-pox they have been reduced to their
> present condition. They yet exercise considerable in-
> fluence over the other tribes near them....(T-104: 596)

In later literature, the Cross Timbers was recognized as the

boundary between the eastern and the western Indians both in Texas and

Oklahoma. In Texas, the Cross Timbers consisted of two timber belts

with a wide band of prairie land between. The Eastern belt was con-

sidered the dividing line as the Handbook of Texas explains:

> In pioneer times the band of timber was a famous
> landmark. It was also a formidable obstacle to travelers
> because of the density of the timber. It served as a
> dividing line between the hunting grounds of the plains
> Indians and East Texas Indians. (T-116: 537)

Randolph Marcy, after passing through the Cross Timbers at six different

points, gave the following description:

This extensive belt of woodland, which forms one of
the most prominent and anomalous features upon the face
of the country, is from five to thirty miles wide, and
extends from the Arkansas river in a southwesterly
direction to the Brazos, some four hundred miles.
(T-152a: 92)

The most comprehensive description of the Cross Timbers, with

details referring particularly to the course of the timber belt north

of the Red river, was made by Josiah Gregg who travelled through the

region in the 1830's. In the course of his detailed observations, he

noted:

The celebrated Cross Timbers, of which frequent mention
mention has been made, extend from the Brazos, or perhaps from the Colorado of Texas, across the sources of
the Trinity, transversing the Red River above the False
Washita, and thence west or north, to the Red Fork of
Arkansas, if not further.

The Cross Timbers vary in width from five to thirty
miles, and entirely cut off the communication betwixt
the interior prairies and those of the great plains....

South of the Canadian, a branch of these Cross Timbers
projects off westward, extending across this stream, and
up its course for 100 miles or so, from whence, it in-
clines northwest beyond the North Fork....(T-214: 254-256)

Taking into consideration both the Trinity river and the Cross

Timbers region, the western line for Caddo territory in Texas has been

drawn as nearly as possible to conform to (a) the watershed between the

Trinity and Brazos rivers, and (b) the western edge of the Grand Prairie

adjacent to the Eastern Cross Timbers. Such a line follows Chambers

Creek north of Corsicana through a notch in the Eastern Cross Timbers

to Joshua, a small town north of Cleburne in Johnson County. From this

point north, the western edge of the Grand Prairie lies west of Fort

Worth and appears to strike the Red river at Sivell's Bend. The western

edge of the "Grand Prairie", the treeless belt between the two Cross

Timbers, has been used as a borderline because the prairie region seems

geologically and topographically allied with the Eastern Cross Timbers,

and clearly differentiated from the Western or "Upper" Cross Timbers.

(T-65: 300) According to the best description available:

72

The western edge of this prairie [Grand Prairie]
projects as an escarpment above the next topographic
feature we here describe. The ragged edge is well
marked, and from it we look down upon the Upper Cross
Timbers to the westward. (T-65: 301)

The western boundary line just described is identical with the western

boundary of Royce area 478* for about twenty-five miles, from Joshua

(North of Cleburne) to the Fort Worth vicinity.

An additional quotation from Gregg suggests that there were breaks

in the Cross Timbers north of the Red river that would make it possible

to draw a line through the forest zone in Oklahoma as a continuation of

the line through the clearly marked "Grand Prairie" separating the

Eastern and Western Cross Timbers south of the Red river in Texas. Gregg,

who was familiar with the Oklahoma terrain, wrote: "The region of the

Cross Timbers is generally well-watered; and is interspersed with ro-

mantic and fertile tracts." (T-214: 254) The topographical map (T-190)

also indicates variations in the Oklahoma timber region that are not de-

fined either in a physiographic or a fegitation map. (T-213: 103, 108)

73

Using the maps just cited, the balance of the western line for

Caddo territory was drawn south to north through the Oklahoma timber

zone, skirting the Arbuckle Mountains then striking northeast across a

ridge to the vicinity of Paul's Valley. The final northeastern portion

of this boundary coincides with a line marking differences in precipita-

tion (T-213: 112) related to a variation in topography. It is interpreted

as an indication of the place where a prong of the Cross Timbers projects

westward along Rush Creek and the Washita river. (T-190) The line just

described lies east of the boundary of the western prairie, a vegitation

zone that extends east to Purcell on the South Canadian river and covers

about the western eighty percent of Jefferson county on the Red river in

southern Oklahoma. (T-213: 108)

Some of the evidence of Caddo use of the Cross Timbers region

does not come to light until later in the nineteenth century. After the

---

*C.C. Royce, Indian Land Cessions of the United States, Eighteenth
Annual Report of the Bureau of American Ethnology (Washington, 1899)
Map 57 "Texas and Portions of Adjoining States".

Texas Indian warfare in 1839, Caddo took refuge in the Cross Timbers region near the Three Forks of the Trinity. This move is interpreted as a flight to the edge of the tribal territory. The Caddo at this time probably located on Caddo Creek east of Fort Worth, noted on the De Cordoba map of 1857. (T-203) The map of explorations near the Red river in 1852 indicates a Caddo trail south of the Arbuckle Mountains, also in the timber zone. (T-152b)

Although no evidence can be submitted, it seems worthwhile to mention that Caddo archaeologists have received reports of an early village site in the forests north of Dallas. The location presents such formidable engineering problems that no investigation has yet been made.* Consideration should also be given to the probable site of the Naoudiche village on a crudely drawn map of 1716 that appears to have been located west of the mouth of the Washita river. This site is probably now submerged in the lake created by the Denison dam. (T-192)

Turning attention to the northern boundary of the Caddo territory, we will first review the historical background of this border region. Espinoza, who was in Texas in the early eighteenth century, and other authorities had stated that the Caddo provinces extended north to the Arkansas river, often called the "Rio de Misouri" in early documents. (T-38: 152) Athanése de Mezières, the source of so much information, referred to the same boundary in 1770 when he was discussing the problem of Osage-Cadohadacho warfare. Writing the Captain-general of Cuba, he stated:

> "Returning to my subject, let me say that the most effective way to establish peace and quiet in the territories of this district will be to forbid the Osage and Cadodachos from crossing the Arkansas river, each confining themselves to the abundant chase which they will find in their respective districts." (T-7: 194)

Although the Arkansas river had ancient status as an inter-tribal boundary, the upper river course became a battle zone in the late eighteenth century. On the South Canadian river, the prairie along the southern bank also was a theatre of Caddo-Osage warfare. (T-47: 189) (T-37: 735)

---

*R.K. Harris, Dallas. Personal Communication November 28, 1971.

Reports indicate that Caddo advanced with security only a limited distance northward into the Ouachita mountains. (T-37: 735) (T-107: 371)
Yet the Osage did not customarily occupy any region south of the Arkansas
river. Thomas Nuthall, who traversed the Ouachita mountains in 1818
and found beacons of an old Osage war trail, observed that the Osage
"occasionally" carry their depredations into the territory of the Caddo.
(T-95: 211, 133)

 Combining and resolving the data on the subject has led to the
conclusion that the northern boundary for Caddo territory east of the
Washita river in Oklahoma should be described as the watershed for the
streams draining toward the Red river. This line runs almost due east
from Paul's Valley, Oklahoma to the vicinity of Hot Springs, Arkansas.
This line encompasses some mountain area in the east as well as the im-
portant--and sometimes raided--prairie hunting grounds on the Blue, Boggy
and Kiamichi rivers.

 Dunbar learned of the Caddo's Oklahoma hunting territory when he
was on the Ouachita river in Arkansas near the mouth of the Little Missouri river in 1804. In the report of his expedition, he wrote:

 This land extends to Red river, and is connected with
 the great prairies which form the hunting grounds of the
 Cadaux nation. (T-27: 735)

Trimble's account written in 1818 conveys the same impression, although
his comprehension of geography was vague and he had not heard of the
Cross Timbers. He also had the American failing for not identifying
Indian tribes. In the following quotation, he was referring not only
to the Caddo tribes, but also to their allies and neighbors on the
Brazos river, the Tawakoni, and probably the Taovoyas we well.

 The game has almost disappeared from the Lower Red River,
 and is not found in any considerably number, until you ascend
 as high as Blue River, where is entered the immense tract of
 Prairie, which extends from the Arkansas to the sources of
 the Trinity, and the Brassos. Those extensive plains are
 covered with the Buffaloe, Elk, Deer, Wild Cows, Hogs, and
 Horses. On the rivers are found the Black Bear.

 The Indians, who reside on Red River, Sabine, Neches,
 Trinity and Brassos, hunt on these Prairies. The white
 people are encroaching on that delightful hunting ground,
 and in the most wanton manner, are destroying the game.

At the time Trimble was writing in Washington, D.C., in August, 1818, federal representatives in St. Louis were arranging with the Quapaw for a cession of most of the hunting ground he described. (Royce area 94) Negotiations were in progress to determine the boundary between Louisiana and Texas, but had not been completed. The following year, 1819, Arkansas territory was established and the federal government tried to remove families such as those indicated by Trimble illegally settled north of Red river. (T-47: 169-170)

Although it is difficult to give an adequate evaluation of nineteenth century observations without full discussion of the historical context, one further quotation will be added concerning Caddo territory. M.M. Kenny wrote a long chapter on the "Indians of Texas" for A Comprehensive History of Texas, published in Dallas in 1898. In the section on the Caddo tribes, Kenny described the territory they occupied, but included within a single region both the territory of the Caddo tribes and the territory of the Tawakoni-Taovayas-Wichita group. For an early Texas historian, this was a reasonable interpretation, since all the Caddo speaking tribes in Texas were grouped together in two main divisions at the time that Texas came into the union. In spite of the fact that his description includes territory later associated with the Wichita as well as original Caddo territory, Kenny's view is of interest. After explaining that the Caddo of Texas belonged to a linguistic family including tribes in North Dakota and on the Platte river, he continued:

> The southern group, the Caddos, occupied a region which may
> be approximately defined as beginning near the mouth of the
> Arkansas River; thence south and east to the Mississippi near
> Red River; thence southwest to the Brazos about the Navasota;
> thence up the Brazos, including a wide range, to the point
> where that stream nearest approaches Red River; thence north
> to a point half-way between Red River and the Arkansas, and
> following that divide southeast to the beginning.

Kenny probably had some insights and information sources that are not available now. It seems worthwhile to point out that Kenny made no allowances for Choctaw encroachment on the eastern border of Caddo territory. His western border includes the Wichita Mountains of western Oklahoma. His northern border, the divide between the Red and Arkansas

rivers agrees with the northern limit of Caddo territory independently
determined through research for this report.

The territorial borders that have been described at length form
somewhat of a square, with the four "corners" near Hot Springs, Arkansas;
Colfax, Louisiana; Bedias, west of Huntsville, Texas; and Paul's Valley,
Oklahoma. Within the area were the villages and hunting grounds of
eight communities of Indians included in the Caddo Tribe, although
there might be reservations concerning the inclusion of the Bidais or
the Kichai. The total population is estimated at around 4,000 people
for the beginning of the American era, or half the 8,000 original figure
for the Caddo population at the beginning of the eighteenth century
according to Swanton's computation. (T-112: 25)

The numbers for individual villages are based on the 1809 report
of Samuel Davenport to Mexican authorities concerning Indians in the
province of Texas. (T-160) (T-200 Map) Davenport, who had handled
the Indian trade in Nacogdoches since 1798, was better informed than
Americans in Louisiana. For each village, Davenport noted the approximate number of men, or heads of households, the common method of census
reckoning in Spanish towns. To arrive at total population estimates,
such numbers are usually converted at a five to one ratio. This procedure gives the following results.

Cadohadacho	1,000
Yatasi & Adai	200
Nadaco	500
Nacogdoches [& Ais]	250
Hainai	300
Nabedachos	400
Kichai	300
Bidai	300

The villages listed so far add up to 3,300 individuals, On the other
hand, Davenport included only villages within the Spanish Province of
Texas. The Cadohadacho "fixed" village he reported was on the Sabine
river in modern Wood County (T-197 Map), probably seventy-five miles
from the Caddo community near Caddo Lake in Louisiana. The latter
village was consistently reported in American documents. The Caddo
Lake village was composed of 100 warriors, 100 other men, and 250 women,

according to Sibley in 1805. (T-105: 721) These figures for adult
population infer a population of 400 or 500 children, and altogether
would double the total number of Cadohadacho. It is reasonable to
expect that there were still two villages of Caddo at the opening of
the American era. Two villages had been in existence in the late
eighteenth century, and two different dates--1790 or 1791 and 1795--
are given for the times Caddo left the big bend area of the Red river.
(T-105: 721) (T-49: 28) Subsequently, two different Caddo locations
were reported in 1818. (T-91: 373) In 1836, after the Caddo had
agreed to leave Louisiana according to the Treaty of 1835, an American
officer visited two villages of Caddo in Texas. (T-53: 926-927) The
visit took place when American troops were in Nacogdoches at the be-
gininng of the Texas revolution for independence from Mexico. Yet
it does not seem reasonable that there would be a one hundred percent
variation in reported population for the Cadohadacho.

78   Another factor contributing to the total numbers for the
Caddo was the influx of immigrant Indians. At the beginning of the
American period, the Caddo began to augment their population by the
admission of immigrant Indian tribes, some of whom remained permanently.
The first group consisted of Coushatta and Alibama who were given a
village site on the Red river due east of the Caddo on the lake.
(T-200 Map) (T-199 Map) The Freeman-Custis expedition in 1806 stopped
at the Coushatta village where they had a conference with the Caddo.
The official War Office report stated:

> This little village has been build within two or three years,
> and consists of 6 or 8 families of stragglers from the lower
> Creek nation, near Mobile. (T-49: 21)

A decade later, the Coushatta village had an estimated population of
350. (T-91: 373)

      Although the population totals for the Caddo cannot be fixed
with precision for the beginning of the American period, round numbers may be used to demonstrate the pattern of land use for hunting.
During the hunting season, village communities dispersed over a
wide geographic area in small groups of ten to twenty persons.

Therefore, a population of 4,000 infers the use of from 200 to 400
hunting locations. Berlandier's report of 1830 stated:

> The Caddo enjoy a highly organized social life. They
> abhor thievery, are honest in their business dealings, and
> have a gift for agriculture. They do a thriving trade in
> furs...(T-6: 108) See also (T-22: 252)

Tribal groups also dispersed over their territory for summer
fishing, berry picking, salt-making, gathering medicinal herbs or
cane for reed mats. Except by chance reporting, few of these locations are even specifically identified. Swanton found a sketch of a
Caddo hunting camp dated March 2, 1849, that "illustrates very well
the manner in which Caddo hunting camps were distributed over the
country before the tribe moved from Texas." [underline added. HT]
(T-112: 153)

One positively identified hunting camp site is Caddo Mills,
in southwestern Hunt County, Texas. In compiling information for the
Handbook of Texas, a local history specialist noted that the town was
named for the Caddo Indians, "who used the area for a camping ground,
until L.T. Johnson erected a sawmill in 1860 and changed the name to
Caddo Mills." (T-116: 266) (T-22: 252)

79

Buffalo hunting was usually a cooperative effort requiring a
large group of horsemen. Pecan Point, near the mouth of the Kiamichi
river was a place where the buffalo crossed the Red river during
their annual migrations. (T-47: 160) A long hunting expedition could
continue for three or four months, and extend to a distance of more
than 200 miles from the village base where a hunter had his house and
garden. (T-20a: 118) (T-106: 11)

The Caddo people also had important but non-utilitarian uses
for their territory. Distinctive ornaments, often made of silver,
were part of their personal attire. One source of silver was a mine
sixty miles upstream on the Kiamichi river in the southern Ouachita
Mountains. This is one of many details concerning the Red river
tributaries reported to Sibley in 1805 by François Grappé, whose
knowledge of the terrain undoubtedly reflects the Caddo's familiarity
with the same environment. The previous year, i.e. 1804, the Indians

had discovered a second silver mine on a creek flowing into the
Kiamichi. (T-105: 729)

When the Mexican boundary commission was in Nacogdoches in
1828, General Teran held an interview with a Caddo delegation. The
following description of a Caddo chief's appearance and his views of
Caddo territory come from Berlandier's account of that conference:

> Few native weigh themselves down with such clumsy,
> heavy ornaments as do the Cado. Most of them wear a sort
> of clip or ring or silver or tin in their noses. From
> this ring hangs a horse or other animal of the same metal
> covering the mouth and often a portion of the chin as
> well. The entire outer rim of the ear is also pierced
> with little holes. In the earlobe they attach pendants
> more than two inches in diameter. All around the rest
> of the ear they fix little rings, or little tubes of
> silver. They wear turkey feathers behind their ears.
> Some of them wear the carefully dried skulls of birds
> instead of metal ornaments....Those of a certain rank
> pull out most of their hair, leaving only an uneven
> crest along the median line. The sides of the head,
> now quite bald, are painted with vermilion in wavy lines
> descending along the side of the neck. (T-6: 106)

80

At the 1828 conference, General Teran also gained an impression of the
Caddo's firm claim to their own territory:

> They proudly recall their ancient lineage and power,
> and claim rights preeminent to those of all the other
> natives over the immense land of Texas. General Teran
> once asked their Chief whether his people's lands lay
> in Mexico or in the United States. Once the chief had
> got the question straight, he answered that he was
> neither on Mexican nor United States territory, but on
> his own land which belonged to nobody but him....

> Although the Cado consider themselves Mexicans,
> the government of the United States of the North main-
> tains an Indian agent, an interpreter and an armorer
> among them. The captain of the nation receives an
> emolument of 50 piastres a year, aside from numerous
> presents. The agent's duty is to see that the Cado
> are respected by the other nations and by the whites.
> He guards the integrity of their territory, while the
> armorer keeps their weapons in good condition. (T-6:
> 107-108)

The preceding quotation indicates the views of the Caddo chief
when he was in Nacogdoches, Texas. An equally positive statement had

been made by the Caddo chief during a council with the Freeman-Custis
expedition on the Red river in 1806. At a meeting which took place
at the newly established Coushatta village, the Caddo chief was under
some strain because he knew that a Spanish detachment was enroute to
intercept the American expedition. Beginning with the welcoming
statement that "he was glad to see them in his land," the chief later
said that:

> Should he find the Spaniards determined to be cross, and
> to spill blood, he would supplicate them not to do so on his
> land: not through fear, because he did not fear man!...If
> entreaty had not the desired effect, he would order the
> Spanish officer immediately to return to his camp, and move
> from the land, and not to trouble the party nearer then
> fifty leagues higher above the old Caddo village (300 esti-
> mated leagues higher than this place). (T-49: 27)

Three hundred leagues would be equivalent to a distance along the Red
river above the Coushatta village of 800 or 900 miles, depending on
use of Spanish of American leagues for measurement.

In summary, at the beginning of the American period in 1804,
the Caddo people had a definite territory in the four state region of
Louisiana, Texas, Oklahoma and Arkansas. To arrive at dimensions, data
has been used from historical narratives, tradition, reports of village
locations and hunting grounds, knowledge of the territory of neighboring
tribes, and claims made by Caddo chiefs. These boundaries do not conflict with the boundaries of any other tribe found in historical literature. In the Appendix to this report, the boundaries of the Caddo
are defined in detail, both in topographic and geographic terms.

81

82

V.
Problems of the Caddo: 1804-1859

The history of the Caddo was swift-moving with elements of human
tragedy during the interval from 1804 when they came under United States
"protection" until August, 1859 when they carried out a forced march
across the hot Texas countryside from a Brazos river reservation to a
new reservation in Oklahoma. After the Caddo had lived hundreds of years
in the same geographic locale, the world around them seethed and eventually
rejected them all within the period of only a half century. The events
of Caddo history, 1804-1846, occurred within a pattern of national and
international history so complex that in the interest of clarity it will
be outlined prior to summarizing the Caddo history.

83

Even in bare outline, the wars and civil disturbances affecting
the Caddo area were so frequent, and population changes so massive that
it is difficult to follow the thread of Caddo history through the course
of these other historical sequences. But it is clear that the Indian
history of the era was largely a reaction to the aggressive, land-hungry
white history characterizing the southwest frontier for the entire period
1804-1859. For this reason, the sketch of major historical themes for
the first part of the nineteenth century in and around the Caddo country
will be presented briefly as a necessary background for comprehending
the Caddo history of the same era.

In 1804, American authorities took over the fort at Natchitoches
naming it Fort Claibourne, and rumors of American intention to rule the
territory to the Sabine river and beyond began to circulate. The next
year, a new Spanish governor of Texas brought troops into East Texas,
reoccupying old Fort Adais and establishing an outpost at Bayou Pierre,
almost on the Red river, with other posts at strategic locations along
the Gulf coast, at river crossings, and increased military support for

San Antonio. (T-130: 127-128) The showdown over the disputed Louisiana-
Texas border took place in 1806 when General James Wilkinson forced the
Spanish troops to retire west of the Sabine. (T-212) The opposing gen-
erals concluded an "agreement" declaring that "neutral ground" existed
between the Arroyo Hondo, the old border of St. Denis' time, and the
Sabine river. (T-136) The status of the Neutral Ground was not settled
until the treaty with Spain was signed in 1819 including the neutral
ground in American territory. In the intervening years, it was a refuge
for border ruffians and the scene of activities questionable to the governments on both sides. (T-212: 70-71 Map) (T-130: 151)

By 1810, the Mexican war for independence from Spain had commenced.
Mexico's political history was not really stable from that year until
1874 when Porfirio Diaz inaugurated thirty-six years of iron rule leading
to the great social Revolution of 1910. Although far from the capital
city, East Texas felt repercussions from most of the overturns of the
Mexican central government. East Texans, "Neutral Ground" characters,
and American citizens of Natchitoches took an active interest in the
Mexican War for Independence. The most significant East Texas participation was the Guttierez-McGee expedition of 1812, provisioned by Samuel
Davenport, that advanced with a force of 1700 to San Antonio and successfully
demanded the surrender of the governor, who was shot along with other
leading officials. (T-43: 135) McGee, an American officer stationed at
Natchitoches, had aspired to set up an independent state that would
join the U.S.A. Guttierez was a refugee in Natchitoches, an early
follower of Hidalgo, Mexico's first independence hero. Indian allies,
unidentified, accompanied this expedition. (T-130: 150-153, 168-169)
Resurgent Spanish Royalists led a wave of reconquest in 1813 that caught
up with McGee's followers and swept all Americans and Mexican "Republicans"
from East Texas. Nacogdoches settlers fled to Natchitoches, and Samuel
Davenport's Indian trading business collapsed. (T-130: 175) (T-212: 66)
(T-43: 135)

Simultaneous with these events, the War of 1812 was in progress
with naval action at New Orleans, and American agents feared that British
agents were at work among the East Texas Indians. In 1814 Andrew Jackson

84

led an army through Creek country in Alabama, and the Creeks sought
Caddo support. Jackson was advised to send a diplomatic message to the
Caddo chief. (T-27: VI, 293) The next invasion of East Texas, the
Long Expedition, was triggered by the Treaty of 1819, with Spain. The
treaty settlement was a disappointment to many Americans who thought
that the nation's diplomats, instead of agreeing on a Red river borderline,
should have demanded the Rio Grande as the border for Louisiana. The
1819 Long expedition started from Natchez, "captured" Nacogdoches, then
declared the independence of Texas and set up a provisional government
whose council included such familiar names as Samuel Davenport, Bernardo
Gutierrez, and John Sibley, the former American Indian agent in Natchitoches.
Long had hoped to get support from LaFitte, the pirate whose island headquarters were off the Texas coast. Davenport and others had been absent
from Nacogdoches for six years, but they had a short stay in East Texas
in 1819, for the town of Nacogdoches was soon abandoned in the face of
attack by a Spanish army. (T-130: 199) (T-43: 139) The Indians interpreted Long's defeat as a Spanish victory over the commander of the entire
army of the United States. Spain's status rose accordingly. (T-19: 198)

      Contemporary with the planning and execution of the Long Expedition
of 1819, other factors were creating a substantial population pressure
along the Louisiana border, spilling over into Texas. Frontier settlers,
including war veterans, began to accumulate in the Caddo country of north
Louisiana and Arkansas right after the war with England ended in 1815 with
a final engagement in Louisiana. A heavily populated area suddenly developed in the Kiamichi and Little river section along the Red river. (T-47:
159-160, 162) This area was included in the county government of the
Missouri Territory, but became part of the Arkansas Territory created in
1819. In late 1818 or perhaps early 1819, land in this Red river region
was surveyed and announced for sale at the Arkansas Post in 1820. (T-47:
166-167) Such a project encouraged the influx of additional white population, although the land sale did not occur.

      In a separate sequence of events, the United States government
was already taking steps to move the Choctaw Indians into this same area.
(T-47: 168) By treaty in 1818, the Quapaw ceded land between the Arkansas

85

and Red rivers.* Negotiations to remove the Choctaw from Mississippi
began in 1818 but were not completed until a treaty was signed in 1820.**
(T-47: 168) In the meantime, the federal government, in 1819, attempted
to remove about 200 families of illegal settlers from a district in Arkansas
territory intended for the Choctaw. Many simply crossed the Red river into
Texas.

In 1820, the year of the Choctaw removal treaty, Miller County,
Arkansas was created with headquarters on the lower Kiamichi river. (T-47:
167) The land surveyed in 1818-1819 was not sold because of plans for the
Choctaw, yet white population still increased north of the Red river.
Foreman, who has studied this frontier in the greatest detail, estimated
that in 1820 there were 5,000 white settlers living in the area of Arkansas
and Oklahoma ceded by the Quapaw and designated for the Choctaw by terms
of the removal treaty. (T-47: 172)

By 1818, an estimated 8,000 immigrant Indians from the north had
forced their way into southwest Missouri. (T-47: 209) Portions of the
86 Cherokee, Shawnee and Delaware tribes, some of whom had moved near St. Louis
during the Spanish era, migrated west of the Mississippi before the federal
government had made adequate arrangements for their accomodation in western
territory. (T-47: 214) Groups from these tribes, and Choctaw as well, had
drifted into the Red river country by 1819, a vanguard of others to follow.
(T-19: 96)

As a result of the mixed white and Indian population influx during
the 1815-1820 period, the general disorder reached alarming proportions.
Settlers and American Indian officials begged for military protection,
but received no aid until 1824 when troops from Louisiana arrived on the
lower Kiamichi to establish Fort Towson. (T-47: 201-204) (T-46: 83)

---

*Quapaw Treaty of August 24, 1818. VII Stat. 176, Royce Area 94 on
Map 21, "Indian Territory and Oklahoma 1". On September 25, 1818 also
at St. Louis, the Osage ceded land north of the Arkansas river, VII
Stat. 183, Royce Area 97, also on Map 21, "Indian Territory and Oklahoma
1". The Oklahoma land cessions are indicated by a series of three maps.
(T-129: 6, 12, 16)

**Choctaw Treaty signed October 18, 1820 at Doaks Stand, VII Stat. 210.

Meanwhile, Mexico achieved independence in 1821. After a colorful
interval under Emperor Augustin Iturbide, who was exiled in 1823, the new
nation in 1824 commenced a hectic history under republican constitutions.
The Mexican land policy, and the land grants acquired by Americans through
adroit personal influence, are the keys to the ensuing history of East
Texas. Stephen Austin, first to achieve success, secured a concession from
the Iturbide government. (T-2: 184) Competition was keen. Most of the
"empresario" grants, or concessions involved contracts for bringing in a
certain number of colonists whom the Mexican government initially believed
would form a bulwark against American encroachment or invasion. Some
grants were annulled, others unfulfilled and therefore voided, but all
represented local power struggles for land. The big year for colonization
was 1825. (T-130: 234) In 1827, political animosities in Nacogdoches
flared up in the "Fredonian War", involving Hayden Edwards who had hoped
to develop the land of the original Hasinai confederacy on the Angelina
and Neches rivers. (T-130: 235-245) In the course of the troubles,
accusations were made that anti-American agents were in collusion with the
Indians, by that time including Cherokee and other immigrant tribes.
(T-13: 139) Again there was a general exodus from Nacogdoches to American
territory. The ultimate Mexican government reaction was to pass a decree
in 1830 prohibiting future immigration from the United States. The background for the abrupt change in policy is summarized in the following
quotation:

> The causes of suspicion and distrust which led to promul-
> gation of this decree begin as far back as the Fredonian Rebel-
> lion at Nacogdoches in 1826, and were continued and augmented
> by the insistent efforts of the United States to purchase Texas,
> by the determination of the colonists to hold slaves, notwith-
> standing their adopted country's reiterated policy of abolition,
> and by the friction which was the inevitable result of racial
> difference and prejudice. (T-73: 421)

The situation in East Texas was tense by 1832, the year Sam Houston
arrived in Nacogdoches. (T-130: 308-309) That year the citizens demanded
that the local Mexican commandant support the "pronouncement" of Santa
Anna. When he refused on grounds of loyalty to the legitimate regime, a
force of 300 "Texians" advanced into the again evacuated town, staging

87

a successful attack that resulted in more than fifty fatalities. Mexican authority in East Texas ended for all practical purposes as the commandant and his surviving military supporters left the province. (T-32: 160) (T-13: 190-192) (T-133: 97)

The full-scale War for Independence from Mexico was under way in 1835 and 1836. In fear of Santa Anna's approaching army, East Texas was depopulated by Anglo inhabitants for the fourth time since 1812 as settlers hastened across the Sabine river. In East Texas annals, this event is called the "Runaway Scrape" of 1836. (T-32: 184) To guard against potential Indian action at the time, American General Edward P. Gaines came with troops from Louisiana and occupied Nacogdoches. (T-133) (T-136) General Gaines' brother, James Gaines, controlled the ferry across the Sabine river and was an important figure in regional politics. (T-32: 70) Early in his East Texas career, James Gaines had joined the McGee Expedition of 1812 and later was employed by Long to negotiate with LaFitte on Galveston Island. (T-32: 135)

88   The Anglo revolution brought independence to Texas in 1836, but a reconquest was threatened in 1842. In 1844, local East Texas factions reached the crisis of a feud called the "Regulator-Moderator War" that subsided only when the opponents resolved their differences to join in fighting Mexico in 1846. (T-32: 197) Contraversy over the slavery issue delayed annexation of Texas to the United States until December 29, 1845. Annexation in turn brought war with Mexico in 1846.

Considering all the conflagrations that have been skimmed over lightly in the previous paragraphs, one can readily understand why a long chapter of Crockett's history of East Texas is simply entitled "Troubles and Wars". (T-32) In writing formal history, Americans usually deal only with the progress of white settlement. Indians are mentioned only when they interfere with this progress; otherwise they are ignored. But throughout the chronicles of formal history in the Caddo area, there is a perpetual concern with what the Indians are doing, or might do. Spanish and Mexican agents appeared to be in contact with the tribes, and there was constant inter-tribal communication.

To complete the outline of Texas non-Indian history for the period
to 1846, a few population figures will be cited. In 1810, the governor of Texas reported that the entire population, other than Indian,
included 3,122 civilians and a military contingent of 1,033 men. East
Texas had three mumicipalities: (1) Trinidad de Salcedo, 91 [This is
a town on the Trinity river obliterated in 1813] (2) Nacogdoches, 655
(3) Payou Pierre, 189. (T-22: 400)

Describing Texas in 1833, Stephen Austin stated that the total
population was 46,500. Under the "Municipality of Nacogdoches, including
the settlements of the Ayish, Trinity, Neches, Attoyac, Tenaha, Sabine and
Pecan Point", he gave a sub-total of 16,700 persons. He added: "The
wandering tribes of Indians and half-civilized persons, whose number
passes twenty thousand, are not included in this enumeration." (T-4: 118-119)

Juan Almonte's statistical report for the Mexican government in
1835 gave lower figures for East Texas. In four municipalities and four
villages, Almonte listed 9,000 persons with an additional 1,600 persons
living outside the towns. The total population of 10,600 applied to the
Department of Nacogdoches, bound on the north by the Red river, the east
by the Sabine river, and on the west by the divide between the Brazos and
Trinity rivers then the divide between the Brazos and San Jacinto rivers.*
(T-4: 207, 197-198)

89

By 1846, the white population had risen to 140,000, with 22,000
slaves. (T-52: 11) Most of this population was in south and coastal
Texas. East Texas still had only two towns of any consequence: San
Augustine with 1,500 and Nacogdoches with 1,000 population. (T-52: 17)
In size, Nacogdoches in 1846, was comparable to the combined civilian
and military community of 1810. The growth of Texas from 1836 to 1846
can be viewed by comparing maps for these dates. (T-207 and T-208)

---

*The Texas province at this time was divided into three departments:
Bexar [San Antonio district], Brazos, and Nacogdoches. The western
boundary for the Department of Nacogdoches above the San Jacinto river
corresponds to the western boundary for Caddo territory in Texas described in this report.

Turning back to the continuity of Caddo History, at the beginning of the American era in Louisiana we find that the Caddo chief
sought out John Sibley in Natchitoches in the fall of 1803 to question
him about the coming of the Americans. The chief had heard from a
Chickasaw that the change of political regime might bring an improvement in prices for furs. Sibley was well-impressed by the "King of
the Caddos", whom he considered "a fine looking man". (T-17: 75)
The two men cooperated in promoting their mutual concerns after Sibley
officially became Indian agent in 1805.

The opening years of the American era were a critical period
in Indian diplomacy because of the dispute between the United States
and Spain over the Louisiana-Texas border. Governor Claibourne of
Louisiana held a council with the Caddo in Natchitoches in September,
1806 shortly after the Freeman-Custis expedition had been intercepted
by a Spanish force just above the bend of the Red river. (T-27: 2-5)
The Spanish force had also struck down an American flag in the Caddo
90 village and warned the Indians not to fly an Americna flag in Spanish
territory. At the time of the Caddo council of 1806, Spanish troops
were posted at Bayou Pierre about eighteen miles from Natchitoches.
(T-27: IV, 8-9) The celebrated "Neutral Ground" agreement was not
concluded until November, 1806. (T-22: 268-269) (T-43: 124-125)

The key event in Indian diplomacy at the beginning of the
American era was a big inter-tribal council in 1807, largely organized
by the Caddo chief. More than three hundred Indians from regions beyond the immediate vicinity of Natchitoches assembled for meetings
that concluded on August 17, 1807 with a treaty agreement. The Caddo
chief came to Sibley on August 9 to announce that "about Three hundred
Indians of different Nations were on their way and would be here
tomorrow." (T-106: 48-49) First to arrive was a delegation of Comanche,
who had sent word in June that they intended to visit Natchitoches
along with the "Great Towiash Chief". The latter did not come for the
council.

By August 13, all the visiting Indians had arrived. The parched
commons of the town could scarcely provide grazing facilities for the

400 horses pastured there. Tribal representation, according to pro-
visioning lists, included: "80 Heitans [Comanche], 18 Tawakenos,
8 Keychies, 45 Nabedaches, 90 Caddos, 34 Nandacos, 16 Inies [Hainai],
24 Nacogdochettos, and 4 Chickesaws." The two Tawakani chiefs declared they never before had seen an American officer or agent.
(T-106: 50-51) The Comanche brought their Spanish flag and asked
to exchange it for an American flag. (T-106: 54) They had already
received generous presents from Governor Cordero in San Antonio.
(T-106: 41-42)

 Captain Zebulon Pike, who had been authorized to make a treaty
with the Comanche if he encountered them in his explorations, was in
Natchitoches at the time of the 1807 Indian Council. (T-43: 127-128)
The moment seemed opportune for a treaty. A spirit of amity prevailed
at the final council on August 18 attended by the Comanche, Caddo,
Tawakoni, Nadaco, Nabedache, Kichai, Hainai and the Ais. (T-106: 55-56)
Sibley delivered a speech indicating that the United States wanted to
have friendly relations with Indians regardless of the international
boundary. He declared that "...we have not come to this country to
harm any of our Red Brethren, but to do them good." The Tawakoni
chief commented, "Time will determine whether this days talk will
prove true." The Kichai chief promised that "...our nation shall be
the last who will transgress the treaty of this day." (T-106: 58, 60,
62)

91

 The concluding speech was made by the Great Caddo Chief, who
addressed the tribes as "my allies". He used the occasion to explain
his recommendations for handling the recent attack on the Nadaco made
by "vagabond Choctaw". (T-106: 22) Commenting that the warrior
responsible had lately been commissioned a chief by the American
government, he asked that three months be allowed for the Choctaw
to obtain satisfaction for the attack. During that time, he himself
would be responsible for seeing that no "mischief" occurred. There
would be no further restraints on Caddo allies if satisfaction was
not obtained before that deadline. The Indians present assented to
this decision. (T-106: 65-66) Difficulties between the Choctaw and
Caddo seem to have been resolved subsequently. (T-106: 69)

The year 1807 also marked the beginning of a period of cooperation between the Cherokee and the Caddo. In March, the first party
of Cherokee ever to come to Natchitoches arrived with Caddo "pilots"
by order of the chief. The Cherokee had "come to see the Caddos &
make friends with them" according to Sibley's journal. Specifically,
the Cherokee arranged an amicable settlement of a misunderstanding
concerning the accidental death of a brother, an incident that had
occurred seven or eight years earlier. (T-106: 16)

In October of 1807, a large party of seventy-four Comanche
and "Panies" came to Natchitoches with their great chiefs. The "Panies"
were probably Taovayas, or "Towiash" in American terminology, who had
not attended the big August council. (T-106: 69) In what was probably
a follow-up of the great council of 1807, a Caddo representative in 1808
went far out on the plains to complete an alliance with the Comanche.
A Spanish captain leading an expedition to Santa Fe in the summer of
1808 reported meeting a Caddo emissary near Dickens, Texas close to
the panhandle district. (T-43: 128) According to the diary account,
"He said his trip to the Comanche [village] had been to parley for
peace--in which he had succeeded." (T-87: 492)

The system of Caddo alliances begun during the De Mezières era
in 1770 appeared strong and even extended in the first decade of the
nineteenth century. During the interval when the War of 1812 and the
Mexican War of Independence were simultaneously in progress, American
authorities relied on the neutrality and friendship of the tribes under
Caddo leadership. (T-53: 905-906) Texas tribes allied to the Caddo
were solicited to join the Spanish Royalist forces as well as expeditions
fitted out in American territory to support the independence cause.

The Caddo chief advised and followed a diplomatically neutral
stance. In the fall of 1812, he visited all the tribes between the
Red river and the San Antonio Road as far west as the Comanche country.
Returning to Natchitoches in February of 1813, he assured Sibley that
not one of the nations visited would have anything to do in the future
with the affairs of the Mexican revolution. He even managed to get
the Comanche to recall the group of their warriors who had been won

over by the Spanish governor. (T-211: 421, 422 fn)

In his reports to the Secretary of War, Sibley indicated
his confidence in the Caddo chief's ability and resources. He wrote:

> It is my present opinion that should any occasion
> justify our government in calling upon the Indians in
> this quarter the Caddo chief with what assistance I
> could afford him could bring into the field from three
> to five thousand as brave Indian warriors under heaven.
> (T-211: 426-427)

A later letter mentioning the Caddo chief stated:

> This man is a very important character and his nation
> generally well behaved people, and the nations to the west
> as far as Rio Grande almost entirely under his influence.
> (T-211: 426-427)

The Caddo were understandably disturbed and resentful when
Americans, most of them disorderly characters, began to congregate
on the upper Red river following the War of 1812. John Sibley had
ended his career as Indian agent in 1815 after ten years of service.
A well-intentioned newcomer, John Jamison had the unpleasant responsibility for handling the border situation. Writing the Secretary
of War in March of 1817, he explained:

> Hordes of hunters and licentious traders have entered
> the Indian villages and camps on Red River above this
> place [Natchitoches] who bids defiance to the laws of the
> United States, of which the Indians have frequently com-
> plained, and it is impossible to restrain them by the
> ordinary course--I have therefore found it necessary to
> call on the Commanding officer of this Post, for a force
> sufficient to expel the intruders. In a day or two we
> shall leave this place with a detachment, and may proceed
> as far as Pecan Point, and I hope we shall be able to
> teach some of those intruders what sort of respect ought
> to be paid to the laws of our Country....

> The disaffection of the Caddo chief (mentioned in my last)
> I believe has arose from the want of protection, and the
> course I am about to take will convince him, that the
> Government will try to remedy the evils he has long com-
> plained of, and perhaps restore confidence. (T-18b: 257-258)

Jamison actually removed a dozen families from land claimed by the Caddo,
but several of the illegal traders escaped. (T-18b: 302) His show
of American force was but a temporary solution to the problem of in-
coming squatters and traders in the border country.

93

The Caddo promoted their own security through expanding offensive and defensive alliances with immigrant tribes. The Coushatta
and Alabama had been the first Indian immigrants to have a village
in their land, moving near the Caddo village in 1804. In 1817, Cherokee
and Delaware also had villages on the Red river, and the Choctaw had
become allies. A new union of tribes opposed to the Osage began to
function in 1817, with all these groups participating. (T-18b: 302)
(T-47: 213) The Cherokee in northern Arkansas were now taking the
leadership against the Osage with Shawnee and Delaware support. Cooperative efforts of the Caddo and Cherokee in the nineteenth century
were not a new development. In 1785, the Caddo and "chiefs of St.
Francis River", who must have been Cherokee, appeared before the Spanish
governor in New Orleans to make peace with the Osage.

Soon after James Miller, the first governor of Arkansas, arrived
at Arkansas Post in December of 1819, he learned that the Caddo had
agreed to aid the Cherokee in their next offensive against the Osage.
In June of 1820, Caddo and Choctaw painted for war, were at the Cherokee
settlements on the Arkansas river. (T-47: 87, 89) Without going into
discussion of the tribal representation in numerous battles of Osage
warfare, evidence suggests that contacts established in these campaigns
led to the appearance of allied immigrant Indians in Caddo territory.
The 1827 map of Texas shows a protective line of villages along the
Red river below Pecan Point: Shawnee, Delaware and Quapaw. On creeks
tributary to the Sabine river, facing the Louisiana border were the
Cherokee and Choctaw. In the hinterland toward the three forks of the
Trinity river were Kickapaw, in a position to serve as "rear guard"
for the Caddo allies in the Angelina-Neches region. (T-201 Map) The
main Kickapoo village was on the Upper Sabine river, but a small group
were near the Shawnee and Delaware. (T-47: 249)

The status of immigrant Indian tribes in Caddo territory was
pointed out by W.A. Trimble in an account included in Jedidiah Morse's
Report to the Secretary of War...on Indian Affairs, published in 1822.
He wrote:

94

> The Coshattas, Delawares, and Cherokees, obtained per-
> mission from the Caddos, to settle on Red River. They
> do not own part of the country. The Coshattas migrated
> from Florida and are believed to be a tribe of the
> Muscogees. (T-91: 257)

The accumulation of immigrant Indians was gradual. Fifty families of

Shawnees from St. Louis moved to the Sulphur Fork region in early 1824,

but additional Shawnee and Delaware were expected that year. (T-19: 612)

In January of 1826, a report from Fort Towson on the Kiamichi indicated

that 170 Shawnee and Delaware had recently passed the post on their way

to Sulphur Ford above the Caddo village in northeast Texas. (T-20a: 185)

The Quapaw were in Caddo territory on a different basis, and

remained only seven years. In 1824, they ceded to the United States

their reserved land between the Saline and Arkansas rivers and agreed

to "join the Caddo".* The whole affair was badly managed. The French-

man conducting the Quapaw to the Red river created the impression that

lands had been purchased from the Caddo to accomodate the Quapaw. Con-

sequently, there was the basis for real misunderstanding when the Quapaw

arrived in early 1826. (T-20a: 237) Although the Caddo chief was

given an emolument for taking in the Quapaw, he assigned them an un-

satisfactory location. They returned to their former homeland and

were ultimately reassigned in Oklahoma territory. (T-47: 210-212)

95

The Cherokee in Texas did not constitute a harmonious element,

but displayed a dangerous factionalism. Part of the tribe was implicated

in the "Fredonian Rebellion" of 1826-1827, the attempt of Edwards colony

settlers of the Nacogdoches district to gain independence from Mexico,

with a reported promise to divide Texas with the Indians. (T-47: 247)

Edwards' grant had been revoked by the Mexican government in October,

1826, an act that was related to local political and land control rivalries.

(T-32: 137) The Cherokee also had thought they had a grant in the same

area, but it was never formally recognized locally. In the course of

the "Fredonian Rebellion", the Cherokee under Chief Bowle killed the

leaders of the Fredonian party within the tribe. (T-47: 247) Immigrant

---

*Quapaw Treaty signed November 15, 1824. VII Stat. 232. Royce Area 121
on map Arkansas 1.

Indians are mentioned as supporting and crushing the uprising. (T-32: 145-146) Native tribes of the Caddo group do not seem to have partici-pated.

By 1827, Americans under the authority of both Mexico and the United States were struggling to control the land on the upper Red river valley, where the international border was not surveyed until 1839-1840. Colonels Ben Milam and Peter Ellis Bean, officials of Texas, were planning to survey lands south of the Red river in an area claimed as Miller County by Arkansas. Arkansas officials in a special session in 1828 created a new Miller County south of Red river and abolished the county north of the river. (T-47: 253, 267, Map before 313) Un-certainty continued as to whether it was in the United States or Texas. (T-46: 84 fn)

The transfer of Miller County and Arkansas settlers to the area south of the Red river was an adjustment to prepare for the arrival of the Choctaw, who did not reach Oklahoma in large numbers until 1834. In 1833, the principal part of the nation had not yet arrived. (T-26: 84) By late 1834, however, an estimated 2,000 were in the Pushmata district west of the Kiamichi river. The more densely populated settlements of Red river district east of the Kiamichi contained a population of 7,000 before they began to move up the river. (T-48b: 26) In 1837, a Chickasaw District was created within the area of southeast Oklahoma originally designated for the Choctaw.* Eastern boundary for the new Chickasaw District was the divide between the Blue and Washita rivers. (T-129: 12 Map) Chickasaw hesitated to advance so far on the prairie, and at first settled among the established Choctaw.

In spite of the changes going on around them, the Caddo and their immigrant Indian allies continued a traditional pattern of existence, insofar as it was possible. In 1829, the combined warrior strength of the Red river group was estimated at 500 to 700 men, who continued to hunt on the southeast Oklahoma prairie, a traditional Caddo hunting ground. (T-47: 277) Grant Foreman has pointed out the customary hunting use of

96

---

*The Chickasaw-Choctaw Treaty of January 17, 1837, was signed at Doaksville, near Fort Towson. VII Stat. 605.

this region prior to the removal of the Choctaw to Oklahoma, and the later
creation of the Chickasaw district. He wrote:

> Bands of Delaware, Shawnee, Kickapoo, Caddo, Uchee, and
> Kanchati had for a number of years occupied the valleys of the
> Blue, Boggy, and Washita and country west as a common hunting
> ground, before the Choctaw had removed above the Kiamichi
> River and the Chickasaw had been assigned that country. (T-46: 98)

In 1830, the Caddo had sent three parties to intercept the Mexican
agent, Colonel Peter Bean, who intended to establish a border post at
Pecan Point. The Pecan Point crossing of the Red river had always been
zealously guarded by the Caddo as access to their hunting range. To
save his life, Colonel Bean returned to his headquarters through Arkansas
and the east side of the Red river. (T-188b: #125)

In 1834, the newly-arrived Choctaw were eager to establish peaceful relations with Indians already living in Oklahoma. Their agent advised them to be accompanied by Caddo if they went to visit plains
Indians, "as the Caddo were accustomed to hunt on the western prairies
and were acquainted with the Indians who lived there." (T-46: 127)
That summer, thirty-three Caddo did meet Colonel Henry Dodge's expedition
at the mouth of the Washita river to serve as guides to the Wichita
and Comanche country. (T-46: 130-131)

The outlook for the Caddo in the Red river region was discouraging
by the 1830's. Ther were hemmed in by a concentration of Choctaw north
of the Red river and constant pressure of white population along the Red
river. The game resources of Oklahoma east of the Boggy river were
severely depleted. John Sibley still retained the confidence of the
Caddo, but he was out of office. His successors apparently tried to
aid and protect the Caddo but were limited in their effectivenes.
George Grey, agent for the Caddo from 1819 to 1828, was also agent for
the Choctaw. During the period from 1821 to 1825, he maintained his
headquarters at the mouth of Sulphur Fork. (T-47: 202) He tried to
remove illegal settlers from Caddo land, but the problem was difficult
when they claimed donations by act of Congress. (T-20a: 90)

The Caddo agency for the next six years was on Caddo Prairie,
further south and nearer the Caddo villages.

97

The two agents following Grey died in quick succession. The
usual gifts and hunting supplied did not reach the Caddo. ' (T-20b: 259)
The Caddo appeared financially desperate, but so were the Nadaco and
Hainai who came over and slaughtered cattle near Bayou Pierre and con-
sumed Caddo stores of food while their hunters were out in the buffalo
range during the winter of 1831. (T-188b: #126)

The last five years of its existence, 1830-1835, the Agency
House was located close to modern Shreveport, less accessible to the
Indian population. (T-53: 908 fn) (T-122: 554 Map) Here, agent
Jehiel Brooks was subject to tremendous pressure from locally powerful
men who wanted Indian land. Brooks did not have the confidence of the
Caddo. Chief Dehakuit addressed a complaint to the President of the
United States in behalf of all the tribes of the vicinity asking for
a new agent, a new interpreter of their choice, and information about
allowances that had been stopped. He asked that the reply be sent to
John Sibley. (T-188b: #128)

98   Brooks was definitely interested in securing a land cession
from the Caddo. For a time after old chief Dehakuit died in 1833,
the Caddo refused to council with Brooks. (T-188b: #133) By the
following year, the pressure for a land cession had increased. The
project for clearing the Great Raft from the Red river had begun,
and land speculators were eager to profit from the opening of the
river. (T-188b: #140) The Caddo had been offered a grant of land in
Mexico near the Guadeloupe river, according to reports of the period,
so they had a destination in prospect if they left their Louisiana
villages. (T-53: 913-914)

Arrangements were made for a treaty that was signed on July 1, 1835.
Circumstances surrounding the treaty were suspicious, beginning with the
fact that the agent wanted to have the proceedings conducted in Washington,
D.C. rather than Louisiana. Later charges of fraud occasioned a long
federal investigation in 1841 and 1842. (T-137: 140) The pages of
conflicting testimony have since been included as evidence in a Caddo
hearing before the Indian Claims Commission in 1954. The evidence does
create the impression that agent Brooks intimidated the Caddo, who

ultimately believed they had no choice but to accept the terms he offered. (T-53: 942) (T-188a)

Only the territory described in the treaty will receive comment in this report. By the 1830's, the Caddo realized that much of their territory in the United States had been taken over by federal legis- lation, as in the Quapaw and Choctaw deals, and by private individuals in defiance of federal law. In 1819, the Indian factor at Sulphur Fork reported that the Caddo chief claimed "all the lands above the raft", interpreted as all land on the Red river above the Shreveport location. (T-19: 70) This statement indicates the extent of white settlement along the river that he recognized.

Later correspondence about the boundaries of Caddo land in Louisiana are vague, although Brooks stated that the geographical markers were well known. George Grey, writing in 1825, described a restricted area that it has not been possible to trace on maps, but he claimed the limits were "best calculated to give satisfaction to all parties." (T-140: 107) Later correspondence referred to the area "assigned" to the Caddo. Comparing maps of the Caddo land cession of 1835 and maps of the "Neutral Ground" creates the impression that the Caddo boundary was drawn to exclude "Neutral Ground" territory where Americans had moved in to establish property claims after 1806. (T-212: 70) The boundary did not refer to Caddo aboriginal territory.*

99

The use of a Bayou Pascagoula marker hear the Coushatta village has no validity. Neither the detailed accounts of early travellers up the Red river nor early maps indicate a "Pascagoula Bayou". No document earlier than the Treaty of 1835 itself has been found that even mentions a Pascagoula Bayou. Inhabitants familiar with the region knew the Pascagoula village and bayou were many miles further south on the Red river than the point marked on the 1835 treaty. (T-140: 80) The treaty boundary was not surveyed by a local person, but by a man from Virginia who doubtless believed what he was told about Louisiana geographics. (T-140)

The departure of the Caddo from Louisiana was delayed and confounded by the outbreak of the Texas War for Independence in October

---

*Treaty with the Caddo, July 1, 1835. VII Stat. 470. (Royce Area 202 on maps Arkansas 1 and Louisiana 1).

of 1835. Many of the details of the subsequent history of the Louisiana
Caddo have been summarized by William Glover and can be followed in
concluding sections of his "History of the Caddo Indians." (T-53:
923-942) The related Caddo tribes in Texas were a major source of
concern for Texans during and following their War for Independence.
The creation of a Committee on Indians and negotiation of Indian
treaties was a first order of business for the new independent government
headed by Sam Houston. Of the first treaties concluded, while war was
in progress, Governor Smith recommended to the council:

> ...the raising of a company of rangers to overawe the Indians,
> and prevent them from becoming allies of the Mexicans; also
> the protection of the civilized Indians in the "just and
> equitable" title which they were generally understood to have
> in their lands. (T-131: 33)

The only one recommended for ratification was with the "Anadarko" and
"Ionies," as the Nadaco and Hainai were henceforth termed by Texans.
This treaty was reported lost from the files and has never been located.

100   After an initial two year term of office, Houston was replaced
by Mirabeau B. Lamarr, formerly of Georgia, who is described as following
an "extermination policy" toward Indians. During his regime, Mexican
agents were in contact with the Texas tribes considered potential
participants in a plot to overthrow the government in 1838. The wars
prosecuted against tribes in East Texas during 1838 and 1839 created
havoc. The Caddo were disarmed and driven back to Shreveport by a
Texas military contingent. In Shreveport, General Thomas J. Rusk made
a treaty whereby Texas would pay for subsistence of the Caddo if they
remained out of Texas. By treaty with the Shawnee, Rusk promised that
they would be paid for improvements on land they had occupied for about
twelve years, but they had to leave Texas.

The Cherokee received much harsher treatment. In a skirmish
in 1839, Chief Bowle was shot and his followers pursued as they fled
west. The general atmosphere was so alarming to all Indians that there
was a general exodus. For the next several years, the Caddo tribes
were dispersed. Some were reported in Arkansas and Texas. (T-174)
One group was followed to a village location at the Three Forks of

the Trinity and attacked. Traditional accounts indicate that part
of the Caddo went to the Cross Timbers, then to Mexico, and finally
returned to the Cross Timbers. (T-186) The presence of Caddo as far
west as Callahan county, and at various points along the frontier of
white settlement is reported in chronicles of "Indian depredations"
often difficult to verify.

In 1843, Shawnee and Caddo were on the lower Washita river.
(T-46: 103) From the frequency of reports, it appears that part of
the Caddo continued to live on the Oklahoma side of the Red river.
Small groups of Delaware and Shawnee remained with the Caddo tribes,
in spite of the program to rid Texas of immigrant tribes carried out
during the Lamarr administration.

When Houston returned to office, he negotiated a series of
peace treaties with the Texas tribes who were concerned about the
availability of hunting supplies and other usual items of Indian trade.
Although discussions were held concerning establishing boundaries
between areas of white occupancy and areas of Indian occupancy, no
firm agreement was ever reached. Surveyors continued to progress up
the rivers, encountering Indian resistence all the way. The progress
of these negotiations, and the advance of the frontier line under
discussion are covered by documents in the Texas Indian Papers.
(T-124, T-125) Citizens of Texas realized they were living in land
still claimed by Indians. Edwards, in his History of Texas published
in 1836, commented on the "50,000 aboriginals who claim that country
lying between the Rio Bravo [Rio Grande] and the Sabine, as their own..."
(T-38: 98)

In the wake of the Texas Indian War, Caddo leaders actively
engaged in a program to achieve peace on the frontier through messages
and councils with Choctaw and Creek chiefs. One of the most important
inter-tribal councils was held on the Deep Fork river, near Eufala,
Oklahoma in 1842. Here, Caddo chiefs met Pierce M. Butler as agent
for the Cherokee, He later came to Texas in May of 1846 as an American Commissioner for the Treaty at Tehuacana Springs of May 15, 1846.
(T-180, T-179, T-176)

101

> Pierce M. Butler described the Caddo chief, Chowawhana, as a "striking man of great personal beauty and commanding appearance, small in stature, yet beautiful and attractive features; dressed in what would be called Indian magnificence--feathers, turbans, and silver bands. Chowawhana deplored the gloomy past, the worse future prospects, and probably fate of the Red People; he approved the council, and advised against hostility among the tribes which would bring the destruction of their race and ruin of their children." (T-129: 50-51)

At the time of the Treaty of May, 1846, the leading spirit among the Caddo tribes was José Maria, an Anadarko whose Indian name was "Aisch," probably a signer of the 1835 Treaty at Shreveport. The principal purpose of this treaty was to establish peaceful relations with the Comanches. Indians brought along from Oklahoma provided indispensible assistance in managing the council. Unfortunately, Butler himself was ill and the less competent M.G. Lewis took charge. Lewis collected on separate sheets of paper the signatures of Indians, unidentified by tribe at the time, and signatures of witnesses, secretaries and interpreters, but contemporary and later disclosures indicate he wrote the treaty after returning to Washington. (T-71) José Maria was among the chiefs who visited the capital city the summer of 1846 as guests of the federal government. Under these circumstances, it is not surprising that the Texas tribes later complained that provisions of the treaty, as they understood the treaty, were not observed. (T-72: 155 fn) The responsibility and procedure for extinguishing Indian title to Texas land still remained a bone of contention between federal and state authorities. David G. Burnet, writing to Robert S. Neighbors, in August, 1847 expressed the prevailing view in Texas:

> The federal government alone is competent to prevent a catastrophe, which, however oppressive to the ancient occupants, is necessarily consequent to the progress of civilization. The State has not the means to extinguish the Indian titles to the specious territory over which they roam in pursuit of the only means of subsistence they know, and which they claim, by the emphatic right of occupancy, for "time immemorial" to them. (T-146: 7)

By the time Texas was annexed to the United States, the Caddo tribes in Texas were congregated on the Brazos river along with the

102

Tawakoni, and a more aggressive division, the Waco. The cluster of
villages near the Clair Fork of the Brazos river was visited by Colonel
Samuel Cooper in 1851, the year before surveys for a reservation were
made in the same area. Colonel Cooper's description of his expedition,
and map drawn by Major H.H. Sibley who accompanied him, provide a
picture of these tribes just before they were confined to the reservation. (T-185a, T-185b)

Colonel Cooper visited the Anadarko, Ioni, Caddo and Keechi
villages, noting the higher location of the Waco and Tawakoni. The
Delaware and Shawnee were situated below Barnard's Trading House by
Comanche Peak, a famous regional landmark. This community was having
great difficulty in raising enough food, and to Colonel Cooper seemed
in "starving condition." He estimated the population at about 1,000,
but of course he did not include the Delaware and Shawnee. The six
villages each had a chief, but were divided into two groups with José
Maria as head chief for the Anadarko, Ioni and Caddo; and the Waco
chief Acoquash as chief of the Wacos, Keechi and Tawakani. (T-185a)
But these tribes had other members living north of the Red river.
There were Waco and Keechi with the Wichita and Comanche near Wichita
Mountains; and Caddo and Keechi on the Washita river within fifteen
miles of the future Fort Arbuckle north of the present Arbuckle
mountains. (T-184a, T-184b)

When the reservation was created in 1854, these tribes were
given the right to hunt for a ten mile area surrounding the reservation.
Hostile whites in the vicinity made life increasingly hazardous for
these Indians. Preparations were made for transfer to Wichita county
in Oklahoma. An unprovoked massacre of Indians sleeping in their
hunting tents was the ultimate tragedy. When their agent learned that
malevolent whites in the vicinity intended complete annihilation,he
hastily gathered the Indians for a march to Oklahoma begun August 1, 1859.
En route, the party was harrassed by whites mascarading as Indians. The
heroic protector of these tribes, Robert S. Neighbors, was killed
before he was able to return to his home from this mission. (T-81)
(T-153) (T-151)

103

The dispersal and gradual re-gathering of the Caddo made a
deep impression on the generations who survived those critical years.
Traditional accounts preserved by contemporary members of the Caddo
Tribe of Oklahoma help to fill in the large gaps of information in
existing documents. According to recollections, one part of the Caddo
lived for a while in limestone caves near the San Marcos river.
(1 M-33) Others who finally came to the Oklahoma reservation had
lived during the previous years in eastern Oklahoma, in the Kiamichi
mountains and in the "Choctaw Country." (1 M-34) One informant in
1968 even identified her father's tribal office by a term phonetically
transcribed as "tum-muh" or "spokesman". This is surely a reference
to the office of "tamma" mentioned in the tribal hierarchy of the
Hasinai tribes of the early eighteenth century. Present day members
of the Caddo Tribe of Oklahoma are familiar with their nineteenth
century history, and trace their ancestry to the Hainai [Texas],
Nadaco, Natchitoches, Yatasi and Caddo divisions, who were aboriginal
104 occupants of a large area in Texas, Louisiana, Arkansas and Oklahoma.
(1 M)

La Harpe's 1719 Post on Red River and Nearby Caddo Settlements

By Mildred Mott Wedel

BULLETIN 30

THE TEXAS MEMORIAL MUSEUM

The University of Texas at Austin

LA HARPE'S 1719 POST ON RED RIVER
AND NEARBY CADDO SETTLEMENTS[1]

By Mildred Mott Wedel[2]

In 1719 Jean-Baptiste Bénard de La Harpe set up a post on Red River, a western tributary of the Mississippi, to establish trade relations with the Spaniards then in Texas and New Mexico. This study proposes a location for the site of this structure built in an Upper Nasoni village above the Great Bend of the Red. Neighboring Caddo settlements were described by the Frenchman in terms that related to his post, so having postulated where it was erected, this paper also suggests the location of settlements of the Kadohadacho, Upper Natchitoches, and the *Nadsoo* or *Natsoo* ("Nanatsoho" in Hodge, 1907-1910, 2: 23). The basic source for data has been La Harpe's 1718-1720 journal.

The information developed here may enable archeologists working in northeast Texas and southwest Arkansas to apply the "direct historic" or "upstreaming" approach in their research, a methodology that has been highly rewarding, particularly in the northern plains, the northeast, and southwest, when carried out with thoroughness and critical skill. This distinctive way of studying archeological materials has been described as moving "from the known to the unknown" (Strong, 1935: 6, 296; W. R. Wedel, 1938). The "unknown" is prehistoric time. The "known" refers to the historic period.

The data for the later period is drawn from documentary sources such as memoirs, letters, official government correspondence, journals, and so on, using the principles of another "approach," the ethnohistoric. To do this, the written records must be critically examined and evaluated in order to determine their kind and degree of validity. Then they must be viewed with the insights of anthropology. The bridge between the "known" and "unknown" is made possible by identification of the village location of a historically recognized people with an archeological site component that gives evidence of Euro-American contact. The soundness of the construct depends upon the skill and care with which it is put together and the amount of historic data and archeological material available (M. Wedel, 1976: 7-11). When this gap has been bridged, a relative chronology displaying cultural continuity of great time depth, anchored to historic times, may be achievable so that a report on the archeological data involved will take on added significance. It is to be hoped that if the arguments presented here regarding Caddo settlement locations are acceptable to professional archeologists, they will proceed to carry further the direct historic approach in their analysis of the archeology of the region. This is a logical procedure and one that could lead to greater insights than have been obtained through study of archeological materials alone.

Jean-Baptiste Bénard, Sieur de La Harpe, first came to the Louisiana colony in 1718 when he was 35 years old. (Note that his surname, not his given name, was Bénard, often mistakenly written "Bernard.") The title he inherited had originally been given to his father, a famed sea captain of St. Malo, France. Having grown up in that city on the English channel, Jean-Baptiste served when 18 in the cavalry of Philip V of Spain. Later, he was to use his knowledge of the Spanish language to advantage in the Red River region. Between 1703 and 1705 he was in South America where presumably he had contact

This paper was read at the Caddo Conference, Nacogdoches, Texas, March 17, 1978.

Research Associate, Department of Anthropology, Smithsonian Institution.

1

with its Indians. His purpose in coming to Louisiana was to claim a concession on Red River where he intended to erect a post from which to establish trade with the New Mexico and Texas Spaniards. He brought from France a group of 40, mostly men from St. Malo or Nearby Rennes, some titled associates, and some indentured workers *(Rolle des Concessionaires,* 1718). Having landed at Dauphin Island, off Mobile, in August 1718, he received that fall the approval of the Council of Louisiana for his venture, as well as the enthusiastic endorsement of LeMoyne de Bienville, governor-general of the Louisiana colony. As a result of his own determination and perseverance, rather than effective assistance from the Company of the West, La Harpe reached the mouth of Red River by January 10, 1719 (M. Wedel, 1971: 41-42). Not until April 1, however, did the Frenchman finally arrive at the mouth of Sulphur River. The rapids and raft of the Red had been largely responsible for his spending three months in the effort to reach this point with his several heavily laden pirogues and flat boats.

Many details of La Harpe's stay in French Louisiana were recorded by him on a day-to-day basis. It would seem that in January 1720, when he was back from Red River and in the lower colony awaiting a ship on which to return to France, he put his scrawled field notes—later evidently discarded—into better form. It appears too that at this time he may have added some incidental information he picked up from Louisiana officials. The only manuscript of La Harpe's 1718-1720 journal that is now extant is in the *Bibliothèque Nationale* of France in Paris (M. Wedel, 1974: 17-25). It is not in La Harpe's handwriting but is part of a copy of several of his documents: the journal of the Red River expedition, journals of two later journeys in Louisiana, and a memoir. I have made my own translation of this Paris copy of the journal, assisted in questionable passages by Monica Heiman of Canyon, Texas and Marie-

Claude Brown of Rennes, France. The translation made by Ralph A. Smith in the *Southwestern Historical Quarterly* (62: 1-4) is of Pierre Margry's printing of the journal (1876-86, 6: 243-306) wherein Margry made inexcusable alterations, deletions, and additions.

The journal contains notations of features La Harpe observed while traveling, happenings of interest, and the direct-line distance and direction he advanced each day. Direction was determined by reading the compass we know he carried. How did he estimate distance? It may be that on clear sections of rivers he used dead reckoning to measure his progress, that is, a measurement based on log-line (a length of rope floated by a chunk of wood at the end) and time. His overland distance estimates also were probably linked to a time reading. We know he had a timepiece of some sort with him because on certain occasions he mentions the hour of the day events occurred. The common league of France was an "itinerary" unit, the equivalent of an hour's travel on foot (Richelet, 1728; La Curne de Sainte-Palaye, 1880: 174; Jones, 1963: 77). In the 1700s the common or land league was recognized as 25 leagues to a degree, or 4444½ meters, which would be slightly over 2.76 miles per league (G. Delisle, 1700 map *L'Amérique//Septentrionale; Société de Gens de Lettres,* 1771, v. 16; E. Littré, 1869 2: 305). The straight-line distance of advance in leagues reported daily by La Harpe was a calculation derived from a number of annotations made during the meandering march of the day. He described this recorded figure as "corrected" or "reduced."

In a 1972-1974 on-the-ground reconstruction of the route taken by La Harpe from his Red River post northwest to a meeting with Caddoan-speaking Indians in the southern plains, my associates— Waldo R. Wedel, Larry Banks, and Quintus Herron—and were greatly impressed when we found that our straight-line map distances consistently correlated with La Harpe's computed straight-

2

line league distances when multiplied by the mileage length of the common league. They did not correlate exactly. The Frenchman with some regularity overestimated his distance by a mile or two. This probably related to his calculation for the "corrected" figure. Understandably, his winding route across high crests of the Ouachita Mountains resulted in excessive direct-line estimates of distance covered, but this was an exception. Only a general description of the course of La Harpe's travel will be presented in this report; it will not indulge in comparative analysis of distance figures. For this it will be necessary to await publication of a longer, more detailed manuscript now in preparation on La Harpe's 1718-1720 experience in the Louisiana colony.

At the mouth of Sulphur River the Natchitoches Indians, who had joined the party downstream, explained to the Frenchman that there was a short cut to the Upper Nasoni Caddo settlement, one that led up the Sulphur and then overland. La Harpe said it was 15 leagues in length, 37 leagues shorter than the Red River course. It was evidently the customary route taken by the Natchitoches when they went to the settlements above the Great Bend, comparable to the trace that led north from the Hasinai Caddo of the Neches and Angelina rivers to the same region.

Therefore, after sending all but one of his boats by the longer route, La Harpe and some of the Indians proceeded up Sulphur River in a pirogue. Less than two days of travel appears to have brought them into the region of Days Creek. This is now the first good-sized tributary to enter the Sulphur on its north side. Its valley, which lies NNW to SSE, has been greatly modified by strip mining for gravel and by expansion westward of the city of Texarkana. The "Nasoni portage" evidently took off to the NNW somewhere near the stream's mouth. For the most part, the path probably followed a crestline to the west of

Days Creek, thereby avoiding the tangled growth of the floodplain that reaches to the creek bank and passing through the woods of oak, walnut, and hickory described by La Harpe. The Frenchman figured the party made about 15 miles, a long day, before it came upon a "beautiful" stream by which it camped. By paralleling Days Creek valley proper (fig. 1), and then Swamppoodle or Cowhorn tributary creeks, the travelers would have come to an east-west divide where in less than a mile Clear Creek heads. This would have been a spring-fed stream—a "spring branch"—which would deserve the adjective "beautiful." Today it flows north into Bringle and Waterworks lakes, which provide the water supply of Texarkana. The next day the men probably followed down Clear Creek coming out of the bluffs near its mouth at McKinney Bayou.

It may have been there that La Harpe was met by the war chief and his entourage of Upper Nasoni and where an initial welcoming ceremony took place. After this, the visitors were mounted on horses and all rode together through "extensive and very beautiful country"—which would have been prairie and woodlands—to the dwelling of the chief (le chef)[3] in the Upper Nasoni settlement. Unfortunately, La Harpe was so engrossed in what was going on after the meeting with the welcoming party that he did not note down direction or leagues advanced on this last lap of his journey to the Upper Nasoni village. Nor did he even comment on whether the Red River was crossed.

A few days later, after some reconnaissance upriver, La Harpe decided to locate his post in the clearing of the "chief" of the Upper Nasoni, evidently the head chief. On April 22 he gave 30 *pistoles* of merchandise in exchange for the land (or for its use, as the chief may have viewed the transaction), to-

[3]Domingo Terán de los Rios called the headman of the Upper Nasoni a *caddí*, adopting the Hasinai Caddo term for this official. La Harpe used *le chef* throughout.

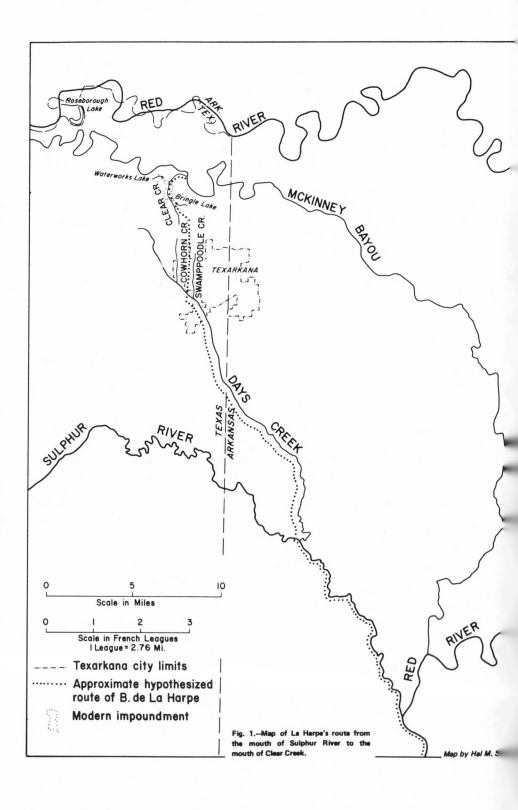

Fig. 1.—Map of La Harpe's route from the mouth of Sulphur River to the mouth of Clear Creek.

RED (ARK) (TEX) RIVER

Roseborough Lake

MCKINNEY BAYOU

Waterworks Lake

CLEAR CR.

Bringle Lake

COWHORN CR.

SWAMPPOODLE CR.

TEXARKANA

SULPHUR RIVER

TEXAS
ARKANSAS

DAYS CREEK

RED RIVER

0   5   10
Scale in Miles

0   1   2   3
Scale in French Leagues
I League = 2.76 Mi.

—·—·— Texarkana city limits

·········· Approximate hypothesized
route of B. de La Harpe

Modern impoundment

Map by Hal M. S

gether with the dwelling and arbors thereon. He supervised the erection there of a 110' by 20' cedar structure (La Harpe *Journal, fol.* 14). Later he surrounded this with a defensive work of some sort, probably a stockade, possibly with a ditch outside (Ibid., *fol.* 15).

La Harpe said his post was on the "left" of the river. Did this refer to the left side in ascending, or was it in descending from his reconnaissance upstream?

When La Harpe queried the assembled chiefs about other Caddo settlements in the region, he was told, "As regards the Kadohadacho they are at two leagues below the Nasoni and the *Natsoo*, and the Natchitoches at 3 leagues above all on the right of the river in [blank]" (*Journal, fol.* 13). Either "ascending" or "descending" might have been appropriate words for the blank space, and, moreover, would have been enlightening. This sentence too is obviously ambiguous, both in respect to the side of the river on which the individual groups were living and in their relationship to each other. Consideration of a related statement in the "Journal Historique Concernant l'Établissement des François à la Loüisianne, " written a few years later under the direction of or by La Harpe (M. Wedel, 1974: 36-67), only adds further uncertainty as to what was intended. This is because of the changed placement of the comma. It reads in the 1831 edition (p. 185): "The Kadohadacho were at this time 2 leagues below the Nasoni, and the *Natsoos* and the Natchitoches 3 leagues above on the right of the river."

Differences in published interpretations of the content of these sentences result from their ambiguity. Herbert E. Bolton (1914: 1: frp. map) placed all four of the Caddo groups on the north bank of Red River, with the Upper Nasoni and Nanatsoho close together, reflecting evidently the journal manuscript sentence. In contrast, John R. Swanton (1942: fig. 1) believed that while the Kadohadacho were downstream from

the Upper Nasoni, the Nanatsoho and Upper Natchitoches were neighbors several miles upstream, as one might interpret the *Journal Historique* passage. And he portrayed the three last-named peoples as all living on the south, that is on the right, of Red River in the modern sense of the usage. Stephen Williams (1964: 548) followed this depiction. J. B. Thoburn of the Oklahoma Historical Society (Lewis, 1924: n. 331-332) located the Nasoni on the south bank, while Ralph A. Smith placed them with the *Nadsoos* on the north, that is, on the right, in ascending (Smith, 1959: map opposite p. 532).

Before considering near whom the Nanatsoho were living and which comma placement was probably correct, let us try to determine with some sense of certainty on which side of the river each of these people lived. The Frenchman always used "right" and "left" in his journal in accordance with the direction he was proceeding, not necessarily as the river was flowing. Therefore, it might have been natural for him to describe the location of the Kadohadacho and Upper Natchitoches as they were encountered in ascending the Red River, that is, on the north side, but one cannot be sure that this was the case.

It is necessary here to seek the help of previous visitors to this locality. Three left records of their stay. The earliest was Henri Joutel, a French soldier, who in 1687 accompanied Father Jean Cavelier when he was ascending to the Illinois country after the murder of his brother, Robert Cavelier de La Salle. Joutel's journal has been lost. The La Galissonnière manuscript copy of the journal, which is in the *Archives Nationales* in Paris, unfortunately lacks the section that dealt with this portion of the journey. Therefore, one must use for primary sources excerpts from the original made by Claude Delisle, the French cartographer, and the Michel published edition of 1713, which is abridged and over-edited. This latter work was inadequately translated into English in

1714. The next recorded visitor was Henri de Tonti who in 1690 was heading south from the Illinois region to look for survivors of the La Salle expedition to the Gulf Coast. He left a 1693 memoir describing his visit to the region and an informative letter to his brother written in 1700 (Delanglez, 1939: 225-226). The following year, 1691, Domingo Terán de Los Rios arrived among the Upper Nasoni in a snowy, cold December. His journal survives, as well as a contemporary map of the area. The published translation of this journal made by Mattie Austin Hatcher is not wholly satisfactory in that there are unnoted omissions and some translation errors.

Do these visitors agree with La Harpe's possible placement of the Kadohadacho on the north bank of the Red? Joutel and Tonti do indeed. Terán makes no mention of them as a people separate from the Upper Nasoni. Joutel visited their main settlement after crossing the Red River from the south to march northeast (Michel, 1713: 28; Delisle, n.d.: 412). In fact, he gave their distance from the Nasoni river crossing as two leagues, which was exactly the same interval given by La Harpe 32 years later. This identity of figures would seem to indicate the same locality was occupied between 1687 and 1719, though there may have been some shifting due to house deterioration and for other reasons. It is likely this was the same settlement visited in March 1690 by Tonti as he went west on the north side of the river, as I interpret his route. His only mention of a river crossing is later, after he left the Kadohadacho. The abandoned "Caddo" site north of the river noted in a post-La Harpe account, that of Thomas Freeman's expedition of 1806 (see later), may correspond also.

The Upper Natchitoches were described by Tonti as being on the Red River in the region of the Upper Nasoni and Kadohadacho. Upon leaving this area, he wrote he crossed a river (presumably the Red) and by bearing a little left came upon what must have been the Hasi-nai Caddo trace, which he then followed south. This would suggest a north bank location in 1690 for the Upper Natchitoches. Therefore, these other documentary sources appear to indicate that La Harpe, when using "right" in his ambiguous statements, intended to place the Kadohadacho and Upper Natchitoches settlements on the north bank of the Red.

As noted earlier, La Harpe wrote of his post in the Upper Nasoni hamlet as on the "left bank" of the Red, thus it would seem on the opposite side from the Kadohadacho and Upper Natchitoches. A south bank location is indisputably confirmed in the Joutel and Terán journals and is illustrated on the Terán map (fig. 2). The small north bank settlement of five holdings opposite the other, also shown on this map, is not reported in the Joutel-related documents or by La Harpe. By 1719 enemy pressures may have caused it to move across the Red.

As to the Nanatsoho in 1719, that depends on which comma one wishes to respect, whether the later position in the *Journal Historique* is considered a correction or a copying error. If they were living near the Upper Natchitoches they were on the north side of the Red, if near the Upper Nasoni, they were on the south. This will be given further consideration later. Since Tonti did not mention their presence in this region in 1690, it is suggested that their move from a former site ten leagues upstream, as reported by La Harpe *(Journal, fol.* 13), occurred between 1690 and 1719.

It may now be seen that the final phrase of the controversial journal sentence—"all on the right of the river"—means in ascending and refers to the Kadohadacho and probably the Upper Natchitoches as on the north, possibly to the Nanatsoho. The Upper Nasoni were unquestionably south of the Red.

Since the locations of the other settlements were given in relation to the Upper

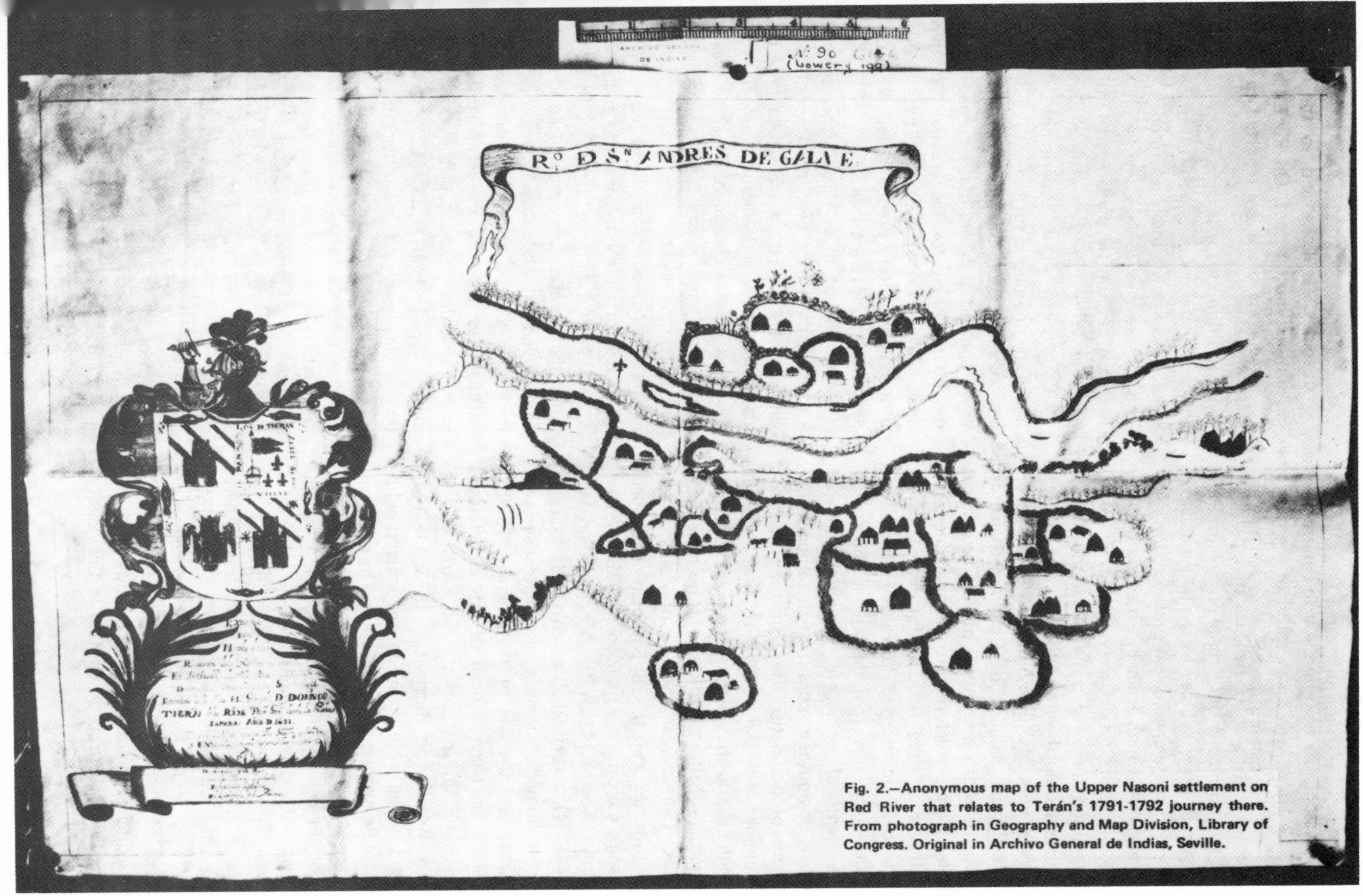

Fig. 2.—Anonymous map of the Upper Nasoni settlement on Red River that relates to Terán's 1791-1792 journey there. From photograph in Geography and Map Division, Library of Congress. Original in Archivo General de Indias, Seville.

Nasoni, the next hurdle is to determine where La Harpe was taken south of the river when the welcoming party escorted him to the dwelling of its chief. Because of La Harpe's failure to record their route, one must look again to other sources for help. First, let us turn to the archeological evidence, for information on which I am indebted particularly to Dee Ann Story, Carolyn Good, and D. L. Hamilton (personal communication). To the north and northwest of the junction of Clear Creek with McKinney Bayou, there are archeological remains of Caddo settlements, two of which are known to have been occupied from prehistoric into historic times. The other may have been. Unfortunately, there has been no thorough, carefully planned archeological survey of the region. The known remnants of settlement, known because of their obviousness, consist of three concentrations of occupation (fig. 3): the Tillson or Summer Hill site (41BW14), near Summer Hill Lake to the north of the creek junction; a group of sites northwest of it near the Clear Lake Cemetery and School, now abandoned, shown on the USGS Barkman TX. quadrangle map, namely Eli Moores (41BW2); Hargrove Moores (41BW39), Mitchell Cemetery (41BW4), and Hatchell (41BW3). Still farther west, immediately northeast of Roseborough Lake, was the site of that name (41BW5), which has recently been destroyed by chisel plowing. One part of the site, Area B, was described (Miroir, Harris et al., 1973: 113-114) as yielding only native-made artifacts with Late Prehistoric Caddo pottery. The southern part of the site, Area A, revealed evidence of both French and Indian occupation. Although many of the trade items seem to relate to a later French occupancy than that of La Harpe, certain glass bead types found there were said to have been used in early 18th century trade. Also within the ceramic concept of Late Prehistoric Caddo, there is sequential evidence for long-continuing habitation before European contact in the vicinity

of old Clear Lake and to the west of its southernmost extent. On the Eli Moores site some glass beads are reported to have been found.

In addition, there is a temple mound on the former oxbow lake just west of old Clear Lake. It is known today as Hatchell Mound. This feature was 25 feet high before excavation. Exploration by the University of Texas and the Works Progress Administration in 1938 revealed eight superimposed floors above the pre-mound surface with evidence of structures on each. Some of these structures were reported as having been burned before mound recapping for the erection of new ones. Throughout the mound, Late Prehistoric Caddo pottery predominated. No European trade goods were seen.

Might one of these three archeologically known hamlets have been the Upper Nasoni village where La Harpe was greeted by the assembled chiefs and where he bought from the head chief a cleared holding? Or was it another site now washed away or covered with silt by the river?

The Frenchman wrote in his journal (fol. 13-13 vo.) that the village was low and sandy, a "musket shot distance" from Red River. He noted the presence nearby of a lake in which he observed fish, undoubtedly an oxbow lake, in former times a channel of the river. No latitude was given for the settlement in the journal. He did record it in the Journal Historique (1831: 179) as 33° 55', a computation as clearly awry as his other latitude calculations.

A musket shot distance is a tricky term to interpret. If restricted to the effective firing distance of a French matchlock musket of that time, it would probably be about 100 yards (pers. comm. Harry Hunter, Division of Military History, Smithsonian Museum of History and Technology; Charles E. Hanson, Jr., Museum of the Fur Trade, Chadron, NE). But there is evidence that La Harpe used it in a more colloquial sense as it is defined in the

8

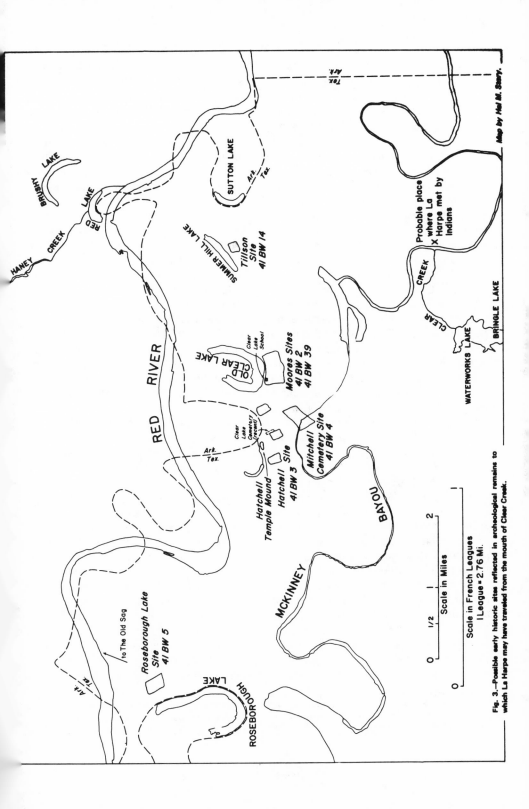

Fig. 3—Possible early historic sites reflected in archeological remains to which La Harpe may have traveled from the mouth of Clear Creek.

HANEY CREEK

BRUSHY LAKE

RED LAKE

SUTTON LAKE
Ark.
Tex.

SUMMER HILL LAKE

Tillson Site
41 BW 14

RED RIVER

Clear Lake School

OLD CLEAR LAKE

Moores Sites
41 BW 2
41 BW 39

Clear Lake Cemetery (recent)

Ark.
Tex.

Hatchell Temple Mound

Hatchell Site
41 BW 3

Mitchell Cemetery Site
41 BW 4

To The Old Sag

Roseborough Lake Site
41 BW 5

Ark.
Tex.

ROSEBOROUGH LAKE

McKINNEY BAYOU

Probable place where La Harpe met by Indians
X

CLEAR CREEK

WATERWORKS LAKE

BRINGLE LAKE

Scale in French Leagues
I League = 2.76 Mi.

0   1/2   1   2
Scale in Miles

Map by Hal M. Story.

Tex.
Ark.

Dictionnaire Quillet (1956: P-Z, p. 1488): *"à peu de distance"* (at a little distance). In the *Journal Historique* (1831: 185), the distance between the chief's holding and the river was changed to "1/8 of a league," (roughly 1/3 to 3/8 of a mile.[4] There is no way of knowing if this is a knowledgeable change made by La Harpe or a conjectured equivalent introduced by a subordinate. In September 1719, when La Harpe approached the encampment of Wichita speakers in the southern plains, he wrote of it as a "musket shot" distance *(Journal,* 1831: *fol.* 19) from a "beautiful" stream they crossed. Having identified, we believe, this creek and La Harpe's probable destination, a map measurement of the distance between is possible. It comes to one and one-half or one and three-fourths miles, depending on how it is figured. Is this the distance the Frenchman had in mind in describing in his journal the interval between his post and the river, or was it shorter? It is clearly evident that none of these descriptive features given by La Harpe of the Upper Nasoni village site is distinctive enough to make possible precise identification of its location.

Again, a survey of written records before and after La Harpe's time is rewarding. For example, two people mentioned a temple mound near the Upper Nasoni village, the Spaniard Terán de los Rios in 1691 and François Grappé who knew the area in the mid-18th century. Joutel earlier may have mentioned the structure even though Michel and Delisle in their excerpts from his journal did not. Or it may not have come to the soldier's attention, perhaps because the Indians preferred that the sacred place be unperceived by the French. Likewise, it was not pointed out to Freeman by his Indian companions in

[4]This is erroneously translated as "half a league" in Bénard de La Harpe's *The Historical Journal of the Establishment of the French in Louisiana,* translated by Joan Cain and Virginia Koenig, edited and annotated by Glenn R. Conrad, the USL History Series No. 3, 1971: 134, Lafayette, La.

1806. La Harpe did not comment on it but analysis of his journal reveals that almost all the information he presented was that which had pertinence for French trade relationships.

The temple mound was a prominent feature of the landscape as Terán came from the southwest into the region seeking the Upper Nasoni. It was described as "a hill which dominated the entire country" with a single structure on top "in which they [the Indians] made offerings to their gods" (Terán, 1691-1692, p. 10). The hill was climbed and from its height the Spaniards viewed on the south of the river the hamlet they sought. On the scaleless, diagrammatic, yet in some respects highly descriptive map (fig. 2) of this Upper Nasoni village made after the 1691-1692 journey, a few habitations appear to the immediate northeast of the temple mound as well as across the Red River. But the largest part of the village lies to the east and southeast of the mound.

François Grappé, of French-Indian descent, was born in a Caddo settlement on this stretch of Red River. His father, Alexis, had carried on trading activities there, possibly as early as 1737. The son continued to live in the region for "upwards of 30 years." In the early 1800s he told John Sibley, Indian agent at Natchitoches, of a hill in the vicinity of his birth where the Indians "pay a devout and sacred homage" (Sibley, 1805b: 729). It was a mile from a handsome lake that was about five miles in circumference, around which Caddo had lived "from time immemorial." If the temple mound in the case of both Terán and Grappé was Hatchell Mound, as seems probable, then the main Upper Nasoni hamlet illustrated on the Terán map south of Red River could coincide with the area of the Hatchell-Mitchell-Moores complex of archeological village and cemetery sites. Grappé's distance of a mile between the temple mound and village would also fit the general Moores-Mitchell site locality.

A study of later maps of this stretch of the

river is additionally instructive. The key map is one drawn by Nicholas King, entitled "Map of the Red River in Louisiana, Protracted from the Courses and Distances given in Mr. Thos. Freeman's Journal of a survey thereof made in June 1806." Evidently the northern section of the large original map, the part pertinent to this study, was not received by the National Archives when the other two sections were acquired. However, a reduced printed version of the entire map is available in that repository. This survey was made in connection with an exploring expedition sent up Red River by President Thomas Jefferson in 1806. Apparently the "journal" referred to in the map title is not the "Account" that exists in the Library of Congress, which seems to be a cumulative document drawn from the notes of several party members. It does not contain the requisite detailed data from which a map of Red River could be drawn. Without the primary surveying data of the original Freeman journal, the map itself becomes the only source for the 1806 channel course of the Red (fig. 4) as recorded by Freeman using a compass and probably the log-line and time method of determining distance.

Of course, there is a great difference between the course of the Red today and that in 1806. However, one can relate the 1806 pattern of the channel from Little River west to the area of today's Roseborough Lake to the pattern recorded on 1840 and 1842 Arkansas quadrangle maps which have the additional features of range, latitude, and longitude as they appear on modern maps (fig. 5). This is because the river course had changed very little between 1806 and 1838 in this region, especially in the stretch containing the archeological sites that were described above. When this comparison is made, there is no problem in identifying on King's map the meander that became Roseborough Lake in 1872, the long meander near which Hatchell Mound was located, and the meander that became Sutton Lake. The 1806 channel curve indicated today by Red Lake even shows the entry of Red Branch or Haney Creek.

In the textual "Account" of the Freeman expedition three "Caddo" village sites are noted above the Great Bend, all abandoned by 1806. Having passed the former site of a "Caddo" village on the north side of the Red, quite possibly that of the Kadohadacho as mentioned earlier, they came to another on the south side, presumably viewed before the Hatchell meander was navigated. There they saw a lake "round which," their Indian companions told them (Account [1806]: 84), "the Caddos had cornfields, when they occupied their principal village which was situate, in the prairie just above it. This lake is about two miles in length and parallel to the river." On the related King map the lake is shown to the southeast of the meander near which Hatchell Mound would then have been standing. The words "Principal Caddo village" extend from west of it to the southeast. The label is undoubtedly out of proportion, indicating too large an area, but it suggests that when the village was described as in the prairie "above" the lake, this meant not upstream but an upper terrace. The close proximity of the village and lake is reminiscent of that described by La Harpe in 1719 and of that related by Grappé to Sibley, cited above, when he noted the lake's nearness to the "Caddo" village occupied from "time immemorial" and, additionally, gave its distance from the temple mound as one mile. Latitude taken by Freeman, probably near the river, was 33°34'42" (Account [1806], p. 84), a reading acceptable for the Red River downstream from the Hatchell mound meander.

Apprehensive of a threatened confrontation with Spaniards, Freeman's party made a deposit of food, ammunition, instruments, and journals on the north side of the Red on high ground between the river and a lake which I suggest was the feature called The Old Sag. This correlation is based on King's pre-

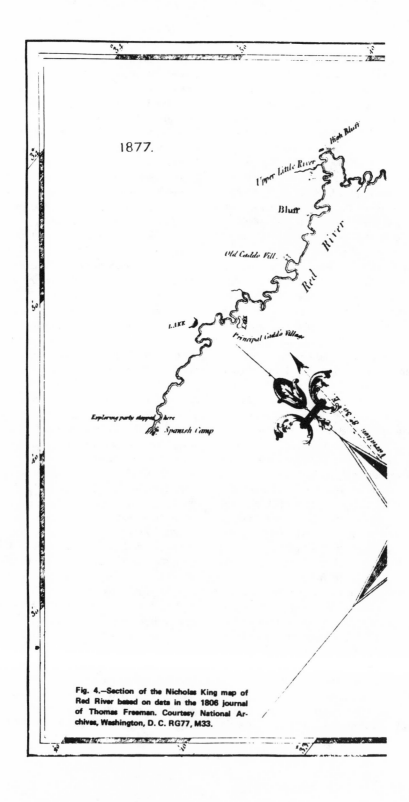

1877.

High Bluff

Upper Little River

Bluff

Old Caddo Vill.

Red River

LAKE

Principal Caddo Village

Exploring party stopped here

Spanish Camp

Fig. 4.—Section of the Nicholas King map of Red River based on data in the 1806 journal of Thomas Freeman. Courtesy National Archives, Washington, D. C. RG77, M33.

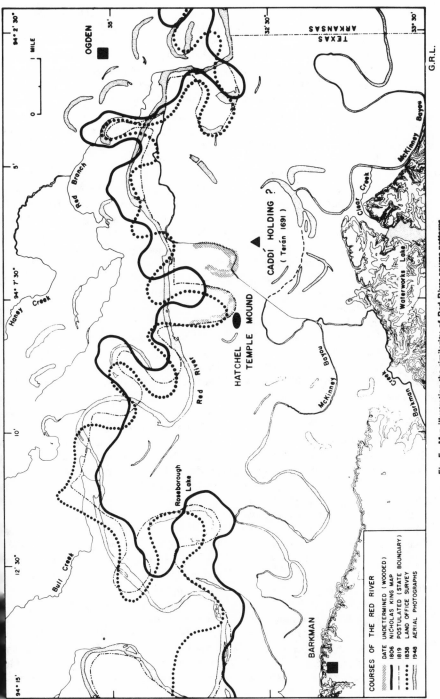

Fig. 5.—Map illustrating the similarity of Red River course patterns from 1806 to 1838 and their relation to the modern channel.

sumed representation of the lake, which in its lengthwise curving shape is the reverse of ox-box lakes in the locality that represent old meanders to the north of Red River. The Old Sag is today a marshy curving stretch, over a mile long, which relates to a Haney Creek tributary and thus curves south as shown on the 1950 USGS Odgen TX-AR quadrangle map.

On the opposite (south) side of the river, according to the Indians (Account [1806]: 85-86), "The French once had a small military post; and there also was one of the principal villages of the Caddos." This seems to refer to a third concentration of Caddo habitations. And if one looked across the Red River southward from a point well above the river bed, probably not far from the present course and south of The Old Sag, Roseborough Lake site would be seen.

It will be recalled that this site produced a large amount of French goods, the preponderance of which was characteristic of the middle and late 18th century. It is reasonable to believe this was the location of the French village that developed sometime in the mid-1700s, probably drawn there by the presence of Alexis Grappé's trading post and the garrison that protected it. This French occupation is reported by both Sibley and members of the Athanase de Mézières' 1770 expedition as being associated with a Caddo Indian settlement. In none of these statements is there mention of a large lake nearby. It may well be that François Grappé's specific birthplace at "Caddo Old Towns," as Sibley called it (Sibley, 1805a: 170), was here at the Roseborough site.

Therefore, in view of the preceding information, I suggest that the Upper Nasoni hamlet visited by Joutel in 1687, viewed by Tonti in 1690, visited by Terán in 1691-1692, and by La Harpe in 1719, was the abandoned locality described by Grappé-Sibley in 1805 and the first south bank "Caddo" site noted by Freeman in 1806. This village, east of the temple mound, was probably the main concentration of Upper Nasoni from 1687 to 1720, as well as in prehistoric times. The Roseborough Lake site probably does not have an equal time depth.

Where, then, might Bénard de La Harpe's post have been built? What has been called the Hatchell meander in this report must have been located in 1719 north of the southern extremity it reached by normal meander cutting before being blocked off at its neck in the 19th century. This occurred just before the waters reached to the temple mound. The map associated with Terán's journey (fig. 2) exhibits a more northern channel location in 1691 by depicting habitations between the mound and the river. The caddi's holding of that time was not among them, however, but was more to the southeast. If La Harpe's "musket shot" distance between his post site and the Red signified only half a mile or less, this when measured south from a river course then farther north might indicate a position on a low terrace which was later washed away by the advancing meander channel. If, on the other hand, a distance of one and one-half miles or so was intended, then a site on the higher secondary terrace would seem to be indicated where sandy soils are mixed with clays and loams. This latter position might accord with the general Mitchell Cemetery-Moores locality as did the village location considered in relation to the temple.

With diffidence I suggest that old Clear Lake, a former channel of the Red (fig. 3) was the lake described by La Harpe, Grappé and Freeman as adjacent to the village. This would mean it was already an oxbow lake in La Harpe's time, but one that had been cut off fairly recently since it was described a two leagues or 4-5 miles long. Grappé described it to Sibley (1805b:76) as oval and about five miles in circumference. In the interim of some 86 years, it would have been

14

filling with sediment and plant growth. On 19th century headright maps of Bowie County, Texas, a small lake (Carter's Lake) is drawn where a remnant of Clear Lake might be expected. Now the area is dry except for rain ponds at certain times and a diversion channel that runs from McKinney Bayou through the eastern portion of the old lake bed to the Red River. If this interpretation is accepted, then we have the temple, Upper Nasoni settlement, and lake in the same locality and in the relationships to each other that were described in the documentary literature. La Harpe's post would have been erected in this vicinity.

The small amount of European trade goods found in the Hatchell-Clear Lake locality has caused some who would relate them to the 1719 French intrusion to question the validity of the postulation that La Harpe's fort was located there. First, it should be pointed out that these French were here for only about six months altogether. Second, when the value of trade goods distributed by La Harpe to the Natchitoches, Wichita, Red River Caddo, Hasinai, and other visitors is totaled, the Upper Nasoni are found to have received less than one-sixteenth of that which he dispensed, including perishable items. We have no idea how much trade merchandise he brought to the area. In four, possibly five, boats he was carrying additionally at least 31 men and miscellaneous equipment. Moreover, we know that in June of 1720 (La Harpe *Journal, fol.* 29 *vo.* - 30) La Harpe was at Biloxi trying to get remuneration from Charles LeGac, director general of the Company of the Indies, for leftover merchandise he wanted to sell to the company, merchandise originally taken to his Red River post but then brought down, along with his armament evidently, and other equipment, to Natchitoches for deposit. The Company of the Indies had replaced the Company of the West during La Harpe's absence upriver. La Harpe's project had been financed almost entirely

by him, costing 10,000 *livres,* according to his claim. He was trying to salvage as much as he could when he closed his concession operation. The military detachment also seems to have returned downstream at that time (La Harpe *Journal, fols.* 25-*vo.*). Little evidence of La Harpe's presence at the Upper Nasoni village is likely to be found.

Now what about the Roseborough Lake site? Was it another Upper Nasoni hamlet or was it the new location of the *Nadsoo* or Nanatsoho village established between 1690 and 1719? At present I incline toward the latter interpretation. This would accord with the comma in the *Journal* which placed this group near the Upper Nasoni rather than the Upper Natchitoches. Adjoining the Indian village would have been the French one with its mill, Grappé's trading post, and the garrison very probably established by Louis Juchereau de St. Denys after he became resident commander at Natchitoches in 1722. The "old French fort" in the Roseborough Lake locality mentioned in documents of the 1770 Mézières and 1806 Freeman expeditions probably referred to this military post that may have existed continuously from the 1720s to 1763 when the territory became Spanish. The term does not necessarily have to refer to La Harpe's post, and I do not believe it did.

Having suggested the location of the main prehistoric and historic Upper Nasoni settlement, consideration may be given to where the Kadohadacho site was in 1719. It will be recalled that it was two leagues (about five and one-half to six miles) from the Upper Nasoni crossing of the Red, where pirogues were kept, which in turn was about four miles, probably east or northeast from the village (Delisle, n.d.: 139). The route overland north of the Red was generally to the ENE and NE. The distances and directions guide us into the region of Temple, Arkansas, which was named for a family and not the presence of a temple mound. If this site was the same "round prairie" of Grappé and Freeman, then it is marked on the King map (fig. 4), presumably as Freeman located it in his survey notes. Comparing river course patterns on that 1806 map and an 1840 Arkansas public land survey quadrangle sheet, we find the 1806 site marked to the northeast of an old river meander that by 1838, when it was surveyed, had become an oxbow lake called Muddy Lake. A remnant of it is still so named on the modern Homan NSGS quadrangle map. This area conforms also to the eight-mile overland distance to Little River recorded by Freeman (Account [1806], p. 79). As Dr. Frank Schambach of the Arkansas Archeological Survey points out (personal communication), this is another region where only the obvious archeological features are known. There has not been a thorough planned survey. This site, if it has not been destroyed by construction or farming activities, has yet to be found.

The Upper Natchitoches north bank settlement upstream three leagues or 8-9 miles from the Upper Nasoni, probably an overland distance, is also unknown. It is possible that cultural remains may still exist in the region. The search is complicated by the paucity of fact regarding the location, our ignorance of the exact 1719 river course, and Corps of Engineers construction work of some time back in the area.

Finally, there remains the problem of the old *Nadsoo* site, ten leagues or about 25-30 miles upriver by water in 1719 from the Up-per Nasoni village. It was described by La Harpe as in a fine situation with a bluff jutting into the river that would have been suitable for establishment of a fort (*Journal, fol.* 13). On lower terraces was fertile land for growing crops. He also observed prairie nearby, springs, and fruit trees, probably plum. The pre-1700 occupation would not be expected to contain European trade materials beyond possibly a few items of Spanish origin. Might this correspond to the pre-contact complex at the Bowman site (3LR46)? This site in Little River County, Arkansas is no longer on the river but lies about one and one-half miles to its north, bounded on the east and south by an old river channel, Choctaw Bayou.

In conclusion, as a result of this ethnohistoric study, it should be possible for archeologists to identify the historic Upper Nasoni cultural complex. Comparison of archeological materials found south of old Clear Lake with those of the Roseborough Lake site may enable researchers to suggest more confidently than is now possible whether this was a Nanatsoho or another Upper Nasoni hamlet. Furthermore, careful searching may yet reveal both the Kadohadacho and Upper Natchitoches sites so that their cultural complexes can be identified with some assurance. Then the move back into prehistory could begin. This development would probably be of more importance than determination of the exact site of La Harpe's post.

ACKNOWLEDGMENTS

I am deeply grateful for the help received from Waldo R. Wedel, Archeologist Emeritus, Smithsonian Institution, and Larry Banks of the Southwest Division of the Corps of Engineers, in the preparation of this manuscript. Appreciation is also extended to G. Robert Lewis, Department of Anthropology, Smithsonian Institution, and Hal M. Story, Texas Memorial Museum, for the maps they drew (as initialed) to accompany this study, an important complement to the text. The published form has benefited materially from the thoughtful editing of Dr. William W. Newcomb.

17

REFERENCES CITED

Account of the Red River in Louisiana, drawn up from the
[1806] returns of Messrs. Freeman and Custis to the War
Office of the U. S. who explored the same, in the
year 1806. Peter Force collection, Ser. 8D, no.
53, Manuscript Div., Library of Congress.

Bénard de La Harpe, Jean-Baptiste
1718-   Journal Du Voyage De la Louissianne fait Par Le
1720   Sr Bernard *[sic]* De La harpe Et Des DeCouvertes
Quil a fait Dans la Party De l'ouest De Cette
Colonie, *(copie)*. Bibliothèque Nationale, MSS.
Français, 8989: *fols.* 1-36.

Bénard de La Harpe, Jean-Baptiste
[1720s] Journal Historique Concernant l'Etablissement
des François à la Loüisianne tiré des Memoires
de M$^{rs.}$ d'Iberville & de Bienville. Commandants
pour le Roi audit Pays et sur les descouvertes et
recherches de M. Bernard *[sic]* de la Harpe, nommé
au Commandement de la Baye de St. Bernard.
Dedié et presenté au Roi. Par . . . le chevalier de
Beaurain, ... 1766. MS. Div., Library of Congress, 215-2654. (See M. Wedel, 1974: 63-67.)

Bénard de La Harpe, Jean-Baptiste
1831   Journal Historique de l'Etablissement des Français à la Louisiane. A. -L. Boimare, ed. New
Orleans and Paris: Hector Bossange.

Bolton, Herbert E.
1914   *Athanase de Mézières and the Louisiana-Texas
Frontier 1768-1780.* 2 vols. Cleveland: Arthur H.
Clark Co.

Delisle, Claude
post-   Extr. du voiage de m. de la salle dans l'amérique
1688   Sept^{le} en l'annee 1684 pour y fe [faire] établissement dans la partie qu'il en avoit auparavent découverte. Henri de Joutel. Archives Marines, Archives du Service Hydrographique, v. 115^9: 11-13.

Delisle, Guillaume
1700   L'Amérique//Septentrionale (map).

Dictionnaire Quillet de la Langue Française.
1956   Paris.

Hatcher, Mattie Austin, transl.
[c. 1932] The Expedition of Don Domingo Terán de los
Rios into Texas (1691-1692). Preliminary Studies
of the Texas Catholic Historical Society, 2/1
(Jan.): 3-48.

Hodge, Frederick W., ed.
1907-   *Handbook of American Indians North of Mexico.*
1910   Smithsonian Institution, Bureau of American
Ethnology, Bull. 30. 2 vols.

Jones, Stacy V.
1963   *Weights and Measures: An Informal Guide.*
Public Affairs Press, Washington, D. C.

Joutel, Henri
1684-   Relation du Voyage de M. de la Salle dans le nord
1687   de l'Amérique Septen^{ale} en 1684 pour y faire un
Etablissement dans la partie qu'il en avoit aupara-
vant découverte. Ms. in La Galissonnière coll. Imperfect copy. Archives Marines, Archives du Service Hydrographique, 67-1.

La Curne de Sainte-Palaye
1880   *Dictionnaire Historique de l'Ancien Langage
François ou Glossaire de la Langue Françoise
depuis son origine jusqu'au siècle de Louis XIV.*
Paris: H. Champion.

Lewis, Anna
1924   "La Harpe's First Expedition in Oklahoma, 1718-
19." Chronicles of Oklahoma, 2:331-49.

Littré, É.
1869   *Dictionnaire de la Langue Française.* Paris: Li-
brairie de L. Hachette et Cie.

Margry, Pierre
1876-   *Découvertes et Établissements des Français dans
1886   l'ouest et dans le sud de L'Amérique Septentrionale (1614-1754). Memoires et documents
originaux . . . Paris: Jouest et Sigaux. 6 vols.*

Michel, M. de
1713   *Journal Historique du Dernier Voyage que seu
M. de la Sale fit dans le Golfe de Mexique, pour
trouver l'embouchure, et le cours de la Riviere de
Missicipi, nomée à present la Riviere de Saint
Loüis, qui traverse la Louisiane.* Paris: Chez
Estienne Robinot.

Miroir, M. P., R. King Harris, et al.
1973   Bénard de La Harpe and the Nassonite Post.
Bulletin of the Texas Archeological Society,
44:113-67.

Richelet, Pierre
1728   *Dictionnaire de La Langue Françoise, Ancienne
et Moderne.* Paris: Chez Jacques Estienne.

Rolle des Concessionaires et passagers quy passent sur le
[1718]   vaisseau le victoire commandé par M. Derosset
apartenant à messieurs de la comp^ie doccident
Destiné pour la louisianne. Archives Nationales,
Colonies, F5, B37. May 25.

Sibley, John
1805a   Letter to William Dunbar, d. April 2, Natchitoches,
in Mrs. Dunbar Rowland, Life, Letters and Papers
of William Dunbar of Elgin, Morayshire, Scotland,
and Natchez, Mississippi. Jackson: Mississippi
Historical Society Press, 1930.

Sibley, John
1805b   Letter to Gen. Henry Dearborn, d. April 5, Natchitoches, *in* American State Papers: Indian Affairs,
1 (1832): /25-30.

Smith, Ralph A.
1958-   Account of the Journey of Bénard de la Harpe:
1959   Discovery Made by Him of Several Nations Situated in the West. Southwestern Historical Quarterly, 62/1-4.

Société de Gens de Lettres
1771   *Le Grand Vocabulaire François*. Paris: Hôtel de
Thou.

Strong, William Duncan
1935   An Introduction to Nebraska Archeology. Smithsonian Miscellaneous Collections, v. 93/10.

Swanton, John R.
1942   Source Material on the History and Ethnology of
the Caddo Indians. Smithsonian Institution, Bureau of American Ethnology, Bull. 132.

Terán, de los Rios, Domingo
1691-   Descripción y Diario . . . Transcript in Bancroft
1692   Library of MS. in Archivo General y Publico de
Mexico, Historia, vol. 27.

Tonti, Henri de
[1678-   [Mémoire presented to Count de Pontchartrain,
1687]   Minister of Colonies 1693]. Bibliothèque Nationale, MSS. Français, n. a., 7485: 103-18, *copie*.
See also L. P. Kellogg, ed., Early Narratives of the
Northwest, 1634-1699: 286-322.

Tonti, Henri de
1700   Letter to his brother, d. March 4, Ft. Mississippi,
in Mid-America, v. 10 n. s., n. 3 (July 1939):
220-35. Copy.

Wedel, Mildred Mott
1971   J.-B Bénard de la Harpe: Visitor to the Wichitas
in 1719. Great Plains Journal, 10/2:37-70.

Wedel, Mildred Mott
1974   The Bénard de La Harpe Historiography on French
Colonial Louisiana. Louisiana Studies, 13/1.

Wedel, Mildred Mott
1976   Ethnohistory: Its Payoffs and Pitfalls for Iowa
Archeologists. Journal of the Iowa Archeological
Society, 23: 1-44.

Wedel, Waldo R.
1938   The Direct-Historical Approach in Pawnee Archeology. Smithsonian Miscellaneous Collections,
97/7.

Williams, Stephen
1964   The Aboriginal Location of the Kadohadacho
and Related Tribes *in* Explorations in Cultural
Anthropology, ed. by Ward H. Goodenough,
pp. 545-570.

THE ABORIGINAL LOCATION
OF THE KADOHADACHO
AND RELATED TRIBES

Stephen Williams

INTRODUCTION[1]

The purpose of this paper is to present the available data on the original location of the Kadohadacho and related tribes of the Red River region and to trace their movements during the period of recorded history. A brief archaeological section attempts to connect the prehistory with the findings of the historic period.

With regard to terminology, the use of either "Caddo tribe" or "Caddo nation" is too confusing to be useful in this presentation of data bearing on the aboriginal occupants of Louisiana and Arkansas. In its place, I have adopted the system used by Swanton (1942, 1952) in his Bureau of American Ethnology publications. I shall refer specifically to the three major confederacies in this general area: Hasinai, Kadohadacho, and Natchitoches. I must confess some misgivings about the political implications in the term "confederacy," and the true nature of these groups along the Red River needs the kind of scrutiny recently given the Cherokee state and the Iroquois Confederacy (Fenton and Gulick, 1961), although data are few. Undoubtedly the Natchitoches Confederacy is the weakest grouping, since it is most obviously a late gathering together of fairly disparate tribes. Swanton himself came to a wide use of the term "confederacy" with reference to these groups only in his last publication (1952). He used it sparingly in his major work on the Caddo (Swanton, 1942). Further, to use the term "Caddo Indians" without any qualification is merely to refer to Indians of the Caddoan linguistic stock who formerly resided in this general area. This type of reference is likewise too imprecise and will be avoided wherever possible.

The Kadohadacho Confederacy was originally made up of five tribes: Kadohadacho, Petit Caddo, Upper Natchitoches, Upper Nasoni, and Nanatsoho (Swanton, 1942, pp. 12–13, 1952, pp. 317–320). The Upper

Yatasi and the Cahinnio joined the confederacy later, in the period before 1800. The Hasinai Confederacy was made up of at least ten tribes including the Hainai, Nacogdoche, Anadarko, and Lower Nasoni (Swanton, 1952, pp. 315–317). The Natchitoches Confederacy was made up of the Doustioni, Ouachita, and Natchitoches. The Lower Yatasi joined them at a later date (Swanton, 1952, pp. 205–207).

The Hasinai have been the subject of a recent and thorough study by William J. Griffith, who gives some credence to the existence of an operational, if loose, organization of tribes which might be termed a confederacy (Griffith, 1954, pp. 63–67). Since their aboriginal location and history is easily distinguished for most of the period under discussion, I shall not deal with the Hasinai in detail. The Adai, the Eyeish, and the Kichai, three other distantly related Caddoan groups living in the general area, will be mentioned only in passing.

The Kadohadacho have been treated adequately by Swanton with regard to social and material culture, although data presented on political organization (Swanton, 1942, pp. 170–174) unfortunately pertain almost exclusively to the Hasinai. The source material on aboriginal location is not as systematically analyzed and presented (Swanton, 1942, pp. 29–121), especially with regard to the crucial 1780–1803 period, and will, therefore, be the main subject of this paper.

THE SPANISH–FRENCH PERIOD (1542–1800)

Shortly after the death of their leader, De Soto, Luís de Moscoso led the Spanish survivors of this first expedition into the southern United States westward and came among the Caddoan tribes on the Red River about the middle of July, 1542. Near the Red River, the only tribal name readily identifiable from the expedition account is Nasoni [Nissohone], but it seems quite certain that they passed into the territory of the Hasinai Confederacy to the west, only to return later in desperation via the same route on their way to the Mississippi.

Not until some one hundred and forty years later did explorers again venture into this part of the Red River region. This time, in 1687, it was a French expedition under the leadership of La Salle. He had penetrated from the southwest to the Hasinai territory the previous year and was determined on this occasion to reach the Mississippi. However, ill fortune befell him on the outskirts of the Hasinai territory, for he and his nephew were murdered by members of his own party. Seven survivors, including Joutel, made for the Mississippi River from the main Hasinai village. Traveling northeast they arrived at the towns of the Kadohadacho at the Great Bend of the Red River. The first village they visited was the Upper Nasoni on the south side of the river; they crossed the river and after some travel arrived at the Kadohadacho (1) village. There they met two Cahinnio Caddo who accompanied them east to their own village near the Ouachita River in Arkansas.

After hearing of the murders, Henri de Tonti, one of La Salle's lieutenants, set out to find the surviving Frenchmen, some of whom were his former companions. He reached Natchitoches on February 17, 1690, and going further north, he encountered the Yatasi [Yataches] on March 16. He finally arrived at the village of Kadohadacho on March 28. Here he learned of two other villages united in the same confederacy: the Upper Natchitoches and the Upper Nasoni. He went west in vain to the Hasinai village of Nacogdoche [Nacendichi], for he found the remaining Frenchmen from the La Salle expedition had been murdered by the Indians. He returned east via the Kadohadacho village.

Hoping to offset the advantage of the early French arrival in the Red River region, the Spanish began to set up missions among the Hasinai in 1690. In the following year, Domingo Terán de los Rios was sent to look over the surrounding country and arrived among the Kadohadacho on November 29, 1691. Despite snow and sleet, a week was spent exploring around the towns; a map of one settlement survives (Swanton, 1942, plate 1). For lack of supplies the proposed missions could not be founded, and Terán returned to the Hasinai country.

French interest in the region continued, and in 1700, Le Moyne d'Iberville, founder of the Louisiana colony at the mouth of the Mississippi, sent his brother Bienville to look over the Red River region. Bienville was accompanied by Louis Juchereau de St. Denis, a young Canadian who was to become famous for his exploits in this region. They reached the Red River at the village of Doustioni, near that of the Lower Natchitoches. They ascended the river until they reached the settlement of the Yatasi, where they inquired about the Kadohadacho, whose village lay to the north. Being told the length of time required to reach them, Bienville's party turned back. Almost immediately, however, St. Denis was ordered back to keep a check on the Spanish, and he returned to the Lower Natchitoches country. There he obtained a guide who took him into the Kadohadacho Confederacy at the Great Bend of the Red River.

The Lower Natchitoches had left their old village in 1702 because of crop failure. After considerable movement, including settlement among the Acolapissa, they returned north with St. Denis, and a new French post was set up at the old village site in the fall of 1714. From here, St. Denis made several trips to visit Spanish outposts among the Hasinai in the period from 1705 to 1719.

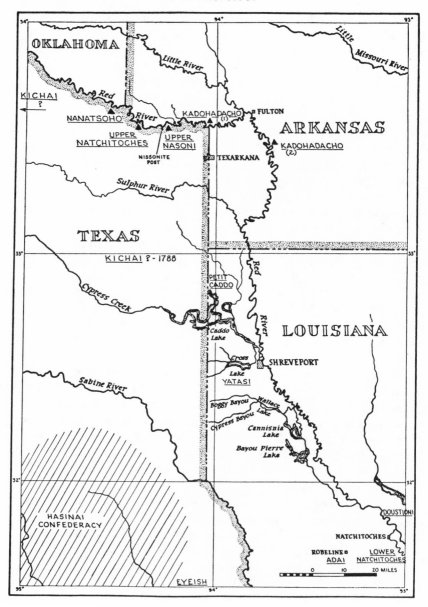

FIGURE 1.   Tribal locations. 1542–1790.

The next major French expedition into the country of the Kado-hadacho left New Orleans on December 17, 1718, with Bernard de La Harpe at its head. He arrived in Natchitoches, now an established post, in January, 1719. At the post he found both Natchitoches and Doustioni Indians, as well as some Lower Yatasi who had come there in 1717 after trouble with marauding Chickasaws. He and his men then began the ascent of the Red River, passing through the nearby Adai territory and finally arriving at the Sulphur River on April 1. He traveled up this river for some distance and then overland to the Upper Nasoni village, instead of making the longer trip via the Red River. There he met with the chiefs of the Kadohadacho, Nanatsoho, and Upper Natchitoches towns. A few days later he ascended the river to an abandoned village of the Nanatsoho.

Back in the Upper Nasoni village, he learned that the Upper Yatasi were living there. This second section of the Yatasi had left its homeland to the south for the same reason as the Lower Yatasi, and La Harpe hoped to restore the Yatasi to their former lands.

On April 25, 1719, his supplies having arrived by boat, he began establishing a French post close to the Upper Nasoni village. Often called the Nissonite post, this fort (Figure 1) was really no more than a house surrounded by a stockade, but it served as an effective barrier to Spanish advances down the Red River from 1719 to 1762. A regular trading route was set up from the Natchitoches post to this frontier post via depots at the Yatasi and Petit Caddo villages.

On July 1, 1720, St. Denis was appointed commandant of the Natchitoches post. He remained a powerful figure on the French-Spanish frontier until his death in 1744. During his administration French trade with the Indians throughout the Red River region flourished, and the Spanish found these alien traders even among their own Hasinai Indians (Griffith, 1954, pp. 139–142).

Cession of the area to Spain, begun in 1762, was not finally completed until 1769. The French population continued to occupy the territory, and all in all the shift made little difference to the aboriginal occupants, as one administration was much like the other.

In 1769, Athanase de Mézières, a former French military official, was appointed lieutenant governor of the Natchitoches District which included the Kadohadacho region. From his headquarters in Natchitoches, De Mézières became an important figure on the Louisiana-Texas frontier, rivaling St. Denis, whose daughter he married. He immediately began to ensure good trade relations with the Indians, and reports (Bolton, 1914, vol. 1, pp. 80–85) that he had the following traders among the Indians:

Morière with the Yatasi; Du Pain with the Petit Caddo; and Grappe at the Kadohadacho village, where he was living in the old French fort.

On April 21, 1770, De Mézières met in council with the chiefs of the Kadohadacho and Yatasi (Bolton, 1914, vol. 1, pp. 89, 157–158). They made an agreement with him to cede him their lands and also promised not to aid warring Indians, such as the Wichita and Comanche. In return the Spanish promised to give them yearly presents.

In the fall of the same year, De Mézières (Bolton, 1914, vol. 1, pp. 92–93, 206–215) undertook to bring peace to the warring tribes to the north and made an expedition from Natchitoches to the principal town of the Kadohadacho. On the way he passed through the villages of the Yatasi and Petit Caddo. The main Kadohadacho town was called San Luiz de Cadodachos by the Spanish (probably the one formerly called the Nasoni village, Figure 1), and here De Mézières received some promises from the Indians to keep the peace.

About 1777 the Osage to the north began to make continual war on the exposed position of the Kadohadacho on the upper Red River. In the same year an epidemic swept through eastern Texas and western Louisiana (Griffith, 1954, p. 152). Besides killing hundreds of Indians, the epidemic also killed many Europeans, and De Mézières at Natchitoches lost his wife and two children in a single week. These pressures on the Kadohadacho took their toll, and in 1779 there was talk among them of leaving their great northern village (Bolton, 1914, vol. 1, p. 84; vol. 2, p. 250).

De Mézières traveled widely over the Southwest and was a strong arm for Spanish control of the Indians in this whole region. He died November 2, 1779, and our sources are the worse for it. However, by later accounts, we know that the period which followed his death was of grave significance for the Kadohadacho.

According to Kinnaird (1946, p. xxxi), "The depredations of the Great Osage and the Little Osage tribes gave Spain her most serious Indian problem west of the Mississippi." The problem was frequently mentioned in the correspondence of the commandant of Natchitoches, Louis de Blanc, to the Spanish governor in New Orleans, Esteban Miró. Despite attempts at peace treaties, no effective means of stopping the Osage were found. In 1787 the Spanish officials at Natchitoches asked for presents (including guns to be used against the Osage) for the three Indian nations under their jurisdiction: the Kadohadacho, the Petit Caddo, and the Kichai. "The Yatasi and the Natchitoch are excluded, and do not deserve to be included among the recipients of presents" (Kinnaird, 1946, p. 198). This exclusion of the Yatasi and the Lower Natchitoches must have been based on solely political grounds, since both groups were still extant as separate entities in the following American period.

The Kichai, a relatively small group of Caddoan speakers whose homeland was west of the Kadohadacho and north of the Hasinai, were forced by Osage raids to move near the Petit Caddo in 1788 (Kinnaird, 1946, p. 259). Sometime during that same year the Kadohadacho were also required to change the location of their village, since with numbers reduced by epidemics, they could no longer hold out against the onslaught of the Osage. In February, 1790, they took refuge in the Petit Caddo village (Kinnaird, 1946, p. 316).

The main conclusions of this survey of the period from 1542 to 1780 are shown in Figure 1.

The best evidence for these locations may be summarized as follows:

Kadohadacho:
> Joutel, 1687; Tonti, 1690; Terán, 1691; St. Denis, 1700; La Harpe, 1719; De Mézières, 1770.

Lower Natchitoches:
> Tonti, 1690; Bienville, 1700; St. Denis, 1700; La Harpe, 1719; De Mézières, 1769.

Yatasi:
> Tonti, 1690; Bienville, 1700; St. Denis, 1700; La Harpe, 1719; De Mézières, 1770.

Upper Natchitoches:
> Tonti, 1690; La Harpe, 1719.

Nanatsoho:
> Tonti, 1690; La Harpe, 1719.

Upper Nasoni:
> Moscoso, 1542 (?); Joutel, 1687; Tonti, 1690; La Harpe, 1719.

Petit Caddo:
> De Mézières, 1770.

Adai:
> Bienville, 1700; St. Denis, 1731; De Mézières, 1778.

Three small groups appear and then disappear during this period. The Cahinnio Caddo, whose homeland was on the middle reaches of the Ouachita River in central Arkansas (Figure 3), moved northwest toward the Arkansas River in Oklahoma, and in 1771, one of their chiefs attended a peace parley at Natchitoches in the company of other northern tribes, including the Kichai and Tawakoni. I have been unable to trace the Cahinnio after this date. Swanton (1942, p. 7) suggests that they ultimately joined the Kadohadacho; a suggestion which accords with the data on the pressure applied to small groups in this general locality by the Osage. The Doustioni (Figure 1) occur as a separate entity only during the early part of the eighteenth century. Evidently they then amalgamated with their close neighbors, the Lower Natchitoches. Part of the Ouachita Caddo came west from their homeland on the lower Ouachita (Figure 3) in 1690 to join likewise with the Lower Natchitoches, and Swanton (1942, p. 12) suggests that the rest probably followed suit later in this period. Archaeology reflects both the occupancy of the lower Ouachita during historic times and the occurrence of trade from Natchez to Natchitoches via this region.

I have depended heavily on Swanton's coverage (1942, pp. 31–67) of the early Spanish and French exploration up to the period of 1770. His conclusions and identification compare well with those of Bolton (1914, vol. 1, pp. 43–45; 1916, map). The precise location of villages for this period has not been attempted as the data are much too generalized. Even the exact position of many of the American-period villages is still an unsolved problem as will be discussed later. The only solution would seem to lie in careful topographic surveys. The location of the Hasinai Confederacy follows Bolton (1908, p. 256; 1912, map), Swanton (1942, fig. 1), and Griffith (1954, maps at end).

The data reviewed suggest a gradual abandonment of the five original villages which made up the Kadohadacho Confederacy prior to the well-documented shift to the south from 1788 to 1790. The Nanatsoho village (Figure 1) appears to have been abandoned by the time of La Harpe's visit in 1719; and in the latter part of the century, reference is usually made to *the* principal Kadohadacho village, the San Luiz de Cadodachos of the Spanish and the Upper Nasoni village (the Nissonite post) of the French, suggesting but a single major town remaining. However, indications on the Nicholas King map of 1806 (Swanton, 1942, plate 2) show three recently deserted villages in this region. This map and the accompanying journal will be discussed more fully in their proper chronological position in the next section.

THE AMERICAN PERIOD (1803–1835)

Transfer of the Louisiana Territory from France to the United States in 1803 brought the remaining members of the Kadohadacho Confederacy under new sovereignty. As we have seen, a shift in the location of these tribes had apparently occurred in the latter part of the eighteenth century. Further supporting evidence will be presented below.

At President Jefferson's direction much new information was gathered concerning the land and Indian inhabitants of the vast Louisiana Purchase. It included a report by Dr. John Sibley, dated April 5, 1805, at Natchitoches. Aided by information derived from Mr. François Grappe, a long-time resident among the Indians, Sibley (1832) presented a historical sketch of the Indian tribes in Louisiana in this document. According to him, the Kadohadacho lived on Sodo Bayou [now called Caddo Lake] about 35 miles west of the main branch of the Red River. They had only lived there since 1800. They had formerly lived far to the north on the south bank of the Red River at a beautiful prairie with a lake in the middle "which had been the residence of their ancestors from time immemorial." Sibley (1832, p. 721) said that the French had a fort [the Nissonite post] there for many years, and that the Indians had left the village about 1791, a date which agrees very well with the Spanish information just presented.

Sibley (1832, pp. 721–722) indicated that the Yatasi lived on Stony Creek about halfway between the Kadohadacho and Natchitoches, and that the Spanish exercised control over the area where the Yatasi lived at that time. They had been reduced in number until only about fifty remained in 1805. The Adai lived below the Yatasi on Lake Macdon about twenty miles above the old Spanish post named for them. The Natchitoches lived in 1805 at a village about 25 miles above the town named for them. Only thirty-one of them remained as an independent unit. Alabamas, immigrants from the east, were split into two sections with one group living near the Kadohadacho (Figure 2), where they were accepted with friendship. Koasati were also migrants from the east. In 1805, Dr. Sibley was appointed Indian Agent for the Red River Agency. He operated out of Natchitoches, as the Spanish had done before him.

As interest in the Red River region increased, it became apparent that more precise information on this frontier would be required, particularly to locate the Spanish boundaries, which were not yet settled. Accordingly, an expedition was sent up the Red River in 1806, with Thomas Freeman (a surveyor) and Dr. Peter Custis (a naturalist) as its leaders. They proceeded up the river from the Mississippi with a small military force of seventeen men and two officers, stopping at Natchitoches. On June 26, the party arrived at the Koasati [Coashutta] village (Figure 2), which was on the main channel of the Red River. There were only six or eight families there.

While they were at this village, the Kadohadacho chief arrived with forty warriors. From them the explorers learned that their village was now located on a small creek flowing into a lake about 50 miles from the Koasati village and that they had lived there eleven years (1795). The chief said they had formerly lived far up the river on a large prairie but were driven from there by the Osage.

The expedition started up the river again on the 11th of July with

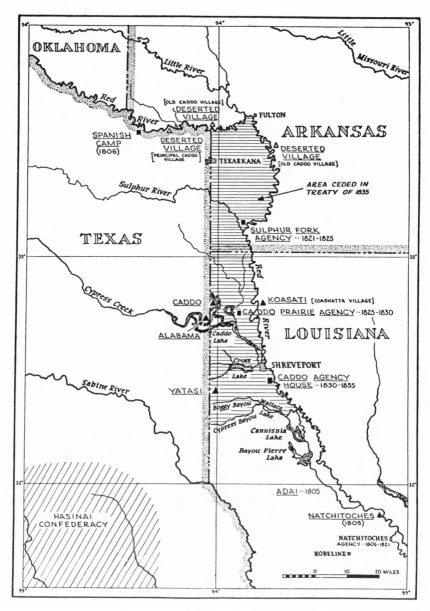

FIGURE 2. Tribal locations. 1803–1835.

three Kadohadacho guides. On the 19th, 125 miles above the Koasati village, they passed a prairie which was the site of an old Kadohadacho village (Figure 2), deserted following a massacre of most of its inhabitants by the Osage. The Indians with the party visited the old site of what was said to have been the largest of their old villages [evidently Kadohadacho (2) in Figure 1]; vestiges of the old houses were still visible.

On the 25th of July, about 20 miles above the mouth of the Little River they came to a prairie on the north side of the river. Here also were the remains of a considerable Kadohadacho village (Figure 2), with some of the posts of the huts still in evidence. This was Kadohadacho (1) in Figure 1.

News of a Spanish force waiting to meet them further up the river was brought by Indian messengers, and they prepared for any eventuality. On the evening of the 26th, the party arrived at a lake south of the river. This site (Figure 2) was the former location of the principal Caddo village (Upper Nasoni), and they were told that the French once had a small military post there (the Nissonite post).

After a little further reconnaissance, the position of the Spanish camp was established (Figure 2). Following a brief parley, the American expedition, being a much smaller force, began descending the river on July 30 (Freeman and Custis, 1806). The location shown for the Spanish camp is close to that of the Upper Natchitoches town and would have been a logical camp site.

The results of this expedition were quite significant. Besides the expedition journal cited above, we have the excellent map drawn up from observations made by the party. Made by Nicholas King, this map presents by far the most accurate picture of the Red River that was available for many years. It shows the three deserted Kadohadacho villages (Figure 2) and has served as a valuable aid in determining tribal locations prior to 1790 (Figure 1).

William Darby, a trained mathematician, began a mapping survey of the state of Louisiana in 1811. He traveled extensively in the state in his efforts to make a good map, and in 1816, he published what was considered at the time to be the best map of the state along with a book (Darby, 1816b, 1816a) entitled *Geographical Description of the State of Louisiana*. He located the Caddo, the Yatasi, and the Koasati villages on his map. The Yatasi region should be quite accurately drawn since he actually visited it.

In 1815 Thomas Gales became Indian agent on the Red River for a single year. Little is known of his administration. He was a former military man and administered from Natchitoches (Glover, 1935, p. 907). The next year, 1816, John Jamison took over the agency in Natchitoches.

He had correspondence with the United States factor (trader), John Fowler, who was an army man stationed at Sulphur Fork. Both Fowler and Jamison mention the influx of new Indians including Cherokee, Delaware, Koasati, and Choctaw into the region. Near the end of his administration he suggested moving the agency to Kiamicha, in present day Oklahoma, far above the Great Bend of the Red River.

Jamison died in the fall of 1819, and on December 1 of that year, Capt. George Gray was appointed Indian agent for the Red River region. The agency had not been moved, although such a move had been authorized, and Gray was told to survey the area and select a good spot. He chose the Sulphur Fork post, where a small military command was stationed. This move was completed in 1821 (Figure 2). Gray found that he also had to deal with the Quapaw and Shawnee, who were moving into or through the region.

In December, 1824, because of trouble with whisky among the Kado-hadacho and Koasati, Gray suggested that the agency be moved south in order to give him better control over the situation (Carter, 1953, vol. 19, pp. 739–740). This move was approved, and by December, 1825, he was established at Caddo Prairie (Figure 2). This was not a good location because the Red River Raft, a mass of trees and debris which clogged the main channel of the river, caused yearly floods which inundated the agency lands.

The amount of surviving correspondence for about a twenty-year period from a single small agency staggers the novice ethnohistorian. Carter (1953, 1954) has published some of it in the Territorial Papers cited above, but quite a bit remains unpublished.[2] Of particular ethnographic interest is the following letter by George Gray from the National Archives:

George Gray, Indian Agent, to James Barbour, Secretary of War

Caddow Prairie   Red River
Ind. Agency.   4th Dec. 1825

Sir.

In consequence of the Murder of a Caddow yesterday, I am induced to write you for instructions how to proceed against the Murderers. Two nights since Three Caddows of bad fame crossed the Lake and came to an encampment of about Ten families of Caddows, within one and a half miles of my House and there shot a Caddow Man without any provocation, and immediately returned over the Lake, and I am informed the only reason they give for this improper murder, is that this Caddow they have murdered, is what they term a Wizard and that they believed, He had the power of puting any of the Indians to death he thought proper by Blowing on them and this is a general idea, those people have amongst them and that He had the same power of restoring life. This Murder has been in consequence of many deaths amongst the Caddows, this last Fall and Summer and the Murdered Man has been generally accused with the cause of their Death. The Caddow Chief is now on a Hunting excursion and will not return for Three Months, and it is my opinion that the Murderers will not be given up by the Caddow Chief. The murder of this man will be a popular thing amongst the Caddows, or at least amongst, a greater propotion [sic] of them. It is impossible I can do anything with the Murderers, without assistance, or would it be best to let the Caddow Chief settle, the business in his own way—

I shall await your answer. —

I have the honr. to be
Respectfully.
your ms. Obe. Hum. Servant

/s/ G. Gray, Ind. Agent

Some months later (April 6, 1826), Gray wrote the Secretary of War that he had reconciled the Caddo and got them to "bury the hatchett" (Carter, 1954, pp. 225–227). This description of a Kadohadacho shaman's malevolent power and his fate accords well with magical powers of blowing recounted in recent Caddo studies (Parsons, 1941, p. 32) and with the reported killing of a practitioner who acquired the reputation of being evil among the Hasinai (Griffith, 1954, p. 90).

Gray had considerable trouble with other Indian groups who were being pushed into the region by pressure from the east. Among these were Quapaws, Choctaws, Alabamas, and Koasati (Carter, 1954, pp. 479–483). He held his position for nine years and died on the job, a courageous but dispirited man, on November 2, 1828. With Gray's death, Thomas Griffith came into the job for a short period (1828–1830), only to die in office. He retained the agency at Caddo Prairie (Glover, 1935, p. 908).

Following the successive deaths of Gray and Griffith, Jehiel Brooks was appointed as Indian agent in 1830. Finding the buildings in disrepair and the Caddo Prairie location untenable, Brooks suggested a move to higher ground. He selected a spot south of Cross Lake on the bluffs overlooking the Red River valley. It was there that the agency house remained until after the treaty in 1835 (Figure 2).

Brooks was Indian agent during a rather turbulent period. He makes constant reference in his letters to other Indians coming into the region, including Quapaw, Shawnee, Delaware, Choctaw, and Chickasaw. Unfortunately, no very precise locations are given, and no documents similar to Sibley's report exist for the period immediately preceding the treaty. This dearth of precise locations applies also to the Natchitoches and Adai, who were under continual pressure from white settlement. Glover (1935, p. 898) felt sure that all the remnants of the former

Kadohadacho and Natchitoches Confederacies had gathered near Caddo Lake by the time of the treaty in 1835, despite Sibley's report only thirty years earlier showing at least the Adai and Natchitoches as separate entities. This assumption would seem to be reasonable, and no direct evidence has been found to the contrary.

On July 2, 1834, Brooks was notified that he was no longer Indian agent, and he returned to Washington where he was instructed as to how to treat with the Kadohadacho concerning the land they then occupied. He returned to the Red River in the latter part of May, 1835. With their numbers decreased and white settlers on the increase, the surviving members of the once powerful Kadohadacho Confederacy met at the agency house and signed a treaty (Swanton, 1942, pp. 89–92) with the United States on July 1, 1835, ceding their former lands for $80,000. Figure 2 shows the extent of this cession. They agreed to leave Louisiana and go into Texas.

The main conclusions of this survey for the period 1803 to 1835 are shown in Figure 2. The eighteenth-century shift of the Kadohadacho from their former residence above the Great Bend of the Red River is further documented by Sibley in 1805 and the Freeman-Custis expedition in 1806. Newcomb (1960, map 2) shows Caddo far to the north in 1840, but this is surely an error for this late date. That three major villages were still occupied from 1770 to 1788 seems well established by the expedition journal and map. The Kadohadacho moved (from 1790 to 1795) to a location near the lake which now bears their name (Swanton, 1942, p. 94, 1952, p. 319; Glover, 1935, pp. 897–898). This village on Caddo Lake was called "Timber Hill" (Mooney, 1896, p. 1094). The Alabamas and Koasati had villages nearby (Darby, 1816; Tanner, 1827; Baker, 1839).

The Adai remained near their former homeland in the vicinity of the present city of Robeline, Louisiana (Swanton, 1942, p. 7). The Lower Natchitoches had moved up the river from their old home near the French post, the site of the present town of Natchitoches. The Kichai remained in east Texas, where earlier (1788 and 1790), in a position northwest of Natchitoches, they had served as a barrier to the Osage raids on local cattle ranches (Kinnaird, 1946, pp. 256, 295). By the time of Sibley's report (1805) some or all of them were on the east bank of the Trinity River (Figure 3), and they later joined the Wichita.

The Upper Nasoni, the Upper Natchitoches, the Nanatsoho, and Petit Caddo had disappeared as separate entities by this time and had become amalgamated with the Kadohadacho into the so-called "Caddo nation" (Swanton, 1942, p. 94; Glover, 1935, pp. 897–898). Their total numbers were severely reduced, and at the time of the treaty they numbered about five hundred. This figure contrasts with an estimated two thousand or more for the Kadohadacho in 1700 (Swanton, 1942, p. 23).

AFTER THE TREATY (1835–1961)

The period immediately following the treaty was one of frequent moves for the Kadohadacho or the "Caddo nation," as the remnants of the different bands were known. Swanton (1942, pp. 94–114) has dealt with these moves in detail. By 1840 most of the survivors were in west Texas, where they had joined with the Anadarko and Hainai of the old Hasinai Confederacy (Glover, 1935, pp. 923–937).

In May of 1846, the chiefs of the Kadohadacho and other tribes, including the Anadarko, signed a treaty with the United States at Council Springs, Texas, and the United States was acknowledged as their protector. A tract of land along the Brazos River was finally set aside in 1854 for the use of the tribes which had signed the treaty. It became known as the Lower Reserve. The Kadohadacho and their allies made considerable progress here during the next four years, but pressure from white settlers was too great. For fear they would be massacred by the whites, the Indians of the Lower Reserve were moved north in July and August of 1859 to the Indian Territory (Wright, 1951, p. 51).

The Wichita Agency, including Kadohadacho, Anadarko, Hainai and Wichita, was established by the War Department in October, 1859, near its present location in Oklahoma. On August 21, 1861, Albert Pike, commissioner of the Confederate States to the Indian nations, concluded a treaty with the Kadohadacho chiefs and other tribes of the Wichita Agency. A "Caddo Battalion" served as scouts and rangers in the Confederate Army under the command of Showetat (Little Boy), who was known as the Caddo George Washington. This battalion was one of the last Confederate Indian forces to surrender at the end of the war in July, 1865. A large part of the Caddo remained loyal to the Union and went north to Kansas, where they stayed until 1867 (Wright, 1951, pp. 51–52).

By 1868, all the tribes had returned to the agency in Oklahoma, and a few years later, in 1872, the agency boundaries were defined by the government in agreement with the Wichita. Under the Severalty Act of 1901, every Caddo man, woman, and child was allotted 160 acres of land within the agency, and the surplus land was opened to white settlement (Wright, 1951, pp. 52, 56).

The modern Caddo are the descendants of the Kadohadacho, the Hainai, and the Anadarko, and all are counted in the census as Caddo.

Also on the same reservation are Kichai and Tawakoni, both speakers of a Caddoan language (Wright, 1951, p. 53).

Anthropological fieldwork has been carried out on the Oklahoma reservation since the beginning of this century. Dorsey (1905) collected folklore and a series of Caddo myths. In 1912, Swanton (1931) obtained data on Caddo social organization and found that a distinction between the Kadohadacho and Hasinai could still be made on linguistic grounds. Some years later, Lesser and Weltfish (1932) studied the Caddoan language and also made a distinction between the language of the Kadohadacho and Hasinai. During the 1920s Elsie Clews Parsons did some fieldwork in Oklahoma and also obtained data from a Caddo in New York City. Her work (1941) is the most comprehensive available in terms of modern ethnology and shows how little of their old culture is left. She also reported dialect differences and noted some remaining knowledge of the older tribal divisions. It would seem that future work must focus on ethnohistory and archaeology. Most recent interest in the Caddo nation has been stimulated by their current claim before the Indian Claims Commission.

ARCHAEOLOGICAL IMPLICATIONS

Terminological problems seem to adhere to this area at all time levels. I have tried to avoid misusing the simple term "Caddo" but have found it necessary when referring to the heterogeneous groups of tribes which came together following the 1835 treaty. I have used the term "Caddoan" mainly to refer to members of that language family. In the archaeological literature the term "Caddo" or "Caddoan" is often used, with quotes (Krieger, 1946) and without (Suhm and Krieger, 1954; Davis, 1961a), both geographically for the four-state area and culturally for most archaeological remains which have well-developed pottery. Thus to say that a site is "Caddoan" has very different connotations from similar usage elsewhere in the eastern United States, where terminology avoids linking historic peoples with prehistoric sites before such linkage has been established. For example, the Davis site (Newell and Krieger, 1949) (Figure 3) is "Caddoan" and therefore presumed to be ancestral to the historic Hasinai of the same region without the detailed analysis needed to prove the genetic and historic connections already assumed by the terminology. Other more neutral terms for the area have been suggested (Orr, 1952, p. 239) but not accepted.

This is not a quibble. Present archaeological interpretation of the "Caddoan area" (cf. Davis, 1961a, pp. 6–12) is bogged down in terminology. Some outside help and a fresh approach seems called for

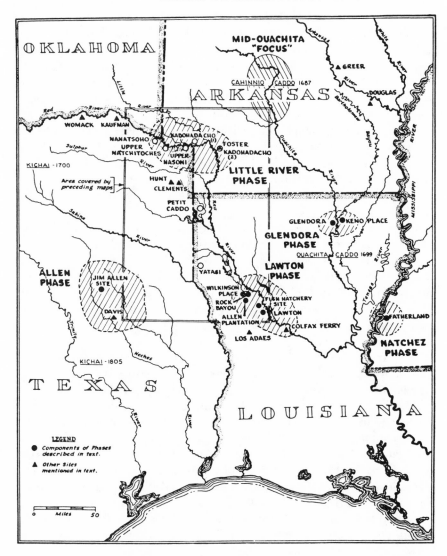

FIGURE 3.   Historic archaeological phases in the Red River region.

(Williams, 1960). Therefore it is without apology that I offer the following revision of the historic "phases" (Willey and Phillips, 1958, pp. 22–24) of the Red River region based on the ethnohistorical findings detailed above.[3]

The Red River region abounds in archaeology, and some important finds have been made on the prehistoric level (Moore, 1912; Harrington,

1920; Webb, 1959). Unfortunately, none of the major villages of the Kadohadacho have been positively located. Webb (1959, pp. 1–7) has recently reviewed the ethnohistorical situation in brief with results compatible with those presented above. He reaffirms his tentative findings (Webb, 1945, pp. 78–79) that the Foster Place is the second Kadohadacho village (Figure 1) found deserted by the Freeman-Custis expedition (Figure 2). However, the Foster site (Figure 3) contains *no* historic artifacts. Its major component is of the Belcher focus, evidently a completely prehistoric complex despite one very late C^{14} date (Webb, 1959, p. 207). This enigma, for the location of the site fits the historic data exceptionally well (Webb, 1945, pp. 78–79), must be solved in the ground. The Hasinai, on the other hand, seem to offer few classificatory problems.

Allen Phase. This phase, representing the historic Hasinai Confederacy, was extracted from the Frankston focus by Suhm and Krieger (1954, pp. 219–221). The type component is the Jim Allen site, Cherokee County, Texas, and seven other components have been listed (Figure 3). *Patton Engraved* is a characteristic pottery type and European trade items occur. The temporal range is estimated at A.D. 1600 to 1835, but some components of this phase were probably still in existence after 1835, as the Kadohadacho joined the Hasinai in Texas after the cession of their treaty lands in Louisiana. The combined tribes began a westward movement toward the Brazos late in that decade.

Lawton Phase. This is a new phase extracted from the old Glendora focus, which Krieger (in Davis, 1961a, pp. 12–13) recently admitted was much too large a unit. The Lawton phase (Figure 3) is identified with the Natchitoches Confederacy, and the type components are the Lawton site, Natchitoches Parish, Louisiana (Webb, 1945), and the nearby Fish Hatchery site (Walker, 1935). Other components include the Allen Plantation, the Wilkinson Place, and the Rock Bayou site, all in Natchitoches Parish (Ford, 1936, pp. 72–97). The characteristic pottery type is *Natchitoches Engraved*, and trade vessels from the east include *Fatherland Incised*, a Natchez type. European items include glass beads, brass bells, and bracelets. The temporal position is estimated as A.D. 1650 to 1805, since amalgamation with the Kadohadacho near Caddo Lake to the north seems to have taken place about this latter date, as described above.

A newly discovered site in this locality, Colfax Ferry (16-Na-15), Natchitoches Parish, Louisiana (Figure 3), is very rich in trade goods including 35,000 glass beads and many German silver ornaments (Webb, 1962). However, the aboriginal pottery is not definitive, making the cultural assignment difficult. A coin and some mutilated Spanish mill dollars seem to date the site after 1800. It is probably not of Caddoan affiliation, since many disparate groups were crowding into this region at this time, as the Indian agent's accounts to Washington make very clear, and Webb has shown that Pascagoula and Biloxi were in this very locality during the American Period.

The Adai, another Caddoan group and one which is considered slightly divergent (Swanton, 1952, pp. 196–197), were located west of the Natchitoches (Figures 1 and 2). The Spanish mission and the nearby military post in their area were important frontier positions with regard to French activities in the eighteenth century. Newcomb (1960, map 1) seems to have slightly misplaced them, showing them north of the Yatasi on the Red River. The Mission site (Los Adaes, Figure 3) has been tested (F. H. West in Davis, 1961a, p. 33) but the material has not been analyzed. I recently stumbled across a small surface collection from the site at the Marksville, Louisiana, Museum which included some blue and white china sherds and shell-tempered aboriginal ware. More archaeological research on the Adai is to be hoped for, since documentary evidence is meager and uncomplimentary (Swanton, 1942, p. 125), despite the amount of time Spanish missionaries and military men spent among them.

Little River Phase. This phase is named for the stream which flows into the Red River near Fulton, Arkansas, just above the Great Bend. It is a tentative phase, ethnographically identified with the Kadohadacho Confederacy as documented historically above. The main components would be the five major villages of the Kadohadacho Confederacy (Figure 1); three located in Bowie County, Texas, one in Little River County, and one in Hempstead County, Arkansas (Figure 3). Other components should include the historic villages of the Petit Caddo and Yatasi in Caddo Parish, Louisiana. It may seem unwise to postulate a phase ahead of the data, but the documentary evidence is so clear that these components must exist, unless they have been destroyed by action of the river or by European construction activities. The temporal range of the phase should be A.D. 1542 to 1788, and considerable trade goods should be found, for lists of Spanish presents given to the Kadohadacho include pounds of glass beads and other nonperishable items such as knives, copper mirrors, and copper wire (Bolton, 1914, vol. 1, p. 144). A component, the Yatasi village, lasts very late and is clearly shown on maps of the period 1816 to 1839, but it, too, is undiscovered. No *historic* sites have been found around Caddo Lake, the final Louisiana home of the Kadohadacho, although a rather careful search has been made (C. H. Webb, personal communication). Thus it is strange but true that no historic archaeological sites pertaining to the Kadohadacho Confederacy have been found within the treaty lands which were ceded in 1835 by their direct descendents.

It is most logical to look for the archaeological antecedents of this tentative Little River phase among the components of the Texarkana focus (Suhm and Krieger, 1954, pp. 203–209) or possibly those of the late Belcher focus (Webb, 1959), although the lack of trade goods at the Foster Place has been mentioned above.[4]

Glendora Phase. Since Orr's (1941) original definition and Krieger's (1946; Suhm and Krieger, 1954, pp. 221–225) extensive use of the term, the Glendora phase ("focus" in Caddoan area terminology) has been a catchall for sites with historic materials in Arkansas and northwestern Louisiana. I have already withdrawn from it the components from around Natchitoches (my Lawton phase) and would limit the Glendora phase to the archaeological remains of the Ouachita Caddo (Figure 3). The type components of the phase are Glendora and Keno (Moore, 1909) in the Ouachita Valley, Louisiana. Other components usually included are the Douglas and Greer sites (Moore, 1908) in the lower Arkansas Valley, Arkansas (Figure 3), but I feel that this extends the phase beyond useful limits. Characteristic pottery is well illustrated by Moore. Aboriginal trade ware includes *Fatherland* and *Natchez Incised.* European trade items were found in a number of graves, including glass beads and ornaments of brass.

This reduction in size of the Glendora phase attempts to bring the historic archaeology more in line with the known ethnographic distribution detailed above. The Cahinnio Caddo (Figure 3) have been left much as they were (Hodges, 1945; 1957). The Mid-Ouachita "focus" is certainly archaeologically distinct from other late prehistoric complexes in the area; and a historic phase has yet to be named and defined for this important intermediate region, which served as a way station on an important trade route to the Mississippi, according to early documentary evidence.

Other untidy bits of important data consist of four unplaced historic components. The Hunt and Clements sites in Cass County, Texas, do not fit the location of any known Caddo villages, as has been pointed out by others (Suhm and Krieger, 1954, pp. 225–227). The Kaufman site, Red River County, Texas (Harris, 1953), is an historic McCurtain focus component, whose ethnohistoric identification is uncertain, although undoubtedly of Caddoan affiliation (Krieger, in Davis, 1961b). The Womack site in Lamar County, Texas, has more trade goods than Kaufman (Suhm and Krieger, 1954, p. 222), but it is a bit too far up the Red River to be one of the major villages of the Kadohadacho Confederacy as named and located here (compare Figures 1 and 3, and also Jelks, in Davis, 1961b). Until some components of the tentative Little River phase, to which they are geographically closest, are discovered and described, their phase assignment will have to be withheld.

An alternative hypothesis, based more on geography than anything else, suggests identifying some of these four components—Hunt, Clements, Kaufman, Womack—with early (prior to 1800) historic sites of the Kichai (Swanton, 1952, pp. 321–322). I have mentioned above the list of presents suggested in 1787 for the tribes of the Natchitoches district including the Kichai. Besides guns, the list included such other nonperishable items as "twenty-five pounds of glass beads: sky blue, black, and white:" (Kinnaird, 1946, p. 198), so that if the gifts were made, as one has every reason to believe they were (Kinnaird, 1946, p. 259), historic sites in this region of the period 1770 to 1790 should be quite rich in European trade goods despite the disquieting lack of information on such items from the would-be components of the putative Little River phase proposed above. Krieger (in Davis, 1961b) recently discussed the problem of trade materials in the Caddoan area, but could offer no reason for their great scarcity except in very late sites (post-1800), as demonstrated by the Colfax Ferry site.

Nevertheless, I feel that this Kichai hypothesis has some merit, especially for the Hunt and Clements components, whose location in Cass County, Texas, jibes very well with the Kichai intention to move in 1787 to a place 6 leagues (Figure 2) from the Petit Caddo (Kinnaird, 1946, p. 259). Further historic evidence for such a position near the Petit Caddo may be found in the modern Louisiana town of Keatchie, De Soto Parish, which is thought (Reed, 1927, p. 34) to be of Caddoan derivation. This location is considerably south and east of that shown in Figure 1, but fits the Spanish documentary evidence even better than the locations of the Hunt and Clements components.

The Kichai's documented friendship with the Kadohadacho might well have stemmed both from a former location on the Red River, where the Kaufman and Womack sites are situated, and from their common suffering in this rather exposed position at the hands of the Osage. Furthermore, Sibley (1832, p. 722) says that their former homeland was near the headwaters of the Sabine (Figure 3). It may be noted that although very full data on these four sites are not available in the literature (with the exception of Kaufman), all have some pottery types in common. This is not very strong supporting evidence, but it at least suggests that further analysis of this new hypothesis may be of value. As already suggested, Hunt and Clements may represent a separate focus (Suhm and Krieger,

1954, p. 226); Webb (1955, p. 262) has even tentatively used the term Hunt focus for the sites.[5]

One final tag-end are the Eyeish. They seem to suffer from lack of attention and a particularly unsavory reputation (Swanton, 1942, p. 125) although they had a Spanish mission among them from 1716 to 1773 and were on the route from the French post at Natchitoches to the Spanish post at Nacogdoches. Their archaeology is virtually unknown, although Jelks (in Davis, 1961b) suggests that one historic site may have been found.

The historic archaeology of the Red River region does at least have a firm anchor to the northwest. The large Spanish Fort site (Krieger, 1946, pp. 161–164; Steen, 1953), located astride the Red River has recently been affirmed as a Taovayas site of the Wichita Confederacy (Jelks in Davis, 1961a, p. 31). Thus, with the Wichita on the northwest, the Hasinai on the west, and the Natchez on the southeast, these three newly formed or revised phases, Lawton, Little River, and Glendora, fill out the picture of this important region and seem to equate well with the documentary evidence now available. Now all that remains to be done is more historic archaeology, as Webb (1960, p. 53) has recently suggested.

CONCLUSIONS

The aboriginal location of the Kadohadacho Confederacy for the period 1542 to 1789 has been ascertained (Figure 1). These conclusions agree with the findings of previous workers in ethnography (Bolton, 1914, 1916; and Swanton, 1942) and in archaeology (Ford, 1936; and Webb, 1959). In 1789 the remaining members of the Kadohadacho Confederacy moved south and by 1795 were located in a single village north of Caddo Lake (Figure 2). An unpublished letter from a Caddo Indian agent gives details of witchcraft among these people in 1825. The Yatasi and the Lower Natchitoches were still living in separate villages about this time, but by 1835 all these tribes participated in a treaty of cession with the United States government (Glover, 1935) and left Louisiana for Texas, where they joined remnants of the Hasinai Confederacy. All these Caddoan tribes are presently amalgamated in Oklahoma.

The historic archaeology of this Red River region may be divided into at least four separate phases: the Allen phase (Hasinai Confederacy), the Lawton phase (Natchitoches Confederacy), the tentative Little River phase (Kadohadacho Confederacy), and the Glendora phase (Ouachita Caddo). The hypothesis that certain hitherto unplaced components may represent some historic villages of the Kichai has been put forward. The Adai and the Eyeish remain virtually unknown.

Notes

[1] The original draft of this paper was prepared in 1955 for use of the Justice Department in the Caddo case before the Indian Claims Commission, and I should like to acknowledge bibliographic information obtained from the unpublished research of Charles H. Lange, anthropologist for the claimants.

[2] Most of this material is not of pure ethnographic interest, but would be useful in chronicling War Department Indian policy and detailing of some minor tribal conflicts. George Gray stands out as an individual deserving of further study. Jehiel Brooks merits attention for less attractive reasons, since his activities on the Red River ultimately led to Federal court action in an early example of conflict of interest.

[3] An earlier version of this suggested revision of historic phases was presented at the Fifth Caddo Conference at Norman, Oklahoma, in 1958 (Davis, 1961b). I have benefited from critical comments by the conference participants and have incorporated information provided by them.

[4] Current research on historic archaeology in this area is being carried on by R. K. Harris of Dallas, M. P. Miroir of Texarkana, and J. Dan Scurlock of Austin. They have tentatively located three of the Kadohadacho villages. The Roseborough Lake site in Bowie County, Texas, has been identified as the Upper Nasoni village, which is consistent with the ethnohistorical data presented here. Harris is presently preparing a report on this site.

[5] Webb (personal communication) feels that there is little merit in this Kichai identification because the archaeological remains show few Plains traits such as those found in other Wichita sites. Thus the Little River phase affiliation appears to be the more likely alternative.

References

Baker, R. Phillips
1839. Map of the Valley of the Red River.
Bolton, Herbert E.
1908. The Native Tribes about the East Texas Missions, *Texas State Historical Association Quarterly*, 11, no. 4:249–276.
1912. The Spanish Occupation of Texas, 1519–1690, *Southwestern Historical Quarterly*, 16, no. 1:1–26.
1914. *Athanase De Mézières and the Louisiana-Texas Frontier, 1768–1780.* 2 vols. Cleveland: Arthur H. Clark Company.
1916. *Spanish Explorations in the Southwest, 1542–1706: Original Narratives of Early American History.* New York: Scribner.
Carter, Clarence Edwin
1953. *The Territory of Arkansas, 1819–1825.* The Territorial Papers of the United States, 19. Washington.
1954. *The Territory of Arkansas, 1825–1829.* The Territorial Papers of the United States, 20. Washington.
Darby, William
1816a. *A Geographical Description of the State of Louisiana. . . . Being an Accompaniment to the Map of Louisiana.* Philadelphia: John Melish.
1816b. *Map of the State of Louisiana.* Philadelphia: S. Harris.

Davis, E. Mott

   1961a. *Proceedings of the Fourth Conference on Caddoan Archeology.* Bulletin of
   the Texas Archeological Society, 30:1–33.

   1961b. *Proceedings of the Fifth Conference on Caddoan Archeology.* Bulletin of the
   Texas Archeological Society, 31:74–143.

Dorsey, George A.

   1905. *Traditions of the Caddo.* Carnegie Institution of Washington, Publication 41.

Fenton, William N., and John Gulick

   1961. *Symposium on Cherokee and Iroquois Culture.* Bureau of American Ethnology, Bulletin 180.

Ford, James A.

   1936. *Analysis of Indian Village Site Collections from Louisiana and Mississippi.*
   Anthropological Study No. 2. New Orleans: Louisiana Department of Conservation.

Freeman, Thomas, and Peter Custis

   1806. *An Account of the Red River in Louisiana.* (Drawn up from the returns of
   Messrs Freeman and Custis to the War Office of the United States, who explored the same in the year 1806.) Washington.

Glover, William B.

   1935. A History of the Caddo Indians, *Louisiana Historical Quarterly,* 18, no. 4:
   872–946.

Griffith, William Joyce

   1954. *The Hasinai Indians of East Texas as Seen by Europeans, 1687–1772.* Philological and Documentary Studies, 2, no. 3. New Orleans: Middle American Research Institute; Tulane University.

Harrington, M. R.

   1920. *Certain Caddo Sites in Arkansas.* Indian Notes and Monographs, Miscellaneous Series, 10. New York: Museum of the American Indian, Heye Foundation.

Harris, R. K.

   1953. *The Sam Kaufman Site, Red River County, Texas.* Bulletin of the Texas Archeological Society, 24.

Hodges, T. L., and Mrs. Hodges

   1945. Suggestion for Identification of Certain Mid-Ouachita Pottery as Cahinnio
   Caddo. *Bulletin of the Texas Archeological and Paleontological Society,* 16:98–
   116.

Hodges, Mrs. T. L.

   1957. The Cahinnio Caddo: A Contact Unit in the Eastern Margin of the "Caddo
   Area." *Bulletin of the Texas Archeological Society,* 28:190–197.

Kinnaird, Lawrence

   1946. Spain in the Mississippi Valley, 1765–1794. Post War Decade, 1782–1791,
   Washington: *Annual Report of the American Historical Association for the
   Year 1945,* 3, pt. 2.

Krieger, Alex D.

   1946. *Culture Complexes and Chronology in Northern Texas with Extension of
   Puebloan Datings to the Mississippi Valley.* University of Texas Publications,
   No. 4640.

Lange, Charles H.

   1954. A Report on Data Pertaining to the Caddo Treaty of July 1, 1835: The Historical and Anthropological Background and Aftermath. (Unpublished.)

Lesser, Alexander, and Gene Weltfish

1932. Composition of the Caddoan Linguistic Stock. *Smithsonian Miscellaneous Collections*, 87:1–15.

Mooney, James

1896. The Ghost Dance Religion, *Annual Report of the Bureau of American Ethnology*, 2, pt. 2.

Moore, Clarence B.

1908. Certain Mounds of Arkansas and Mississippi, *Journal of the Academy of Natural Sciences of Philadelphia*, 13, pt. 4:482–557.

1909. Antiquities of the Ouachita Valley, *Journal of the Academy of Natural Sciences of Philadelphia*, 14:1–170.

1912. Some Aboriginal Sites on Red River, *Journal of the Academy of Natural Sciences of Philadelphia*, 14:481–644.

Newcomb, William W., Jr.

1960. *Indian Tribes of Texas*. Bulletin of the Texas Archeological Society, 29:1–34.

Newell, H. Perry, and Alex D. Krieger

1949. *The George C. Davis Site, Cherokee County, Texas*. Society of American Archaeology, Memoirs, 5.

Orr, Kenneth G.

1941. The Eufala Mound: Contributions to the Spiro Focus, *Oklahoma Prehistorian*, 4, no. 1:2–15.

1952. Survey of Caddoan Area Archaeology. In James B. Griffin (ed.), *Archaeology of Eastern United States*. Chicago: The University of Chicago Press, pp. 239–255.

Parsons, Elsie Clews

1941. *Notes on the Caddo*. American Anthropological Association, Memoirs, 57.

Reed, William A.

1927. *Louisiana Place-names of Indian Origin*. University Bulletin, Louisiana State University, 19, no. 2.

Sibley, John

1832. Historical Sketches of the Several Indian Tribes in Louisiana, South of the Arkansas River, and between the Mississippi and River Grande. *American State Papers, Class II, Indian Affairs*, 1:721–731.

Steen, Charlie R.

1953. *Two Early Historic Sites on the Southern Plains*. Bulletin of the Texas Archeological Society, 24:177–188.

Suhm, Dee Ann, and Alex D. Krieger

1954. *An Introductory Handbook of Texas Archeology*. Bulletin of the Texas Archeological Society, 25.

Swanton, John R.

1931. The Caddo Social Organization and Its Possible Historical Significance, *Journal of the Washington Academy of Science*, 21, no. 9:203–206.

1942. *Source Material on the History and Ethnology of the Caddo Indians*. Bureau of American Ethnology, Bulletin 132.

1952. *Indian Tribes of North America*. Bureau of American Ethnology, Bulletin 145.

Tanner, H. S.

1827. Map of Louisiana and Mississippi .

Walker, Winslow M.

1935. A Caddo Burial Site at Natchitoches, Louisiana. *Smithsonian Miscellaneous Collections*, 94, no. 14:1–15.

Webb, Clarence H.

1945. A Second Historic Caddo Site at Natchitoches, Louisiana. *Bulletin of the Texas Archeological and Paleontological Society,* 16:52–83.

1955. Comments concerning the East Texas Section of "An Introductory Handbook of Texas Archeology." *Bulletin of the Texas Archeological Society,* 26:259–271.

1959. *The Belcher Mound: A Stratified Caddoan Site in Caddo Parish, Louisiana.* Society for American Archaeology, Memoirs, 16.

1960. A Review of Northeast Texas Archeology. *Bulletin of the Texas Archeological Society,* 29:35–62.

1962. Early 19th Century Trade Material from the Colfax Ferry Site, Natchitoches Parish, Louisiana, *Southeastern Archaeological Conference Newsletter,* 9, no. 1:30–33.

Willey, Gordon R., and Philip Phillips

1958. *Method and Theory in American Archaeology.* Chicago: The University of Chicago Press.

Williams, Stephen

1960. Review: *The Belcher Mound: A Stratified Caddoan Site in Caddo Parish, Louisiana,* by Clarence H. Webb, *American Journal of Archaeology,* 64:304–305.

Wright, Muriel H.

1951. *A Guide to the Indian Tribes of Oklahoma.* Norman: University of Oklahoma Press.

SOCIO-CULTURE

CADDOAN KINSHIP SYSTEMS

Alexander Lesser
Hofstra University
(Professor Emeritus)

The Caddoan language family includes four major languages with some dialectic subdivisions. The four languages are Pawnee, Wichita, Kitsai, and Caddo. The Pawnee language is spoken in three dialects: Pawnee proper, the dialect of the three south bands of the Pawnee—Chawi, Pitahawirata, and Kitkahahki; the Skiri Pawnee, which is spoken by the Skiri band; and the Arikara, the dialect of the Arikara tribe. The Wichita language is spoken by eight of the nine bands of the Wichita; viz., all the bands save the Kitsai. This includes the following, which I believe as complete and accurate a list of former Wichita bands as can be obtained today: *tokáns, tawakarú^(w'), wéku', isĩ·s, tiwá·, itá, kɩrikɩris·, akwi·ts.* Dialectic divergence, which has been hinted at for Waco and Tawakoni (viz., the *tawakarú^(w')* and *wéku'* bands), seems on the basis of data which can be secured today to have been merely differences of idiomatic usage. Kitsai is the language of the *tikitsas* band of the Wichita. Caddo, as spoken today, is essentially the language of the *kado'adátc'^(u)* band of the Caddo. There were eight bands of the Caddo tribe: Hainai (with a large branch called *nabadaitcu), nadárko, nacidóc, yát'as, nak'ohodótsi, háic, kayamaíci,* and *kado'adátc'^(u).* According to Caddo tradition, all bands differed dialectically from one another in their speech, except for the two branches of the Hainai, which are said to have spoken the same dialect. While it is impossible today to obtain systematic linguistic data on the band differences of the Caddo, occasional differentiations recalled by older natives indicate that at least in the case of

---

*Originally read at the annual joint meetings of the American Anthropological Association and the American Folk-Lore Society at Vassar College, Poughkeepsie, December 29, 1929. The material on which the paper is based was obtained in the field and includes kinship terminologies with related data from all known dialects of the Caddoan stock.

Hainai and Kadohadacho, traditional belief is accurate, and Hainai may prove the most divergent of the band dialects. In kinship, even where terms are phonetically identical, a difference of systematic usage is recalled and will be discussed briefly below.

Kinship material was obtained independently from all the major groups: the Arikara, Skiri, and South Band Pawnee; the Wichita; the Kitsai; and the Caddo and Hainai.

From a linguistic standpoint, the Caddoan terms of kinship can be characterized by the small number of kinship stems, and the generally meager development of distinctions of relative age, sex of relative, and sex of speaker. Superficially, the number of stems used amount to the following: Pawnee, Skiri, and Arikara each have 15; Kitsai, 17; Wichita, 15; Caddo, 18; and Hainai, 16. Analysis indicates that these numbers will be reduced, since some terms are differently inflected forms of the same verb stem.

From the standpoint of systematic usage, four systems are represented in the Caddoan terminologies. One system of usage may be said to include the kinship of Wichita and Kitsai, in spite of some differences in terms. Another system is identical throughout for the usage of the South Band Pawnee, the Skiri, and the Arikara. A third system, on present evidence, must be associated with usage of the Kadohadacho and Anadarko bands of the Caddo; while a fourth seems to have been in use among the Hainai. I shall speak of these systems as the Kitsai, the Pawnee, the Caddo, and the Hainai.

There is a curious resemblance of features between the Kitsai and Pawnee systems, which requires for purposes of presentation that they be considered together. Elsewhere I have commented several times on the fact that Pawnee kinship includes all those features which may be taken as characteristic of the Crow kinship type which occurs so widely in North America, and particularly in three areas reasonably contiguous to the Pawnee tribes, viz., among the Crow and Hidatsa, in the Southeast, and in the Southwest. There are, however, striking features of Pawnee kinship which are absent in the Crow type, and apparently are alien to it. If the Crow type be said to include features denominated *A*, the Pawnee system may be abstractly stated as *A plus B*, the divergent features being denominated *B*. The *B* features of the Pawnee system are all present in detail in the Kitsai system (i.e., in the kinship of the Kitsai and the Wichita), while features *A* are absent. Thus from a conceptual point of view, we may say that Pawnee kinship is a combination of the Kitsai system and the Crow-type system.

To outline the features of the Kitsai and Pawnee systems, then, it will be well to call attention first to the complex summarized as *B* traits, which represent all essentials of the Kitsai system, and then to consider the traits summarized as *A*, which added to *B* constitute the Pawnee system.

To avoid needless repetition, it might be stated at the outset that in both the Kitsai and the Pawnee systems, as well as in the Caddo and the Hainai systems—that is, throughout the kinship usage of all Caddoan groups—the familiar principles of levirate and sororate kinship classification appear. Thus the father's brother and father are equated conceptually as 'fathers'; the mother's sister and mother are equated conceptually as 'mother'; and a man's brother's children are as his own and a woman's sister's children are as her own. Finally, children of siblings of like sex—that is, children of two brothers, or children of two sisters—are siblings to each other. These features are carried through the systems consistently for all collateral lines, and it may be assumed in the following discussion that usage with respect to parents, siblings, and children is always intended to apply also in these obvious classificatory extensions.

It may also be added, in connection with the above, that the levirate and sororate marriage customs, of which these kinship classifications are the correlate and the expression, are in one form or another universal for Caddoan peoples.

Kitsai System

The Kitsai type shares the classificatory features just mentioned with all Caddoan usage. In addition, while there are special terms for mother's brother and father's sister, the children of these are siblings to each other, making all cousins, cross as well as parallel, 'brothers' and 'sisters.' The Kitsai, exceptionally, preserves a nephew/niece term, evidently reciprocal to the mother's brother term, which, according to the memory of my oldest informants, is an isolated usage and does not function systematically. By this I mean that while an uncle-nephew/niece usage is present in Kitsai, but absent in

Wichita, it has no effect upon other usages. Children of nephew or niece in Kitsai are as children of others of the child generation, 'grandchildren.' Thus in both Wichita and Kitsai usage, one has the following as consanguinities: (a) grandparents; (b) fathers, mothers, uncles, and aunts; (c) siblings; (d) children; and (e) grandchildren. In consanguinities, the peculiar and characteristic features which I referred to as of *B* type are that parents of grandparents are addressed and spoken of by parent terms, and children of grandchildren are addressed and spoken of by child terms. Thus reading up from ego's generation of siblings, we have conceptually: parents, grandparents, parents, grandparents, and so on. Reading down, we have: children, grandchildren, children, grandchildren, and so on.

In affinal relationships five basic concepts summarize the Wichita and Kitsai systematic usage. These concepts are: (1) husband; (2) wife; (3) males married into the family; (4) spouses of males married out of the family; and (5) person of same sex as speaker married into same family as speaker. Inverting somewhat the order in which I have stated these concepts, I shall discuss first the last three (i.e., 3-5).

Wichita and Kitsai, as well as all the Pawnee groups, are basically matrilocal. Both the earth lodge of the Pawnee and the large grass houses of the Wichita accommodated extended families of many persons, and these families always included—if these generations were represented among the living members of the family—maternal grandparents, parents, married and unmarried daughters, and unmarried sons. Thus, from the standpoint of the individual family, one might say that the community consisted of in-marrying males, and that the males of the household might be called out-marrying males. Females are in all essentials rooted to the parental home, while males are migratory as regards permanent residence. In Pawnee two terms, *kustáwehtsu?* and *tskúrus,* differentiate and group all relatives-in-law who are affected by the principle of residence. Thus in-marrying males—designated by the term *kustáwehtsu?*—would include son-in-law, a man's sister's husband, and a man's niece's husband, a man's granddaughter's husband. These in-married males, in turn, use the same stem with different pronominal form for the reciprocal relations of wife's parents, wife's brother, wife's uncle and wife's grandfather. The form *tskúrus,* on the other hand, includes the daughter-in-law, a woman's brother's wife, a man's nephew's wife, and a woman's grandson's wife; while these designated individuals use other pronominal forms for reciprocation to the husband's parents and husband's sister. It will be seen that one concept is applied always to males, the other always to females; but this is not because of any sex differentiation in the terms: *kustawehtsu?,* so far as it is translatable, refers merely to 'the one sitting among us', *tskúrus* to 'the outsider.' The grouping by sex is a reflex of the fact of strict unilocal residence usage.

The concept of person of same sex as speaker; married into same family as speaker, is used with reference to two unrelated males married to sisters, or two unrelated females married to brothers. In Wichita and Kitsai, it may also be applied to a man and his granddaughter's husband, or a man and his wife's grandfather, or to a woman and her grandson's wife, or to a woman and her husband's grandmother. These last usages are in some cases in Wichita and Kitsai preferred to the distinctions based on the two preceding concepts, which in some cases overlap in application.

These three concepts are not carried through with the same rigid consistency in Wichita, Kitsai, and Pawnee. Pawnee is most consistent, in that it has no other usage for parents-in-law (except for the vocative use of 'old man' and 'old woman') than those based on the concepts of in-marrying males and wives of out-marrying males. Kitsai and Wichita, however, have special terms for parent-in-law, and have in addition other terms than those based on the above two concepts, which in some cases may be used optionally instead of these terms.

The affinity concepts of husband and wife are applied throughout Wichita, Kitsai, and Pawnee in the same manner. The Pawnee terms are merely different pronominal forms of the same stem. Thus, if the Pawnee term for 'wife' is said to mean 'I have or own you,' or 'the one I have or own,' the Pawnee term for husband would mean 'He has or owns me.' Wichita and Kitsai stems may be independent forms for husband and wife; based on present data they can be considered so, although further linguistic analysis may show them to be formed in a parallel manner to the Pawnee. Nevertheless, to repeat, the usage of these terms is fundamentally the same for all three groups.

The regular singular, subject pronoun forms for 'wife' are applied directly by a man to the wife's sister, the wife's grandmother, and the wife's granddaughter, as well as his own wife; the form for 'husband' is applied directly by a woman to the husband's brother, the husband's grandfather, and the husband's grandson, as well as her own husband. In addition, dual pronominal forms—viz., meaning 'our wife,' 'our husband'—are applied by a man to his brother's wife, his grandson's wife, and his grandfather's wife (not own grandmother), and by a woman to her sister's husband, her granddaughter's husband, and her grandmother's husband (not own grandfather).

These usages are not merely terminological. It was pointed out earlier that levirate and sororate customs are universal for Caddoan groups. For Wichita, Kitsai, and Pawnee, both levirate and sororate occurred during life as well as after death; that is, it was customary for a woman to consider her husband's brothers as her husbands, just as it was customary for a man to consider his wife's sisters as his wives. Thus a true fraternal polyandry existed here, as well as a true sororal polygyny. The sororate during life was very frequent, as genealogies vividly illustrate.

The levirate was not so openly considered a marriage. Nevertheless, it was a custom of Wichita, Kitsai, and Pawnee parents, in the course of their instruction of their sons, to teach younger brothers to love an older brother's wife as an own wife. It was, as well, the custom for the younger brother, while still immature, to go to live with his older married brother. A Wichita informant stressed that the older brother tells his younger brother, "This is our wife," and that he would permit the younger brother to live with her as such. The same informant stated as his positive knowledge a case of such fraternal polyandry existing today among the Wichita: two classificatory brothers (viz., through parallel cousinship) were living with the same woman as wife. A Chawi informant stated that the older brother offered the younger brother his wife when he had demonstrated his manhood by conspicuous bravery; and that he would tell his brother to go places with the wife. Pawnee informants agreed that this usage was true for several younger brothers as well as for only one. A Skiri informant said that when a married son has gone away for any length of time, his younger brother is sent to live with the wife and take care of her. This custom is, incidentally, also present among the Comanche.

Thus the usage of spouse terms for spouses of siblings is not a mere joking relationship, although joking goes along with it. In addition to this form of joking, the most pronounced joking relationship among the Wichita, Kitsai, and Pawnee, is grandparent-grandchild joking, particularly with reference to marriage, and particularly with reference to each other's spouses. This joking is indiscriminate; that is, grandmothers as well as grandfathers joke with grandsons, grandfathers as well as grandmothers joke with granddaughters. The joking may be humorous, critical, and vulgar; and it is never resented, but taken in kind.

While it may seem an extreme statement, this grandparent-grandchild joking is no more a mere joking relationship than the sibling-in-law customs. A Wichita informant stated that a man could marry a grandson's wife or a brother's granddaughter, or a grandfather's wife who was not an own grandmother. Naturally these customs are not practiced today as they were in earlier times, so that it is futile to expect genealogical substantiation in records of contemporary families. An aged Kitsai informant stated the following possibilities: a grandson could marry a grandfather's widow, depending on considerations of age and absence of close blood-relationship; with the consent of the girl, a grandfather could have intercourse with his grandson's wife; and among both Kitsai and Wichita, a man could marry either his sister's or his brother's granddaughter.

The Pawnee evidence is more conclusive, though it is here tied up with other complications of Pawnee kinship to be discussed later. Statements include general agreement among a very large number of old Pawnee that in former times marriages of those who called each other by grandparent-grandchild terms are very frequent, though not obligatory. Statements bearing on this particular point are that a grandfather's wife, who was not an own grandmother, joked and had sex relations with the husband's grandson. It was said that a woman could marry her sister's grandson and that a woman joked with her husband's grandfather as if she were his wife, and could live with him. Also mentioned was a specific case in which a man married his brother's granddaughter. In connection with the latter case, the informant added that this situation was common in the old days.

This freedom of discussion and action between relatives of alternate generations is reflected in another curious fact. When the question of marrying a son or daughter is considered in a household, it is the boy's grandfather and the girl's grandmother who not only deal for the young people to be married, but who are the ones to talk it over with them and get their views. A Kitsai informant explained this fact by the statement that parents never discussed such things with their children, but that grandparents, who joked with the children, did, so that when the girl had to be asked about her acceptance of a certain boy, it was the grandmother who talked to her about it.

Up to this point I have discussed those features of Kitsai and Wichita kinship (and their parallel forms in Pawnee) which I refer to as *B* features. In summary, they include the peculiar alternation of parent-grandparent and child-grandchild terms above and below the ego's generation respectively, and the differentiation of affinity relationships under five concepts. I have added comments on the sociological status of these usages. These features, called *B*, are common to Wichita, Kitsai, and Pawnee.

Pawnee System

Pawnee kinship, to repeat, adds to features *B*, features denominated *A*, by which are meant the features of the Crow-type system. These are briefly as follows:

Cross-cousins are not siblings. On the mother's brother's side they are children and on the father's sister's side they are mother and father. In other connections, I have tried to show that these shifts flow from a kinship identification of the mother's brother and the sister's son as 'brothers.' All extensions of usage of Pawnee kinship follow the Crow-type in these features consistently, with several added features. Thus, wherever in extensions of usage, a grandchild term appears, the children of such are as own children, and the parents of grandparents, in ascending generations, are as mothers and mother's brothers. In affinal usage, the special marriage to be associated with the Crow-type—namely, a marriage of a man to his mother's brother's wife, or conversely of a woman to her husband's sister's son—is one of the most general customs of the Pawnee. James R. Murie early pointed out that the uncle's wife was the one who instructed a youth in things sexual, and that when the uncle died, if the nephew was unmarried, he married the widow. It might be added that among the Pawnee, the custom of sending a younger brother to live with an older married brother is extended to include a boy's mother's brother—a custom which is further sociological substantiation of the point of view I have taken, that is, that the mother's brother and sister's son are in Crow-type usage equated conceptually as 'brothers.'

Caddo and Hainai Systems

The other two types of Caddoan usage, the Caddo and the Hainai, can be discussed here only briefly. They agree in certain negative characteristics, as opposed to both the Kitsai and the Pawnee types; viz., there is no alternation of terms in ascending and descending generations; there is no complicated extension of usage of the spouse terms; and there is no grandparent-grandchild joking.

Fundamentally the same terms and usages are employed by both the Caddo and Hainai, with one striking exception, which seems to me to give a different slant to the Caddo.

The Hainai is the simpler. In the speaker's generation it merges all collateral relatives, including cross and parallel cousins, in the concept of siblings; and it groups all relatives of generations beyond grandparents, and beyond grandchildren, in the concepts of grandparents and grandchildren respectively. One complicated usage stands out: it is the existence of special terms for the mother's brother, and for a man's sister's child, whether boy or girl. The terms themselves must be very old, as they are undoubtedly related to the stems for these concepts in all other Caddoan dialects. Usage requires that the children of either nephew or niece be grouped as nepotic relatives with their parents. That is, the term *pa'haṭisi* refers not only to a man's sister's son and daughter, but to a man's sister's grandson and granddaughter. Thus it follows that for a man or woman the father's or mother's mother's brother is as a mother's brother. So far as can be found out today from the only living Hainai with any memory of the language or usage, there are no indications in the rest of the kinship usage which might clarify this peculiar concept of uncle and nephew/niece. The uncle's probably a diminutive construction based on the term for grandmother; while the Caddo or Hainai grandfather in the same way uses a term for both his grandson and granddaughter which is a diminutive construction based on the grandfather term. This usage, with its trend toward reciprocity, and particularly in the manner of the linguistic formation of terms, is foreign to the Caddoan languages and kinship systems except in this isolated case, and is definitely like such usage further west, as among the Tonkawa and in the Pueblos.

Summary

From a descriptive standpoint there are four kinship systems present among the Caddoan tribes: the Kitsai, Pawnee, Caddo, and Hainai. Kitsai and Pawnee usage are related in such a way that all of the characteristic features of Kitsai usage are present in Pawnee usage, in addition to those features which characterize the widely distributed Crow-type of usage. Caddo and Hainai kinship usage show traces of influence from the west.

In the Pawnee and Kitsai systems we found a striking inter-relation of conceptual categories within the systems and behavior distinctions in the life of the people; these included not only familiar joking relationships and marriages, but the unique and strong development of grandchild-grandparent joking with its corresponding marriages, and furthermore, a striking interrelation of the concepts of relatives by affinity and the principles of residence usage among these tribes.

The historical inference suggested by the Pawnee and Kitsai kinship systems and usage is that the Kitsai, with its parallels in Wichita, represents the older Caddoan system and usage, and that the Pawnee "Crow-type" features are later additions or changes.

BIBLIOGRAPHY

Lesser, Alexander
    1929 Kinship Origins in the Light of Some Distributions. *American Anthropologist* 31: 710-730.
    1930 Levirate and Fraternal Polyandry Among the Pawnee. *Man* 30:98-101.

THE CADDO AND ASSOCIATED TRIBES

CADDO TRIBAL SYNONYMY

Asinais—an old French name, from *Hasinai.*

Caddo—popular name, from *Kä'dohadä'cho.*

Cadodaquio—Joutel (1687), another form of *Kä'dohadä'cho.*

Cenis—old French name used by Joutel in 1687; from *Hasinai.*

Dä'sha-i—Wichita name.

Dĕ'sa—another form of *Dä'sha-i.*

Hasi'nai or *Hasi'ni*—the proper generic term for at least the principal Caddo divisions, and perhaps for all of them. It is also used by them as synonymous with "Indians."

Kä'dohädä'cho—the name of the Caddo proper, as used by themselves.

Ma'se'p—Kiowa name; "pierced nose," from *mak'on*, nose, and *sep*, the root of a verb signifying to pierce or sew with an awl.

Na'shonit or *Na'shoni*—Comanche name, frequently used also by the neighboring tribes to designate the Caddo; the Nassonite of the early French writers on Texas.

Nez Percé—French traders' name; "pierced nose."

Ni'ris-häri's-ki'riki—another Wichita name.

Otä's-itä'niuw'—Cheyenne name; "pierced nose people."

Tani'bänĕn, Tani'bänĕnina, Tani'bätha—Arapaho name; "pierced nose people," *tani*, nose.

CADDO TRIBAL SIGN

"Pierced nose," in allusion to their former custom of boring the nose for the insertion of a ring.

SKETCH OF THE CADDO

The Caddo are the principal southern representatives of the Caddoan stock, which includes also the Wichita, Kichai, Pawnee, and Arikara. Their confederacy consisted of about a dozen tribes or divisions, claiming as their original territory the whole of lower Red river and adjacent country in Louisana, eastern Texas, and southern Arkansas. The names of these twelve divisions, including two of foreign origin, have been preserved as follows:

Kä'dohadä'cho (Caddo proper).

Nädä'ko (Anadarko).

Hai'-nai (Ioni).

Nä'bai-dä'cho (Nabedache).

Nä'kohodo'tsi (Nacogdoches).

Näshi'tosh (Natchitoches).

Nä'ka῾na'wan.

Hădai'-i (Adai, Adaize).

Hai'-ĭsh (Eyeish, Aliche, Aes).

Yä'tăsi.

I'măha—a band of Omaha, or perhaps more probably Kwâpâ, who lived with the Kä'dohadä'cho, but retained their own distinct language.

There are still a few living with the Caddo, but they retain only the name. It will be remembered that when the Caddo lived in eastern Louisiana the Arkansas or Kwâpâ were their nearest neighbors on the north, and these Imaha may have been a part of the Kwâpâ who lived "up stream" (*U'mañhañ*) on the Arkansas. The Caddo call the Omaha tribe by the same name.

Yowa'ni—originally a band of the Heyowani division of the Choctaw. They joined the Caddo a long time ago, probably about the time the Choctaw began to retire across the Mississippi before the whites. Some few are still living with the Caddo and retain their distinct language. There is evidence that some Koasati (Cooshatties) were mixed with them.

The Kä'dohadä'cho seem to be recognized as the principal Caddo division, and the generic term *Hasi'nai* by which the confederates designate themselves is sometimes regarded as belonging more properly to the three divisions first named. According to their own statements some of the dialects spoken by the several divisions were mutually unintelligible. At present the Kädohadächo and Nädäko are the ruling dialects, while the Näbaidächo, Näkohodotsi, Hädai'-i, and Hai'-ish are practically extinct. The Kichai, Bidai, and Akokisa, who formerly lived near the Caddo on the eastern border of Texas, did not belong to the confederacy, although at least one of these tribes, the Kichai, is of the same stock and is now on the same reservation.

The Caddo have ten gentes: *Na'wotsi*, Bear; *Tasha*, Wolf; *Ta'nähä*, Buffalo; *Ta'o*, Beaver; *Iwi*, Eagle; *Oät*, Raccoon; *Ka'g'aih*, Crow; *Ka'gähänĭn*, Thunder; *Kĭshi*, Panther; *Sûko*, Sun. The Bear gens is the most numerous. The Buffalo gens is sometimes called also *Koho'* or Alligator, because both animals bellow in the same way. These of a particular gens will not kill the animal from which the gens takes its name, and no Caddo in the old times would kill either an eagle or a panther, although they were not afraid to kill the bear, as are so many of the western tribes. The eagle might be killed, however, for its feathers by a hunter regularly initiated and consecrated for that purpose.

The original home of the Caddo was on lower Red river in Louisiana. According to their own tradition, which has parallels among several other tribes, they came up from under the ground through the mouth of a cave in a hill which they call *Cha' kani'nä*, "The place of crying," on a lake close to the south bank of Red river, just at its junction with the Mississippi. In those days men and animals were all brothers and all lived together under the ground. But at last they discovered the entrance to the cave leading up to the surface of the earth, and so they decided to ascend and come out. First an old man climbed up, carrying in one hand fire and a pipe and in the other a drum. After him came his wife, with corn and pumpkin seeds. Then followed the rest of the people and the animals. All intended to come out, but as soon as the wolf had climbed up he closed the hole, and shut up the rest of the people and animals under the ground, where they still remain. Those who had come out sat down and cried a long time for their friends below, hence the name of the place. Because the Caddo came out of the ground they call it *inä'*, mother, and go back to it when they die. Because they have had the pipe and the drum and the corn and pumpkins since they have been a people, they hold fast to these things and have never thrown them away.

From this place they spread out toward the west, following up the course of Red river, along which they made their principal settlements. For a long time they lived on Caddo lake, on the boundary between Louisiana and Texas, their principal village on the lake being called Sha'chidi'ni, "Timber hill." Their acquaintance with the whites began at a very early period. One of their tribes, the Nädäko, is mentioned under the name of Nandacao in the narrative of De Soto's expedition as early as 1540. The Kädohadächo were known to the French as early as 1687. The relations of the Caddo with the French and Spaniards were intimate and friendly. Catholic missions were established among them about the year 1700 and continued to exist until 1812, when the missions were suppressed by the Spanish government and the Indians were scattered. In the meantime Louisiana had been purchased by the United States, and the Caddo soon began to be pushed away from their ancient villages into the western territory, where they were exposed to the constant inroads of the prairie tribes. From this time their decline was rapid, and the events of the Texan and Mexican wars aided still further in their demoralization. They made their first treaty with the United States in 1835, at which time they were chiefly in Louisiana, southwest of Red river and adjoining Texas. They afterward removed to Brazos river in Texas, and to Washita river in Indian Territory in 1859. When the rebellion broke out, the Caddo, not wishing to take up arms against the government, fled north into Kansas and remained there until the close of the war, when they returned to the Washita. Their present reservation, which they hold only by executive order and jointly with the Wichita, lies between Washita and Canadian rivers in western Oklahoma, having the Cheyenne and Arapaho on the north and west and the Kiowa, Comanche, and Apache on the south. In 1893 they numbered 507.

In person the Caddo are rather smaller and darker than the neighboring prairie tribes, and from their long residence in Louisiana, they have a considerable admixture of French blood. They are an agricultural tribe, raising large crops of corn, pumpkins, and melons, and still retaining industrious habits in spite of their many vicissitudes of fortune. They were never buffalo hunters until they came out on the plains. They formerly lived in conical grass houses like the Wichita, but are now in log houses and generally wear citizen's dress excepting in the dance. The old custom which gave rise to the name and tribal sign of "Pierced Nose" is now obsolete. In 1806 Sibley said of them, "They are brave, despise danger or death, and boast that they have never shed white man's blood." Their former enemies, the prairie tribes, bear witness to their bravery, and their friendship toward the whites is a part of their history, but has resulted in no great advantage to themselves, as they have been dispossessed from their own country and are recognized only as tenants at will in their present location.

They and the Wichita received the new doctrine from the Arapaho, and were soon among its most earnest adherents, notwithstanding the fact that they were regarded as the most advanced of all the tribes in that part of the country. It may be that their history had led them to feel a special need of a messiah. They have been hard and constant dancers, at one time even dancing in winter when there was nearly a foot of snow upon the ground. Their first songs were those which they had heard from the Arapaho, and sang in corrupted form, with only a general idea of their meaning, but they now have a number of songs in their own language, some of which are singularly pleasing in melody and sentiment.

THE WICHITA, KICHAI, AND DELAWARE

Closely associated with the Caddo on the same reservation are the Wichita, with their subtribes, the Tawakoni and Waco, numbering together 316 in 1893; the Delaware, numbering 94, and the Kichai (Keechies), numbering only 52. Of these, all but the Delaware, who are Algonquian, belong to the Caddoan stock. The Wichita and their subtribes, although retaining in indistinct form the common Caddoan tradition, claim as their proper home the Wichita mountains, near which they still remain. Sixty years ago their principal village was on the north side of the north fork of Red river, a short distance below the mouth of Elm creek, in Oklahoma. They live in conical grass houses and, like the other tribes of the stock, are agricultural. They call themselves *Ki'tikiti'sh*—they are called *Tawe'hash* by the Caddo and Kichai—and are known to most of their other neighbors and in the sign language as the "Tattooed People" (*Do' kănă*, Comanche; *Do'gu'at*, Kiowa), from an old custom now nearly obsolete. For the same reason and from their resemblance to the Pawnee, with whose language their own has a close connection, the French called them *Pani Pique's*.

The Kichai or Keechie, or *Ki'tsäsh*, as they call themselves, are a small tribe of the same stock, and claim to have moved up Red river in company with the Caddo. Their language is different from that of any of their neighbors, but approaches the Pawnee.

The Delaware are a small band of the celebrated tribe of that name. They removed from the east and settled with the main body in Kansas, but drifted south into Texas while it was still Spanish territory. After a long series of conflicts with the American settlers of Texas, before and after the Mexican war, they were finally taken under the protection of the United States government and assigned to their present reservation along with other emigrant tribes from that state.

SONGS OF THE CADDO

1. HA'YO TĂ'IA' Ă'Ă'

Nä'nisa'na, Nä'nisa'na,
Ha'yo tă'ia' ă'ă',
Ha'yo tă'ia' ă'ă',
Na'wi hă'iă' i'nă',
Na'wi hă'iă' i'nă'.

Translation

Nä'nisa'na, Nä'nisa'na,
Our father dwells above,
Our father dwells above,
Our mother dwells below,
Our mother dwells below.

" Our mother" here refers to the earth.

2. WŮ'NTI HA'YANO' DI'WITI'A

Nä'nisa'na, nä'nisa'na,
Wŭ'nti ha'yano' di'witi'a ha'yo',
Wŭ'nti ha'yano' di'witi'a ha'yo',
A'ă ko'ia' ha'yo',
A'ă ko'ia' ha'yo',
Wŭ'nti ha'ya'no ta'-ia' ha'yo',
Wŭ'nti ha'ya'no ta'-ia' ha'yo'.

Translation

Nä'nisa'na, nä'nisa'na,
All our people are going up,
All our people are going up,
Above to where the father dwells,
Above to where the father dwells,
Above to where our people live,
Above to where our people live.

3. Nṵ'na Ï'tsiya'

He'yawe'ya! He'yawe'ya!
Nṵ'na Ï'tsiya' si'bocha'ha',
Nṵ'na Ï'tsiya' si'bocha'ha',
Wṵ'nti ha'yano' ha'nïn gṵ'kwṵ'ts-a',
Wṵ'nti ha'yano' ha'nïn gṵ'kwṵ'ts-a',
He'yahe'eye'! He'yahe'eye'!

Translation

He'yawe'ya! He'yawe'ya!
I have come because I want to see them,
I have come because I want to see them,
The people, all my children,
The people, all my children.
He'yahe'eye! He'yahe'eye!

This song was composed by a woman named Nyu'taa. According to her story, she saw in her trance a large company approaching, led by a man who told her he was the Father and that he was coming because he wished to see all his children.

4. Na'tsiwa'ya

Na'tsiwa'ya, na'tsiwa'ya,
Na' ika'—Wi'ahe'e'ye',
Na' ika'—Wi'ahe'e'ye',
Wi'ahe'e'ye'ye'yeahe'ye',
Wi'ahe'e'ye'ye'yeahe'ye'.

Translation

I am coming, I am coming,
The grandmother from on high, *Wi'ahe'e'ye'*,
The grandmother from on high, *Wi'ahe'e'ye'*,
Wi'ahe'e'ye'ye'yeahe'ye',
Wi'ahe'e'ye'ye'yeahe'ye'!

This song also was composed by the woman Nyu'taa. In her trance vision she fell asleep and seemed (still in the vision) to be awakened by the noise of a storm, when she looked and saw approaching her the Storm Spirit, who said to her, "I come, the grandmother from on high." The Caddo call thunder the "grandmother above" and the sun the "uncle above."

5. Na'-iye' ino' ga'nio'sït

Wa'hiya'ne, wa'hiya'ne,
Na'-iye' ino' ga'nio'sït,
Na'-iye' ino' ga'nio'sït.
Wa'hiya'ne, wa'hiya'ne.

Translation

Wa'hiya'ne, wa'hiya'ne,
My sister above, she is painted,
My sister above, she is painted.
Wa'hiya'ne, wa'hiya'ne.

This is another song composed by Nyu'taa, who herself explained it. In this trance vision she saw a spirit woman painted with blue stripes on her forehead and a crow on her chin, who told her that she was "her sister, the Evening Star." While singing this song Nyu'taa was sitting near me, when she suddenly cried out and went into a spasm of trembling and crying lasting some minutes, lifting up her right hand toward the west at the same time. Such attacks were so common among the women at song rehearsals as frequently to interfere with the work, although the bystanders regarded them as a matter of course and took only a passing notice of these incidents.

6. NA'A HA'YO HA'WANO

Nä'nisa'na, nä'nisa'na,
Na'a ha'yo ha'wano,
Na'a ha'yo ha'wano.

Translation

Nä'nisa'na, nä'nisa'na,
Our father above (has) paint,
Our father above (has) paint.

This refers to the sacred paint used by the participants in the Ghost dance, and which is believed to confer health and the power to see visions.

7. WŪ'NTI HA'YANO KA'KA'NA'

Nänisa'na, nänisa'na,
Wû'nti ha'yano ka'ka'na' ni"tsiho',
Wû'nti ha'yano ka'ka'na' ni"tsiho',
Aa' ko'ia' ta'-ia' ha'yo',
Aa' ko'ia' ta'-ia' ha'yo',

Translation

Nä'nisa'na, nänisa'na,
All the people cried when I returned,
All the people cried when I returned,
Where the father dwells above,
Where the father dwells above.

This song was composed by a girl who went up to the spirit world and saw there all her friends, who cried when she started to leave them again.

8. NA'WI I'NA

Nä'nisa'na, nä'nisa'na,
E'yahe'ya, e'yahe'ya, he'e'ye'!
E'yahe'ya, e'yahe'ya, he'e'ye'!
Na'wi i'na ha'yo ä'ä—He'yoi'ya, he'e'ye'!
Na'wi i'na ha'yo ä'ä—He'yoi'ya, he'e'ye'!

Translation

Nä'nisa'na, nä'nisa'na,
E'yahe'ya, e'yahe'ya, he'e'ye'!
E'yahe'ya, e'yahe'ya, he'e'ye'!
We have our mother below; we have our father above—*He'yoi'ya, he'e'ye'!*
We have our mother below; we have our father above—*He'yoi'ya, he'e'ye'!*

This song was composed by a woman named Niaha'no', who used to have frequent trances in which she would talk with departed Caddo and bring back messages from them to their friends. "Our mother below" is the earth. (See page 1096.)

9. NI' IKA' NA'A

Ni' ika' na'a ha'na',
Ni' ika' na'a ha'na';
Na'a-a' ha'na',
Na'a-a' ha'na'.

Translation

There are our grandmother and our father above,
There are our grandmother and our father above;
There is our father above,
There is our father above.

By "grandmother" is meant the storm spirit or thunder. (See Caddo song 4.)

10. HI'NA HA'NATOBI'NA

Hi'na ha'natobi'na i'wi-na',
Hi'na ha'natobi'na i'wi-na',
Na' iwi' i'wi-na',
Na' iwi' i'wi-na';
Na'nana' ha'taha',
Na'nana' ha'taha'.

Translation

The eagle feather headdress from above,
The eagle feather headdress from above,
From the eagle above, from the eagle above;
It is that feather we wear,
It is that feather we wear.

This refers to the eagle feather worn on the heads of the dancers. (See song number 12.) This song is in the Hai-nai dialect.

11. NA' ĂĂ' O'WI'TA'

Na' ăă' o'wi'ta',
Na' ăă' o'wi'ta',
Na' kiwa't Hai'-nai',
Na' kiwa't Hai'-nai'.

Translation

The father comes from above,
The father comes from above,
From the home of the Hai-nai above,
From the home of the Hai-nai above.

This song, like the last, was composed by one of the Hai-nai tribe, and refers to the silent majority of the band in the spirit world.

12. Na' iwi' o'wi'ta'

Na' i - wi' o' - wi' - ta', na' i - wi' - o' - wi' - ta'; do'-hya di'-wa - bo'n na' na' i-wi' o' - wi'-ta',

do'-hya di'-wa - bo'n na' na' i-wi' o' - wi'-ta'; na'-ha' na'-da-ka'-a', na'-ha' na'-da-ka'-a'.

Na' iwi' o'wi'ta',
Na' iwi' o'wi'ta';
Do'hya di'wabo'n na' na' iwi' o'wi'ta',
Do'hya di'wabo'n na' na' iwi' o'wi'ta';
Na'ha' na'daka'a', Na'ha' na'daka'a'.

Translation

See! the eagle comes,
See! the eagle comes;
Now at last we see him — look! look! the eagle comes,
Now at last we see him — look! look! the eagle comes;
Now we see him with the people,
Now we see him with the people.

This refers to what the Caddo call the "return of the eagle feathers" in the Ghost dance. With the Caddo, as with other tribes, the eagle is a sacred bird, and in the old times only the few medicine-men who knew the sacred formula would dare to kill one for the feathers. Should any-one else kill an eagle, his family would die or some other great misfor-tune would come upon him. The formula consisted of certain secret prayers and ritual performances. Among the Cherokee the eagle killer's prayer was a petition to the eagle not to be revenged upon the tribe, because it was not an Indian, but a Spaniard, who had killed him — an indication of the vivid remembrance in which the cruelty of the early Spaniards was held among the southern tribes. To further guard against the anger of the eagles, the Cherokee eagle killer, on his return to the village, announced that he had killed, not an eagle, but a snowbird, the latter being too small and insignificant to be dreaded. The eagle-killing ceremony among the northern prairie tribes has been already described under Arapaho song 47. The Caddo eagle killer always took with him a robe or some other valuable offering, and after shooting the eagle, making the prayer, and pulling out the tail and wing feathers he covered the body with the robe and left it there as a peace offering to the spirit of the eagle. The dead eagle was never brought home, as among the Cherokee. The last man of the Caddo who knew the eagle-killing ritual died some years ago, and since then they have had to go without eagle feathers or buy them from the Kiowa and other tribes. Since Sitting Bull came down and "gave the feather" to the leaders of the dance the prohibition is removed, and men and women alike are now at liberty to get and wear eagle feathers as they will.

13. A'NANA' HANA'NITO'

A'nana' hana'nito' ni'ahu'na — *He e'ye'!*
A'nana' hana'nito' ni'ahu'na — *He'e'ye'!*
A'nana'sa'na'? A'nana'sa'na'?
Ha'yo ha'nitu' ni'ahu'na — *He'e'ye'!*
Ha'yo ha'nitu' ni'ahu'na — *He'e'ye'!*
A'nana'sa'na'? A'ana'sa'na'?

Translation

The feather has come back from above — *He'e'ye'!*
The feather has come back from above — *He'e'ye'!*
Is he doing it? Is he doing it?
The feather has returned from on high — *He'e'ye'!*
The feather has returned from on high — *He'e'ye'!*
Is he doing it? Is he doing it?

This refers to the return of the eagle feathers, as noted in the preceding song. The question "Is he doing it?" is equivalent to asking, "Is this the work of the father?"—an affirmative answer being understood.

14. NA' IWI' HA'NAA'

Na' iwi' ha'naa',
Na' iwi' ha'naa';
Wû'nti ha'yano' na'nia'sana',
Wû'nti ha'yano' na'nia'sana'.
Na'ha na'ni'asa',
Na'ha na'ni'asa'.

Translation

There is an eagle above,
There is an eagle above;
All the people are using it,
All the people are using it.
See! They use it,
See! They use it.

This song also refers to the use of eagle feathers in the dance.

15. WI'TĈ' HA'SINI'

E'-ye - he'! Nä'-ni - sa' - na,　　E'-ye - he'! Nä'-ni - sa' - na.　　Wi' - tû'　Ha' - si - ni'

di' - wi - ti' - a' - a',　wi' - tû'　Ha' - si - ni' di' - wi - ti' - a' - a'　　ki'-wat ha'- i - me' He'-

e'-ye'! Ki-wat ha'-i-me' He'-e'-ye'! Na'-ha-yo' na', Na'-ha-yo' na' - ä'-ä' ko'-i-ä',

He' - e'-ye'! I'-na ko'-iä', He' - e' ye'! I'-na ko'-iä', He' - e'-ye'!

E'yehe'! Nä'nisa'na,
E'yehe'! Nä'nisa'na.
Wi'tŭ' Ha'sini' di'witi'a'a'.
Wi'tŭ' Ha'sini' di'witi'a'a'
Ki'wat ha'-ime' — Ho'e'ye'!
Ki'wat ha'-ime' — He'e'ye'!
Na'hayo' na',
Na'hayo' na'ä'ä' ko'iä' — He'e'ye'!
I'na ko'iä' — He'e'ye'!
I'na ko'iä — He'e'ye'!

Translation

E'yehe' ! Nä'nisa'na,
E'yehe' ! Nä'nisa'na.
Come on, Caddo, we are all going np,
Come on, Caddo, we are all going up
To the great village — *He'e'ye'!*
To the great village — *He'e'ye'!*
With our father above,
With our father above where he dwells on high — *He'e'ye'!*
Where our mother dwells — *He'e'ye' !*
Where our mother dwells — *He'e'ye' !*

The sentiment and swinging tune of this spirited song make it one of the favorites. It encourages the dancers in the hope of a speedy re-union of the whole Caddo nation, living and dead, in the "great village" of their father above, and needs no further explanation.

CADDO GLOSSARY

Ăă — father.
Ăă Kakï'mbawiút — "the prayer of all to the Father;" from *aa*, the Father, i. e., God, and *tsimba'dikŭ*, I pray; the Ghost dance, also called *Nä'nisa'na Gao'shăn*, Nä'nisa'na dance.
A'nana — for *Năuă*.
A'nanasa'na — for *Nana'sana*.
Ba'hakosĭn — "striped arrows," from *bah*, arrow; the Caddo name for the Cheyenne. They sometimes call them *Siä'näbo*, from their Comanche name.
Cha"kanĭ'na — "the place of crying;" the traditional first settlement of the Caddo tribes, where they came up out of the

ground, at the mouth of Red river, on the south bank, in Louisiana.
Detse-ka'yăă — "dog eaters;" the Caddo name for the Arapaho.
Di'wabon — we see him; *tsibo'nŭ*, I see him.
Di'witi'ă — we are all going up, we shall all ascend; *tsidiŭ'*, I ascend.
Do'hya — now, at once.
E'yahe'ya! — an unmeaning exclamation used in the songs.
E'yehe'! — ibid.
Ganio'sĭt — he (she) is painted; *atsĭno'sĭt*, I paint myself.
Gao'shăn — a dance; *ga'tsioshăn*, I dance.

Gú'kwúts—my (plural); *gúkwú'nda*, my (singular); *ha'nĭn gú'kwúts*, my children.

Hǎ'-iǎ—he (she) dwells there below. Compare *Ko'iǎ*.

Ha'-imi—large.

Hai'-nai—a tribe of the Caddo confederacy.

Hǎ'naů or *Hǎ'nǎ*—there he is! that is he!

Ha'nani'to—this feather, the feather; *ni'toh*, feather; *ha'taha*, feather (generic).

Ha'natobi'na—a feather headdress; feathers prepared to wear on the head.

Ha'nĭn—children.

Ha'nitu—for *Ni'toh*.

Hasi'ni or *Hasi'nai*—the Caddo; the generic name used by themselves.

Ha'taha—feather (generic); *nitoh*, feather (specific).

Ha'wano—paint.

Ha'yano—people.

Ha'yo—above, on high. Compare *Naha'yo*.

He'eye'!—an unmeaning exclamation used in the songs.

He'yahe'eye'!—ibid.

He'yawe'ya!—ibid.

He'yoi'ya!—ibid.

Hi'na—eagle feathers.

Ika—grandmother; a term sometimes applied to the thunder or storm spirit.

Inǎ'—mother; *na inǎ'*, mother above.

I'tsiya—I have come; *hatsi'ûs*, I come.

I'wi—eagle; also the name of a Caddo gens.

Ka'gǎhǎnĭn—thunder; a Caddo gens.

Ka'g'aih—crow; a Caddo gens.

Kaka'na—they cried; *ha'tsikaka's*, I cry.

Ka'ntsi—"cheats;" the Caddo name for the Kiowa Apache, Lipan, and Mescalero.

Kĭ'shi—panther; a Caddo gens.

Kiwa't—village, town, settlement.

Koho'—alligator; another name for the Ta'nǎhǎ or Buffalo gens of the Caddo.

Ko'iǎ—where he dwells above; *tǎ'-iǎ*, he dwells above; *datsii'ǎ*, I dwell above.

Na—see! look! now!—also coming down from above, as *iwi-na*, the eagle coming down from above.

Nǎǎ'—father above, i. e., God; from *ǎǎ'*, father, and *na*, above, on high.

Na'daka—with the people.

Nahǎ'—that's all! now you see! there now!

Naha'yo—up, above, the plural of *Ha'yo*.

Hasi'ni diwĭti'a na'hayo, all the Caddo are going up, everybody of the Caddo is going up.

Na-iye'—sister above; from *na*, above, in composition, and *iye'*, sister.

Nǎnǎ' or *Nǎ'nǎnǎ'*—that one (demonstrative).

Nana'sána—is he making it?

Na'ni'asa—they are using it; *ha'tsĭna'sa*, I use it.

Na'nia'sana—for *Na'ni'asa*.

Nǎ'nisa'na—an Arapaho word, adopted by the Caddo in the Ghost-dance songs and meaning "my children."

Nǎ'nisa'na gao'shǎn—"Nänisana dance," one of the Caddo names for the Ghost dance, from *gao'shǎn*, a dance, and *nänisa'na* (q. v.), an Arapaho word which forms the burden of so many Arapaho Ghost-dance songs. It is also called *Ǎǎ Kakĭ'mbawiút*, "the prayer of all to the Father."

Na'tsiwa'ya—I am coming.

Na'wi—below; *ha'yo*, above.

Nawotsi—bear; a Caddo gens.

Ni—a syllable prefixed merely to fill in the meter.

Niahu'na—for *Nĭ'tahǔ'nt*.

Nĭ'tahǔ'nt—it has returned. It has come back; *tsĭtsihǔ'nǎ*, I return; *Nĭ"tsiho*, when I returned.

Ni'toh—feather (specific); *ha'taha*, feather (generic).

Nĭ"tsiho—when I returned. Compare *Nĭ'tahǔ'nt*.

Nǔ'na—because.

O'ǎt—raccoon; a Caddo gens.

O'wita—he comes; *a'tsiús*, I come.

Sha"chadĭ'ni—"Timber hill," a former Caddo settlement on Caddo lake, Louisiana.

Si'bocha'ha—I want to see them; *hatsi'bos*, I see.

Súko—sun; a Caddo gens.

Tǎ'-iǎ—he dwells above. Compare *Ko'iǎ*.

Ta'nǎhǎ—buffalo; a Caddo gens.

Ta'o—beaver; a Caddo gens.

Tasha—wolf; a Caddo gens.

Tsaba'kosh—cut-throats; the Caddo name for the Sioux.

Wa'hiya'ne!—an unmeaning exclamation used in the songs.

Wi'ahe'eye'!—ibid.

Wi'tǎ!—come on! get ready.

Wú'nti—all of them.

WICHITA AND CADDO RELATIONSHIP TERMS

By LESLIE SPIER

THE following Wichita and Caddo terms[1] were obtained at Anadarko, Oklahoma, August, 1919, from John Haddon, a Kichai who habitually speaks Wichita, and Bill Edwards, a Caddo of the xasinĕ band,[2] respectively. While I am reasonably sure of the Wichita, I lack confidence in the Caddo, particularly as the unusual separation of collateral from lineal relatives suggested would indicate misunderstanding.

WICHITA[3]

ŏ'kω, grandparent.

dada, father.

nati'áse'i, my father; used only for God (?).

da'tasikitsá, "little father:" father's younger brother; great grandfather.

da'tasiwatsá, "big father:" father's older brother; greatgrandfather (since in the last case relative age cannot be meant; possibly this term and the preceding are used indiscriminately for greatgrandfather).

ŏ'tsiŭ, mother, used by children.

natïkahe'kĭ, "my woman:" mother, father's sister, mother's sister.

natiatsia'tsĭkitsá, my father's sister or my mother's sister, both younger than mother or father (which one is not clear; probably the former); greatgrandmother.

natiatsia'tsiwatsá, my father's sister or my mother's sister, both older than mother or father; greatgrandmother (again relative age can play no part).

---

[1] Published by permission of the American Museum of Natural History.

[2] The Caddo were said to comprise the xasinĕ, kadohadatc, hainaĭ, and anadark' (among others?), between whom there were slight dialectic differences. All now speak the same dialect.

[3] a as in father; ă as in hat; á as in hut; e as in fate; ĕ as in met; i as in pique; ĭ as in pin; o as in note; ŏ as in not; ö as in German schön; u as in rule; ŭ as in put; ω as in law; d and t may be variants of a single intermediate; ' is a weak glottal stop, except after k where it is almost a fortis; ' is a breath.

natĭkaheki neĭkĭti, my father's sister's husband; my mother's husband (i.e. my father).

nakĭri yörtsski, stepfather; father's sister's husband; mother's sister's husband.

natiwatsiŏssi, my mother's brother.

natĭdihŏssi, "my old man:" mother's brother.

natĭŏtsskĭtsi, my mother's brother's wife; son's wife (cf. natĭ'tsĭtsi). This term may sometimes be used by a man for his own or a conceptual brother's wife.

hantoero'ski, man speaking—brother; son of parent's sibling.

nati'rotsĭi, woman speaking—brother, as the preceding.

natitωtsiĭ, man speaking—sister; daughter of parent's sibling.

hantare"eyatsĭ'i, woman speaking—sister, as the preceding. Half-brothers and sisters are siblings; step-brothers and sisters are not related.

nateöĭ, my child; my brother's child; my greatgrandchild: woman speaking—my sister's child. This corresponds to the designation of greatgrandparents as parents. (*natĭyĕ'ki*, my children.)

nateöĭ wirsŭksĕĕ, "my child a boy:" son.

nateöĭ tcĕrĭksĕĕ, "my child a girl:" daughter.

hirotĭĕöĭ, our (dual) child, i.e., man speaking—his own child or that of his brother; woman speaking—her own child or that of her sibling. (Perhaps this is used only in speaking to a non-sibling; cf. *hĭrotiokĭ* and *hirotĭkĭtĭ*.)

natidohöĭ, our (plural) child, i.e., man speaking—his own or one of his brothers' children; woman speaking—her own or one of her siblings' children.

natidohöĭ dodikitsĭrĕĕ, "our child the young man."

natidohöĭ kohek'odĕ'ĕ, "our child the young woman." These words specifying a youth or maiden may also be used with *nateöĭ* and *hirotĭĕöĭ*.

natĭtorĭkĭtsi, man speaking—my sister's son.

natitsĕwatsĭĭ, man speaking—my sister's daughter.

natikĭdĭ, my husband.

hĭrotsiĕkĭdĭ, our (dual) husband, used by two (real or conceptual) sisters to one another. The individual's name is suffixed when a specific reference is desired.

hirotĭkĭtĭ, our (dual) husband, used by two sisters in talking to anyone not their sister.

natsilrokĭkĭdĭ, our (plural) husband, used by three or more sisters among themselves.

natĭok'ĭ, my wife.

hĭrotsio'kĭ, our (dual) wife, used by one brother to another (real or conceptual) of either's wife.

hĭrotiokĭ, our (dual) wife, used by one of two brother's of either's wife in talking with someone not a brother.

natsiorok'ok'i, our (plural) wife, i.e. the wife of any of three or more brothers talking among themselves.

natiĕ'si, my daughter's husband; my (real or conceptual) sibling's daughter's husband; man speaking—my (real or conceptual) sister's husband.

'utckĭtsi,[4] woman speaking—brother's wife.

natĭ'tsĭtsi, my son's wife; my (real or conceptual) sibling's son's wife; my father's brother's wife.

natĭiwaworĭsi, my grandchild; my sibling's grandchild (possibly including those of a man's sister). Where precision is demanded the words for boy, girl, young man or woman given above are suffixed.

natĭĭwoworsĭ nekĭdĭ, "my granddaughter's husband."

natĭĭwoworsĭ nok'ĭ, "my grandson's wife." The grandchild's spouse is jokingly called "husband" or "wife," since this follows from the designation of greatgrandchildren as children.

natsĕiwksi, my parent-in-law.

hirotsiωtsĕωksĭ, our (dual) parent-in-law, used by two (real or conceptual) siblings in speaking to each other about the parent-in-law of either.

hirotsiωtsĕωksĭkĭ, our (dual?) parents-in-law, used by two brothers to one another for the parents-in-law of either or both, i.e., two or four persons.

No exogamous units are said to exist. Nor were the bands or villages exogamous: on the contrary, a certain feeling of band solidarity brought about a tendency toward band endogamy. The children of the parent's brothers and sisters cannot be married; in fact, these conceptual siblings must be treated with all the respect shown to real brothers and sisters. The sororate was practised: this was considered preferable to marriage with women who were not sisters, but it was not obligatory. Usually if a man

---

[4] In a communication Mr. Haddon wrote this "dutch-kits, with the d silent."

married an eldest sister and she left him or died, he would marry a younger sister if it was agreeable to her. A man could marry any of his wife's real or conceptual sisters, but not her aunt or niece. The levirate was practised only to keep a woman who had children in the family.[5] She would marry either an older or younger brother according to choice.

Neither a man nor a woman could talk much to their parents-in-law or the brothers and sisters of these parents-in-law, nor to the wife's or husband's nephews and nieces. Communication was usually carried on through the spouse; but these relatives could be directly addressed in matters of extreme importance. This taboo is rigorously followed even to-day. On the other hand, one may joke freely with a spouse's brothers and sisters. Joking is tabooed with one's parents' siblings and with his siblings' children, but not with grandparents and all those regarded as siblings.

CADDO

ebŭ'l, grandfather.
ĭkŭ'', grandmother.
à'à, father.
àhàhaĭlme', "big father": father's older brother.
àhàĭlt, "little father": father's younger brother; stepfather.
ĭna'', mother
ĭnahaĭlmĕ, "big mother": mother's older sister.
ĭnatil, "little mother": mother's younger sister.
ĭkwĕ'i, stepmother.
àhai', father's sister.
eba'', mother's brother.
ebakĭn, father-in-law; (real or conceptual) daughter's husband.
inka'an, mother-in-law.
tcuhuànŭ, mother's brother's wife; (real or conceptual) son's wife.
ĭne'tĭt, man speaking—older brother; parents' sibling's son older than self. The final syllable *tĭt* is customarily dropped in this and the following terms.
tu'ĭtĭt, man speaking—younger brother; parents' sibling's son younger than self.

---

[5] G. A. Dorsey does not specify the levirate, but indicates that the deceased husband's parents must give their consent before the widow can marry again. (The Mythology of the Wichita, Carnegie Inst., Publ. 21, 1904, 10).

kĭ'nĭĭ or *kĭnĭtsĭ*, woman speaking—brother; parents' sibling's son.

tai'ĭĭĭ, man speaking—sister; parents' sibling's daughter, woman speaking—younger sister; daughter of parents' sibling younger than self.

ie, woman speaking—older sister; parents' sibling's daughter older than self.

dahai', spouse of (real or conceptual) sibling.

saiĕtĕ, "old lady"; wife (non-vocatively).

honĭsti, "old man": husband (non-vocatively).

nătsikwaĭ, spouse (non-vocatively). There seems to be no term for a spouse in direct address.

hanĭ'', son; daughter: (real or conceptual) brother's child; woman speaking—(real or conceptual) sister's child.

pa''tsĭ, man speaking—sister's child (also given for father's sister's daughter, but this seems to be an error).

bŭkkĭntc, man speaking—grandson; greatgrandson.

kahanĭtc, woman speaking—grandson; greatgrandson. Both of these terms probably include the granddaughter and the greatgranddaughter.

The application of the following terms is by no means clear. *Cahŭ't* was given first as meaning "cross-cousin" and even "parallel-cousin," but the final explanations were the following.

cahŭ't, father's father's brother's son's son or daughter, etc. Presumably a cousin in the speaker's generation related through a grandparent.

sa'kĭn, father's father's brother's son's son's son or daughter, etc. Evidently the child of *cahŭ't*.

wahadĭn, father's father's brother's son's son's son's son or daughter, etc., i.e. the child of *sa'kĭn*.

ĭne'ĭĭ, etc., The terms for siblings are applied to the children of *wahadĭn*.

One cannot marry cross or parallel-cousins, nor any *cahŭ't*, *sa'kĭn*, *wahadĭn*, or their children, *ĭnétĭt*, etc. "One boy was at the river and he became deaf and dumb. The old men asked about him and found out his parents were *wahadĭn*." If a man marries the oldest sister of several and she dies, a younger sister may take her place if it is agreeable. There are said to be no exogamous groups, but in conversation with my informant maternal affiliation seemed to be stressed.

Conversation is tabooed between parents-in-law and children-in-law except in cases of serious need.   This is equally binding to all concerned.

University of Washington,
Seattle, Washington.

LINGUISTICS

CADDO TEXTS

Wallace L. Chafe

University of California, Berkeley

These six stories were recorded from the late Mrs. Sadie Bedoka Weller of Anadarko, Oklahoma. Text 1 was recorded in 1959, Texts 2, 3, and 4 in 1961, and Texts 5 and 6 in 1964. The titles I have given them are not Mrs. Weller's, but have been added here for purposes of identification.

Mrs. Weller used the term 'children's story' for the genre represented by the first five of the texts. It can be seen that the first three bear a resemblance to the Uncle Remus type stories associated with the Southeast, in that they are said to explain some prototypical characteristic of an animal: how the turtle got its squares, why the wildcat eats the turkey raw, or why the wolf has yellow eyes. The Caddo regard themselves as a Southeastern Woodlands tribe, and these stories seem appropriate to that area. On the other hand, the borderline nature of the Caddo as the Southeastern people who were in closest contact with tribes to the west may be reflected in the resemblance of Text 2 to a Coyote story; its main interest seems to be in the trick the turkey played on the predatory wildcat. But that influence is even more apparent in Text 3, whose protagonist is Coyote without a doubt. The Caddo use the same word, tá:sah, for both coyotes and wolves, and it is interesting to compare the character in Text 3 with the wolf in Text 4, who has clearly been transplanted from his European encounter with Red Ridinghood into this Native American setting. Text 5 provides another example of an assimilated European fairy tale. Text 6 is very different from the other five, being more purely Native American with its indigenous themes of hunting and magical transformation.

Texts 2 and 4 contain songs. Mrs. Weller believed that both songs were Chickasaw in origin. It is conceivable that the stories as well were originally borrowed from the Chickasaw or another Muskogean tribe.

Caddo words undergo a number of phonological changes in fast speech, and also when they are linked to other words in sentences. Such modifications are not shown here, and words are written as they would be pronounced slowly in isolation. However, accent marks have been placed on word-final syllables that were accented in the text, even though such accents would not be present on words in isolation.

A sketch of Caddo grammar is available in Chafe (1976: 52-82).

Text 1: How the Turtle Got its Squares

1. ahyá?   tikí   bah?nah,   kínkambašúh   wán?ti? tiki.
   In the past far   it is said   liquid (water)   all   far.
                                         was dried up   (i.e., far and wide)

2. bah?nah   ná   č'áyáh,   banít,   dika?háy   wán?ti?
   It is said   that   turtle,   birds,   things   all

3. kah?ukakí:?ah   bah?nah   háhbakán?ín?a?   kahutáyá:bah
   all kinds   it is said   they were counciling concerning

4. síttut,ihah   wáy?šah   dí   wán?ti? dika?háy   kambašú:kah.
   what is the reason still   this   all   things   liquid was
                                                                     dried up.

5. kú?akannidah   kú:ku?.   bah?nah   wa?náh   háyá:nuh
   They didn't find   water.   It is said   each   person

6. háhiyah   wa'náh   hǔšnu'   kac'ihutáy'ah.   bah'nah
     went   each   different   manner (i.e.,   It is said
                                            walking, flying,
                                            swimming).

7. ná   cah   č›áyáh,   háhiyah   kúkidah.   kámbah'wá:wa'
     that   Mr. Turtle   he went   by the   They said,
                                              creek.

8. háwwih   háyá:nuh,   kassáw'k›asáy'   díh'náh   dahká:nit,
     "All right,   person,   be silent   but   shout,

9. háyá:nuh,   nassahkannida'káh   kú:ku'.   bah'nah   háhiyah.
     person,   when you find liquid   water."   It is said   he went.

10. kúsidí,   bah'nah   ha'ímáy   hússayah'ni'a'.   nátti'
      After a while   it is said   big   there is a log!   There

11. bah'nah   dikahí:yah.   kúyatáyánnáhdu'   natdah'ní:way.
      it is said   he got stuck.   He was unable   to get over the log.

12. bah'nah   kúhaišuh   nat'ikáhnah.   bah'nah   nátti'
      It is said   suddenly   he shouted.   It is said   there

13. di:niwsakáh   ná   nabít   kahánná:bah.   náná   kánnutáy'ah,
      one stepped on him   those   others   it was them.   That   is the reason

14. dúhya'   bah'nah,   wa'náh   háhučá:nní'sa'.   bah'nah
      now   it is said   each   he has squares.   It is said

15. daškuhih   natáynahyah   sínátti'   bah'nah   ná
      dark   when it became   then   it is said   that one

16. sah   u'ǔš,   ukkih   hákahut›áyá:sa'.   bah'nah
      Ms.   Owl   really   she was splashing.   It is said

17. háhučambahsáy'usa'.   kúsidí   bah'nah,   ná   sah   nídímbah'náh
      they heard her water.   After a   it is said   that Ms.   one asked her
                                     while   (Flea)

18. bah'nah   ná.   kámbaka'   cihánna'ah'a',   sisih.   bah'nah
      it is said   that one.   She said,   "I will,"   flea.   It is said

19. nítdiyah.   bah'nah   ná   kánkidukáh   sah.   sah   u'ǔš
      she went.   It is said   that one   she bit her   Ms.   Ms.   Owl

20. bah'nah   sínátti'   tučat›i:hahwah.
      it is said   then   she spilled it.[1]

---

[1]The last episode is obscure, but evidently Ms. Owl was washing, Ms. Flea was sent to check on her, bit her, and Ms. Owl spilled her water.

Text 2: Why the Wildcat Eats the Turkey Raw

1. bah?nah   ahyá?   tikí,   cah   wadu?   ukkih   bah?nah
    It is said   in the past far   Mr. Wildcat   really   it is said

2. háh?áw?isdakánná:sa?   kahbahnáînnidan?.   naht,uh   kín?a?nihah.
    he is scooping over   to dig roots.   A garden   he was making.

3. bah?nah   kúsidí   háyá:nuh   níhbahsay.   háy   dika?háy
    It is said   after a   a person   he was heard.   "Hey,   something
                   while

4. wássâ:nihah.   aháy   kánímbaka?.   cibahnáînnidan?.   kánímbaka?
    you are doing!"   "Yes,"   he said to him. "I'm digging   He said to
                                                   roots."   him,

5. dikadâ:nihah.   c,í:nih.   ci:yas?aháh,   kahciháybah.
    "What are you   "Nothing.   I'm going around   looking at things."
    doing?"

6. kánímbaka?   háwwih   ici?.   c,i?ahnahsáh   dahkut,ikáy?ah?a?.
    He said to him,   "All right   then.   (Being) useless, you'll be in my way."

7. witu?   dúhya?,   bah?náh   húh?i?áysa?.   di:yá:nah,
    Just   now   it is said he caught him.   He caught him,

8. di:yuhkah,   kánímbaka?   ku?á:na?   kúhnisah?a?,   táh?í:?a?
    plucked him,   said to him,   "Over there where (my)   she lives
                                                  house is   there

9. náttih.   tû:dah?yat.   náttih   dah?úmbah?nah,   hísi:kasni?
    woman.   Now go there.   Woman   say to her   she should
                                                                  cook you

10. diskah   náná   t,a:yáh?a?.   bah?nah   kúsidí,
    noon   then   I will eat you." It is said after a while

11. háh?áwnánní:yah,   nú?.   bah?nah   áwwissiyah.   bah?nah
    he trotted along   turkey.   It is said he arrived   It is said
                                               there.

12. ná   sah   wadu?   ukkih   bah?náh   háh?áwsa?.   hacihdi?
    that one Ms. Wildcat   really   it is said she was   Baby
                                                   sitting.

13. háhna:wida:wí:?íh?isa?.   ukkih   bah?nah   dáhnáy?áwsa?,
    she is pushing in a   Really   it is said she is singing there
    cradle-hammock.

14. nasa:wí:?íhsa?   bah?nah.   bahsáyhah
    when she pushes   it is said.   She was heard (singing):

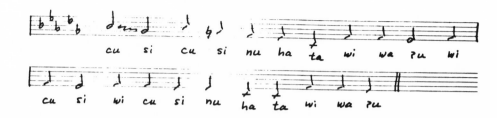

15. ukkih   bah?nah   cah nu?   háy kámbaka?. híkkúyámmáh
    Really   it is said   Mr. Turkey "Hey," he said. "He sent me

16. kassahkúndânna?na?   kišwah.   nassahkúndânna?niháh   sínátti?
    you should make the   parched corn.   When you have made the   then
    granular substance for me   granular substance for
                                                 me

17. ci:yáhdi?a?.   bah?nahway?   kúhakáhtí?   húc›isahkišwánt›a?.
    I will go on."   In fact   quickly   she had the parched corn.

18. dindí:?áh,   bah?nah   iháhdissiyah.   ku?á:na?   tikí
    She pounded it   it is said   he went on.   Over there   far
    for him

19. bah?náh   hákahyah?ni?a?   ha?ímáy   ya?k›uh   kahyač›ah,
    it is said   a log lies   big   tree   log

20. nítdâwtí:yáh.   bah?nah   nátti?   dâ:titi?   hákahyâ:ni?a?.
    fallen tree.   It is said   there   little   he was lying
                                                      deer   in the brush.

21. bah?nah   ná   cah   nú?   bah?nah   íwyuhah
    It is said   that   Mr.   Turkey   it is said   he climbed

22. há:yúh   káynkidáwyahsan.   bah?nah   kúsidí,   awasá:k›uhah   ná
    on top   he stood on it.   It is said after a   he yawned   that
                                                      while

23. dâ:titi?.   bah?nah   háhbahsáy?usa?   kakkudikí:nu?,
    little deer.   It is said   he was heard   "I'm sleepy,
                                      saying,

24. nú?.   ná   cah   nú?   kámbaka?,   háy   wasba:sáyk›awihah.
    (turkey)."[1]   That   Mr.   Turkey   he said,   "My   he knows my name!"
                                                             goodness,

[1]The last syllable of kakkudikí:nu?, which the deer repeated as he yawned,
is the word for turkey.

5. bah?nah   kúsidí   bahsáyhah.   nasa:wasá:k'unáh

   It is said   after a while   he was heard   When he yawned
                                   saying it
                                   (again).

?6. bahsáyhah,   kakkudikí:nu?,   nu?.   nátti?   bah?nah,

   he was heard   "I'm sleepy,   (turkey)." There   it is said
   saying,

?7. c'iyatáy?ah   diskah   nítdiskáwwidáh,   nít?iháhdah   ná,

   just at that time   noon   it was that time   he went by   that one
                                   of day

?8. bah?nah   áwwiśśiyah   kúhnisah?a?   ná   cah   wadu?.

   it is said   he arrived   where the house   that   Mr.   Wildcat.
                                     was

?9. kámbaka?,   nú?   sâ:kasni?ah.   hun?náh   kámbaka?.   dítti?

   He said,   "Turkey did you cook   "No,"   she said.   "Here
                             him?"

30. hít?áwwit   kúmbaka?   sîná   kínah?úmbah?nah   kiśwah

   he came   he told me   like that   you told him   parched corn

31. dahkúndânna?na?.   nátcíndânna?niháh,   dâmbíhnu?náh   náhiyah.

   you make for me.   After I made the   he put the granular he left."
                              granular substance   substance on his
                              for him   back

32. bah?nah   kúsidí   háhunnacánniyah.   ku?á:na?   bah?nah

   It is said   after a while   he followed him.   Over there   it is said

33. ditáyníwdiśśiyah.   ná   ditáyníwdáh,   náná   dúhya?

   he caught up with   That   he caught up   that   now
   him there.   one   with him

34. kánnutáy?ah   kúsibah?uh   háh?i?áhsa?.

   is the reason   raw   he eats him.

Text 3: Why the Wolf Has Yellow Eyes

1. bah?nah   ahyá?   tikí,   k'an?   háhutáywa:nihsa?   nihdáhih.

   It is said   in the past far   ducks   they were playing   at a river.

2. haka?aw?   kínkammač'ah.   wít   wa?náh   nasa?č'ánníwtakáh,

   Deep   it was a water-   Self   each   when he removed his eyes
                   hole.

3. háki?č'ánnáywat'áw?isa?.   sínátti?   wa?náh   nasahwatnukahyukáh,

   he dropped his eyes in   Then   each   when he dove in
   the water.

4. kutí   asáhayt   hác'ih?ič'áncâ:ni?a?.   bah?nah   kúsidí,

   on the other   he emerged   his eyes were back in.   It is said   after a while
   side

5.   ibấh   tá:šah   hússáyʔasuh.   kámbakaʔ   páhciʔ,
    Uncle   Coyote   he was coming!   He said,   "Sister's
                                                                      children,

6.   dikadâ:waʔnihah.   kánímbakaʔ,   cʼíː:nih.   citáywa:nihah,
    what are you doing?"   They said to him,   "Nothing.   We're playing,

7.   kakiʔčʼɛ́nnáywatʼawayʔ,   nátti?   kakihwatnukahyuh   kakiʔčʼɛ́nnidaʔah.
    dropping our eyes in   then   diving in   finding our eyes.
    the water,

8.   kutí   nasʔa:wáyhuh   kûhaʔahat   háhʔaʔčʼɛ́ncâ:niʔaʔ.
    On the other   when you climb   fine   your eyes are back
    side   (out)   in place."

9.   háwwih.   wáyʔ iciʔ   bahʔnahwayʔ   háhwitʼihsaʔ   híyahkáwʔah.
    "All right."   Actually   in fact   he wanted   to eat them.

10.   kámbakaʔ   háwwih   páhciʔ   hícitánnaʔah.   dahkuʔčʼɛ́nníwʔáhah.
    He said,   "All right,   sister's   let me try.   Take my eyes out.
                                            children.

11.   dahkuʔčʼɛ́nnáywatʼawayʔ.   bahʔnah   kúsidí,   diʔčʼɛ́nníwtakáh
    Drop my eyes in the water."   It is said   after a   they took his eyes
                                              while   out

12.   diʔčʼɛ́nnáywatʼáwʔáh,   hawatnukáyhah.   kutí   íwyuhšiyah.
    they dropped his eyes in   he dove in.   On the   he climbed
    the water   other side   (out) there.

13.   bahʔnah   kûhaʔahat   dáhʔicʼɛ́ncâ:niʔaʔ.   bahʔnah   nabít
    It is said   fine   his eyes were in   It is said   "A second
                         place there.   one

14.   yutánnabahnit.   kʼanʔ   kámbahʔwá:waʔ   háwwih   dúhyaʔ
    let's try."   Ducks   they said,   "All right   now

15.   nasahwatnukahyukah   hídiʔčʼɛ́mmaʔá:nih.   bahʔnah   ukkih
    when he dives in   let's catch his eyes."   It is said   really

16.   háhutʼáyá:saʔ   katčahih.   páhciʔ   páhciʔ   kwídáywá:yah.
    he was moving   on the bank.   "Sister's   sister's   where are you?
                                 children,   children,

17.   kútʼaháybah.   bahʔnah   kúsidí,   háhíwá:yah   bahʔnah
    I can't see."   It is said   after a   they went   it is said
                            while

18.   čʼahkaʔayʔ   diʔčʼɛ́nníwáhdah.   náná   waʔnáh   diʔčʼahdawʔnáh
    bone nettle   they brought.   That   each   they hit the socke

19.   kûhʔicʼáhammanʔnaʔ.   kutí   bahʔnah   pakáwtahšiyah.   náná
    in the eye holes.   On the   it is said   he emerged there.   That
                         other side

0. kánnutáy?ah   dúhya?   háh?ič,ánna?ahsa?   hak,ay?ku?.
   is the reason   now   the eyes are   yellow.

ext 4: The Wolf and the Wren

1. ahyá?   tikí   bah?nah   háh?í:?a?,   cínda:kísci?.
   In the past   far   it is said   she lived   a wren.

2. bah?náh   ná   sá:sin?   tut?iyas?niháh   dawat.
   It is said   that one   her mother   she prepared for her   a basket.

3. túmbah?náh   ná   t,i?   čiyuhci?   kahni:dih?á?,   ná
   She told her   that   little   wren   to take it   that

4. dawat   ku?á:na?.   kánímbaka?   nassa?a?ú:dih,   na?ínniyah
   basket   over there.   She told her,   "When you arrive   somewhere

5. a?ihsa?   tá:šah.   bah?nah,   tusdáwá:?áh,   wa?náh   ha?ahat
   he is   wolf."   It is said   she laid it on   each thing   well
                                               a platform for
                                               her,

6. tut?iyas?niháh   nátti?   há:yúh   bah?nah   tusdímbíhnidáh,
   she prepared for her,   then   on top   it is said   she laid for her

7. kakkanduc,ah.   kánnúmbaka?,   ná   dúhya?   nassâybáw?á?   síná
   mud.   She said to her, "That   now   if you see him   like this
                                         one

8. dah?úmbah?nah.   dí   ibát   ci?nadihah.   cičandu?nadihah
   you tell him."   "This   grand-   I'm taking it   I'm taking mud
                                father   to him.   to him

9. t,ánk,uh   kah?a?nih?a?.   bah?náh   háhiyah,   háhiyah.
   pipe   to make."   It is said   she went   she went.

10. ku?á:na?   bah?nah,   hákah?í?asuh.   kánímbaka?   kwídá:dihah.
    Over there   it is said   he was coming.   He said to   "Where are you
                                                      her,   going?"

11. kánnúmbaka?,   ibát   cičandu?nadihah   t,ánk,uh   nah?a?na?.
    She told him,   "Grand-   I'm taking mud   pipe   so he can
                       father   to him   make."

12. ná   tá:šah   kámbaka?,   kúy?a?   hít,usbah.   síná   kut,ihah.
    That   wolf   said,   "Let me see   let me look   Like   I am.
                                                       at it.   that

13. wín?t,á?   kú:?nutah   nast,án?a?na?   t,ánk,uh.   bah?nah
    Also   I like   to make them   pipes."   It is said

14. isikáwní:yáh   way?šah   wán?ti?   dika?háy   dínt,áhnah.
    he put his hand in   indeed   all   things   he ate up on her.

15. bah?nah   sínáttí?   hákíyánniyah.   ku?á:na?   bah?náh
    It is said   then   he chased her.   Over there   it is said

16. hákakkidáwsa?,   ká:k'ay?.   ahaꞩꞩáh   bah?náh   háhnáy?áwsa?.
    he was sitting on a   crow.   Really   it is said   he was singing.
    branch

17. kúsidí,   ná   t'i?   kámbaka?,   hákkutáyní:?asuh
    After a while   that   little   she said,   "He's following me
                  one

18. ná   tá:ꞩah.   sínátti?   bah?nah   kánímbaka?   dá:yahyuh
    that   wolf."   Then   it is said   he said to her,   "You go in

19. kúkku:sú:?a?.   bah?nah   sínátti?,   dí   á:yhah   kúh?isú:?a?.
    where my nose is."   It is said   then   this   she went   where his
                                       one   in   nose is.

20. bah?nah   ukkih   bah?nahway?   ná   cah   tá:ꞩah
    It is said   really   in fact   that   Mr.   Wolf

21. hússaháyní:?asuh.   kámbaka?   sidí   hít?ínámmah.   bah?náh
    he was following!   He said,   "This   she flew."   It is said
                                   way

22. ná   ká:k'ay?   ahaꞩꞩáh   dáhnáy?áwsa?.   kín?a?nihah
    that   crow   really   he was singing   He was making
                            there.

23. kánday.   bah?náh   háhbak'ihsa?
    a wooden bowl.   It is said   he was saying:

24. ahaꞩꞩáh   bah?nah   táh?áwwiꞩꞩiyah   ná   tá:ꞩah   bah?náh
    Really   it is said   when he arrived   that   wolf   it is said

5. háhúmbak'ihsa?,   ná   sídat'ihah.   ahassáh   ha?ímáy

   he is saying to him.   "That   what's the matter   Really   big
                                   with you?

6. háka:sú:dí:t'a?.   kánnúmbaka?   si?ídãnt'a?.   wít   híssahbin?

   you have a bump   He said to him,   "What happened Your-   did you hit
   on your nose."   to you?   self

7. kúkâ:nihsa?   ná   kánday.   hun?náh,   híkku?bin?   na

   where you are   that   wooden bowl?"   "No,   I got hit   by
   making

8. nidún   kwíhcitáywan.   baka?,   nuka?   sah?atáyánnáhdu?wa?

   ball   where I played."   He said,   "Maybe   can you do it

9. kúkâ:suhí?usa?,   bah?nah,   kakúdah?náwkáybah.   kánímbaka?,

   where you blow   it is said,   without feeling pain?"   He said to him,
   your nose,[1]

10. háwwih,   citáyáncáybáw?a?.   bah?nah   ukkih   kudí

    "All right,   I will try."   It is said   really   away

11. náh?ínánniyah,   ciyuhci?.   bah?náh   di:yúníh?nah.

    she flew   wren.   It is said   she escaped.

Text 5: The Old Woman and the Elves

1. bah?nah   ahyá?   tikí   háh?í:?a?   ha?ímáyci?,

   It is said   in the past   far   there lived   old person,

2. sah?ya?ti?.   bah?nah   kayttut'áyáh?áh   dika?háy   háh?a?nihsa?

   It is said   she would make   dika?háy   something   she is doing
                     an effort

3. háhisciyah.   bah?nah   nasayahcudah   bah?nah   áwnáw?a?

   all day.   It is said   when she got   it is said   she sat down
                                     tired

4. kaypbahsáy?unah   nuka?,   kakitánkahyún?a?.   kwí:yáwtáhdih

   she would call   maybe   trying to get help.   No one was
                                                            interested

5. kakitánkahyún?a?.   sínátti?   bah?nah   síttut'ihnah   bah?nah

   in helping her.   Then   it is said,   suddenly   it is said

6. nasáykún?nah   c'i?ahyá?ti?   nasa:nihá:hit   wán?ti?

   when it was evening   in the morning   when she gets up   all

---

[1]I.e., I wonder if you can blow your nose...

7. dika?háy   kúha?ahat.   nídih?abín?,   ha?ahat   wán?ti?
   things   well.[1]   It was swept,   well   all

8. dika?háy   kúhasak'ay   háhunčidín?a?.   dika?háy   wán?ti?
   things   clean   they were lying   Things   all
                                 on the table.

9. kahutánnáwsit.   bah?nah   sínátti?,   títdiscah,   wa?náh
   completely.   It is said   then,   every day   each

10. dika?háy   áwyah?úhdin?ná?   t,i?   nahwa?áh   yahyasatci?
    something   she would save   a little for them   elves
                                to eat

11. hússahánnabahsa?.   bah?nah   nápba?   sáwáwdihah   ha?ahat
    they were the ones!   It is said   at night   they came   well

12. hákit,abí?sa?   hákitacáywatáh?nisa?,   hákincahi?sa?.   bah?nah
    they swept for   they cleaned the place   they washed her   It is said
    her   dishes.

13. dika?háy   wa?náh   kidímmá?wa?.   kúhúmbahsúncidín?a?
    something   each   she would leave   On her willow table
                           on the table.

14. dika?háy   nakkissa?.   nasánk,a?niháh   ha?ahat   háhun?k,í?sa?.
    things   it was to   When she made the   good   she had a fire.
                 lay on.   fire

15. bah?nah   ná   t'i?   yahyasatci?   sahas?náwwáyáhah   nápba?
    It is said   those   little   elves   they would eat   at nigh

16. nasáwáwdáh,   ná   kúhuca?k,a?   nakihas?náwyah,
    when they came,   that   where her wooden   table
                             object is

17. kahbahsúncidínna?ah.   nátti?   bah?nah   síttutáyyakíhnáh,
    that which is a willow   Then   it is said   later on
    table.[2]

18. wáy?sah   wa?náh,   dika?háy   hákimmissa?   nápba?.
    different   each   things   they brought   at night.

19. bah?nah   c,i?ahyá?ti?   hác,ihúnda?a?   dika?háy,
    It is said   in the morning   it's already hung   things,
                             up for her

---

[1]I.e., between the evening and the morning when she got up, everything was taken care of.

[2]I.e., they would eat from her table.

0. | da?, | nú?, | hi?nuh | náw?ci? | kakk'aš?ah. | dika?háy |
   |------|------|--------|---------|-------------|----------|
   | deer, | turkey, | perhaps | bear | leg. | Things |

1. | wa?náh | háhda?a?. | ná | kúkahánná:bah | yahyašatci?. |
   |--------|----------|-----|---------------|-------------|
   | each | hand. | Those | it was just them | elves. |

2. | bah?nah | dihaš?náwyáhdi?nah | tutáyánnah | kwí:yáwtáhdih |
   |---------|--------------------|-----------|---------------|
   | It is said | they fed her | because | no one cared |

3. kakitánkahyún?a?.

   to help her.

ext 6: The Transformed Husband and the Elf

1. | bah?nah | ahyá? | tikí, | háhnámmiht'a?. | wísc'i? | náttih |
   |---------|-------|-------|----------------|--------|--------|
   | It is said | in the past | far | there was a village. | One | woman |

2. | háh?í:?a?. | háyá:nuh | háhúnt'a?. | síttutáyyakíhnáh | bah?nah |
   |------------|----------|-----------|-------------------|---------|
   | she was there. | Person | she had.[1] | Sometime later | it is said |

3. | háhwíswá:yah | ná | šú:wi? | kah?íyáh?ah. | síttutcanna?ahnah |
   |--------------|-----|--------|-------------|-------------------|
   | they two journeyed | that | man | so he could hunt. | A certain number of days |

4. | nuka? | háhíwá:yah, | nuka? | dahaw? | hiwi?. | nappáwdihšiyah |
   |-------|-------------|-------|--------|--------|----------------|
   | perhaps | they journeyed, | perhaps | three | four. | When they arrived |

5. | kwíhándáw?ah | kúh?áw?ih?á? | kahnah?wa?nih?á? | nuka? | na |
   |---------------|--------------|-------------------|-------|-----|
   | at a camp site | where they would camp | to make a fire | perhaps | where |

6. | haš?náwwá:yáh | dika?háy | kúh?akas?ni?wá? | ná | sah | háyá:nuh. |
   |----------------|----------|-------------------|-----|------|-----------|
   | they eat | something | where she would cook | that | Ms. | Person. |

7. | bah?nah | t'i? | pit'uhci? | háhnu?ín?t'a?. | bah?nah |
   |---------|-------|-----------|----------------|---------|
   | It is said | little | terrier | they two had. | It is said |

8. | títdisča?áh | c'i?ahyá?ti? | nasa:nihá:yáh | kaytdiyah. |
   |--------------|--------------|----------------|-----------|
   | every day | in the morning | when he got up | he would go. |

9. | háhwitáyyah | háhwitáyyah | bah?nah | nasáykún?nah |
   |--------------|--------------|---------|--------------|
   | He was gone | he was gone[2] | it is said | when it was evening |

0. | áwwit?a?. | ná | pit'uhci? | kambaka? | háwwih | iyay?. |
   |-----------|-----|-----------|---------|--------|--------|
   | he would return. | That | terrier | said, | "All right, | older sister. |

---

[1] I. e., she had a husband.

[2] I. e., he kept being gone.

11. citáynáhyún'a'.   kaytcí:bah   hikat'a'nihah.   kwít'adihah

    I will follow him.   I'm going to see   what he is doing.   Where he goes

12. dí   dahay'   dúhya'   nasa'yat.   háwwih

    this   brother-in-law now   when he goes."[1]   "All right,"

13. kánímbaka'   dáháybah.   dah'utáyni'at.   bah'nah   kútikí:sah

    she said to her. "Look and see.   Follow him."   It is said   at a distance

14. háhutáyní:yah.   síttutáyyakíhnáh   bah'nah   da'čah

    she followed him.   Sometime later   it is said   gun

15. áwyátáh'nah.   ínámbín'unah.   bah'nah   kutí   dika'háy

    he leaned it.   He rolled (on the   It is said   on the   something
                       ground).   other side

16. húšnu'   sáy'ah.   bah'nah   háhiyah.   ha'ímáy   háhacá:wisa'

    different   he was.   It is said   he went on. Big   there was a
                                                                            clearing

17. bahkahih.   nátti'   bah'nah   ná   dika'háy   hikítdabahsa'

    in the woods.   There   it is said   those   things   whatever they wer

18. naytda:yáhah   bah'nah   háhutámmabín'usa'.   has'nih

    the one(s) that   it is said   they were wrestling.   In the spring
    would eat you

19. kínháy'ah.   sínátti'   bah'nah   ná   t'i'   pit'uhci'

    it was.   Then   it is said   that   little   terrier

20. ahuhnáh   kánnúmbaka'.   iyay'   kíht'úmbaka'

    she went back she said to her.   "Older   I told you
                                      sister,

21. citáyni:dih'a'.   ci:báwnah.   da'čah   áwyátáh'nah

    I would follow him.   I saw him.   Gun   he leaned it

22. ínámbín'unah   sidí   nat'a'nihšiyah   dika'háy   húšnu'

    he rolled   that   after he had done   something   different

23. sáy'ah.   háwwih   sidáwcáh'áh   hí'awihtahyúh,   hasuwah

    he was.   All right,   what do you think, let's go home,   hurry up

24. dáhkacánčidú:ni'.   hatidu'   kakúc'itdisk'anah.   ná

    gather your things.   Hot   before the sun   Those
                                            becomes."

25. háhwíswá:yah   háhwíswá:yah   nat'akacánčidú:ni'ah.   ku'á:na'

    they two journeyed they two journeyed after she gathered   Over there
                                            her things.

_____

[1]Mrs. Weller added later that they were suspicious of the husband because he
was gone all day, but was not bringing back any game.

26. bah?nah   kúsidí   dika?háy   níhbahsáy?   kah?abímbahsáy?

it is said   after a while   something   made a noise   wings fluttering

27. kah?áwwih.   bah?nah   t·i?   yahyašatci?   hákah?ánkisa?.

descending.   It is said   little   elf   he was standing.

28. kwídá?ítdihah.   ciwihtáwáynihah.   hákku?íntáyní:?asuh.   háyá:nuh

"Where are you two   "We're running away.   He's following us.   Person
going?"

29. híkkut'ihah   náná   dika?háy   hússáy?ahsa?   húšnu?.

I had   that   something   he was   different.[1]
                                       (exclamatory)

30. ciwihtahyúnhah.   háwwih   kani?ímbaka?.   bah?nah

We're going home."   "All right,"   he told the two.   It is said

31. kac'ihikún?nah.   ici?   nuka?   háhnu?íš?núnt'a?.   díh?nah

it was late in the   Although   perhaps   they two had had   But
evening.   their lunch.

32. kámbaka?   nátti?   kutí   dah?ínnahsa?   nasawkámmáh

he said,   "There   on the   lie in the brush,   when we hear him
                     other side

33. sínátti?   dí   kúhci:yuhsa?   nátti?   dah?íttáwka?ahni?.

then   this   where I pluck it   there   you two lie underneath."

34. bah?nah   pítta:bihnáh   ná   nátti?   bahšúnčippá:?áh

It is said   they two lay down   those   there   he piled branches
                                         on them

35. nátti?   bah?nah   ná   kúhní:?náy?ahsa?   kúh?iyuhsa?

there   it is said   those   with feathers   with the pluckings

36. ná   nú?.   bah?nah   háhut'áyá:sa?   ná

(from) that   turkey.   It is said   he was engaged in   that

37. yahyašatci?   kahdáysahwa?.   wáy?   háhwíttáwka?ah?a?

elf   roasting.   Indeed   they two were lying underneath

38. kúhní:t'isdatčah.   bah?nah   kúha?ahat   daškuhih   kaháynah

where the feathers   It is said   just   dark   having become
were piled.

39. kúsidí   níhbahsay?   kah?í:kuh.   háh?í:?asuh   háh?í:?asuh

after a while   he was heard   roaring.   He was coming   he was coming

40. kúná:nuh   háhbašwabáwsa?.   bah?nah   ná   yahyašatci?

plainly   they heard him.   It is said   that   elf

---

[1]I. e., "I had a husband but he turned out to be some other kind of thing."

41. háh⁷áwsa⁷.   kúsidí   bah⁷nah   dammínnáhsukâ:nihah.
    he was sitting.   After a while   it is said   he made a notch in a branch.

42. níttáhsukâ:nihah.   nattáhsukâ:niháh   bah⁷nah   cáwáy
    He went ahead and made a   After he had made the it is said   bow
    notch.   notch

43. háhu⁷nín⁷a⁷.   bah⁷nah   kúsidí   áwwidáh,   kánímbaka⁷.
    he had lying.   It is said   after a   he arrived,   he said to him,
                                        while

44. t'úsa⁷íkkáybáwnáh   dí   háyá:nuh.   t'ámmahwihtáhdáh   dítti⁷
    "Did you see the two   those   people.   Did the two pass by   here

45. ínniyah.   kánímbaka⁷   núkka⁷.   ná   ici⁷   hikatda⁷ah
    somewhere?"   He said to him, "I don't   That   indeed   what is it
                                      know.

46. kutí   háhní:⁷na:ni⁷a⁷   hikat⁷ínka⁷áy⁷ah   ná.
    on the other there are feathers   what is lying under-   that?"
    side   neath

47. bah⁷nah   kwíh⁷áwsáycahah   háki:cahsiyah   ná   yahyasatci⁷.
    It is said   as he was about to jump   he shot him   that   elf.
                                           there

48. bah⁷nah   kutí   áwwí:siyah   kínnakâ:ca:wáy⁷hah.
    It is said   on the other   he fell there.   He started to jump over
                 side   the fire.

49. bah⁷nah   áwsahyáh,   kúka⁷ukí:huhnáh   húki:cahsa⁷   bah⁷nah
    It is said   he got down,   he started back   he was shot   it is said
                                                       just then

50. kutí   áwwí:siyah.   bah⁷nah   ha⁷ahat   tun⁷k'a⁷nihah
    on the other he fell there.   It is said   well   he built up the
    side   fire

51. takáhdi⁷náh   ná   dika⁷háy.   bah⁷nah   sínátti⁷   ná
    he burned him   that   thing.   It is said   then   those

52. píttáwháydáh   bah⁷nah.   háhas⁷náwwáyáhsa⁷   nú⁷   háhwa⁷áhsa⁷.
    the two got up   it is said.   They ate a meal   turkey   they ate.

53. nappa⁷áhcúh⁷náh,   sínátti⁷   kani⁷ímbaka⁷   háwwih.
    After they ate,   then   he said to the   "All right.
                                          two,

54. kúsah⁷ítdikíh,   tucaáynih   c'i⁷ahyá⁷ti⁷   dah⁷ihtáhdi⁷a⁷.
    Go to sleep,   enough time   in the morning   you two can go on.

55. ci:káyá⁷t'awih⁷a⁷   ná   kaht'áwíkkáybah   háhinassah.
    I will sit by the fire   there   to watch over you   through the night.

6. ya?awihtanayaht'anah.   c'i?ahyá?ti?   tikí   dah?wihtáhdi?a?.
    You two rest.   In the morning   early   you can go on."

7. háwwih   kánímbaka?.   bah?nah   r.á   kúsibít   pítdikí:náh
    "All right,"   they said to him. It is said   those both   they two went
                                                                     to sleep

8. dí?ci'   húhúnt'a?.   c'i?ahyá?ti?   tikí   bah?nah
    dog   she with it.   In the morning   early   it is said

9. kwíhut?iyah?wá:yúh   ná   nú?   bah?nah   náná   t'a?
    what they had left from   that   turkey   it is said   that   also
    it

0. piht'áhnah.   wáy?   ahnah   bah?nah   dáskát
    they two ate.   Indeed   they them-   it is said   bread
                                  selves

1. háhnu?ín?t'a?.   dí   kaniwihtiháh   kwíhut?iyah?ú:kih.
    they two had.   Those   he gave them   what he had left.

2. háhwíswá:yah   háhwíswá:yah.   bah?nah   tikí   ku?á:na?,
    They two journeyed   they two journeyed.   It is said   far   over there

3. kánímbaka?   ná   yahyasatci?.   ná   dí   dúhya?
    he said to them   that   elf.   "Now   this   now

4. hákah?íswá:yah.   ku?á:na?   nasah?áwítníwdih   ínniyah
    you two are journeying. Over there   when you two arrive   somewhere

5. dah?i:dakáywa?ut   ha?ímáy   kahdahsukah?i?.   ná   kúhdahsukah?a?
    look for a tree   big   with a hollow   That   in the hollow place
                                      place.

6. nátti?   dah?wít?yahyuh.   nac'issah?ít?yáyhah   ná   pit'uhci?
    there   go in.   When you go in   that   terrier

7. hí?it'aw?   naswacih.   sínátti?   dahsú:du?á?   díh?nah
    let him sit   by the door.   Then   the tree will   but
                                                close up

8. dí   kaytámmak'í?   kúkahucaáynih   ná   pit'uhci?
    this   hole will be   enough for it   that   terrier
             there

9. kúh?isu:sáy?wa?.   nátti?   bah?nah   háhwíswá:yah
    for her nose to stick   Then   it is said   they two journeyed
    out."

70. háhwíswá:yah   ná   háhisciyah.   bah?nah   kúha?ahat
    they two journeyed   that   all day.   It is said   just

71. kahikún?nah   pihdanda?káh   ná   kahdahsukah?í?   pít?yayhah
    in the evening   they two found   that   with the hollow   they two went
                           the tree   place   in

72. kûsikiki?îmbah?nah.   bah?nah   ná   sah   háyá:nuh   kúha?ahat

    just as they had been   It is said   that   Ms.   Person   just
    told.

73. háh?áwyahdatčah   háh?ikkihsa?   ná   pit·uhci?   háh?áwsa?

    she leaned back   she slept   that   terrier   she sat

74. kuká?kah.   ná   nu?uhti?   yahyasatci?   hússahyá:sa?.

    in front.   That   nearby   elf   he was there!

75. hušnu?   t·a?   nú?   di?încí:?ah.   ná   c·ippihcaš?ah.

    Different   also   turkey   he killed for   Those   they two were on
    the two.   their way.

76. nadahaw?   c·ittu?îtcač·ah.   háhwíswá:yah   háhwíswá:yah

    The third   it was the day.   They two journeyed they two journeyed.

77. kánímbaka?   ná   nayahyasatci?.   t·awihtánáyátdírmáw?ni?a?.

    She was told   that   by the elf.   "I'll accompany you two.

78. tikí   háysi?   nassah?áwít?níwdih   kiwat.   bah?nah

    Far   still   when you two arrive   home."   It is said

79. bitiht·i?   kiwát   kahwítniwit   sínátti?   bah?nah

    close to   home   they two being   then   it is said
    there

80. ná   sah   náttih   dínnihah   ná   nayahyasatci?   ná   čawáy,

    that   Ms.   Woman   she was given   that   by the elf   that   bow

81. bá?   t·ana?.   kánímbaka?   háwwih.   dika?háy   ínniyah

    arrow   also.   He said to her,   "All right.   Some   somewhere

82. nassah?yankadínda?ah.   nassah?áwnit·a?   dá?,   nú?,   náw?ci?,

    when you find charred wood.   If you want   deer,   turkey,   bear,

83. dika?háy   hikatda?ah?a?,   tú?   dah?yankadíncah.

    something   whatever it will be,   go ahead   shoot the charred wood.

84. nassah?yankadíncahkáh   dáw?k·anah   nakakáwnit·a?.   hikatda?ah?a?

    When you have shot the   name   whatever you   Whatever it wil
    charred wood   want.   be

85. náná   dah?at·ih?a?.   ní?ítdiscah   wa:sah   kúsah?anah?núh?a?.

    that   you will have.   Someday   never   you will not be
    hungry."

86. bah?nah   háhwíswá:yah   háhwíswá:yah.   bitiht·i?   kiwát

    It is said   they two journeyed they two journeyed.   Close to   home

87. kahwítniwit,   sínátti?   bah?nah   íncahkah,   kahyankadíncah

    they two being there,   then   it is said   she shot some-   charred wood.
    thing lying,

8. bah'nah   wayah   ka'uht'uh   pînhahyú:náh,

   It is said   much   meat   they two took home,

9. pítnîwdiss̆ah   háyyûhnáh   sikíhúnt'a'.   ná   kúsinah.

   they two arrived there   she told   what had   That   is all.
                                                   happened.

SMITHSONIAN MISCELLANEOUS COLLECTIONS
VOLUME 87, NUMBER 6

COMPOSITION OF THE CADDOAN LINGUISTIC STOCK

BY
ALEXANDER LESSER and GENE WELTFISH
New York, N. Y.

(PUBLICATION 3141)

CITY OF WASHINGTON
PUBLISHED BY THE SMITHSONIAN INSTITUTION
MAY 14, 1932

The Lord Baltimore Press
BALTIMORE, MD., U. S. A.

COMPOSITION OF THE CADDOAN LINGUISTIC STOCK[1]

By ALEXANDER LESSER and GENE WELTFISH

New York, N. Y.

CLASSIFICATION

The Caddoan linguistic stock, named after the language of the Caddo, is composed of four major languages, Pawnee, Wichita, Kitsai,[2] and Caddo. Of these, the Kitsai had never developed dialectic differentiation; the Wichita and Caddo probably each included several dialects, but as at present spoken are known only in one form; and the Pawnee today occurs in three dialects. On the basis of present knowledge, the broad relationships of the four languages can be indicated as follows: Pawnee, Wichita, and Kitsai are, in relation to each other, about equally divergent, save that Kitsai in phonetic structure and some forms is probably closer to Pawnee than Wichita is to Pawnee. All three, however, are mutually unintelligible. Caddo is the most divergent of the four languages. The general interrelationships of these languages and their dialects can be summarized by the following table:[3]

---

[1] Based on field research for the Committee on American Indian Languages.

[2] The authors have preferred this spelling of Kichai. Kitsai approximates more closely the phonetic character of the native name.

[3] In the transcription of native names and words of this treatment, the authors have followed the recommendations embodied in Phonetic Transcription of Indian Languages, Smithsonian Misc. Coll., vol. 66, no. 6, September, 1916. Briefly summarized, the characteristics represented are as follows:

Consonants:

b, m, n, h, and y have their usual values.

p, t, and k (except in Caddo) are intermediates, neither quite sonant nor quite surd. Pawnee final t is nasalized, indicated by superior n (t[n]). Caddo t is surd d sonant; Caddo k is, however, intermediate.

s is throughout surd, somewhat more sibilant than English s.

c is the usual sound of sh in English show.

x closely approximates the ch of German ich.

r in Pawnee and Arikara is a single trilled r made with the tip of the tongue on the alveolar ridge (see also Boas, Handbook of American Indian Languages, Bull. 40, Bur. Amer. Ethnol., pt. 1, p. 17, 1911); in Kitsai and Wichita where a distinct n occurs, the r more nearly approximates the English r, but it is never made as far back in the mouth or trilled as strongly. Caddo r is more strongly trilled.

The affricative ts is intermediate where t is intermediate. In Caddo it is surd.

I. Pawnee, Kitsai, and Wichita.

A. Pawnee: a) South Band Pawnee (or Pawnee proper);
spoken by:
pi·tǫhaɯíra·tᵃ
tsąwî·'�
kɩ́tkǫhaxkiˣ
b) Skiri[1] Pawnee
c) Arikara

B. Kitsai: tįkítsɛ's band of the Wichita.

C. Wichita: a) Wichita proper, spoken by:
toka'nɛ
ɩsí·s
tiwá·
ɩtá·
kɩrikɩrí·s
ɑkwi·ts
b) Probably dialectically divergent:
tawakǫrúw'
wéku'

II. Caddo: a) Caddo proper; spoken by:
nada'rko
nacįdóc
ya't'ɑs
nak'ohǫdo'tsi
ha'i·c
kayǫmáici
kado'ǫdátc'ᵘ
b) Hainai; spoken by:
hainai
nabadáịtcu
?c) ? Adai

---

[1] Skiri is used herein for Skidi.   The d of earlier records is the Pawnee r; see the phonetic key above.

---

tc has its usual affricative character in Caddo, while in Arikara it is more intermediate.

w is slightly more rounded than in English.

Vowels:

With a few exceptions, the symbols for vowels indicate the usual continental values as follows: *a* as in father; a (Greek alpha) as u in but; *e* as a in fate; ɛ (Greek epsilon) as e in met; *i* as ee in feet; ɩ (Greek iota) as i in hit; *o* as o in go; *u* as oo in hoot.   Exceptional is ɛ in Pawnee, where in making the sound the lips are very

SUBDIVISIONS

PAWNEE

Of the three Pawnee dialects, that known as South Band Pawnee or Pawnee proper preserves the oldest forms of Pawnee. The dialect of the Skiri differs from the South Band Pawnee primarily in phonetics. Speeds, lengths, and tones differ between these dialects; but most important is the fact that the phonetic changes which have occurred have resulted in Skiri in the loss of a number of vowel and consonant distinctions that are found in South Band Pawnee. As a result, what was already a meager phonetic system in Pawnee proper is still further reduced in Skiri.[1] While it may well be true that historically—as tradition claims—the Arikara dialect diverged from a root which was once common to Arikara and Skiri, nevertheless on the basis of a comparison of the three Pawnee dialects as spoken today, the Arikara divergences should be treated in relation to the Pawnee proper or South Band dialect, rather than in relation to the speech of the Skiri. The phonetic divergence of Arikara can be characterized in two ways: first, there are many shifts of vowels and consonants, numbering many more than those which differentiate Pawnee proper and Skiri; and second, in Arikara enunciation whole syllables are lost to the ear through elision and whispering of the vowels. Today, South Band and Skiri dialects are almost fully mutually intelligible; older natives understand the speech of the other group but reply in their own, while among the young people there is a tendency to develop a mixed dialect which overrides the differentiation of the two. Skiri and Arikara generally insist that they can understand one another, and some do; but

---

[1] Material on which these statements and those referring to the Arikara are based, as well as the details of the phonetic shifts, will be given in an analytic study of comparative text material.

---

wide, the aperture between them forming a very narrow slit; and *e* in Pawnee which does not have the usual diphthongal quality.

ω (Greek omega) of Wichita is the aw of English law.

ai of Caddo is the diphthong of English height.

Diacritical marks:

The glottal catch (') and the aspiration (ʻ) are used in the usual way. Stress accent is indicated by (ʹ) after the syllable (aʹ). Vowel length is indicated by (·) after the vowel (a·); vowel shortness by (‿) under the vowel (a̧). Pitch accents are (á) for high tone, (ȧ) for middle high. Tone combinations occurring in Pawnee are: (â·) high to middle high, (ä·) normal to middle high, (ǎ·) middle high to normal, (á·) middle high to high.

Whispered or slightly articulated sounds are indicated as superior symbols (tº).

for the most part, this seems due more to their control of a smattering of the other dialect than to any inherent possibilities of intelligibility, which are in fact slight because of the character of the phonetic changes which have taken place. Actually an Arikara was not able to understand a Skiri text, but was at once able to grasp the same text in South Band Pawnee and translate or transpose it into Arikara. There is still current among the Pawnee a tradition that the K̦ąwárä·kɩs group of the Pi·tᶏhawíra·tᵃ spoke like the Arikara. It is impossible at the present day to check this tradition, and it seems unlikely that it was true. The few suggestions of linguistic difference between K̦ąwárä·kɩs speech and Pawnee proper which can be obtained, point rather to earlier dialectic differences in the speech of the South Bands. Traditions support this view strongly, all South Band Pawnees of the older generations insisting that when the bands lived apart there were differences in their speech, which disappeared after they came to live together. Texts taken from the oldest living representatives of each band failed to show any vestige of such differences remaining today.

The Pawnees have no name for themselves which includes as a unity the four bands of Tskiri, Tsᶏwí·ⁱ, Pi·tᶏhawíra·tᵃ, and Kɩtkᶏhaxkiˣ. These bands were known to themselves and to each other by their band names. The absence of a general tribal name reinforces other evidence for the fact that the four bands never formed an integrated tribal unity; in fact, they were in former times independent tribal groups. They often banded together for the buffalo hunt and other collective enterprises. But the Skiri, for example, were no more likely to join the three South Bands for a buffalo hunt in the early nineteenth century, than they were to join the Omahas and Poncas. This fact of the essential political independence of each of the bands is too often overlooked, in part because the United States Government has for long dealt with all the Pawnees as one group.

The words "chahiksichahiks" (tsᶏhiksɩtsahiks), often quoted as the name of the Pawnees for themselves[1], has quite a different use. It is not a word for the Pawnees as distinguished from other Indians. tsᶏhiks—is "person", "human being", the generic word, as distinct from words for "man", "woman". In the combination the connective—ɩ—has prepositional value rendered somewhat by the translation "men of men" or "people of people". This combination "men of men" implies "civilization" on the part of the persons

---

[1] Fletcher, A. C., Handbook of American Indians, Bull. 30, Bur. Amer. Ethnol. (cited hereafter as Handbook), pt. 2, p. 214, 1910.

referred to. tsǎhiksti'ᶜ, "he's a man", "he's really a human being", implies the idea that a man's ways are civilized, well-mannered, gentle. A wild, ill-mannered, mean man would be called tsǎhikskaki'ᶜ, "he's not a human being". Thus tsǎhiksįtsahiks is applied by the Pawnees not alone to themselves but also to other Indian groups of .their acquaintance whom they considered civilized, such as the Poncas and Omahas. In a general way it was also used for Indians as opposed to white men.[1]

The name Pawnee is one which was first applied to the Pawnees by white men. It seems unlikely for linguistic reasons that its use came from parí·ku', "horns", as suggested in the Handbook.[2] Our informants claimed that it derived from parí·sᵘ', "hunter" (Skiri dialect). They said that the first Pawnees to meet white men were on the hunt, and that when the white men asked, "Who are you?" an Indian answered, "parĩ·sᵘ'", "a hunter". In the light of this possible derivation, it is interesting to note that the spelling of Pawnee on the early maps is "panis", and also that in more recent years several recorders have written Pawnee "r's" as "n's" because of the peculiar phonetic character of the Pawnee "r". Clearly from "les panis" a derived singular would be pani or Pawnee.[3]

The Skiri derive their name from the word for the wolf. In present day usage this is tskįrⁱxkⁱˣ (adding the diminutive), but it may well have been the shorter form earlier (tskiri). The Skiri were known ʈɔ themselves and to other tribes as "wolves".[4] Their war whoop was the cry of the wolf, and for deception on the warpath and in scouting they dressed as wolves, and signalled each other vocally with wolf cries.[5] In war dances where combat is dramatized the warriors act like wolves. A mythological background for this

---

[1] This usage is also quoted from Hayden, Handbook, pt. 2, p. 216.

[2] Handbook, pt. 2, p. 213.

[3] Some years ago James R. Murie suggested to F. W. Hodge *pares*ᵘ as the origin of Pawnee, and told the same story about it. See Amer. Anthrop., n. s., vol. 17, pp. 215–216, 1915. Apparently the story is a general Pawnee tradition.

[4] Dunbar, J., in Mag. Amer. Hist., vol. 4, p. 259, 1880, offers as explanation of the name Skiri the association of this group of Pawnees with the Loup (Wolf) River, which in turn was so called because of the abundance of wolves along the stream. Pawnees of today still recall that wolves were abundant along the Loup River in early days. It seems reasonable to believe that such a wolf-teeming habitat had an important influence on Skiri Pawnee cultural forms, and thus was indirectly responsible for the name.

[5] Grinnell, G. B., Pawnee hero stories and folk tales (cited hereafter as Grinnell), pp. 245–248, 1890, describes these methods of deception in some detail; the statements made herein are based on information from present-day informants.

conception is furnished by an incident in the story of Lightning's visit to the earth carrying all people in a sack. The Wolf-Star, being jealous of the Evening-Star who has sent Lightning to the earth, sends a wolf to steal Lightning's pack. When the people come out and observe the wolf's strange behavior, they kill him, thus introducing death into the world. Lightning tells them to skin the wolf, and to keep its hide on their sacred bundle. He tells them also that wolves will multiply, and that they shall be known as Tskiri.[1]

While there was no name for the four Pawnee bands together, an old informant stated that in Nebraska the Skiri used to speak of the other three bands together as tɥhä·wɩtⁿ (in South Band dialect the word is tuxrä·wɩtⁿ) which means "village-east". This evidently refers to the position of these bands in relation to the Skiri. The orientation of the Pawnee bands in Nebraska according to present informants was schematically as follows:[2]

```
                        N
W    tskiri    kɩtkɑhaxkiˣ    tsąwî·'ɩ    pi·tɑhawíra·tᵃ    E
                        S
```

It is a matter of interest that contrary to the theoretical statements that the Pawnees always maintained the same orientations of the bands, the band locations in Oklahoma are about as follows:

```
               N
                                   tskiri
W    tsąwî·'ɩ                                    E
         kɩtkɑhaxkiˣ
               pi·tɑhawíra·tᵃ
               S
```

The three bands which spoke South Band dialect or Pawnee proper did not, however, have any name for themselves as a unit group. Nevertheless restrictions upon intermarriage between bands

---

[1] Dorsey, G. A., Traditions of the Skidi Pawnee, Mem. Amer. Folklore Soc.' vol. 8, pp. 17–18, 1904.

[2] Dunbar, op. cit., pp. 257–258, discusses the location of the bands as they were oriented to each other in 1834. While his statements are ambiguous, their most likely interpretation would make the band orientation agree with the statements of our informants. Dunbar also gives tu'-ra-wit-u, eastern villages, as the name applied by the Skiri to the other bands.

Fletcher, A. C., Handbook, pt. 2, p. 214, gives the relative positions exactly as we have recorded them. Grinnell, p. 218, also gives this order. Inasmuch as our records were secured independently from Pawnees who had moved to Oklahoma from Nebraska, and who knew the facts only from memory and tradition, they are important confirmation of the earlier statements.

broke down earlier among the three South Bands, and marriages were tolerated between tsąwî·'ʹ and pi·tǫhawíra·tᵃ at a time when they were still frowned upon between any one of the three bands and the tskiri, indicating a closer affiliation of the peoples of the South Bands.

The name pi·tǫhawíra·tᵃ can be analyzed as meaning "man who goes east": pi·tα—"man", hawíra·tᵃ—"goes east." The latter is a combination derived from ǎ·wιtⁿ—"east" and írǎ·tᵃ—"one who goes."[1]

According to the writings of James R. Murie,[2] the pi·tǫhawíra·tᵃ were formed of two villages: the pi·tǫhawíra·tᵃ proper and the kawǫrǎ·kιs. Informants today state that while these two groups did not live apart, but formed one village, they did speak different dialects, as above noted, and also had independent bundles and ritual and ceremonial performances. The name kawǫrǎ·kιs simply refers to the fact that these were the people who had or owned the kawǫrá'ᵃ bundle, which seems to have been one of the most ancient bundles of the Pawnees, certainly the oldest of the pi·tǫhawíra·tᵃ bundles. An indication of the conceived relationship of the two groups is given by the kinship terms which they used for each other. The kawǫrǎ·kιs called the pi·tǫhawíra·tᵃ tskу̨'rus, "in-law", while the pi·tǫhawíra·tᵃ replied rįkurąkátskу̨'rusu', "they are in-laws to us".

kítkǫhaxki× means literally "little mud lodge". "On a hill", the meaning given by Grinnell[3], has no linguistic basis.

Murie speaks of four divisions of the kítkǫhaxki×:[4] "the kítkǫ-haxki× proper, the little kítkǫhaxki×, the Black Heads, and the karíki·su or 'one who stands in the circle to recite the creation ritual' ". A number of informants agree that there were not four divisions of the kítkǫhaxki× band. Informants state that there were two divisions, the kítkǫhaxki× proper, called kιtkǫhaxkisú-rąriksιsᵘ (rąríksιsᵘ, "real"), and the little kítkǫhaxki×, called

---

[1] Grinnell, p. 216, gives " 'down the stream', or east" as the meaning of this name. There are two usages for east in Pawnee, of which one means "outside through the entrance", referring to the fact that the doorway of the Pawnee earth lodge is oriented toward the Morning Star and the rising sun, hence eastward; while the second usage, ǎ·wιt as above, is related to the stem for floating, hence has a downstream connotation. As all rivers flowed eastward or southeastward from the Pawnee villages in Nebraska, the word has come to be used for east.

[2] Murie, J. R., Ceremonies of the Pawnee. To be published by the Bureau of American Ethnology.

[3] Op. cit., p. 216.

[4] Op. cit.; Grinnell, p. 241, speaks of three.

kɪtkɑhaxkɪ̞ripɑtski (kɪ̞ripɑtski, "small"), and that the latter group split off from the main band not more than three generations ago under a self-made chief, Curly-Chief, téktɕsaxkɑrɪxku. The camp of the kɪtkɑhaxkɪ̞ripɑtski was set up southeast of the main village. The Black Heads (pákskä·titⁿ) was the name of a society; and the karíkiˑsu was the woman's dance or ceremony before the planting of the corn. Between the kɪtkɑhaxkiˣ proper and the little kɪtkɑhaxkiˣ old informants claim there was a slight dialectic difference of speech; but they lived together in one village and as far back as memory and tradition go, their bundles and ceremonies were merged or the same.

The tsɑwîˑ‘ name, according to many Pawnee informants, has the reference "beggars."[1] This could not be established as a linguistic meaning; the closest similarity of the word seems to affiliate it with the stem for "doctoring". Nevertheless, we do not doubt that "beggars" had a relevance which has been lost. People of the other bands claim that the tsɑwîˑ‘ always came asking for meat, hence the name. Wissler, in a footnote to Murie,[2] states: "They are now known as tsɑwîˑ‘ or Chaui, a band sprung from tsákɪtä·ru— ɪtsɑt, coon; wiˑ‘ part of band". This derivation, on close linguistic analysis, does not seem likely; ɪtsɑt and ákɪtä·ru would combine into tsákɪtä·ru in South Band dialect, but ɪtsɑt and wiˑ‘ would combine into tsɑxwîˑ‘ not tsɑwîˑ‘.

The *Arikara* are called· arikɑrä·ru', "horns" or "elk", by the Pawnees, and they call the Pawnees *awáhu*. As the term Arikara is a good Pawnee and Caddoan word, the linguistic derivation of which is clear, it seems unlikely that, as has been contended, the name is not used by the Arikara for themselves.[3] The word means "elk".[4]

---

[1] Grinnell, p. 216, gives "in the middle" as the meaning of tsawiˑ‘. He probably derives this from a confusion of the name with the word tɑwe which means "among".

[2] Op. cit.

[3] Gilmore, M. R., The Arikara Book of Genesis, Pap. Michigan Acad. Sci., Arts, and Lett., vol. 12, p. 95, 1929.

[4] The Handbook, under the synonymy of Arikara, lists: "starrahe" from Bradbury's Travels in the Interior of America, and "star-rah-he" from Lewis and Clarke, the latter given by the explorers as the people's own name. Phonetically this is a good Caddoan (Pawnee or Arikara) word (tstarahi), and its suggestive correspondence to the "harahey" "arahey" of Coronado's expedition makes this a plausible alternative derivation of the Coronado name to awahi, the Wichita name for the Pawnees (see below). In the case of awahi, the possibility is that Wichitas spoke of Pawnees to the Spaniards, in that of "star-rah-he" that Turk or some other Pawnee told them about the Arikara.

The word given by Gilmore[1] as the Arikara name for themselves, "sanish" is saxnᵢc, paralleling the South Band word tsaxriks, meaning "person"; and "san-sanish" is clearly the Arikara analogue of the Pawnee tsaxriksᵢtsaxriks (tsąhiksᵢtsahiks) discussed above.

Awahu, the name used by the Arikaras for the Pawnees means "left behind"; it also occurs as the name of one of the Arikara villages.[2] Traditionally it is said to reflect the movements of the peoples, the fact that the Arikaras moved on to the north in the Pawnee migrations and left the Pawnees behind.

While the Arikara spoke of the Pawnees as *awahu*, they also knew the bands by their individual names. These they rendered as follows: stciˑri (tskiri);[3] wiˑtᵃhawíraˑᵃt (piˑtąhawíraˑtᵃ); tᵢtkᵃhaxtc (kᵢtkąhaxkiˣ); sąwíˑɑt (tsąwîˑᵗ).

KITSAI

This Caddoan language is known only as the speech of one small tribe of that name.   It was in recent historic times closely affiliated with the Wichita peoples, and Wichitas will be found consistently to give the Wichita name for the Kitsai as one of the bands of the Wichita tribe, although all are aware of the difference in speech. In culture the Kitsai became so similar to Wichita that it is almost impossible today to find characteristics that differentiate them.

The Kitsai language is closely related to both Pawnee and Wichita.   Comparisons of the three indicate that it is intermediate to the two others.   Many of the Kitsai forms show a striking relation to the Pawnee, while others bear as pronounced a resemblance to Wichita forms.   Kitsai resemblances are clearest with South Band Pawnee, and comparison with that Pawnee dialect indicates that these two—South Band Pawnee or Pawnee proper and Kitsai— have been most conservative in retaining old Caddoan forms of the northern Caddoan languages—Pawnee, Kitsai, Wichita.

The Kitsai language is practically extinct today.   Of six individuals reputed to know it, one woman knows some simple vocabulary, another seems to understand but is never known to express herself in the language; one man who pretends to speak some Kitsai has its words and forms inextricably confused with a smattering of Pawnee (Wichita being his native speech).   Thus only three can

---

[1] Op. cit.

[2] On Arikara village names see Gilmore, M. R., Notes on Arikara tribal organization, Indian Notes, vol. 4, no. 4, pp. 344–345, October, 1927.

[3] *Tschihri*, quoted in the Handbook, pt. 2, p. 216, from Maximilian as the Arikara name for the Pawnee, is clearly the Arikara version of tskiri, as here given.

be said to know any Kitsai, and these habitually talk in Wichita and use no English at all. Of these the man can control Kitsai in its simple forms well; one woman who speaks Kitsai and Wichita is not linguistically gifted in either, and is rather subnormal in intelligence; while one woman, Kai Kai, is thoroughly bilingual in Wichita and Kitsai, with a genuine talent for clear thought in language, and it is from her that a knowledge of Kitsai has been obtained and preserved. It may be said that only while she lives is Kitsai still existent; and she is now past 83.

So far as the Kitsai are known to other Caddoans as a group distinct from the Wichita-speaking peoples, they are known by phonetic variants of their own name.[1] The Wichita speak of the language as kí·tsɛ·s, while their own pronunciation is kitsías; their full name tikítsịas. The Pawnees call them kï·tsas. Their own name is said by Kai Kai to mean "going in wet sand"; while the Pawnees translate their version of it as "water turtle."

The Kitsai designate the various groups of the Wichita by the regular Wichita band names, and the Pawnees as awą́hi, the same name as that used by the Wichita for the Pawnee.

WICHITA

The Wichita language is spoken by eight of the nine bands of the Wichita tribe, all bands save the tikítsɛ·s or Kitsai. Today it consists of one dialect only, and there is no evidence in the speech as used by different Wichitas of former subdivision or divergence. But by tradition, and some casually remembered words and expressions, it seems probable that at least two of the Wichita bands spoke Wichita that was dialectically divergent to a minor degree.

Information obtained and cross-checked with a number of informants yielded the following list of former Wichita bands. It is probably as complete and accurate a list as can be secured at this late date: toka'nɛ, ɩsí·s, tiwá·, ɩtá·, kịrikịrí·s, ɑkwi·ts, tawakɑrú·ʷ·, wéku' (and tikítsɛ·s). James Mooney[2] lists nine bands, some of which are immediately identifiable with those above: thus kɩtikɩtish (kɩrɩkɩrish) for kịrikịrí·s; akwesh for ɑkwi·ts; tawakoni (tawakarehu) for tawakɑrú·ʷ·; and waco for wéku'. "kirishkitsu", although it is evidently intended for a Wichita-speaking group, may be an old Wichita name for the tikítsɛ·s: in which case it is kík'i·skitsu, meaning "water turtles", and forming an analogy to the meaning which

---

[1] Unless "kirishkitsu", as mentioned below is the old Wichita name for the Kitsai.

[2] Handbook, pt. 2, p. 947.

is given by the Pawnee proper for the Kitsai name. "Tawehash" may be a variant of tiwá·, possibly resulting from dialectic differences of pronunciation; the synonymy of the Handbook includes several Spanish variants, such as Teguayos, which seem to support this view.[1] "Yscani," suggested by Mooney on the evidence of Bolton as possibly another name for the wéku', an idea which is supported by the disappearance from historical records of the name Yscani at the time wéku' makes its appearance, nevertheless accords too closely with toka'nɛ or ɪsí·s or both taken together. Further the reason for the late appearance of wéku' seems more probably as suggested below. Of Mooney's names, we have no record of "kishkat" and "asidahetch". The words can however be recognized as good Caddoan. Of the names in the list above Mooney lacks any suggestion of ɪtá·. One old informant suggested as an additional band name nɛtɛkwω'·kǫrikʷ•, "the laughing people", but others claimed this was the name of a village, not of a band.

Traditions and statements of informants today agree that the tawakǫrúʷ' and wéku' (towaconi and waco) spoke somewhat differently from people of the Wichita bands, although mutual intelligibility is affirmed. Discussion of the speech of these two bands with contemporary Wichitas arouses laughter, apparently because many of the turns of expression of the tawakǫrúʷ' and wéku' speech as grasped in Wichita phonetics have different meanings from those intended, and sound ludicrous. One or two expressions still recalled, though how accurately can not be determined, support this view, indicating a real dialectic difference which has been lost: a few others suggest as more probable difference of idiomatic usage as the distinction between the speech of these two bands and that of the others. As the wéku' and tawakǫrúʷ' were the westernmost groups of the Wichita, and somewhat apart from the others, it seems reasonable that local differences should have existed.

The name generally given as the Wichita name for themselves is kɪrikɪrí·s, the name of one of the bands. The origin of the term Wichita is open to some dispute. One tradition is that the first native met by a white man, asked who he was, replied "wɪts ɪtá", "a man, that's what I am", whence the name. The suggestion is sound linguistically; but in view of informants' statements that ɪtá· was the name of a Wichita band, it may be that Wichita is a combination of wɪts—"man", and ɪtá—this group name, viz., ɪtá·—

---

[1] Handbook, pt. 2, pp. 705-706.

men.[1] Actually there seems no Wichita name for the tribe as a whole.

Meanings have not been obtained for all the band names of the Wichita, and the full understanding of these must await thorough analysis of the Wichita language.

ιsí's means "awls", and was used for this group of the people because of their skill in the use of awls.

αkwi·ts is "dull teeth", said to refer to the fact that the old people of the band had dull teeth.

tawakɐrúʷ‘ "neck of land in the water" refers to the character of the place where these people lived.

kιrikιrí·s "coon eyes", "raccoon eyes", is understood by the Pawnee proper as kιrikū·ruks "bear eyes".

wéku' is said by informants to be derived from wéhiko, which latter is evidently the Wichita rendition of Mexico as pronounced by the Spanish; it was used for the people of this band because, according to tradition, they were always fighting with the Mexicans. They are spoken of as "Indians who were always scouting around". They are said to have originally been part of the tawakɐrúʷ‘, without a village to themselves, but later to have lived independently. If this origin of the name be correct, it is clearly not an ancient Wichita or Caddoan name, which may explain why it does not appear unmistakably in historical records until after 1820.[2]

The Wichita refer to the Pawnee as awa'hi; apparently this is the same designation as the awáhu of the Arikara. There is no evidence that use of awa'hi is recent; but the significance of this identity of Wichita and Arikara names for the Pawnee, in view of the traditional explanation of its meaning as given by the Arikara, must await further study.

It seems possible that this awa'hi is what was intended by the "Harahey" and "Arahey" of the Spanish accounts of Coronado's expedition into Wichita and Pawnee country.[3] The country to which Coronado was led has been identified as Wichita country, and there the people told the Spaniards about a land and people to

---

[1] Nevertheless the same kind of misunderstanding occurred in the case of the Pawnee. Grinnell, p. 240, says of the Pawnees, "the southern tribes call them pi-ta'-da". This is evidently pí·tɐtat which means "man, that's what I am", and phonetically and morphologically is exactly equivalent to the Wichita wιts ιtá.

[2] Cf. Handbook, pt. 2, p. 887.

[3] James R. Murie some years ago made this same suggestion to F. W. Hodge. See Amer. Anthrop., n. s., vol. 17, pp. 215–216, 1915.

the north, Harahey, whose customs and houses were similar to their own; evidently they spoke of the awa'hi.[1]

CADDO

Caddo, as spoken today, is essentially the language of the kado'-adátc'ᵘ band, which seems to have gradually eliminated whatever former dialectic differentiation existed, in favor of a common speech. All traditions of older living Caddos point to a time when the various bands lived apart and each spoke a somewhat divergent dialect; some even claim that these were not mutually intelligible, but there is little evidence for this view.

There were in all eight branches of the Caddo tribe which are remembered by present day natives as speaking Caddoan: hāīnāī, nabadāītcu, nada'rko, nacįdóc, ya't'ɑs, nak'ohodo'tsi, ha'i·c, kayɑmāíci, and kado'ɑdátc'ᵘ. To these should probably be added the Adai.

James Mooney lists 12 bands of the Caddo confederacy.[2] Of these he identifies one (Imaha) as a small band of Kwapa, and another (Yowani) as a band of Choctaw. Of the remaining 10, 9 will be found readily identifiable with the names in the above list; only Mooney's "Nakanawan" is absent. Mooney states that the kado'ɑdátcu'ᵘ, nada'rko, and hāīnāī called themselves collectively hasinai "our own people". While this may have been used by Caddos for some groups of the people collectively, it seems doubtful that it included just these three, since nabadāītcu and hāīnāī are closely associated together as speaking the same dialect, and as forming the most divergent branch of the Caddo.

According to informants' statements, at one time all bands of the Caddo spoke divergent dialects, save the hāīnāī and nabadāītcu, whose speech was identical; in fact they claim that the nabadāītcu was a branch of the Hainai rather than of the Caddo in general. Hainai was the largest band numerically, kado'ɑdátcu'ᵘ the second largest.

The divergence of Hainai dialectically from Caddo proper is supported by a little evidence still obtainable in the form of a few remembered differences in words. These are of two types: slight phonetic differences of a dialectic character; and complete difference of word. In some cases the latter type of difference suggests adoption of foreign words, particularly of Spanish words; such occur

---

[1] Nevertheless the possible relation of "harahey" to the Arikara "star-rah-he", as above mentioned, cannot as yet be dismissed.

[2] 14th Ann. Rep., Bur. Amer. Ethnol., p. 1092, 1897.

prominently for words which must be relatively recent in use, such as the word for horse. In Caddo proper, the vocabulary shows instances of multiple synonymy, and more than one word for the same object, which may prove to have resulted from two factors: adoption of foreign words, as Spanish, and preservation of usages of a number of the Caddo bands in the contemporary Caddo proper. Hainai kinship terms and usages also differ from those of Caddo proper.

Adai is preserved to us in the form of brief vocabularies.[1] Those words which can be summarily identified with Caddoan stems indicate that Adai is probably a divergent dialect of the Caddo.

Linguistically the Caddo is most divergent of the Caddoan languages in three directions: phonetics, vocabulary and morphology. In vocabulary, it shows, as above suggested, a mixture of stems and words from a number of alien sources.

NOTE ON NAMES APPEARING IN THE CORONADO NARRATIVE[2]

It is well known that Coronado, while in the Pueblos in 1540–1541, heard from captive Plains Indians of the lands to the east; and that "Turk", his guide into the Plains, was probably a Pawnee. The name Quivira, used in the Spanish accounts for the land along the eastern Plains to which they were led, is evidently the Pawnee word kíwịra. This word is not one which was ever employed as a name for any definite tribe or country. It means "different", "strange". It seems plausible that Turk in trying to describe to the Spaniards the country to the east, explained "it's different", etc., meaning different as to flora, fauna and ways of life from the pueblo country in which the Spaniards then were. If this was the case, kíwịra would have been correctly used for his meaning.

---

[1] Latham, R. G., Opuscula, pp. 402–405 (50 words), London, 1860.

Latham, R. G., Natural history of the varieties of Man, pp. 366–367 (48 words), London, 1850.

Latham, R. G., Elements of comparative philology, pp. 468–470 (45 words), London, 1862.

Gallatin, A., Synopsis of the Indian Tribes of North America, Amer. Antiq. Soc. Trans. (135 words from the Sibley manuscript).

Trans. Amer. Ethnol. Soc., vol. 2, pt. 1, pp. 95 and 97 (60 words from Sibley), 1848.

Gatschet, A. S., A migration legend of the Creek Indians, p. 42, Philadelphia, 1884. Refers to a list of 300 words gathered in 1802 by Martin Duralde, which is now in the Library of the American Philosophical Society in Philadelphia. We have not seen this last Adai vocabulary.

[2] Winship, G. P., The Coronado expedition, 1540-1542, 14th Ann. Rep., Bur. Amer. Ethnol., pt. 1, 1896.

While in Kansas, the Coronado expedition was told by the natives about a land and people to the north similar in ways of life to themselves. The Spaniards recorded the name given them as Harahey or Arahey. We have discussed the possible derivations of this name under Arikara and Wichita above. It has generally been accepted that the country to which Turk first brought the Spaniards was Wichita country. No doubt the statements of Spanish accounts that the houses were made of grass is part of this evidence. But there survives among the Pawnees a tradition to the effect that long ago their lodges were grass-covered, and that only as they came into colder northern regions did they cover the lodges with mud. Thus it seems to us possible that it was to a relatively southern group of Pawnee villages that Turk led the Spaniards, and that Harahey was intended to refer to the Arikara further north. This cannot be substantiated, however, by present usage of the Pawnee for the Arikara.

Coronado and his men were told that the nation was ruled by Tatarrax. This is certainly a Pawnee word, tátąra·k—forming the first person inclusive plural of all Pawnee verbs. The most probable form for which it was intended is tátąra·k^{ux}, "one of us is present (sitting)". It is, however, not a personal name.[1]

Ysopete, the name of the Plains Indian who supplanted Turk in the confidence of the Spaniards, seems to be a Wichita word.

---

[1] James R. Murie considered Tatarrax as probably intended for táturash (tá·tųras), "I found it", stating that a Pawnee with that name died after the removal of the tribe to Oklahoma. See note by F. W. Hodge in Amer. Anthrop. n. s., vol. 17, pp. 215–216, 1915.

ANTHROPOLOGY.[1]

ANTHROPOLOGICAL NEWS. — The following vocabulary of the Caddoquis, or Caddo, language was received from Judge J. F. H. Claiborne, of Natchez, Miss., who writes, " It was prepared and sent to my uncle, Gov. Claiborne, of Louisiana, by Dr. Sibley, agent for the Caddos, an educated gentleman. The southern Indians held this tribe in great respect for its supposed antiquity. It was known as the Father tribe."

Among the Smithsonian Comparative Vocabularies, now in charge of Major J. W. Powell, is a short one of the Caddo, No. 444, by Dr. D. J. Macgowan, taken in 1865.

All that remains of this once flourishing tribe are gathered on the Witchita agency, in the Indian Territory. The agent, Mr. A. C. Williams, reports their numbers at 467 persons, principally

[1] Edited by Prof. OTIS T. MASON, Columbian College, Washington, D. C.

engaged as farmers and stock-raisers. They are a quiet and inoffensive people, most of whom have adopted the habits of civilized life.

Dr. Sibley's vocabulary was taken in 1804, when the Caddos were located on Red river, from Alexandria to Natchitoches, and follows the French orthography:

Fire, niquor
Water, cou cou
Earth, ouadat cequeteot
Air, yanour
Wind, havetour
Sky, quarchator
Sun, faquor
Moon, nis
Star, suoquas
Light, binaquor
Darkness, dasquoee
Day, nayañon
Night, naba
Heat, atedot
Cold, acourdot
Smoke, cousour
Cloud, carchavesa
Fog, cou sour quabariou
Rain, quaveour
Snow, ijna
Hail, tarsour
Ice, quitousour
Frost, devchea
Dew, cabariou
Rain-bow, nachnuvoin
Thunder, adenine
Lightning, avoidgnauia
Yesterday, nieschur
To-day, douria,
To-morrow, cearia
A day, ouiche deschar
A month, ouiche nis
A year, ouiche adavyour
Spring, asnis
Summer, yaar caades
Autumn, nibba
Winter, chei
Man, chouve
Woman, nateg
Boy siarches
Girl, nategches
Child, anin
Father, a-sin
Mother, sasin
Brother, nayin
Sister, dardin
Husband, arnouu
Wife, danayei
Son, anin quarcounté
Daughter, natichetez
The body, catocse
Head, quantour
Hair, bahat
Beard, sounnieites

Face, chanqua'er
Eye, chaor
Nose, souour
Cheek, chaminni
Chin, soun
Mouth, lip, ouar
Tooth, taor
Tongue, adetour
Ear, bistor
Neck, nachée
Arm, minni
Wrist, a
Hand, cenour
Finger, cebinour
Belly, binni
Back, chabaches
Side, quocher
Bubby, dantour
Nipple, dante echanqua
Thigh, quasour
Leg, casosce
Foot, nasour
Toe, senbitour
Skin, nousches
Nails, ceonour
Bone, narquour
Blood, baor
Life, quava
Death paquaca
Food, deace nouyour
Meat, quaoutour
Fat, acayou
Lean, nargou
Bread, dasquat
Indian-corn, quaces
Milk, sou-sou
Egg, nosbiquor
House, sahor
Mammoth, douriates
Buffalo, tanaa
Elk, oueyat
Deer, da
Bear, naoeches
Wolf, tacha
Panther, quiches
Wildcat, ouado
Polecat, vueiet
Fox, couons
Beaver, chestaor
Raccoon, hot
Opossum, narcous
Hare, diot
Squirrel, siouar
Flying-quirrel, detes.

Ground-squirrel, chiouva aquared
Mole, cequouva
Bird, banit
Eagle, ioy
Hawk, souit
Owl, ouous
Turkey, nou
Swan, sartos
Wild-goose, quinar
Duck, can.
Turkey-buzzard, souquates.
Raven, ouvar
Crow, caquail
Black-bird, quacho
Crane, douno
Pigeon, ouáas
Pheasant, ounani
Partridge, colati
Mocking-bird, quathile quatou
Red-bird, laodoucé
Snake, quiqua
Lizzard, taquon
Butterfly, banous
Fly, quouni
Fish, bata
Frog, quidau
Gold, sounar aquayguo
Silver, sounar aquayou
Copper, dedot noustor
Stone, siguor
Wood, youcour
Gum, guaruoadat
Mountain, ouadat iniquo
Hill, chuquaet
Valley, nicquedaic
Sea, eiquot aicmaie.
Lake, eiquot
Pond, quanmachar
River, baat
Creek, nidday quayarda sar
Spring, quayardacha
Grass, adeitour
Tree, quardacha
Pine, devoas
Cedar, betes
Sycamore, quiour
Ash, quiquor
Elm, da auve
Beech, aligonqua danquone
Birch, saibatocha
Oak, ba
Chestnut, nouba
Hickory, nar
Walnut, sciar
Locust, danani
Mulberry, baie
Vine, sasour
Tobacco, yaar
Joy, quavrinout
Sorrow, gouienout
One, gauenie
Two, bit
Three, daauo

Four, evui
Five, de cequan
Six, danqui
Seven, bi cequan
Eight, daauo cequa
Nine, ivui cequa
Ten, benaar
Eleven—twenty,the numerals double
Twenty, benar bit
Thirty, benaar daauo
Forty, benaar evui
Fifty, benaar decequan
Sixty, benaar danqui
Seventy, benaar bicequa
Eighty, benaar davuecequa
Ninety, benaar ivuicequa
Hundred, ouische aa sour
Two hundred, carquaniauosit
Horse, detama
Dog, deches
White, aquayou
Black, adeguo
Green, barnou sar
Blue, a sarquour
Yellow, aquaij quo
Red, atenou
Good, hanhat
Bad, avouna
Large, quarquavevour
Small, ayortetes
High, ayou
Low, naver,
Narrow, sidites
Old, anistes
Young, siarte
New, souroun
Hard, aiequai
Soft, achounou
Sweet, abe save
Sour, abasquo
Bitter, aquccho
Hot, atedos
Cold, acourdas
Dry, adaqui
Wet aquarquo
Strong, adasquar
Weak, aicquaie quoiace
Pretty, hanhat
Ugly, aouna
Sick, auequarion
Brave, ches soues
Cowardly, che inij inij
Wise, ouin anet
Foolish, quarnous quourdetaui
I, quarches
You, naquaya
He, deer
She, annas
They, davre
This, deschez
That, déhé
To eat, naquiar
To drink, naquarqua

To sleep, youdic
To laugh, saqua
To cry, nasaquaqua
To sing, yourneiyoeu
To whistle, youdanou
To smell, nasoeunout
To hear, youquaibe
To see, nasaibe
To speak, nasacoupinte
To walk, nasavear
To run, nasaninic
To stand, daarni
To sit, dataue

To lie down, darsa
To smoke a pipe, darquavra
To love, sendamane
To hate, atedo ciyer
To strike, younbin
To kill, youques
To dance, youvechan
To jump, avesaria
To fall, navvania
To break, yoniouva
To bend, darquven
Yes, aaie
No, aounna

THE CLASSIFICATION OF THE CADDOAN LANGUAGES [1]

ALLAN R. TAYLOR

Department of Linguistics, University of California, Berkeley

Two and one-half centuries elapsed following colonization of America before the native languages of the continent came to be regarded as anything more than a practical necessity for commerce and evangelism. However, by the second half of the eighteenth century, intellectual curiosity about language had become a part of European scientific thought. America, long a European outpost, offered hundreds of languages and dialects which invited scientific investigation. Credit for the first work on relationships among North American languages belongs to Dr. Jonathan Edwards,[2] but it is to Albert Gallatin that we owe our first really thorough and rigorous classification.[3]

In the Gallatin classification the present Caddoan family [4] appears distributed through three families: Adaize, Caddo, and Pawnee. The eventual union of these three into a single stock took many years, and involved several scholars, both European and American. The intention of the present paper is to assemble and present a bibliography for those languages now known to be Caddoan and to outline the course of thinking on the question of the genetic affinity of the various languages.

Although occasional Caddoan forms may be found scattered through early administrative and missionary writings, largely Spanish,[5] it was

---

[1] The attention of the reader is called to the author's comparative Caddoan, due to appear in the near future in the *International Journal of American Linguistics*. In this article are assembled more than 100 cognate sets, and some conclusions concerning Proto-Caddoan are advanced. I wish to extend sincere thanks to Mrs. Margaret Blaker, Archivist of the Bureau of American Ethnology, for furnishing me an inventory of the Caddoan manuscripts in the Bureau, and the Library of the American Philosophical Society for useful information regarding its collection of early vocabularies.

[2] *Observations on the language of the Muhhekaneew Indians*, first published in 1788. The work is an early monument in Algonquian scholarship, and is still an interesting document. It was reprinted twice; the best known, and most useful, of the three printings is the 1823 edition annotated by John Pickering. Dr. Jonathan Edwards was the son of the eminent Puritan divine of the same name; the younger Edwards had a sound speaking knowledge of Mohican which he gained from residence as a child among the Stockbridge Indians.

[3] A synopsis of the Indian tribes within the United States east of the Rocky Mountains, and in the British and Russian possessions in North America, *Trans. and Collections Amer. Antiquarian Soc.* 2, Cambridge, 1836. Born in Switzerland, Gallatin became interested in the American aborigines from the time of his arrival during the American Revolution. Problems of linguistic classification occupied him at least from the beginning of the 1820's until the end of his life in 1849. Gallatin himself prepared a 600-word vocabulary list (1824–1825) which he used in his comparisons; the list was circulated for him by James Barbour, the Secretary of War, to all Indian agents, military outposts, and missionaries with whom the War Department maintained correspondence. Gallatin personally collected material for Creek, Chicasa, and Natchez, all of which he published in his study. Another great contribution of Albert Gallatin was the

1842 founding of the American Ethnological Society. John Wesley Powell took Gallatin's Synopsis to be the foundation of American comparative linguistics: "There is no safe resting place anterior to Gallatin, because no scholar prior to his time had properly adopted comparative methods of research, and because no scholar was privileged to work with so large a body of material. It must further be said of Gallatin that he had a very clear conception of the task he was performing, and brought to it both learning and wisdom. Gallatin's work has therefore been taken as the starting point, back of which we may not go in the historic consideration of the systematic philology of North America" (Indian linguistic families of America north of Mexico, *7th Annual Report of the Bureau of American Ethnology*, 1885–1886: 10, Washington, 1891).

[4] The Caddoan stock has been defined most recently by Alexander Lesser and Gene Weltfish, The composition of the Caddoan linguistic stock, *Smithsonian Misc. Coll.* 87(6), Washington, 1932. The languages included in this stock are the following: Arikara, Pawnee, Wichita, Kitsai, Adai, and Caddo. Arikara was spoken in several permanent villages on the upper Missouri in North Dakota; Pawnee was spoken aboriginally by four politically independent bands living in southern Nebraska and northern Kansas; Wichita, Kitsai, and Caddo were spoken by numerous bands in Texas, with some of the Caddo groups also living in western Louisiana. Adai was spoken by a very small group in western Louisiana.

[5] It was nevertheless the Sieur de la Salle who first collected a word list for a Caddoan language. The list was of the Hasinai dialect of Caddo, and was elicited in 1687: ". . . et de plus [il] avoit soin de prendre tousjours quelques mots de leur langue qu'il escrivoit. Il en prit aussi de ceux-là. . . ." ("Relation de Joutel," in Pierre Margry, *Découvertes et établissements des français dans l'ouest et dans le sud de l'Amérique Septentrionale* 3: 305, Paris, 1879–1888). By contemporary testimony (1690, "Interrogations faites à Talons," Margry, *op. cit.*,

---

Americans who first collected specimens of Caddoan speech for scientific study. Just prior to the cession of Louisiana to the United States (1803) an American doctor named John Sibley went to Louisiana, apparently with the intention of settling in the still Spanish territory as a rancher.[6] After the territory passed briefly to France and then to the American flag, Sibley came to the attention of the American government through the new American governor of Louisiana, William Charles Coles Claiborne. Since Sibley had already gained some familiarity with the territory of the Red River as far north as Natchitoches he was appointed surgeon's mate for the troops stationed at Natchitoches (1804), then Indian agent for Orleans Territory and the region south of the Arkansas (1805).[7]

It is to Dr. Sibley that we owe our first word lists of Caddoan languages, although by the date of publication of some of his materials he must partially yield to George Gray, a successor of his as Indian agent. Sibley was furnished vocabulary blanks by Jefferson, and he collected vocabularies of Adai and Caddo; he apparently also collected a vocabulary of Natchitoches, for he wrote a letter to Jefferson[8] which was to cover the vocabulary of this language. The list must never have reached Washington, however, for Gallatin mentions that as of 1836 a Natchitoches list was still wanting.[9] For Caddo, Gallatin elected to publish mostly Gray's vocabulary, because of its greater length, although he included nineteen Sibley forms in the published list. Sibley's full list, collected in 1804,

was published in 1879 in the *American Naturali[s]* This list of just under two hundred items was se[t] by Sibley to Governor Claiborne, and Claiborne nephew had it published approximately seventy five years later. When compared with Caddo [a]s spoken today, the poor quality of the lists of bot[h] Sibley and Gray is apparent—phonetic accurac[y] in recording Indian languages was still many year[s] in the future. As a result, what is virtually th[e] only value of these lists is their occasional recor[d] of semantic shift, as for example Gray's *nushto* "animal skin," contemporary núst²uw "pape[r] book."[10]

In addition to these two lists there are two othe[r] early Caddo vocabularies in print. The longer, als[o] poorly recorded, was collected about 1853 b[y] Captain Randolph Marcy; it was published b[y] Schoolcraft. The other is very short, consisting [of] only twenty words collected by Lieutenant Ami[e] Weeks Whipple, published in volume III [of] Whipple's 1856 *Reports*.

To round out the Caddo corpus there are thre[e] relatively modern lists, which, because they a[re] better recorded, are of potentially greater valu[e] James Mooney, in his monumental study of th[e] ghost-dance, gives a short but useful glossary fo[r] Caddo ghost-dance songs. Next to appear wer[e] the Caddo kinship terms published by Leslie Spie[r] in the *American Anthropologist* in 1924. Mos[t] recently, Elsie Clews Parsons gives numerou[s] Caddo forms, transcribed either by herself or b[y] Gladys Reichard, in her ethnographic work *Note[s] on the Caddo*. Additional Caddo is probably t[o] be found in manuscript in the papers of Parson[s] Reichard, and Da Cruz.[10a]

The first vocabularies for the Pawnee branch [of] Caddoan have the distinction of being the onl[y] ones among the early Caddoan lists which wer[e] collected by scientists; in the case of Arikara th[e] collector was even a linguist of some sophisticatio[n]

The fact that this branch of the family receive[d] superior treatment is no accident, since thes[e] Indians lived in the northern portion of the Louisi ana Purchase, the part of the new territory whic[h] was most thoroughly explored in the early nine

---

619) the Spanish Franciscan missionaries also collected Hasinai vocabularies in the course of their efforts to learn the language of their prospective converts. None of these lists survive.

[6] Cox, Isaac Joslin, The early exploration of Louisiana, *University Studies*, ser. 2, 2: 14, University of Cincinnati, 1906. Sibley's emigration to Spanish territory may have been due to his having been accused of attempted bigamy in the United States (*Jefferson papers* 150, May 26, 1805).

[7] Cox, *op. cit.*, 37.

[8] *Jefferson papers* 154, December 14, 1805.

[9] As a consequence the only "Natchitoches" which we now possess is that recalled by one of Swanton's informants, Caddo Jake, an elderly man who had not spoken the dialect for decades. Swanton gives a short comparative Natchitoches/Kadohadacho vocabulary in his *Source material on the history and ethnology of the Caddo Indians, Bur. Amer. Ethnol. Bull.* 132: 15, Washington, 1942. When the forms are not entirely different, they are virtually identical. Owing to the unfavorable conditions under which the list was collected, it is of uncertain reliability. Comparative Caddoan studies may eventually permit an assessment of its validity.

[10] The modern word is from Daniel Da Cruz, A pro visional analysis of segmental phonemes in Caddo, Insti tute of Language and Linguistics of Georgetown Univer sity, 1957. The paper remains unpublished.

[10a] Extensive new Caddo materials were collected b[y] Dr. Wallace L. Chafe between 1959 and 1962. Thes[e] materials, still in manuscript, were gathered while D[r] Chafe was associated with the Bureau of America[n] Ethnology.

eenth century. The first scientific expedition into the area was the famous Lewis and Clark Expedition of 1804–1805.[11] Another such expedition was organized toward the end of the second decade of the century and placed under the command of Major Stephen Harriman Long. Its purpose was the scientific and military reconnaissance of the still largely unknown territory. The party left Pittsburgh by Ohio steamer in 1819, including among its experts a painter and two topographers in addition to the two members of most interest here. One of these was the expedition zoologist. Dr. Thomas Say. The other, the surgeon-botanist-geologist Edwin James, joined the expedition the spring following its departure from the East.

By historical accident it is to both these men [12]

---

[11] The earliest Pawnee list seems to have been taken by Captain Meriwether Lewis, commander of the expedition. This list, along with other Indian linguistic material, was turned over to President Jefferson at the expedition's return. Most of Jefferson's Indian vocabularies were later lost in the James River while being shipped from Washington to his home in Virginia. A few sheets were recovered (now in the Library of the American Philosophical Society), but the "only morsel of an original vocabulary among them was Captain Lewis's of the Pani language" (Jefferson to Barton, September 21, 1809; Jefferson papers 188). Jefferson regretted the loss keenly, particularly since some of the material was from dialects which had become extinct during his own lifetime.

[12] Thomas Say was one of the earliest descriptive entomologists and conchologists produced by our young nation. He also participated in the founding of New Harmony, Indiana, which was his official home from 1825 until the end of his life (1834). Among his many correspondents was the collector of the first Arikara list, who spent his first American winter in Say's home in New Harmony before journeying to the prairies the following summer.

Following the Long Expedition, Edwin James spent several years on the frontier as an assistant surgeon in the United States Army. He was stationed at Prairie du Chien (Wisconsin) and Mackinac (Michigan), and like his contemporary Henry R. Schoolcraft he had a great interest in the languages of the Indians of the area. James composed, during this period, several Ojibwa spellers, published an Ojibwa New Testament (1833), and also published the autobiography of a famous Ojibwa interpreter, John Tanner, which contains considerable material of ethnohistorical and (secondary) linguistic interest. James also had some acquaintance with Menomini. After retiring from public service, Edwin James participated actively in the anti-slavery movement, and his farm in Iowa was a station of the underground railway.

One feat for which James deserves to be remembered was his ascent of Pike's Peak, the first known ascent by white man, which he accomplished in July, 1820, while on the Long Expedition. Long named the peak James

that we are indebted for our first published Pawnee material. This vocabulary, as well as vocabularies of five Siouan languages (Oto, Kansa, Omaha, Yankton, Hidatsa), was collected by Say, and appeared in *Account of an Expedition from Pittsburgh to the Rocky Mountains, Performed in the Years 1819–1820 by Order of the Honorable John C. Calhoun, Secretary of War, Under the Command of Major Stephen H. Long*, which was published by James in 1823 as the semi-official report of the expedition. The American edition of the work was published in Philadelphia; another edition was printed in London the same year. All the Say vocabularies were utilized by Gallatin and reprinted in his 1836 study.

The Say vocabulary seems to have been the only Pawnee vocabulary in print until the appearance in the 1860's of the lengthier and greatly superior vocabularies published by Dr. Ferdinand Vandeveer Hayden.[13] The first of these appeared in 1863 in *On the Ethnography and Philology of the Indian Tribes of the Missouri Valley*. Hayden's source for the Pawnee list was a missionary to the Skiri, the Reverend William Hamilton. After independent field work, Hayden published additional Pawnee (also Omaha and Winnebago) materials in 1868, intended by himself as an interim study to a fuller sequel to the 1863 work. This work was apparently never published.

The early edge which Pawnee had over the other Caddoan languages was further increased during the late nineteenth and early twentieth centuries by the labors of such scholars as Dunbar, Fletcher, Densmore, and Weltfish. Thanks

---

Peak in his honor, but by popular usage the peak came to be called Pike's Peak. A somewhat lower peak in northern Colorado, not far from the peak named for Long, is now called James' Peak.

[13] Hayden was a geologist, but of himself he noted in the introduction to his 1868 work that ". . . no pursuit has ever given me greater pleasure than the study of the languages and customs of our native tribes, and it would be my choice to give my undivided attention to those researches, but all my labors in that direction must ever be incidental to other duties." Unfortunately for Hayden's reputation, it has recently been established (1949) that much of the ethnographic portion of the 1863 work is lifted virtually verbatim from a manuscript written by a contemporary upper Missouri trader, Edwin Thompson Denig. The Denig manuscript was discovered in the Missouri Historical Society library by John Ewers and published with the title *Five Indian tribes of the upper Missouri*, Norman, Oklahoma, 1961. Hayden's failure to give Denig adequate credit is all the more curious in view of his acknowledgment of his source for the Pawnee vocabulary.

largely to Dr. Weltfish, we possess today an abundance of well-recorded Pawnee.

The first Arikara list did not become available for inspection until some time after it became generally known that Arikara was a Pawnee dialect.[14] It was nonetheless a valuable contribution to Caddoan linguistics, for it stood for years as the most accurately recorded Arikara material. The collector of this list, Alexander Philipp Maximilian, Prince of Wied-Neuwied, justly deserves a place in the history of American linguistics, both for his vocabularies and for his careful field technique. Maximilian was unlike nearly all his predecessors, and most of his successors before Gatschet, in that he had had philological training, and furthermore, again like Gatschet, he was a polyglot. Moreover, he had a clear conception of the nature of the problem and of his task as a recorder, in addition to which he brought to North America the whole of his experience as a field collector in Brazil. Because he felt that any traveler who was in a position to do so was obliged to contribute to the knowledge of the languages and mores of exotic peoples, he availed himself of every opportunity to collect data; as a result he presented to the world in 1837 a set of 23 North American vocabularies of varying length together with the outline of a Mandan grammar, begun during the winter spent in the Mandan villages, 1833–1834.[15]

Maximilian's procedure would do credit in its spirit to any field-worker. Throughout his vocabularies he indicated the source of the material (i.e., native speaker, Indian, but of another tribe, trader, etc., sometimes even giving the name of his informant) and in his orthography he specified when his symbols were not to have the standard German values of the Latin alphabet. He was no less careful in his attempts to indicate prosodic features, describing such things as speed and tenseness of articulation. He tried to indicate vowel length, indicated position of stress, and did not fall into the trap of dividing "words" into "syllables," a practice which he deplored: "A word divided in the English style into its com-

ponent parts could be correctly pronounced neithe by a German nor a Frenchman; besides, ever language has its own intonation, not common t others."[16] Anticipating that some field contact would be very brief, he chose a twenty-item lis of common terms which he elicited first "in orde to make a comparison and draw conclusions re garding the relationship of the tribes."

There can hardly be any doubt that, if thi aristocratic countryman of Boas had decided t become a professional Americanist, modern Amer ican linguistics would enjoy a tradition both riche and older by half a century.

Maximilian's list, published abroad and in Ger man, was followed very shortly (1841) by anothe Arikara list, also published abroad, but in an En glish language work. The list was collected b the painter George Catlin[17] and published in hi *Letters and Notes on the Manners, Customs, an Conditions of the North American Indians.* Thi list is inferior to that of the German prince; th recordings show missed voiceless vowels and res onants, incorrectly recorded vowels and conso nants (misprints may be partially responsible), an inaccurate or absolutely incorrect glosses, as fo example, the Arikara word for "woman" trans lated as "she," the word for "man" translated a "moon."

The next Arikara list was published by Hay den in his 1863 work on the philology of th tribes of the upper Missouri. These three list

---

[14] Gallatin announced Arikara to be such in his 1836 work, page 129. His authority, not identified specifically, was said to be Indian tradition and the testimony of interpreters.

[15] Maximilian's Mandan materials even included the beginnings of a comparative study of two different Mandan dialects—a study impossible in this century, and quite likely impossible even shortly after the visit of the German prince, since the Mandans were virtually wiped out by smallpox in 1838.

[16] The vocabularies and grammar were published i the German account of Maximilian's expedition. Th work was translated almost immediately, and it was late reprinted by Thwaites in his *Early western travels* 22 23, 24. This and the following quote appear on pag 205 of volume 24 of this edition. Maximilian also too copious notes on fauna, flora, and geology of the region through which he traveled; his painter companion, Kar Bodmer, made a number of paintings and sketches which are today of great ethnological value.

[17] "These words have all been written down by mysel from the Indians' mouths, as they have been correctl translated by me" (*Letters and notes on the manners customs, and conditions of the North American Indian* 2: 236, London, 1841). This statement by Catlin i probably not true. According to Robert Gordon Latham the British amateur ethnologist and linguist, the list wa collected by Kenneth Mackenzie, an official of the Ameri can Fur Company (see Miscellaneous contributions to th ethnography of North America, *Trans. Philol. Soc.* 2: 32 London, 1846). Catlin was in London for several year beginning in 1840, and he must have told Latham per sonally who had actually collected the list. Mackenzi collected numerous lists for languages of the upper Mis souri tribes; Gallatin cites him as authority for four o the lists published in 1836.

(Maximilian, Catlin, and Hayden), collected within twenty years of each other, and the kin terms given by Morgan, were all the Arikara in print until the turn of the century. The only other original vocabulary for Arikara in print appeared in 1909. This list was published by Edward S. Curtis in his series of luxurious volumes on the American Indian. Although this material is recorded in a somewhat cumbersome transcription (utilized in printing the numerous vocabularies given by Curtis), it is accurate enough to permit use in comparison.

The only Arikara in manuscript known to this writer outside of the Bureau of American Ethnology was collected since Curtis by Dr. Gene Weltfish, and Dr. Melvin Gilmore; more recently materials have been gathered by Dr. Wallace Chafe and by the present author.

Chronologically last to appear were vocabularies of Wichita, its subdialect Waco (Hueco), and Kitsai. Whereas the first lists for the Pawnee branch were collected by scientists and missionaries, the lists for Wichita, Waco, and Kitsai were gathered by army officers.

The first Wichita list to reach print was collected in 1852 by Captain Marcy during the course of an official exploration of the Red River country of Texas and Louisiana. The list of seventy items was published together with a longer Comanche list as Appendix H to Marcy's report. Marcy is also the source of Schoolcraft's Wichita vocabulary, which was printed together with the Caddo vocabulary mentioned above.

For a number of years these two Marcy lists (there are very few identical glosses in the two lists, so that there is little duplication; it appears that there was some attempt to make the two lists complementary) were the only Wichita available. Apparently next was Spier's short list of Wichita kinship terminology which was published in the *American Anthropologist* in 1924. Very soon after this (1930) came the ethnography and vocabulary of Edward Curtis, in volume 19 of *The American Indian*. This vocabulary, as in the case of Curtis' Arikara vocabulary mentioned earlier, can be used in comparison. Following Curtis the Wichita were apparently not revisited until 1949, the first year of the field work of Karl Schmitt and Paul L. Garvin.[18] The Garvin material is the first really accurately recorded Wichita material which

has been published, and furthermore Garvin's notes are apparently the only Wichita in manuscript outside the Bureau of American Ethnology of the Smithsonian Institution.

Vocabularies of Kitsai and Waco did not appear until 1856, with the publication of Amiel Weeks Whipple's report. As in the case of the first Caddo and Wichita lists, these are so badly recorded that only the most general information can be derived from them. These appear to be the only published data for these two Caddoan languages; Kitsai exists in manuscript in the field notes of Dr. Alexander Lesser.

It is a tribute to the care and rigor of Gallatin that his 1836 classification of the languages now known to be Caddoan remained unchanged for a number of years. Nothing could be done until more material was collected and published. Even the appearance in 1853 of Marcy's Wichita did not help: it did not show conclusive resemblances to anything then known. In 1856, however, the Whipple vocabularies of Kitsai and Waco were published, and then the way was opened for new work on classification.

The discovery of the Pawnee affinity of Kitsai, Waco, and Wichita was made by a professor of Oriental literature at Union Theological Seminary, William Wadden Turner.[19] The discovery (although Professor Turner would go no farther than to term the relationship probable) was announced in 1856 in chapter five of the "Report upon the

---

[18] The kin terms which Schmitt published were transcribed by Garvin, so that linguistic field work was actually performed only by Garvin.

[19] This relationship had actually already been affirmed in print by Josiah Gregg as early as 1844: "The Pawnees and Rickaras of the north, and the Wacoes, Wichitas, Towockanoes, Towyash and Keechyes, of the Red River, are of the same origin" (*Commerce of the prairies, or the journal of a Santa Fé trader during eight expeditions across the great western prairies and a residence of nearly nine years in northern Mexico*, 251, New York, 1844). No linguistic evidence was cited, although Gregg had language specifically in mind: "The origin of the American Indians has been discussed by too many able writers for me to enter into it here: nor will I attempt to show the general traits of similarity that are to be observed in their various languages: yet it may interest an occasional reader, to be informed of the relations of consanguinity which subsist between many of the different Indian tribes" (*op. cit.*, 250).

William Wadden Turner was born in England, but came to this country as a child. He learned the printer's trade in his youth, and after becoming a scholar he had the reputation of being the most skillful proofreader in the United States. Master of Arabic, Hebrew, and Sanskrit, and a translator from German as well, Turner turned to exotic languages towards the end of his life. He published a Chinook manual in 1853, and a work on Yoruba by him was issued by the Smithsonian Institution in 1858. He died in 1859 at the age of forty-nine.

Indian Tribes," itself part three of the third volume of Whipple's 1856 *Report*.

The accompanying Kichai and Hueco vocabularies ... enable us to make a comparison with the Pawnee proper; the result of which is that these languages really do, in all probability, belong to the Pawnee stock. ... The Wichita vocabulary of Captain Marcy, which I was formerly [1853] unable to place, here also finds its appropriate location.[20]

Turner supported his claim with fifteen cognate sets, arranged in a table according to English gloss, using Pawnee (Say), Arikara (Maximilian), Kitsai, Wichita, and Waco (Whipple). The key to the solution of the problem was Kitsai (although to a lesser extent Waco also). This is partially due to the fact that Whipple's vocabularies were fuller, and so contained some words cognate with Pawnee which were missing in Marcy's Wichita list. Even more important, however, is the fact that these languages, particularly Kitsai, show strong lexical resemblances now to Pawnee, now to Wichita.

In the same paper, Professor Turner took up the question of possible wider affinity for the now enlarged Pawnee family. Turner suggested six possible cognate sets in which single Caddo forms were compared to forms with the same meaning from the Pawnee languages, including Kitsai and Waco.[21] Turner offered these only tentatively, suggesting that the apparent affinity might be due either to "relationship or to long and intimate intercourse."[22]

Writing in 1854, the great German Americanist Johann Carl Eduard Buschmann[23] was not so cautious:

The Caddo is an entirely independent language which I found to be related to no other. ... With Wichita alone Caddo has some words in common (some few also with Waco or Kitsai) which, unless the agreement rests on chance, might be borrowed by each from the others: Caddo from Wichita when the word is found in the Pawnee family, and Wichita from Caddo when the word is foreign to this family.[24]

Buschmann was quite unable to assemble cognate sets which satisfied him, although he presented several possible ones. Once again, just as before the Kitsai and Waco vocabularies were secured, it became apparent that the maximum possible conclusions had been drawn from the available data.

After 1859—the date of publication in Berlin of Buschmann's *Spüren der aztekischen Sprache*— no further attempt at classification was made for nearly twenty years. The next to appear was a classification published in England in 1878. This work, *Stanford's Compendium of Geography and Travel*, included an appendix entitled "Ethnology and Philology of America," and its cautious tone places it within the earlier rather than the later period of Caddoan studies. In this contribution the "Pawnee family" has Caddo as its fourth branch, but placed there with the significant qualification "here grouped provisionally with the Pawnees, the affinity not being clearly established."[25] and meticulous attention to all the Caddoan materials available to him marks him as one of the most painstaking scholars who ever worked on these languages. Regarding Buschmann, Powell states "Many of the results obtained may have been considered bold at the time, but recent philological investigations give evidence of the value of many of the author's conclusions" (*7th Annual Rept. Bur. Amer. Ethnol.*, 19).

[20] Report upon the Indian tribes, 68.

[21] Gatschet (*Migration legend of the Creek Indians*, 42, Philadelphia, 1884) credits Robert Gordon Latham with being first to suspect Caddo relationship to Pawnee. In the passage which he cites in Latham, the latter suggests that "a language may be Pawni without ceasing to be Caddo, and Caddo without losing its place in the Pawni group. ... The true explanation of this lies in the highly probable fact that the Caddo and Pawni are members of one and the same class" (Addenda and Corrigenda to the reprint of: On the languages of northern, western, and Central America, in *Opuscula, Essays chiefly philological and ethnographical*, 400, London, 1860; the essay itself was written more than a decade earlier). Since Latham mentions Turner's paper in the next sentence, it must be suspected that he got his idea from Turner. Turner deserves the credit, since he not only suggested Caddo-Pawnee affinity, but attempted to support it with cognates.

[22] Report upon the Indian tribes, 70.

[23] Buschmann's greatest Americanist contributions were in Uto-Aztekan and Athapascan studies, but his sober

[24] "Die Caddo-sprache ist eine ganz selbständige Sprache, die ich mit keiner anderen verwandt gefunden habe. ... Mit der Wichita allein hat das Caddo einige Wörter (davon ein paar zugleich mit Waco oder Keechi) gemein; welche, wo die Uebereinstimmung nicht auf dem Zufall beruht, jede von der anderen aufgenommen haben kann: das Caddo von der Wichita dann, wenn das Wort der letzteren in der Pawnee-Sprachfamilie steht; die Wichita von dem Caddo, wenn das Wort dieser Familie fremd ist" (*Die Spüren der aztekischen Sprache im nördlichen Mexico und höheren amerikanischen Norden*, 448, Berlin, 1859.)

[25] The *Compendium* is credited by Powell to Augustus H. Keane, although it seems in reality to have been a translation (by Keane) and expansion (by H. W. Bates) of Hellwald's *Die Erde und Ihre Völker*, Stuttgart, 1877-1878.
In the section on Pawnee it is noted (page 477) that the Pawnees were included "by H. H. Bancroft and other high authorities" in the Shoshone family. This placement is rejected, since "L. H. Morgan, after careful study, pronounces the Pawnee to be a stock, that is, an inde-

The real turning point in the classification of the Caddoan languages was reached in 1884, when Albert Gatschet described [26] "the great family of Pani Indians." Caddo, for the first time, was unambiguously classed as cognate with Pawnee and its congeners. In 1891 was published Daniel Garrison Brinton's *The American Race*, called by Truman Michelson "the first systematic classification of the aboriginal languages of both North and South America." [27] Also dated 1891, but not actually distributed until 1892, was "Indian Linguistic Families of America North of Mexico," the famous classification completed under the directorship of John Wesley Powell, published in the *7th Annual Report of the Bureau of Ethnology*.

The Brinton classification was characterized by its author as the work of several years: "The outlines of the classification and the general arrangement of the material . . . [are] those . . . for several years . . . adopted in . . . lecture courses before the Academy of Natural Sciences at Philadelphia" [28] In this classification all the Caddoan languages except Adai, in effect the Caddoan stock of Powell, were grouped together (pages 95–97) as the "Pani stock," number 8 of Brinton's North Atlantic Group.

The Powell classification appeared in 1892,

somewhat as an anticlimax, although two lasting contributions to Caddoan linguistics were made in it. In the first place the name of the stock was established as *Caddoan*, and second, a bibliography for the family was given.

One addition to the Caddoan stock has been made since the Powell classification. This is Adai, a language of Louisiana which became extinct sometime in the first half of the nineteenth century. Justification for the inclusion of Adai in the Caddoan stock has never been published.

Gallatin, Brinton, and Powell regarded the language as constituting an independent stock. However, in establishing a separate Adaizan family, Powell did not rule out the possibility of Caddoan affinity for the language. Nevertheless, that he was basically unsympathetic to the idea [29] is shown by his observation that "the amount of material . . . necessary to establish its relationship to Caddoan is not at present forthcoming, and it may be doubted if it ever will be. . . ." More recently, Swanton [30] accepted Caddoan affinity for Adai. The most recent opinion can only be termed somewhat ambivalent: Lesser and Weltfish list Adai as perhaps Caddoan (indicated by query before the name in their table on page 2), but at the same time they add that "those words which can be summarily identified with Caddoan stems indicate that Adai is probably a divergent dialect of the Caddo." [31] The problem, then, remains essentially as in 1891.

That the difficulties connected with Adai are grave cannot be doubted. The chief problem, as noted by Powell, is the paucity of Adai materials, accompanied by the only slightly lesser problem of interpretation of such materials as there are. Only one manuscript is known to have been prepared in the field, the 1802 list by Sibley, [32] of which Gallatin published 147 words in 1836. Other scattered

---

pendent language, having no known affinities with any other." My research failed to discover any claim for "Shoshone" affiliation of Pawnee by Bancroft or anyone else. A statement in Morgan's *Ancient society*, 165, New York, 1877, may have been the authority for the reference to Morgan: "these tribes [Pawnee and Arikara], with the Huecos and some two or three other small tribes residing on the Canadian river . . . speak an independent stock language."

Another notable misclassification, more recent than that reported of Bancroft, was George Bird Grinnell's assignment of the Lipans and Tonkawas to the Caddoan stock (*Pawnee hero stories and folk tales*, 218–222, New York, 1890). Grinnell did this on Indian authority, which alleged similarity in language, naming customs, and singing style among the groups in question. Actually the Lipans (Athabascan) had long been confused with the Pawnees owing to the alternative spelling of their name as *Le panis*.

[26] See footnote 21; Gatschet, *loc. cit.*

[27] *Dictionary of American Biography* 3: 50. Concerning Brinton, Michelson wrote "He never was a field worker and remained a closet anthropologist, apparently never finding the necessity of coming into close contact with primitive peoples. On the other hand he delved into the libraries of Europe as well as of this country. It is also to be remarked that he utilized the results of field workers in his writings and spoke appreciatively of them."

[28] *The American race*, x, New York, 1891.

[29] Credit for development of the idea must go to Gatschet, whose "People and language of the Adai of Louisiana," BAE manuscript number 254, remains unpublished. Dorsey also seems to have studied the problem. *Cf.* BAE manuscript 255.

[30] Swanton, John R., Indian tribes of North America, *Bur. Amer. Ethnol. Bull.* 145, Washington, 1952.

[31] Lesser and Weltfish, Composition of the Caddoan stock, 14.

[32] Albert Gatschet, on page 42 of *A migration legend of the Creek Indians*, Philadelphia, 1884, wrongly attributes the manuscript to Martin Duralde. The manuscript in the possession of the American Philosophical Society Library is a copy by Duponceau of the Sibley original. The numerous other Adai citations of Powell and Lesser and Weltfish all stem from Sibley via Gallatin.

Adai might be located in the correspondence and other writings of the Misión de los Adayes, which existed between 1715 and the end of the same century, but such material would require a great deal of research, and might not be worth the effort. Hence hope for a solution rests virtually entirely with the Sibley materials and such internal consistencies as they possess. Judging from Sibley material amenable to present-day verification, the list is poorly recorded. On the other hand, if Adai is Caddoan, and if it stands closest to Caddo as guessed by Lesser and Weltfish, then field work on Caddo might yield enough cognate sets to permit correspondences to be established. Proto-Caddoan reconstructions based on the other languages may also be of great eventual use.[33] For the present nothing more can be said than that the final question in Caddoan classification has not yet been answered.

The balance of this paper contains a bibliography of all primary Caddoan linguistic sources in print known to this writer. In order to be listed the work must contain Caddoan linguistic material together with identification of the terms, generally by translation. Not included is the five-volume collection by George A. Dorsey of Caddoan folklore (in English),[34] although some volumes, particularly those on the Skiri Pawnee and Wichita have some Caddoan words scattered throughout. I have also not included lists put together secondarily from various of the listed primary sources, nor preliminary materials later reprinted in fuller treatments.

CATLIN, GEORGE. 1841. Letters and notes on the manners, customs, and conditions of the North American Indians. London. [Arikara vocabulary on pages 262–265 of volume 2.]

CLAIBORNE, JUDGE J. F. H., and OTIS T. MASON. 1879. Anthropological news. *Amer. Naturalist* 13: 788–790. [Caddo vocabulary collected by John Sibley.]

CURTIS, EDWARD S. 1909. The North American Indian 5. (The Mandan. The Arikara. The Atsina.) Cambridge. [Arikara vocabulary, pages 169–177.]

———

[33] In the study mentioned in footnote 1, two Adai forms are compared, successfully it is hoped, with reconstructed Caddoan forms.

[34] Traditions of the Skidi Pawnee, *Memo. Amer. Folklore Soc.* 8, 1904. Traditions of the Arikara, *Carnegie Inst. Wash.* 17, 1904. Mythology of the Wichita, *Carnegie Inst. Wash.* 21, 1904. Traditions of the Caddo, *Carnegie Inst. Wash.* 41, 1905. The Pawnee, mythology (Part I), *Carnegie Inst. Wash.* 59, 1906. Notes on Skidi Pawnee Society, *Field Mus. Nat. Hist.* 27, 1940. (This work was composed with the collaboration of a Skidi, James Murie.)

——— 1930. The North American Indian 19. (The Indians of Oklahoma. The Wichita. The Southern Cheyenne. The Oto. The Comanche. The Peyote Cult.) Cambridge. [Pages 230–237 contain a Wichita vocabulary; in both this and the preceding work additional lexical items for the languages are to be found *passim* throughout the text.]

DENSMORE, FRANCES. 1929. Pawnee music. *Bur. Amer. Ethnol. Bull.* 93. Washington. [Pawnee song texts distributed throughout the work.]

DUNBAR, JOHN BROWN. 1880, 1882. The Pawnee Indians, their history and ethnography. *Mag. Amer. Hist.* 4: 241–281; 5: 321–385; 8: 734–756. [Numerous Pawnee lexical items are given throughout the series of articles.]

——— 1890. The Pawnee language. *In:* Pawnee hero stories and folk tales, by George Bird Grinnell, 409–437, New York. [A word and paradigm description of Pawnee grammar; page 411 has a comparative table of Pawnee, Arikara, Wichita, Waco, Caddo, and Kitsai.]

FLETCHER, ALICE C. 1902. The Hako, a Pawnee ceremony. *22nd Annual Report Bur. Amer. Ethnol. 1900–1901.* Washington. [Pawnee song texts throughout the work.]

GALLATIN, ALBERT SMITH. 1836. A synopsis of the Indian tribes within the United States east of the Rocky Mountains, and in the British and Russian possessions in North America. *Trans. and Coll. Amer. Antiq. Soc.* 2. Cambridge. [Adai vocabulary of John Sibley, Caddo vocabulary of George Gray and John Sibley, pages 305–367; Caddo verbal paradigm page, 272; supplementary Caddo vocabulary, 383–397; Caddo sentences, pages 409, 411, 413.]

GARVIN, PAUL L. 1950. Wichita I: Phonemics. *Internat. Jour. Amer. Ling.* 16: 179–184.

GRINNELL, GEORGE BIRD. 1913. Some Indian stream names. *Amer. Anthropologist,* n.s., 15: 327–331. [Pawnee names for rivers and streams in their former territory in Nebraska, pages 330–331.]

HAYDEN, FERDINAND VANDEVEER. 1863. Contributions to the ethnography and philology of the Indian tribes of the Missouri Valley. *Trans. Amer. Philos. Soc.* 12: 231–461. Philadelphia. [Pawnee vocabulary, pages 347–351, Skiri dialect; Arikara vocabulary, pages 356–363.]

——— 1868. Brief notes on the Pawnee, Winnebago, and Omaha languages. *Proc. Amer. Philos. Soc.* 10: 389–421. Philadelphia. [Pawnee grammatical notes and vocabulary, pages 390–406.]

JAMES, EDWIN. 1905. Account of an expedition from Pittsburgh to the Rocky Mountains, performed in the years 1819–1820 by order of the Honorable John C. Calhoun, Secretary of War, under the command of Major Stephen H. Long. *In:* Early western travels: 1748–1846, ed. by R. G. Thwaites, 17. Cleveland. [Pawnee vocabulary collected by Thomas Say, pages 290–298, numbers on page 305.]

LESSER, ALEXANDER, and GENE WELTFISH. 1932. Composition of the Caddoan linguistic stock. *Smithsonian Misc. Coll.* 87(6). Washington. [Names of Caddoan tribal divisions, some of which are translated.]

MARCY, RANDOLPH B. 1853. Exploration of the Red River of Louisiana in the year 1852. Washington. [Wichita vocabulary on pages 307–308.]

MAXIMILIAN, ALEXANDER PHILIP, PRINCE OF WIED.
1839–1841. Reise des Prinzen Maximilian zu Wied
Neuwied in das Innere Nord-Amerika in den Jahren
1832 bis 1834. Coblenz. *In English in:* Early western travels: 1784–1846, ed. by R. G. Thwaites, **24**.
Cleveland. 1906. [An Arikara vocabulary is given
on pages 210–214, a Pawnee vocabulary on pages
293–294.]

MOONEY, JAMES. 1896. The ghost-dance religion, and
the Sioux outbreak of 1890. *14th Annual Rept. Bur.
Amer. Ethnol. 1892–1893,* part 2. Washington. 1896.
[A Caddo glossary is given on pages 1102–1103.]

MORGAN, LEWIS HENRY. 1871. Systems of consanguinity
and affinity of the human family. *Smithsonian Contributions to Knowledge* **17**. Washington. [Morgan
schedules for Republican and Grand Pawnee, *Arikara*
nos. 34, 35, 36 of Table II, 293–382.]

MURIE, JAMES R., and GEORGE A. DORSEY. Notes on
Skidi Pawnee society. *Field Museum Nat. Hist.,
Anthropol. Ser.* **27**. Chicago. [Skiri kin and other
terms *passim,* especially pages 83–87.]

PARSONS, ELSIE CLEWS. 1941. Notes on the Caddo.
Memo. Amer. Anthropol. Assoc. **57**: 1–76. [Caddo
lexical items distributed throughout the article.]

SCHMITT, KARL. 1952. Wichita kinship past and present. Norman, Oklahoma. [Wichita kin terms, pages
1–2, comments on terms collected by Spier.]

SCHOOLCRAFT, HENRY ROWE. 1853. Historical and statistical information respecting the history, condition,
and prospects of the Indian tribes of the United
States **5**. Philadelphia. [Caddo and Wichita vocabularies collected by Randolph Marcy, pages 709–
712.]

SPIER, LESLIE. 1924. Wichita and Caddo relationship
terms. *Amer. Anthropologist,* n.s., **26**: 258–263.

SWANTON, JOHN R. 1942. Source material on the history and ethnology of the Caddo Indians. *Bur.
Amer. Ethnol. Bull.* **132**. Washington. [Natchito-
ches/Yatasi and Kadohadacho comparative vocabulary, page 15.]

WELTFISH, GENE. 1936. The vision story of Fox Boy.
Internat. Jour. Amer. Ling. **9**: 44–75. [South Band
Pawnee text with grammatical analysis.]

—— 1937. Caddoan texts. *Publ. Amer. Ethnol. Soc.* **17**.
New York.

WHIPPLE, AMIEL WEEKS. 1856. Reports of explorations and surveys to ascertain the most practicable
and economical route for a railroad from the Mississippi River to the Pacific Ocean, 1853–1854, **3**.
Washington. [Part 3 of volume 3, separately pagi-
nated from the preceding portions, is entitled: Report
upon the Indian tribes; vocabularies of Waco and
Kitsai are given, pages 65–68, Caddo vocabulary,
page 70.]

PHYSICAL ANTHROPOLOGY

Reprinted from AMERICAN JOURNAL OF HUMAN GENETICS
Vol. 12, No. 1, March, 1960
Printed in U.S.A.

Blood Groups of Caddoan Indians of Oklahoma

MARGERY P. GRAY AND WILLIAM S. LAUGHLIN

Blood Groups of Caddoan Indians of Oklahoma

MARGERY P. GRAY AND WILLIAM S. LAUGHLIN

Department of Anthropology, University of Wisconsin, Madison, Wisconsin

INTRODUCTION

TRIBES CLASSIFIED as belonging to the Caddoan linguistic family present problems in tracing their prehistoric movements and locations. In the latter part of
the 19th Century the Pawnee were moved from central Nebraska to northern
Oklahoma and the Caddo were moved from Texas and Louisiana up to central
Oklahoma to an area claimed at that time by the Wichita. At present, the Pawnee are concentrated in the vicinity of Pawnee, Oklahoma. The Wichita and
Caddo are located in the vicinity of Anadarko, Gracemont and Binger, Oklahoma. All three tribes have undergone drastic population reductions since white
contact. Population estimates based on Mooney's 1780 figures list 10,000 Pawnee and 13,400 Red River Caddoans (Caddo, Wichita, Kichai and Waco)
(Kroeber, 1947). At the time of contact, the Pawnee were composed of 4 endoga-
mous bands: Skidi, Kitkahaxhi, Pitahauriata, and Chaui. The largest, Skidi,
maintained 13 villages (Lowie, 1954). The old band endogamy broke down with
the enforced move from Nebraska. Each band still maintains a cemetery in the
vicinity of Pawnee even though the biological significance of band membership
has disappeared. The present tribal roles list about 1500 Pawnee but many of
these are less than ¼ Pawnee. A total of 160 Pawnee were blood typed.

The Caddo are the remnants of a loose federation of groups whose territory
extended from the west bank of the Mississippi River in Louisiana and along the
Red River in Texas (Kroeber, 1947). It is not known how far north the Caddo
extended. At the present time the Caddo number not more than 250 with many of
those being hybrids. Of the 250, 61 Caddo were blood typed.

At the time of contact, the Wichita were apparently occupying an area which
brought them in contact with the Caddo to the south. The northern limit is un-
defined except that it is known that they extended up into Kansas (Kroeber,
1947). The latest census lists 515 individuals of which 235 are listed as 4/4
Wichita, 122 as 3/4 Wichita, 76 as 1/2 Wichita, 68 as 1/4 Wichita, and 14 as not
more than 1/8 Wichita. A total of 137 Wichita were blood typed.

At the present time the Pawnee and Wichita maintain close cultural ties in
the form of reciprocal hand games, dances, and gift exchanges. No such ties
were detected between the Pawnee and Caddo. The cultural affinities of the
Caddo and Wichita may be a reflection of having lived in the same area since
moved by the government or may have extended back into prehistory.

This project was supported by the Wenner Gren Foundation and the Graduate School of
the University of Wisconsin.
Received July 13, 1959.

86

Human groups form Mendelian populations if they set themselves apart from surrounding groups and maintain their distinctiveness by language or social customs which encourage marrying within the group. Boundaries of such populations will be sharp or diffuse depending on the strength of social pressures. If the size of an intra-breeding population is small, many of its members will be related to one another. Collecting genealogical information on nuclear families will prevent sibs, and parents and offspring from being included in a sample; however, extensive biological relationships of extended families will be missed and mistakenly be presumed to be absent. The extent of intrarelationship in a small group makes it impossible to obtain an adequate sample of unrelated individuals. Since random mating is not possible in a small group, it is impossible to select a random sample. Sub-sample is the term that will be used in this paper. Since the degree of relationship of individuals included in the sample has a marked effect on phenotype frequency (Table 1), the coefficient of relationship between all individuals was determined. The greatest coefficient of relationship (r) allowed in the computation of gene frequencies of Caddo, Wichita, and Pawnee was $r = .125$. The coefficient of relationship was computed by the formula $r = \frac{1}{2}^n$ where n = the number of biological links connecting any two individuals. As an example, the value of r between parents and offspring would be .500. A smaller value of r would have reduced the sample size to the point where statistical calculations would have been impossible for any of the three groups.

Since gene frequencies estimated from the present sub-samples were to be compared with gene frequencies of other groups, attention was paid to the extent that tribal membership followed biological membership. There is an increasing tendency for Indian tribes to adopt entire families of non-Indians. In the present instances, individuals of Mexican ancestry could not have been excluded on purely morphological grounds.

"Full bloods" in the present samples reported all four grandparents with the same tribal affiliation. Tribal samples are composed of "full bloods" plus Pawnee, Wichita or Caddo—Indian hybrids. All Indian-non-Indian hybrids were excluded since their biological backgrounds were not as clear.

The Pawnee tribal sample is composed of "full bloods" plus Wichita, Ponca, Kiowa, Oto, Sauk and Fox, Cree, Cherokee, Potawotomi, Osage, Blackfoot, Quapaw, Iowa, Arapaho, Wyandotte and Chinook hybrids. The Wichita tribal sample is composed of "full bloods" plus Caddo, Pawnee, Kiowa, Commanche, Seneca, Creek and Delaware hybrids. The Caddo tribal sample is composed of "full bloods" plus Wichita, Commanche, Delaware, Choctaw, Seminole, Shawnee, Chickasaw and Kiowa hybrids. With the exception of one individual (¾ Pawnee-¼ Chinook), the three tribal samples show no biological affiliation with Western or Southwestern tribes. There were no Pawnee-Caddo in the present samples even though the Caddo are as geographically close to the Pawnee as are the Wichita.

TABLE 1. INFLUENCE ON PHENOTYPE FREQUENCIES BY
INCLUSION OF CLOSE RELATIVES

Phenotypes	PAWNEE "Full Blood"				WICHITA "Full Blood"			
	Entire Sample		Sub-sample (maximum r. 125)		Entire Sample		Sub-sample (maximum r. 125)	
	No.	%	No.	%	No.	%	No.	%
O	45	44.6	23	50.0	29	46.8	10	43.5
A	54	53.5	21	45.6	27	43.6	11	47.8
B	2	1.9	2	4.3	3	4.8	1	4.3
EB	0	0.0	0	0.0	3	4.8	1	4.3
Total	*101*		*46*		*62*		*23*	
MS	29	28.7	17	37.0	10	16.1	4	17.4
MNS	17	16.8	4	8.7	16	25.8	5	21.7
NS	1	1.0	1	2.1	8	12.9	2	8.7
Ms	33	32.8	15	32.6	13	21.0	3	13.0
MNs	20	19.8	8	17.4	11	17.7	7	30.4
Ns	1	1.0	1	2.1	4	6.4	2	8.7
Total	*101*		*46*		*62*		*23*	
CCDee	26	25.7	10	21.7	13	21.0	3	13.0
CcDEe	30	29.7	15	32.6	25	40.3	6	26.1
ccDEE	14	13.9	6	13.0	8	12.9	5	21.7
CcDee	7	6.9	2	4.3	7	11.3	3	13.0
ccDEe	8	7.9	5	10.1	6	9.7	4	17.4
CCDEe	6	5.9	3	6.4	3	4.8	2	8.7
CcDEE	9	8.9	4	8.7	0	0.0	0	0.0
ccDee	1	1.0	1	2.1	0	0.0	0	0.0
CCDEE	0	0.0	0	0.0	0	0.0	0	0.0
Total	*101*		*46*		*62*		*23*	
Fy(a+)	94	93.0	42	91.3	55	88.7	21	91.3
Fy(a−)	7	6.9	4	8.7	7	11.3	2	8.7
Total	*101*		*46*		*62*		*23*	
K+	4	4.0	2	4.4	0	0.0	0	0.0
K−	97	96.0	44	95.6	62	100.0	23	100.0
Total	*101*		*46*		*62*		*23*	
Le(a+)	0	0.0	0	0.0	0	0.0	0	0.0
Le(a−)	101	100.0	46	100.0	62	100.0	23	100.0
Total	*101*		*46*		*62*		*23*	
P+	95	94.0	44	95.6	50	80.6	19	82.6
P−	6	5.9	2	4.3	12	19.3	4	17.4
Total	*101*		*46*		*62*		*23*	

The following sera were used: Anti-A and B—saline tube test, *Ulex europeus* lectin (anti-H)—saline tube test (Boyd, 1954), Anti-M and N—saline tube test, Anti-D—albumin rapid tube test, Anti-D—saline capillary test (Chown, 1944), (All saline capillary tests were run by the technique of Chown, (1944).) Anti-C —albumin rapid tube test, Anti-C—saline capillary test, Anti-c—albumin rapid tube test, Anti-E—albumin rapid tube test, Anti-E—saline capillary test, Anti-e —albumin rapid tube test, Anti-Fy[a]—Coombs test, Anti-Kell—Enzyme capillary test (Gray, 1959), Anti-Le[a]—saline tube test, Anti-P—saline tube test, and Anti-S—saline capillary test.

Blood samples were drawn from the ear into saline and tested within 12 hours with the samples made up in the diluent appropriate to each serum. Positive and negative reactions were checked against a cell panel obtained from Knickerbocker Biosales. One example of a weak D antigen was found using the Chown capillary method. This was not termed a D[u] since the tube reaction using albumin anti-D was within the normal range of agglutination.

The observed and expected phenotype frequencies are listed in Table 2. Gene frequencies are listed in Table 3. ABO frequencies were computed by Bernstein's formulae and adjusted by Bernstein's correction. The variances and standard errors were derived using the formulae presented in Boyd (1956). The MNS and Rh gene frequencies were estimated by maximum likelihood methods derived by Boyd (1954) and Boyd (1958) respectively. Gene frequencies were not computed for the Duffy, Kell, Lewis and P groups since only one anti-serum was available for each system and each of these systems is known to consist of multiple alleles.

In spite of the small numbers in the Caddo and Wichita "full blood" sub-samples, the internal consistency for ABO and Rh groups is good. No definite reason can be offered as to why the Pawnee MNS observed frequencies diverge the most from expectation as the Pawnee sub-samples were the largest of the three groups tested.

Since the anthropologist is beset with sampling problems due to population size and structure, it is advisable to use efficient estimates of gene frequencies (Table 4). The Rh frequencies for the two Pawnee sub-samples are not greatly altered by the use of maximum likelihood estimates; however, considerable change in frequencies is apparent for the two Wichita sub-samples. The reverse situation is true for the MNS frequencies. Two rounds of maximum likelihood calculations produce significant changes in the Pawnee MNS estimates.

Limiting factors influence the tracing of prehistoric migrations of inter-tribal affiliations of American Indians by the comparison of blood group gene frequencies. The Pawnee and Wichita suffered severe reduction in numbers over a

TABLE 2. BLOOD GROUP PHENOTYPE FREQUENCIES OF PAWNEE,
WICHITA AND CADDO INDIANS

Phenotypes	PAWNEE						WICHITA						CADDO					
	"Full Blood"			Tribal Status			"Full Blood"			Tribal Status			"Full Blood"			Tribal Status		
	% Obs	N Obs	N Exp	% Obs	N Obs	N Exp	% Obs	N Obs	N Exp	% Obs	N Obs	N Exp	% Obs	N Obs	N Exp	% Obs	N Obs	N Exp
ABO																		
O	50.0	23	23.4	57.5	46	46.4	43.5	10	9.7	55.1	27	26.5	94.4	17	17.0	70.2	33	33.0
A	45.6	21	20.5	40.0	32	31.6	47.8	11	11.3	40.8	20	20.4	5.6	1	1.0	29.7	14	14.0
B	4.3	2	1.5	2.5	2	1.5	4.3	1	1.4	2.0	1	1.5	0.0	0	0.0	0.0	0	0.0
AB	0.0	0	0.5	0.0	0	0.5	4.3	1	0.6	2.0	1	0.5	0.0	0	0.0	0.0	0	0.0
Total		46	45.9		80	80.0		23	23.0		49	48.9		18	18.0		47	47.0
MNS																		
MS	36.9	17	8.4	30.0	24	17.0	17.4	4	4.0	18.4	9	7.3	22.2	4	4.1	31.9	15	15.4
MNS	8.7	4	5.0	12.5	10	9.6	21.7	5	5.4	18.4	9	9.2	11.1	2	1.8	12.8	6	5.2
NS	2.2	1	0.7	1.2	1	1.1	8.7	2	1.8	6.1	3	2.8	0.0	0	0.1	0.0	0	0.3
Ms	32.6	15	22.5	38.8	31	38.22	13.0	3	3.3	22.4	11	13.6	27.8	5	6.0	29.8	14	15.4
MNs	17.4	8	8.4	16.2	13	12.9	30.4	7	5.8	30.6	15	12.9	38.9	7	5.0	25.5	12	9.3
Ns	2.2	1	0.9	1.2	1	1.1	8.7	2	2.6	4.0	2	3.1	0.0	0	1.0	0.0	0	1.4
Total		46	45.9		80	79.9		23	22.9		49	48.9		18	18.0		47	47.0
Rh																		
CCDee	21.7	10	8.4	23.8	19	16.3	13.0	3	3.0	16.3	8	8.7	27.8	5	4.7	29.8	14	12.9
CcDEe	32.6	15	15.8	35.0	28	29.8	26.1	6	7.5	38.8	19	17.6	22.2	4	4.5	31.9	15	15.0
ccDEE	13.0	6	6.7	15.0	12	12.9	21.7	5	4.2	16.3	8	8.3	5.8	1	0.8	6.4	3	3.9
CcDee	4.4	2	4.1	3.8	3	6.6	13.0	3	2.7	8.2	4	4.9	11.1	2	2.9	6.4	3	5.1
ccDEe	10.9	5	3.8	11.2	9	5.9	17.4	4	3.1	12.2	6	4.8	5.5	1	1.1	8.5	4	2.8
CCDEe	6.5	3	3.3	5.0	4	4.0	8.7	2	0.8	6.1	3	1.9	16.6	3	2.3	8.5	4	4.1
CcDEE	8.7	4	3.0	5.0	4	3.5	0.0	0	1.0	2.0	1	1.9	16.6	3	0.9	6.4	3	2.3
ccDee	2.1	1	0.5	1.2	1	0.7	0.0	0	0.6	0.0	0	0.7	5.5	1	0.4	2.1	1	0.5
CCDEE	0.0	0	0.3	0.0	0	0.2	0.0	0	0.0	0.0	0	0.1	0.0	0	0.3	0.0	0	0.3
Total		46	45.9		80	79.9		23	22.9		49	48.9		18	17.9		47	46.9
Duffy																		
Fy(a+)	91.3	42		87.5	70		91.3	21		91.8	45		77.7	14		85.1	40	
Fy(a−)	8.7	4		12.5	10		8.7	2		8.1	4		22.2	4		14.8	7	
Total		46			80			23			49			18			47	
Kell																		
K+	4.3	2		3.7	3		0.0	0		0.0	0		0.0	0		0.0	0	
K−	95.6	44		96.25	77		100.0	23		100.0	49		100.0	18		100.0	47	
Total		46			80			23			49			18			47	
P																		
P+	95.6	44		95.0	76		82.61	19		79.6	39		77.8	14		79.5	39	
P−	4.3	2		5.0	4		17.39	4		20.4	10		22.2	4		20.5	8	
Total		46			80			23			49			18			47	
Lewis																		
Le(a+)	0.0	0		0.0	0		0.0	0		0.0	0		0.0	0		0.0	0	
Le(a−)	100.0	46		100.0	80		100.0	23		100.0	49		100.0	18		100.0	47	
Total		46			80			23			49			18			47	

short period of time followed by a gradual population increase so that the possibility of considerable genetic drift cannot be discounted. Some tribes such as the Caddo, Kansa, Iowa and Missouri did not recover from the effects of white contact so that adequate samples can no longer be obtained. A sample of living

TABLE 3. ABO, MNS, AND RH GENE FREQUENCIES
FOR PAWNEE, WICHITA AND CADDO INDIANS

Genes or Chromosomes	PAWNEE		WICHITA		CADDO	
	"Full Blood"	Tribal Sample	"Full Blood"	Tribal Sample	"Full Blood"	Tribal Sample
ABO	n = 46	n = 80	n = 23	n = 49	n = 18	n = 47
p	.264 ± .050	.226 ± .036	.307 ± .082	.243 ± .070	.029 ± .028	.162 ± .099
q	.022 ± .015	.012 ± .010	.044 ± .034	.020 ± .014	.000	.000
r	.714 ± .051	.762 ± .041	.649 ± .105	.736 ± .048	.972 ± .028	.838 ± .099
MNS						
mS	.128 ± .042	.140 ± .028	.185 ± .049	.126 ± .017	.174 ± .037	.237 ± .040
ms	.699 ± .050	.691 ± .037	.380 ± .065	.527 ± .042	.576 ± .096	.571 ± .047
nS	.044 ± .008	.052 ± .002	.101 ± .019	.096 ± .018	.009 ± .000	.018 ± .000
ns	.129 ± .029	.117 ± .021	.333 ± .057	.251 ± .036	.241 ± .038	.174 ± .025
Rh						
CDe (R_1)	.426 ± .053	.451 ± .040	.363 ± .071	.422 ± .048	.513 ± .094	.523 ± .052
cDE (R_2)	.383 ± .051	.402 ± .040	.428 ± .072	.413 ± .033	.207 ± .075	.289 ± .048
cDe (R_o)	.106 ± .033	.092 ± .024	.159 ± .054	.118 ± .033	.154 ± .069	.104 ± .033
CDE (R_z)	.085 ± .030	.055 ± .017	.050 ± .033	.047 ± .017	.126 ± .070	.083 ± .052

TABLE 4. DIFFERENCE IN GENE FREQUENCIES CALCULATED BY TWO METHODS

Genes or Chromosomes	PAWNEE				WICHITA			
	"Full Blood"		Tribal Status		"Full Blood"		Tribal Status	
	Mourant	M. L.	Mourant	M. L.	Mourant	M. L.	Mourant[1]	M. L.[2]
CDe (R_1)	.441	.426	.455	.451	.293	.363	.394	.422
cDE (R_2)	.398	.383	.405	.402	.358	.428	.394	.413
cDe (R_o)	.091	.106	.089	.092	.229	.159	.136	.118
CDE (R_z)	.070	.085	.051	.055	.120	.050	.076	.047
mS	.233	.128	.202	.140	.171	.185	.133	.126
ms	.593	.699	.630	.691	.394	.380	.520	.527
nS	.045	.044	.048	.052	.107	.101	.111	.096
ns	.129	.129	.120	.117	.328	.333	.236	.251

[1] Mourant, E. A. (1954).
[2] Boyd, W. C. (1954).

tribal members may not adequately represent the tribe of the same name in existence 500 years before. Tribal roles may list considerable numbers but the affiliation of an undetermined number may be cultural or political and not biological.

In the area under investigation, comparative blood group data for linguistically or geographically related tribes is not extensive so that little can be said concerning gene clines. Many of the earlier studies concentrated on areas instead of tribal background so that the frequencies may represent composite samples

TABLE 5. ABO AND RH ALLELE AND FY(A+) FREQUENCIES
OF SEVERAL AMERICAN INDIAN TRIBES

Tribe or Area	Investigator	Number	ABO			Rh							Phenotype % Fy(a+)
			p	q	r	R_1	R_2	R_z	R_o	r''	r'	r	
Blackfoot	Chown, 1953	39	.608	.000	.392								97.44
Blood	Chown, 1953	241	.582	.010	.407	.469	.401	.038	.000	.026	.000	.064	93.24
Stoney	Chown, 1955	155	.161	.000	.839	.484	.349	.019	.021	.029	.000	.097	88.39
Sarcee	Chown, 1955	95	.281	.000	.718								92.13
Chippewa	Matson, 1954	161	.064	.000	.936	.315	.587	.019	.000	.079	.000	.000	98.22
Navaho	Brown, 1958	106	.241	.000	.759	.375	.261	.026	.338	.000	.000	.000	
Apache	Brown, 1958	179	.234	.000	.766	.362	.264	.005	.369	.000	.000	.000	
Pima	Brown, 1958	489	.100	.001	.899	.444	.263	.051	.126	.035	.081	.000	2.72[1]
Cherokee Agency, N. C.	Snyder, 1926	250	.088	.041	.863								
Cherokee	Pollitzer, 1958	136	.018	.004	.978								
Choctaw-Chickasaw Sanatorium	Snyder, 1926	137	.048	.004	.947								
Ponca Agency Whiteage, Okla.	Snyder, 1926	100	.058	.016	.917								
Wichita Tribe	p[2]	49	.243	.020	.736	.422	.412	.047	.118	.000	.000	.000	91.84
Pawnee Tribe	p	80	.226	.012	.761	.451	.401	.055	.092	.000	.000	.000	87.50

[1] Sample size of 184.
[2] Present study.

of several tribes. In the only recent study, Pollitzer (1958) found 95% type O among full blood Cherokee living in North Carolina. It does appear that the Wichita and Pawnee have a much higher frequency of type A that other Southeastern tribes or tribes with Southeast cultural affiliation, which may indicate a northern Plains affiliation (Table 5) despite evidence to the contrary. Lowie (1954) believes that, on the basis of cultural and archaeological evidence, the Pawnee and Wichita can be connected with the Southeast and, in turn can be related linguistically to the Cherokee. The MNS distribution of the Pawnee and Wichita do not provide much in the way of comparative information since early studies did not include these factors and the present study shows some internal inconsistency. The frequency of R_o is higher than that observed for northern tribes (Brown, 1958). The Fy^a distribution is similar to that observed for northern tribes (Chown and Lewis, 1953, 1955; Matson, Koch and Levine, 1954) and shows little resemblance to that observed for the Southwest (Brown, Hannah, Dahlberg, and Strandskov, 1958). The few K+ individuals probably represent the result of white admixture even though this information does not appear in their family histories. Two of the three K+ individuals in the Pawnee tribal sample are first cousins. Two Le (a+) individuals were found in the otal series but both of these were less than 1/4 Indian and were not included in he sub-samples.

SUMMARY

Blood group gene frequency data are presented for the Caddo, Wichita and Pawnee Indians, all belonging to one linguistic stock and all located in Oklahoma. The non-random structure of small American Indian tribes is presented n the form of an inter-tribal genealogy. The effects of tribal structure on sampling and phenotype frequencies is discussed. Gene frequency estimates for MNS and Rh grounps are derived by both inefficient, and efficient maximum likelihood methods with the latter giving, in several instances, quite different estimates. While tribes belonging to the Caddoan linguistic stock are placed in the Southeastern culture area, their gene frequencies indicate a northern biological relationship.

ACKNOWLEDGMENTS

We wish to express our appreciation to Mr. James Sun Eagle, Chief of the Pawnee Tribe, Mr. Frank Miller, tribal leader of the Wichita Tribe, and Mr. Wilbur Williams, tribal leader of the Caddo Tribe for their assistance and co-operation in contacting tribal members and checking family histories. We are indebted to Dr. H. A. Hudgins, Area Medical Director, U. S. Public Health Service and his staff for their assistance and for providing laboratory facilities at Pawnee. Dr. Kenneth Richter and Dr. Alice Brues of the Department of Anatomy, University of Oklahoma Medical School provided laboratory facilities. Dr. Griffitts of the Dade Reagents, Inc., and Dr. Bruce Chown of the Rh Laboratory very kindly provided anti-sera. Appreciation is also expressed to Mrs. Rene Bock and Miss Sonja Homme for technical assistance in the field.

REFERENCES

BOYD, W. C. 1939. Blood Groups. *Tabulae Biologicae* 17: 113–240.

BOYD, W. C., AND SHAPLEIGH, ELIZABETH. 1954. Diagnosis of subgroups of blood groups A and AB by use of plant agglutinins (lectins). *J. Laborat. Clin. M.* 44: 235–237.

BOYD, W. C. 1954. Maximum likelihood method for estimation of gene frequencies from MNS data. *Am. J. Human Genet.* 6: 1–10.

BOYD, W. C. 1956. Variances of gene frequency estimates. *Am. J. Human Genet.* 8: 24–38.

BOYD, W. C. 1958. Gene frequency estimates for MNS data when four sera are used or for Rh data when five sera are used but all individuals are positive with Anti-D. (unpublished).

BROWN, K. S., HANNA, B. L., DAHLBERG, A. A., AND STRANDSKOV. H. H. 1958. The distribution of blood group alleles among Indians of southwest North America. *Am. J. Human Genet.* 10: 175–195.

CHOWN, B. 1944. A rapid, simple and economical method for Rh agglutination. *Am. J. Clin. Path.* 14: 114–115.

CHOWN, B., AND LEWIS, M. 1953. The ABO, MNSs, P, Rh, Lutheran, Kell, Lewis, Duffy and Kidd blood types and the secretor status of the Blackfeet Indians of Alberta, Canada. *Am. J. Phys. Anthrop.* 11: 369–383.

CHOWN, B., AND LEWIS, M. 1955. The blood group and secretor genes of the Stoney and Sarcee Indians of Alberta, Canada. *Am. J. Phys. Anthrop.* 13: 181–189.

GRAY, M. P. 1959. Use of bromelin in blood typing. *Am. J. Laborat. Clin. M.* (in press).
KROEBER, A. L. 1947. *Cultural and Natural Areas of Native North America.* Berkeley, Calif. Univ. California Press.
LOWIE, R. H. 1954. *Indians of the Plains.* New York: McGraw-Hill.
MATSON, G. A., KOCH, E. A., AND LEVINE, P. 1954. A study of the hereditary blood factors among the Chippewa Indians of Minnesota. *Am. J. Phys. Anthrop.* 12: 413–426.
MOURANT, A. E. 1954. *Distribution of the Human Blood Groups.* Springfield, Ill.: C. C Thomas
POLLITZER, W. S. 1958. (unpublished).

ARCHAEOLOGY

Changing Archeological Methods and Theory In the Transmississippi South

CLARENCE WEBB

EXCITING CHANGES have taken place in archeological method and theory over the forty years that King Harris and I have been engaged in the discipline. For most of that time we have been primarily concerned with archeological studies in Texas, Louisiana, Oklahoma, and Arkansas, the states that share the diagonal axis of the Red River. Much of this territory is incorporated in the Caddoan area and much of it is in the Trans-Mississippi South, a biogeographical construct introduced by Frank Schambach (1970) at the Thirteenth Caddo Conference held at the Balcones Research Center in 1971. The Trans-Mississippi South incorporates as a natural area the oak-hickory southeastern Woodland environment that occurs west of the lower Mississippi Valley, interposed between the valley and the plains; it largely coincides with the four-state Caddoan archeological area, with some extension beyond its usual boundaries. Most of the interests that King Harris and I have shared are encompassed within the two constructs—archeological and physiographic— but to some extent our studies have ranged from the low plains to the Mississippi.

Forty years ago nearly all who engaged in archeology in this area were amateurs—untaught, self-taught, or with rudiments of the craft taught by individuals who had academic connections in other, sometimes related, fields. Professors J. E. Pearce and W. C. Holden in Texas, Fred Kniffen in Louisiana, S. C. Dellinger in Arkansas, J. Willis Stovall in

Oklahoma, Major Webb in Kentucky, Wrench in Missouri, and Jones in Alabama, had their training in such fields as history, geography, zoology, or sciences other than archeology. Nevertheless, they did some creditable archeological work, established museums, laid the groundwork for departments of anthropology in their institutions, and fostered the early careers of professionals such as Tom Campbell, Robert Bell, Bob McGimsey, Bill Haag, Tom Lewis, David DeJarnette, and Jim Ford. Credit should also go to some of the pioneers who were active in local archeological societies, the Houston society and several others, and contributed to such publications as Frank Watts's *Central Texas Archaeologist* of the 1930s and the *Dallas Record*, which Robert Hatzenbuehler and King Harris took turns editing in the 1940s.

The Texas Archeological and Paleontological Society was the pioneer of the statewide organization, and its bulletin has the longest record of continuous publication in the field. The society was established before 1930 under the leadership of Cyrus N. Ray, the crusty but indomitable spirit of Abilene, and it continued under his presidency, with the bulletin under his editorship, for nearly two decades. In 1940 W. C. Holden became editor, and he has had a number of distinguished successors. In 1953 the Texas Archeological and Paleontological Society became the Texas Archeological Society.

The original name was an indication that paleontology was an important part of the society's early interests, as was geology. The society's activities centered in the plains of western Texas and the panhandle. Early man and the extinct animals that he hunted were focal. E. H. Sellards, Glen Evans, Grayson Meade, Ray, and Holden were frequent contributors to programs and publications. Ray attracted well-known students of early man, geology, and the Southwest, encouraging them to visit the area, do field work, and participate in programs of the society. The programs were sometimes more noted for heat than for light, but times were never dull. Involved were people like Warren Moorehead, Ernest A. Hooten, J. Alden Mason, Frank Bryan, Harold Gladwin, M. R. Harrington, E. S. Renaud, Ales Hrdlicka, W. C. McKern, A. E. Jenks, and Lloyd A. Wilford, the latter two (Jenks and Wilford, 1938) concerned with the Sauk Valley skeleton research. One of James B. Griffin's early pottery descriptions, that of sherds from the Abilene area (1935), was published in the *Bulletin*. (He has recently said, "I knew very little about it at the time and even less now.") This paper included a description and chemical analysis by Frederick Matson, of the University of

Michigan, of a white aplastic temper that Matson showed to be calcium phosphate, presuming it to be derived from limestone beds or fossil bone. Later, Alex Krieger and I showed a microscopic study that this temper of Leon Plain pottery in central Texas and of ceramics in East Texas and northwestern Louisiana is crushed bone.

The methodology of the early excavations and studies in central and western Texas related largely to the geological and extinct animal associations, and to the morphology of the projectile points. The absence of relatively exact time markers and, sometimes, the vagaries of excavation led to heated discussions.

In the mid-1940s, during a trip to the Texas Panhandle, Krieger, my son, and I participated briefly with Glen Evans in an excavation of the Plainview bison kill (Sellards et al., 1947). We were taken by Floyd Studer and Judge Pipkin to visit the Alibates quarries and the Antelope Creek ruins, where I observed for the first time the curious West Texas custom of the individuals' leasing of archeological search rights on entire ranches—and the avid defending of them.

During the mid-1930s a minimal amount of work occurred in East Texas, southern Arkansas, and northwestern Louisiana. A. T. Jackson was excavating burial sites and houses in East Texas and securing collections for the Austin Museum, including pottery and pipes and ornaments, about which he wrote descriptive articles in the *Bulletin of the Texas Archeological and Paleontological Society* (Jackson, 1933, 1934, 1935). The archeology of Titus County was reported by Goldschmidt (1935), following a summer's work by a field party from the University of Texas. He first presented evidence of cultural stratigraphy in the Caddoan area of East Texas, began the identification of Titus Focus, and discounted the prior opinion by Jackson that cultural subareas in East Texas corresponded to the four major river systems. Dickinson (1936), Lemley (1936), and Lemley and Dickinson (1937) published reports of the Crenshaw site in southwestern Arkansas and of studies along Bayou Macon in the southeastern part of that state. In 1936 King Harris was on the program of the Texas society at its Abilene meeting, with a description of sites on the upper Trinity River. This was my first meeting, and, I believe, my first acquaintance with King.

Elsewhere, many of the excavations and explorations were specimen-related, made on behalf of museums or by nonprofessionals for private collections. Dellinger was exploring the Ozark bluff shelters of northern Arkansas. Numerous local or regional collectors were actively digging into graves and collecting, buying, or manufacturing artifacts up and down the Mississippi Valley (an activity that is still going on); museum people had to develop some expertise in detecting fraudulent objects. The Great Depression stimulated the hunting and selling of pottery; Mississippi pots from the St. Francis, wagonloads of pottery from the Carden Bottoms on the Arkansas River, and many thousands of artifacts from Poverty Point site found their way into museums and private collections throughout the nation. Toward the latter part of this period the great "mining" rape of Craig Mound at Spiro took place. Museum directors as well as amateurs and admitted artifact dealers were contaminated by the loot, but—to their credit—some hardy individuals and tough societies resisted the temptation to exploit the sites and opposed the looting process. For example, Henry Hamilton (1952) and Harry Trowbridge (1938) traced many of the Spiro objects and recorded them for archeology.

With the Depression came Works Progress Administration (WPA) archeology and the first large influx of professionally trained archeologists into the area. The first relief labor program was at the Marksville site in Louisiana, under Frank M. Setzler and James A. Ford; but the real prototype was the Tennessee Valley Authority (TVA) series of explorations and excavations in the Norris, Wheeler, and Pickwick Basins, between 1934 and 1939. This was organized and directed by Major William S. Webb. For the first time huge crews exposed entire villages and completely excavated mounds or immense shell middens. To the credit of Major Webb, within eight years of the program's inception there resulted three massive reports (W. S. Webb, 1938, 1939; W. S. Webb and DeJarnette, 1942), completely illustrated, with special sections on physical anthropology and osteology by Funkhouser, Newman, and Snow; ceramics by Griffin and Haag; tree-ring dating by Florence Hawley; molluscs by J. P. E. Morrison; geology by Walter Jones; and ethnographic and comparative artifact studies and conclusions by Webb or DeJarnette.

In the Trans-Mississippi South the WPA methods and results were more variable and less spectacular. The economic need for the use of manpower sorely tried the newly found expertise of professional archeologists in managing budgets, in transporting and supervising raw crews numbering from dozens to hundreds, in doing a massive volume of archeological work, and in handling specimens that numbered into the multiplied thousands. There is little wonder that scant attention was paid to processual debris and debitage, small floral and faunal remains, and other minutiae. There were floods of specimens and skeletal material, stacks of excavation reports, maps, and logs, and masses of photographs and drawings. Storage facilities were packed, analyses lagged far behind, and final publications were scarce or late—some are still waiting in the wings or are stored in attics.

Out of this exasperating welter of sweat and worry, however, some outstanding beginnings of analysis and synthesis did result. Kniffen brought Ford to Louisiana State University and with his help imported, for the WPA program, trained individuals who were destined to become well known in their own right. Included in the group were Gordon Willey, John Cotter, George Quimby, R. S. (Stu) Neitzel, Arden King, Edwin Doran, and Carlisle Smith. Ford (1936) had used an unwieldy system of pottery sherd classification in his analysis of collections from Louisiana and Mississippi, and had employed it in establishing the sequence of Marksville, Coles Creek, Deasonville, Tunica, Caddo, and Natchez ceramic complexes. Out of his and Willey's dissatisfaction with the system and their experiences in the Southwest, they worked out the binomial system of pottery nomenclature with Griffin in the 1937 Conference on Pottery Classification for the Southeastern United States. Ford and Willey (1941) used this system in the Louisiana WPA projects between 1938 and 1941. It was adopted by the nascent Southeastern Archeological Conference (Haag, 1939), later used by Caldwell and Waring in Georgia, and eventually became standard throughout the eastern United States.

I had been encouraged by Griffin and Ford to develop pottery types in northwestern Louisiana. I used the binomial system (i.e., "Belcher Engraved") in a report of pottery types from the Belcher Mound, published in the *Bulletin of the Texas Archeological and Paleontological Society* (C. H. Webb and Dodd, 1941)—the first use of this system for Caddoan ceramics in the bulletin. Later I assisted Krieger in extending the binomial or trinomial (i.e., "Holly Fine Engraved") system throughout the Caddoan area.

Ford and his coworkers in central Louisiana, and Phillips, Ford, and Griffin (1951) in the Lower Mississippi Valley Survey used the techniques of meticulous stratigraphic study, vertical as well as horizontal distribution of artifacts, resolution of artificial and natural levels, histograms and overlays in presentation of data, pottery sherd seriation (previously used, but reintroduced by Ford), and correlation of cultural occupations with Fisk's monumental river geology reports to establish the prehistoric sequences of the lower valley. The Poverty Point-Tchefuncte-Marksville-Troyville-Coles Creek-Plaquemine-Natchez or the alternate Poverty Point-Tchula-Marksville-Baytown-Coles Creek Early and Late Mississippian sequences served as fulcrums around which other cultural complexes of the eastern United States have been oriented or with which they have been compared.

In Oklahoma, excavations were conducted at the Spiro group and other prehistoric Caddoan sites, also in pre-Caddoan Archaic and early ceramic sites in the Arkansas River valley and eastern Oklahoma (Orr, 1952; Bell and Baerreis, 1951). Hopewell related materials were reported and the Fourche Maline complex of Late Archaic and Early Woodland sites was outlined. By long-range comparisons, Fourche Maline was assumed to cover a Poverty Point-Tchefuncte-Marksville time span. Among the workers in Oklahoma were Forrest Clements, Kenneth Orr, David Baerreis, Lynn Howard, Rodney Cobb, and Phil Newkumet.

Concurrent with the Oklahoma archeological activities during the late 1930s were the WPA excavations in East Texas which included the George C. Davis site near Nacogdoches and the Hatchel Mound near Texarkana. McAllister was department chairman at the University of Texas, T. N. Campbell was department archeologist, and Perry Newell was field archeologist for the Davis excavations between 1939 and 1942. Krieger came to the university as research associate in 1941, completed the Davis publication (Newell and Krieger, 1949) after Newell's death, established artifact types that later appeared in the Texas handbook, and developed cultural entities and chronologies for Texas and the Caddoan area. J. Charles Kelley, Campbell, and Donald J. Lehmer were working in southwestern and central Texas.

Between 1935 and 1942 Monroe Dodd, Jr. and I made surface collections in northwestern Louisiana, excavated a small cemetery at Smithport Landing (C. H. Webb, 1963) which demonstrated early Caddoan nonceremonial burial and village wares, salvaged two large burial pits at the Gahagan site (C. H. Webb and Dodd, 1939), and were excavating the Belcher Mound (C. H. Webb, 1959) as another salvage program. I exchanged visits with Ford and Willey, then with Newell and Krieger. At Ford's recommendation we excavated the Belcher Mound by the peeling technique, rather than the then popular "cake-slicing" technique, completely exposing the occupations and house floors one at a time. I believe that this was the first Caddoan mound to be so excavated.

The concept of interrelationships over the four-state area was beginning to ferment. Eventually, in January, 1942, Krieger and Newell from Texas, Baerreis and Cobb from Oklahoma, and Beecher and I from Louisiana spent a weekend together at my home studying archeological data. We confirmed or established ceramic types, compared materials from the several states, and laid the groundwork for areal cooperation that culminated, in 1946 and after World War II, in the First Caddo Conference (symposium) at the University of Oklahoma (Krieger, 1947).

This initial conference, under the cochairmanship of Alex Krieger and Kenneth Orr, set several patterns that were followed at Caddo conferences for many years: (1) no written papers; (2) round table discussions with one or more leaders for each chosen topic; (3) full audience participation; (4) representation from each of the states and from outside of the area; and (5) a minimum of formality. The expressed purposes of the meetings were to assemble data relative to the definition of cultural units, to seek agreement on these identities and their relationships, to integrate them with those found in surrounding areas, to discuss the broader implications of these correlations in terms of the Southwest, Mississippian, the Southeast, the Plains, and Mexico, and to try to define the major unsolved problems in the area.

An attendance of forty-one persons at the first conference included representatives from the four states. Those from outside of the area were: Chapman, the Hamiltons, and Wrench from Missouri; Spaulding and Trowbridge from Kansas; Deuel, MacNeish, and McGregor from Illinois; Neumann from Indiana; Griffin from Michigan; Dr. and Mrs. Mera from New Mexico; and Armillas, Du Solier, and Noguera from Mexico. King Harris and I participated, and we have attended most, if not all, of the subsequent Caddo conferences, which in 1978 totaled twenty-one. Griffin continued to attend frequently, and often he, Krieger, and Ford led spirited discussions of cultural and temporal relationships between Caddoan, Mississippian, and Lower Valley manifestations. As they came to the area or developed within it, others took over frequently as discussion leaders: Robert Bell, Hester and Mott Davis, C. R. McGimsey, Don Wyckoff, Michael Hoffman, Dee Ann (Suhm) Story, Hiram Gregory, James Brown, Frank Schambach, Harry Shafer, Terry Pruitt, Ned Woodall, and Martha Rolingson.

The Caddo conferences and other meetings in the area after the mid-1940s often reflected archeological trends that were occurring throughout the eastern United States. There was, of course, the desire to use artifacts and excavation findings for the reconstruction of culture history, replacing the collection of artifacts for esoteric pleasure. Then a lot of new ground was broken in artifact typology, in the attempt to advance from cumbersome individual artifact description to the establishment of *types* (comparable to the *species* concept in botany and zoology) as more effective tools. With the introduction of the binomial or trinomial system in nomenclature, much additional study entered into questions of how attributes should be quantified in the formulation of types. Arguments were, and still are, rife over subjective versus mathematical formulations, the latter concept emphasized by Spaulding (1953) and reinforced by the advent of computer technology. In artifact classification there are those who lump types and those who prefer to split types in finer detail; there are arguments over relative values of attributes. Some people, such as Ford, Willey, and I working in Louisiana; Krieger, Suhm, and Jelks in their papers in the Texas handbook; and Bell and Perino in their studies in the Oklahoma projectile point handbooks, prefer to establish types as simple and sharp tools. Others, including Phillips, Williams, Brain, Halley, and Belmont in working with the Harvard University surveys in the Yazoo and Tenas Basins; Duffield, Johnson, and McClurkan in dealing with East Texas lithics; and Schambach in studying Arkansas ceramics, have preferred the type-variety concept, with further study of modes, in their attempts to clarify changes in time and relationships in space. Still other serious students have questioned artifact formulation by named types and varieties lest this method might interfere with the recognition of individual and local technologies.

Similarly, there have been varying ideas of the ways in which artifact types and other cultural traits should be manipulated or combined in the demonstration and comparison of prehistoric culture units. The Texas and Caddoan taxonomists initially adopted the McKern Midwestern system of site (component)-focus-aspect-phase-pattern (the latter two seldom used). Progressively, however, they modified the original purity by adding, overtly or covertly, temporal and historic connotations. Students in the Lower Mississippi Valley and eastward have modified the McKern system to use the site (component)-phase-period formulation of cultures and chronologies, sometimes expressing their restiveness by substituting terms like *stages* or *characterizations*. The words *period* and *complex* have meant different things to different people.

On a larger scale, discussions of trends, broad sweeps of cultural transmission, and even grandiose generalizations have been essayed or proposed. The WPA era resulted first in the establishment of local and regional chronologies; then came an outstanding series of syntheses and interpretations. Griffin, Ford, Willey, Phillips, William H. Sears, Joseph R. Caldwell, Jesse D. Jennings, and Alex Krieger were prominent in these endeavors. The outstanding volume of a quarter-century ago was *Archaeology of Eastern United States*, edited by Griffin (1952) and dedicated to Fay-Cooper Cole. Others have followed, including the Rice Institute symposium, which resulted in the publication of *Prehistoric Man in the New World*, edited by Jennings and Norbeck (1964). Ford (1952) published the results of one of the early attempts at widespread comparisons and demonstrations of culture movements—from Florida to the Caddoan area—in his "Measurements of Prehistoric Design Developments in the Southeastern States." Krieger's (1946) "Culture Complexes and Chronology in Northern Texas, with Extension of Puebloan Datings to the Mississippi Valley," and Bell's study of Caddoan extensions into the plains are other examples.

Many debates have centered around the concepts of independent invention versus culture diffusion, or of man-the-innovator versus man-the-culture-bearer. The latter was one of the favorite arguments between Jim Ford and me, with Ford expounding on Leslie White's culture diffusion theory and with me holding for my concept of individualistic and humanistic action.

King Harris and I contributed to the knowledge of the Caddo-European contact period along Red River. His studies were of sites like Roseborough Lake, Womack, and Kaufman (Harris, 1953, 1967; Harris and Harris, 1967; Harris et al., 1965; Skinner et al., 1969) in the northeastern corner of Texas, south of Red River and above the Fulton Bend. Although the materials he worked with included both native and trade objects, perhaps King's finest contribution was an exhaustive compilation of trade bead types and datings. My work was in the Natchitoches area, with reports of late Caddoan pottery types, presumably from the Natchitoches tribe, and trade materials (C. H. Webb, 1945). Later reports from the Colfax Ferry site concerned a 1790-1805 occupation by Pascagoula-Biloxi groups. Hiram Gregory

(Gregory and Webb, 1965) joined me in describing trade bead types from the Natchitoches vicinity and subsequently wrote his doctoral dissertation (1973) at Southern Methodist University on the Spanish post at Los Adaes, with a careful study of European beads, ceramics, and other trade or native objects found in his exploration at the site.

At the other end of the time spectrum, Harris and I were involved in studies of early man in the Trans-Mississippi South. Wilson W. Crook, Jr. and Harris (1952, 1954) described two sequent Archaic cultures near Dallas. Then they discovered and reported the Lewisville site (Crook and Harris, 1957, 1958), with radiocarbon dating of charcoal from a hearth reported to be older than 38,000 B.C. The date and site have elicited much discussion and some controversy, especially since a Clovis point was found in Hearth 1. In recent years there has been less reluctance to accept a date this early for man in the Americas, as radiocarbon datings much earlier than the accepted range for Clovis have been reported from other sites, including recent datings of approximately 16,000 years ago from rock shelters in Pennsylvania and Tennessee.

King and I shared an interest in San Patrice culture. I had initially described San Patrice points and Albany type sidescrapers from northwestern Louisiana in the *Bulletin of the Texas Archeological and Paleontological Society* (Webb, 1946). Lathel Duffield's published findings (1963) at the multicomponent Wolfshead site in East Texas indicated San Patrice antedated Archaic horizons. He also gave some evidence of the associated tool types and delineated three varieties of San Patrice type. More recently (Webb, Shiner, and Roberts, 1971) we reported isolated San Patrice components, stratigraphically below Archaic materials, at the John Pearce site near Shreveport. Here the San Patrice varieties *Hope* and *St. Johns* were associated with side-notched Keithville points, Albany sidescrapers, and a complete assemblage of microlithic tools made from flakes and blades. King Harris found a San Patrice point in the Wood Pit site at a level deeper than material from which a radiocarbon date of approximately 4000 B.C. was secured (personal communication). Gagliano and Gregory (1965) and C. H. Webb (1948) had previously demonstrated the presence of a wide variety of Paleo-Indian point types in Lousiana, including Clovis, Folsom, Angostura, Scottsbluff, Plainview, Meserve, Dalton, San Patrice, and Pelican types.

The third field in which King Harris and I have collaborated concerns the Poverty Point culture. Although this culture is primarily centered in the Lower Mississippi Valley and adjoining portions of the Gulf Coast, it reached the Ouachita River to the west and influenced late Archaic cultures across southwestern Arkansas to the Red River. Following brief reports (Webb, 1944, 1948) that I made in *American Antiquity*, and later the Jaketown report of Ford, Phillips, and Haag (1955) and the Ford and Webb (1956) publication by the American Museum of Natural History, many of us have joined in pursuing this intriguing culture. The work of the Lower Mississippi Valley Survey has continued under the sponsorship of Peabody Museum, Harvard University, with Phillips's (1970) monumental Lower Yazoo Basin report. Other aspects of Poverty Point have been investigated by Stephen Williams and Jeffrey Brain. Before his untimely death, Ford (1966) published a stimulating article outlining the Formative Period in the southeastern United States, and then later a widely acclaimed book (Ford, 1969) which compared Poverty Point, Adena-Hopewell, Olmec, and Chavin cultures of the American Formative during the millennium before the time of Christ.

Poverty Point has now (C. H. Webb, 1977) been documented as a widespread culture of the American Formative, involving five river systems and more than 125 documented sites, with its cultural climax and politico-religious center at the index site.

Many other people have contributed to studies of Poverty Point: in Louisiana, Sherwood Gagliano, Jon. L. Gibson, William Haag, Hiram Gregory, Donald G. Hunter, William G. Neitzel, Robert Neuman, William Baker, Carl Alexander, Richard Shenkel, Carl Kuttruff, and many other members of the Louisiana Archaeological Society; in Arkansas, Frank Schambach, Cynthia Weber, Martha Rolingson, Dan Morse, Harvey McGehee, and others of the Arkansas Archaeological Society; in Mississippi, John Connaway, Sam McGahey, Richard Marshall, L. B. Jones, Thomas H. Koehler, and dozens of members of the Mississippi Archaeological Association in the Yazoo Basin and on the Gulf Coast. Beyond these states, our study of the cultural influence and trade connections has involved professional and nonprofessional students in Missouri, Tennessee, Florida, and most of the southeastern tier of states. The Poverty Point collections of King Harris and several of his Dallas friends were among the eighteen collections Ford and I classified and tabulated during the 1960s. Additionally, King (personal communications) found earth ovens and a bead-maker's kit at the site which were important additions to the technology; he also reported on jasper bead-making in Walker County, Alabama (Harris, 1950).

In the most recent epoch in the archeology of the Trans-Mississippi South there is involvement in archeological surveys and feasibility studies in conjunction with river basin, dam site, highway, and other kinds of public—or private—earth-altering operations. Contract archeology is an outstanding example of applied science. It has the advantages of governmental funding of research and publication, and the affording of employment to many graduate students and full-time archeologists. It demonstrates to the government and to the public the important role of archeology in developing and preserving the national and state heritage in history and prehistory. But it has the disadvantages of confining efforts largely to limited studies and restricted excavations at the expense of problem-oriented research, and it can condition departments, universities, and legislatures to depend on federal financing, with the attendant possibilities of restrictive or unimaginative directives or the withdrawal of support.

The establishment of a state archeologist's office in each of the states and the development of active state archeological societies have been important advances. With the latter have come society-sponsored field schools and supervised excavations. Also, in Arkansas there are training programs for amateurs which offer certification of training accomplishments and qualification for certain degrees of independent responsibilities. This program is being watched with interest by other state societies. C. R. McGimsey and Hester Davis came to Arkansas in connection with river basin salvage and were appointed to university positions. They worked with an active state archeological society to develop a favorable atmosphere in the state legislature. This has resulted in funding to support a statewide network of regional survey offices and anthropological staffing of the state universities.

Don G. Wyckoff has been most prominently associated with the Oklahoma River Basin Survey Project and the Oklahoma Research Institute for more than a dozen years. He and his associates have produced an outstanding series of survey reports. In East Texas, Robert Stephenson, Edward Jelks, Lathel Duffield, E. Mott Davis, Curtis Tunnell, and others have been connected with river basin surveys. Departments of Anthropology at the University of Texas at Austin, Southern Methodist University, Texas A&M University, and Stephen F. Austin University have been active in East Texas studies.

The burgeoning expansion of archeological programs during the last two decades has been paralleled, nationally and regionally, by a spirit of introspection and inquiry into motives, methodology, and mission. The social anthropologist, elevated to an atmosphere of social awareness and surrounded by an aura of rightness (if not righteousness), looks down at the dirt archeologist and demands to know how immediate and relevant his work is. The archeologist, possibly feeling guilty because he enjoys his work and forgetting that the pursuit of knowledge does not have to be immediately relevant in order to be useful, responds by trying to orient his science toward individual people rather than toward cultural-historical situations. Let us hope that the injection of sociology into archeology will have happier results than those achieved by sociologists in government, education, welfare, and the judicial-correctional systems.

The theoreticians are looking for a new paradigm. Readers of archeological literature have become accustomed to this word, which the dictionary translates as "show side by side," as a pattern or an example; but in reference to anthropology or archeology Leone (1972) expands the term to mean "a theory or set of propositions assumed or known to govern the operation of an isolated body of phenomena." A paradigm is a set of laws to some, a guiding and shining light to others. One might also get acquainted with words like strategy (as "excavation strategy"), models, systems analysis, cultural dynamics, interaction spheres, ecotones, manufacturing trajectory, exchange hypothesis, functionalism, and pragmatism—they are all present in archeological literature today.

What is the "new archeology"? For a reasonably balanced presentation of the subject, I recommend *Contemporary Archaeology: A Guide to Theory and Contributions*, a compilation of thirty-three essays, edited by Leone (1972). A more in-depth study is *New Perspectives in Archeology* by Binford and Binford (1968). There is also other good work by Flannery, Service, Sahlins, Deetz, Levi-Strauss, and—nearer to dirt archeology—Struever. These seem to typify the modern schools that challenge Leslie White, Kroeber, and Taylor, just as these latter challenged, but never supplanted, the original American anthropological theoretician Franz Boas. From our area and especially with regard to research design in contract archeology there are the studies of Raab and Klinger (1977) or Schiffer and House (1975).

There is dissatisfaction with the results of former periods of archeology, which have been described by Willey (1968) as speculative (up to the mid-nineteenth century), descriptive (to the early twentieth century), descriptive-historic (to 1950) and comparative-historic (since 1950). Willey and Phillips (1958) said "the ultimate aim of archaeology is science but at the present stage the practice has more of the character of history."

The present desire, as I fathom it, is to replace the study of culture history with the study of culture process, thence to deduce or formulate the laws and dicta of culture change and the dynamics of cultural transformation, which will then be made available (confidently) as guidelines for society. To be relevant, it is said, the reconstruction of the prehistoric past must be applied to man's future.

Specifically, Binford and Binford (1968) states that processual archeology is the deductive generation of multiple hypotheses from general anthropological theory that are then tested by sophisticated quantitative methods. This is the hypothetico-deductive approach; with it, to quote Leon (1972), "People are now said to be doing science as opposed to writing history, deducing as opposed to inducing, testing hypotheses (models) as opposed to speculating, and so on down the whole litany of procedural requirements for being legitimate as opposed to tainted." The present view seems to be that the new archeology can handle a new range of problems, like social organization, ecological relationships, demographic and paleonutritional assays, and the relationships of material culture to technology and economics. These are laudable aims to which all archeologists should address themselves as the opportunities are presented, but the attempt to force them in the face of inadequate evidence can produce ludicrous results. It remains to be seen how much better the results of the new school are than those of the old (anything before 1960); so far, I have seen more words than results.

An unfortunate aspect of the new dogma is the conviction—sometimes implied, too often expressed—that traditional archeology was erroneous or futile, that only the new approach is scientific, that no excavation is worthwhile unless it is problem-oriented, that scientific results can be secured in the excavation of a site only if the work is done according to modern sampling theory, that deduction is scientific and induction is not (even though the terms are often confused), and that anyone who practices anything other than the new archeology is, ergo, doing "bad" archeology. After fifty years in one science and forty in another, with some experience in research in each and with much contact with excellent scientists in both, I must observe: (1) no individual or school of thought has a corner on the market for earnestness or intellect; (2) most scientists worth their salt use both deduction and induction; (3) much of scientific progress is about 80 percent dogged perseverence and 20 percent sound methodology, intuition, and luck (witness for perseverence Ehrlich's 605 chemical compounds before he found the 606th that was the "magic bullet," and for a combination of luck and brilliance the almost accidental discovery of penicillin by Fleming); (4) there are many paths to science and most breakthroughs represent the apex of a large pyramid of antecedent studies and clarifications; and (5) unfortunately, most scientists who seek to elevate their own stature by attacking or deriding their contemporaries are suffering feelings of insecurity or inferiority.

History may be no more futile than process. Moreover, anyone reporting on human behavior would do well to remember the newspaper reporter's dictum, "who, what, where, when, why—and how." And, if history *can* be separated from process and human behavior, I happen to prefer history. King Harris and I feel we have paid our debt to society by service rendered in our other professions; archeology is to us a pure intellectual joy, and no polemics can succeed in making us feel guilty.

There is no question that many methods are now available, often from other sciences, to assist and excite the archeologist. Radiocarbon dating has stabilized chronology, and other isotopes are reaching into the distant past. In our area Du Bois is doing outstanding work with archeomagnetic studies at Oklahoma, and Bell, at the same institution, is measuring hydration of obsidian from El Inga. Cynthia Weber arranged for thermoluminescence studies of Poverty Point baked clay objects by Aitken and Huxtable at Oxford, England. Palynology, flotation techniques, paleonutritional techniques, tree-ring dating in this area, specialized studies of flint knapping, the application of computer techniques, and many other advances offer avenues of approach for the future. This is a time for experience-sharing and cooperative working in an exciting science, not for procedural bickering and theoretical snobbishness.

BIBLIOGRAPHY

BELL, R. E., and BAERREIS, D. A. 1951. "A survey of Oklahoma Archaeology." *Bulletin of the Texas Archeological and Paleontological Society* 22:7-100.

BINFORD, S. R., and BINFORD, L. R., eds. 1968. *New Perspectives in Archeology*. Chicago: Aldine Publishing Co.

CAMPBELL, T. N. 1959. "A List of Radiocarbon Dates from Archaeological

Sites in Texas." *Bulletin of the Texas Archeological Society* 30:311-20.

CROOK, W. W., JR., and HARRIS, R. K. 1952. "Trinity Aspect of the Archaic Horizon: The Carrollton and Elam Foci." *Bulletin of the Texas Archeological and Paleontological Society* 23:7-38.

————— 1954. "Traits of the Trinity Aspect Archaic: Carrollton and Elam Foci." *The Record* 12 (1):2-16.

————— 1957. "Hearths and Artifacts of Early Man near Lewisville, Texas, and Associated Faunal Material." *Bulletin of the Texas Archeological and Paleontological Society* 28:7-97.

————— 1958. "A Pleistocene Campsite near Lewisville, Texas." *American Antiquity* 23:233-46.

DICKINSON, S. D. 1936. "Ceramic Relationship of the Pre-Caddo Pottery from the Crenshaw Site." *Bulletin of the Texas Archeological and Paleontological Society* 8:56-70.

DUFFIELD, L. 1963. "The Wolfshead Site: An Archaic-Neo-American Site in San Augustine County, Texas." *Bulletin of the Texas Archeological Society* 34.

FORD, J. A. 1936. *Analysis of Indian Village Site Collections from Louisiana and Mississippi.* Department of Conservation, Louisiana Geological Survey, Anthropological Study no. 2.

————— 1952. *Measurement of Some Prehistoric Design Developments in the Southeastern States.* Anthropological Papers of the American Museum of Natural History, vol. 44, no. 3.

————— 1966. "Early Formative Cultures in Georgia and Florida." *American Antiquity* 31(6):781-99.

————— 1969. *A Comparison of Formative Cultures in the Americas.* Smithsonian Contributions to Anthropology, vol. 11. Washington, D.C.: Smithsonian Institution Press.

—————; PHILLIPS, P.; and HAAG, W. G. 1955. *The Jaketown Site in West-Central Mississippi.* Anthropological Papers of the American Museum of Natural History, vol. 45, no. 1.

—————, and WEBB, C. H. 1956. *Poverty Point: A Late Archaic Site in Louisiana.* Anthropological Papers of the American Museum of Natural History, vol. 46, no. 1.

—————, and WILLEY, G. B. 1941. "An Interpretation of the Prehistory of the Eastern United States." *American Anthropologist* 43(3):325-63.

GAGLIANO, S. M., and GREGORY, H. F. 1965. "A Preliminary Survey of Paleo-Indian Points from Louisiana." Louisiana Studies, vol. 4, no. 1. Louisiana Studies Institute, Northwestern State University.

GOLDSCHMIDT, W. R. 1935. "A Report on the Archaeology of Titus County." *Bulletin of the Texas Archeological and Paleontological Society* 7:89-99.

GREGORY, H. F. 1973. "Eighteenth Century Caddoan Archeology: A Study in Models and Interpretation." Ph.D. dissertation, Southern Methodist University.

———, and WEBB, C. H. 1965. "European Trade Beads from Six Sites in Natchitoches Parish, Louisiana." *Florida Anthropologist* 18 (3), pt. 2, pp. 15-44.

GRIFFIN, J. B. 1935. "Report on Pottery Sherds from near Abilene, Texas." *Bulletin of the Texas Archeological and Paleontological Society* 7:57-69.

———, ed. 1952. *Archeology of Eastern United States.* Chicago: University of Chicago Press.

HAAG, W. G. 1939. "Description of Pottery Types." *Newsletter of the Southeastern Archaeological Conference* 1(1-6).

HAMILTON, H. W. 1952. "The Spiro Mound." *Missouri Archaeologist*, vol. 14.

HARRIS, R. K. 1950. "Preliminary Report on Site 3 Walker County, Alabama." *The Record*, vol. 9, no. 2 (November-December 1950).

———. 1953. "The Sam Kaufman Site, Red River County, Texas." *Bulletin of the Texas Archeological Society* 24:43-68.

———. 1967. "Reconnaissance of Archaeological Sites in Fannin, Lamar and Red River Counties, Texas." In *The Archaeological, Historical and Natural Resources of the Red River Basin*, edited by Hester Davis. University of Arkansas Museum.

———, and HARRIS, I. M. 1967. "Trade Beads, Projectile Points and Knives." In *A Pilot Study of Wichita Indian Archeology and Ethnohistory*, edited by E. B. Jelks, pp. 129-63. Report to The National Science Foundation, grant 964.

———; HARRIS, I. M.; BLAINE, J. C.; and BLAINE, J. L. 1965. "A Preliminary Archaeological and Documentary Study of the Womack Site, Red River County, Texas." *Bulletin of the Texas Archeological Society* 36:287-363.

JACKSON, A. T. 1933. "Some Pipes of East Texas." *Bulletin of the Texas Archeological and Paleontological Society* 5:69-86.

———. 1934. "Types of East Texas Pottery." *Bulletin of the Texas Archeological and Paleontological Society* 6:38-57.

———. 1935. "Ornaments of East Texas Indians." *Bulletin of the Texas Archeological and Paleontological Society* 7:11-28.

JENKS, A. E., and WILFORD, L. A. 1938. "The Sauk Valley Skeleton." *Bulletin of the Texas Archeological and Paleontological Society* 10:136-68.

JENNINGS, J. D., and NORBECK, E., eds. 1964. *Prehistoric Man in the New World.* Published for Rice University by University of Chicago Press.

KRIEGER, A. D. 1946. *Culture Complexes and Chronology in Northern Texas, with Extension of Puebloan Datings to the Mississippi Valley.* University of Texas Publication no. 4640.

————. 1947. "The First Conference on the Caddoan Archaeological Area." *American Antiquity* 12(3):198-207.

LEMLEY, H. J. 1936. "Discoveries Indicating a Pre-Caddo Culture on Red River in Arkansas." *Bulletin of the Texas Archeological and Paleontological Society* 8:25-55.

————, and DICKINSON, S. D. 1937. "Archaeological Investigations on Bayou Macon in Arkansas." *Bulletin of the Texas Archeological and Paleontological Society* 9:11-47.

LEONE, M., ed. 1972. *Contemporary Archaeology: A Guide to Theory and Contributions*. Carbondale: Southern Illinois University Press.

NEWELL, H. P., and KRIEGER, A. D. 1949. *The George C. Davis Site, Cherokee County, Texas*. Memoirs of the Society for American Archaeology, no. 5.

ORR, K. G. 1952. "Survey of Caddoan Area Archaeology." In *Archeology of Eastern United States*, edited by James B. Griffin. Chicago: University of Chicago Press.

PHILLIPS, P. 1970. *Archaeological Survey in the Loyer Yazoo Basin, Mississippi, 1949-1955*. Papers of the Peabody Museum of Archaeology and Ethnology, Harvard University, vol. 60.

————; FORD, J. A; and GRIFFIN, J. B. 1951. *Archaeological Survey in the Lower Mississippi Valley, 1940-1947*. Papers of the Peabody Museum of Archaeology and Ethnology, Harvard University, vol. 25.

RAAB, L. M., and KLINGER, T. C. 1977. "A Critical Appraisal of 'Significance' in Contract Archaeology." *American Antiquity* 42(4):629-34.

SCHAMBACH, F. 1970. "Pre-Caddoan Cultures in the Trans-Mississippi South: A Beginning Sequence." Ph.D. dissertation, Harvard University.

SCHIFFER, M. B., and HOUSE, J. H. 1975. *The Cache River Archaeological Project: An Experiment in Contract Archaeology*. Arkansas Archeological Survey, Publications in Archeology, Research Series, no. 8.

SELLARDS, E. H.; EVANS, G. L.; MEADE, G. E.; and KRIEGER, A. D. 1947. "Fossil Bison and Associated Artifacts from Plainview, Texas." *Bulletin of the Geological Society of America* 58:927-54.

SKINNER, S. A.; HARRIS, R. K.; and ANDERSON, K. M., eds. 1969. *Archaeological Investigations at the Sam Kaufman Site, Red River County, Texas*. Southern Methodist University Contributions in Anthropology, no. 5.

SPAULDING, A. C. 1953. "Statistical Techniques for the Discovery of Artifact Types." *American Antiquity* 18:305-13, 391-93.

TROWBRIDGE, H. M. 1938. "Analysis of Spiro Mound Textiles." *American Antiquity* 4(1):51-53.

WEBB, C. H. 1944. "Stone Vessels from a Northeast Louisiana Site." *American Antiquity* 9(4):386-94.

————. 1945. "A Second Historic Caddo Site at Natchitoches, Louisiana." *Bulletin of the Texas Archeological and Paleontological Society* 16:52-83.

————. 1946. "Two Unusual Types of Chipped Stone Artifacts from Northwestern Louisiana." *Bulletin of the Texas Archeological and Paleontological Society* 17:9-17.

————. 1948. "Evidences of Prepottery Cultures in Louisiana." *American Antiquity* 13(3):227-32.

————. 1956. "The Role of the Nonprofessional in the Local Society." *American Antiquity* 23(2), pt. 1, pp. 170-72.

————. 1959. "The Belcher Mound: A Stratified Caddoan Site in Caddo Parish, Louisiana." *Memoirs of the Society for American Archaeology,* no. 16.

————. 1963. "The Smithport Landing Site: An Alto Focus Component in De Soto Parish, Louisiana." *Bulletin of the Texas Archeological Society* 31:143-87.

————. 1974. "Can the Professional and the Amateur Archaeologist Co-operate?" *Louisiana Archaeology* 1:1-7.

————. 1977. *The Poverty Point Culture.* Geoscience and Man, School of Geoscience, Louisiana State University, vol. 17.

————, and DODD, M., JR. 1939. "Further Excavation of the Gahagan Mound: Connections with a Florida Culture." *Bulletin of the Texas Archeological and Paleontological Society* 11:29-126.

————. 1941. "Pottery Types from the Belcher Mound Site." *Bulletin of the Texas Archeological Society* 13:88-116.

————; SHINER, J. L.; and ROBERTS, E. W. 1971. "The John Pearce Site (16CD56): A San Patrice Site in Caddo Parish, Louisiana." *Bulletin of the Texas Archeological Society* 42:1-49.

WEBB, W. S. 1938. *An Archaeological Survey of the Norris Basin in Eastern Tennessee.* Bureau of American Ethnology Bulletin no. 118.

————. 1939. *An Archeological Survey of Wheeler Basin on the Tennessee River in Northern Alabama.* Bureau of American Ethnology Bulletin no. 122.

————, and DeJARNETTE, D. L. 1942. *An Archaeological Survey of Pickwick Basin in the Adjacent Portions of the States of Alabama, Mississippi and Tennessee.* Bureau of American Ethnology Bulletin no. 129.

WILLEY, G. R. 1968. "One Hundred Years of American Archaeology." In *One Hundred Years of Anthropology,* edited by John O. Brew. Cambridge: Harvard University Press.

————, and PHILLIPS, P. 1958. *Method and Theory in American Archaeology.* Chicago: University of Chicago Press.

MATERIAL CULTURE AND
THE ARTS

DENVER ART MUSEUM

100 W. 14th Ave. Parkway, Denver, Colorado 80204

Department of Indian Art

NORMAN FEDER, *Curator*

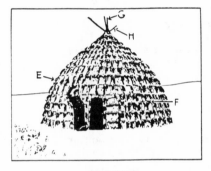
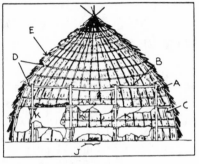

EXTERIOR   INTERIOR

(Cleveland Museum of Natural History)

Leaflet No. 42   -   February 1932

3rd Printing, June 1957

Reprinted January, 1973

THE GRASS HOUSE OF THE
WICHITA AND CADDO

Reprinted June, 1975

GRASS HOUSES were used by the southern branches of the Caddoan linguistic stock, that is, the Wichita and Caddo groups, and a long list of now vanished tribes once living in Arkansas, western Louisiana and eastern Texas. About 1,350 Indians, the remnants of many of these tribes, are now living in western Oklahoma. They were still using the grass house 25 years ago, but information is lacking as to whether any are now used.

The exact extent of the grass house in very early times cannot definitely be stated. In the north of the area it was certainly in use in 1541, when Coronado reached the Wichita on his search for gold. Descriptions of the houses found in the expedition's records might well have been applied to those of the 19th century. For the south there is the description of Joutel, one of La Salle's men, who reached the Caddo country after the murder of his master in 1687. His narrative gives a very full and clear account of the grass houses, their construction and contents.

For further information about the Wichita group see leaflet 40. For a list of all the Caddoan tribes see page 183, volume 1, of the Handbook of American Indians, Bulletin 30 of the Bureau of Ethnology.

FRAMEWORK

HEAVY BEAMS. A circle from 15 to 40 feet in diameter was drawn on the ground. Around its circumference were set up from 8 to 16 forked top logs 12 to 15 feet high (A). These logs were usually cedar. Other logs (B) were laid across the tops of these uprights and were firmly tied in place with slippery elm bark ropes.

WALL RIBS. Another circle was drawn on the ground outside of the main beams, about 4 feet from their bases. On this outer circle were set from 50 to 75 long, slender cedar poles (C), which leaned inwards and rested on the transverse beams of the main framework, to which they were tied. The tops of these poles were tightly fastened together.

Rows of slim peeled willow rods (D) were next tied to these ribs at right angles to them. These horizontal ribs were about 2 feet apart. They were fastened in place with elm bark cord.

THATCHING. Bunches of long, coarse grass (E) were tied to the horizontal ribs in a series of overlapping layers, the work beginning at the bottom of the structure.

When this thatch was in place a second series of horizontal ribs (F) was put in place on top of the thatch, to keep it firmly in place. At each crossing of the horizontal and vertical ribs an ornamental tuft of grass was tied, the line of tufts following the invisible upright ribs.

PEAK. At the top of this cone-shaped structure a sharp peak (G) of tightly bound grass bundles was set up. It was about 3 feet high. At the base of this peak short poles (H) projected to the four points of the compass. The peak was 15 to 25 feet above ground.

ENTRANCES were formerly four in number, facing the compass points. They were about 2 feet wide and 3½ to 5 feet high. Two of them, those to the north and south, were only used during certain ceremonies. But in more recent years only the eastern and western ones have been made. The south entrance seems to have lasted longer than the north. The east entry is used in the morning and the west in the afternoon. These openings were closed with panels made by tying bunches of grass to willow frames. They were not hinged, but were set to one side either within or outside the building.

SMOKEHOLE. The smoke from the central fireplace escaped through a small hole in the roof a little to the east of the peak.

SYMBOLISM. The four projecting beams at the peak were symbolic of the compass points, where were the paths down which the gods came to help man. The peak typified the heavenly home of the mysterious force which filled all nature.

INTERIOR ARRANGEMENTS

FIREPLACE. In the middle of the floor a shallow excavation was made for the fire (J). A 17th century account says that the fire was not allowed to go out, being made of large trees which were constantly pushed into the firepit as they burned away. Anyone who came in the building took care of it. The fireplace was considered to be extremely sacred, and was treated with great reverence by all.

BEDS. Around the walls and between the large upright posts were a series of beds (K). These were platforms, 3 or 4 feet wide, and 2 to 3 feet from the ground, made of cane in the southern parts of the area and of willow rods in the north. On them were placed rush mats, dressed skins and buffalo robes. Upper berths were often constructed for sleeping places or for storage. The spaces between the lower berths were also used for storage. There were six beds in most houses, but twelve or more might be found.

Each berth, or pair of berths, was provided with skin curtains which could cut it off from the rest of the room. These curtains were often painted with war scenes.

CORN MORTAR. Halfway between the fireplace and the western door stood the family corn mill. This was a section of log, a foot and a half in diameter and four feet long, firmly implanted in the ground. In the upper end a deep hollow was dug out. In this hollow the corn was reduced to meal by pounding it with long, heavy wooden pestles. Usually several women pounded together.

NUMBER OF OCCUPANTS. Though small houses of this type were made for single families, most of them were occupied by several groups, as many as a dozen being mentioned for the large houses found by the French. The fire was common to all, but each family was assigned to several of the berths, mat partitions being hung between the several sections. On and under the berths and on the beams above were stored the mats, clothing, tools, weapons and the pottery, basketry and wooden utensils of the family.

VILLAGES. As these tribes were agriculturalists they located their villages on sites near land suitable for farming. As many as 70 or 80 houses were grouped fairly close together in favorable localities, such as the lower slopes of well-watered valleys. All around were the fields. These villages were permanent. If for any reason it became necessary to abandon them they were burned. The presence in the tribe of an official appointed to pick new sites indicates that such removals did come about. When the tribes went on buffalo hunts they lived in skin tipis like those used by the Plains tribes. See leaflet 19.

FORTIFICATIONS. In reference 4 there is an account of the method of fortifying the houses. In localities where attacks from hostile tribes were to be feared the floors were excavated to a depth of 2 feet and 3-foot earthworks were thrown up around the outside of the house, thus making a 5-foot embankment behind which the villagers could fight. The thick grass walls were impenetrable by arrows. As a precaution against fire-arrows the grass thatch was well dampened. As these villages had no place in which to gather horses in the event of an attack this process of fortifying the houses died out when horses and firearms became widespread.

OTHER STRUCTURES

WORK ARBOR. Near each house, unless the owners were very poor, was built an arbor in general construction much like the house, but of different shape. These arbors were rectangular and but 8 or 10 feet high. The thatch covered the roof, but failed by 4 feet of reaching the ground. Inside was a low platform on which the Indians worked and rested during the heat of the summer.

A smaller arbor was long ago used as a sleeping place for the young girls of the tribe.

DRYING FRAME. A platform of poles was made, perhaps 10 by 20 feet, and far enough above the ground to necessitate the use of a ladder made of a single notched log. Corn, meat and skins were laid on this platform to dry and from it were hung drying pumpkin strips.

SWEAT HOUSE. This low domed hut of logs and earth or mats was used for the sweat bath so common among the Plains and many other tribes.

Compiled from the following sources by F. H. Douglas:

BUREAU OF AMERICAN ETHNOLOGY.
1. Article on the Grass House—Fletcher. Page 505, Vol. 1, of the Handbook of American Indians, Bulletin 30.
2. Article on the Caddoan Stock—Fletcher. Page 182, Vol. 1, of the Handbook of American Indians, Bulletin.
3. Villages of the Caddoan Tribes West of the Mississippi—Bushnell. Bulletin 77, pages 179-183.

SMITHSONIAN INSTITUTION.
4. Indian Forts and Dwellings—Doyle. Annual Report 1876, page 460.

CARNEGIE INSTITUTION OF WASHINGTON.
5. The Mythology of the Wichita—Dorsey. Publication 21, pages 4-7.

CLEVELAND MUSEUM OF NATURAL HISTORY, CLEVELAND, OHIO.
6. Indian Homes—Madison. Pages 20-21.

Pictures 1, 3, 6; accounts of early explorers, 3; general description of the Wichita, 5; descriptions of grass houses, 1, 5, 6.

THE OASHUNS OR DANCES OF THE CADDO

Eugene Heflin

The majority of the Caddo Indians now live around Anadarko, Lookeba, Binger and Gracemont in Caddo County, Oklahoma. Some of them have moved out of the county and some have moved out of the state; a few have moved to Oklahoma City to work at Tinker Field or in other employment. At certain times of the year, usually July or August, the Caddo are host to about four days of intertribal dancing. Some of these dances are quite ancient, for there are records of them as far back as the 18th century when the Kadohadacho or Caddo proper of northeast Texas, southwest Arkansas, northwest Louisiana, and the Hasinai of east Texas danced them.

Maurice Bedoka, Caddo-Delaware (the Delaware have been a part of the Caddo tribe since adopted at a council in 1874), told the author at one of these dances in 1938 that he was certain of only two original dances - the Note-hie-oashun or Turkey Dance and the Scalp Dance or Round Dance, the others having been borrowed or adopted from other tribes. On the other hand, Swanton (1942) was told by the Caddo in 1912 that the original dances were the Turkey Dance, the Duck Dance and the Skunk Dance. Records show that the Skunk Dance was danced by the Creeks, the Alibama and Koasati. The Duck Dance is apparently Muskogean and is called Fuchuse by the Choctaw; it was formerly danced by the Choctaw of Bayou Lacomb, St. Tammany's Parish, Louisiana. The Turkey Dance was originally the Scalp Dance but was later changed to the Turkey Dance because the Caddo believed the turkeys started it.

The author was doing motion picture work for Dr. J. Willis Stovall of the University of Oklahoma when he first witnessed these dances at Whitebread Creek, about three and one-half miles north of Gracemont, Oklahoma. This four day meeting was to show appreciation to the Great Spirit, Ko-na-ka-ay or Naa, Father Above, for abundant crops. A large clearing along the blackjacks, tall oaks and hackberry trees served as a ko-na-cha-ka-wa-ah-sa or dance ground. Logs served as seats for the spectators.

The drum or ka-e-ko was of the large dance type and was suspended in the air by four posts driven into the ground. A smaller hand drum was also used. There were seven drummers. Several dances were given, some at night; these included the Squat Dance, Fish Dance, Soldier Dance, Corn Dance, Alligator Dance and Swing. The following remarks, however, will be limited to dances which are typically Caddo or attributed to the Caddo.

Stanley Edge, assuming the role of tuma or crier, began calling for the women to enter the Turkey Dance. This dance took place each day, just before noon. Concerning its origin, the Caddo say that a young warrior was hunting through the woods one day when he heard beautiful music. Tracing it to the source, he discovered a number of turkey hens singing and dancing around a group of gobblers. He watched and listened until he had memorized their songs; later he informed his tribe of his discovery and told them that he had learned a new dance.

The Turkey Dance was a dance for women only. They wore one-piece dresses, usually of calico, with long sleeves and aprons tied around the waist. In addition to this, they wore shawls or blankets and a plaque tied to their hair braid. This plaque was decorated with small round mirrors and ribbon pendants or streamers attached with brass tacks.

The leader of the dance, Mrs. Alice Cussens, presented the drummers with tobacco. Three Caddo men beating a small water drum made of willow and buckskin represented the gobblers. The dance then started with the women representing the turkey hens and doing a turkey trot around the gobblers. The women suddenly began kicking up dirt around the gobblers, supposedly hunting something to eat. One informant, Maika Martin (Silvermoon) said this was strictly a women's dance; however, at this time men were brought into the dance. Each woman could pick out a man to dance with her by pelting him with a stone pebble, and, if he were struck, he had to dance with her. If she missed him and he ran away, she could grab some article that belonged to him, and it was necessary for him to pay some sort of fine or token to get it back.

The other dances were held at night. The Caddo Round Dance was given first. This dance represents an old scalp dance that was brought from Louisiana. It formerly took place when scalps were brought into the kiwat or village at night. The dance was started by the women who stood in a half-circle about the drummer and choir for the first song. At the second song, the men joined in, alternating with the women, and all joining hands and dancing around the fire in a circle. Inkanish calls this dance Nutty-auschien; Silvermoon, Nutti-oashun or gunigah'niasiwa.

The following dance was called the Gagi-go-ani or Grab Dance. The women started the dance by forming a circle around the drummers, moving back and forth, and singing with them. They sang to the men on the sidelines, inviting them to come in and grab them. The men would strike matches to see whom they wanted, and then they grabed the person desired.

One dance in which all joined in regardless of age or sex was the Kay-ka-hie-oashun or Snake Dance. This is not an original Caddo dance but one copied from the Louisiana Choctaw who called it Siente Hitkla. The dancers formed a single line, first the men, then the women, and then the boys and girls. They danced a serpentine course, moving about, coiling and becoming a tighter unit until they could no longer move; then they ceased dancing.

Another dance, the Duck Dance or Ki-nuc-oashun was apparently borrowed from the Choctaw of Bayou Lacomb, Louisiana. The men and women formed two lines facing each other. Two partners then passed under the arms of another couple, imitating a duck walking.

The Bell Dance, called Ka-ke-chun-e-shin, was one of the final dances and was given toward morning. Thirty or forty men formed a line which faced toward the east. White men who were present could join in this dance, also. The leader, shaking a strap decorated with sleigh bells, started forward singing and dancing. All men joined in, and as they started around the fire, the women fell in behind the men they wanted to dance with and took their hands. Each faced the direction ahead, one hand forward and the other one back.

PLATE 19

Women Dancing Turkey Dance Around Ralph Murrow

PLATE 20

Top: Caddo Stomp Dance
Bottom: Grab Dance; left to right - Ralph Murrow, Mrs. Amos Longhat
and Jimmy Bobb

HOUSE TYPES AMONG THE CADDO INDIANS

By Clarence H. Webb

Considerable historical and archaeological evidence exists concerning dwellings of the various Caddoan tribes, but very little of this relates to the Kadohadacho or Caddo proper in the region of their historic confederation on Red River in northwest Louisiana and southwest Arkansas.

The simplest Caddoan house type, which was frequently described by French and Spanish travelers of the 16th and 17th centuries, was the grass lodge, which persisted among the Wichitas up to within recent years. Fletcher (1) states that in making these beehive shaped houses, a circle was drawn on the ground, along which a number of crotched posts were set, beams being laid across the crotches. Closely-placed poles were leaned inward across the beams, the tops drawn together and tied, and willow rods laced across them. A close thatch of grass was laid and bound down with similar rods. Surmounting the peak of the house were two rods crossed to indicate the cardinal points. For ceremonial houses, four openings or doors were left on the sides corresponding to the cardinal points; for the ordinary dwellings, openings on the east and west sides were used in the mornings and afternoons, respectively.

Joutel (2) described similar dwellings among the Cenis and the Assonis, stating that their cabins were in groups of seven to fifteen, separated by their fields. Houses of the Cenis were large, sometimes 60 feet in diameter, accommodating eight to ten families.

Professor Bolton (3), in "Texas of the Middle Eighteenth Century," published a drawing of a Caddo village near Texarkana, in 1691, showing beehive-shaped grass houses as described above, also a second type, which had grass thatched roofs and mud-plastered walls. Similar wattle-and-daub construction of round and oval dwellings is seen in a photograph of a Caddo village by Soule (1868-72) which is reproduced by courtesy of the Smithsonian Institution (Plate 8, No. 1). Members of the tribe are seated beneath a platform of the type used to dry the corn.

A third type of house, used by the Pawnees and other Caddoan tribes of the Plains area, was the earth lodge. Fletcher (1) states that after digging a circular excavation of 2 to 4 feet, a grass-thatched structure was built, using two circles of supporting posts, then covered with sod. A single entrance on the east side, also sod covered, projected 6 to 10 feet from the wall. Skin curtains closed the entrance way and, during the winter season, were also placed around the inner circle of supporting posts, making a smaller room around the fire.

Inside arrangements of the lodges have been described by Joutel (2), Father Manzanet (4) and others. The floors were smoothed and hardened; in the center a small excavation accommodated a fire, the smoke from which escaped through a small hole in the roof.

Beds or couches were placed around the walls, separated by partitions of buffalo skins, which also served for blankets. Large shelves above the door and on the opposite side of the lodge held hampers and baskets of cane or bark, in which shelled corn, nuts, beans, acorns, and other foods were stored. Pottery and other household utensils were also placed on these platforms or shelves.

Larger ceremonial structures were made in similar fashions. Jackson (5), who excavated a circular house floor in the Asinai area which evidently represented one of the ceremonial fire-temples, quotes the description by Father Manzanet of the house of the Governor of the Nabedache, a large grass lodge as described above. In the center of the house was a fire which was never extinguished and from which the fires of all the surrounding households were kindled. Similar fire houses were stated to be at the Neches and among the Nacogdoches and Nasonis.

To the east of the Caddo area, Swanton (6) states that the "fire temple" was a characteristic feature of lower Mississippi culture. The Natchez and Taensas built oval temples, with vertical walls of wattle-work, peaked roofs covered with cane mats and surmounted by carved figures of three birds. Inside each temple, a fire was kept burning continuously by elders of the tribe, appointed for this

PLATE 8
1. Photograph of a Caddo Camp by Soule (1868-1874).
2. Floor plan, House 1, Belcher Mound B.

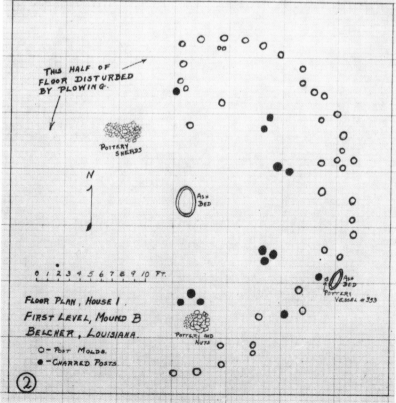

THIS HALF OF
FLOOR DISTURBED
BY PLOWING.

POTTERY
SHERDS

N

ASH
BED

0 1 2 3 4 5 6 7 8 9 10 FT.

FLOOR PLAN, HOUSE 1.

FIRST LEVEL, MOUND B

BELCHER, LOUISIANA.

O - POST MOLDS.

● - CHARRED POSTS

ASH
BED

POTTERY
VESSEL #353

POTTERY AND
NUTS

Plate 9

specific duty. Dry hickory and oak logs were used and only the ends of the logs were lighted, to keep the fire from blazing too brightly.

Farther afield, the council houses of the Cherokees and Creeks were very large, "capable of accommodating several hundred people," according to Bartram (7). A large central post was surrounded by two or three circular rows of upright posts, the roof covered with bark layers, occasionally mud coated. The Chickasaws and possibly the Choctaws of Mississippi were stated to have built earth lodges similar to those of the Pawnee.

Turning to archeological evidence, besides the description of the east Texas fire-site by Jackson, the most pertinent is that of Harrington (8), who excavated many sites between the Red and Ouachita rivers in southwest Arkansas, where the preponderance of artifacts was Caddoan. In some thirty instances, at nine sites, he mentioned either floor levels in mounds, with post molds, fire places or charred timbers; or floors on the ground level, covered with a small mound of earth, one to three feet high. There seemed to be little uniformity of detail, the shapes being square, oval, round, rectangular and square or rectangular with rounded corners; sizes varied from 16 feet square to 33 feet in diameter; fire pits were central, eccentric or sometimes lacking. Of the five structures where entrances were identified, one each faced east, west, southeast and southwest, while the fifth had entrances to both southeast and southwest. In the six instances where post molds were described, only a single row or circle was found.

Charred timbers, cane, grass and wattle-work were found in many instances, covered with one to five feet of sand or clay, indicating a widespread custom of burning the houses on deserting them. Harrington apparently considered all of these structures to be the remains of earth lodges, covered with earth from the collapsed house, with additional earth used in some instances to build the mound higher. It is significant that his assistant, Alanson Skinner, (9)

described the one house which he excavated as a burned grass lodge, although its details were not greatly different from others described by Harrington.

House I, Belcher Mound Site

During the past four years, Mr. Monroe Dodd and the author, with the assistance of various friends, have conducted excavations in a small mound site on a lateral stream in the Red River Valley near Belcher, located twenty miles north of Shreveport, in Caddo Parish. A complete report is being prepared for publication and those interested in detailed features are referred to this report. For the purpose of the present description of house types, it suffices to note that we have uncovered four habitation levels in Mound B, with a structure on each level, immediately superimposed and separated by about two feet of sand fill between each level, with a fifth structure on the surface immediately adjoining Mound B. No trade objects have been found and pottery types all fall within the Caddo classification as given by Ford (10).

Houses 1 to 4 occurred in the succeeding levels of Mound B and are numbered from the surface downward. The floor of House 1 lay under an 8 to 12 inch layer of soil, the lower 4 to 6 inches of which was black humus containing many sherds, small segments of charred timbers and cane, masses of baked clay, mud-dauber nests and other debris. This refuse material was especially abundant on the slopes of the small mound and around the outer circle of post molds. The structure outline was incomplete, as the western half had been disturbed by deep plowing. The eastern half (Plate 8, No. 2), was a semicircle of post molds, 15 feet in radius, the molds being 6 to 9 inches in diameter, 1 1-2 feet in depth and spaced at intervals of approximately 2 feet. Grouped post molds and heavy masses of burned clay in the northeast segment suggested this point as the entrance. No projecting post molds were found.

A second circle of grouped post molds, most of which contained charred segments of cypress posts, was found 6 to 7 feet within the outer circle. These posts were 7 to 10 inches in diameter, larger than the outer molds, and evidently served as roof supports.

In the center of the structure there was a bed of extremely white ashes, 2 by 2 1-2 feet in size and nearly a foot in depth. It was de-

---

PLATE 9

1. Floor plan, House 2, Belcher Mound B.
2. Photograph of Eastern half of House 2.

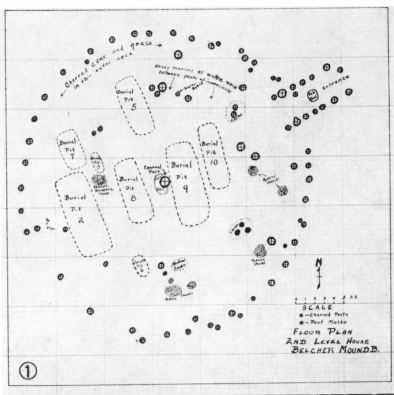

Charred cane and grass
in this outer area

Heavy masses of wattle work
between posts or inner circle

Wattle work inner circle

Main entrance

Burial
Pit
5

Burial
Pit
7

Burial
Pit
13

Central
Post

Burial
Pit
10

Burial
Pit
8

Burial
Pit
9

Burial
Pit
2

Burial
Pit

N

0 1 2 3 4 5 FT.
SCALE
● —Charred Posts
● —Post Molds

FLOOR PLAN
2ND LEVEL HOUSE
BELCHER MOUND B.

①

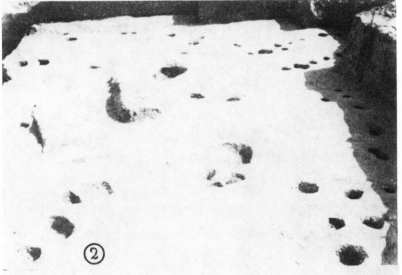

②

Plate 9

void of sherds or animal bones, although these occurred in abundance around a smaller ash bed which lay just outside the outer circle of post molds. An intact small pottery jar and fragments of a pipe !ay near this outside fire bed.

At two points on the house floor (Plate 8, No. 2) heavy masses of pottery sherds lay together. Four vessels, including two large olla types, were reconstructed from one of these sherd masses. The second mass was found to be a single large jar, crushed in situ, with an inverted and unbroken bowl nearby. Around these were charred hickory nuts. The positions of these objects suggests that they fell or were crushed when the lodge burned.

House II, Belcher Mound B

Approximately 2 1-2 feet below floor 1, separated by a practically sterile sand fill, lay a level floor of packed white sand, which could be perfectly delineated because of the charred materials which had fallen on it. The absence of a humus layer indicated that the building had not been used very long before it was burned. Almost immediately underlying the semicircle of House 1 was a circle of post molds (Plate 9, No. 1) which could be completed for its entire circumference. The circle was mathematically exact, no mold varying more than 6 inches from a perfect circle, 30 feet in diameter.

Parallel lines of post molds, 3 feet in width, formed an entrance way (Plate 10, No. 1) which projected 7 feet from the northeast segment of the circle. Seven posts were used on each side of the entrance way. A large or double mold marked the point where the entrance joined the outer wall of the structure. The extra mold inside the doorway, with the inset terminal mold on the north line, may represent posts to support a bench, as Skinner (9) suggested of a similar occurrence in the Flower's mound structure; or, possibly, supports for doors. It is mentioned of the Natchez ceremonial structures, that entrances were kept carefully closed to prevent children from entering these lodges.

The floor of the entrance way was of hard packed sand, which extended inside the lodge toward the central fire. In the middle of the entrance there was a 10 inch square bed of white ash, (Plate 10, No. 1) possibly the result of some ceremony related to entering or leaving the lodge.

An inner circle of molds (Plate 9, No. 1) was spaced as in House 1, apparently 8 groups which were 5 to 8 feet apart. Strong (11) reports 4 to 8 central posts in the Pawnee lodges, stating that their number and location had ceremonial significance. Some of the groups in House 2 were destroyed by burial pits, but it is to be noted that the north and south groups are exactly on the compass line through the center of the structure. Shallow cache pits, containing only pottery sherds, surrounded several of these grouped molds. Over and around this inner circle of post molds lay masses of burned clay which showed impressions of poles, sticks and grass. Many had one side quite smooth, often greenish in color, as though covered with a green wash. The abundance of this material around the inner circle of molds suggests a wall or partition dividing the inner room from the outer portion of the building. Over the outer portion of floor, between the two circles of posts, heavy masses of charred materials lay on the floor—a layer of grass usually next the house floor, then a layer of split cane, then poles and sticks. This probably was roof material and must have inverted in falling, as masses broke loose from the burning structure, otherwise the relative position of the materials is difficult to understand. It is unlikely that the roof was sod covered, since this sod would have fallen between the house floor and the grass-cane layers when they inverted.

Several inset post molds between the two circles suggest seats, bunks or partitions.

In the exact center of the structure there was a large post mold, 12 inches in diameter and 18 inches deep, partially surrounded and covered by an oval shaped bed of very white ash (Plate 10, No. 2), identical with that of House 1. In both instances the ash was so white and free of charcoal or burned materials as to have the appearance of lime. It is probable that carefully selected ash or oak wood was used and the fires carefully tended, as reported of the Natchez. The large post must have been temporary, such as those used by the Asinai in constructing their lodges, otherwise the fire would not have been built on this spot.

PLATE 10

1. Entrance way, House 2, Belcher Mound B. Notice ash bed and inset post molds.
2. Central ash bed and large post molds, House 2.
3. Floor plan, House 3, Belcher Mound B.

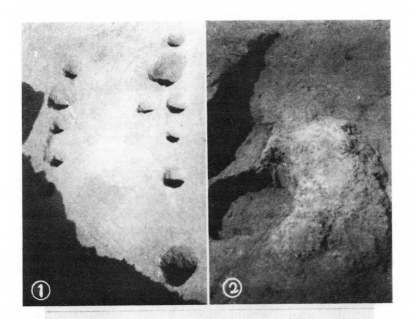

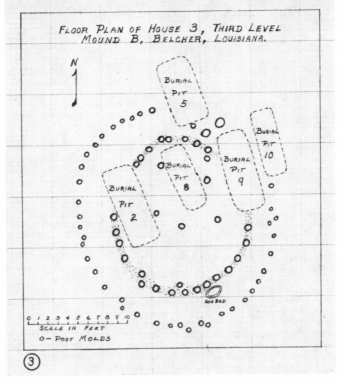

FLOOR PLAN OF HOUSE 3, THIRD LEVEL
MOUND B, BELCHER, LOUISIANA.

N

BURIAL
PIT
5

BURIAL
PIT
10

BURIAL
PIT
8

BURIAL
PIT
9

BURIAL
PIT
2

ASH BED

0 1 2 3 4 5 6 7 8 9 10
SCALE IN FEET
O— POST MOLDS

③

Plate 10

Six large masses of sherds lay on the floor, from which a dozen nearly complete vessels were assembled. Sherds of a single vessel were often found in three or four separate heaps and, after these vessels were completed, comparatively few sherds remained. These facts suggest that the vessels were broken shortly before destruction of the building and were thrown or swept into the separate heaps. At one place in the back half of the house, sherds of two entire vessels were found with fragments of charred basketry and charred seeds. In other places a small pipe and a water bottle, both intact, lay on the floor.

The floor was cut through by eight burial pits which started from the fill between floors 1 and 2. Details will be found in the complete report. The pottery found in these burials, as well as the sherds on House floors 1 and 2, was of the highly developed Caddo type.

House III, Belcher Mound B

The flat summit of a small circular mound was found two feet beneath the floor of House 2. The mound was covered in its entirety with a cap of charcoal-streaked red clay, about 1 foot in thickness. Two circles of post molds were found (Plate 10, No. 3), the inner circle of 5 to 8 inch molds, about 2 feet in depth, forming an irregular oval, 13 by 15 feet in diameters. The outer circle of smaller molds, 3 to 4 inches in diameter and only 1 foot in depth, slanted slightly inward. It was 20 by 22 feet in diameter, and both circles were interrupted by the second floor burial pits, which apparently cut through the entrance way on the northeast side. The absence of charred materials or post suggests that the building may not have been burned, as were the other structures. Internal post molds were irregularly placed. A small ash bed, surrounded by sherds and animal bones, lay between the circles of molds on the south side. A moderate number of sherds was found on the floor and the slope of the small mound.

House IV, Belcher Mound B

The mound described above was found to overlie the remains of a burned structure (Plate 11), which had been built on the original ground surface, 3 feet under House floor 3 and 8 feet beneath the summit of Mound B. This surface was of clay, stained dark with humus. House 4 wreckage consisted of heavy masses of baked clay daub over the central areas of the house; charred timbers, split cane and grass over the outer portions. In a straight line along each wall, charred timbers projected upward 1 to 1 1-2 feet into the covering sand. Their molds extended down into and through wall trenches, for a total depth of 2½ feet (Plate 12, No. 2). The trenches, 8 to 10 inches wide and 18 inches deep, extended the length of each wall, failing to meet at the corners by about 3 feet, this space being filled in by three post molds, 4 to 6 inches in diameter, to produce a rounded corner. Red clay to the height of one foot was banked against the outside of each wall. The structure was 24 feet wide, 20 feet 8 inches in length (Plate 12, No. 1).

The front wall had two trenches with a 3 foot opening in the center, from which projected a 7 foot long entrance, similar to that of House 2. The entrance floor had been built up one foot to form a ramp or incline, declining to floor level within the structure. Atop the ramp, midway of the entrance, was a small white ash bed (Plate 11), identical in size and relative position to that of the House 2 entrance. Projecting laterally from the ends of the doorway were one foot high walls of clay (Plate 11), paralleling the front wall of the structure. Outside of the right wall, a smooth, crescentic bank of clay, 2 feet high, 8 to 9 feet long and 3 to 4 feet wide, faced toward the southeast.

The structure contained two large ash beds. Near the center of the house, a shallow basin of yellow clay, 3 to 3 1-2 feet in diameter, contained very white ashes. In the northwest corner of the structure, there was a larger ash bed with many sherds and deer bones. Spaced on opposite sides of this fire bed were four post molds, probably representing cooking supports.

By the opposite (south) wall of the house, 4 post molds formed a 4 1-2 foot square, probably a platform of some type. Just within the doorway, closely placed molds formed an irregular circle, but these started beneath the clay ramp and may have represented some earlier structure. A large clay pipe of modified platform type lay in the wreckage of the back wall.

Two large burial pits started just beneath the clay cap of House floor 3, Pit 11 cutting through and six feet below House floor 4,

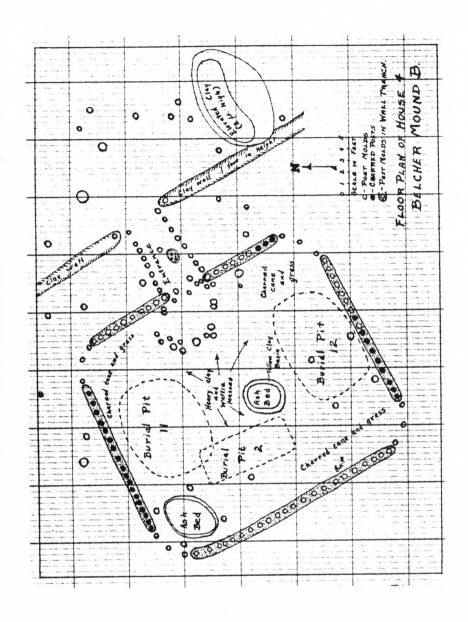

PLATE 11

Floor plan, House 4, Belcher Mound B.

Pit 12 extending just to this floor. The pottery, although Caddoan in type, differed from that of the first and second levels, being scanty in amount, cruder in manufacture and plainer in ornamentation.

House V, Belcher Site

About 15 feet northwest of Mound B, another circle of post molds was discovered (Plate 13, No. 1). The center of this structure lay under 6 inches of topsoil and humus; the periphery sloped downward slightly and, immediately beyond the circle of post molds, the black humus layer dipped downward for 2 feet, forming a small house mound (Plate 12, No. 3).

The outer circle was 36 to 37 feet in diameter, of 6 to 8 inches molds, spaced 2 to 2 1-2 feet apart. The western segment of the house had washed into the small stream. The entrance was in the northeast segment, formed by a number of grouped posts on each side of a steep ramp, in the center of which was a large mold filled with very black loose charcoal and ash. No projecting entrance way was found.

An inner circle of grouped post molds resembled those of Houses 1 and 2. Many irregular molds occurred. Two small cache pits, 1 1-2 to 2 feet in diameter, contained sherds, shells, bones and baked clay material. Several disturbances indicated burial pits, but these have not been investigated.

A single ashbed was found in the exact center of the structure, about 2 feet in diameter and surrounded by scattered sherds. On the house floor and in the covering humus were a moderate number of sherds, 8 to 10 diminutive arrow points, 2 ear ornaments, several whetstones, fragments of flaked stones, numerous flakes, a few pieces of charred timbers and moderate amounts of baked clay daub material. Sherds and daub material were more abundant in the post molds and down the slopes of the house mound.

House I, Greer Site, Gibsland

About 3 miles east of Gibsland, Bienville Parish, Louisiana, a mixed Coles Creek-Caddo site lies along Black Bayou, on the Ed Greer farm. In 1938 a burial was struck by the plow, and with the assistance of Mr. Greer, we uncovered the skeleton, finding no artifacts in association. We noticed a layer of very white sand and on following this, uncovered numerous molds (Plate 13, No. 2), which probably represent two separate structures. The floor was formed by a layer of firm white and yellow sand under about 8 inches of cultivated soil. Post molds were 5 to 12 inches in size, 1 to 1 1-2 feet in depth, containing dark humus and occasional sherds. No charred materials were found.

A definite entrance way projected from the southeast side of the structure, near the burial, and a possible entrance way was on the northeast side. Three fire beds and three small cache pits were found, the cache pits containing sherds, shells and animal bones. No other artifacts were discovered.

Fire Pit A was large, 5 by 4 feet, containing a thick layer of very black ash and humus, with a few sherds. Opposed post molds suggested cooking supports. We were amazed, after removing two feet of the black ash, to break through into a cache pit beneath the fire bed which had been dug into the hard clay for a depth of about 4 feet, the pit was 2 1-2 feet in diameter. It contained a number of Caddo sherds, but no whole artifacts. This is the first deep cache pit of the Nebraska type (11) found in this area, so far as we know.

We conclude that this structure is Caddoan, rather than the earlier Coles Creek, because the sherds found on the floor, in the pits and post molds were almost exclusively Caddoan in type.

Discussion

Mound B at Belcher affords interesting evidence of temporal sequence in house types. The first people who lived here built a rectangular house on the level ground, using the trenching technic for placement of the wall posts, then covering the house with poles, split cane mats and sedge grass. The trenching technic, a method not previously found in this area, was reported for the circular structures at Deasonville, Mississippi, by Collins (12). It was also described by Cole and Deuel (13) for rectangular houses of the Middle Mississippi phase in Fulton County, Illinois. Numerous

---

PLATE 12
1. Photograph of House 4, Belcher Mound B.
2. Wall trench with post molds, House 4.
3. Photograph of House 5, Belcher Site.

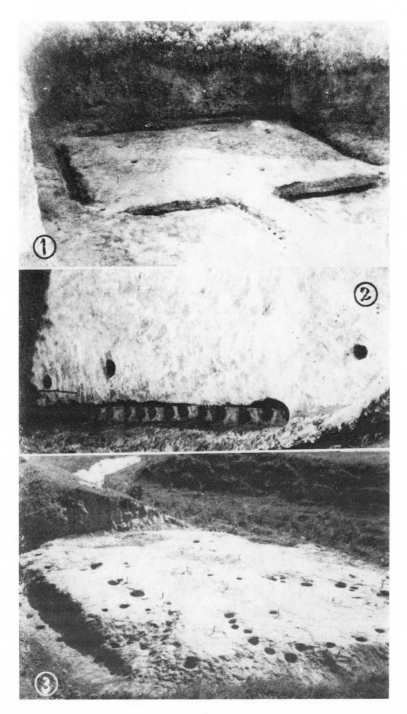

Plate 12

rectangular structures at various sites in the Norris Basin of Eastern Tennessee, as described by Webb (14), exhibited the trenching technic. They also showed centrally placed ceremonial ash beds in prepared clay basins, and construction of cane, grass and wattle-and-daub, these materials being preserved by incomplete burning. House 4 differed from the Norris basin structures in having a projecting doorway and having the burial pits cut through the fallen debris. Horizontal log molds found in the trenches of the Norris Basin structures and the clay seats or pedestals inside these structures were lacking in House 4 at Belcher. However, the 2-foot-high, crescentic ridge of clay in front of House 4 may have served as a seat.

Incompleteness of data allows us to draw few conclusions from the small structure (House 3) which surmounted the first small mound heaped over the remains of House 4. It lacked a centrally placed firebed and is the only structure found at Belcher which showed no evidence of burning. The unique feature of this floor is the complete capping over of the small mound with the layer of red clay before construction of House 3.

The people who built Houses 1, 2 and 5 had the culture traits of the later Caddos, who had developed a high degree of proficiency in pottery making. It is probable that they were intrusive into this area, displacing at Belcher the crude pottery makers of floor levels 3 and 4. It is interesting to note, as we have discussed in our complete report, that the simpler incised straight line type of Caddo pottery is widespread over this area, the highly developed engraved curved line pottery complex appearing much less frequently. Dickinson and Lemley (15) in Arkansas and Goldschmidt (16) in East Texas, present evidence of this same intrusion of engraved, curved-line Caddo wares into an indigenous complex of inferior pottery with incised designs.

These later Caddos built circular structures using an outer circle of grouped posts for roof supports, with coverings of poles, stakes, split cane and grass. Wattle-and-daub, often plastered with a green slip (Skinner (9) also found green coloration of the clay plastering) was used for the walls. The central fire bed, the ash bed of the doorway and the lack of cooking fires in Houses 1 and 2 suggest that they were ceremonial structures, identical with the "eternal fire" lodges of the Asinai and Natchez.

The constructional features mentioned above are quite similar to the structures of the historic Pawnees, Cherokees and Creeks, previously described. There is no evidence of excavated floors such as the earth lodges of the Pawnees had, but the projecting doorway is quite similar in type. The cache pit of House 1 on the Greer site suggests Plains affinities.

The question of earth lodges among the southern Caddo tribes is an interesting one. The Chickasaws and Choctaws among southern tribes were stated to have built earth lodges, similar to the Pawnees of the midwest. Webb (14) concluded that the square structures excavated in the Norris Basin area gave evidence of having had sod covered roofs, which on collapse of the burning buildings, covered over and preserved the charred materials. Harrington (8) reached similar conclusions of the Caddo structures in southern Arkansas, and Fowke (17) attributed to collapsed Caddo earth lodges the thousands of low mound-like elevations seen over a wide area of Arkansas, Missouri, Louisiana, eastern Oklahoma and East Texas.

With respect to these mound-like elevatior.s, Fowke's conclusions were based on incomplete observations. Hundreds of them in North Louisiana have been cut through during road construction, and none of those examined by local geologists or ourselves show any evidence of habitation. They dot the hills of this area, often miles from water courses, and are attributed by geologists to some peculiar erosional feature of geological formation.

The following reasons lead us to believe that at Belcher the structures were not earth lodges:

1. The surface structures, Houses 1 and 5, were covered with a relatively thin humus layer, showing no evidence of heaped up earth.

PLATE 13

1. Floor plan, House 5, Belcher Site.
2. Floor plan House 1, Greer farm, Gibsland, Louisiana. Notice numerous molds, fire beds and cache pits.

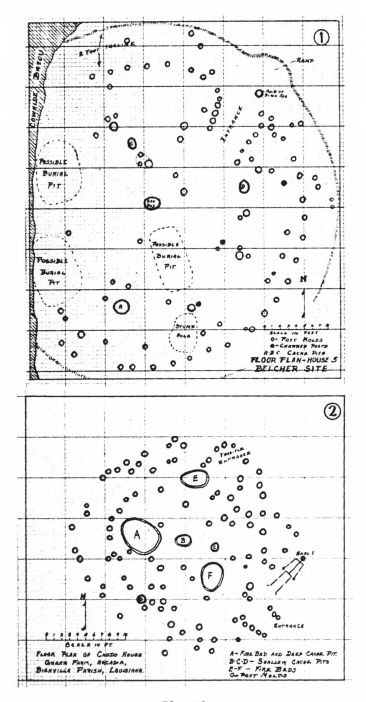

Plate 13

2. The earth covering the deeper structures was a clear sand, instead of the clay or sod which would be expected had they been earth lodges.

3. The sand immediately overlying the fallen burned structures had the same appearance as the higher sand fill.

4. The burned clay daub material which appeared with the house debris was tightly pressed, showing imprints of sticks, cane and grass. One surface was usually smooth, indicating its use as an adobe or plaster in wall construction.

5. The greater abundance of charred materials around the periphery suggests that earth was thrown on the collapsed structure as it burned.

6. Inversion of the roof sections, with grass lying directly on the floor, then cane, then poles, would not be expected if the roof had been sod covered.

We advance the hypothesis that when death of important personages, epidemics, war, or depreciation of the buildings made it desirable to construct a new lodge, the Caddos had the custom of burning the old structure, probably intentionally breaking the potteries used therein (House 2) and, as a part of the ceremony, gathering around the burning structure to heap on earth as it collapsed. Additions of soil built up a higher mound, on which the new temple was built. There is an obvious analogy with the custom among the Aztecs of Central Mexico, of destroying their houses, furnishings and potteries at the end of their 52 year cycle and building new temples on successively higher pyramids. The presence of burial pits dug through the covered ruins, before building a new structure, suggests that death of these individuals was responsible for or connected with destruction of Houses 2 and 4 at Belcher.

Conclusions

1. Historical evidence indicates that grass lodges and lodges with wattle-daub walls and grass thatched roofs were the prevailing types of structures among the southern Caddoan tribes.

2. House remains from a mound site within the historic Caddo area indicate several types of houses, with the custom of burning the houses when deserting them or before building new structures.

3. The highest type of Caddo culture at this site is associated with circular structures, where split cane and grass roofing, wattle-and-daub walls are constructional features.

4. A simpler and apparently earlier type of Caddoan pottery culture is associated with a rectangular house, which presents the Middle Mississippi feature of wall posts set in trenches.

5. No definite evidence of the earth lodge type of house was found.

6. Deep cache pits and burials through the floor while in use, do not seem to be prevalent in this area, although burial pits are cut through the ruins of burned structures.

The Children's Clinic,
Shreveport, Louisiana.

Bibliography

1. Fletcher, A. C., in Handbook of American Indians, by F. W. Hodge, Bureau of American Ethnology, Bull. 30, p. 505.

2. Joutel, Relation, pp. 341, 343, 345, quoted by Harrington, M. R., Certain Caddo Sites in Arkansas, Museum of the American Indian, Heye Foundation, N. Y., 1920, pp. 247-248.

3. Bolton, Texas in the Middle Eighteenth Century, quoted by Harrington, op. cit., pp. 250-251.

4. Father Manzanet, quoted by Jackson, A. T., A Perpetual Fire Site, Bull. of the Texas Archeological and Paleontological Society, Abilene, Texas, 1936, pp. 159-160.

5. Jackson, A. T., op. cit., pp. 134 to 172.

6. Swanton, J. R., Indian Tribes of the Lower Mississippi Valley and Adjacent Coast of the Gulf of Mexico, Bull. 43, Bur. Amer. Ethnol., pp. 59-60, 1911.

7. Bartram, Wm., Travels Through North and South Carolina, Georgia, East and West Florida, pp. 366-367, London, 1792. Quoted by Collins, H. B., Excavations at a Prehistoric Indian Village Site in Mississippi, United States National Museum, Vol. 79, pp. 1-22, 1932.

8. Harrington, M. R., op. cit.

9. Skinner, Alanson, An Ancient Town or Chief's House of the Indians of Southwestern Arkansas, in Harrington, M. R., op. cit. pp. 291-297.

10. Ford, J. A., Analysis of Indian Village Site Collections from Louisiana and Mississippi, Anthropological Study No. 2, Department of Conservation, Louisiana Geological Survey, 1936.

11. Strong, W. D., An Introduction to Nebraska Archeology, Smithsonian Miscellanous Collections, Vol. 93, Washington, D. C. 1935.

12. Collins, H. B., op. cit.

13. Cole, Fay-Cooper and Deuel, T., Rediscovering Illinois, University of Chicago Press, 1937, pp. 111-119.

14. Webb, W. S., An Archeological Survey of the Norris Basin in Eastern Tennessee, Smithsonian Institution Bull. No. 119, Washington, D. C., 1938.

15. Dickinson, S. D. and Lemley, H. J., Evidences of the Marksville and Coles Creek Complexes at the Kirkham Place, Clark County, Arkansas. Bull. of the Texas Archeological and Paleontological Society, Vol. 11, 1939, p. 138.

16. Goldschmidt, W. R., A Report on the Archeology of Titus County, Bull. of the Texas Archeological and Paleontological Society, Vol. 7, 1935.

17. Fowke, Gerard, Archeeological Investigations (II), 44th Annual Report, Bureau of American Ethnology, Washington, D. C., 1928, p. 408.

OVERVIEW

Some Comments on Anthropological Studies Concerning the Caddo

DEE ANN STORY

BECAUSE MUCH OF MY INTEREST in the Caddo has been generated by R. K. Harris, it is in appreciation of his generous sharing of ideas and information that I have written this essay on the subject.

It is widely agreed (Fletcher, 1959a, p. 179; 1959b, p. 638; Powell, 1966, pp. 88, 134; Swanton, 1942, pp. 5-6) that the word *Caddo* is derived from a native term for *chief*, either directly from *kä-ede* or as an abbreviated form of *kä-dohädä'cho* (real chiefs). Since the French customarily shortened tribal names by using only the first syllable of the proper term, it is most probable that *Caddo* stems from their usage (Mildred Wede, letter dated Feb. 3, 1975).

Unfortunately, there is no similarly simple anthropological explanation of the term. *Caddo* and *Caddoan* have come to have linguistic, ethnographic, archeological, and even geographical connotations. They have served to designate (1) a linguistic family, (2) a subdivision of related dialects within the family, (3) a collective term for perhaps as many as twenty-five tribes or bands, (4) a possible confederacy on the Red River, (5) a tribe or band within that possible confederacy, (6) certain prehistoric and historic archeological manifestations, and (7) the geographic region containing these archeological remains. A paper which could untangle and disassociate even some of the usages is obviously desirable, though probably at least several decades too late. As an alternative, this brief essay attempts to place anthropological concern with the

46

Caddo into a broad perspective and to evaluate critically the current status of research on the Caddo. Throughout, the focus is on *Caddo* and *Caddoan* as they have been applied to historic Indian groups and archeological remains in Northeast Texas, Northwest Louisiana, Southwest Arkansas, and Southeast Oklahoma.

LINGUISTIC STUDIES

It was through linguistics that *Caddo* initially assumed a broad and significant anthropological meaning. Taylor (1963a, 1963b) and Chafe (1973) provide excellent discussions of *Caddo* as a linguistic construct.

Although a Caddo (Hasinai) word list was apparently collected as early as 1687 by Henri Joutel, it was not until Americans gathered data in the early 1800s that a systematic analysis could begin (Taylor, 1963a, p. 51). The first important classification of American Indian languages did not appear until 1936, when Albert Gallatin published *A Synopsis of Indian Tribes within the United States East of the Rocky Mountains, and in British and Russian Possessions in North America* (Powell, 1966, pp. 88-99; Taylor, 1963a, p. 51). This remarkable work identified twenty-eight linguistic groups and laid the foundation for the many classifications which followed. Adaize, Caddo, and Pawnee were included in the Gallatin scheme as separate languages. By the 1850s the relatedness of Pawnee and Caddo began to be perceived, usually by reference to the "great Pawnee" or "Pani" family. The affinity of the two languages is recognized by Powell's oft-cited 1891 classification, but under the rubric Caddoan rather than Pawnee. As Powell (1966, p. 135) explained:

> The Pawnee and Caddo, now known to be of the same linguistic family, were supposed by Gallatin and many later writers to be distinct, and accordingly both names appear in the Archaeologia Americana as family designations. Both names are unobjectionable, but as the term Caddo has priority by a few pages preference is given to it.

Powell lists the principal tribes comprising the Caddoan linguistic family as including Pawnee, Arikara, Wichita, Kichai, and Caddo.

Adai appears in both Gallatin and Powell as a distinct language, although Powell (1966, pp. 121-22) acknowledges that it could be affiliated with Caddoan. Since Adai is available only as an internally inconsistent list of about 250 words collected by Sibley in 1802 (Powell, 1966, p. 122), its classification remains an unsolved problem. Swanton (1942, p. 6) accepts it as Caddoan, while Lesser and Weltfish (1932, pp. 2, 14) are ambivalent. They conclude that it was probably a divergent dialect of Caddo. Linguistic placement of the Eyeish (or Hais), a group sometimes culturally identified as Caddo, is impossible. Sibley (1922, p. 12) indicated that he collected a vocabulary from an "Aiche" woman in exchange for a shawl. The list apparently has not survived and Eyeish has long been an extinct language.

In essence then, the definition of the Caddoan family has changed little since 1891. As presented by Lesser and Weltfish, (1932, p. 2) it includes:

I. Pawnee, Kitsai, Wichita
   A. Pawnee
      1. South Band or Pawnee proper
      2. Skiri
      3. Arikara
   B. Kitsai
   C. Wichita
      1. Wichita proper
      2. Tawakaru, Weku
II. Caddo
   A. Caddo proper
   B. Hainai
   C. Adai?

Lesser and Weltfish characterize the relationship between these languages as follows:

Pawnee, Wichita, and Kitsai are, in relations to each other, about equally divergent, save that Kitsai in phonetic structure and some forms is probably closer to Pawnee than Wichita is to Pawnee. All three, however, are mutually unintelligible. Caddo is the most divergent of the four languages.

The possibility that the Caddoan family of languages bears a remote generic relationship to other major linguistic groups, particularly to Iroquoian and Siouan, has been suggested from time to time for over a century (Chafe, 1973, pp. 1190, 1193). The most famous and controversial grouping was that proposed by Edward Sapir in 1929 (pp. 138-39). In this classification Sapir lumped the languages spoken by North American Indians into six great stocks or suprafamilies. Iroquoian and Caddoan were joined into one subgroup, which was classed with Siouan and a number of other languages into a stock called Hokan-Siouan. Documentation supporting a relationship between Caddoan and either Iroquoian or Siouan, however, was not published until 1973. In this year Chafe presented evidence of what were judged to be genetically derived similarities between these groups and suggested that the resulting stock be termed Macro-Siouan. Other more distant ties have been proposed, especially for Siouan (and by extension Caddoan); but, like Sapir's Hokan-Siouan stock, they are still highly speculative.

From this review it should be evident that classification problems—primarily the composition and internal relationships of the Caddoan family, and secondarily the broader and more ancient affiliations—have been the dominant concerns in Caddoan linguistics. There are, to be sure, some exceptions such as the kinship inferences drawn by Spier (1924), Troike's (1957) acculturation study, which relied heavily on linguistic data to document interaction between Tonkawa and Hasinai groups, Chafe's (1968) use of Caddoan examples in dealing with phonological theory, and the areal-typological approach of Sherzer (1973). It nonetheless remains true that linguistic attention to the Caddo, and to the Caddoan family of languages, has been on the whole quite meager. Sound descriptive data are still sorely lacking and detailed, anthropologically oriented linguistic research is necessarily severely hampered. Encouragement, however, is to be found in Chafe's observation that Caddo survives as a language and that among its speakers are "remnants of the earlier dialect differences . . . distributed among them in a manner that could repay further study." (1973, p. 1165).

ETHNOGRAPHIC STUDIES

By the early 1890s, when the Caddo were first visited by an anthropologist, James Mooney (1896, pp. 1092-1103; Swanton, 1942, p. 118), they had suffered greatly from more than two hundred years of Spanish, French, and Anglo-American pressure. Perhaps it is because they were so disturbed that the Caddo largely escaped the flurry of field work conducted among American Indians, particularly by Bureau of American Ethnology personnel and students of Franz Boas. The little field work that has been published (Mooney, 1896; Dorsey, 1905a, 1905b; Parsons, 1941; Swanton, 1931, 1942; Spier, 1924) is based generally on brief visits and few informants. It also has tended to be narrowly focused, emphasizing only certain aspects of cultural behavior, such as folk tales (Dorsey, 1905a) or participation in the Ghost Dance (Mooney, 1896). Sadly, there is no detailed well-balanced ethnology derived from intensive, firsthand observation and interview by a trained professional. Elsie

Clews Parsons's *Notes on the Caddo*, which is based mainly on data obtained in the 1920s from an informant then living in New York City, remains the most inclusive, up-to-date description of Caddo culture.

Fortunately, the documentary sources have not been equally neglected, and it is primarily from observations made from the late seventeenth through mid-nineteenth centuries that we know the various groups now commonly identified as Caddo. The two major monographs, John R. Swanton's *Source Material on the History and Ethnology of the Caddo Indians* (1942) and William J. Griffith's *The Hasinai Indians of East Texas as Seen by Europeans, 1687-1772* (1954), are ultimately derived from these documents. In addition, there are numerous historical studies (see, for example, bibliographies by Glover, 1935; Castañeda, 1936-58; Swanton, 1942; Griffith, 1954; Neuman and Simmons, 1969) which contain invaluable information. While the primary and secondary ethnohistoric accounts are far too voluminous and complex to be reviewed in this essay, a few general observations are offered.

Perhaps most importantly, the limitation of Caddo as an ethnohistoric construct should be stressed. Although this point was clearly made a decade ago by Williams (1964, p. 545), it merits reiteration. Caddo is a concept of convenience which for the period ca. A.D. 1690-1800 has come to include about twenty-three, or perhaps twenty-five, distinct bands or tribes. Ignoring the difficult problems of correlating names and locations given in the documents at different times and by different observers, these groups are most often identified (Swanton, 1942, pp. 7-14; Newcomb, 1961, pp. 200-202) as:

Near or above the Great Bend of the Red River:
    Kadohadacho   Upper Natchitoches
    Upper Nasoni   Nanatsoho

Near San Augustine, Texas:
    Eyeish

Between the Great Bend and Vicinity of Natchitoches:
    Yatasi
    Petit Caddo

Vicinity of Natchitoches, Louisiana:
    Lower Natchitoches
    Doustioni

Near Robeline, Louisiana:
Adai

Ouachita River, near Arkadelphia, Arkansas:
Cahinnio

Lower Ouachita River:
Ouachita

On the Upper Neches and Angelina Drainages (the so-called "Hasi-nai" or "Tejas" Indians):

Nabiti	Neche
Nadaco	Nacogdoche
Lower Nasoni	Nabedache
Hainai	Nacono
Nacao	Nechaui
Nacachau	

The justifications for lumping these groups together have never been discussed in detail but apparently include linguistic affinity, geographical distribution, native statements of relatedness, and historical events. That the groups were in fact very similar culturally and that most of them were organized in terms of confederacies (Bolton, 1908, p. 251; Swanton, 1942, p. 7) has not been challenged seriously enough. *Confederacy* is a term almost certainly inappropriate when applied to the groups in the Natchitoches area. In the case of others, particularly those in the Great Bend region of the Red River, confederacy may be appropriate, but it could be a late phenomenon, resulting from pressure by Europeans or Osages.

As a single sociopolitical entity, Caddo does not emerge until after the 1850s after there had been much displacement, reduction in numbers, and considerable amalgamation with other groups. It was in 1874, while on the reservation of the Wichita and Affiliated Tribes near Fort Cobb, Oklahoma, that the remnants of the various Caddo groups, along with the Delaware and probably other Indians, formally agreed to unite and be known thereafter as the Caddo Indians (Foreman, 1946, p. 284). The uncritical projection of this unity into the past is an obvious over-simplification, especially when we are generating hypotheses against which prehistoric archeological data are to be tested. Significant cultural variations in both time and space could well have existed among the various tribes, and observations made at a specific village at a specific time should not be taken to apply necessarily to all places and times. Given the time span involved, we should also be prepared for differences in acculturation stemming from variations in the European cultures and displaced Indians with whom the various Caddo groups were associated. Whenever possible, specific dates and names should be used rather than *Caddo* and generalized cultural descriptions.

In view of the desirability of particularizing our approach in terms of more functional social entities—Hainai, Kadohadacho, Village of El Loco, etc.—it is regrettable that the historic sources pertaining to specific tribes or settlements are not equally rich in ethnographic details. At a fairly early date some groups, such as the Cahinnio and Ouachita (Swanton, 1942; Williams, 1964, p. 546), disappear from the documents as distinct entities. Others, for example the Nechaui (Hatcher, 1927, p. 215; Bolton, 1908, p. 267), are known only as names and vague locations. By contrast, it is the Hasinai—the so-called principal tribes resident in the Upper Neches and Angelina drainages (Bolton, 1908, pp. 253-55)—that between ca. 1690 and 1840 experienced the most prolonged and intimate contact with Europeans, especially the Spanish and Anglo-Americans. The most in depth descriptions are for the Hasinai groups; but even these accounts are disturbingly few. Swanton makes this quite clear when he discusses the sources from which he compiled his monograph (1942, pp. 2-3):

> In the subjoined material there are but a few original notes, the greater part, as the title [of his monograph] implies, being a compilation from the productions of earlier writers, including mainly the letters and reports of the missionaries Francisco Casañas de Jesus Maria Francisco Hidalgo, Isidro de Espinosa, and José de Solís, the Historia and Memorias of Juan Agustín Morfi, and the relations of La Salle's companion, Henri Joutel.

We have come to depend very heavily upon Spanish sources, both as primary documents and, more often, as known through translations and historic interpretations. This situation introduces certain geographical and temporal limitations, as well as a Spanish (especially missionary) cultural screen through which the recorded native behavior has been filtered. One has to suspect that this reliance upon Spanish material reflects the outstanding archival research of such competent historians as Eugene Bolton (1908, 1912, 1914, 1915) and Carlos Castañeda (1936-1958), and that the French and Anglo-American accounts have not been as thoroughly combed for tidbits of ethnographically relevant information.

As with the language of the Caddo, much remains to be learned about their culture(s). The almost 1,800 persons now listed on the tribal roll (Marquis, 1974, p. 167) merit attention, not to seek survivals of the past but to understand the Caddo as a viable segment of contemporary society. Historically significant information can come only from the historic documents, and we must view the work of Swanton and Griffith as beginnings, not ends. New sources surely remain to be discovered and old ones, especially the primary accounts, need to be critically reexamined and more carefully utilized. The ethnohistoric research presently underway by Mildred Wedel, who is working with the badly neglected French sources, and by T. N. Campbell, who is combing materials pertaining to Texas Indians, is certain to provide new information and new perspectives.

PHYSICAL ANTHROPOLOGY STUDIES

Published information on the biology of Caddo populations has been derived primarily from analyses of skeletal remains from archeological sites. The concern with living groups has been quite limited and to my knowledge includes only Hrdlicka (1908), Dixon (1923), and Gray and Laughlin (1960). Hrdlicka reports on pathological and genetic anomalies observed by reservation personnel. The Caddo appear only in his table 9, in a listing (item 40) that uselessly includes them with nearby Oklahoma tribes: the Kiowa, Apache, Wichita, and Comanche. Dixon's treatment of the Caddo[1] in his book *The Racial History of Man* (1923, pp. 423, 426-29) is also cursory and is based mainly on unpublished metric data collected by Franz Boas for the Chicago World's Columbian Exposition of 1893. On the strength of head and nose form, Dixon classed the Caddo as basically a "Plains" type but, along with the Tonkawa, as displaying features which represented a survival of physical elements once dominant on the southern plains.

Using blood group gene frequencies, Gray and Laughlin almost forty years later reached essentially the same conclusion, with more specific and useful samples. This most recent study is the only one of the three to deal with the living Caddo in a fashion that today might

[1] The few crania also included by Dixon as Caddo (1923, p. 428) are based on observations published by Allen in 1896. In examining this reference I found that Allen identified the skulls in question as "Arickaree." The basis for this identification and exactly what Dixon meant by *Caddo* are not specified.

be called significant. It represents an interesting, though clearly problem-fraught, attempt to unravel the genetic affiliations of the Caddoan-speakers: the Pawnee, Wichita, and Caddo.

Whether studies are biological or cultural, however, it is almost certainly too late to extract much of the past from the living Caddo. Growth and nutrition research would seem to be far more promising and relevant both to the Caddo and to contemporary physical anthropology. As yet there is little indication that such studies are being conducted or even contemplated.

By contrast, the health status of prehistoric populations—insofar as it can be assessed from skeletal remains—has been a fairly consistent concern in the analysis and interpretation of materials from archeological sites. Particular attention has been given diseases affecting the mouth and teeth (Colquitt and Webb, 1940; Webb, 1944; Goldstein, 1948; Keith, 1973), with interesting inferences for modern dentistry being pointed out in one study (Colquitt and Webb, 1940, p. 2417). Observations on other kinds of pathologies and on mortality rates typify most recent papers, at least when the skeletal collection is in fair condition. Good examples are to be found in Brues (1958, 1959), Butler (1969a), and Buikstra and Fowler (1975).

Detailed study of the crania is another well-established tradition in the analysis of Caddoan, and other, skeletal remains. It is especially evident in the works of the earlier researchers, most notably Hrdlicka (1909, 1912, 1927, 1940) and to a lesser degree Goldstein (1941) and Stewart (1940). Determination of racial affinity was apparently one of the major objectives of the seemingly endless observations and measurements possible on well-preserved skulls. Evidence of cranial deformation has also been consistently sought, as deformation has long been recognized as being frequent in collections from Caddoan sites. Usually it is only one of many observations made (e.g., Butler, 1969b); but one paper (Bennett, 1961) deals solely with cranial deformation among Caddo Indians, and two others (Neumann, 1941; Stewart, 1941) have utilized Caddoan materials in establishing types of deformation. Somewhat surprisingly, deformation has attracted little interest from a behavioral point of view. Bennett has attempted to define the practices which probably produced various types of modification to the skull and has briefly presented distributional data, concluding that deformation was a matter of individual choice. Gregory (1963) has published a brief note on skull deformity as a means of enhancing personal appearance.

No one appears to have tried to determine, however, whether or not cranial deformation co-varies with certain cultural traits. Is it, for example, closely associated with artifacts believed to signify special social position?

More commonly asked questions concern the affiliations of the skeletal remains found at archeological sites (e.g., Stewart, 1940; Brues, 1958). Neumann (1952, 1954), in the most encompassing classification of Amerindian material developed thus far, has defined eight varieties. Maples (1962) is apparently one of the few to compare Caddoan series with Neumann's types. Using skeletal remains from eight Caddoan sites in Texas (Sanders, Womack, Hunt, Farrar, Allen, Hatchel, Moore, and Mitchell), Maples noted, among other conclusions, (1962, pp. 25-26) a close morphological relationship with Neumann's Walcolid and Lenapid varieties. However, a more recent study (Long, 1966) has convincingly cast doubt on the validity of Neumann's varieties. It is thus unlikely that such affiliations are of any real significance. The typological approach to skeletal remains has simply never been very productive.

The problems confronting any sort of meaningful analysis of skeletal remains are manifold and difficult to surmount. Ideally, a study should be based on a population in a biological sense, and should examine this population in terms of the genetic and environmental factors that interact in complex ways to affect the phenotypic characteristics of its members. The most serious problems are (1) the extraction of a valid population sample from the archeological record, (2) the uncertainty surrounding the heritability of many skeletal attributes, (3) the physical limitations in the reaction of the skeleton to environmental conditions (especially disease, nutrition, and injury), and (4) the frequently poor preservation of bones in archeological sites. Some of these problems we must accept as inherent; others can at least in part be overcome, particularly if there is a closer interaction between the physical anthropologist and the archeologist. The objectives of an analysis must be more explicitly and more realistically related to both the nature of the sample and the levels of confidence possible.

The crucial definition of a breeding population must depend heavily upon a critical evaluation of the cultural evidence. On an archeological level this is most effectively conceived as a cultural problem rather than a biological problem. In the Caddoan area the recognition of the parameters of population is facilitated by (1) the widespread occurrence of cemeteries which may yield large samples from a definable spatial context, and (2) the common inclusion of offerings in graves which aid temporal and cultural alignments within and beyond one site. The tendency, however, to equate a cemetery sample with a population is not necessarily justified. It may result in an improbable biological assemblage of materials for study, or a disadvantageous reduction in sample size. In view of the need for statistically adequate samples, the possibility of ranging beyond one site should always be considered. Well-documented and well-curated skeleton collections are of key importance and should be receiving far more attention than they have received to date. Moreover, the scientific value of fragile skeletal remains could probably be enhanced by archeologists familiarizing themselves with up-to-date techniques of preservation, and by having a physical anthropologist visit the site to advise on collecting procedures and to make a preliminary *in situ* analysis.

Given reasonable preservation and sample size, we should expect a skeletal analysis at a minimum to yield demographic data, to draw inferences on health status, and to comment on the relative homogeneity or heterogeneity of the sample, as a whole and as sorted in sex categories. When these data are integrated with information on cultural behavior, such as mortuary practices, social organization, and subsistence patterns, they become highly useful. When they stay isolated in an appendix they are of little value to either physical anthropology or archeology.

ARCHEOLOGICAL STUDIES

Whether measured by the published literature or by the number of researchers currently active, it is evident that the dominant anthropological concern with the Caddo has been from the perspective of archeology. It is equally apparent that much of Caddoan archeology remains poorly explained. Well-sampled and well-reported sites are relatively few in number, and data lacking good contextual associations are major sources of information.

As an archeological term *Caddoan* has interrelated cultural and spatial dimensions. The Caddoan area centers geographically near the Great Bend of the Red River and encompasses much of the contiguous portions of Arkansas, Louisiana, Oklahoma, and Texas. It does not coincide with a commonly recognized natural region, nor does it lend itself to simple geographical reference.[2] It is an area delineated by the extent

---

[2] These circumstances have no doubt contributed to the occasional, confused usage of "Caddoan area" in distributional studies of non-Caddoan remains (e.g., Orr, 1952). A workable solution to this terminological problem was proposed by Frank Schambach

of certain archeological remains—in actual practice, primarily ceramics —which are presumed to represent the Kadohadacho, Hasinai, etc., and their prehistoric cultural ancestors. The defining ceramics are difficult to characterize in general but are more or less distinctive in specific temporal, spatial, and functional contexts—at the type level and at the attribute level.

Other archeological traits which have been listed as characteristically Caddoan (E. M. Davis, 1961, pp. 86-89; Hoffman, 1969, p. 43) include circular houses with temporary center posts, certain clay pipe forms, and shaftlike burial pits with elaborate offerings. These, however, are even less serviceable than pottery. They vary greatly by kind of settlement as well as by time and place of occurrence. Even more importantly, it is being increasingly recognized (e.g., Brown, 1975) that material traits alone contribute little to the understanding of social entities and relationships, political organizations, or economic adaptations.

The ways in which Caddoan archeological remains are characterized and explained are very much functions of the conceptualizations and methodologies in vogue at the time of study. There have been about seventy years of investigation, and Caddoan archeology, like Caddoan culture, has a history of development. Since reasonably inclusive and up-to-date summaries of this history are available (H. A. Davis, 1969; E. M. Davis, 1970; Neuman, 1970; Hoffman, 1970; Wyckoff, 1970), this review will briefly discuss what I see as three major phases in Caddoan research. These are presented in roughly historical sequences and are admittedly generalized characterizations based largely on published materials.

The first several decades of fieldwork in the Caddoan area focused on the recovery of specimens for display and for answering very broadly framed questions about lifeways of the past. It was a time of basic discovery, with the quantity and quality of artifacts found serving as the main measures of success of an excavation. The emphasis was on large sites and, even more particularly, on the cemeteries they contained. Contextural relations were often poorly recorded and nonartifactual debris (faunal remains, chipping debitage, and the like) were only incidentally collected, or completely ignored. This specimen-oriented approach domi-

at the 1971 Caddo Conference. In an as yet unpublished paper read at this conference, Schambach introduced Trans-Mississippi South as a natural area and defined the Caddoan area as a cultural province which occurs in portions of the Trans-Mississippi South. (See Webb, this volume.)

nated much of the institutionally supported fieldwork from the time of
C. B. Moore in the late 1900s to the close of the WPA at the outbreak
of World War II. It still continues today, mainly in the form of the
unwitting private collector.

In spite of the sampling biases and the often skimpy documentation,
the collections amassed during this early era of Caddoan archeology are
major resources for study. They are the contributions of many individuals,
only a few of whom can be singled out here. C. B. Moore and M. R.
Harrington certainly deserve mention as pioneer researchers. Moore is
especially remembered for his prompt and lavishly illustrated publications of 1908, 1909, and 1912. These reports attracted attention to a
region that had largely escaped serious notice, and they remain as the
sole or primary sources of published information on a number of important sites, including Gahagan, Haley, Friday, and Foster on the Red
River, and Glendora and Keno on the Ouachita River.

M. R. Harrington, commissioned in 1916-17 by the Heye Foundation
to continue Moore's work, was apparently the first in print (1920) to
associate archeological remains with a historic Caddo Indian group, the
"true Caddo" (Kadochacho), and to make interpretations by reference
to ethnohistoric accounts. Subsequent historic associations (Jackson,
1934; Walker, 1935; Dickinson, 1941; Webb, 1945; Harris, 1953)
seemed to cinch Harrington's pronouncement and, though periodically
criticized (Krieger, 1947; E. M. Davis, 1961) "Caddo" and "Caddoan"
have become deeply entrenched in the archeological literature.

The years following Harrington's work in southwestern Arkansas saw
a gradual increase in fieldwork, as well as a shift toward more locally
based excavations by both private individuals and institutionally affiliated
archeologists. The late 1930s were especially active times, with major
WPA excavations being conducted in eastern Oklahoma and northeastern
Texas. Public work projects in Louisiana and Arkansas, however, resulted
in few or no investigations at Caddoan sites. Rather, this task fell to
dedicated nonprofessionals such as Clarence H. Webb and Harry J.
Lemley.

By the outbreak of World War II and the termination of the WPA
program, cultural complexities in the Trans-Mississippi South and Caddoan archeology were becoming apparent. For example, pre-Caddoan
material had been identified in Arkansas (Dickinson, 1936; Dickinson
and Lemley, 1939); a Caddoan sequence was being developed in Louisiana (Webb and Dodd, 1941); comparative studies of materials from

Caddoan sites in Texas had been undertaken (e.g., Jackson, 1933, 1934, 1935, 1938); and Caddoan culture complexes were beginning to be defined in Oklahoma (Orr, 1941).

From the recognition that Caddoan archeology could not be explained as a single culture complex emerged a second major phase of research, one of systematic description and synthesis. This cultural-historical approach crystallized in the early 1940s and reached a peak in the summaries published in the 1950s (Bell and Baerreis, 1951; Orr, 1952; Suhm, Krieger, and Jelks, 1954). It had been stimulated by a new generation of highly trained archeologists who had begun their professional careers (many on WPA projects) and who were formulating new approaches to artifact typologies (e.g., Rouse, 1939) and to cultural taxonomies (e.g., McKern, 1939), as well as publishing broad chronologic schemes (e.g., Ford and Willey, 1941).

The way to systematic ordering of Caddoan archeology was led by one such archeologist from the University of California at Berkeley, Alex D. Krieger. Krieger came to Texas in the late 1930s as supervisor of the WPA Austin lab. In 1941 he began his comparative Caddoan studies, and by 1943, in a paper presented at the Third Round Table Conference in Mexico City (Krieger, 1944), was able to outline two major time periods, the Gibson (early) and Fulton (late) aspects, and twelve foci. The definition and chronologic placement of Caddoan complexes, particularly their alignment with the better established sequences in the Southwest, Lower Mississippi Valley, and Mesoamerican, became dominant themes in many of Krieger's subsequent publications. His broad command of New World prehistory and his ability to synthesize a wide variety of information are quite evident in his two major contributions to Caddoan archeology: *Cultural Complexes and Chronology in Northern Texas* (1946) and *The George C. Davis Site* (Newell and Krieger, 1949).

In Texas, Krieger provided a continuity with the WPA investigations. In Oklahoma, it was Kenneth G. Orr and David A. Baerreis. Orr is best known for his analysis of the Spiro Site (1946) and his summary article on Caddoan archeology (1952). Baerreis has also published on Caddoan materials in the Arkansas River drainage (1954, 1955, 1957). In 1951, he collaborated with Robert E. Bell to produce a good example of the syntheses of this period, "A Survey of Oklahoma Archeology."

While Oklahoma and Texas were centers of institutionally supported research during the 1940s and on into the early 1950s, significant contributions were also being made by amateurs and by professionals working outside the Caddoan area. The latter include most notably James A. Ford and James B. Griffin, both of whom injected an invaluable perspective (see especially Ford, 1951; Griffin, 1950, 1952, 1961). Particularly outstanding among the nonprofessionals active during this period are C. H. Webb in Louisiana, R. K. Harris in Texas, and Dr. and Mrs. T. L. Hodges in Arkansas.

By the late 1950s fieldwork in the Caddoan area was again on the increase, largely as a result of renewed federal support of archeological projects in Arkansas, Oklahoma, and Texas. What had begun in 1946 as modestly funded reservoir surveys, generally under the auspices of the Smithsonian Institution (e.g., Bell, 1948; Stephenson, 1948), had by 1958 shifted to cooperative agreements between local institutions and the National Parks Service, and to expanded survey and excavation programs. The opportunities to answer many unresolved questions of typology, taxonomy, and chronology seemed close at hand.

Gradually, however, it was becoming evident that not all of the weaknesses were in the data. E. B. Jelks, for example, noted in his analysis of Texarkana Reservoir excavations (1961, p. 74):

> Differences in quantitative representation of pottery types at Knight's Bluff, Sherwin, and the Hatchel Site (type site of the Texarkana Focus) emphasize a general observation that a focus (as that classifactory unit has been applied in the Caddoan Area) is not necessarily a closely integrated complex of traits found with little or no variation from site to site.

The time-space constructs were not adequately expressing, much less explaining, the observable variations between and within sites. From dissatisfaction with the limited objectives of the taxonomic approach arose new directions in American archeology. The most significant of these crystallized in the early 1960s, mainly in the writings of Lewis L. Binford (1962a, 1962b). Known variously as processual, scientific, and new archeology, it basically takes the position that the residue of the past can be comprehended only in the context of generalizing principles of human behavior. The strategies of processual archeologists have been classed (Flannery, 1973) as falling into two camps: one which seeks covering laws of human behavior and tests them by statistical correlation, the other which seeks regularities of human behavior in the framework of systems theory.

The new archeology has had a profound impact on Caddoan research, even though there are still relatively few full-blown processual studies, such as James A. Brown's analysis of Spiro mortuary behavior (especially Brown, 1971, 1975) and segments of the Lake Palestine project (Gilmore, 1973; Anderson et al., 1974). This is most evident in the increased concern with nontemporal dimensions of artifacts (e.g., Woodall, 1969; Shafer, 1973), subsistence systems (e.g., Keller, 1974), intrasite variability (e.g., Story, 1972), settlement patterning (e.g., McCormick, 1973), and, in general, interpretations framed in behavioral terms. There is new optimism but there are also new and complex demands. Projects are certain to become more costly and time-consuming and to require specialized facilities and expertise that are presently difficult to obtain. Since the still *in situ* sample for study is daily being reduced, it is imperative we quickly and intelligently meet the new challenges of what we have come to call Caddoan archeology.

BIBLIOGRAPHY

ALLEN, H. 1896. "Crania from the Mounds of the St. Johns River, Florida: A Study Made in Connection with Crania from Other Parts of North America." *Journal of the Academy of Natural Sciences of Philadelphia* 10 (4): 367-448.

ANDERSON, K. M.; GILMORE, K.; McCORMICK, O. F. III; and MORENON, E. P. 1974. *Archaeological Investigations at Lake Palestine, Texas.* Southern Methodist University Contributions in Anthropology, no. 11.

BAERREIS, D. A. 1954. "The Huffaker Site, Delaware County, Oklahoma." *Bulletin of the Oklahoma Anthropological Society* 2:35-48.

————. 1955. "Further Material from the Huffaker Site, Delaware County, Oklahoma." *Bulletin of the Oklahoma Anthropological Society* 3:54-68.

————. 1957. "The Southern Cult and the Spiro Ceremonial Complex." *Bulletin of the Oklahoma Anthropological Society* 5:23-38.

BELL, R. E. 1948. "Recent Archeological Research in Oklahoma." *Bulletin of the Texas Archeological and Paleontological Society* 19:148-54.

————, and BAERREIS, D. A. 1951. "A Survey of Oklahoma Archaeology." *Bulletin of the Texas Archeological and Paleontological Society* 22:7-100.

BENNETT, K. A. 1961. "Artificial Cranial Deformation among the Caddo Indians." *Texas Journal of Science* 13 (4): 377-90.

BINFORD, L. R. 1962a. "Archaeology as Anthropology." *American Antiquity* 28 (2): 217-25.

————. 1962b. "Archaeological Systematics and the Study of Cultural Process." *American Antiquity* 31 (2): 203-10.

BOLTON, H. E. 1908. "The Native Tribes about the East Texas Missions." *Texas State Historical Association Quarterly* 11 (4): 249-76.

———. 1912. "The Spanish Occupation of Texas, 1519-1690." *Southwestern Historical Quarterly* 16 (1): 1-26.

———, ed. 1914. *Athanase de Mézières and the Louisiana-Texas Frontier, 1768-1780.* 2 vols. Cleveland: Arthur H. Clark Co.

———. 1915. *Texas in the Middle Eighteenth Century.* Reprint. Austin: University of Texas Press, 1970.

BROWN, J. A., 1971. "The Dimensions of Status in the Burials at Spiro." In *Approaches to the Social Dimensions of Mortuary Practices,* ed. J. A. Brown, pp. 92-112. Memoirs of the Society for American Archaeology, no. 25.

———. 1975. "Spiro Art and Its Mortuary Context." Dumbarton Oaks Conference on Death and the Afterlife in Pre-Columbian America (Oct. 17, 1973), pp. 1-32.

BRUES, A. M. 1958. "Skeletal Material from the Horton Site." *Bulletin of the Oklahoma Anthropological Society* 6:27-32.

———. 1959. "Skeletal Material from the Morris Site (CK-39)." *Bulletin of the Oklahoma Anthropological Society* 7:63-70.

BUIKSTRA, J., and FOWLER, D. 1975. "An Osteological Study of the Human Skeletal Material from the Bentsen-Clark Site." Appendix in *The Bentsen-Clark Site, Red River County, Texas: A Preliminary Report,* by L. Banks and J. Winters. Texas Archeological Society, Special Publication no. 2, pp. 79-97.

BUTLER, B. H. 1969a. Appendix I: "Analysis of the Human Skeletal Remains." In *Archaeological Investigations at the Sam Kaufman Site, Red River County, Texas,* ed. S. A. Skinner, R. K. Harris, and K. M. Anderson. Southern Methodist University Contributions in Anthropology, no. 5, pp. 115-36.

———. 1969b. Appendix III: "The Skeletal Material from the Bison Site, Area B." In *Archaeological Excavations in the Toledo Bend Reservoir, 1966,* by J. N. Woodall. Southern Methodist University Contributions in Anthropology, no. 3, pp. 84-93.

CASTAÑEDA, C. E. 1936-1958. *Our Catholic Heritage in Texas, 1519-1936.* 7 vols. Austin: Van Boeckmann-Jones Co.

CHAFE, W. L. 1968. "The Order of Phonological Rules." *International Journal of American Linguistics* 34:115-46.

———. 1973. "Siouan, Iroquoian, and Caddoan." In *Current Trends in Linguistics,* ed. T. A. Sebeok. *Linguistics in North America* 10:1164-1209. New York: Mouton.

COLQUITT, W. T., and WEBB, C. H. 1940. "Dental Diseases in an Aboriginal Group." *Tri-State Medical Journal* 12 (4): 2414-17.

DAVIS, E. M. 1961. "Proceedings of the Fifth Conference on Caddoan Archeology." *Bulletin of the Texas Archeological Society* 30:77-143.

_____ 1970. "Archeological and Historical Assessment of the Red River Basin in Texas." *Archeological and Historical Resources of the Red River Basin*, ed. H. A. Davis. Arkansas Archeological Survey, Publications on Archeology, Research Series, no. 1, pp. 25-65.

DAVIS, H. A. 1969. "A Brief History of Archeological Work in Arkansas up to 1967." *Bulletin of the Arkansas Archeological Society* 10 (1-3): 2-8.

DICKINSON, S. D. 1936. "Ceramic Relationships of the Pre-Caddo Pottery from the Crenshaw Site." *Bulletin of the Texas Archeological and Paleontological Society* 8:56-69.

_____ 1941. "Certain Vessels from the Clements Place, an Historic Caddo Site." *Bulletin of the Texas Archeological and Paleontological Society* 13:117-32.

_____, and LEMLEY, H. J. 1939. "Evidences of the Marksville and Coles Creek Complexes at the Kirkham Place, Clark County, Arkansas." *Bulletin of the Texas Archeological and Paleontological Society* 11:139-89.

DIXON, R. B. 1923. *The Racial History of Man*. New York: Charles Scribner's Sons.

DORSEY, G. A. 1905a. *Traditions of the Caddo*. Carnegie Institution of Washington, Publication no. 41.

_____ 1905b. "Caddo Customs of Childhood." *Journal of the American Folk-Lore Society* 18:226-28.

FLANNERY, K. V. 1973. "Archeology with a Capital S." In *Research and Theory in Current Archeology*, ed. C. L. Redman, pp. 47-53. New York: John Wiley & Sons.

FLETCHER, A. C. 1959a. "Caddo." In *Handbook of American Indians North of Mexico*, ed. F. W. Hodges, pt. 1, pp. 179-83. American Bureau of Ethnology Bulletin no. 30 (1907). Reprint.

_____ 1959b. "Kado Hadacho." In *Handbook of American Indians North of Mexico*, ed. F. W. Hodges, pt. 1, pp. 638-39. American Bureau of Ethnology Bulletin no. 30 (1907). Reprint.

FORD, J. A. 1951. *Greenhouse: A Troyville-Coles Creek Period Site in Avoyelles Parish, Louisiana*. Anthropological Papers of the American Museum of Natural History, vol. 44, pt. 1.

FORD, J. A., and WILLEY, G. R. 1941. "An Interpretation of the Prehistory of the Eastern United States." *American Anthropologist* 43 (3): 325-63.

FOREMAN, G. 1946. *The Last Trek of the Indians*. Chicago: University of Chicago Press.

GALLATIN, A. 1836. "A Synopsis of the Indian Tribes within the United States East of the Rocky Mountains, and in British and Russian Possessions in North America." In *Transactions and Collections of the American Antiquarian Society (Archeologia America)*, vol. 2.

GILMORE, K. K. 1973. "Caddoan Interaction in the Neches Valley, Texas." Ph.D. dissertation, Southern Methodist University.

GLOVER, W. B. 1935. "A History of the Caddo Indians." *Louisiana Historical Quarterly* 18 (4): 872-946.

GOLDSTEIN, M. S. 1941. "Crania from East Texas." *News Letter of the Southeastern Archaeological Conference* 2 (4): 5.

———. 1948. "Dentition of Indian Crania from Texas." *American Journal of Physical Anthropology*, 6 (1): 63-84.

GRAY, P. M., and LAUGHLIN, W. S. 1960. "Blood Groups of Caddoan Indians of Oklahoma." *American Journal of Human Genetics* 12 (1): 86-94.

GREGORY, H. F. 1963. "Skull Deformation: An Indian Beauty Mark." *Louisiana Studies* 2 (3): 52-53.

GRIFFIN, J. B. 1950. Review of "The George C. Davis Site, Cherokee County, Texas." *American Anthropologist* 52:413-15

———. 1952. "An Interpretation of the Place of Spiro in Southeastern Archaeology." In W. H. Hamilton, "The Spiro Mound." *Missouri Archaeologist* 14:89-106.

———. 1961. "Relationships between the Caddoan Area and the Mississippi Valley." In "Symposium on Relationships between the Caddoan Area and Neighboring Groups," ed. E. M. Davis. *Bulletin of the Texas Archeological Society* 31:27-51.

GRIFFITH, W. J. 1954. "The Hasinai Indians of East Texas as Seen by Europeans, 1687-1772." Reprinted from Middle American Research Institute, Tulane University Publication no. 12. *Philological and Documentary Studies* 2 (3): 41-168.

HARRINGTON, M. R. 1920. "Certain Caddo Sites in Arkansas." Museum of the American Indian, Heye Foundation, Indian Notes and Monographs, Miscellaneous Series, no. 10.

HARRIS, R. K. 1953. "The Sam Kaufman Site, Red River County, Texas." *Bulletin of the Texas Archeological Society* 24:43-68.

HATCHER, M. A., trans. and ed. 1927. "Descriptions of the Texas or Asinai Indians I: Fray Francisco Casañas de Jesus Maria to the Viceroy of Mexico, August 15, 1691. *Southwestern Historical Quarterly* 30 (3): 206-18.

HOFFMAN, M. P. 1969. "Prehistoric Developments in Southwest Arkansas." *Bulletin of the Arkansas Archeological Society* 10 (1, 2, & 3): 37-49.

———. 1970. "Archaeological and Historical Assessment of the Red River Basin in Arkansas." *Archeological and Historical Resources of the Red River Basin*, ed. H. A. Davis. Arkansas Archeological Survey, Publication on Archeology, Research Series, no. 1, pp. 135-94.

HRDLICKA, A. 1908. *Physiological and Medical Observations among Indians of Southwestern United States and Mexico.* Bureau of American Ethnology Bulletin no. 34

————. 1909. Report on an Additional Collection of Skeletal Remains, from Arkansas and Louisiana. In C. B. Moore, "Antiquities of the Ouachita Valley." *Journal of the Academy of Natural Sciences of Philadelphia* 14:171-249.

————. 1912. Report on Skeletal Remains from a Mound on Haley Place near Red River, Miller County, Arkansas. In C. B. Moore, "Some Aboriginal Sites on Red River." *Journal of the Academy of Natural Sciences of Philadelphia* 14, 2d ser., pt. 4, pp. 639-40.

————. 1927. "Catalogue of Human Crania in the United States National Museum Collection." *Proceedings of the United States National Museum,* vol. 69, art. 5.

————. 1940. "Catalog of Human Crania in the United States National Museum Collections: Indians of the Gulf States." *Proceedings of the United States National Museum* 87:315-464.

JACKSON, A. T. 1933. "Indian Pipes of East Texas." *Bulletin of the Texas Archeological and Paleontological Society* 5:69-86.

————. 1934. "Types of East Texas Pottery." *Bulletin of the Texas Archeological and Paleontological Society* 6:38-57.

————. 1935. "Ornaments of East Texas Indians." *Bulletin of the Texas Archeological and Paleontological Society* 7:11-28.

————. 1938. "Fire in East Texas Burial Rites." *Bulletin of the Texas Archeological and Paleontological Society* 10:77-113.

JELKS, E. B. 1961. *Excavations at Texarkana Reservoir, Sulphur River, Northeastern Texas.* Bureau of American Ethnology Bulletin no. 179; River Basin Survey Papers no. 21, nos. 1-78.

KEITH, K. D. 1973. "The Paleostomatology at the Moore Site (Lf-31), LeFlore County, Oklahoma." *Bulletin of the Oklahoma Anthropological Society* 22:149-57.

KELLER, J. E. 1974. "The Subsistence Paleoecology of the Middle Neches Region of Eastern Texas." Ph.D. dissertation, University of Texas, Austin.

KRIEGER, A. D. 1944. "Archaeological Horizons in the Caddo Area." In *El Norte de Mexico y el Sur de Estados Unidos,* pp. 154-56. Sociedad Mexicana de Anthropologia.

————. 1946. *Culture Complexes and Chronology in Northern Texas.* University of Texas Publication no. 4640.

————. 1947. "The First Symposium on the Caddoan Archaeological Area." *American Antiquity* 12 (3): 198-207.

LESSER, A., and WELTFISH, G. 1932. "Composition of the Caddoan Linguistic Stock." Smithsonian Miscellaneous Collections 87 (6): 1-5.

LONG, J. K. 1966. "A Test of Multiple-Discriminant Analysis as a Means of Determining Evolutionary Changes and Intergroup Relationships in Physical Anthropology." American Anthropologist 68 (2) pt. 1: 444-64.

MAPLES, W. R. 1962. "A Morphological Comparison of Skeletal Material from Sanders Focus and from Fulton Aspect." Master's thesis, University of Texas at Austin.

MARQUIS, A. 1974. A Guide to America's Indians. Norman: University of Oklahoma Press.

McCORMICK, O. F. III. 1973. The Archaeological Resources in the Lake Monticello Area of Titus County, Texas. Southern Methodist University Contributions in Anthropology, no. 8.

McKERN, W. C. 1939. "The Midwestern Taxonomic Method as an Aid to Archaeological Culture Study." American Antiquity 4 (4): 301-13.

MOONEY, J. 1896. "The Ghost-Dance Religion and the Sioux Outbreak of 1890." Annual Report of the Bureau of American Ethnology 14(2).

MOORE, C. B. 1908. "Certain Mounds of Arkansas and of Mississippi." Journal of the Academy of Natural Sciences of Philadelphia 13 (4).

—————. 1909. "Antiquities of the Ouachita Valley." Journal of the Academy of Natural Sciences of Philadelphia 14 (1): 5-170.

—————. 1912. "Some Aboriginal Sites on Red River." Journal of the Academy of Natural Sciences of Philadelphia 14, 2d ser. (4): 526-636.

NEUMAN, R. W. 1970. "Archaeological and Historical Assessment of the Red River Basin in Louisiana." Archeological and Historical Resources on the Red River Basin, ed. H. A. Davis. Arkansas Archeological Survey, Publications in Archeology, Research Series, no. 1, pp. 3-24.

—————, and SIMMONS, L. A. 1969. A Bibliography Relative to Indians of the State of Louisiana. Department of Conservation, Louisiana Geological Survey, Anthropological Study no. 4.

NEUMANN, G. K. 1941. "Types of Artificial Cranial Deformation in the Eastern United States." (abstract). News Letter of the Southeastern Archaeological Conference 2 (4): 3-5.

—————. 1952. "Archeology and Race in the American Indian." In Archeology of the Eastern United States, ed. J. B. Griffin, pp. 13-34. Chicago: University of Chicago Press.

—————. 1954. "Measurements and Indices of American Indian Varieties." In Yearbook of Physical Anthropology 1952, ed. J. N. Spuhler, pp. 213-55. Wenner-Gren Foundation for Anthropological Research.

NEWCOMB, W. W., JR. 1961. The Indians of Texas, from Prehistoric to Modern Times. Austin: University of Texas Press.

NEWELL, H. P., and KRIEGER, A. D. 1949. The George C. Davis Site, Chero-

kee County, Texas. Memoirs of the Society for American Archaeology, no. 5.

ORR, K. G. 1941. "The Eufaula Mound: Contributions to the Spiro Focus." *Oklahoma Prehistorian* 4 (1): 2-15.

————. 1946. "The Archaeological Situation at Spiro, Oklahoma: A Preliminary Report." *American Antiquity* 11 (4): 228-56.

————. 1952. "Survey of Caddoan Area Archeology." In *Archaeology of Eastern United States*, ed. J. B. Griffin, pp. 239-55. Chicago: University of Chicago Press.

PARSONS, E. C. 1941. *Notes on the Caddo*. Memoirs of the American Anthropological Association, no. 57.

POWELL, J. W. 1966. *Linguistic Families of America North of Mexico*. Bureau of American Ethnology, 7th Annual Report, 1885-1886, ed. P. Holden, pp. 1-142. Lincoln: University of Nebraska Press, Bison Books. Reprint.

ROUSE, I. 1939. *Prehistory in Haiti: A Study in Method*. Yale University Publication in Anthropology no. 21.

SAPIR, E. 1929. "Central and North American Languages." *The Encyclopaedia Britannica*, 14th ed. 5: 138-40.

SCHAMBACH, F. n.d. "The Trans-Mississippi South: The Case for a New Natural Area West of the Lower Mississippi Valley and East of the Plains." Paper presented at the 1971 Caddo Conference, Balcones Research Center, Austin, Texas.

SHAFER, H. J. 1973. "Lithic Technology at the George C. Davis Site, Cherokee County, Texas." Ph.D. dissertation, University of Texas at Austin.

SHERZER, J. 1973. "Areal Linguistics in North America." In *Current Trends in Linguistics*, ed. T. A. Sebeok. *Linguistics in North America* 10: 749-95, New York: Mouton.

SIBLEY, J. 1922. *A Report from Natchitoches in 1807*. Edited, with an introduction, by A. H. Abel. Indian Notes and Monographs, Museum of the American Indian Heye Foundation.

SPIER, L. 1924. "Wichita and Caddo Relationships Terms." *American Anthropologist*, n.s. 26 (2): 258-63.

STEPHENSON, R. L. 1948. "Archaeological Survey of McGee Bend Reservoir: A Preliminary Report." *Bulletin of the Texas Archeological and Paleontological Society* 19:57-73.

STEWART, T. D. 1940. "Some Historical Implications of Physical Anthropology in North America." In *Essays in Historical Anthropology of North America* (published in honor of John R. Swanton). Smithsonian Miscellaneous Collections 100: 15-50.

————. 1941. "The Circular Type of Cranial Deformity in the United States." *American Journal of Physical Anthropology* 28:343-51.

68 TEXAS ARCHEOLOGY

STORY, D. A. 1972. "A Preliminary Report of the 1968, 1969, and 1970 Excavations at the George C. Davis Site, Cherokee County, Texas." Report of Field Research Conducted under National Science Foundation (GS-273 and 3200) and Interagency Contracts between The University of Texas at Austin and the Texas Building Commission and Texas Historical Survey Committee.

SUHM, D. A.; KRIEGER, A. D.; and JELKS, E. B. 1954. "An Introductory Handbook of Texas Archeology." *Bulletin of the Texas Archeological Society* 24:144-227.

SWANTON, J. R. 1931. "The Caddo Social Organization and Its Possible Historical Significance." *Journal of the Washington Academy of Sciences* 21:203-6.

————— 1942. *Source Material on the History and Ethnology of the Caddo Indians.* Bureau of American Ethnology Bulletin no. 132.

TAYLOR, A. R. 1963a. *The Classification of the Caddoan Languages.* Proceedings of the American Philosophical Society, vol. 107, pp. 51-59.

————— 1963b. "Comparative Caddoan." *International Journal of American Linguistics* 29 (2): 113-31.

TROIKE, R. C. 1957. "Tonkawa Prehistory: A Study in Method and Theory." Master's thesis, University of Texas at Austin.

WALKER, W. M. 1935. *A Caddo Burial Site at Natchitoches, Louisiana.* Smithsonian Miscellaneous Collections, vol. 94, no. 14.

WEBB, C. H. 1940. "House Types among the Caddo Indians." *Bulletin of the Texas Archeological and Paleontological Society* 12:49-75.

————— 1944. "Dental Abnormalities as Found in the American Indians." *American Journal of Orthodontics and Oral Surgery* 30 (9): 474-86.

—————.1945. "A Second Historic Caddo Site at Natchitoches, Louisiana." *Bulletin of the Texas Archeological and Paleontological Society* 16:52-83.

WEBB, C. H., and DODD, M., JR. 1941. "Pottery Types from the Belcher Mound Site." *Bulletin of the Texas Archeological and Paleontological Society* 13:88-116.

WILLIAMS, S. 1964. "The Aboriginal Location of the Kadohadacho and Related Tribes." In *Explorations in Cultural Anthropology,* ed. W. H. Goodenough, pp. 545-70. New York: McGraw-Hill.

WOODALL, J. N. 1969. "Cultural Ecology of the Caddo." Ph.D. dissertation, Southern Methodist University.

WYCKOFF, D. G. 1970. "Archaeological and Historical Assessment of the Red River Basin in Oklahoma." In *Archeological and Historical Resources of the Red River Basin,* ed. H. A. Davis. Arkansas Archeological Survey, Publications in Archeology, Research Series, no. 1, pp. 67-134.

EARLY HISTORIC HASINAI ELITES: A MODEL FOR THE MATERIAL CULTURE OF GOVERNING ELITES

Don G. Wyckoff
Timothy G. Baugh

ABSTRACT

Archaeologists are writing more about prehistoric political structures and their role in maintaining or changing social and cultural systems. Because material culture is complexly integrated with many other cultural subsystems, a theoretical problem exists in correlating prehistoric material remains to specific governing positions or levels of organization. As an initial step toward resolving this problem, we examine the historical records on one society's governing elites, their material culture, and what might be expected to occur in the archaeological record.

French and Spanish chroniclers recorded many observations of the Caddo people in east Texas and adjacent Louisiana. This study concentrates on those records covering the A.D. 1687-1721 period. Most of these accounts describe people in the Hasinai confederacy, a loose alliance of villages in east Texas. These descriptions allow identification of 7 potentially elite positions in Caddo society. Analysis of their duties and interrelationships reveals that 3 socially prominent people made decisions affecting all members of their society. The *xinesi* (priest), *caddi* (headman), and *canahas* (elders) are the recognized governing elite during this period. Each position is combined to form a hierarchy in a ranked society. Historical references are interpreted to indicate the *xinesi* and *caddi* occupy inherited positions, probably ambilineal with a patrilineal bias, whereas the *canahas* is an elected or achieved position. Each governing elite position has specific associations of contexts and material goods. Although there is limited preservation of the latter, a series of archaeologically testable hypotheses about the 3 governing positions and their respective material culture is offered. These hypotheses await future research and data collection in the Caddo area for validation.

Introduction

Proposals for identifying the existence and operation of prehistoric political systems have been presented by several authors (Rathje 1970; Sears 1968; Trigger 1974). These proposals originate primarily from studying the material remains of large-scale, complex societies. Ruled by

Mid-Continental Journal of Archaeology, Vol. 5, No. 2
0146-1109/80/0052-0004 $03.15/0

political and/or religious elites, these cultures are considered to have a sociopolitical structure equivalent to a state level (Flannery 1972; Sears 1968:140–151). As a result, these proposals emphasize sets of evidence that are uncommon in less complex, ranked societies. Such societies are potentially precursory sociopolitical systems to a state (Haviland 1977; C. Jones 1977; Marcus 1974; Murra and Morris 1976). While studying less complex social and political systems, however, archaeologists have recognized several major problems. These include: (1) distinguishing different hierarchical levels of elites (Trigger 1974:99–100); (2) operationalizing the study of elite recruitment and maintenance through time (Rathje 1970); (3) establishing relationships between material objects and prehistoric social units that might be classified as elite (Trigger 1974:98–99); and (4) identifying elites, especially when burial contexts and their contents are emphasized (Ucko 1969).

The first two problems are addressed by presenting information from ethnohistorical and ethnographic accounts. From these a general model of Caddo society and elites has been established. The difficulties of correlating these data with archaeological remains, as stated in the latter two problems, are still tremendous. This is a result of poor preservation of organic remains and archaeologists' inability (due to cost, time, logistics, or a combination of these) to completely excavate a site. Thus the critical need is to maximize the correlation between a general model and the findings from actual excavations. Before this can be accomplished, however, the general model itself must be defined for archaeological examination, testing, and evaluation. To accomplish this task, a model from ethnohistoric materials available for the Caddoan-speaking, farming people native to east Texas, northwest Louisiana, southwest Arkansas, and southeast Oklahoma (Bolton 1908; Newcomb 1961:270–313; Swanton 1942:7–16; Wedel 1978; Williams 1964) is proposed. Villages of these groups were visited and documented by Spanish and French explorers, missionaries, traders, and governmental officials between A.D. 1541 and 1803 (Glover 1935; Swanton 1942:29–120).

Ethnohistoric Materials

Because most of the information used to generate this model comes from ethnohistoric documents, a note of caution is necessary. Indirect sources (i.e., dictionaries, genealogies, kinship terminologies, and marriage data) are frequently the most reliable for such an undertaking inasmuch as these tend to be subject to fewer errors than direct sources (i.e., chronicles, letters, reports, and diaries). However, direct sources are the most commonly available documents for the Caddo, and these sources often exhibit a biased view- depending on the nationality and professional position of the observer. To illustrate the former, Iberian prejudices against the Moors, and hence against dark-skinned peoples and infidels, were rampant among Spanish administrators, military officials, and missionaries of the sixteenth and seventeenth centuries. These were readily transferred to the New World as is indicated in several passages dealing with the Caddo. For example, when Fray Espinosa attempted to persuade the proper authorities that the Hasinai were imminently worthy of being brought into the Christian fold, he wrote:

> I feel compassion for the Asinais (Hasinai) Indians and the numerous other nations who are located on this northern frontier, because, as a general rule, they are well made and much whiter than the Mexicans and Tlascaltecans. They are naturally civilized and have good minds; but all these gifts are disfigured by their great idolatries and the superstitions with which the devil has deceived them (Espinosa in Hatcher 1927:158).

Professional background was also reflected in individual observations and commentaries. Explorers attempted to create interest in their endeavors by embellishing, and sometimes even fabricating, the value of their findings. Missionaries were more concerned with the presence or absence of religious beliefs and morals, and military officials were attempting to collect population figures for intelligence purposes (Swanton 1928a:678–679). Civil authorities were not much more attuned to native culture than explorers or missionaries. These state representatives frequently tried to impose institutions from Mesoamerica, the Carib-Arawak region, or feudal Spain on the aboriginal cultures of the American Southeast. The Spanish captain who accompanied Fray Espinosa, Don Domingo Ramon, provided the following commentary:

> All of the Indians having convened, I addressed them through an interpreter, getting them to understand the purposes of our coming to their country, which was for the salvation of souls; that they should recognize absolutely their only King, who is God and their natural master, Don Philip the Fifth, who sent them these gifts as a sign of his love, through His Excellency, Señor Duke of Linares, Viceroy of New Spain, under whose orders I have come to this country; that it was, therefore, necessary for their good political government that they should elect a Captain General among themselves, which should be done at their discretion. They talked for some time, and soon afterwards a young man, less than a Captain, was chosen by the Spaniards because they always elect the younger in order that the government may last longer. The Indians said that they wanted this one for their Captain General. To him in the name of His Majesty I delivered my cane and approved said election, giving him one of my best jackets to improve his appearance, which made the Indians very happy and contented (Foik 1933:21).

Not only did the Spaniards here establish a new political office among the Hasinai, but they circumvented the traditional system by not selecting an already recognized headman, leader, or elder.

Except for such overtly displayed biases, the writers of direct sources also intermingle information without citing references (administrative documents, letters, hearsay, or direct observations). In some cases, such materials may confuse different groups or refer to several at the same time without distinguishing specific bands or villages (Whitecotton 1968:27). In addition, the more notable or larger villages tend to be overly represented in the literature, whereas the smaller and less conspicuous groups are either totally absent or only nominally described (Swanton 1928a:679). Finally, errors may result during transcription when a scribe misreads or mistakenly copies a wrong letter or word. Such mistakes may result in a completely different meaning than originally intended by the actual observer (Bolton 1908:259, n. 5). This type of error may be most readily minimized by consulting the original document whenever possible.

Ethnographic Perspective

The Caddo are affiliated linguistically with several Prairie-Plains societies including Arikara, Pawnee, and Wichita (Lesser and Weltfish 1932; Chafe 1976:527–531). Accordingly, they are most closely related to Wichita with 3000 years of minimum separation (yms), then to Pawnee with 3300 yms, and finally to Arikara with 3500 yms (Hughes 1968:79–85). Evaluation of the validity of these dates is not attempted; rather the relative chronological relationships as indicated by glottochronological estimates are accepted (Table 1).

Despite linguistic affiliations to these Plains societies, Swanton (1928a:717) states that the Caddo clearly show evidence of an underlying structure common to the Gulf Area. Nevertheless, the social organization of the eastern and western Caddo differ substantially; the former are similar to the Muscogee (Creek) while the latter resemble the Natchez (Swanton 1931a:206). Because the majority of the ethnohistoric materials between A.D. 1680 and 1725 concentrate on the members of the western Caddo (especially the Hasinai Confederacy), this study focuses there. The Hasinai alliance was composed of 8–11 villages located in the upper Neches and Angelina River valleys of east Texas (see Fig. 1). Griffith (1954:58) lists 9 such villages plus 2 potential affiliates: the Hainai, Nabedache, Nacogdoche, Nasoni (lower), Nadaco (Anadarko), Neche, Nacono, Nechaui, Nacao, and possibly Nabiti (Namidish) and Nacachau. Swanton (1946:89, 136, 154–156, 158, 162; see also Swanton 1942:12; Mooney 1896:321–323) also notes 11 villages, but replaces Nabiti with Guasco. Population estimates for the Confederacy range around 4500 individuals (Bolton 1908:274–276; Griffith 1954:58; Swanton 1942:25).

Hasinai villages tended to have a core area surrounded by hamlets. Each hamlet consisted of 7–15 houses and was circumscribed by fields of corn (Bolton 1907:50, 1908:272). Spanish missionaries attempted to influence this settlement pattern by reducing these hamlets into a single concentrated village or pueblo. As Bolton (1908:273) points out, reduction "was a chief aim of the [Spanish] government and the missionaries, and failure to accomplish this was a primary cause of abandonment, after fifteen years of effort."

The Hasinai technological system was basically direct. Each village could satisfy its own needs in terms of producing tools, pottery, and food. Trade also played an important role in this aspect of the physical environment. Although there is no direct evidence, trade may account for the initial formation of the alliance itself, and trade did have an important impact on Hasinai technology and economy. By the time of contact, trade with the Jumano Apache resulted in the Hasinai acquiring numerous horses that were used for bison hunting. Once contact was established with the French, trade muskets became an important exchange item, although they never completely replaced the bow and arrow because of the latter's greater accuracy and firepower. Indeed, one of the major trade items offered by the Hasinai was Osage orange or, as the French call it, *bois d'arc* (Swanton 1928a:692).

Hasinai economy centered around 4 basic subsistence activities: farming, hunting, collecting, and fishing (see Fig. 2). Horticulture production was the core activity. Two types of maize, several varieties of beans, squash, and sunflowers were grown. The first type of maize to be planted each spring may have been a variety of popcorn. The chroniclers refer to this as a small or little corn (*el maiz pequeño*), for it grows less than 3 ft (1 *vara*) in height (Casañas in Hatcher 1927:211; Espinosa in Hatcher 1927:156; Swanton 1942:131, 276). Planted in the latter part of April, this early variety matures in about 6 weeks. Its harvest is followed by the planting of flour corn which ripens in 2–3 months (Casañas in Hatcher 1927:211; Espinosa in Hatcher 1927:156). Seeds from these crops were smoked and dried to provide stock for future plantings, a technique that acted as insurance against isolated crop failures. By the time the first Europeans arrived in the Hasinai villages, watermelons, peaches, and other fruit orchards may have become an integral part of the horticultural inventory (Swanton 1942:131–133).

Although men aided with the clearing and cultivation of fields, much of the gardening was performed by women. Horticultural products were supplemented with game animals, and hunting was primarily the duty of men. The most important game animal seems to have been deer with bison placing a close second, especially during the protohistoric period. Deer were stalked by individual hunters who wore antlers and skillfully imitated the animals' movements. Bison, on the other hand, were hunted communally as well as individually. For example, the entire villages of the Nasoni and Nacogdoche moved out onto the buffalo prairies during the winter. The Hasinai and Neche, however, left a keeper of the fire (*Xinesi*?) behind "so the fire would not go out if wood failed" (Espinosa in Hatcher 1927:169). Smaller family units were known to exploit bison at other times of the year (see Massanet in Bolton 1916:374).

Unlike the Plains tribes, the Hasinai also hunted bear. Such hunts were held during the winter months when dogs can easily find bruins hibernating in hollow trees. Once located, the bruin was flushed out by fire. The sluggish bear was then pelted with a volley of arrows from the hunters as he backed out of his hole, and was often dead before he hit the ground. These animals were hunted for their tallow, rather than flesh or skins, as it was used as a preservative and oil (Espinosa in Hatcher 1927:157; Swanton 1928a:693).

Collecting and fishing also provided a valuable resource base for the Hasinai. Women collected roots, herbs, berries, grapes, and acorns throughout much of the year (Espinosa in Hatcher 1927:152–153; Casañas in Hatcher 1927:211; Swanton 1942:132–133). During the spring "the Indians go with their families to certain spots and stay for some days, living on fish" (Espinosa in Hatcher 1927:153).

Overall the economic pattern of the Hasinai reflected a changing trend. A greater dependence on bison became evident as the Hasinai, with the acquisition of horses, began to rely more heavily on an annual bison hunt (Swanton 1946:265). The exact causes for this shift are uncertain, yet certain ecological premises, both physical and social, may be invoked. As Europeans began to displace more and more Southeastern cultures to the west, various pressures were exerted on the Hasinai. First, the woodland bison rapidly became extinct (Swanton 1928a:693). The Hasinai then switched their focus to the prairie bison as their major food source. At the same time, intergroup relations became more strained as population pressures resulted in an increasing number of encroachments on the eastern boundaries of the Caddo.

These shifts in the physical and social environment were reflected in the Hasinai social system as well. A comparison of the Hasinai (Caddo) terminology system for kinship with those of the other Caddoan-speaking groups indicates some differences. The sedentary Pawnee and Arikara had a Crow system in which separate terms are used for the matrilateral and patrilateral cross-cousins (Schmitt and Schmitt 1951; Weltfish 1971:30–35). The less sedentary Wichita had a system more closely resembling that of the nomadic Plains societies (Schmitt and Schmitt 1952), and generally, Murdock (1965:229) places many of these societies in a Matri-Hawaiian system. This is somewhat of a misnomer, however, because the overall pattern tends to be generational only in ego's own generation. In other words, cross-cousins were known by the same term as parallel cousins or as brother and sister. Yet in the first ascending generation, a bifurcate merging system was employed (for further discussions of Plains kinship systems, see Maxwell 1978; Baugh 1979). The Caddo system differs from the Crow system of the Pawnee and Arikara as well as the generational/bifurcate merging system of the Wichita. Anthropologists agree that the Caddo had an Iroquois terminology system in which cross-cousins were equated yet distinguished from parallel cousins (Lesser 1979; Parsons 1941:11–24; Spier 1924).

The Caddo descent system is sometimes said to be "asymetric" (Brain 1971:222, n. 2; White and others 1971:387, n.3). In this sense, asymetric refers to preferred descent being with the mother's lineage unless the father is of a higher rank, in which case the sons belong to the father's lineage and the daughters to the mother's. This is somewhat similar to the Natchez system. However, examination of the terminology structure of the Natchez again reveals a Crow system (Swanton 1911:107–108, 1928b:91–96; Haas 1939), and this is typical of the kinship systems of a number of Southeastern groups (for Creek see Swanton 1928b:80–88; for Cherokee see Gilbert 1955:289–291; for Choctaw see Swanton 1931b:84–90 and Eggan 1937; and for Yuchi see Eggan 1937 and Speck 1909:68–70). This information indicates that the Caddo do indeed stand alone when compared to other Southeastern societies (Swanton 1928a:717).

From this it may be argued that the Iroquois system of the Caddo represents a transitional phase toward a more nomadic Plains-like structure similar to that of the Wichita. In other words, the merging of matrilateral and patrilateral cross-cousins into a single term may represent the first step to including them under the same term for parallel cousins, and hence a generational system. This is underscored by the absence of an Iroquois kinship system in any other Southeastern or even Plains society (Murdock 1965:244). It may be argued further that an "asymetric" system of descent is a nebulous concept at best and represents nothing more than a system based on options from which the best alternative is selected. It can be said, therefore, that Caddo descent might also have been undergoing a change to a more ambilineal type of system similar to that of the Wichita.

The changes brought about in Hasinai technology and economy through contact and trade may thus be correlated with a simultaneous transformation in social structure. During this process, Hasinai society is attempting to readjust and maintain a harmonic regime "in which the rule of residence is similar to the rule of descent" (Levi-Strauss 1969:215). Indeed, the Caddo present an interesting example for the study of social change, for they represent a fairly well-documented case of structural change without a breach in continuity (Radcliffe-Brown 1965). At this point, however, all Caddo social change should not be explained in ecological terms alone, for it is possible that other less well-defined factors may have played a major role — such as an imbalance in the movement and distribution of goods— which could result in a structural collapse of the ranking system. Whatever the causes may be, there is enough difference between protohistoric and prehistoric Caddo society to make extrapolation and interpretation from the former period into the latter highly problematic.

Archaeological evidence indicates that Caddo people continuously inhabited the four-state region since at least the A.D. 800s, if not several thousand years before (Davis 1970; Hughes 1968; Newell and Krieger 1949; Orr 1952; Story and Valastro 1977; Webb 1958; Wyckoff 1974). Changes in settlement patterns and site complexity suggest marked changes in the

Caddo tradition occurred through time. Some probably resulted from prehistoric modification of the Caddo sociopolitical system (Bell and Baerreis 1951:96–97; Brown and others 1978; Krieger 1947:211–216; Orr 1952:251–252; Story 1972; Webb 1959). Between A.D. 1775 and 1835, historical records (Glover 1935; John 1975:487–766; Sibley 1832; Swanton 1942:71–89) document even more dramatic changes in Caddo society and culture. Sustained Euroamerican contact during this period resulted in: intensive warfare with the Osage to the north as well as Southeastern groups (i.e., Chickasaw and Natchez) that were pushed westward; in population decimation by disease and warfare; and in the eventual loss (during the 1840s) of all Caddo traditional homelands (Swanton 1942:89–99; Williams 1964:559–660).

Given the prehistoric, historical, and ethnographic evidence for changes in material culture and the sociopolitical system, a model of Caddo elites cannot be developed that would be applicable throughout the Caddo continuum. It is better, therefore, to focus on data that may provide an ethnohistorical model, and its material culture counterpart, of Caddo elites during the period of A.D. 1687–1721. Subsequent missionizing, trading, and Spanish-French administration increased in scale and intensity, thus altering the extant Caddo sociopolitical system even further. This temporally restricted model may: (1) identify Caddo social subunits which can be considered elite in character; (2) distinguish a hierarchical structure for these positions; (3) delimit the systemic relationships and functions of these subunits and their components; and (4) establish parameters on the material culture associated with—and potentially recoverable through excavation—the respective elite subunits. This model provides a data base and develops hypotheses by which prehistoric sociopolitical process and change in the Caddo area can be evaluated. More importantly this model will provide hypotheses about political structure and process that can be tested with material culture recovered from appropriate periods in the Caddo area.

Social Elites

For the purposes of this study, it is useful to identify the political structure and process in Hasinai society, but some basic concepts must be established first. Service (1962:18 19) indicates that society consists of an ordered set of relations between human beings. Barth (1969:9) notes that the concept of society is "highly abstract" and represents an "encompassing social system within which smaller, concrete groups and units may be analyzed." A small, concrete group within the western Caddo social system, the Hasinai elite, will be examined here.

A definition of elite is essential to this study. Mosca (1939:50) indicates that all societies consist of 2 classes: those who rule and those who are ruled. Pareto (1935) similarly emphasizes a dichotomy between those with and those without power. As Bottomore (1974:9) suggests, both Mosca and Pareto "were concerned with elites in the sense of groups of people who either exercised directly, or were in a position to influence very strongly the exercise, of political power." Pareto (1935:1423-1424) further distinguishes between a governing and nongoverning elite as follows: (1) the governing elite is represented by those individuals who actually hold power and make political decisions; and (2) the nongoverning elite is represented by small communities of intellectuals or nonmanual laborers. This paper attempts to determine if protohistoric (A.D. 1687-1721) Hasinai society had governing and/or nongoverning elites.

Identification of Hasinai Elites

Research Design

Although Swanton (1942) has compiled an exhaustive monograph on Caddo history and ethnology, this study focuses on data collected from original sources, namely, English translations of French and Spanish documents. The objective is to record all references relating to western Caddo political structure. We prefer not to depend on Swanton's (1942:159 173) interpretations or quotations which were selected to emphasize his view of Caddo society and political structure. By this means we present a synchronic study of Hasinai political process and its archaeological implications during the period A.D. 1687-1721. This research will furthermore document and compare the diversity concerning potentially different positions and functions as they are described by early French and Spanish chroniclers.

Results

Table 2 presents a chronological listing of French and Spanish references for Hasinai elite positions. It describes their functions and, when possible, their interrelationships as well as the dates, chronicler, and reference. Some of these sources, however, may refer to the Kadohadacho, and such exceptions are noted.

A review of Table 2 reveals a considerable amount of variation in Spanish and French terms (or their translations) as applied to several recognized status positions. Differences can be partially resolved by comparing terms and the contexts or responsibilities attributed to them. Such a comparison suggests the correlations shown in Table 3. These correlations compare favorably to the Hasinai political organization (see Fig. 3) described by Casañas (Hatcher 1927:215 216).

Seven potentially elite positions are identified in Table 3 and illustrated in Fig. 3. Only Casañas (Hatcher 1927:215 217, 286, and 295 296) lists and briefly describes each of these. However, 25 years later, Espinosa (Hatcher 1927:154–178) mentions and discusses the activities of 6 positions, excluding only the *chaya* or pages from his 1715 report on the Hasinai. Given the duties, responsibilities, and relationships of these 7 positions (Table 2), Hasinai society during the A.D. 1687–1721 period does indeed contain both governing and nongoverning elites. There is evidence, furthermore, for both a hierarchical structure and a politico-religious dichotomy among these positions.

The Governing Elite

The key positions of the Hasinai governing elite are the *xinesi*, *caddi*, and *canahas*. On certain occasions the *amayxoya* might also be linked to this group. A review of Table 2 indicates that the *xinesi* functions primarily as a religious leader, yet he is also the only person for whom the *caddi* and *canahas* hold allegiance and respect. Casañas (Hatcher 1927:215–217) reports that the *xinesi* corresponds to a "petty king" and does not participate in the manual labor of planting, harvesting, hunting, or house building. Among his reported duties (Table 2) are: (1) maintaining the temple containing the sacred perpetual fire; (2) acting as a religious leader for 2 or more of the formally allied villages; (3) mediating between the deities and the people, especially the nominal decision makers for each village; and (4) leading and participating in certain special rites (i.e., first fruits, harvest, and naming ceremonies). Through his mediation with the deities, the *xinesi* is able to call assemblies of village leaders (composed of *caddices* and elders) and relate his perception of the people's present and future welfare. During these assemblies he is able to solicit, even demand, solemn covenants from the governing bodies. Thus he greatly influences the decision-making process and thereby affects the entire population (Hatcher 1927:290–292).

In each village, assemblies of the headman (*caddi* or governor) and elders (*canahas*, captains or leading old men) perform governmental operations. The Spanish recognized these officials as "nobles from the mass of the people" (Massanet in Bolton 1916:382). Several references (Massanet in Bolton 1916:378; Casañas in Hatcher 1927:216; Joutel 1962:133 and 139) indicate the *canahas* are hamlet representatives. LaHarpe (Smith 1958:250–251) reports a principal chief or headman for each village in an alliance. This *caddi* or *desza* was recognized by the Europeans as having a distinguished status. Massanet (Bolton 1916:381) translates *desza* to indicate something on the order of a "Great Lord and superior to all." Casañas (Hatcher 1927:213–217) reports the *caddi* is highest in rank and "like a governor ruling and commanding his people." Sociopolitical responsibilities for the *caddi* (Table 2) include: (1) joining with the *caddices* of allied villages to settle intervillage disputes. Such settlements include the authority to punish or expel offenders; (2) calling assemblies of the village elders for decisions affecting the entire village; (3) setting specific dates for house construction; (4) hosting of occasional village feasts; and (5) providing house and patio space, as well as food, for the harvest ceremonies. In combination with the *canahas* (village elders) the *caddi* also is involved with: (6) forming the official village body to greet and welcome visitors; (7) conducting the calumet (smoking of the peace pipe) ceremony; (8) dividing gifts from foreign emissaries among the general populace; (9) conducting councils for the raising of a war expedition and selecting its leader; (10) hosting war victory (Turkey dance ?) ceremonies; and (11) helping sponsor and officiate at the planting and harvest ceremonies.

As this list of functions and responsibilities reveals, the village is the major political unit in Hasinai society. Even though each is basically autonomous, there are points of articulation (i.e., number 1 above) that form a wider cooperative network. Such characteristics are commonly associated with a ranked society (Fried 1967:119). Although this first feature attributes strong authority to the headman, we should be aware that power to carry out such decisions is absent. In other words, a leader rules by example rather than by sanction. One important example provided by the headman is that of generosity through the redistribution of goods. Fried (1967:134) maintains that this activity also has important ramifications in the economic and production spheres. By acting as a host and feast sponsor the headman is essentially regulating the economic cycle and encouraging "maximum output by a number of his followers" (Fried 1967:134).

The remaining elite position involved in the decision-making process is the warrior (*amayxoya*). Concerning this position Casañas (Hatcher 1927:217) writes: "All men who have achieved some victory in war are called *amayxoya* in addition to their own names. This means 'great man.' The arms and banners they must carry are the skins and the scalps of the enemies they have killed." LaHarpe (Smith 1958:256–258) notes that the position of warrior is an honorific title attained by bravery and daring in combat. Each village elects a "war chief" from the *amayxoya* ranks (Espinosa in Hatcher 1927:175–176). One function of the village war chief is to meet strangers (M. Wedel 1978:3), although a group of warriors usually accompanies the war chief inasmuch as a certain degree of risk is involved (Joutel 1962:107; Massanet in Bolton 1916:363). When the war chief leads a raiding expedition, he has, furthermore, total command over all of the participants. The selection of an overall war leader thus reflects a strong egalitarian tendency among the Hasinai during this period, yet at the same time, these officials may have a great deal of authority invested in them during particular situations.

It may be useful at this point to examine the limited evidence for a dialectic of war and peace among the Hasinai. Many Southeastern societies have such a dialectic, one that is frequently associated with a moiety system and the colors of red and white (Swanton 1928a:695, 1946:664). Although the western Caddo do not have a moiety structure, certain evidence indicates that such a dichotomy once existed. For example, when LaHarpe (Smith 1958:256) visits the Upper Nasoni (Kadohadacho), "the four nations celebrated the calumet to the white chief, who is the war chief of the Natchitoches whom I had brought with me in order to be my guide." This comment is somewhat confusing because white is equated with peace in most Southeastern societies. Indeed, Ramon indicates that this may hold for the western Caddo as well:

> They then took out a long pipe, which they had for peace only, and they filled it with tobacco, placing a fire in the center. The Captains began to smoke, and the first puff was blown toward heaven, the second to the east, the third to the west, the fourth to the north, the fifth to the south, and the sixth to the earth. This was a demonstration of true peace. The bowl of the pipe has many white feathers, which also decorate the stem from one end to the other, being more than a yard long. (Foik 1933:20)

Although this seems to imply that the color white represents peace, neither Ramon nor LaHarpe provides a verified contrast to these observations. Hence, the existence of any such dialectic among the western Caddo may be doubtful.

Concerning the Southeast, Newcomb (1974:45) maintains that "The White People, or the People of Peace, did not take the initiative in warfare, and their towns served as sanctuaries for murderers and even enemies. The People of Alien Speech, also known as the Red or War People, were considered to be aggressors and did not provide sanctuary." Penicaut (Swanton 1942:188) observes the following upon his visit to the Hasinai in 1714:

> They returned from the war (with the Kichai) the day after we arrived at their village. They numbered a hundred and fifty men armed and mounted. . . . They brought with them two prisoners out of six which they had taken; they had eaten four on the way back. These two prisoners were placed in the town square in the midst of a guard of twelve savages for fear that they might enter one of their cabins, for it is the custom of these savages that, if a prisoner, escaping by force or craft, enters one of their cabins, his life is spared and he is henceforth reputed to belong to their nation.

Although these comments are inconclusive as to an extant dualistic structure among the Hasinai, they are indeed suggestive. Future research into the structural analysis of Hasinai myths might provide more insights into this intriguing problem of Caddo ethnology.

The Nongoverning Elite

There is no available evidence that either the *chaya* or *tammas* are an integral part of the actual decision-making process. Instead, they are apparently an echelon of personnel who carry out decisions made by the *caddí* and *canahas*.

Massanet (Bolton 1916:378; Casis 1899:304) refers to the captains (which are correlated with *canahas*) and indicates that, by Hasinai custom, they are supposed to bring their pages when they are called to assembly by the governor (*caddi*). Casañas (Hatcher 1927:216) reports the *chaya* are subordinate to the *canahas* and do everything they tell them to do. In contrast, the *tanmas* or *tammas* are responsible to the *caddi* (Hatcher 1927:154), and their duties are to: (1) promptly carry out orders (Hatcher 1927:216); (2) notify all families who are to assist with house building, what supplies they are to bring, and when to arrive at the selected spot (Hatcher 1927:154); (3) punish those who are idle or late during house building (Hatcher 1927:155); and (4) collect the first growths of tobacco and take them to the *caddi* who will use them in various ceremonies (Hatcher 1927:171). This evidence suggests that the *chaya* and *tammas* represent individuals who ensure that the village is informed of assembly decisions and that these decisions are carried out. Therefore, they may be considered as members of the nongoverning elite.

The remaining position of potential elite affiliation is the *conna*, or shaman, and it is also included with the nongoverning elite. Major descriptions of the *conna* are provided by Casañas (Hatcher 1927:295-296) and Espinosa (Hatcher 1927:165-169). Both chroniclers emphasize the *conna's* shamanistic characteristics, especially the practices of curing, divination, and astrology. Certain notations of Espinosa, however, (Hatcher 1927:165-167) imply identical attributes for the *conna* and *xinesi* or *caddí*. (1) have seats higher than the captains; (2) "take the measure for building the houses"; (3) are "present at the blessing of the new building"; and (4) are "first at the function of feasting." It is uncertain whether Espinosa, a Franciscan priest, has mistakenly mixed these attributes or whether he perceives the native "medicine men" and religious leaders in the same manner– namely, as hindrances to his missionizing. Espinosa expresses a low opinion of the "medicine men" (Hatcher 1927:167), and such an attitude is apparently common among Franciscan missionaries (Spicer 1962:298). Both Casañas and Espinosa record one aspect for the *conna* that is not reported for the *xinesi* or *caddi* (Table 2). The *conna* may be killed by village or family members if a sick relative is not cured and the *conna* is subsequently suspected of witchcraft. This is a critical factor for eliminating the *conna* from the governing elite.

Recruitment and Ranking

Recruitment and ranking are interrelated factors integral to understanding maintenance of the Hasinai villages' elite positions. Both are partially couched within the elite's basis of power. A review of the available information (Table 2) indicates that the Hasinai elite's power derives from their forming an incipient theocracy.

Although not as formally dramatic as their Natchez contemporaries (Albrecht 1946; Swanton 1911:100–107, 138–163), the Hasinai leadership between A.D. 1687 and 1721 is a governing elite consisting of a religious head (*xinesi*) and village or confederacy assemblies. The latter include the *caddices* and *canahas* who deal with the more mundane matters affecting the village or confederacies. However, both the *caddices* and *canahas* participate in such religiously influenced rituals as rain invocations, planting ceremonies, first fruits or harvest ceremonies, elite funerals, and, to a lesser extent, war victory dances (Table 2). Casañas (Hatcher 1927:213, 216) reports the *xinesi* and *caddices* are officials who practice monogamy and that they are the only officials with elevated seats in their houses. Also, Espinosa (Hatcher 1927:171–172) indicates a small replica of the *xinesi*-maintained temple occurs at a captain's (*caddi* ?) house and is used during the harvest ceremony. Such symbols and ritual participation probably serve to link and continually validate these officials' positions relative to those of the *xinesi*.

Given the Hasinai governing elite's positions and theocratic character, two questions come to mind: how are these positions filled, and what is their internal structure? The relationships between the *xinesi*, *caddi*, and *canaha* have already been discussed and illustrated (Fig. 2), primarily from Casañas' perception (Hatcher 1927:215–217) of the Hasinai confederacy's political structure. Notations provided by Massanet (Bolton 1916: 378–381) and Espinosa (Hatcher 1927:156) seem to reaffirm a hierarchical order from most to least powerful of: *xinesi* (priest); *caddi* (principal village headman); and *canaha* (captains or elders), respectively.

The Xinesi

Most chroniclers refer to a single *xinesi* for each village or confederacy (Table 2), and this position is therefore interpreted as the apex of the governing elite hierarchy. There are clues, however, that the situation may have been more complex. For example, de Tonti (1690), referring to the *Cadadoquis*, states: "We went together to their temple, and after the priests invoked God, they conducted me to the cabin of their chief" (Falconer 1975:87). Hildalgo (1710), while among the *Tejas*, notes: "When they kill a deer they never cut it up until the priest of the pueblo arrives. He cuts it up. The Indians had rather lose it than to cut it open before their priest arrives" (Hatcher 1927:52). Espinosa (1715–1717), discussing *Tejas* funeral rituals, comments: "All gather together, the mourners, men and women stretched upon their beds. A leader among the holy men appears and speaks a few words to them" (Hatcher 1927:163). For baptism, Espinosa indicates that "As soon as a child is born the saints begin to go through various ceremonies with it, which seem to show a desire to represent baptism.

When the new born child is six or eight days old, they inform one of their priests" (Hatcher 1927:164). These citations contain implications for several priests existing in the entire confederacy, perhaps one for each village. If this is the case, the priestly subunit in the governing elite may contain different status positions with related and somewhat similar responsibilities; the *conna* or shaman could be an integral part of the priesthood.

Available source material does not provide sufficient information to fully resolve questions about the priesthood's internal structure. A *grand xinesi*, the *xinesi*, and shamen are variously mentioned by Casañas, Hidalgo, Espinosa, and Morfi (Table 2). The last 3 chroniclers indicate the *xinesi* is the high, leading, or chief priest, but they do not clearly distinguish priests of lower status. Espinosa appears to categorize both the priest and the "medicine men" into one class, i.e., villains who hinder the Church's mission (Hatcher 1927:165). It is interesting to note that Morfi, who is highly dependent on Espinosa's writings (Swanton 1942:129), both equates (Swanton 1942:160) and distinguishes (Swanton 1942:230) between the priest and the "medicine men."

A contextual study of Casañas' writings (Hatcher 1927:217, 290–293, 299–301) reveals an interchange between the terms *grand xinesi* and *xinesi* rather than referring to 2 priestly subdivisions. But Casañas also reports (Hatcher 1927:286) the *xinesi* has a subordinate who rallies entire villages, as well as sacristans, to help care for the fire temple (Hatcher 1927:291). Also, Casañas (Hatcher 1927:293) records that the *xinesi* consults with 2 old women who are in his house, and one of them causes the *xinesi* to change a previous decision.

A review of the pertinent documentation suggests that the Hasinai priest subunit probably contains more positions than just the *xinesi*. These may be assistants who help care for the main temple, and there may be lower-status priests present in each major village. Unfortunately, the data do not allow more precise definitions or descriptions of these positions or their internal relationships. With regard to the *conna*, or shamen, this study accepts Casañas' distinction of them. They are therefore not included among the governing elite.

The *xinesi* is commonly described (Table 2) as an old man, and Morfi (Swanton 1942:60) suggests that blindness is a customary attribute of this official. At the time of the *xinesi's* death the position is reportedly filled through direct descent, inasmuch as "the nearest blood kin to him becomes his successor" (Casañas in Hatcher 1927:215). While the nature of descent is not specified, Swanton (1942:168) indicates a "matrilineal character" prevailing in Hasinai social organization. Information on *caddi* succession does not seem congruent with matrilineality, however, and this may be due to a shift to an ambilineal system.

Though not specified, *xinesi* recruitment may involve blood relatives who are serving as temple assistants or village priests. It is possible that

Espinosa's (Hatcher 1927:167) description of initiation rituals for new "medicine men" actually refers to *xinesí* recruitment. *Xinesí* recruitment may have undergone a change in character late in the period under study. Both Aguayo and Morfi (Table 2) note that the *Nocono* (Nacono) are led by a headman who is also the high priest. It is not clear how this method of succession transpires, but the ritual participation of the *caddices* noted prior to 1721 may have provided some religious training necessary to attain and maintain this position.

The Caddices

Historical accounts (Table 2) document that several *caddices* are represented within a confederacy, but Casañas (Hatcher 1927:216) reports only one *caddi* (governor or principal leader) for each village assembly. Except for a *Cadadoquis* (Kadohadacho) or female governor, mentioned by de Tonti (Falconer 1975:86), all the *caddices* are males. They are occasionally described as being very old (LaHarpe in Smith 1958:250–252). Age combined with oratory ability and esteem (Hatcher 1927:218; Swanton 1942: 171–172) may have been the criteria employed to rank respective *caddices* in those situations where 2 or more assemble.

Caddi succession is reportedly by inheritance. As Casañas (Hatcher 1927:216) notes, "The office of *caddi* also descends through the direct line of blood relationship." According to Espinosa (Hatcher 1927:175), "His office is perpetual and one of his sons or relatives inherits it when he dies." Morfi reports that "This office is perpetual and hereditary in the oldest son, or, in his absence, in the next brother, or nearest kin" (Swanton 1942:171). If Espinosa and Morfi are correct, the preferred *caddi* inheritance may have been patrilineal. This is contrary to the matrilineal character attributed by Spier (1924) and Swanton (1942:168), and it tends to support this study's construct of ambilineal inheritance and succession.

The Canahas

Though not consistently reported as *canahas*, certain references (Table 3) to elders, leading men, old men, captains, and chiefs are correlated with this position. These officials are major constituents in village assemblies and apparently participate in confederacy assemblies as well. As Casañas (Hatcher 1927:216) notes, one of their primary duties is to relieve the *caddi* in governing. These officials are commonly described as elderly males; there are no references to female *canahas*. There is also evidence that these people are ranked in certain situations. Though the criteria are not discussed, both Espinosa (Hatcher 1927:156) and Morfi (Swanton 1942:129 130) report that crops are communally planted for such officials in an order determined by the governing assemblies. Such ranking may be age-based. Casañas (Hatcher 1927:218) indicates the speaking order in tribal assemblies is based on age, the eldest being first. There is no specific description of *canahas* recruitment or succession. Morfi (Swanton 1942:171–172) mentions captains or chiefs having limited authority being elected by acclamation. This could be interpreted as referring to the *canahas*, but inasmuch as Morfi does not say so explicitly, it is problematic to assume that election was the primary means of *canahas* recruitment.

Summary of Recruitment and Ranking

The *xinesi* and *caddi* share several recruiting and ranking characteristics. The somewhat minimal data may be interpreted to indicate that both positions are represented by several individuals within each village and confederacy. Certain references support the contention that each position's representatives are graded or ranked. Age may be the primary basis for this ranking, but an individual's abilities and charisma may also have been an integral part of the selection process for the *caddices*.

Both the *xinesi* and *caddi* positions may be filled through either succession or inheritance. However, these two means would differ from one another. Succession may occur either by the oldest village priest for the entire confederacy becoming *xinesi* (representing age grading) or by selecting a closely related, highly qualified *caddi* (representing ambilineal succession, but with a patrilineal bias?). Direct inheritance, on the other hand, may operate by initiating a youth (related to the present *xinesi*?) into the priesthood and training him for that position. Regardless of how selection occurs, it is evident that by the end of the period under study one person could hold both positions of *xinesi* and *caddi*.

Also among the western Caddo governing elite are the *canahas*, nobles, or village elders. Like the other 2 governing positions, they are ranked according to age, but evidently attain their assembly positions through election.

Because they are not full-time governing elites, the *amayxoya* (warriors) have not been discussed in this section. This position is attained through daring or bravery during warfare, thus enabling one to acquire prestige, provided that there is proper validation of these deeds. An *amayxoya* may be selected as the village "war chief," and it is likely that becoming an established *amayxoya* provides an access to one of the full-time governing positions.

Material Culture of the Hasinai Governing Elite

Having determined the structure, duties, and maintenance of the Hasinai governing elite, the second research goal of this study is to document the material culture. Swanton (1942:127–159) has discussed much of the historically reported Caddo material culture, but he has not systematically presented such data for the Hasinai governing elites. Available historical documents have therefore been reviewed in order to record as many material culture references as possible for the *xinesi*, *caddi*, and *canahas* positions between A.D. 1687–1721.

The Results

A chronological listing of material culture notations for the 3 elite positions is presented in Table 4. Except where noted, these references pertain to the villages in the Hasinai confederacy of eastern Texas. Morfi's descriptions have not been emphasized in this section because so much of Morfi's writing is only a slight paraphrasing of Espinosa that it embodies few substantive additions.

To facilitate study and comparison of the Table 4 data, the material traits in Table 5 have been listed as items present, absent, inapplicable, or having no data for the governing elite positions. The temple has been added as a special context since the *xinesi* functions here as well as in his and others' residences. Table 5 also refers to the assembly. This term applies to the actual governing body (*caddices* and *canahas*) and the special structure used by this body. Finally, the material attributes in Table 5 are itemized under 5 major categories: (1) Contexts and their spatial relationships; (2) Architectural details; (3) Building furniture and furnishings; (4) Ceremonial accouterments; (5) Attire and personal goods.

Although the literature was examined thoroughly, the material culture listed in Table 5 cannot be considered as complete. The early explorers and missionaries provide very uneven descriptions of the observed contexts and materials. Because they were treated as special ambassadors, these chroniclers were primarily hosted by the *caddices* and *canahas*, but there are few specific descriptions of the latter's residence or its furnishings. The missionaries were acutely interested in the temples and adjacent houses for the 2 heavenly children, but they do not provide much detail on the *xinesi's* residence, its contents, or his attire.

The Governing Elite's Material Culture:
Implications for Western Caddo Archaeology

Even a cursory review of Table 4 should demonstrate the vital role played by the varied material goods of Hasinai governing elite. A prolonged inspection of these data, however, raises some questions: (1) Does the recorded material culture identify the governing elite's hierarchical structure? (2) Can this material be archaeologically recovered and related to this hierarchical structure?

Identifying the Hierarchical Structure
Through Its Material Culture

Initially we should emphasize that no single attribute can be considered as diagnostic for any of the 3 governing elite positions. Instead, the shared attributes in Table 5 may support the implication that very complex relationships do exist between material culture and these 3 positions. An analysis of Tables 4 and 5 provides evidence for limited constellations of material attributes being associated with each elite position. These constellations would be larger and more diverse, however, if the residence and attire descriptions were of comparable detail for all positions. Because of the lack of sufficient historical detail, it has been concluded that an hierarchy within each position cannot be delimited solely on the basis of material culture.

The *xinesi* has been regarded as the religious head of an incipient theocracy that the links dispersed hamlets (and clans?, Swanton 1942:163-166) into a village and several villages into a confederacy. Persons filling this position have very special residence and activity patterns, centering on the temple and adjacent houses of the heavenly children. These special contexts contain unique paraphernalia used and maintained by the *xinesi*. Attributes listed (Table 5) as present for the temple or *xinesi* include certain salient material associations for this position: isolated temple-residence complex; wooden or split-cane altars; pottery incense burners; headgear of skins and feathers; and coffers containing stone and wooden animal effigies. Also noted, however, are such mundane items as pottery vessels, cane mats, storage boxes, and wooden benches.

The *caddi's* theocratic ties are believed to be exemplified by the temple replica in his residence and by his use of the special elevated seats mentioned also for the *xinesi*. As a political-religious leader, the *caddi* is similarly distinguished by a specially situated residence-ritual compound with attendant structures and furnishings (Table 5). Other integral material attributes for the *caddi* include: pipes used in calumet ceremony; a ceremonial stool; and special validating gifts from Spanish and French emissaries.

Canahas are interpreted as the lowest ranking members of the governing elite. They share few of the distinctive residence or ritual-related material attributes cited (Table 5) for the *xinesi* and *caddi*. *Canahas* are residents of the dispersed hamlets and farmsteads frequently described during this period (see Fig. 4). They do not have a spatially distinct residence-ritual compound as is associated with the *xinesi* and *caddi*. *Canahas* live temporarily in a special house (elongated rather than circular?) when called to the *caddi's* compound, and they apparently hold assemblies with the *caddices* in yet another structure. *Canahas* are integral participants in many ceremonies and have distinctive accouterments for these occasions (Table 5). They are also expected to provide the *xinesi* with a special seat and bed when he visits their houses. Although the material-position associations mentioned above are limited in number and nature, a review of the available data indicates that they result primarily from individuals occupying and fulfilling duties associated with particular slots in the governing hierarchy.

Caddo Governing Elites:
Archaeological Construct or Reconstruction?

The final goal of this research is to assess how well archaeologists might be expected to recover, analyze, and model data from almost 300 years ago that is relevant to governing elites. Increasingly archaeologists are recognizing that political systems are significant components in the processes behind cultural change and continuity. A political system can integrate the social, religious, and economic systems, and in a sense it comprises one adaptive mechanism for a society. At a certain level of organization, this mechanism can function well. With growing complexity, self-serving interests, and environmental stress, a political organization may not be capable of being effective, thus causing its own collapse—one that might include hardships for the society (Flannery 1972:418–424). Given this component's potential significance in prehistoric examples of adaptive inadequacy, the definition of political structure becomes an archaeological problem of considerable concern. If archaeologists are to discuss, examine, and analyze egalitarian, rank, stratified, and state levels of political organization, it becomes important to constantly evaluate data basic to these terms. This evaluation may initially involve proposing models that mirror or approximate previously existing governmental systems; this section presents one such proposal.

At some stage in their research, archaeologists must necessarily focus their attention on recovering material remains of past human activity. In this regard, the historical documents dealing with the Caddo provide a valuable perspective on some of the material culture for the governing elite. Table 5 is a list of what might be found. Unfortunately, what might occur is seldom related to what is found.

An inspection of Table 4 results in an overwhelming realization that the reported artifacts are predominantly organic in nature. Wood, cane, hides, hair, bone, and feathers are prominent in the furnishings, accouterments, and garb of the *xinesi, caddi,* and *canahas.* These raw materials are rarely preserved in the warm, humid, acidic, and oxidized soils common to east Texas and adjacent Louisiana. A few examples of comparable organic artifacts have been reported for 3 sites: G. C. Davis in Texas (Newell and Krieger 1949; Story 1972), Belcher in Louisiana (Webb 1959), and Mounds Plantation in Louisiana (Webb and McKinney 1975). These sites are interpreted as ceremonial centers dating from prehistoric periods (A.D. 900

to 1500) of the Caddo cultural continuum. Recovered organic artifacts typically come from unique preservation contexts consisting of elaborately furnished burial tombs in specially built earthen mounds.

Tombs placed in specially constructed earthen mounds are not contexts documented for the A.D. 1687–1721 period of the Caddo tradition. There are a few reported nonmound sites which probably relate to Caddo occupations of this period (Anderson 1972; Duffield and Jelks 1961; B. Jones 1968; Miroir and others 1973; Scurlock 1962; Woodall 1969). Most of these sites have not been extensively excavated, and none have yielded organic artifacts similar to those reported for the governing elite. Given these limitations, drawing a historical analogy with archaeological finds has been difficult, and archaeologists may not be able to develop models that mirror or replicate the structure, content, and operation of Hasinai governing elites in the late seventeenth and early eighteenth centuries.

A more useful model is one which synthesizes the historical data on elite structure, function, process, and material remains with what might be archaeologically recovered. Such a model is a construct of testable hypotheses which can be examined as more archaeological data become available. Points of observed incongruity should be critically examined for their potential contribution to improving the model. Such examination may also make it easier for archaeologists to define and explain past governmental systems.

The presented model for the Hasinai political system of A.D. 1687 to 1721 entails recognizing it as a form of theocracy. Its primary structure consists of 3 hierarchical positions, each probably composed of several individuals who are internally ranked according to various criteria. At the apex is the *grand xinesi*, a male head priest who attends a major religious center and whose mediation with the deities provides him with a basis of power to place demands on the whole society. The immediately subordinate position is the *caddi*, an official imbued with some religious sanctity but more involved with decisions on the mundane affairs of society. The lowest-governing officials are the *canahas*, persons interpreted as elderly representatives from the many hamlets and farmsteads dispersed over the controlled region.

These positions organize and sanctify a variety of annual ceremonies deemed essential for the society's material and spiritual welfare. Such celebrations offer opportunities for the redistribution of excess food and certain material goods. The *caddices* and *canahas* also meet as assemblies to decide on seasonal bison hunts to the north and northwest, to plan raids on groups (including other Caddoan-speaking villages) considered as enemies, and to welcome foreign emissaries.

The Hasinai governing elites are documented to have performed rituals and tasks attendant to their positions in rather specific settings. These associations provide the basis for postulating the presence of elite-related contexts and materials in the eastern Texas-western Louisiana region. The postulations listed below appear relevant for western Caddo archaeological sites dating from the seventeenth and early eighteenth centuries.

1. The overall settlement pattern should consist primarily of single farmsteads, small hamlets, and a few large villages dispersed along the major stream valleys (Fig. 4).

2. Within or between these valley settings may occur areas with sparse evidence of habitation. Such locations may be boundary zones established between clans, villages, or confederacies.

   a. Analyses of ceramics from the adjacent settled locales may reveal evidence for 2 different pottery-making and decorating traditions which could result from socially different patterns of residence and training (Woodall 1972).

3. Within or near a boundary zone will be found a site that covers 2 or 3 acres. This site will not be close to other hamlets or farmsteads, and it will contain evidence for a minimum of 4 circular, pole-frame buildings that have been burned. This site will be the *xinesi's* temple-residence complex.

   a. The temple will have a much larger diameter than the others; it will have a central fireplace, probably of larger size than in other structures, and there may be discernible evidence for an eastern entryway. Adjacent to this building may occur an ashy midden containing disarticulated human bones and broken pottery vessels distinguished by a thick char on their interiors. These vessels may be incidentally broken pottery incense burners. Chemical analysis of the char may substantiate this identification if the results indicate the presence of animal fats and vegetal fiber.

   b. Probably less than 100 yards from the temple will occur a smaller structure that should be the *xinesi's* residence. It should be distinguished by a central hearth and an eastern entryway. Posthole alignments within the structure may denote where bedposts were implanted. A midden area may occur near this house and should contain such domestic trash as ash, sherds of diverse vessel forms, charred vegetal food, and faunal remains. Because the *xinesi* is allowed to choose meat cuts from deer, deer bones from this midden may show a nonrandom preference for certain elements. Because the *xinesi* is not directly involved with hunting, there may be relatively few projectile points deposited at this site.

   c. A cemetery will occur in proximity to the residence or temple. An outstanding feature should be one or more pits containing only the remains of human skulls (from the deposition of the trophy skulls). Other components of the cemetery may be the *xinesi*, family members, and other relatives. With the *xinesi's* death, the residence doorway is blocked and he is buried nearby. Analysis of the skeleton should reveal that it is a male in the older age bracket for the population. His burial associations will most likely be personal or domestic goods and not items directly related to his position.

d. Within 100 yards of the temple should occur evidence for the house locations for the 2 heavenly children. Both structures are smaller than the temple, and both should have sparse evidence of domestic activities around them.

4. Located within, and perhaps near the center of, each inhabited watershed should be a partially isolated site of approximately 2 to 3 acres. This place will be distant from, but readily accessible to, other hamlets. It will contain evidence for at least 3 buildings and a plazalike area between them. An arbor may be nearby. This complex of structure locations and distinct spatial arrangements is the *caddi's* residence and the scene of many village ceremonies. More than likely, all structures will show evidence of having been burned.

a. The *caddi's* residence will be the largest structure at this site; its floor space will probably equal that observed for the temple. Architectural details should include the circular pattern of the exterior walls' postholes, an eastern entryway, a central hearth, and numerous postholes within half of the floor space. The latter result from forked posts implanted for the many beds observed in this half of the house. The remaining floor area may be relatively free of postholes and provide traces of tools and debris from domestic activities. A small circle of postholes may occur within this structure that result from the construction of a temple replica within the house.

b. Perhaps 30 to 60m east of the *caddi's* residence will occur a second structure location. The intervening space will show few subsurface cultural disturbances, even though this plaza-like area was used for dances and rituals attended by major segments of the village population.

c. The second structure will exhibit smaller dimensions than the *caddi's* residence. It will probably have traces for both western and eastern entries, exhibit a central hearth, and show evidence for many interior posts (bed supports). The structure's exterior posthole pattern may be more elongated than circular, thus substantiating that this was the long house used to lodge the *canahas* when they were assembled by the *caddi*.

d. Not far to the east of the elongated structure will occur the smaller lodging for the *canahas'* attendants. This third structure should be circular in outline, have an interior hearth, and probably exhibit both eastern and western entries. It, too, may contain many interior postholes resulting from posts implanted for constructing beds.

e. Adjacent to one side of the plaza may occur 4 postholes delimiting the supports for a large, cane-covered arbor. There will probably not be any features (e.g., hearths or ash beds) associated inside or adjacent to this context.

f. Near the plaza's margin, a circular alignment of postholes may occur. These should mark the location of the small, grass-covered hut used by elderly dancers during the harvest or first fruits ceremony.

g. Somewhere near this residential-ritual complex should occur a cemetery area for the site's residents, perhaps including the *caddi*. This official was typically an older male. Grave associations at this cemetery will primarily consist of personal goods that probably reflect differences in sex rather than status. If a *caddi* is buried there, the associations might include native pottery and arrowpoints as well as such special items as metal axes, metal knives, glass beads, or a silverheaded cane. The latter would represent a special gift presented by either the Spanish or French to those native individuals occupying influential positions in a village or confederacy.

h. Either one extensive or several middens will occur near this site. These may attain considerable depth and should contain quantities of debris. Their contents will represent deposits resulting from the site's daily residents as well as special guests and visitors attending the ceremonies.

i. Pottery vessels and sherds from this site may exhibit larger vessel dimensions than are normal for the small hamlets and isolated farmsteads. There may also occur a larger ratio of pottery vessels per structure than other sites. Both observations could result because the collection and storage of grains, nuts, and other foodstuffs for feasting and other village ceremonies is an integral function of this site.

5. Within a mile of the *caddi's* center may occur a site containing a single building that is large in diameter. The structure should be circular, have an eastern doorway and a central hearth. This structure housed the *canahas* and *caddi* when they assembled to discuss village matters. Because it does not function as a residence, there should be few interior postholes resulting from the placement of post-supported beds.

a. The description for one assembly house indicates it is surrounded by fields, so other structures should not be in close proximity.

    b.   Any nearby midden should contain ash, but only a very limited variety of material remains.

6.   Located among the farmsteads, hamlets and few villages will occur structures inhabited by the *canahas*. These houses will be virtually indistinguishable in size and form from those of nongoverning persons. They will not have the large dimensions noted for the *caddi's* residence. They should be circular, have interior central hearths, and doorways to the east. Interior postholes may be more numerous than in nearby houses because these officials provided a special bed used only by the visiting *xinesi*. Nearby should occur a midden area and a cemetery.

    a.   The midden should contain trash resulting primarily from daily domestic activities.

    b.   The cemetery may contain individuals from all houses in the hamlet or village, but these may show spatial clustering potentially attributable to kin groupings. Deceased *canahas* should be men representing the older segment of the age spectrum of this society. Burial associations may be similar to those of the *caddi*; namely, personal goods that might include special pipes and gifts from foreign emissaries.

7.   Hamlet clusters may include structure locations that are comparable in size to that of the temple. If such locations yield contextual and artifactual evidence similar to that from the temple complex, it should be possible to postulate that there are village priests as well as a *xinesi*.

The expectations offered above are rather simplistic in nature, but they provide a basis for testing our ability to identify the positions of power in early Caddo society. Such an evaluation cannot come from excavating only historic burials. Instead, it will involve surveys, limited field testing, and large-scale excavation throughout several watersheds. Such research designs have not been carried to fruition, but Anderson's (1972) survey in the upper Neches is an important first step.

Summary

Archeologists' growing interest in studying political systems and their articulation with prehistoric social maintenance and change demands sharpened analytical approaches to data recovery and interpretation. Constant evaluation of how well the recovered evidence supports the interpretation is also important. This research has focused on evaluating the correlation between material culture and positions of governing power. Using historical documents, a model for governing elites in the Caddo villages and confederacies of A.D. 1687 to 1721 has been presented. Three hierarchical positions have been identified, their interrelationships defined, and their duties examined. Historical references to material culture provide some basis for believing each position has particular associations of contexts and material goods. After allowing for preservation problems, a series of archaeologically testable hypotheses about these 3 governing elite positions and their respective material culture have been offered. The actual testing of these hypotheses awaits evidence collected from thorough surveys and follow-up excavations within watersheds located in the Caddo homelands.

Acknowledgments

The initial draft of this paper was stimulated by Dr. Joseph Whitecotton's class "Elites in Society" at the University of Oklahoma. Dr. Whitecotton has provided many useful comments and insights as well as constructive criticisms toward the improvement of this work. Other individuals who have read over the manuscript and provided invaluable comments include John Moore, Dee Ann Story, Rain Vehik, Clarence Webb, and Mildred Wedel. Marie Gilbert, Kandra Kline, and Pam Odell aided with the typing of the final manuscript. Any errors contained herein belong solely to the authors. Because of their interest and understanding of Caddo culture and history, we wish to dedicate this paper to the memory of Sadie Bedoka Weller and Melford Williams.

Oklahoma Archaeological Survey
University of Oklahoma

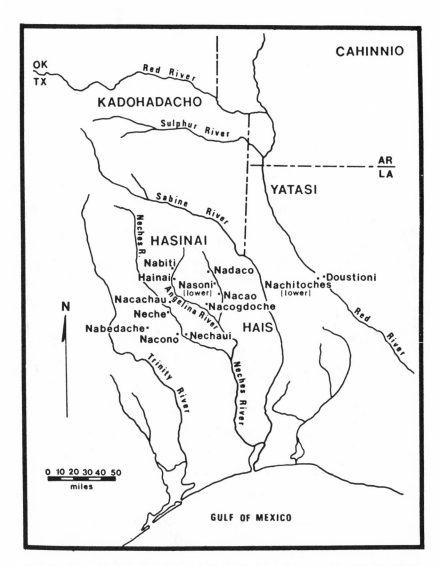

Fig. 1. Protohistoric location of Hasinai Confederacy villages and related Caddoan speaking groups (after Swanton 1942:8).

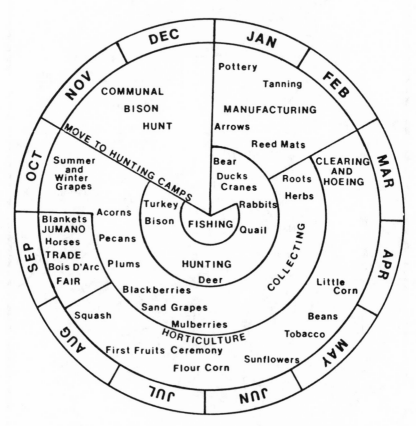

Fig. 2.   Schematic economic cycle chart for the Hasinai.

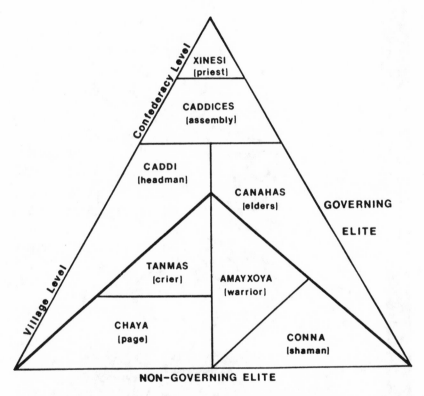

Fig. 3. Diagram of governing and non-governing elite structure among the late seventeenth and eighteenth-century Hasinai.

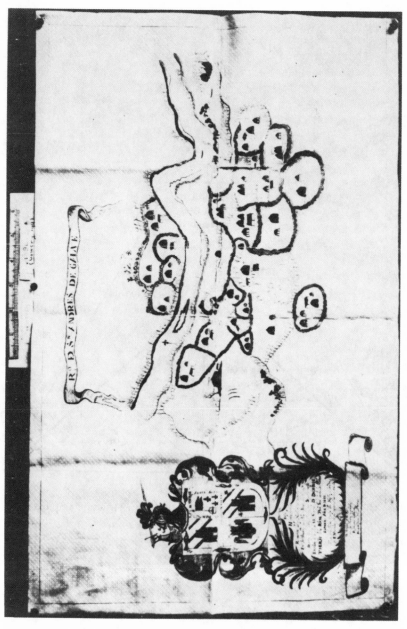

Fig. 4.   Dispersed settlement pattern of the Upper Nasoni (Kadohadacho) village on Red River as mapped by an anonymous cartographer of the Teran (1691 1692) expedition. Photo courtesy of the Geography and Map Division, Library of Congress (original in Archivo General de Indias, Seville).

TABLE 1

Glottochronological Dates for Caddoan-speaking Societies
in Minimum Centuries (after Hughes 1968:83)

	Caddo	Wichita	Pawnee	Arikara
Caddo	—	30	33	35
Wichita	30	—	14	20
Pawnee	33	14	—	5
Arikara	35	20	5	—

TABLE 2

Historical References to Hasinai Status Positions and Their Responsibilities

Status identification	Reported Context and/or responsibilities	Date	Chronicler	Reference
Chief and Elders	A contingent formally meets members of La Salle's party. Twelve elders are surrounded by youths and warriors.	1687	Joutel	Joutel 1962:108
Chief	Has a larger cottage where public rejoicings and great assemblies are held.	1687	"	" :109
Elder	Presides over corn-ripening ceremony.	1687	"	" :113
Group of Elders	Meet and greet members of La Salle's party.	1687	"	" :115
Elders	Conduct council concerning war expedition.	1687	"	" :118
Chief	War party returns to his dwelling and celebrates their victory.	1687	"	" :126

TABLE 2 CONT.

Status identification	Reported Context and/or responsibilities	Date	Chronicler	Reference
Elders	One acts as an orator and master of ceremonies for the post raid rituals.	1687	"	" :127
Chief	Offers to accompany French expedition to the village of the Assonys.	1687	"	" :130
Chief and Elders	Joutel taken to chief's dwelling and elders are notified.	1687	"	" :130
Chief and Elders	Assony people come out to meet the French and go back to their village to notify elders. Taken to chief's cottage where elders wash the visitors' faces. Four chiefs from different villages make speeches to the Frenchmen.	1687	"	" :133
Elders	Meet the Frenchmen in their cottage to seek aid in fighting their enemies.	1687	"	" :134
Chief	Among *Cadodaquio* (Kadohadacho), the French are taken to chief's cottage, and he provides supplies for their journey to the *Cahainihoua* (Cahinnio) village.	1687	"	" :137
Elders	Among *Cahainihoua* (Cahinnio), the French are met by elders who held a calumet ceremony.	1687	"	" :139
Governor	De Leon's party meets Tejas (Nabedache) war chief and 8 of his Indians on the Guadalupe River.	1689	Massanet	Bolton 1916:363
Governor	The following year De Leon's party again meets the Tejas (Nabedache) governor and 14 or 15 of his Indians west of Trinity River. Massanet presents the governor with clothing, "so that his people might see how highly we thought of him."	1690	"	" :376
Governor	Guides the Spaniards to his village. On their arrival he and others kiss Massanet's robe. The governor invites him into his house which is round.	1690	"	" :377

TABLE 2 CONT.

Status identification	Reported Context and/or responsibilities	Date	Chronicler	Reference
Captains and their Pages	Are lodged in a long house when called by the governor to a meeting. Pages have a smaller house nearby in which they are lodged.	1690	"	" :378
Pages	Law provides each captain shall bring his page when the governor assembles the captains.	1690	"	Casis 1899:304
Governor	Each week 10 women do his housework. They bring firewood, clean the patio and house, carry water, and grind corn.	1690	"	Bolton 1916:378 -379
Minister	Tejas (Nabedache) always had an old Indian who was minister and presents offerings to God and pretastes food at ceremonies. He has a house reserved for sacrifices of food, and it is entered very reverentially. He does not sacrifice to idols.	1690	"	" :380
Captains, Governor, and Minister	Captains and governor himself treat the minister with much consideration. Governor sends out captains with orders to pay honor to Indian priest and bring him with them. They sing and dance for 3 days in his honor before he arrives.	1690	"	" :380
Minister	Blesses first food by directing it to 4 cardinal points.	1690	"	" :381
Governor	Is called desza, Great Lord and Superior to all, to distinguish him from other captains.	1690	"	" :381
Governor	Sends his brother and 2 other relatives as envoy with the Spanish. Governor admonishes, "Do not permit anyone to demand service from these men . . . nor to make them work," due to their rank. They are nobles among the mass of people.	1690	"	" :382
Chiefs	While among the Nachitoches, chiefs of 3 nations (Nachitoches, Ouasita, and Capiche) assemble and speak to the French.	1690	de Tonti	Falconer 1975:85

TABLE 2 CONT.

Status identification	Reported Context and/or responsibilities	Date	Chronicler	Reference
Governor	de Tonti arrives at the Cadadoquis (Kadohadacho) village. A woman governor and other dignitaries greet the French; she weeps and asks the French for aid to revenge the death of her husband.	1690	"	" :86
Priests	The French arrive at a temple where priests invoke God and then take de Tonti to the chief's cabin.	1690	"	" :87
Caddi	The *Caddi* is sent a portion of each dish before a feast is actually initiated.	1690-91	Casañas	Hatcher 1927:212
Chief and Caddi	If chief is a feast host he may invite the whole village to his house; *caddi* goes with all the rest. The *caddi* takes a portion from every dish and throws part of it into the fire, part on the ground and to each side. He retires to a corner where he speaks, consecrating the whole harvest to God.	1690-91	"	" :212 -213
Caddi	Is highest in rank.	1690-91	"	" :213
Grand Xinesi and Caddices	Only these officials have elevated seats in their houses and their sayings and actions are carefully heeded.	1690-91	"	" :213
Caddi	On the last day of the war dance he comes forward to encourage the warriors.	1690-91	"	" :214
Grand Xinesi	The Indians are obedient to him since he compares to a "petty king." He holds office by direct line of descent. If one dies, his nearest blood kin succeeds. To him 9 tribes (*Nabadacho, Necha, Nechavi, Nacono, Nacachau, Nazadachotzi, Cachae, Nabiti,* and *Nasayaha*) are subject.	1690-91	"	" :215 -216
Canahas	Are officials who aid in governing. They relieve the *caddi,* publish his orders, and frighten people into submission if they do not obey orders.	1690-91	"	" :216

TABLE 2 CONT.

Status identification	Reported Context and/or responsibilities	Date	Chronicler	Reference
Chaya	Are subordinate to *canahas* and do everything the *canahas* tell them to do.	1690–91	"	" :216
Tanmas	Are officers who promptly execute orders and whip idlers.	1690–91	"	" :216
Canahas	Call the old men to the home of *caddi* to discuss any matter. Also, when hunting or raiding, they fix place for *caddi* to rest, eat, and sleep. They prepare peace pipe for *caddi*.	1690–91	"	" :216
Xinesi and Caddices	Each official has one wife, designated by the title of *aquidau*.	1690–91	"	" :216
Amayxoya	Man who attains recognition for some victory in war.	1690–91	"	" :217
Xinesi and Caddi	During planting time all tribal members plant a small garden for the *xinesi* but they generally furnish all of his food and clothing. They plant crops for each *caddi*, then move on down the ranks.	1690–91	"	" :217
Caddices and Grand Xinesi	*Caddices* work like the rest but *grand xinesi* never goes out for anything except to take a walk or make certain visits. *Xinesi* has special bench and bed in all *caddices* houses as well as other nobles. He must always be above the rest.	1690–91	"	" :217
Xinesi, Caddices and leading men	People have great respect for these officials.	1690–91	"	" :218
Caddi and Elders	*Caddi* calls old men together to make decisions. Each may speak in turn according to age.	1690–91	"	" :218
Grand Xinesi	People have remarkable respect and obedience for him. "Everybody tries to keep him satisfied" through gifts and by hunting for him. "All obey because they fear his frown . . . they agree that his proposition is very reasonable."	1690–91	"	" :218

TABLE 2 CONT.

Status identification	Reported Context and/or responsibilities	Date	Chronicler	Reference
Caddi	Must be notified by a girl's parents when she is given away in marriage.	1690–91	"	" :283
Xinesi	"These allied tribes do not have one person to govern them. . . . They have only a *xinesi*. He usually has a subordinate who gathers together four or five tribes who consent to live together and to form a province."	1690–91	"	" :286
Grand Xinesi	Has no idols but communicates with 2 heavenly children who live in his house. He uses them to coerce people to bring corn and other things he needs. "He calls all the tribes to his house and gives orders to all the *caddices* and the old men to come into the house where he keeps the two children. This house is much larger than the one where he lives."	1690–91	"	" :290
Xinesi	Keeps a fire burning day and night. Offers incense to 2 spiritual children. Uses ceremony to relate childrens' wishes to tribal leaders.	1690–91	"	" :291
Governor	Found in an enclave with the old men discussing an epidemic among the *Asinai*.	1690–91	"	" :295
Medicine Men	Are present in the tribes and are called *conna*.	1690–91	"	" :295 -296
Conna	May be killed by the people if they have poor luck in curing diseases.	1690–91	"	" :296
Leading Men and Imposter Priests	Go through many ceremonies when one of them dies. Gives description of such ceremonies. Two Indians are chosen to serve as priests.	1690–91	"	" :297
Imposter Priests	Serve only during burial of ranked individuals, mainly those of chiefly status.	1690–91	"	" :298

TABLE 2 CONT.

Status identification	Reported Context and/or responsibilities	Date	Chronicler	Reference
Grand Xinesi	Is not buried until 2 days after his death. All 9 tribes must perform the proper ceremonies.	1690–91	"	" :298
Grand Xinesi and Caddices	Casanas appeals to Viceroy for a favored Native leader to become "the chief of the whole province," for he is now "no more than a *caddi*," along with 8 other *caddices* and is subject to a *grand xinesi*.	1690–91	"	" :299
Caddices and Xinesi	*Caddices* "have never known a higher authority than that of a *xinesi*."	1690–91	"	" :300
Caddices and Grand Xinesi	The people arrange certain feasts at different times during the year to honor *caddices* and *grand xinesi* to celebrate victories of their ancestors. Gifts are brought by captains (*caddices*?) to the *xinesi*.	1690–91	"	" :301
Chenesi	Home fires brought from the house of the high priest known as *chenesi*. He assumes voices of 2 children from God and asks for what he needs for their use. He threatens people with snake bites if they are disobedient.	1710	Hidalgo	Hatcher 1927:51
Captain	Harvest ceremony is held at his house and its patio. They build a special straw hut near the captain's house for 12 dancers who are old men.	1710	"	" :52
High Priest	Deer are not butchered until village priest arrives. He cuts it up and selects a portion which is sent to him. Corn and bean crops are handled in the same manner. "Each one and each family gives a portion of everything to the high priest."	1710	"	" :52
Chief	Penicaut is met and received by chief of *Nassitoches* as well as one for the *Colapissas*.	1712	Penicaut	Penicaut 1953:145

TABLE 2 CONT.

Status identification	Reported Context and/or responsibilities	Date	Chronicler	Reference
Chief	Penicaut saves *Nassitoches* chief from death.	1712	"	" :146
Chiefs	St. Denis assembles chiefs of *Doustiony* and *Nassitoches*. He asks them to settle and plant crops.	1712	"	" :149
Chiefs	*Assinais* chiefs agree to provide guides to Spanish settlements on Rio Grande.	1712	"	" :151
Eldest Men	Among *Assinais*, 4 of eldest men ritually incise prisoners to drain their blood which is caught in plates and cooked by 2 other old men.	1712	"	" :155
Captains and Caziques	Spanish meet 34 *Asinai* with 5 being captains. They go to a large arbor where they smoke "a pipe adorned with many white feathers as a sign of peace." Spanish give gifts to *caziques*, and captains divide them among the Indians.	1715	Espinosa	Hatcher 1927:151
Caddi and Tammas	For house building, *caddi* sets the day and orders overseers (*tammas*) to notify all households to aid and what supplies to bring. *Tammas* sleep at proposed site.	1715	"	" :154
Tammas	Punish those who arrive late at house building.	1715	"	" :155
Captains	House owners hold a feast upon the works completion. Captains are fed first. When a captain builds a new house the feast is more elaborate.	1715	"	" :155
Chenesi and Principal Captains	Everyone helps with the planting. *Chenesí*, the leading priest who cares for the fire temple, has his fields planted first, then the "principal captain and afterwards for all the rest in the order as fixed by captains in their assemblies."	1715	"	" :156
War Leaders	Are chosen by the men.	1716	Hildago	Hatcher 1927:57
Chenesi	The *Asinai* worship fire and have a perpetual fire in a special house. They have appointed an old man as chief priest (*chenesi*) to keep it up always. This house is halfway between *Naichas* and *Ainais* and common to both.	1716	Espinosa	Hatcher 1927:160

TABLE 2 CONT.

Status identification	Reported Context and/or responsibilities	Date	Chronicler	Reference
Old Men	Fire temple serves as an assembly place for the old men who gather for consultations, war dances, and when rain is needed.	1716	"	" :160
Priests and Captains	In funeral ceremony, captains sit according to order, and food is then offered to the priest who performs an offering to the fire and patrons.	1716	"	" :163
Priest	Is involved in a naming ceremony for an infant.	1716	"	" :164
Medicine Men	Spanish priest detests infestation of doctors or medicine men. They practice curing, have a role in blessing new houses, and are "first at the function of feasting." They are highly respected by everyone but may be killed if cure fails.	1716	"	:165 -167
Captain	His house serves for general meeting of those going to war.	1716	"	" :169
Saint (Priest)	Leads prayers and rituals before the eating of new corn.	1716	"	" :169
Captain	Before planting, mats are made and given to a captain who offers them in the fire temple to insure good crops. Ceremony ends in house of captain where there is a small fire temple.	1716	"	" :169 -170
Tamma and Captains	Tamma is an official who collects first ripe tobacco and delivers it to his captain who must bless the first fruits.	1716	"	" :171
Chenesi	An old man acts as chenesi during the harvest feast and meets with captains and men at the captain's house with the small fire temple. Chenesi orders young men to hunt while he and old men pray. Harvest ceremony is described in detail.	1716	"	" :171 -172

TABLE 2 CONT.

Status identification	Reported Context and/or responsibilities	Date	Chronicler	Reference
Captains	"All of these people have their principal captains." This office is perpetual, being inherited by a son or relative when he dies.	1716	"	" :175
Chief Captain	Even a very young son may inherit his father's office. A council of *caziques* is furnished him during his youth and they carry him to all meetings where he is assigned the highest seat.	1716	"	" :175
War Chief	Is elected and during a campaign is obeyed totally.	1716	"	" :176
Caziques	Intervillage disputes are settled by an assembly of all *caziques* who can punish or expel offenders.	1716	"	" :178
Cazique and Captains	Come out of a village to greet newcomers.	1716	"	" :178
Cazique	Spanish governor is carried by the principal *cazique* and in a ceremony the governor is made a captain-general among them.	1718	"	" :180
Chief	Of *Oulchiones* nation is sought for aid in cutting logs for a trading post.	1719	LaHarpe	Smith 1958:84
War Chief	Of *Natchitoches* with 12 warriors guides the French.	1719	"	" :86
War Chief and Notables	LaHarpe is met by the *Nassonites* and 6 village notables.	1719	"	" :250
Chief	Of *Nassonites* is 70 years old.	1719	"	" :250
Chiefs	One each for *Cadodaquious, Nadsoos,* and *Natchitoches.*	1719	"	" :251
Chief	Of *Cadodaquious* is an old man, ca. 80 years. He is a most eloquent haranguer, urging the village groups to accept French protection.	1719	"	" :251 -252
Elders	Locate the nearest Spanish settlements.	1719	"	" :252

TABLE 2 CONT.

Status identification	Reported Context and/or responsibilities	Date	Chronicler	Reference
War Chief	Honorific title conferred for bravery among *Nachitoches*.	1719	"	" :256 -258
Nobleman	Of *Nassonite* tells of metallic stones in mountains north of *Cadodaquious*.	1719	"	Smith 1959:371
Chiefs	Of *Nadaco* nation come to smoke calumet.	1719	"	" :372
Chief	Great *Naouydiche* chief and his warriors testify to their friendship and celebrate calumet with the French.	1719	LaHarpe	Smith 1958:385
Chief also a High Priest	*Nacono* tribe is led by a chief who is also high priest. He is blind, a reported custom for this position. He makes a long speech in support of the Spanish.	1721	Morfi	Swanton 1942:60
Principal Chief	"In each of the Texas tribes there is a principal chief whom they respect and obey. This office is perpetual and hereditary in the oldest son, or, in his absence, in the next brother, or nearest of kin."	1721	"	" :171
General and Captains	Each nation (village) elects a general who is subordinate to the superior chief and commands in war. Captains are elected by acclamation, but have limited authority.	1721	"	" :171 -172
Chief	Authority is in proportion to eloquence, valor, or esteem by which he is held by nation.	1721	"	" :172
Cazique and Chiefs	Spanish party is met by *cazique* of *Aynay* village. He is recognized as head of *Assinais* nation and is accompanied by 8 of the chief Indians.	1721	Aguayo	Buckley 1911:42
Chief	Of *Neches* arrives and smokes pipe of peace with Spanish.	1721	"	" :43
High Priest (also Chief?)	Spanish party is met by 100 *Nocono* led by a high priest and chief who acts as a spokesman.	1721	"	" :44
Chief	Chescas is chief of *Aynay*.	1721	"	" :44

TABLE 3

Correlation of Hasinai Status Terminology*

Chronicler	Position a	Position b	Position c	Position d	Position e	Position f	Position g
Joutel (1687)		Chief	Elders				
Massanet (1689–90)	Minister	Governor	Captain	Page			
de Tonti (1690)	Priest	Chief & governor					
Casañas (1690–91)	Xinesi & grand xinesi	Caddi	Canahas & leading men	Chaya	Tammas	Amayxoya	Conna
Hidalgo (1710)	Chenesi & high priest	Captain	Old men			War leader	
Penicaut (1712)		Chief(s)	Eldest men				
Espinosa (1715)	Chenesi & priest	Caziques, caddi, & captain	Captains		Tammas	War chief	Medicine men
La Harpe (1719)		Chief	Notable elders			War chief	
Morfi (1721)	High priest	Chief					
Aguayo (1721)	High priest	Chief cazique & chief	Chiefs				

* Based on comparison of status terms and their attributed responsibilities as listed in Table 2.

TABLE 4

Historical References to the Material Culture of Hasinai Governing Elite

Status identification	Material culture description	Date	Chronicler	Reference
Elders	Wear goat (deer?) skins painted in several colors and pieces of white linen. Also wear plumes of colored feathers and carry square sword blades, clubs, bows and arrows. Their faces are daubed black or red.	1687	Joutel	Joutel 1962:108
Chief	His cottage is small and is a quarter league from a larger cottage used for public assemblies and ceremonies.	1687	"	" :109
Assembly	This larger hut is furnished with mats for sitting. Fields occur around this hut.	1687	"	" :109
General Populace	General description of houses and their construction: circular (60' diameter) of implanted poles lashed together at top, woven with lath, and covered with weeds (grass?). Are burned down when abandoned.	1687	"	" :110
Elder	Places basket of corn on a special stool during harvest ceremony.	1687	"	" :113
Elder	During assembly, pottage is boiled in a great pot which is then placed on a ceremonial stool.	1687	"	" :113
Elders	Take Frenchmen to their cottage where they sit on mats and smoke.	1687	"	" :115
Chief (deceased)	Has one of largest huts in village. Is not burned down after his death.	1687	"	" :115
Chief and Prime Men	Chief's hut is used for victory ceremony after a raid. Trophy heads are brought here for first ceremony and taken to huts of other prime men.	1687	"	" :126

TABLE 4 CONT.

Status identification	Material culture description	Date	Chronicler	Reference
Chief and Prime Men	For victory ceremony their huts are cleaned and many mats are placed on floor for the elders. Trophy heads are brought in by warriors' wives and after rituals are placed all around the interior.	1687	"	" " :127
Elder Master of Ceremonies	During victory ceremony he takes food in a vessel and smokes a pipe.	1687	"	" " :127
Chief	Among *Nahordikhe*, his cottage is part of hamlet.	1687	"	" " :130
Elders	Among *Nahordikhe*, they bring mats for Frenchmen to sit on.	1687	"	" " :130
Chief	Rides a horse and smokes with Frenchmen.	1687	"	" " :132–133
Chief	Earthen vessel is used to wash Frenchmen's faces at his cottage. Then they are seated under a low (4) scaffold of wood and cane.	1687	"	" " :133
Assembly	Among *Cadadoquio*, men have short hair soaked with oil and lint dyed red.	1687	"	" " :138
Chief	Among *Cahinnio*, his cottage had bearskins on the floor for sitting.	1687	"	" " :139
Elders	Among *Cahinnio*, they bring bows and hides of buffalo, otter and deer.	1687	"	" " :139
Elders	Among *Cahinnio*, they smoke long calumet pipe with attached feathers. Ceremony also involves gourd rattles and a tripod of red sticks.	1687	"	" " :140

TABLE 4 CONT.

Status identification	Material culture description	Date	Chronicler	Reference
Governor	Invites 26 Spaniards to live in his house since it has room for them all.	1690	Massanet	Bolton 1916:377
Governor	Has circular house built of stakes and covered with grass thatching. It is 20 varas (1 vara = 2.75 feet) high. Has no windows but with an open door. Over this on the inside is a shelf. Perpetual fire is kept in the middle of house. Ten beds are in half the house; each has a reed rug laid on 4 forked sticks and is covered with buffalo skins. At foot and head of each is a canopy of brilliantly colored reed mats. Other half of house has shelves (2 varas high) holding large reed baskets (of corn, nuts, acorns, and beans) and earthen pots. Also, there are 6 wooden mortars for grinding corn in rainy weather; corn is ground outside when weather is nice.	1690	"	" :377–378
Governor	Has wooden benches brought out onto the patio in front of his house.	1690	"	" :378
Captains	Have long house across the patio and opposite door of governor's house. They stay in this house when the governor calls an assembly. Behind this house is a smaller lodge for captains' pages.	1690	"	" :378
Governor	Has a little wooden bench in front of the fire in his house.	1690	"	" :379
Minister	Has a house reserved for sacrifices.	1690	"	" :380
Chief	Of village has a shrine with several images.	1690	DeLeon	" :403
Priests	Among *Cadodaquis*, they are found in a temple.	1690	de Tonti	Falconer 1975:87
Grand Xinesi and Caddices	Have privilege of sitting on an elevated seat which only these officials have in their houses. These seats are like tables; they have legs rather than the the one-piece benches.	1690–91	Casañas	Hatcher 1927:213

TABLE 4 CONT.

Status identification	Material culture description	Date	Chronicler	Reference
Caddí	Has pouch for tobacco and a pipe of peace.	1690–91	"	" :216
Grand Xinesí	Has human skulls hanging in a tree near his house.	1690–91	"	" :217
Caddí and Nobles	Their houses contain a special bench for seating a visiting Xinesí. They also have a high bed (alcove-like) where Xinesí may rest or sleep.	1690–91	"	" :217
Xinesí	Calls Caddices and elders to his house where he keeps 2 heavenly children. This house is much larger than where he lives. People are seated around a perpetual fire. There is a tablelike seat 2 sq. varas in size. At its side reed boxes used to store what people bring. Priest has gourd rattles.	1690–91	"	" :290–291
Xinesí	Temple door has a covering. Temple also contains a mortar on which priest grinds grain for 2 heavenly children. His home is about 100 paces away.	1690–91	"	" :292
Xinesí	He wears deerskin.	1690–91	"	" :292
Xinesí	Two heavenly children are kept in a round wooden box with parchmentlike cover that has a hole in it.	1690–91	"	" :292
Leading Men	At their death a coffin is made in which a bow and arrow are placed. Burial is always near the house. An axe is used to mark the grave spot. Some personal goods are placed with the body. After covering the grave a fire is built on top, and a pot of water is left there.	1690–91	Casañas	Hatcher 1927:297–298
Xinesí	At his death a tall pole topped by a grass globe is placed in front of his door.	1690–91	"	" :299
Chenesí	Fire for people's houses comes from the house of this high priest.	1710	Hidalgo	Hatcher 1927:51

TABLE 4 CONT.

Status identification	Material culture description	Date	Chronicler	Reference
Captain and Elders	Harvest ceremony is held in captain's house and on his patio. Nearby is a little straw hut for the dancers. Dancers are elders and they wear plumes. Houses have doors to the east.	1710	"	" ":52
Leaders	Conduct calumet ceremony with pipe smoking.	1712	Penicaut	Penicaut 1953:150
Elders	Drain human blood into plates and then cook it.	1712	"	" ":155
Grand Chief (Xinesi)	Among *Natchitoches* the temple contains wooden bird figures outside and over the door. Inside are 3 coffers containing wooden and stone figures of dragons, serpents, and toads.	1712	"	Swanton 1942:155, 216
Priest	Has a temple with perpetual fire as well as large and small idols.	1716	Hidalgo	Hatcher 1927:55–56
Captains and Leading Men	Take Spaniards to a very large arbor which has coarse cloth carpets. Also have beautifully painted deerskins and a pipe adorned with white feathers.	1715–17	Espinosa	Hatcher 1927:151
Captains and Leading Men	Have larger grass thatched, circular houses than the rest of the people.	1715–17	"	" ":155
Chenesi	His temple is located half-distance between the *Naichas* and *Ainais*.	1715–17	"	" ":160
Chenesi	Maintains the temple which is set apart and in which there is a perpetual fire. Building is "large, round, and thatched" and contains altar of reed mats. A bed holds 3 finer mats. On one side of a door are benches holding rolled reed mats. In front of the bed is a wooden bench with 4 legs on which there is tobacco, a pipe with feathers, and earthen vessels which serve as incense (fat and tobacco) burners.	1715–17	"	" ":160–161

TABLE 4 CONT.

Status identification	Material culture description	Date	Chronicler	Reference
Chenesi	Temple fire is 4 large logs pointing to 4 principal directions. Ashes from fire accumulate outside and in these the bones of their enemies are buried.	1715–17	"	" :161
Chenesi	At gunshot distance from temple are 2 smaller houses for the heavenly children. These contain 2 small chests on a wooden altar. Chests contain black wooden platters with feet; platters are carved like animals (duck, alligator, or lizard). Also in chests are many feathers, crowns of skin and feathers, flutes of carved crane bones, and flutes of reeds.	1715–17	"	" :161
Priest	In funeral for those killed in fighting, gifts (arrows, bows, beads, clothing, etc.) are gathered, rolled in fine deerskins and mats, and burned outside the house.	1715–17	Espinosa	Hatcher 1927:163
Priest	During infant-naming ceremony, he has a special seat and uses a large vessel to bathe the child.	1715–17	"	" :164
Elders	They drink a portion of laurel tea and use eagle wings in dances and songs. A fox tail is used in a ritual to foresee the future.	1715–17	"	" :168–169
Priests	Cover themselves with white dirt in a ceremony before young men go deer hunting.	1715–17	"	" :170
Captain	In planting ceremony, he takes cane mats to fire in temple. In his house is a smaller fire temple around which they make hoes of black walnut before planting.	1715–17	"	" :170–171

TABLE 4 CONT.

Status identification	Material culture description	Date	Chronicler	Reference
Priest, Captains and Old Men	Participate in harvest ceremony at captain's house where they sit on benches and smoke pipes. Food is collected in 2 large containers.	1715–17	"	" :171–173
Priest, Captain and Old Men	In harvest ceremony, a large bonfire is built in a large circle of green cane stuck in ground outside captain's house. Old men dress in buffalo robes and receive food in earthen vessels. During dancing, gourd rattles and hollow-log drums are used.	1715–17	"	" :171–173
Leaders and People	Hang trophy skulls in a tree and conduct special ceremony when these are buried. Build a number of fires; have musicians and singers painted black. Ceremony lasts through night. At morning they cover themselves with white dirt, take skulls to cemetery near fire temple, and bury them. Afterwards, they take food offerings to this grave for a period of time.	1715–17	"	" :174
Chief Captain	Has highest seat.	1715–17	"	" :174
Chief	Among Nassonite, he has a dwelling near which is an arbor. Here, LaHarpe and people feast on bread, boiled corn, bear, bison, and fish.	1719	LaHarpe	Smith 1958:250–251
Chiefs and Elders	Celebrate calumet with smoking of pipe.	1719	"	" :255
Priest	Hasinai's main fire temple reportedly destroyed by Yojuane (Tonkawa).	1719	"	Smith 1959:376
Chief	Among Naouydiche, he celebrates calumet with La-Harpe.	1719	"	" :385
Chief	Aguayo gave an Aynay cazique a cane with a silver head.	1721	Aguayo	Buckley 1911:43

TABLE 4 CONT.

Status identification	Material culture description	Date	Chronicler	Reference
Principal Captain, Caciques, Elders and Officers	Wear ceremonial attire to greet ambassadors from other tribes.	1721	Morfi	Swanton 1942:177
Medicine Man (Priest ?)	Clothing of "his ministry decorated with big bunches of feathers, adding necklaces made with skins of coral-col-ored snakes, which are very showy and of bright colors." Have feather fans, whistles, and a carved stick shaped like a rattlesnake.	1721	"	" :223

TABLE 5

Correlation of Material Culture Attributes with Hasinai Governing Elite Positions and Special Buildings

Attributes	Temple	Xinesi	Caddi	Canaha	Assembly (Caddi & Canahas)
Contexts and spatial relationships					
separate from village	+				+
residence part of village	+	+[1]	+[2]	−	−
residence separate from temple	+	+	+	+	+
special houses nearby	+	−	+	−	0
arbor near residence		−	+	−	−
patio adjacent to residence	0	0	0	+	+
fields occur nearby	0	0	+	−	−
buried near temple	0	0	−	+	+
buried near residence	+	+	+	+	−
trophy skulls in nearby tree	+	0	−	−	−
trophy skulls buried nearby	+	0	−	−	−
nearby accumulation of ash and human bones	+	0	−	−	−
Architectural details					
building circular of pole frame covered with thatch	+	+	+	+	+
noncircular structure	−	−	−	−	−
structure larger than most	+	−	+[3]	+	+
wooden animal effigies over entry	+	−	+[4]	−	−
door covered	+	−	−	−	−
door faces east	0	0	+	+	0
door blocked at death	−	+	−	−	−
shelf over door on interior	−	0	0	0	0
perpetual fire in center	+	+	+	+	0
perpetual fire of 4 cardinally pointed large logs	+	0	0	0	0
structure burned when abandoned	+	+	+	+	+
nearby arbor of wood and cane	−	+	+	−	0
nearby hut of straw for dancers	−	−	−	−	−
nearby circle of implanted green cane	−	−	+	−	−

TABLE 5 CONT.

Attributes	Temple	Xinesi	Caddi	Canaha	Assembly (Caddi & Canahas)
Building furniture and furnishings					
special elevated seats (like tables)	+	+	+	–	–
special bench and bed for *xinesi*	–	+	+	+	o
reed floor mats for sitting	+	o	+	+	+
bearskin rugs for sitting	–	–	+[5]	–	–
ceremonial stool	o	o	+	o	o
earthen vessels	+	o	+	+	+
beds of reed rugs over 4 forked poles covered with bison hides	–	o	+ +	o	–
colored reed canopy by beds	–	o	+	o	–
Building furniture and furnishings					
reed baskets filled with corn	+	o	+	o	o
reed storage boxes	+[6]	o	+	o	o
wooden mortars	–	–	+	–	–
wooden bench on patio	–	o	+	o	o
little wooden bench by fire	+	o	+	o	o
wooden benches	+	–	+	o	o
replica of fire temple and shrine with images	–[7]	–	–	–	–
round wooden box with parchmentlike cover	+[7]	–	–	–	–
coffers containing wooden and stone effigies of animals	+	–	o	–	–
altar of reed mats	+	–	–	–	–
benches holding reed mats	+	o	o	o	o
tobacco	+	o	+	o	+
pipe with feathers	+	o	+	o	+
gourd rattles	+	o	+	o	o
incense burners (pots of fat and tobacco)	+	–	–	–	–

TABLE 5 CONT.

Attributes	Temple	Ximesi	Caddi	Canaha	Caddi Canaha	Assembly (Caddi & Canahas)
wooden platters shaped like animals	+?	−	−	−	−	−
various colored feathers	+?	−	−	−	−	−
crowns of skin and feathers	+?	−	−	−	−	−
carved crane bone flutes	+?	−	−	−	−	−
reed flutes	+?	−	−	−	−	−
a bonnet of skin and feathers	+?	−	−	−	−	−
chests	+?	−	−	−	−	−
wooden altar	+?	−	−	−	−	−
Ceremonial accouterments						
infant-naming						
special seat and large vessel	−	+	−	−	−	−
Calumet						
long pipe with feathers	−	−	0	+[a]	−	0
earthen vessel to wash face	−	−	0	+[a]	−	0
pipe case of skin (wild goat?)	−	−	0	+[a]	−	0
tripod of red sticks	−	−	0	+[a]	−	0
otter skin and gourd rattles	−	−	−	+[a]	−	0
Planting						
cane mats	+	0	0	0	−	−
black walnut hoes	−	0	+	0	−	−
Harvest						
benches, pipes, large pots	−	+	+	+	+	−
basket of corn on ceremonial stool	−	−	+	+	+	−
vessel of pottage on ceremonial stool	−	−	+	+	+	−
large circle of green cane	−	−	0	+	+	−
bison robes	−	−	−	0	+	−
gourd rattles	−	−	−	0	+	−

TABLE 5 CONT.

Attributes	Temple	Xinesi	Caddi	Canaha	Assembly (Caddi & Canahas)
hollow log drums	–	–	0	+	–
Forecasting					
fox tail	–	–	0	+	+
eagle wing fans	–	–	0	+	+
Victory					
trophy heads first displayed	–	+	+	–	–
trophy heads later displayed	–	–	+	+	–
many mats placed	–	+	+	+	–
vessel of food	–	+	+	+	–
pipe and tobacco	–	+	+	–	–
trophy heads finally displayed	+	+	–	–	–
Funeral of leading men					
coffin made	–	+	+	0	–
bow and arrow pit in coffin	–	+	+	0	–
personal clothes put in grave	–	+	+	0	–
leave goods on grave	–	+	+	0	–
leave tobacco, fire, and water on grave	+	+	–	–	–
goods of war dead burned	–	;	–	–	–
Human sacrifice					
earthen vessels to catch and cook blood and meat	–	;	+	+	–
Attire and personal goods					
painted goat (deer?) skins and white linen	–	;	+	+	–

TABLE 5 CONT.

Attributes	Temple	Xinesi	Caddi	Canaha	Assembly (Caddi & Canahas)
plumes of colored feathers	–	–	+		–
swords, clubs, and bows/arrows	–	–	+	+	–
faces painted red or black	–	–	+	+	–[9]
short hair soaked in oil and red lint	–	–	+	0	+
pipe	–	+	0	0	0
deerskin clothing	+	0	0	–	–
silver headed cane	0	+	–	–	–
bunches of colorful feathers	0	–	–	–	–
snakeskin necklaces	0	–	–	–	–
feather fans	0	–	–	–	–
stick carved like rattlesnake	0	–	–	–	–

Key: +, present; –, absent; 0, no data; blank does not apply; [1] Village priest, [2] reported for *Nahordikhe*, [3] long house near *Caddi* (see Massanet), [4] Joutel reports a chief's cottage is small, [5] Joutel reports for *Cahinnio*, [6] Casanas indicates mortar but doesn't specify wood, [7] Espinosa describes for 2 houses of heavenly children near temple, [8] Joutel describes for *Cahinnio*, [9] Joutel reports for *Cadadoquio* assembly of men.

TABLE 6

Material Remains Common to Hasinai Elites

I. *Xinesi* Temple-Residence Complex.

   A. General Data:

      1. Size ranges from two to three acres.
      2. Location is an interzonal boundary between major cultural units.

   B. Types of Structures:

      1. Residence:
        a. is circular with an approximate diameter of 60 feet.
        b. should have evidence of burning.
        c. has an east entryway blocked by pole(s).
        d. has a central hearth.
        e. has interior postmolds located on one side.
        f. artifacts include pottery vessels of diverse forms and types, a limited range of lithic implements, and European trade items (such as brass and silver disks).

      2. Temple:
        a. is circular with a diameter larger than 60 feet.
        b. has a large central hearth.
        c. may contain logs with only one burned end.
        d. artifacts include sherds from incense burners indicated by thick char deposits on interior, stone zoomorphic effigies, and crane bone flutes.

      3. Sanctuaries:
        a. consist of two circular structures less than 60 feet in diameter.
        b. are related to the maintenance of the two Heavenly children.
        c. are located within 100 yards of temple.
        d. contain little evidence of domestic artifacts.

   C. Types of Features:

      1. Midden:
        a. is located outside of residence structure.
        b. contains sherds of diverse forms and types and a limited range of lithic artifacts.
        c. should have a nonrandom correlation of deer bones.

      2. Ash deposit:
        a. is usually found in a pit located outside of temple structure.
        b. should contain large ash deposits with several human crania and other disarticulated bones.
        c. artifacts may include sherds with thick char deposits, broken crane bone flutes and stone zoomorphic effigies.

      3. Cemetery:
        a. contains a small number of individuals.
        b. may have stone or metal axe placed as a grave marker for important individuals.
        c. artifacts may include pottery vessels and European trade items such as glass beads, brass objects, and silver disks.

II. *Caddi* Residence Complex.

   A. General Data:

      1. Size ranges from two to three acres.
      2. Location may be near the center of occupied river basin.

B. Types of Structures:

1. Residence:
    a. is the largest structure at the site.
    b. is circular and is approximately 60 feet in diameter.
    c. has an east entryway.
    d. has a central hearth.
    e. contains numerous small, interior postmolds on one side of the structure.
    f. artifacts include sherds of less diverse types than *Xinesi's* residence, a wider variety of lithic implements, and European trade items such as gun parts, gunflints, strike-a-lights, etc.

2. Visitor's house:
    a. is circular to elongated with a diameter less than 60 feet.
    b. contains two entryways located on the east and west sides.
    c. has a central hearth.
    d. has numerous small, interior postmolds located on both sides of the structure.
    e. artifacts are similar to 1f, but may possibly have a wider variety of projectile points.

3. Attendants' house:
    a. is smaller than the visitor's house.
    b. also has two entryways on the east and west sides.
    c. has a central hearth.
    d. should contain several small, interior postmolds on both sides of the structure.
    e. artifacts should be few in number.

4. Circular Area:
    a. may have been used by participants during various ceremonies.
    b. consists of circular alignment of postmolds.
    c. contains very few artifacts.

C. Types of Features:

1. Plaza:
    a. is located between the residence and visitor's house.
    b. is approximately 100 to 200 feet on a side.
    c. has a compact surface.

2. Arbor:
    a. is found on one side of the plaza area.
    b. has a minimum of four postmolds indicating a square-to-rectangular outline.
    c. should contain no other features and very few artifacts.

3. Cemetery:
    a. should contain several burials.
    b. will have most important individuals denoted by grave offerings such as a lithic or metal axe, gun parts, metal knives, glass beads, and possibly the silver head of a cane.

4. Middens:
    a. are generalized areas located outside of structures and features.
    b. contain disarticulated animal bones and possibly ash deposits.
    c. contain various types of broken artifacts.

III. Assembly Complex.

A. General Data:

1. Size may range up to an acre.
2. Location is less than a mile from the *caddi's* residence.

TABLE 6 CONT.

Material Remains Common to Hasinai Elites

B. Assembly Structure:

    1. is the only structure found in this area.
    2. is a large circular structure with a diameter greater than 60 feet (?).
    3. has an east entryway.
    4. contains few if any interior postmolds.
    5. contains a limited number of artifacts.

C. Midden:

    1. is located outside of assembly structure.
    2. contains large ash deposits, but with limited variety of artifacts.

IV. *Canahas'* Residence Complex:

A. General Data:

    1. Size is equal to or greater than five acres.
    2. Locations are within and scattered throughout occupied river basin.

B. Types of Structures:

    1. Residences:
        a. are indistinguishable on the basis of size.
        b. have east entryways.
        c. have central hearths.
        d. contain numerous small, interior postmolds on one side of the structure.
        e. *canahas'* residence may contain artifacts similar to *caddi's*.

C. Types of Features:

    1. Middens:
        a. are located outside of structures.
        b. contain broken artifacts indicating normal daily activities.
        c. may contain ash deposits.

    2. Cemetery:
        a. contains a large number of burials.
        b. may show spatial clustering of related individuals.
        c. contains the *canahas'* burial with grave offerings similar to the *caddi's*.

References

Albrecht, Andrew C.
1946 Indian-French relations at Natchez. *American Anthropologist* 48(3):321-354.

Anderson, Keith M.
1972 Prehistoric settlements of the upper Neches river. Texas Archeological Society *Bulletin* 43:121-197.

Barth, Fredrik
1969 Introduction in *Ethnic groups and boundaries: The social organization of cultural differences*, edited by Fredrik Barth; pp. 9-38. London, Allen and Unwin.

Baugh, Timothy G.
1979 A structural perspective of Plains Indian society: Comments on Maxwell's "The evolution of Plains Indian kin terminologies: A non-reflectionist account." *Plains Anthropologist* 24(84):171-175.

Bell, Robert E. and David A. Baerreis
1951 A survey of Oklahoma archaeology. Texas Archeological and Paleontological Society *Bulletin* 22:7-100.

Bolton, Herbert E.
1907 Various Hasinai entries in Handbook of American Indians north of Mexico, edited by Frederick Webb Hodge. Bureau of American Ethnology *Bulletin* 30(2):1-8, 34, 49-50.
1908 The native tribes about the east Texas missions. Texas State Historical Association *Quarterly* 11(4):249-276.
1916 *Spanish exploration in the Southwest, 1542-1706.* New York, Scribner's.

Bottomore, T. B.
1974 *Elites and society.* Middlesex, Penguin Books.

Brain, Jeffrey P.
1971 The Natchez "paradox." *Ethnology* 10(2):215-222.

Brown, James A., Robert E. Bell and Don G. Wyckoff
1978 Caddoan settlement patterns in the Arkansas River drainage in *Mississippian settlement patterns*, edited by Bruce Smith, pp. 169-200. New York, Academic Press.

Buckley, Eleanor C. (trans.)
1911 The Aguayo expedition into Texas and Louisiana, 1719-1722. Texas State Historical Association *Quarterly* 15(1):1-65.

Casis, Lillia M.
1899 Translation of letter of Don Damian Manzanet to Don Carlos de Siguenza relative to the discovery of the Bay of Espiritu Santo. Texas State Historical Association *Quarterly* 2(4):253-312.

Chafe, Wallace L.
1976 Siouan, Iroquoian, and Caddoan in *Native languages of the Americas*, Vol. 1, edited by Thomas A. Sebeok, pp. 527-572. New York, Plenum Press.

Davis, Hester A. (ed.)
1970 Archeological and historical resources of the Red River Basin. Arkansas Archeological Survey *Research Series* 1.

Duffield, Lathel F. and Edward B. Jelks
  1961 The Pearson site, a historic Indian site in Iron Bridge Reservoir, Rains County, Texas. University of Texas, Department of Anthropology *Archaeology Series* 4.

Eggan, Fred
  1937 Historical changes in the Choctaw kinship system. *American Anthropologist* 39:34–52.

Falconer, Thomas (trans.)
  1975 *On the discovery of the Mississippi: With translation from original manuscript of memoirs relating to discovery of the Mississippi by Robert Cavelier de la Salle and the Chevalier Henry de Tonti.* Austin, Shoal Creek Publisher.

Flannery, Kent V.
  1972 The cultural evolution of civilizations. *Annual Review of Ecology and Systematics* 3:399–426.

Foik, Paul J.
  1933 Captain Dom Domingo Ramon's diary of his expedition into Texas, 1716. Texas Catholic Historical Society *Preliminary Studies* 2(1).

Fried, Morton H.
  1967 *The evolution of political society: An essay in political anthropology.* New York, Random House.

Gilbert, William H.
  1955 Eastern Cherokee social organization in *Social anthropology of North American tribes*, edited by Fred Eggan, pp. 281–338. Chicago, University of Chicago Press.

Glover, William B.
  1935 A history of the Caddo Indians. *Louisiana Historical Quarterly* 18(4):872–946.

Griffith, William Joyce
  1954 The Hasinai Indians of east Texas as seen by Europeans, 1687–1772. *Philogical and Documentary Studies* 2(3), Middle American Research Institute, Tulane University.

Haas, Mary R.
  1939 Natchez and Chitimacha clans and kinship terminology. *American Anthropologist* 41(4):597–610.

Hatcher, Mattie A. (trans.)
  1927 Descriptions of the Tejas or Asinai Indians, 1691–1722. *Southwestern Historical Quarterly* 30(3):206–218, 30(4):283–304, 31(1):50–62, 31(2):150–180.

Haviland, William A.
  1977 Dynastic genealogies from Tikal, Guatemala: Implications for descent and political organization. *American Antiquity* 42(1):61–67.

Hughes, Jack T.
  1968 *Prehistory of the Caddoan-speaking tribes.* Ph.D. dissertation, Department of Anthropology, Columbia University. University Microfilms International.

John, Elizabeth A. H.
1975 *Storms brewed in other men's worlds: The confrontation of Indians, Spanish, and French in the Southwest, 1540-1795.* College Station, Texas A&M University Press.

Jones, Buddy C.
1968 *The Kinsloe focus: A study of seven historic Caddoan sites in northeast Texas.* M.A. thesis, Department of Anthropology, University of Oklahoma.

Jones, Christopher
1977 Inauguration dates of three late Classic rulers of Tikal, Guatemala. *American Antiquity* 42(1):28-60.

Joutel, Henri
1962 *A journal of La Salle's last voyage.* New York, Corinth Books.

Krieger, Alex D.
1947 Cultural complexes and chronology in northern Texas. University of Texas *Publication* 4640.

Lesser, Alexander
1979 Caddoan kinship systems. *Nebraska History* 60(2):260-271.

Lesser, Alexander and Gene Weltfish
1932 Composition of the Caddoan linguistic stock. *Smithsonian Miscellaneous Collections* 87(6):1-15.

Levi-Strauss, Claude
1969 *The elementary structures of kinship.* Boston, Beacon Press.

Marcus, Joyce
1974 The iconography of power among the Classic Maya. *World Archaeology* 6(1):83-94.

Maxwell, Joseph A.
1978 The evolution of Plains Indian kin terminologies: A non-reflectionist account. *Plains Anthropologist* 23(79):13-29.

Miroir, M. P., R. King Harris, Jay C. Blaine and Janson McVay
1973 Bénard de la Harpe and the Nassonite Post. Texas Archeological Society *Bulletin* 44:113-167.

Mooney, James
1896 The Ghost-dance religion and the Sioux outbreak of 1890. Bureau of American Ethnology, *Fourteenth Annual Report (1892-93),* Part 2.

Mosca, Gaetano
1939 *The ruling class.* New York, McGraw-Hill.

Murdock, George Peter
1965 *Social structure.* New York, The Free Press.

Murra, John V. and Craig Morris
1976 Dynastic oral tradition, administrative records and archaeology in the Andes. *World Archaeology* 7(3):269-279.

Newcomb, William W., Jr.
1961 *The Indians of Texas: From prehistoric to modern times.* Austin, University of Texas Press.
1974 *North American Indians: An anthropological perspective.* Pacific Palisades, CA., Goodyear Publishing Co.

Newell, H. Perry and Alex D. Krieger
    1949   The George C. Davis site, Cherokee County, Texas. Society for
           American Archaeology *Memoirs* 5.
Orr, Kenneth G.
    1952   Survey of Caddoan area archaeology in *Archaeology of eastern
           United States*, edited by James B. Griffin, pp. 239-255. Chicago,
           University of Chicago Press.
Pareto, Vilfredo
    1935   *The mind and society*, Vols. I-IV. New York: Harcourt, Brace.
Parsons, Elsie Clews
    1941   Notes on the Caddo. American Anthropological Association
           Memoir 57. (Supplement to *American Anthropologist* 43(3), part
           2.)
Pénicaut, André
    1953   *Fleur de lys and calumet. Being the Penicaut narrative of French
           adventure in Louisiana*, edited by Richeobourg G. McWilliams.
           Baton Rouge, Louisiana State University Press.
Radcliffe-Brown, A. R.
    1965   Introduction in *Structure and Function in Primitive Society*, pp.
           1-14. New York, The Free Press.
Rathje, William L.
    1970   Socio-political implications of lowland Maya burials: Methodology
           and tentative hypotheses. *World Archaeology* 1(3):359-374.
Schmitt, Karl and Iva Osanai Schmitt
    1951   Arikara field notes. On file with the Department of Anthropology,
           University of Oklahoma, Norman.
    1952   *Wichita kinship past and present*. Norman, University of Oklahoma
           Press.
Scurlock, J. Dan
    1962   The Culpepper site, a late Fulton Aspect site in northeastern Texas.
           Texas Archeological Society *Bulletin* 32:285-316.
Sears, William H.
    1968   The state and settlement patterns in the New World in *Settlement
           archaeology*, edited by K. C. Chang, pp. 134-153. Palo Alto,
           National Press.
Service, Elman R.
    1962   *Primitive social organization: An evolutionary perspective*. New
           York, Random House.
Sibley, John
    1832   Historical sketches of the several Indian tribes in Louisiana, south
           of the Arkansas River, and between the Mississippi and River
           Grande. *American State Papers*, Class II, *Indian Affairs* 1:721-731.
Smith, Ralph A. (trans.)
    1958   Account of the journey of Bénard de la Harpe: Discovery made by
           him of several nations situated in the west. *Southwestern Historical
           Quarterly* 62(1):75-86, 62(2):246-259.
    1959   Account of the journey of Bénard de la Harpe: Discovery made by

him of several nations situated in the west. *Southwestern Historical Quarterly* 62(3):371–385.

Speck, Frank G.
    1909   Ethnology of the Yuchi Indians. University of Pennsylvania Museum, *Anthropological Publications* 1(1):1–154.

Spicer, Edward H.
    1962   *Cycles of conquest: The impact of Spain, Mexico, and the United States on the Indians of the Southwest, 1533–1960.* Tucson, University of Arizona Press.

Spier, Leslie
    1924   Wichita and Caddo relationship terms. *American Anthropologist* 26:258–263.

Story, Dee Ann
    1972   A preliminary report of the 1968, 1969, and 1970 excavations at the George C. Davis site, Cherokee County, Texas. *Report* submitted to the National Science Foundation.

Story, Dee Ann and Sam Valastro, Jr.
    1977   Radiocarbon dating and the George C. Davis site, Texas. *Journal of Field Archaeology* 4(1):63–89.

Swanton, John R.
    1911   Indian tribes of the lower Mississippi Valley and adjacent coast of the Gulf of Mexico. Bureau of American Ethnology, *Bulletin* 43.
    1928a Aboriginal Culture of the Southeast. Bureau of American Ethnology, 42nd *Annual Report*, 1924-25, pp. 673–726.
    1928b Social organization and social usages of the Indians of the Creek Confederacy. Bureau of American Ethnology, Forty-second *Annual Report*, 1924-25, pp. 23–472.
    1931a The Caddo social organization and its possible historical significance. Washington Academy of Science *Journal* 21(9): 203–206.
    1931b Source material for the social and ceremonial life of the Choctaw. Bureau of American Ethnology, *Bulletin* 103.
    1942   Source material on the history and ethnology of the Caddo Indians. Bureau of American Ethnology *Bulletin* 132.
    1946   The Indians of the southeastern United States. Bureau of American Ethnology *Bulletin* 137.

Trigger, Bruce
    1974   The archaeology of government. *World Archaeology* 6(1):95–106.

Ucko, Peter J.
    1969   Ethnology and archaeological interpretation of funerary remains. *World Archaeology* 1(3):260–280.

Webb, Clarence H.
    1958   A review of northeast Texas archaeology. Texas Archeological Society *Bulletin* 29:35–64.
    1959   The Belcher Mound: A stratified Caddoan site in Caddo Parish, Louisiana. Society for American Archaeology *Memoirs* 16.

Webb, Clarence H. and Ralph R. McKinney

1975   Mounds Plantation (16CD12), Caddo Parish, Louisiana. *Louisiana Archaeology* 2:39-127.

Wedel, Mildred Mott
1978   La Harpe's 1719 post on Red River and nearby Caddo settlements. The Texas Memorial Museum *Bulletin* 30.

Weltfish, Gene
1971   *The lost universe: The way of life of the Pawnee.* New York, Ballantine Books.

White, Douglas R., George P. Murdock and Richard Scaglion
1971   Natchez class and rank reconsidered. *Ethnology* 10(4):369-388.

Whitecotton, Joseph W.
1968   *The valley of Oaxaca at Spanish contact: An ethnohistorical study.* Ph.D. dissertation, Department of Anthropology, University of Illinois. University Microfilms International.

Williams, Stephen
1964   The aboriginal location of the Kadohadacho and related tribes. In *Explorations in cultural anthropology*, edited by Ward H. Goodenough, pp. 545-570. New York: McGraw-Hill.

Woodall, J. Ned
1969   *Cultural ecology of the Caddo.* Ph.D. dissertation, Department of Anthropology, Southern Methodist University.
1972   Prehistoric social boundaries: An archeological model and test. Texas Archeological Society *Bulletin* 43:101-120.

Wyckoff, Don G.
1974   *Caddoan culture area: An archaeological perspective. Caddoan Indians* (1):25-279. New York, Garland Publishing.